Mac OS® X Tiger™ All-in-One Desk Reference For Dummies®

Cheat Sheet

Finder Keyboard Shortcuts

Key	Function
⌘+A	Selects all items in the active window
⌘+C	Copies selected items
⌘+D	Duplicates the selected item(s)
⌘+E	Ejects the selected volume
⌘+F	Displays the Find dialog
⌘+H	Hides All Finder windows
⌘+I	Shows info for selected item or items
⌘+J	Shows the view options for the active window
⌘+K	Displays the Connect to Server dialog
⌘+L	Creates an alias for the selected item
⌘+M	Minimizes the active window
⌘+N	Opens a new Finder window
⌘+O	Opens (or launches) the selected item
⌘+R	Shows the original for selected alias
⌘+T	Adds the selected item to the Sidebar
⌘+V	Pastes items from the Clipboard
⌘+W	Closes the active window
⌘+X	Cuts the selected items
⌘+Z	Undoes the last action (if possible)
⌘+,	Displays Finder Preferences
⌘+1	Shows the active window in icon mode
⌘+2	Shows the active window in list mode
⌘+3	Shows the active window in column mode
⌘+[	Moves back to the previous Finder location

Key	Function
⌘+]	
⌘+Del	Moves sele... Trash
⌘+↑	Show enclosing folder
⌘+`	Cycles through windows
⌘+?	Displays the Mac OS X Help Viewer
⌘+Shift+A	Takes you to your Applications folder
⌘+Shift+C	Takes you to the top-level Computer location
⌘+Shift+G	Takes you to a folder that you specify
⌘+Shift+H	Takes you to your Home folder
⌘+Shift+I	Connects you to your iDisk
⌘+Shift+Q	Logs you out
⌘+Shift+N	Opens a new untitled folder in the active window
⌘+Shift+U	Takes you to your Utilities folder
⌘+Shift+Del	Deletes the contents of the Trash
⌘+Option+H	Hides all windows except the Finder window
⌘+Option+N	Opens a new Smart Folder
⌘+Option+T	Hides the Finder window toolbar
⌘+Option+Space	Opens the Spotlight window
⌘+ Space	Opens the Spotlight menu
F9	Shows all open windows using Exposé
F10	Shows all open windows for the current application using Exposé
F11	Hides all windows to display the Desktop using Exposé
F12	Displays your Dashboard widgets

For Dummies: Bestselling Book Series for Beginners

Mac OS® X Tiger™ All-in-One Desk Reference For Dummies®

Cheat Sheet

Strange-Looking Menu Keys

Symbol	Key
⌘	Command
^	Control
⇧	Shift
⌥	Option
⌦	Del

Mark's Mac OS X Maintenance Checklist

Task	Schedule
Check for updates with Software Update	Once a day (automatically, if you like)
Back up (Backup/Retrospect Backup)	Once a day or once a week
Defragment (Micromat TechTool Pro/ Micromat Drive 10)	Once a week
Repair Disk Permissions (Disk Utility)	Once a week
Scan for viruses (Intego VirusBarrier X)	Once a week (with automatic scanning)
Check all volumes (Disk Utility/ Micromat TechTool Pro)	Once a month
Check for the latest drivers for your hardware	Once a month (or after installing new hardware)
Delete temporary Internet cache files (Allume Systems Spring Cleaning)	Once a month

For Dummies: Bestselling Book Series for Beginners

Mac OS® X Tiger™
ALL IN ONE DESK REFERENCE
FOR
DUMMIES®

by Mark L. Chambers

WILEY

Wiley Publishing, Inc.

Mac OS® X Tiger™ All-in-One Desk Reference For Dummies®

Published by
Wiley Publishing, Inc.
111 River Street
Hoboken, NJ 07030-5774
www.wiley.com

WILEY

About the Author

Mark L. Chambers has been an author, computer consultant, BBS sysop, programmer, and hardware technician for more than 20 years — pushing computers and their uses far beyond "normal" performance limits for decades now. His first love affair with a computer peripheral blossomed in 1984 when he bought his lightning-fast 300 BPS modem for his Atari 400. Now he spends entirely too much time on the Internet and drinks far too much caffeine-laden soda.

With a degree in journalism and creative writing from Louisiana State University, Mark took the logical career choice: programming computers. However, after five years as a COBOL programmer for a hospital system, he decided there must be a better way to earn a living, and he became the Documentation Manager for Datastorm Technologies, a well-known communications software developer. Somewhere in between writing software manuals, Mark began writing computer how-to books. His first book, *Running a Perfect BBS*, was published in 1994 — and after a short decade or so of fun (disguised as hard work), Mark is one of the most productive and best-selling technology authors on the planet.

Along with writing several books a year and editing whatever his publishers throw at him, Mark has also branched out into Web-based education, designing and teaching a number of online classes — called *WebClinics* — for Hewlett-Packard.

His favorite pastimes include collecting gargoyles, watching St. Louis Cardinals baseball, playing his three pinball machines and the latest computer games, supercharging computers, and rendering 3-D flights of fancy with TrueSpace — and during all that, he listens to just about every type of music imaginable. Mark's world-wide Internet radio station, *MLC Radio* (at www.mlcbooks.com), plays only CD-quality classics from 1970 to 1979, including everything from Rush to Billy Joel to the Rocky Horror Picture Show.

Mark's rapidly expanding list of books includes *iMac For Dummies, 4th Edition; Building a PC For Dummies, 4th Edition; Scanners For Dummies, 2nd Edition; CD & DVD Recording For Dummies, 2nd Edition; PCs All-in-One Desk Reference For Dummies, 2nd Edition; Mac OS X Tiger: Top 100 Simplified Tips & Tricks; Microsoft Office v. X Power User's Guide; BURN IT! Creating Your Own Great DVDs and CDs; The Hewlett-Packard Official Printer Handbook; The Hewlett-Packard Official Recordable CD Handbook; The Hewlett-Packard Official Digital Photography Handbook; Computer Gamer's Bible; Recordable CD Bible; Teach Yourself the iMac Visually; Running a Perfect BBS; Official Netscape Guide to Web Animation;* and the *Windows 98 Troubleshooting and Optimizing Little Black Book.*

His books have been translated into 14 different languages so far — his favorites are German, Polish, Dutch, and French. Although he can't read them, he enjoys the pictures a great deal.

Mark welcomes all comments and questions about his books. You can reach him at mark@mlcbooks.com, or visit MLC Books Online (his Web site) at www.mlcbooks.com.

Dedication

This book is dedicated to my oldest daughter, Erin Chambers — "Version 1.0" — with all the love and happiness I can give her.

—Mark Chambers

Author's Acknowledgments

It's high time I express my heartfelt thanks to everyone who helped produce the book you're holding!

Copious thanks are due (again) to the technical editor, Greg Willmore (along with his equally Mac-savvy sons Matt and Chris), who checked each and every word of this Desk Reference for technical accuracy . . . and that, my friends, is no easy job, especially when you consider that Tiger was in "squeaky" beta during the development of this book! I was very lucky to have the help of such a knowledgeable technical editor. Mondo kudos also to my friend Teresa Artman for her outstanding work as copy editor.

A book of this size places a huge burden on the publisher's Composition Services team because those folks have to design over 700 pages and then prepare both the copy and the high-resolution figures. Again, as in the past, the work they've done is wonderful, and I appreciate the hard work of *everyone* on the Composition Services team.

As with all my books, I'd like to thank my wife, Anne, and my children, Erin, Chelsea, and Rose, for their support and love — and for letting me follow my dream!

Finally, I turn to the two people at Wiley who literally made this book possible: my friend Bob Woerner, the acquisitions editor whom I've been lucky enough to know for several years now; and Mark Enochs, my uber-patient (and **remarkably** calm) project editor, whom I was lucky enough to work with for the first time on the Tiger edition of this tome. Their talents and ongoing assistance made this project a joy instead of a job as they gave me all the support that every author craves. Many, many thanks to you both from a *very* grateful Mac owner!

—Mark Chambers

Publisher's Acknowledgments

We're proud of this book; please send us your comments through our online registration form located at www.dummies.com/register/.

Some of the people who helped bring this book to market include the following:

Acquisitions, Editorial, and Media Development

Project Editor: Mark Enochs

(Previous Edition: Linda Morris)

Senior Acquisitions Editor: Bob Woerner

Senior Copy Editor: Teresa Artman

Technical Editor: Greg Willmore

Editorial Manager: Kevin Kirschner

Media Development Manager: Laura VanWinkle

Media Development Supervisor: Richard Graves

Editorial Assistant: Amanda Foxworth

Cartoons: Rich Tennant (www.the5thwave.com)

Composition Services

Project Coordinator: Nancee Reeves

Layout and Graphics: Andrea Dahl, Denny Hager, Stephanie D. Jumper, Melanee Prendergast, Heather Ryan

Proofreaders: John Greenough, Leeann Harney, Jessica Kramer, Carl Pierce, Dwight Ramsey, Evelyn Still

Indexer: Richard T. Evans

Special Help: Matt Willmore, Chris Willmore

Publishing and Editorial for Technology Dummies

Richard Swadley, Vice President and Executive Group Publisher

Andy Cummings, Vice President and Publisher

Mary Bednarek, Executive Acquisitions Director

Mary C. Corder, Editorial Director

Publishing for Consumer Dummies

Diane Graves Steele, Vice President and Publisher

Joyce Pepple, Acquisitions Director

Composition Services

Gerry Fahey, Vice President of Production Services

Debbie Stailey, Director of Composition Services

Contents at a Glance

Table of Contents

Book II: Customizing and Sharing 165

Chapter 1: Building the Finder of Your Dreams 167

Chapter 2: Giving Your Desktop the Personal Touch 185

Introduction

*E**legant.***

I remember the first moment that I moved a mouse across a Mac OS X Desktop — at that time, it was the beta of version 10.0 — and I very well remember the word *elegant* as my first impression. (My second impression was *UNIX done better.*)

That's really saying something because I'm an old operating system curmudgeon: I cut my computing teeth on Atari, Commodore 64, and TRS-80 Model III machines, and I still feel much at home in the character-based environment of DOS and UNIX. Of course, I've also used every version of Windows that His Gateness has produced, including the much-improved Windows XP. And yes, I've used Mac OS since before the days of System 7, using a Macintosh SE with a 9-inch monitor (and a built-in handle).

But out of this host of operating systems, could you really call one *elegant* before now? (Even Mac OS 9 didn't deserve such a description although it did provide the foundation of convenience and simplicity.) Mac OS X — now at version 10.4, affectionately called *Tiger* — is something different: It's a fine-cut diamond amongst a handful of semi-precious stones. It's the result of an unnatural marriage, I'll admit . . . the intuitive, graphical world of Mac OS 9 paired with the character-based stability and efficient multitasking of UNIX. Who would have thought that they would work together so well? Mac OS X performs like a Ferrari, and (unbelievably) it looks as good, too.

Therefore, you can imagine just how excited I was to be asked by my friends at Wiley to write this book and how I immediately jumped at the chance to write a comprehensive guide to Apple's masterpiece. The book that you hold in your hands is a classic *For Dummies* design — it provides you the step-by-step instruction (plenty of which my editors agree is humorous) on every major feature of Mac OS X — but it also goes a step further from time to time, delving into why something works the way that it does or what's going on behind the scenes. You can chalk that up to my sincere admiration for everyone in Cupertino and what they've perfected.

What you *won't* find in this Desk Reference is wasted space. All the new features of version 10.4 are here, including the latest iChat AV, Dashboard, Spotlight, the new Automator application, the latest versions of all the *iApps* (including GarageBand), and the new incarnations of the Finder and Apple Mail. Everything's explained from the ground up, just in case you've never touched an Apple computer before. By the time you reach the final pages, you'll have covered advanced topics such as networking, AppleScript, Internet security . . . and yes, even an introduction to the powerful world of UNIX that exists underneath.

I sincerely hope that you'll enjoy this book and that it will act as your guide while you discover all the wonderful features of Mac OS X Tiger that I use every day. Remember, if a Windows-enslaved acquaintance still titters about your iMac, I'll understand if you're tempted to drop this weighty tome on his foot.

 The official name of the latest version is (portentous pause here, please) Mac OS X version 10.4 Tiger. But who wants to spit out that mouthful every time? Throughout this book, I refer to the operating system as *Mac OS X,* and when I discuss something that's particular to the latest version, I call it *Tiger.*

What's Really Required

If you've got a Mac that's either running Mac OS X version 10.4 (Tiger) or is ready to be upgraded to it, you're set to go. Despite what you might have heard, you *won't* require any of the following:

✦ **A degree in computer science:** Apple designed Mac OS X for regular people, and I designed this book for people of every experience level. Even if you've never used a Mac before, you'll find no hostile waters here.

✦ **A fortune in software:** I do describe additional software that you can buy to expand the functionality of your Mac; however, that section is only a few pages long. *Everything else* covered in this book is included with Mac OS X Tiger — and by the size of this volume, you get a rough idea of just how complete Mac OS X is! Heck, many folks buy Macs just because of the free software you get, like iMovie HD and iPhoto 5. (Tough cookies to the vast Unwashed Windows Horde.)

✦ **An Internet connection:** Granted, you're not going to do much with Apple Mail without an Internet connection, but computers *did* exist before the Internet. You can still be productive with Mac OS X without receiving buckets of spam.

Oh, you will need a set of Mac OS X version 10.4 installation discs, unless Tiger came pre-installed on your Mac. Go figure.

About This Book

Although this book is a Desk Reference, you can also read it in a linear fashion (straight-through) — probably not in one session, mind you. (Then again, Diet Coke is cheap, so it *is* possible.) The material is divided into seven mini-books, each of which covers an entire area of Mac OS X knowledge. For example, you'll find mini-books on networking, the Apple Digital Hub suite of applications, customizing your Desktop, and Internet-related applications.

Each self-contained chapter discusses a specific feature, application, connection, or cool thing about Mac OS X. Feel free to begin reading anywhere or skip chapters at will. For example, if you're already using an Internet connection, you won't need the chapter on adding an Internet connection. However, I recommend that you read this book from the front to the back, like any good mystery novel. (Watch out, oncoming spoiler: For those that want to know right now, Bill Gates did it.)

Conventions Used in This Book

Even *For Dummies* books have to get technical from time to time, usually involving commands that you have to type and menu items that you have to click. If you've read any of my other *For Dummies* books, you'll know that a helpful set of conventions is used to indicate what needs to be done or what you see onscreen.

Stuff you type

When I ask you to type a command or enter something in a text field (like your name or phone number), the text appears like this: **Type me.**

Press the Return key to process the command or enter the text.

Menu commands

When I give you a specific set of menu commands to use, they appear in the following format: Edit⇨Copy.

In this example, you should click the Edit menu and then choose the Copy menu item.

Display messages

If I mention a specific message that you see on your screen, it looks like this on the page: This is a message displayed by an application.

In case you're curious about computers

No one expects a book in the *For Dummies* series to contain techno-jargon or ridiculous computer science semantics — especially a book about the Macintosh, which has always strived for simplicity and user-friendliness. I hereby promise that I'll do my absolute best to avoid unnecessary techno-talk.

For those who are interested in what's happening under the hood, I provide sidebars that explain a little more about what's doing what to whom. If you'd rather just have fun and ignore the digital dirty work, please feel free to disregard these additions (but don't tear sidebars out of the book because there's likely to be important stuff on the opposite side of the page).

How This Book Is Organized

I've done my best to emulate the elegant design of Mac OS X by organizing this book into seven mini-books, with cross-references where appropriate.

Book 1: Introducing Mac OS X

This mini-book begins with an invigorating chapter explaining exactly why you should be so happy to be a Mac OS X owner. Then I provide an introduction to the basic tasks that you'll perform — things like copying files, running programs, and the like. Because Sherlock 3 and the Address Book are such important elements of Mac OS X, I also cover them in this mini-book. You'll also find coverage of Tiger's new Spotlight search engine, a guide to normal Mac OS X maintenance and troubleshooting, and instructions on using the Mac OS X Help system.

Book 11: Customizing and Sharing

Who wants to stick with the defaults? The material in this mini-book leads you through the steps that you need to customize Mac OS X to your specific needs and desires . . . everything from a tweak to your background or screen saver to a description of how to set up and administer multiple accounts on a single Macintosh. You'll also find coverage of the different settings that you can change in System Preferences, which is an important place in Mac OS X.

Book 111: The Digital Hub

Sweet! This mini-book jumps right in among the crown jewels of the Digital Hub: iTunes, iPhoto, iDVD, iMovie, QuickTime, GarageBand, and the DVD Player. Taken as a suite, these applications allow you to plug in and use all sorts of electronic gadgets, including digital cameras, digital video (DV) camcorders, and MP3 players — plus, you can edit or create your own DVDs, audio CDs, and movies.

Book 1V: The Typical Internet Stuff

This mini-book contains just what it says. But then again, it's easy to get enthusiastic about Apple Mail, the latest version of Apple's instant messaging application (iChat AV), and the online storage provided by iDisk. I also cover Safari, Apple's hot-rod Web browser. Finally, you'll discover more about the built-in Internet firewall and how you can use it to safeguard your Mac from Internet undesirables.

Book V: Networking in Mac OS X

Ethernet, Bluetooth, Bonjour, and AppleTalk are lurking in this mini-book. I explain them step-by-step, in language that a normal human being can understand. Find out how to use wireless networks like AirPort Extreme from Apple as well as how to share an Internet connection with other computers in a local network.

Book VI: Expanding Your System

Time to take things up a notch. In this mini-book, I discuss the hardware and software that everyone's adding to Mac OS X and why you might (or might not) need such toys. Memory (RAM), hard drives, printers, USB, and the newest FireWire 800 . . . they're all discussed here in detail. Consider this a banquet of expansion information.

Book VII: Advanced Mac OS X

I know that I told you earlier that I was going to avoid techno-talk whenever possible, yet I also mentioned the advanced things that you'll find in this mini-book, like using UNIX within Mac OS X and using Automator to build your own custom script applications that handle repetitious tasks. If you don't mind immersing yourself in all that's technical, read here for the skinny on hosting a Web site and communicating with Mac OS X by using your voice and your handwriting.

Icons Used in This Book

The icons in this book are more than just attractive — they're also important visual cues for stuff that you don't want to miss.

Okay, so Mark's Maxims aren't marked with an icon, per se. However, they represent way-important stuff, so I call your attention to these nuggets in bold, like this:

> **Something *Really* Important Is Being Said that will likely affect your person in the near future. Pay attention, commit those Maxims to memory, and you'll avoid the pitfalls that the rest of us have hit on the way.™**

The Tip icons flag short snippets of information that will save you time or trouble (and, in some cases, even cash).

These icons highlight optional technical information for folks like me. If you also used to disassemble alarm clocks for fun when you were 6 years old, you'll love this stuff.

Always read this information next to this icon first! Something looms ahead that could put your hardware or software at risk.

Look to the Remember icons for those tidbits that you need to file away in your mind. Just remember to remember.

Follow these road signs for all the cool updates and innovations in Mac OS X version 10.4 Tiger.

Book I

Introducing Mac OS X

The 5th Wave   By Rich Tennant

"Come here, quick! I've got a new iMac trick!"

Contents at a Glance

Chapter 1: Shaking Hands with Mac OS X

In This Chapter

✔ Understanding the advantages of Mac OS X

✔ Checking your system requirements

✔ Upgrading from earlier versions of Mac OS

✔ Installing Mac OS X

✔ Running Mac OS X for the first time

*I*t's human nature to require instant gratification from your software. I've seen it countless times: Someone runs a program, immediately feels comfortable with it, and then spends the rest of his days using that program religiously. Or another person plays with the same program for 120 seconds and dismisses it as too difficult or too confusing. It's rather like watching a fancy fashion show runway in Rome or Paris: There had better be eye appeal pretty quickly, or the bucks won't flow.

Ditto for modern computer operating systems. An operating system is the basic software that determines the look and feel of your entire computer and usually extends to the programs that you run as well. Microsoft felt the pinch of an old-fashioned operating system when Windows 98 and Windows Me were starting to appear rather plain-looking. MS promptly released Windows XP, where menus fade in and out like fireflies on a summer night, little puppies help you find files, and animation abounds. To be honest, however, updating a PC by upgrading to Windows XP is a little like putting on a polyester sports coat over the same tired old T-shirt and jeans — most of what changes is on the *outside*.

Apple doesn't work that way. Sure, Mac OS X looks doggone good. Forget the minimum requirement of shirt and shoes because this operating system is wearing an Armani suit. What's really exciting for Macintosh owners around the world, however, is the heart that beats *beneath* the pretty form. Mac OS X is quite literally an operating system revolution, delivering some of the most advanced features available on any personal computer in use today while remaining as easy to use as the first Macintosh. (And yes, I do own, use, and enjoy both PCs and Macs — what's important to me is which computer does the job the fastest in the easiest manner.)

Now, I'm not going to just haul off and proclaim that Mac OS X can run rings around — well . . . you know, the *W* word — without solid proof. In this chapter, I introduce you to the advantages of Mac OS X and why it's such a step ahead for those running Windows. I also cover the hardware requirements that you'll need to run Mac OS X version 10.4 (Tiger) as well as guidelines on switching from Windows. Finally, I familiarize you with the steps that you'll encounter the first time that you fire up the Big X.

Convince Me: Why Mac OS X?

Apple pioneered the graphical approach to computing with the appearance of the first Macintosh, so you'd expect Mac OS X to be simple to use — and indeed it is. For many folks, that's Job One. If you're one of those people, you can happily skip this section without need of further evidence because Mac OS X is undoubtedly the easiest operating system on the planet to use. (And believe me, I'm not knocking simplicity. Computers are supposed to be getting easier to use, and techno-nerds like me are supposed to be rendered unnecessary as computers advance.) Here is the mantra of the Mac — and the first of Mark's Maxims for this volume:

One Mouse, One Button, One King.™

Still with me? Need more testimony? Or perhaps you're just curious about the engine under the hood. Then read on — and if you're a Macintosh owner, feel free to gloat! (If you're a PC owner, there's always eBay.)

Pretty to behold

Let me illustrate with a screenshot or two: Figure 1-1 illustrates a typical screen from a day spent in Mac OS v. 9.2, the capable — albeit rather old-fashioned — version of the Mac OS operating system that shipped in the days before Mac OS X.

Compare that screen with a similar screen from the latest version of the Big X, as shown in Figure 1-2. As you can see, everything's streamlined in appearance, with maximum efficiency in mind. Tasteful 3-D abounds, from the drop-shadowed windows to the liquid-look scroll bars. Icons look like miniature works of art. Macintosh owners appreciate outstanding design — and can recognize the value of a great computer, even if it is lime-green (or looks like half of a white basketball). After all, many Mac owners are professionals in the graphic arts, and Apple provides the hardware that they need — like the top-of-the-line, liquid crystal display (LCD) used with the 20" flat-panel iMac G5 or the killer performance of the latest Power Mac G5 with dual processors (*liquid-cooled* processors, no less).

Take a look at what's going on behind the curtain — the Great Oz is actually pretty busy back there.

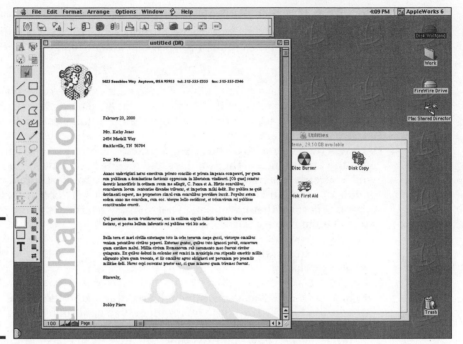

Figure 1-1:
Mac OS 9.2
was a
workhorse,
true, but it
wasn't a
work of art.

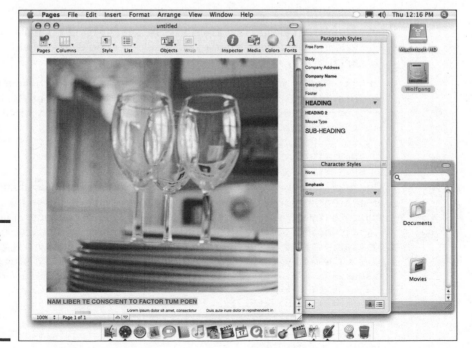

Figure 1-2:
Eye-
catching?
You bet!
Mac OS X
Tiger is a
knockout.

The allure of Aqua

The Apple software developers who introduced us to Mac OS X designed this new look from the ground up. They call it *Aqua,* and it's Tiger's standard user interface.

Whoops, I just realized that I slipped a ten-cent example of techno-babble into that previous paragraph. Let me explain: A *user interface design* determines how things look throughout both the operating system itself and all applications that are written to run under an operating system (OS). This includes the buttons that you push, the controls that you click or move, and even the appearance of the windows and menus themselves. For example, if you've already begun to use Mac OS X, you've probably stopped right in the middle of a task and exclaimed to yourself, "Why, Self, look at that cool 3-D contour effect on that menu bar!" That shapely contour is a tiny part of the Aqua user interface design.

Aqua also extends to the placement of controls and how they're shown to you. For example:

✦ Mac OS X uses Aqua *sheets* (which are attached to their parent dialogs and windows) to prompt you for input, like confirming when you're about to close a document without saving it. Unlike Windows, multiple programs can have multiple sheets open, so you can continue to work in other applications without being rudely forced to answer the query immediately.

✦ Aqua's file selection controls, like the one in Figure 1-3, make it much easier to quickly navigate to a specific file or folder from within an application.

✦ The *Dock* is another Aqua addition, replacing some of the functions of the old Control Strip and the Launcher from Mac OS 9. The Dock launches your favorite applications, indicates what's running on your Mac, and allows you to switch between those programs — and all in a strip that you can relocate and customize at will. I talk about the Dock in greater detail later in Book II, Chapter 2.

Consider Aqua as the *look-and-feel* of Mac OS X and virtually all applications that it runs; you'll discover how to use these Aqua controls in the pages to come. Of course, Mac owners really don't have to worry about Aqua itself; the Aqua guidelines are a roadmap for those writing applications for Mac OS X. Programs written to the common Aqua interface standard will be easier for you to use, and you'll become a proficient power user of that program much faster.

Figure 1-3:
A typical file
selection
dialog
(done right
in Aqua).

The quality of Quartz

The second ingredient in the visual feast that is Mac OS X is *Quartz Extreme* —
again, I must ask your forgiveness, good reader, because I have to get a
tad technical again. Quartz Extreme is a *graphics engine:* It's the portion
of Mac OS X that draws what you see on the screen (in the Aqua interface,
natch). Think of the engine in your car, which is responsible for making your
car move. Whether your Mac is running Microsoft Word or simply idling at
the Desktop waiting for you to finish your soda, Quartz Extreme is at work
displaying icons, drawing shapes, exhibiting the Finder, and animating things
in the Dock.

What sets Quartz Extreme apart from the ho-hum graphics engine that
Windows uses? It's all about international programming standards . . . you
know, those things that Microsoft would much rather that you forget. To wit:

✦ **PDF:** The Quartz Extreme engine is built around the Acrobat Portable
Document Format (*PDF* for short) developed by Adobe. If you've been
spending any time at all on the Internet in the last two or three years,
you know that PDF files have emerged as the standard for displaying
and printing the highest-quality electronic documents. Plus, Adobe has
released a version of the free Acrobat Reader (www.adobe.com) for just
about every computer on this green Earth. This means that text and
graphics displayed in Quartz Extreme are razor sharp, resizable, and easily

portable from one computer to another. In fact, Mac OS X displays PDF files without even requiring Acrobat, using the built-in Preview application. Figure 1-4 shows a complex PDF document that I opened in Mac OS X.

✦ **OpenGL:** Gamers will get really excited about this one: Quartz Extreme also uses the OpenGL graphics acceleration standard, which delivers the fastest 3-D graphics on the planet. (Think photo-realistic, high-resolution graphics drawn in the blink of an eye.) In fact — and this is a really cool trick — if you have an advanced 3-D card, OpenGL is even used to produce the Desktop in Mac OS X Tiger.

In English, that means that today's top-of-the-line, 3-D gaming and 3-D graphics acceleration can take care of drawing *everything;* forget about waiting for windows to close or menus to appear, even when you're creating the world's biggest honking spreadsheet or building a presentation the size of Baltimore. As the Chairman of the Board would say, "We're talkin' fast, baby, like a rocket ship to the moon!"

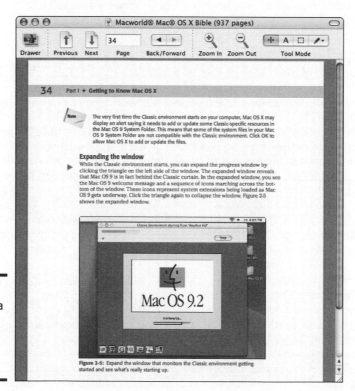

Figure 1-4: Yep, that's a PDF document, not a scanned image!

Stable, stable, stable

"So it's elegant in design. That's great, Mark, but what if Mac OS X crashes? Aqua and Quartz Extreme aren't worth a plug nickel if my mouse doesn't move and I lose my document!" Believe me, I couldn't agree more; I make my living from computers, and every time that a misbehaving program locks up one of my machines, I throw a tantrum that would make Godzilla back off. Lockups shouldn't be tolerated in this day and age . . . and, unfortunately, Mac OS 9 crashed almost as often as Windows 98.

Luckily, the folks who designed Mac OS X were just as interested in producing a rock-solid operating system as they were in designing an attractive look. (Think of Tom Cruise's face on The Rock's body.)

Mac OS X is as hard to crash as the legendary UNIX operating system — that's right, the same reliable workhorse that techno-wizards around the world use to power the Internet, where stability is all-important. In fact, Mac OS X is actually built on top of a UNIX base. It's just well hidden underneath, allowing you and me to focus on our programs and click with a mouse without learning any of those obscure, arcane keyboard commands. You get the benefits of UNIX without a pair of suspenders, a pocket protector, or the hassle of growing a beard. (Not to mention years of computer programming experience.)

Don't forget QuickTime!

If you've recorded or edited digital video (DV), you're probably already familiar with Apple's QuickTime MOV format. QuickTime movies are high-resolution, relatively small in size, and easily created with iMovie HD, which I discuss in Book III, Chapter 4. Although QuickTime isn't "on stage" all the time like Aqua or Quartz Extreme, it's still an important part of Mac OS X: Every time you display a video clip that you've recorded or watch a streaming TV broadcast from a Web site, you use QuickTime. (Note, however, that you don't use QuickTime to watch DVD movies — that job is reserved for the Apple DVD Player.) And hold the phone: Tiger adds support for AVC (Advanced Video Coding) for the best possible display of the latest HD (High Definition) video signals from the expensive hardware that's now appearing at your local electronics Maze o' Wires chain store.

QuickTime is actually not a new Mac OS X feature — it's been around since the days of Mac OS 8 — but the latest versions of Mac OS X includes the free QuickTime Player, which provides support for the latest broadcast and Web video. In fact, you can set up your own TV station on the Web with the tools included in the Professional QuickTime package.

Apple calls this UNIX foundation at the heart of Mac OS X by another nifty title: *Darwin.* I could tell you that Darwin provides the latest in 64-bit memory support and CPU management, but if you're a normal human being, your eyes will glaze over. Suffice it to say that Darwin makes the best use of your computer's memory (RAM) and your computer's brain (CPU). Rest assured that your Web server will stay up even if your misbehaving Virtual Birdcalling simulation decides to run amok. (Emus running amok . . . how dreadful.)

Yes, yet another standard is at work here — uh-oh, Overlord Gates is truly angry now! For those who *do* have a beard and are curious about such things, Darwin uses a FreeBSD kernel, so it also inherits all the protocol standards that have made UNIX the foundation of today's Internet. You can find more about FreeBSD at www.freebsd.org. Because Mac OS X is developed as an open source project, software engineers outside Apple can actually contribute ideas and code, just like UNIX continues to evolve over time. (And yes, you'll even discover how to access the UNIX command prompt from Mac OS X later in Book VII, Chapter 1!)

To get an idea of just how well-armored Mac OS X is, consider Figure 1-5. See how one program, which I call Titanic 1.0, has locked up like San Quentin. Under Mac OS 9, your only chance at recovering anything would involve divine intervention. However, in Mac OS X, my Pages application is unaffected because it has a completely protected area of system memory to play in. *Hint:* I show you how to force a misbehaving application to go away a little later in Book I, Chapter 3.

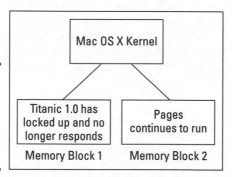

Figure 1-5: Mac OS X keeps applications separate for a reason.

By the way, Darwin makes it easy for UNIX software developers to quickly and easily *port* (or modify) all sorts of UNIX applications to work under Mac OS X. I think that you'll agree that a wider selection of applications is a good thing.

Multitasking and multithreading for normal human beings

And now, for your entertainment, a short one-act play. (Yes, really.)

A Shakespearean Moment of Multitasking and Multithreading

Our play opens with Julius Caesar shaking his head in disgust at his Mac OS 9 Desktop.

> **Caesar:** Anon, I am only one mortal, yet my Desktop doth abound with portals to applications of all different mien. Tell me, foul beast, why thy spirit seems slow and sluggish, and my Excel spreadsheet doth crawl on its belly!

[Enter Romeo, a cocky and rather brash young Apple software developer.]

> **Romeo:** Dude, the problem is, like, your operating system. Y'see, older versions of Mac OS ended up constantly, like, shifting your computer's attention from one app to another — Excel has to cooperate with everything else that's running in the background, like a good little corporate boy. It's less efficient and very, very '90s. Upgrade to Mac OS X, and you get *pre-emptive multitasking* — the app you're actually using, like, gets the lion's share of the processing time, and everything runs smoother when you need it. That's the way UNIX works.

> **Caesar:** Verily, your strange tongue doth annoy me. Guards, behead him — then obtain for me this Mac OS X.

> **Romeo:** I'm outta here — I've got a hot date — but don't forget, like, Mac OS X also uses *multithreaded processing,* so your Mac can handle different operating system tasks at the same time. It's kind of like your computer can both walk and chew gum at the same time: fast, fast, fast!

[Exit Romeo — rather swiftly — stage right.]

Fin

As the play closes, we can only hope that Romeo is fast as well. (I told you it was a short play.)

The definition of Internet-savvy

Remember the classic iMac advertisements that touted the one-plug approach to the Internet? That entire campaign was centered on one idea: that the Internet was *supposed* to be easy to use. The folks at Microsoft sat up and took notice when the iMac proved so incredibly successful, and Windows XP actually reduced some of the overwhelming folderol that you had to encounter just to connect to the Internet — but Mac OS X still wipes the floor with XP when it comes to easy and complete Internet connectivity. For example:

✦ **Easy configuration:** Mac OS X sets up your entire Internet connection with a simple wizard of four screens. As long as you've got the right information handy (which your Internet service provider [ISP] should supply), it's a snap to set up.

✦ **iDisk:** What if I told you that for a reasonable yearly subscription fee, Apple can provide you with a chunk of Internet-accessible, private hard drive space — and that you can access this hard drive space from any-where on Earth with an Internet connection? Absolutely, unbelievably, massively cool. This neat trick is called *iDisk,* and I cover it later in detail in Book IV, Chapter 4.

✦ **All the Internet behind-the-scenes stuff:** The Internet is basically built on a number of *protocols* (read that as *rules for exchanging all sorts of data*) — and, as I mention earlier, UNIX machines dominate the Internet. Ergo, adding Mac OS X to your Macintosh also provides you with support for just about every Internet protocol on the planet. Even if you don't know them by name or write your own software, the applications that you buy can use them.

✦ **A gaggle of great Internet applications:** Mac OS X ships with all sorts of Internet magic built in. For example, there's *Sherlock* — a supercharged search program that also acts as a doorway to information channels, which I discuss in Book I, Chapter 5. You also get instant Internet and local network communication with iChat AV (which I cover in Book IV, Chapter 3), Safari (covered in Book IV, Chapter 5), and Apple Mail, a standard-issue, battle-ready e-mail program (which I discuss in Book IV, Chapter 2). Yup, it's all free.

✦ **And Apache, sweet Apache:** Friends, as a Webmaster myself, I can tell you that I was visibly moved — well, at least *exceptionally* excited — when I learned that Mac OS X included the industry-standard Apache Web server, which runs over half of the sites on the Web! (Yep, that includes `www.apple.com`.) Get all the details in Book VII, Chapter 4.

Lots of free goodies

You don't just get Internet applications when you latch your fingers onto a box o' Mac OS X — you can start doing all sorts of neat stuff without invest-ing one extra dollar in more software!

Remember, what you receive along with Mac OS X depends on whether you're buying a boxed copy, upgrading from an older version of Mac OS, or receiving the Big X already installed on a new Macintosh. With that in mind, check out the possibilities.

✦ **This is the iLife:** This suite of easy-to-use integrated programs is practically as well known as the Macintosh itself these days: iDVD, iPhoto, iTunes, GarageBand, and iMovie HD. Each of these stellar programs is covered in full in Book III. If you've got a digital camera, an MP3 player, a USB musical keyboard, or a DV camcorder, you're going to be a very happy individual. I promise.

✦ **AppleWorks:** If you've bought a new Macintosh with Mac OS X pre-installed, you've also received *AppleWorks* (Apple's answer to Microsoft Office). Good stuff, indeed. If you don't want to spend the bucks on Office 2004 and you don't need the complex gewgaws and baroque architecture of Word and Excel, I can guarantee you that AppleWorks is powerful enough to satisfy your office productivity yearnings.

✦ **The obligatory games:** Apple couldn't have picked two games that are a better match: the finger-exercising arcade challenge of Marble Blast Gold and the immersive 3-D fun of Nanosaur 2. Because this book isn't a game guide, I leave you to explore these two programs at your leisure.

Naturally, there are others that I haven't mentioned here — in fact, bundled programs like Quicken for Mac have entire *For Dummies* books devoted to them — but that gives you a taste of what's included.

It even runs the old stuff

Convinced yet? Before I go, I should mention one more outstanding feature of Mac OS X that will undoubtedly please dyed-in-the-wool Mac users: When properly configured, the Big X can run virtually all software written for older versions of Mac OS 8 and 9! (It's rather like Windows XP running Windows 98 programs without the hassle and the deluge of error messages.) The good folks at Cupertino are sharp enough to ensure that you can run legacy software if necessary. These applications are called *Classic* programs; to run a Classic application, Mac OS X actually launches a virtual Mac OS 9 session.

If you're a new Mac owner, you can promptly forget about this feature — everything that you'll be buying and using from now on will be written for the Big X, and the latest Mac models no longer include Mac OS 9.2. (It's kind of like an appendix.)

What Do 1 Really Need to Run the Big X?

I've written six other *For Dummies* books — I know, it's getting to be a habit (and a career) — and I always find the "Hardware Requirements" section a hard one to write. Why? Well, I know what Apple claims as the minimum hardware requirements necessary to run Mac OS X. But, on the other hand, I know what *I* would consider the minimum hardware requirements, and they're substantially different. Oh, well, let me list the bare bones, and then I'll give you my take on what you really need. (Naturally, if Mac OS X Tiger is already pre-installed on your computer, feel free to tear out this page and create a handful of celebratory confetti.)

From *The World According to Jobs*, the minimum requirements are

✦ **Hardware:** You'll need any Mac with a G3, G4, or G5 processor — except for older Macs without internal FireWire hardware and a DVD drive (these older machines aren't supported in Mac OS X Tiger). Other than those exceptions, this means that just about any iMac, eMac, Mac Mini, iBook, Power Mac G3/G4/G5 is *technically* eligible to play (although you might find the performance of a G3 running Tiger to be unacceptable). I should also mention that Mac OS X doesn't support most third-party CPU upgrade cards out of the box. Again, note that you'll need a DVD drive to install Tiger.

✦ **RAM:** You'll need at least 128MB of memory (RAM). At today's low prices, that's like buying a pizza.

✦ **Hard drive territory:** Although svelte by Windows standards, Mac OS X still needs about 2GB of free space on your hard drive.

From *The World According to Chambers*, the minimum requirements are

✦ **Hardware:** I recommend a Mac with at least a 500 MHz G4 processor. Remember, this is *my* take on what you'll need to really take advantage of Mac OS X Tiger, and again, I have to say that I don't think it performs well enough on older, slower G3 computers. Of course, if your Mac is lucky enough to sport a G5 processor, it can use Mac OS X to run rings around a pokey Pentium 4 PC.

✦ **RAM:** Don't settle for anything less than 512MB. Again, with memory as cheap as it is these days, this is like adding extra cheese to that pizza.

Time for a Mark's Maxim:

Any techno-nerd worth the title will tell you that the *single most important key* to performance in today's operating systems is RAM — yep, it's actually more effective than a faster processor!™

If you've got any extra spending cash in between your sofa cushions, spend it on RAM. (Up to an Earth-shaking 8GB of RAM on the latest Power Mac G5 racehorses!)

✦ **Hard drive territory:** I'd recommend having 4GB free.

Upgrading from Earlier Versions of Mac OS

Because the installation of Mac OS is as simple as loading a DVD and double-clicking an icon, there's not much to tell. What's important is the steps that you should take care of *before* you start the installation. I cover those in the next section. Pay heed, or pay later. I won't go into detail about the actual installation because there really aren't any details to speak of — you'll answer a question or two, and then hop up to get another cup of coffee or another caffeine-laden soda while the installer does the rest. Would anyone expect any different from Apple?

Back up — PLEASE back up

I know you're anxious to join the In crowd, and Apple makes the upgrade process as non-invasive and as safe as possible, but SNAFUs like power loss and hard drive failures do happen. With a full backup of your system on CD or DVD (or even to an external hard drive), you can rest assured that you'll get your precious files and folders back in pristine shape if tragedy strikes. To be honest, you need to back up your system on a regular basis anyway. Promise me now that you'll back up your system, won't you?

I recommend a good commercial back-up program like Retrospect Backup from Dantz Development Corporation (www.dantz.com).

Snuff out disk errors

Before you upgrade, I recommend using the Mac OS 9 Disk First Aid utility one last time — upgrading a disk with errors will take longer. You'll find Disk First Aid in the Utility folder.

On the plus side, Mac OS X comes with its own disk check-up program, called *Disk Utility,* which I cover later in the book in Book I, Chapter 7. Ain't technology grand?

Plug it, Road Warrior

You're on the road with your iBook, and you've just bought your copy of Mac OS X. You're thinking of installing your brand-spanking new operating system. . . . Stop! NOW.

Pet peeve number 1 . . .

The round object that you load into your CD-ROM or DVD-ROM drive is a *disc,* **not** a *disk,* like your hard drive or that flimsy floppy that the Windows horde still uses. Anyone who pretends to talk oh-so-knowingly about a *CD-ROM disk* or *DVD disk* is a dweeb, and you should steer as far away from that dweeb as possible in the future.

Before you decide to upgrade your Mac notebook, consider what will happen if that magical vessel containing all your files should flicker and. . . . No, on second thought, don't even *visualize* it. (Even if the battery is fully charged.) If you're installing a Mac OS X upgrade on a PowerBook or an iBook, make sure that it's plugged in and receiving its share of good, clean AC power from a handy, nearby wall socket. The installation process could take an hour, and there'll be constant hard drive and DVD drive activity — think "Attack of the Energy Draining Installation from Planet Lithium." You **don't** want to try this while your notebook is operating on battery power.

Heck, a techno-purist would probably recommend that you attach your Macintosh to an uninterruptible power supply (UPS) for the installation process, but I'm not quite *that* paranoid about power outages.

Keep one thing in mind while installing Mac OS X: If you format the *destination drive* — the drive where you'll install Mac OS X — you'll lose everything that it stored. No big surprise there, and the installation program will warn you profusely about this beforehand. There's really no reason to do so unless you just crave a *clean* installation (an installation of a new operating system on a newly formatted drive, compared with an upgrade of your existing Mac OS System files). Oh, and don't forget to use Mac OS Extended format.

Personalizing the Big X

After the installation has completed and you've rebooted the beast, stand back and watch those beautiful rounded edges, brushed stainless steel surfaces, and liquid colors appear. But wait — you're not quite done yet! Mac OS X needs to be personalized for you, just like your toothbrush or your SUV's six-way power seat; therefore, use the Setup Wizard that automatically appears the first time that you boot Mac OS X Tiger.

These wizard screens change periodically — and they're completely self-explanatory — so I won't march you through each one step by step. However, here are a few tips that will provide a bit of additional over-the-shoulder help while you're setting things up.

✦ **How rude!** If you're outside the United States or other English-speaking countries, you should know that Mac OS X defaults to US formats and keyboard layouts. Rest assured, though, because Mac OS X does indeed provide full support for other languages and keyboard configurations. To display these options in the list boxes, click the Show All button at the bottom of the wizard screen.

✦ **Accounts are important.** When Mac OS X asks you to create your account, don't forget your password — oh, and they're case-sensitive, too, so *THIS* is different from *this* or *ThiS*. It's a good idea to enter a pass-word hint, but don't make that hint too easy to guess. For example, *My first dog's name* is probably preferable to *Plays Seinfeld on TV*. Mac OS X will use the name and password that you enter to create your account, which you'll use to log in if you set up a multi-user system for several people. (More on this later in Book II, Chapter 4.) *Never* write down your passwords, either; such crib sheets work just as well for others as for you.

✦ **I need to fix that.** You can click the Back button at any time to return to previous wizard screens. Mac OS X, being the bright child that it is, automatically saves your choices for you, so when you click Continue to return, everything is as you left it.

✦ **Extra stuff.** Whether you decide to accept the news, offers, and related-product information from Apple is your decision. However, it's only right that I point out that you can find this same information on the Apple Web site, so there's no need to engorge your e-mail Inbox unless you so desire. (In other words, I turned this off.)

✦ **Local area network (LAN) connections.** If you're connecting your Mac to a Transmission Control Protocol/Internet Protocol (TCP/IP) network (or you're using an Internet router that uses Dynamic Host Configuration Protocol [DHCP]), it's a good idea to click Yes when you're asked whether you should use the configuration supplied by the existing server.

DHCP automatically provides the computers on the network with all the settings that they need to connect. If that sounds like ancient Sumerian, find out more in Book V, Chapter 1.

✦ **Do create your .Mac account!** Apple's .Mac service just plain rocks — especially the iDisk storage that you receive. Again, more on this in Book IV, Chapter 4, but take my word for it. Join up, trooper. (The trial subscription is free, and it's easy to upgrade to a full membership if you decide that you like the .Mac benefits.)

✦ **Have your Mail settings handy.** If you set up your trial .Mac account, you can set up your @mac.com address without any bother — again, this is A Good Thing. However, if you're setting up an existing account, make sure you have all those silly settings and numbers and names that your ISP supplied you with when you signed up. This stuff includes your e-mail address, mail server variety, user account ID, password, and outgoing mail server.

Chapter 2: Navigating and Running Programs

In This Chapter

⮑ Restarting, sleeping, and shutting down Mac OS X

⮑ Using windows

⮑ Using menus

⮑ Recognizing and selecting icons

⮑ Using the keyboard

⮑ Running applications

⮑ Switching between programs

⮑ Opening, saving, and quitting within an application

A s the folks in Cupertino will tell you, "It's all about the graphics." They're right, of course — Mac OS X is a highly visual operating system, and using it without a mouse is like building Hoover Dam with a pocketknife. (And not a particularly sharp pocketknife, either.) Therefore, most of this chapter will require you to firmly grasp the little rodent — I introduce you to little graphical bits like icons and menus, and you discover how to open windows that can display anything from the contents of a document to the contents of your hard drive.

On the other hand, any true Macintosh power user will tell you that the keyboard is still a useful piece of hardware. Because I want you to be a bona fide, well-rounded Mac OS X power user, I also demonstrate those key combinations that can save you time, effort, and possible tennis elbow from all that mouse-wrangling.

Finally, I lead you through the basic training that you'll need to run your programs: how to start them, how to open and save documents, and how to quit an application as gracefully as Fred Astaire on his best day.

Restarting, Sleeping, and Shutting Down

First things first. As the guy on the rocket sled probably yelled, "This is neat, but how do you stop it?" Call 'em The Big Three — Sleep, Restart, and Shut Down are the Mac OS X commands that you use when you need to take care of other business. All three appear on the friendly Apple menu (🍎) at the top-left corner of your Desktop (as shown in friendly Figure 2-1).

Each of these options produces a different reaction from your Mac:

✦ **Sleep:** There's no need for a glass of water or a bedtime story when you put Mac OS X to *Sleep,* which is a power-saving mode that allows you to quickly return to your work later. ("Waking up" from Sleep mode is much faster than booting or restarting your computer, and it can conserve battery power on laptops.) Depending on the settings that you choose in System Preferences — which I discuss in Book II, Chapter 3 — your Mac can power-down the monitor and spin-down the hard drives to save wear and tear on your hardware. You can set Mac OS X to automatically enter Sleep mode after a certain amount of inactivity. To awaken your slumbering supercomputer, just click the mouse or press any key on the keyboard. PowerBook and iBook owners can typically put their laptops to sleep by simply closing the computer, and wake the beast by opening it back up again.

✦ **Restart:** Use Restart if your Mac has suddenly decided to work "outside of the box" and begins acting strangely — for instance, if your Universal Serial Bus (USB) ports suddenly lock up or your FireWire drive no longer responds. Naturally, you'll need to save any work that's open. You also elect to restart Mac OS X when you switch start-up volumes. (Many applications and Apple software updates require a restart after you install them.)

✦ **Shut Down:** When you're ready to return to the humdrum, real world and you're done with your Mac for the time being, use the Shut Down option. Well-behaved Mac applications will automatically prompt you to save any changes that you've made to open documents before the computer actually turns itself off. If you've configured your Mac with multiple accounts, you can shut down Mac OS X from the login screen as well.

**Book I
Chapter 2**

**Navigating and
Running Programs**

Figure 2-1:
Choose your
path from
the Apple
menu.

Besides the Apple menu command, many Macs have a Power key on the keyboard that you can press to display the dialog that you see in Figure 2-2. If you change your mind and decide to tie up loose ends before you leave, click the Cancel button to return to Mac OS X.

Figure 2-2:
Will that be
Restart,
Sleep, or
Shut Down?

Are you sure you want to shut down your computer now?

Restart   Sleep   Cancel   Shut Down

If your Mac has a Drive Open key that you use to load and eject discs (like the new G5 iMacs and G5 Power Macs), you can hold down the Control key and press the Drive Open key to display the same options.

Actually, we're not finished just yet. . . .

I should probably also mention the other guys: the Log Out command (which you can find under the Apple menu) and the User Switch menu (at the right side of the Finder menu).

✔ Choose Log Out when you're running your Mac with multiple users and you want to completely pass control over to another person. All your programs will quit, and the other person can take over by logging in with his/her account. Mac OS X then reconfigures itself with the other user's preferences.

✔ If you've enabled Fast User Switching, another user can log in from the User Switch menu. However, your applications do not quit, you don't have to formally log out, and you can take control back when the other user is finished. (Hence the words *Fast* and *Switching* in the name.) To turn on this feature, display the Accounts panel in System Preferences, click Login Options, and then select the Enable Fast User Switching check box. (More on Fast User Switching appears in Book II, Chapter 4.)

A Window Is Much More Than a Frame

"And in the beginning, there was the window." Like older Mac operating systems, most of what you'll do in Mac OS X occurs within these fancy rectangular frames. And, as you might imagine, a number of controls are at your disposal that you can use to control the size, shape, and appearance of these potent portals. In this section, I'll — well, to be blunt, I'll do windows. (No squeegee jokes, if you please.)

Opening and closing windows

Windows are generally opened automatically. Usually, a window gets opened by an application (when you first run it or it needs to display a document) or by Mac OS X itself (when the Finder opens a window to display the contents of your hard drive). The *Finder,* by the way, is the application that Mac OS X runs to display the operating system's menus and windows.

Some programs even let you open new windows on the fly: For example, Figure 2-3 illustrates a window in its purest form: a new Finder window. To display this window on your own Mac, choose File⇨New Finder Window or press ⌘+N. From here, you can reach any file on your Mac or even venture onto the Internet.

Close button

Figure 2-3:
You're ready
to navigate
with this
Finder
window.

The Command key has both an Apple (🍎) and a rather strange-looking
symbol (⌘) on it that I often call the Spirograph.

When you're finished with a document or you no longer need a window
open, you can close it to free that space on your Desktop. To close a window
in Mac OS X, move your mouse pointer over the Close button; it's the red
circular button at the top-left corner of the window (refer to Figure 2-3). An X
appears on the button when you're in the zone. When the X appears, just
click the mouse.

If you've been living the life of a hermit in a cave for the last decade or so,
pressing the mouse button is called *clicking the mouse.* In the Apple universe, a standard mouse has only one button; if you're using a trackball
or an uber-mouse with a right mouse button, a right click usually acts the
same as holding down the Control key while you click with a standard Apple
mouse.

Most Mac applications don't want you closing a window willy-nilly if you've
changed the contents without saving them. For example, try to close a document window in Word or AppleWorks without saving the file first. The program
will ask you for confirmation before it closes the window containing your
Great American Novel. Most programs also have a Close command on their
File menu.

To close all windows that are displayed by a particular program, hold down the Option key while you click the Close button on one of the windows. Whoosh! They're all gone.

Scrolling windows

Often there's more stuff in a document or more files on your hard drive than you can see in the space available for a window. Guess that means it's time to delete stuff. No, no, *just joking!* You don't have to take such drastic measures to see more in a window.

Just use the scroll bars that you see in Figure 2-4 to move through the contents of the window. You click the scroll bar and drag it — for the uninitiated, that means clicking the bar and holding down the mouse button while you move the mouse in the desired direction. Alternatively, you can click in the empty area above or below the bar to scroll pages one at a time.

Minimize button

Zoom button

Scroll bars

Figure 2-4: You can use the scroll bars to boldly go — well — anywhere in a window.

Depending on the type of application that you're using, you might be able to scroll a window with your arrow keys as well — or perhaps use the Page Up and Page Down keys to move through a window.

Minimizing and restoring windows

The multitalented Figure 2-4 also displays another control that you can use with a window: the Minimize button. When you *minimize* a window, you eliminate it from your Desktop and store it safely in the *Dock* — that strip of icons that appears along the bottom (or the side) of your Mac OS X Desktop. In fact, a minimized window appears as a miniature icon in the Dock, so you can actually keep an eye on it (so to speak). Figure 2-5 illustrates a minimized window from Safari, which is actually displaying my Web site at www.mlcbooks.com. To minimize a window, move your mouse pointer over the yellow Minimize button at the top-left corner of the window — a minus sign appears on the button — and then click.

You're gonna love this "Easter Egg" hidden in Mac OS X — if you hold down the Shift key whilst you minimize, the window shrinks in *cool* slow motion. (Who says operating systems have to be totally serious, anyway?)

When you're ready to display the window again on your Desktop — a process called *restoring* the window — simply click the thumbnail icon representing the window in the Dock, and Mac OS X automagically returns it to its former size and location.

Figure 2-5:
Note the
miniature
Web page in
the Dock —
minimizing
at work.

By the way, some — note that I said *some* — applications continue to run when minimized, while others will simply stop or pause until you return them to the Desktop. Such is the crazy world we live in.

Zooming windows

Zooming windows has a kind of Flash Gordon sound to it, don't you think? It's nothing quite that exciting — no red tights or laser guns — still, when you're trying to view a larger portion of a document, *zooming* is a good thing because it expands the window to the maximum practical size for the application that you're using. In some cases, zooming a window fills the entire screen; at other times, the extra space would be wasted, so Mac OS X zooms the window to the maximum size that shows as much content as possible (without any unnecessary white space). In fact, the Zoom button can even be disabled by an application that doesn't want you to muck about with the window; for example, I own a game or two that don't allow zooming.

To zoom a window, move your mouse pointer over the green Zoom button at the top-left corner of the window. Again, Figure 2-4 struts its stuff and illustrates the position. (Man, that is one versatile figure.) A plus sign appears on the Zoom button. Click to expand your horizons.

After you've finished with a zoomed window, you can return it to its previous dimensions by clicking the Zoom button again.

Toggling toolbars

If you're wondering what that little lozenge-shaped button is at the right corner of many Mac OS X application windows, I won't leave you in suspense: It toggles the display of the window's toolbar on and off. A *toolbar* is a strip of icons that appears across the top of a window that you can click to perform common commands, like changing the display format or printing the current document. (The toolbar in Figure 2-4, for example, features icons to move Back and Forward, among others.) You'll encounter more toolbar technology throughout the book.

Moving windows

Unlike the rather permanent windows in your home, you can pick up a window and cart it to another portion of the Desktop. Typically, this is done when you're using more than one application at a time, and you need to see the contents of multiple windows. To grab a window and make off with it, click the window's *title* bar — the strip at the top of the window that usually bears a document or application name — and drag the window to the new location. Then release the mouse button to plant it firmly in the new location.

By the way, some applications allow you to arrange multiple windows in a graceful swoop with a single click on a menu. Click the Window menu and choose Arrange All to perform this magic.

I talk about Exposé later in the section, "Switching 'Twixt Programs with Aplomb." This cool feature helps you organize a large number of open windows on your Desktop. You can use it to display all open application windows so that you can pick the one you want . . . or even display all the windows opened by a specific application.

Resizing windows

Next, consider how to change the width or height of your window. To change the dimensions of a window to your exact specifications, move your mouse pointer over the lower-right corner of the window (which is usually marked with a number of slashed lines to indicate its status as a control), click, and drag until the window is the size that you prefer.

Switching windows

Before I move to other graphical wonders of Mac OS X, it's important that you master how to switch between windows on your Desktop. First, remember this old Norwegian saying (or is it one of Mark's Maxims?):

> **Only *one* can be active at once.™**

What our Oslo friends are communicating is that only one window can be active at any time. The active window appears on top of other windows, and it's the one that you can edit by typing or by moving your mouse. (It also sports Close, Minimize, and Zoom buttons in color.) Other windows that you have open might be minimized, as I describe earlier in "Minimizing and restoring windows," or they can be inactive (mere ghosts of themselves) and remain on your Desktop. Mac OS X dims inactive windows so that you can tell they're hanging around . . . but you can't use them at the moment. Figure 2-6 illustrates a number of open windows, with the iTunes window active.

I know you're going to get tired of hearing me say this, but here I go again: Certain applications will continue to run while their windows are inactive, like File Transfer Protocol (FTP) clients and such. Most programs, however, stop or pause until you make their window active.

Figure 2-6:
Many are open, but only one is active.

And how do you switch to — *activate* — a different window in Mac OS X? Again, Exposé allows you to activate another window, but if the window is currently visible, you can simply click on any part of that window. I generally click the window's title bar if it's visible, but any part of the inactive window will do. The window that you click leaps like a proud stallion to the fore, and the previously active window now skulks in the background.

You can still use a window's Close, Minimize, and Zoom buttons even when it's inactive.

Menu Mysteries Explained

Next, I move on to menu control in Mac OS X. *Menus* are handy drop-down controls that allow you to select commands that are grouped together logically. For example, an application's File menu will usually allow you to create or open a document, save a document to disk, or quit the program. To pull down a menu, click the desired menu group name on the bar at the top of the screen and then click the desired menu option from the extended menu.

Figure 2-7 illustrates the Safari menu: Note the submenus designated by right-arrow icons. When you move your mouse pointer over a submenu command, you get another set of even more specific menu commands — in this case, the Services submenu command displays commands like Mail and Grab.

Some applications allow you to create your own custom menus; naturally, configuring a new menu system takes some time to learn, but imagine the productivity gains that you'll enjoy! For example, my menus in Microsoft Word 2004 for Mac feature only the commands that I use often — they're sleeker and easier to navigate. (However, you have to stop short of claiming that you wrote the application. And yes, I already checked with Microsoft, which got downright snippy about it.)

Mac OS X also provides another type of menu: contextual. A *contextual menu* appears when you hold down the Control key and click certain items on the screen, revealing commands that relate specifically to that item. (Unfortunately, the items that sport contextual menus vary from application to application, so it's best to check the documentation for a program before you spend countless hours Control-clicking everything onscreen.) The same items in the Control-click menu appear when you select an item and then click the Action drop-down list box, which looks like a mechanical gear.

Figure 2-7: Drilling deeper into Safari's Services menu.

As I mention earlier, many manufacturers sell mice, trackballs, and other pointing things that include a secondary mouse button. This is decidedly a Windows trait — remember, Apple feels that a second mouse button is mere filigree — but if you have one, the device might display contextual menus when you click the secondary button. (This is often called *right-clicking* because the left mouse button is typically the primary button.) Then again, you might launch Aunt Harriet into a geosynchronous orbit, so double-check the manual for your pointing thing on the default button assignment (and how to change it, if necessary).

You'll note that many commands in menus have keyboard shortcuts. Because I'll be holding forth on this subject in the upcoming section, "Keyboard Shortcuts for the True Power User," I'll hold off on describing them here.

Icons 'R Us

Icons are more than little pictures. They're . . . well . . . actually, I guess they are little pictures. However, these graphical WUDs (that's short for *Wonderful User Devices*) are really representations of the components of your Mac OS X system, and therefore they deserve a section of their own.

For complete details on what any icon is, what it represents, and what it will do, click the icon once to highlight it and then press ⌘+I. This displays the Info dialog that you see in Figure 2-8, which tells you what kind of icon it is, where the item it represents is actually located, and how big it is. You'll also see a version number for applications — a handy way of quickly checking what version of a program you're running — and when the file was created and last modified. The Info dialog also offers other settings and options that you can display by clicking in the General drop-down list box, and I cover them in other parts of the book.

Hardware

Mac OS X uses icons to represent the various hardware devices of your computer, including your

✦ Hard drive

✦ CD or DVD drive

✦ Printer

✦ iPod

Figure 2-8:
The complete lowdown on my Apple Backup application.

You get the idea. Just double-click a hardware icon to display the folders and files that it contains, like with your hard drive and CD/DVD drive.

Generally, you'll only encounter hardware icons on your Desktop or in Finder windows. Figure 2-9 illustrates some of the hardware icons that live in my system.

Figure 2-9:
A wealth of different hardware icons.

Programs and applications

These are the fancy icons, folks. Most applications have their own custom icons, and double-clicking one will typically whisk you on your way. Mac OS X also includes a generic icon or two for applications that don't include their own custom icon. Figure 2-10 illustrates a number of my favorite program icons from all sorts of Mac OS X applications.

Running a program in Mac OS X can be as simple as double-clicking the application icon — more on this later in the section, "Houston, We're Go to Launch Programs."

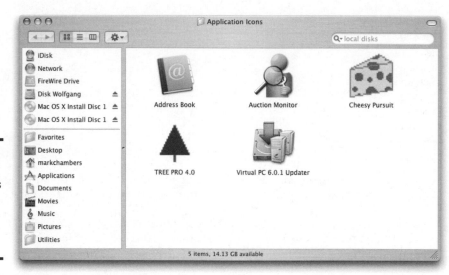

Figure 2-10: Most Tiger applications are represented by custom icons.

Files

Your hard drive will contain many thousands of individual files, and the Big X tries to make it as easy as possible to visually identify which application owns which file. Therefore, most applications use a special icon to indicate their data files. For example, Figure 2-11 illustrates several documents and data files created by a range of applications: Microsoft Word, AppleWorks, QuickTime, Safari, and Adobe Acrobat. Some cheeky applications even use more than one icon to differentiate between different file types, like documents and templates in Microsoft Word.

Figure 2-11:
File icons
generally
give you a
visual clue
about their
origin.

There are also a number of generic file icons that indicate text files, including RTF (short for rich text format) documents and PDF (Portable Document Format) documents, which use the Adobe Acrobat format.

You can open most documents and data files by double-clicking them, which automatically launches the proper application and loads the document.

Folders

Folders have a 3-D look in Mac OS X — and, as you can see in Figure 2-12, some applications even customize their folder icon!

To open a folder within Mac OS X, just double-click it. (Alternatively, you can click it once to select it and then press ⌘+O.) Discover more about how to control the look of folder contents in Book II, Chapter 1.

Figure 2-12:
A selection of different generic and custom folder icons.

Aliases

An *alias* is a strange beast. Although it might look like a standard icon, upon closer examination, you'll notice that an alias icon sports a tiny curved arrow at the base, and the tag `alias` usually appears at the end of the icon name. Figure 2-13 has roped in a variety of aliases for your enjoyment, along with one or two actual icons for comparison.

Essentially, an alias is a link to something else on your system. For example, a Photoshop alias can run Photoshop just like the actual program icon, but it takes up only a scant few bytes on your hard drive. (If you're a Switcher who's just crossed over from the Windows Wilderness, think *shortcut* — Windows shortcuts work in a similar manner.) The alias file is just big enough to hold the location of the actual file or folder, allowing it to yell at Mac OS X: "Hey, the Human actually wants you to run *this* or open *that thing* over there!"

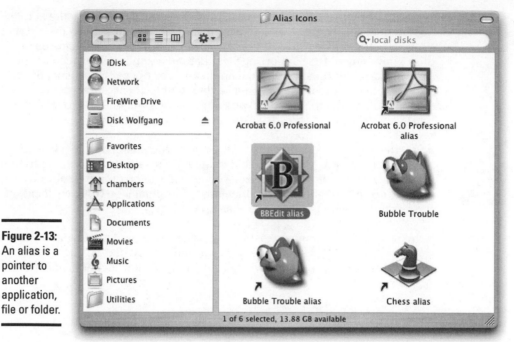

Figure 2-13:
An alias is a
pointer to
another
application,
file or folder.

Aliases come in handy for a number of reasons:

✦ **They allow you to launch applications and open files and folders from anywhere in your system.** For example, you might want an alias icon in your MP3 folder that runs Roxio Toast so that you can launch Toast and burn an audio CD without laboriously navigating to the Roxio folder, which could be nested in goodness-knows-how-many layers of subfolders.

✦ **They can be easily deleted when no longer needed without wreaking havoc on the original application, file, or folder.** If you decide that you'd rather use iTunes to burn audio CDs, you can simply delete the Toast alias without trashing Toast itself.

✦ **Their tiny size allows you to add multiple aliases (and mucho convenience) for a single application without gulping down hard drive space.**

You might be wondering, "Why use aliases when I can just copy the actual application, file, or folder to the desired spot?" Well, indeed you can do that. However, the application might not work in its new location because you didn't copy any of the supporting files that most applications need to run. (An alias actually runs the original application or opens the original file or folder, so things should work just as if you double-clicked the original icon.) Additionally, remember that copying applications willy-nilly throughout your hard drive will eat up territory like a horde of angry Vikings.

If you dislike the alias hanging off the end of the icon name, feel free to rename it (as I show you in the next chapter). The alias will continue to function nicely no matter what moniker you give it. (If you create an alias by holding down ⌘+Option whilst dragging the original icon to a new location, the alias name won't include the alias appendage.)

If the original file no longer exists, an alias naturally no longer works, either. However, Mac OS X is sharp enough to automatically "fix" an alias if you rename or move the original file, pointing it to the new location. *Slick!*

Selecting Icons for Fun and Profit

You'll often find yourself performing different actions on one icon — or a number of icons at one time. For example, you can copy or move files from one location on your hard drive to another or delete a group of files that you no longer need. (The idea of drag-and-drop file management using icons originated on the Macintosh, but I'll wait until the next chapter to describe these operations in detail.) For now, focus on the basics of selecting one or more icons, which specifies which files and folders that you want to use for whatever you're going to do next.

Selecting a single icon

First, here are the various ways that you can select a single icon for an impending action:

✦ **Place your mouse pointer over the file and click once.** Mac OS X darkens the icon to indicate that it's selected — a mysterious process called *highlighting*.

✦ **Type the first few letters of the icon's name.** After you type enough characters to identify the icon uniquely (whether it be one or a dozen), Mac OS X highlights the icon that matches the text string.

✦ **If an icon in a window is already highlighted, you can move the high-light to the next icon across by pressing the right-arrow key.** Likewise, the other three directional arrow keys move the highlight in the other directions. To move through the icons alphabetically, press Tab to go forward and Shift+Tab to go backward.

Selecting multiple icons

To select a gaggle of icons for an action, use one of these methods:

✦ If the icons are next to each other, click and drag within the window (and not directly on a specific item) to highlight them all. While you drag, Mac OS X displays a selection box, and any icons you touch with that box will be highlighted when you release the mouse button (as shown in Figure 2-14). Think "lasso," and you'll get the picture.

✦ You can also select multiple adjacent icons by clicking the first item to highlight it and then holding down the Shift key while clicking the last icon in the series that you want to select.

If the icons are *not* next to each other, you can hold down the ⌘ key while you click each item that you want to select.

Just selecting an icon doesn't launch or do anything . . . you're just marking your territory.

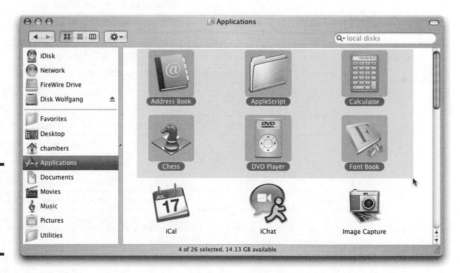

Figure 2-14:
Dragging a
selection
box in
Mac OS X.

Keyboard Shortcuts for the True Power User

Virtually all Mac OS X applications have their own *keyboard shortcuts* — a ten-cent term for a key combination that performs the same operation as a menu command or a toolbar button. Although the mouse might seem the easier path when controlling your Mac, it's not always the fastest. Those hardy souls who venture to learn common keyboard shortcuts can zip through a spreadsheet or warp through a complex outline at speeds that no mere rodent-wrangler could ever hope to attain.

With that in mind — and with the goal of "pumping you up" into a power user — I hereby present the most common keyboard shortcuts for the Big X in Table 2-1. I've also sprinkled other keyboard shortcuts liberally through the book when I discuss other applications, but these combinations are the classics that appear virtually everywhere.

Table 2-1		Common Mac OS X Keyboard Shortcuts
Combination Key	*Location*	*Action*
⌘+A	Edit menu	Selects all (works in the Finder, too)
⌘+C	Edit menu	Copies the highlighted item to the Clipboard
⌘+H	Application menu	Hides the application
⌘+M	Window menu	Minimizes the active window to the Dock (works in the Finder, too)
⌘+O	File menu	Opens an existing document, file, or folder (works in the Finder, too)
⌘+P	File menu	Prints the current document
⌘+Q	Application menu	Exits the application
⌘+V	Edit menu	Pastes the contents of the Clipboard at the current cursor position
⌘+X	Edit menu	Cuts the highlighted item to the Clipboard
⌘+Z	Edit menu	Reverses the effect of the last action you took
⌘+?	Help menu	Displays the Help system (works in the Finder, too)
⌘+Tab	Finder	Switches between open applications
⌘+Option+M	Finder	Minimizes all Finder windows to the Dock
⌘+Option+W	Finder	Closes all Finder windows

By the way, I should mention that many keyboard combinations use three different keys instead of just two. When these shortcuts appear in a menu, they look something akin to Egyptian hieroglyphics, but you need only hold down the first two keys simultaneously and press the third key. Common "strange" key symbols that you'll see in both the Finder and most applications are shown in Table 2-2.

Table 2-2	Arcane Key Symbols	
Action	*Symbol*	
Control	⌘	
Command	⌘	
Del	⌦	
Option	⌥	
Shift	⇧	

Houston, We're Go to Launch Programs

The next stop on your introductory tour of Mac OS X is the launch pad for your applications — although the Finder is useful, you'll likely want to actually do something with your Mac as well.

Running applications from your hard drive

You can launch an application from your hard drive by

✦ Navigating to the corresponding application folder — by either clicking or double-clicking drive and folder icons — and double-clicking the application icon.

✦ Double-clicking a document or data file that's owned by the application. For example, double-clicking an MP3 audio file will run iTunes.

✦ Double-clicking an alias that you've created for the application. (Get the skinny on aliases in the earlier section, "Aliases." I'll wait.)

✦ Clicking the application's icon in the Dock (more on adding items to the Dock in Book II, Chapter 2).

✦ Selecting the application icon and pressing the ⌘+O keyboard shortcut.

✦ Adding the application to your Startup items list. (I cover this in more detail later in Book II, Chapter 3.)

Running applications from a CD-ROM or DVD-ROM

After you load a CD-ROM or DVD-ROM, you can display its contents by double-clicking the disc icon that appears on your Desktop. A Finder window opens and shows the files that reside on the disc (see Figure 2-15).

After you locate the application you want to run on the disc, you can launch it by double-clicking it or selecting it and pressing ⌘+O.

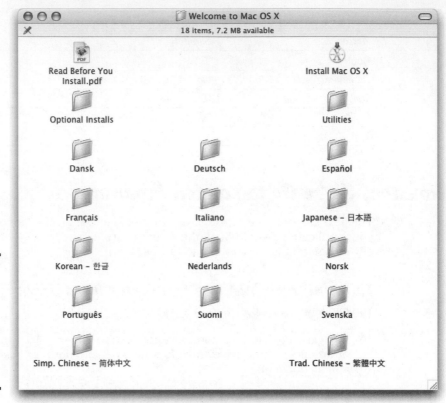

Figure 2-15: The Finder shows the contents of a disc when you double-click the icon.

Switching 'Twixt Programs with Aplomb

You might think that juggling multiple applications will lead to confusion, fatigue, and dry mouth, but luckily Mac OS X makes it easy to jump between programs that are running on your Mac. Use any of these methods to jump from open application to application:

✦ **Press ⌘+Tab.** If you've got a dozen windows open, this can get a bit tedious, which leads us to one of Tiger's sassiest features, brazenly named Exposé and shown in Figure 2-16. (Am I stretching things a bit? You say that technology doesn't compare to the glamour of Hollywood? Then take in a Steve Jobs keynote address at the yearly Macworld convention! The man is a superstar. Poor Bill. . . .)

✦ **Press F9 to show all open application windows using Exposé; then click the one that you want.** Figure 2-16 illustrates the tiled window display on my Mac after I press F9. Your cursor changes into the traditional (and so very elegant) gloved hand. Move the cursor on top of the window that you want to activate — the window turns blue when it's selected — and click once to switch to that window. You can specify which keys you want to use to control Exposé within System Preferences.

✦ **Press F10 to show all open windows from the application that you're currently using; then click the one that you want to activate.** This Exposé function is great for choosing from all the images that you've opened in Photoshop or all the Safari Web pages littering your Desktop!

✦ **Click anywhere in the desired application window to make it the active window.**

✦ **Click the application icon in the Dock.** All applications that are running have an icon in the Dock, and the icon will have an up arrow beneath it to indicate that the application is open.

Along with the window switch, an astute observer will notice that the application menu bar will also change to match the now-active application.

Besides the F9 and F10 hot keys that I just discussed, Exposé provides one more nifty function: Press F11, and all your open windows scurry to the side of the screen, as shown in Figure 2-17. (Much like a herd of zebras if you dropped a lioness in the middle.) Now you can work with drives, files, and aliases on your Desktop — and when you're ready to confront those dozen application windows again, just press F11 a second time.

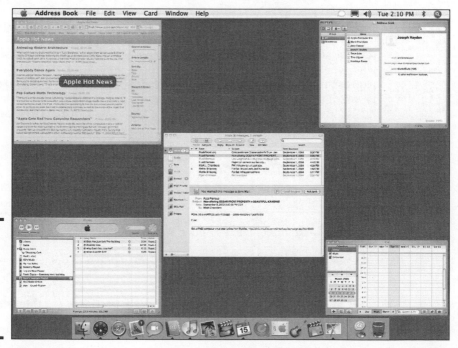

Figure 2-16:
Exotic
Exposé
displays
thumbnails
of all open
windows.

Figure 2-17:
Scat,
windows!
I want my
Desktop.

Opening and Saving Your Stuff in an Application

Almost all Mac OS X applications open and save documents in the same way, whether you're typing a quick letter to your mom with AppleWorks or expressing your artistic side with Painter. Therefore, I'm going to take a moment to outline the common procedures for opening and saving documents. Believe me, you'll perform these two rituals dozens of times a week, so no nodding off.

Opening a document

First, the simple way to load a document: Double-click that document in a Finder window, and . . . well, that's it. (This is my preferred method because I'm an ALT — short for *Admitted Lazy Techno-wizard* — who would rather use complex hand movements to pour myself another Diet Coke.)

To open a document the hard way — from inside an application — here's the plan:

1. **Choose File⇨Open or press that handy ⌘+O key combination.**

Your Mac OS X program is likely to display the attractive Open dialog that you see in Figure 2-18.

2. Navigate to the location of the document that you want to open.

The drop-down list allows you to jump directly to common locations — such as the Desktop, your Home folder, and your iDisk — as well as places that you've recently accessed (Recent Places).

If the target folder isn't in your drop-down list, move the slider at the bottom of the dialog to the far left to display your hard drives, CD-ROM/DVD drives, and network locations.

3. Click the habitat where the file will be found.

You'll note that the right column(s) will change to show you the contents of the item that you just clicked. In this way, you can cruise through successive folders to find that elusive document. (This somewhat time-consuming process is somewhat derisively called *drilling* — hence, the importance of using Recent Items, or dragging files, locations, and applications into the sidebar at the left of the Finder.)

4. When you sight the document that you want to load, either double-click it or click once to highlight the filename and then click Open.

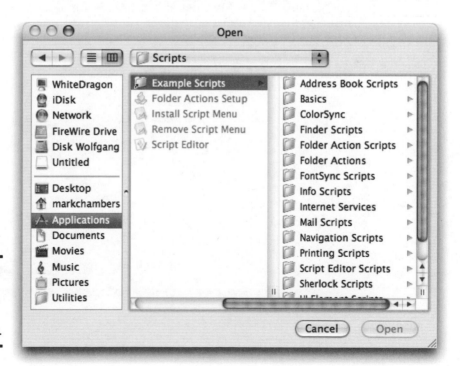

Figure 2-18:
The soon-to-be-quite-familiar Open dialog.

"Hey, the Open dialog can be resized!" That's right, good buddy — you can expand the Open dialog to show more columns and find things more easily. Click and drag the bottom-right corner of the Open dialog to resize it.

Saving a document

To save a document, follow these steps:

1. **Choose File⇨Save.**

   If you've previously saved this document, your application should immediately overwrite the existing document with the new copy, and you get to return to work . . . end of story. If you *haven't* previously saved this document, the program will display a Save dialog that's usually very similar to the Open dialog; it generally has a few more options, however, so stay frosty.

2. **Navigate to the location where you'd like to save the document and then type a filename.**

   Often, you can use a default name that's already provided by the thoughtful folks who developed the software. Note that you might be given the chance to save the document in several different formats. For example, Figure 2-19 illustrates the AppleWorks Save dialog; you can click the File Format drop-down list to choose other formats, such as RTF, HyperText Markup Language (HTML), and even bargain-basement text.

3. **Click Save (or OK, depending on the application).**

Figure 2-19: Saving a work of art in AppleWorks.

If an application offers a Save As menu option in the File menu, you can in effect copy the document by saving a new version of the document under another name. Save As comes in particularly handy when you want to retain the original version of a document.

Quitting Programs

If I had a twisted and warped sense of humor, I'd simply tell you to quit applications by pulling your Mac's power cord from the wall socket. (Luckily, I don't.) There are, however, more sane ways to exit a program — use one of these methods instead:

✦ Press the ⌘+Q keyboard shortcut.

✦ Choose File⇨Quit.

✦ Control-click (or right-click) the application icon on the Dock and click Quit on the pop-up menu that appears.

✦ Click the Close button on the application window. Note, however, that this doesn't always completely close down the application. For example, Safari stays running even if you close the browser window.

Chapter 3: Basic OS X Housekeeping

In This Chapter

✔ Copying, moving, and duplicating files

✔ Deleting and recovering files

✔ Renaming files

✔ Finding specific files

✔ Locking files

✔ Using Apple menu commands

✔ Using Services, the Go menu, and menu icons

✔ Listening to audio discs and recording data discs

✔ Printing within Mac OS X applications

After you master basic Mac spell-casting — things like selecting items, using menus, opening and saving documents, working with windows, and launching an application or two — it's time to delve deeper into Mac OS X. (Can you tell I'm a Dungeons & Dragons old-timer?)

In this chapter, I discuss file management, showing you the hidden power behind the friendly Apple menu. I also discuss some of the more advanced menu commands, how to print within most applications, and how to listen to an audio CD on your Mac. (It makes a doggone good stereo.) Finally, I introduce you to the built-in CD/DVD recording features within the Big X.

The Finder: It's the Wind beneath Your Wings

So what exactly is the Finder anyway? It's a rather nebulous term, but in essence, the *Finder* gives Mac OS X the basic functions that you'll use for the procedures that I outline in this chapter. This UberOS has been around in one guise or another since the days of System 6 — the creaking old days when a Mac was an all-in-one, tote-able computer with a built-in screen. Come to think of it, some things never change.

The Finder is always running, so it's always available — and you can always switch to it, even when several other applications are open and chugging away. Figure 3-1 illustrates the Dock with the rather perspective-crazy Finder icon at the far left side.

Action button

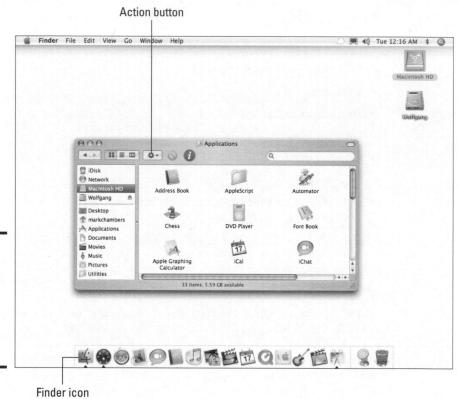

Figure 3-1:
The Finder is always there, supporting you with a unique smile.

Finder icon

Is that icon supposed to be one face or two faces? I'm still confused, and I've been using the Mac now since 1991.

Don't forget that Mac OS X gives you a second method of doing everything I cover in this chapter: You can use Terminal to uncover the UNIX core of Mac OS X, employing your blazing typing speed to take care of things from the command line. Of course, that's not the focus of this book, but for those who want to boldly go where no Mac operating system has ever gone before, you'll find more in Book VII, Chapter 1. Despite what you might have been led to believe, power and amazing speed are to be found in character-based computing.

Copying and Moving Files and Folders

Here's where drag-and-drop makes things about as easy as computing can get:

✦ **To copy a file or folder from one window to another location on the same drive:** Hold down the Option key and click and drag the icon from its current home to the new location. (*Note:* You can drop files and folders on top of other folders, which puts the copy inside that folder.) If you're copying multiple items, select them first (read how in Book I, Chapter 2) and then drag and drop the entire crew.

"Is the Desktop a valid target location for a file or folder?" You're darn tootin'! I recommend, though, that you avoid cluttering up your Desktop with more than a handful of files. Instead, create a folder or two on your Desktop and then store those items within those folders. If you work with the contents of a specific folder often, drag it into the column at the left side of any Finder window, and you can open that folder from the Finder with a single click — no matter where you are! (Alternatively, drag the folder to the Dock and drop it there, and you can open it with a single click from anywhere.)

✦ **To copy items from one window to a location on another drive:** Click and drag the icon from the window to a window displaying the contents of the target drive. Or, in the spirit of drag-and-drop, you can simply drag the items to the drive icon, which places them in the root folder of that drive.

✦ **To move items from one window to another location on the same drive:** Simply drag the icon to the new location, whether it be a window or a folder.

Mac OS X provides you with a number of visual cues to let you know what's being copied or moved. For example, dragging one or more items displays a ghost image of the items, and when you've positioned the mouse pointer over the target, Mac OS X highlights that location to let you know that you're in the zone. If you're moving or copying items into another Finder window, the window border is highlighted to let you know that Mac OS X understands the game plan.

In case you move the wrong thing or you port it to the wrong location, press ⌘+Z to undo the previous action.

If the item that you're dragging already exists in the target location, you get a confirmation dialog like the one you see in Figure 3-2. You can choose to replace the file, leave the existing file alone, or stop the entire shooting match.

Figure 3-2:
To replace,
or not to
replace —
the choice
is yours.

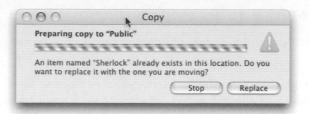

Cloning Your Items — It's Happening Now!

No need for sci-fi equipment or billions in cash — you can create an exact duplicate of any item within the same folder. (This is often handy when you need a simple backup of the same file in the same folder or when you're going to edit a document but you want to keep the original intact.)

Click the item to select it, and then choose Finder➪File➪Duplicate. To distinguish the duplicate from the original, Mac OS X adds the word *copy* to the end of the duplicate's icon name; additional copies have a number added to the name as well.

Alternatively, aficionados of the keyboard can hold down the Option key and drag the original item to another spot in the same window — when you release the button, the duplicate appears.

Heck, if you prefer the Control key, you can hold it down while clicking the item, and then choose Duplicate from the contextual menu that appears. Decisions, decisions. . . .

Oh, and don't forget that Action button (it looks like a little gear with a downward-pointing arrow) on the Finder toolbar (refer to Figure 3-1). You could also click the Action button and choose Duplicate from the drop-down list.

When you duplicate a folder, Mac OS X automatically duplicates all the contents of the folder as well. Remember that this could take some time if the folder contains a large number of small files (or a small number of large files). Groucho would've loved computers!

Deleting That Which Should Not Be

Even Leonardo da Vinci made the occasional design mistake — his trash can was likely full of bunched-up pieces of parchment. Luckily, no trees will be wasted when you decide to toss your unneeded files and folders; this section shows you how to delete items from your system.

By the way, as you'll soon witness for yourself, moving items to the Trash doesn't necessarily mean that they're immediately history.

Dragging unruly files against their will

In Mac OS X, the familiar Macintosh Trash can has been moved to the right edge of the Dock — in fact, it's now a spiffy-looking wire can instead of the old clunker that the Mac faithful remember. You can click and drag the items that you've selected to the Trash and drop them on top of the wire can icon to delete them. When the Trash contains at least one item, the wire can icon changes to appear as if it were full of trash.

You can also add a Delete icon to your Finder toolbar — for all the details, see Book II, Chapter 1.

Deleting with the menus and the keyboard

The mouse isn't absolutely necessary when deleting items. Your other options for scrapping selected files include

✦ Choosing File from the Finder menu and choosing the Move to Trash menu item

✦ Pressing the ⌘+Delete keyboard shortcut

✦ Clicking the Action button on the Finder toolbar and selecting Move to Trash from the drop-down list

✦ Holding down Control while clicking the item to display the contextual menu and then choosing Move to Trash from that menu

Emptying That Wastepaper Basket

As I mention earlier, moving items to the Trash doesn't actually delete them immediately from your system. Believe me, this fail-safe measure comes in handy when you've been banging away at the keyboard for several hours and you stop paying close attention to what you're doing. (I usually also blame lack of Diet Coke.) More on how to rescue files from the Trash in the next section.

Like any folder, you can check the contents of the Trash by clicking the Trash icon in the Dock.

After you double-check the Trash contents and you are indeed absolutely sure you want to delete its contents, use one of the following methods to nuke the digital Bit Bucket:

✦ **Choose Finder from the Finder menu and choose the Empty Trash menu item.**

✦ **Choose Finder from the Finder menu and choose Secure Empty Trash.**

Believe it or not, if you use the standard Empty Trash command, you haven't completely zapped that refuse! Some third-party hard drive repair and recovery programs will allow an uncool person to restore items from the Trash. Use the Secure Empty Trash method for those sensitive files and folders that you want to immediately and irrevocably delete — the data is overwritten with random characters, making it impossible to recover. (A great idea for that Mac you want to sell on eBay, no?)

✦ **Press the ⌘+Shift+Delete keyboard shortcut.**

✦ **Click the Trash icon in the Dock, hold down the mouse button, and choose Empty Trash from the menu that appears.**

✦ **Hold down Control while clicking the Trash icon in the Dock and then choose Empty Trash from the contextual menu that appears.**

Depending on the method that you select and the settings that you choose in System Preferences (which I cover in Book II, Chapter 3), Mac OS X might present you with a confirmation dialog to make sure that you actually want the Trash emptied.

WAIT! I Need That After All!

In the adrenaline-inducing event that you need to rescue something that shouldn't have ended up in the scrap pile, first click the Trash icon in the Dock to display the contents of the Trash. Then rescue the items that you want to save by dragging them to the Desktop or a folder on your hard drive. (This is roughly analogous to rescuing your old baseball glove from the family garage sale.)

Feel free to gloat — if someone else is nearby, ask her to pat you on the back and call you a lifesaver.

Renaming Your Items

You wouldn't get far in today's spacious virtual world without being able to change a moniker for a file or folder. To rename an item in Mac OS X, use one of these two methods:

✦ **With the mouse:** Click once on an icon's name (or just press Return). Mac OS X highlights the text in an edit box — type the new name and then press Return when you're done.

You want to wait a few seconds between clicks, as opposed to a rapid-fire double-click.

✦ **From the Info dialog:** Select the item and press ⌘+I to display the Info dialog; then click the triangle next to Name & Extension. Click in the name field, drag the mouse to highlight the text that you want to change, and type the replacement text.

Naturally, the first method is the easiest, and it's the one that I use most often.

Adding a Dash of Color

Tiger also provides the ability to *color-code* files and folders to help you organize and recognize your data in a hurry. For example, why not assign the green label color to the files and folders that make up your current project? Or, if you need to mark a file for immediate attention, assign it the red label color.

To assign a label color to selected files and folders, you have three options:

✦ Click the Action button on the Finder toolbar and then click the desired color.

✦ Hold down Control while you click on the selection and then choose the color from the pop-up menu.

✦ Click File and choose that perfect shade from the menu.

Displaying the Facts on Files and Folders

The Finder's Info dialog is the place to view the specifics on any highlighted item (including drives and aliases). Select an item and press ⌘+I, click the Action toolbar button and select Get Info from the list, or choose the Finder's File menu and then choose Get Info (see the results in Figure 3-3). If you select more than one item, the Info dialog combines as many properties as possible to give you a summary.

Mac OS X displays the General information panel when you first open the Info dialog, but other panels are usually available (depending on the type of selected items). To display the other panels, click the panel that you want to see.

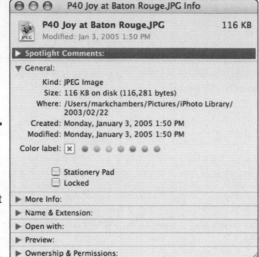

Figure 3-3:
The General
Information
panel
appears first
when you
display the
Info dialog.

For most types of files and folders, the Info dialog can tell you

✦ **Kind:** What type of item it is — for example, whether it's a file, folder, drive, or alias — and what program automatically launches when you open the selected item

✦ **Size:** The total size of the item (or items) that you select

✦ **Where:** The actual path on your hard drive where the item is located

✦ **Dates:** The date when the item was created and was last modified

✦ **Version:** The application version number

✦ **Permission:** The privileges that control who can do what to the file — more on this later in Book II, Chapter 6 — and whether a file is locked in read-only mode

Some of this information you can change, and some can only be displayed. To banish the Info dialog from your Desktop, click the dialog's Close button.

For the rest of this section, I describe a number of tasks that you can accomplish from the Info dialog.

If you use a specific document over and over as a basis for different revisions, you can enable the Stationery Pad check box on the General information panel to use the file as stationery. Opening a stationery file automatically creates a new, untitled version of the file in the linked application; this can save you steps compared with duplicating the file or using the Save As procedure that I show you in Book I, Chapter 2.

Adding comments

Mac OS X provides you with a comment field where you can add additional text that's stored along with the file (and can be matched with Spotlight). I use this feature to record the version number of manuscript chapters and programs that I create during the course of writing books.

To add a comment, follow these steps:

1. **Display the Info dialog for the item by pressing ⌘+I or choosing File⇨ Get Info.**

2. **Click in the Spotlight Comments box and type the comment text.**

   If you need to expand the Spotlight Comments section of the Info dialog, click the triangle next to the Spotlight Comments heading. The arrow rotates and the Spotlight Comments box appears.

3. **Close the Info dialog to save the comment.**

Displaying extensions

Extensions are alien creatures to most Mac owners. However, these three- or four-character add-ons that follow a period at the end of a filename have been a mainstay in the DOS, Windows, and UNIX environments for years. An extension identifies what program owns a specific file, and therefore which application launches automatically when you double-click that file's icon. Examples of common extensions (and the applications that own them) include

- ✦ .pdf: Adobe Acrobat
- ✦ .doc: Microsoft Word
- ✦ .pages: Apple Pages
- ✦ .key: Apple Keynote
- ✦ .psd: Adobe Photoshop
- ✦ .jpeg or .jpg: Preview, or your image editor
- ✦ .tiff or .tif: Preview, or your image editor
- ✦ .htm or .html: Safari, or your Web browser of choice

Why would someone want to see a file's extension? It comes in handy when a number of different types of files are linked to the same application. For example, if you install Adobe Photoshop, both JPEG and TIFF images have the same icon, so you can't tell one from the other. With extensions displayed, it's easy to tell what type of file you're looking at.

Follow this procedure to hide or display extensions with your filenames:

1. **Display the Info dialog for the item by pressing ⌘+I or choosing File⇨ Get Info.**

2. **If you need to expand the Name & Extension section of the Info dialog, click the triangle next to the Name & Extension heading.**

3. **To display the extension for the selected file, clear the Hide Extension check box to disable it.**

4. **Close the Info dialog to save your changes.**

Choosing the application to launch with a file

So what's the plan if the wrong application launches when you double-click a file? Not a problem: You can also change the linked application from the Info dialog as well. (I told you this was a handy toy box, didn't I?) Follow these steps to choose another application to pair with a selected file:

1. **Click the Action button on the Finder toolbar and click Show Info to display the Info dialog for the item.**

2. **Click the triangle next to the Open With heading to expand it.**

3. **Click the drop-down list button, and Mac OS X displays the applications that it feels are best suited to open this type of document.**

4. **Select the application that should open the file.**

To go completely hog-wild and choose a different application, select Other from the drop-down list. Mac OS X opens a Choose Other Application dialog where you can navigate to and select the application you want. (If the application is not recognized as *recommended*, click the Enable list box and choose All Applications.) After you highlight the application, click Add.

5. **To globally update all the documents of the same type to launch the application that you chose, click the Change All button.**

Mac OS X displays a confirmation dialog asking whether you're sure about making this drastic change. Click Continue to update the other files of the same type or click Cancel to return to the Info dialog.

6. **Close the Info dialog to save your changes.**

Locking files against evildoers

"Holy Item Insurance, Batman!" That's right, Boy Wonder: Before I leave the friendly land of the Info dialog, every Mac owner needs to learn how to protect files and folders from accidental deletion or editing. By locking a file, you allow it to be opened and copied — but not changed, renamed, or sent to the Trash. Locked items appear in the Finder with a small padlock attached to the icon.

To lock or unlock a file, you have to have ownership of the file. I cover privileges in Book II, but on a Mac where you've configured only one administrator account, you should already have ownership. Follow this procedure:

1. **Display the Info dialog for the item.**

2. **Select the Locked check box to enable it.**

The Locked check box is in the General section of the dialog.

3. **Close the Info dialog to save your changes.**

Creating an Alias

I mention aliases in Book I, Chapter 2. As I discuss in that chapter, an *alias* acts as a link to an application or document that actually exists elsewhere on your system (a handy trick to use when organizing items on your hard drive). You have a number of different ways to conjure an alias after you select an item:

✦ Choose File from the Finder menu and choose the Make Alias menu item. (You have to move the alias yourself.)

✦ Press the ⌘+L keyboard shortcut. (Again, you have to move the new alias to its new location.)

✦ Click the Action button on the Finder toolbar and then click Make Alias.

✦ Hold down Control while clicking the selected item and then choose Make Alias from the contextual menu that appears.

In addition, you can hold down the ⌘+Option key combination and drag the item to the location where you want the alias.

Although Mac OS X does a great job in tracking the movements of an original and updating an alias, some actions can break the link. For example, if you delete the original, the alias is left wandering in search of a home. However, all is not lost — when you double-click a broken alias, Mac OS X offers to help you fix the alias. This involves browsing through your system to locate a new original.

Using the Apple Menu

The Apple menu is a familiar sight to any Mac owner. Although Apple contemplated removing it during the original development and beta cycle for Mac OS X version 10.0, the ruckus and cry from beta-testers ensured that it remains today. It's amazing how reassuring that little fellow can be when you boot the Big X for the first time.

In this section, I cover the important things that are parked under the Apple menu.

Using Recent Items

If you're like most of us — and I think I'm safe in assuming that you are — you tend to work on the same set of applications and files (and use the same network servers) during the day. Normally, this would be somewhat of a pain because each time you sit down in front of the keyboard, you have to drill down through at least one layer of folders to actually reach the stuff that you need. To make things easier on yourself, you could create a set of aliases on your Desktop that link to those servers, files, and applications . . . but as you move from project to project, you'd find yourself constantly updating the aliases. As Blackbeard the Pirate was wont to exclaim, "Arrgh!"

Ah, but Mac OS X is a right-smart operating system, and several years ago Apple created the Recent Items menu to save you the trouble of drilling for applications and files (and, with the arrival of Tiger, network servers as well). Figure 3-4 illustrates the Recent Items menu from my system. Note that the menu is thoughtfully divided into Applications, Documents, and Servers. When you open documents or launch applications, they're added to the list. (Accountants will revel in this First In, First Out technology.) To launch an application or document from the Recent Items menu — or connect to a network server — just click it.

To wipe the contents of the Recent Items menu — for example, if you've just finished a project, and you want to turn over a new digital leaf — click Recent Items and choose the Clear Menu item.

You can specify the number of recent items that will appear in the menu from System Preferences; display the Appearance icon and click the Applications, Documents, and Servers list boxes in the Number of Recent Items field. (More on this in Book II, Chapter 3.)

Also, remember the trick that I mention earlier: You can drag any folder or server into the Sidebar column at the left of the Finder window, adding it to that exclusive club that includes your Home folder, Applications folder, and media folders.

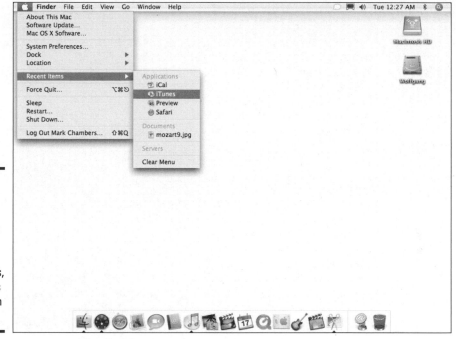

Figure 3-4:
Use the
Recent
Items menu
to access
files,
applications,
and servers
you've been
using.

Playing with the Dock

You know how Air Force One acts as the mobile nerve center for the president? And how The Chief can jet all around the world and take all his stuff along with him? Well, the Dock is kind of like that. Sort of.

If you want your Dock to go mobile as well, click the Apple menu and choose the Dock item to display the submenu. Here's a rundown of the options that you'll find:

✦ **Magnification:** Click Turn Magnification On/Off to toggle icon magnification when your pointer is selecting an icon from the Dock. With magnification on, the icons in the Dock get really, *really* big . . . a good thing for Mr. Magoo or those with grandiose schemes to take over the world. Check out the rather oversized icons in Figure 3-5. (The amount of magnification can be controlled from the System Preferences Dock settings, which I explain in Book II, Chapter 3.)

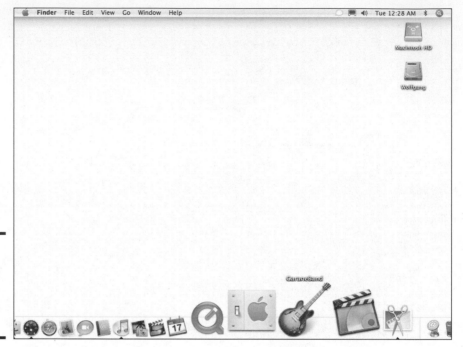

Figure 3-5:
Now those, my friend, are some pumped-up icons.

✦ **Hiding:** Click Turn Hiding On/Off to toggle the automatic hiding of the Dock. With hiding on, the Dock disappears off the edge of the screen until you move the mouse pointer to that edge. (This is great for those who want to make use of as much Desktop territory as possible for their applications.)

You can press ⌘+Option+D to toggle Dock hiding on and off from the keyboard.

✦ **Position:** Click one of three choices (Position on Left, Bottom, or Right) to make the Dock appear on the left, bottom, or right of the screen, respectively.

✦ **Dock Preferences:** Click this to display the System Preferences Dock settings, which I explain in Book II, Chapter 3.

Bad program! Quit!

Once in a while, you're going to encounter a stubborn application that locks up, slows to a crawl, or gets stuck in an endless loop — although Mac OS X is a highly advanced operating system, it can still fall prey to bad programming or corrupted data.

Luckily, you can easily shut these troublemakers down from the Apple menu. Just choose Force Quit to display the Force Quit Applications dialog that you see in Figure 3-6. (Keyboard types can press ⌘+Option+Esc.) Select the application that you want to banish and then click the Force Quit button; Mac OS X requests confirmation, after which you click the Force Quit button again.

Figure 3-6:
Forcing an
application
to take a
hike.

If you select Finder in the Force Quit Applications dialog, the button changes to Relaunch. This allows you to restart the Finder, which comes in handy if your system appears to be unstable. (This is much faster than actually restarting your Mac.)

Forcing an application to quit will also quit any open documents that you were working with in that application, so *save your work* (if the program will allow you to save anything). If you relaunch the Finder, some programs might restart as well.

Tracking down your version

This isn't a big deal, but if you choose About This Mac from the Apple menu, Mac OS X displays the About This Mac dialog that you see in Figure 3-7. In case you need to check the amount of memory or the processor in an unfamiliar Mac, the About This Mac dialog can display these facts in a twinkling. However, I primarily use it to check on the Mac OS X version and build number as well as to launch the Apple System Profiler (which I discuss in full in Chapter 7 of this mini-book). Click the More Info button to launch the Profiler.

Figure 3-7:
Display your
Mac's
memory,
processor,
and Big X
version.

Apple includes a button that launches Software Update to both the About
This Mac dialog and the Apple menu . . . sheesh, they must really want you
to keep your Big X up to date, I guess.

Specifying a location

Mac OS X allows you to create multiple network locations — think of a location as a separate configuration that you use when you connect to a different
network from a different locale. For instance, if you travel to a branch office,
you'd assign a location for your desk and a location for the remote branch. A
student might assign one location for her home network and another for the
college computer lab network.

A location saves all the specific values that you've entered in the System
Preferences Network settings, including IP address, AppleTalk Zones, proxy
servers, and the like. If all this means diddly squat to you, don't worry — I
explain this in Book V, Chapter 1. For now, just remember that you can
switch between locations by choosing Location from the Apple menu, which
displays a submenu of locations that you can choose from.

Availing Yourself of Mac OS X Services

In Mac OS X, Services allow you to merge information from one application
with another. To Mac old-timers, that might sound suspiciously like the
Clipboard; however, services can also include functionality from an application, so you can create new documents or complete tasks without running
another program! Services can be used in both the Finder and Mac OS X
applications.

To illustrate, here's a fun example:

1. **Launch TextEdit (you'll find it in your Applications folder) and type these words:** Hello from your Macintosh!

2. **Highlight those words.**

3. **Click the TextEdit menu — don't switch to the Finder, use the TextEdit Application menu — and choose Services.**

4. **From the Services submenu, choose Speech and then choose Start Speaking Text.**

After you've chuckled a bit at your Mac's accent, consider what you just did — you ran the Speech application from within TextEdit, using the selected words! Pretty slick, eh?

A glance at the other Services that show up from within most applications gives you an idea of just how convenient and powerful Mac OS X Services can be — I often use Services to take care of things like

✦ **Sending an e-mail message** from an e-mail address in a text file, AppleScript document, or the Address Book (via the Mail Service)

✦ **Capturing a screen snapshot** within an application (using the Grab Service)

✦ **Sending a file to a Bluetooth-equipped PDA or cell phone** within an application (using the Send File to Bluetooth Device service)

Remember, you can access the Services menu from a Mac OS X application by picking that program's Application menu (sometimes called the *named menu*). For instance, in the demonstration earlier, I use the TextEdit menu that appears on the TextEdit menu bar. In Microsoft Word, I would click the Word menu.

Geez, I think the computing world needs another word for menu — don't you?

Many third-party applications that you install under Mac OS X can add their own commands under the Services menu, so be sure to read the documentation for a new application to see what Service functionality it adds.

Get Thee Hence: Using the Go Menu

Remember the transporter from *Star Trek*? Step on the little platform, assume a brave pose, and whoosh! — you're transported instantaneously to another ship or (more likely) to a badly designed planet exterior built inside a soundstage. Talk about convenience . . . that is, as long as the doggone thing didn't malfunction.

The Finder's Go menu gives you the chance to play Captain Kirk: You can jump immediately to specific spots, both within the confines of your own system as well as external environments like your network or the Internet. (You can leave your phaser and tricorder in your cabin.)

The destinations that you can travel to using the Go menu and the iDisk submenu include the following:

✦ **Back/Forward/Enclosing Folder:** I lump these three commands together because they're all basic navigation commands. For example, Back and Forward operate just like they do in Safari or your favorite Web browser. If you're currently inside a folder, you can return to the parent folder by clicking Enclosing Folder.

✦ **Computer:** This window includes your hard drives, CD and DVD drives, and your network — the same places that appear when you open a new Finder window with the ⌘+N key shortcut.

✦ **Home:** This window displays the home directory for the user currently logged in.

✦ **Network:** Did you guess this displays a window with all of your network connections? Dead giveaway, that.

✦ **iDisk:** This window displays the contents of your Internet iDisk storage (or someone else's). (More on the coolness that is iDisk in Book IV, Chapter 4.)

✦ **Applications:** This window includes all the applications that appear in your Mac OS X Applications folder (a neat *Just the programs, ma'am* arrangement that really comes in handy).

✦ **Utilities:** This window displays all the utilities in your Mac OS X Utilities folder.

✦ **Recent Folders:** This window displays a submenu that allows you to choose from the folders that you've recently opened.

You can also type the path for a specific folder (use the Go to Folder command) or connect to a specific network server (use the Connect to Server command).

Note that most of the Go menu commands include keyboard shortcuts, proving once again that the fingers are quicker than the mouse.

Monkeying with the Menu Bar

Ever stared at a menu bar for inspiration? Fortunately for Mac owners like you and me, people in Cupertino are paid to do just that, and these designers get the big bucks to make the Mac OS X menu bar the best that it can be.

Thus were born menu bar icons, which add useful controls in what would otherwise be a wasted expanse of white.

Using menu bar icons

Depending on your hardware, Mac OS X might install several menu bar icons. The Volume icon is always there by default, along with the Clock display, which is actually an icon in disguise. Figure 3-8 illustrates these standard icons, along with a couple of others.

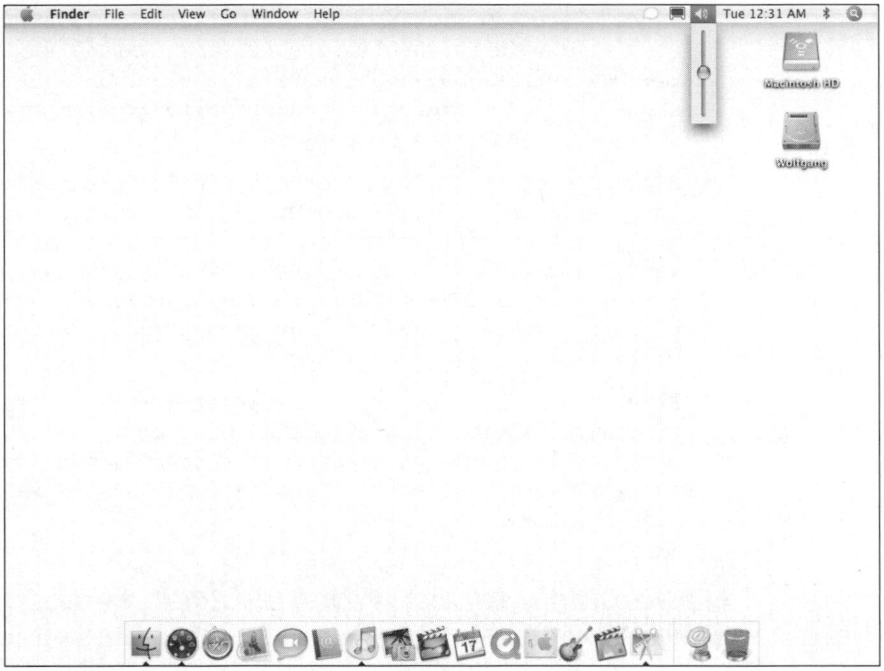

Figure 3-8: Adjust your Mac with a click of these menu icons.

Some icons won't appear unless you turn them on. For instance, the Displays icon won't appear unless you enable the Show Displays in Menu Bar check box within the Displays pane in System Preferences. The Displays menu bar icon, which looks like a monitor, allows you to choose from the recommended resolutions and color depth settings for your graphics card and monitor. For example, the recommended settings for my G5 iMac, which has an LCD monitor, includes 800 x 600, 1024 x 768, or 1680 x 1050 resolutions, and my display can be set to thousands or millions of colors. Typically, it's a good idea to choose the highest resolution and the highest color depth. You can also jump directly to the System Preferences Display settings by clicking Displays Preferences.

To quickly change the audio volume level within Mac OS X, click the Volume icon (it looks like a speaker with emanating sound waves) once to display its slider control; then click and drag the slider to adjust the level up or down. After you select a level by releasing the mouse button, your Mac thoughtfully plays the default system sound to help you gauge the new volume level.

Depending on the functionality that you're using with Mac OS X, these other menu bar icons might also appear:

✦ **Modem status:** You can turn on the display of the Modem status icon from the Internal Modem panel of the Internet Connect application, which I discuss in Book IV, Chapter 1. Click this icon to connect to or disconnect from the Internet by using a modem. You can open the Internet Connect application from the menu bar icon, and the icon can be set to show the time that you've been connected to the Internet as well as the status of the connection procedure.

✦ **AirPort:** If you've installed an AirPort or AirPort Extreme card in your Mac, you can check the status of the AirPort connection; click the AirPort icon to toggle AirPort on or off. The icon displays the relative strength of your AirPort signal, whether you're connected to a Base Station or a peer-to-peer computer network, or whether AirPort is turned off. You can also switch between multiple AirPort networks from the menu.

✦ **PPoE:** The display of this icon is controlled from the Ethernet panel of the Internet Connect application. Click this icon to connect to or disconnect from the Internet using *Point-to-Point over Ethernet* (PPoE), which is a type of Internet connection offered by some digital subscriber line (DSL) providers.

Doing timely things with the Clock

Even the Clock itself isn't static eye candy on the Mac OS X menu bar — I told you this was a hardworking operating system, didn't I? Click the Clock display to toggle the icon between the default text display and a miniature analog clock.

You can also open the System Preferences Date & Time settings from the icon. From within the Date & Time settings, you can choose whether the seconds or day of the week are included, whether the separators should flash, or whether Mac OS X should display the time in 24-hour (military) format. More on this in Book II, Chapter 3.

Mark's totally unnecessary Computer Trivia 1.0

"Where the heck did *mounting* come from, anyway? Sounds like a line from a John Wayne Western!" Well, pardner, the term dates back to the heyday of Big Iron — the Mainframe Age, when giant IBM dinosaurs populated the computing world. Sherman, set the WayBack Machine. . . .

At the time, disks were big, heavy, removable cartridges the diameter of dinner plates (and about as tall as a 100-count spindle of CD-Rs). The acolytes of the mainframe, called computer *operators*, would have to trudge over to a cabinet and swap disk cartridges whenever the program stopped and asked for them — that's right, those mainframes would actually stop calculating and print, "I need you to mount cartridge 12-A-34, or I can't go any further. Have a nice day." (Can you imagine what it would be like loading and unloading a hard drive every time you needed to open a folder?)

Anyway, even though eons passed and minicomputers appeared — which were only the size of a washing machine — the terms *mounting* and *unmounting* still commonly appeared in programs. This time, the removable volumes were 8-inch floppy disks and tape cartridges. Because UNIX and its offspring Linux date from the Minicomputer Age, these operating systems still use the terms.

Eject, Tex, Eject!

Mac OS X makes use of both static volumes (your Mac's hard drive, which remains mummified inside your computer's case) and removable volumes (like USB Flash drives and CDs/DVD-ROMs). Mac OS X calls the process of loading and unloading a removable volume by old-fashioned terms — *mounting* and *unmounting* — but you and I call the procedure *loading* and *ejecting*.

I won't discuss loading/mounting a removable volume — the process differs depending on the computer because some Macs need a button pushed on the keyboard, others have buttons on the drive itself, and some drives have just a slot, with no button at all. However, there are a number of standard ways of unloading/unmounting/ejecting a removable volume:

✦ **Drag the Volume icon from the Desktop to the Trash,** which changes to an Eject icon to help underline the fact that you are *not* deleting the contents of the drive. Let me underline that with a Mark's Maxim because Switchers from the Windows world are usually **scared to death** by the concept of dragging a volume to the Trash.

 Have no fear — in the Apple universe, you *can* drag removable volumes to the Trash with aplomb.™

✦ **Click the Volume icon and use the ⌘+E keyboard shortcut.**

✦ **Click the File menu and choose Eject.**

✦ **Click the Eject button next to the device in the Finder window sidebar.**

✦ **Hold down Control and click the Volume icon to display the contextual menu; then choose Eject.**

✦ **Press your keyboard Eject key (if it has one) to eject a CD or DVD from your built-in optical drive. (If you're using a keyboard without a Media Eject key, press F12 instead.)**

You can't unmount a static volume from the Desktop — you have to use the Disk Utility application — so your internal hard drive icon will stay where it is.

Common Tasks Aplenty

Okay, I admit it — this section is kind of a grab bag of three very common tasks. However, I want to walk you through these three procedures early in the book. Most Mac owners will want to listen to and record CDs as soon as Mac OS X is installed, and you'd be amazed how much information still flows across the Internet in plain, simple text.

Therefore, hang around and take care of business.

Opening and editing text files

Text files would seem to be another anachronism in this age of formatted Web pages, rich text format (RTF) documents, and word processors galore. However, virtually every computer ever built can read and write in standard text, so text files are often used for

✦ **Information files** on the Internet, like FAQs (Frequently Asked Question files)

✦ **README and update** information by software developers

✦ **Swapping data** between programs, like comma-delimited database files

Here's the quick skinny on opening, editing, and saving an existing text file:

1. **Navigate to your Applications folder and launch TextEdit.**

2. **Press ⌘+O to display the Open dialog.**

3. **Navigate to the desired text file and double-click the filename to load it.**

You can also open an existing text file by dragging its icon from the Finder window to the TextEdit icon.

4. **Click the insertion cursor anywhere in the file and begin typing. Or, to edit existing text, drag the insertion cursor across the characters to highlight them and type the replacement text.**

   TextEdit automatically replaces the existing characters with those that you type. To simply delete text, highlight the characters and press Delete.

5. **After you finish editing the document, you can overwrite the original by pressing ⌘+S (which is the same as choosing File⇨Save), or you can save a new version by choosing File⇨Save As and typing a new, unique filename.**

6. **To exit TextEdit, press ⌘+Q.**

Listening to an audio CD

By default, Mac OS X uses iTunes to play an audio CD. Although I cover iTunes in complete detail in Book III, Chapter 2, take a moment to see how to master the common task of playing an audio CD (just in case you want to jam while reading these early chapters). Follow these steps:

1. **Load the audio CD into your Mac's CD-ROM/DVD-ROM drive.**

   An Audio CD volume icon appears on your Desktop.

2. **Mac OS X automatically loads iTunes and displays its spiffy window.**

3. **Click the Play button at the upper left of the iTunes window to begin playing the disc at the beginning. To play an individual track, double-click the track name in the iTunes window.**

4. **To adjust the volume from within iTunes, drag the Volume slider to the left or right — it's under the Play button.**

5. **To eject the disc and load another audio CD, click the Eject CD button at the lower-right of the iTunes window.**

6. **To exit iTunes, press ⌘+Q.**

The first time that you run iTunes, you're asked to configure the program and specify whether Mac OS X should automatically connect to the Internet to download the track titles for the disc you've loaded. I recommend that you accept all the default settings and that you allow automatic connection. Is simple, no?

Recording — nay, burning — a data CD

Mac OS X offers a built-in CD recording feature that allows you to burn the simplest form of CD: a standard data CD-ROM that can hold up to approximately 660MB of files and folders, and can be read on both Macs and PCs running Windows, UNIX, and Linux. (To burn an audio CD, use iTunes, as I show you in Book III, Chapter 2.). Naturally, you'll need a Mac with a CD or DVD recorder.

Adding the perfect font with Font Book

Need to install a font in Mac OS X, or perhaps you'd like to organize your fonts into collections based on their theme or their designer? If so, you're talking about *Font Book,* which is the font organizer that ships with Tiger. To open Font Book, visit your Applications folder and double-click the Font Book icon.

Press ⌘+O (or choose File⇨Add Fonts) to import a new font into your system, or simply drag the font file from a Finder window into the Font Book window. **Remember:** Tiger can accept both TrueType and OpenType PostScript fonts. When it's been added, your new font can be categorized by dragging it into one of your *collections,* thus making that font easier to locate and display. Individual fonts and entire collections can be enabled or disabled (by using the plus and Disable buttons at the bottom of the Font Book window), so that you can "turn on" only those fonts that you need for a specific application or project. The Font Book window also comes fully equipped with a Search box, so you can find any font by name.

If you're interested in recording all the exotic CD and DVD formats available today, I can heartily recommend the best book on CD and DVD recording on the shelves: *CD & DVD Recording For Dummies,* 2nd Edition, written by (surprise!) yours truly (Wiley). *CD & DVD Recording For Dummies* is a comprehensive recording guide that shows you how to burn all types of audio, data, and video by using the latest PC and Mac hardware and the best software on the planet (Roxio Easy Media Creator for the PC and both iDVD and Toast for the Mac). I can honestly say that it's a good read.

Back to the story! To record a disc, follow these steps:

1. **Load a blank CD-R, DVD-R, or CD-RW into your drive.**

We'll assume for this demonstration that you're using a write-once CD-R. Mac OS X displays an Untitled CD volume icon on your Desktop. (It's marked with the letters CDR so you know that the disc is recordable.) You'll be prompted for permission to open it.

2. **Double-click the Untitled CD icon to display the contents — it'll be empty, naturally.**

The window tells you that you have 660.7MB of space remaining on the disc.

3. **Click and drag files and folders to the CD window as you normally do.**

4. **Rename any files or folders as necessary — remember, after you've started recording, this stuff is etched in stone, so your disc window should look just like the volume window should look on the finished CD-ROM.**

5. **Click File on the Finder menu and choose Burn CD.**

6. **The Big X displays a confirmation dialog. If you've forgotten something, you can click the Cancel or Eject button.**

Otherwise, click the Burn button and sit back and watch the fun.

Unfortunately, Mac OS X doesn't support recording from the Finder for many of the external and third-party drives available for the Macintosh. If you can't burn from the Finder, I recommend that you buy a copy of Roxio Toast recording software (www.roxio.com).

All You Really Need to Know about Printing

To close out this chapter, I turn the attention to another task that most Mac owners need to tackle soon after installing Mac OS X: printing documents. Because basic printing is so important (and in most cases, so simple), allow me to use this final section to demonstrate how to print a document.

Most of us have a Universal Serial Bus (USB) printer — the USB being the favored hardware connection within Mac OS X — so as long as your printer is supported by Mac OS X, setting it up is as easy as plugging it in to one of your Mac's USB ports. The Big X does the rest of the work, selecting the proper printer software driver from the Library/Printers folder and setting your printer as the default power of the universe.

Before you print, *preview!* Would you jump from an airplane without a parachute? Then why would you print a document without double-checking it first? Click Preview, and Mac OS X opens the Preview application to show you what the printed document will look like. (Once again, some upstart programs have their own built-in Print Preview mode.) When you're done examining your handiwork, close the Preview application to return to your document.

To print from within any application using the default page characteristics — standard 8½-x-11 inch paper, portrait mode, no scaling — follow these steps:

1. **Within your application, click File and choose Print — or press the ⌘+P keyboard shortcut.**

2. **Mac OS X displays the Print dialog that you see in Figure 3-9.**

Some applications use their own custom Print dialogs, but you should see the same general settings.

3. **Click in the Copies field and enter the number of copies that you need.**

You can also enable or disable collation, just like those oh-so-fancy copiers.

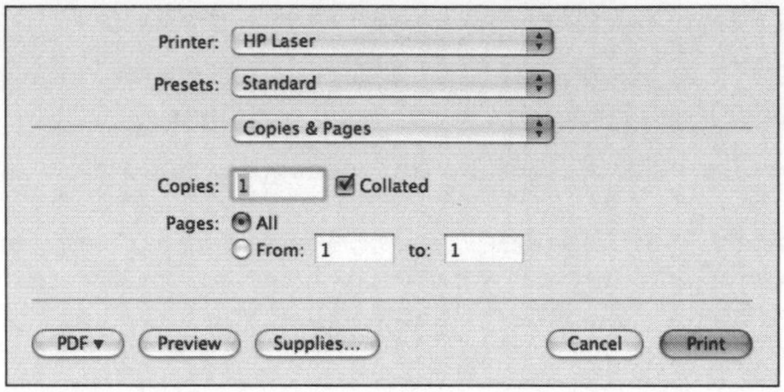

Figure 3-9: The Print dialog is available from any application with any real guts.

4. Decide what you want to print.

- *The whole shootin' match:* To print the entire document, use the default Pages radio button setting of All.

- *Anything less:* To print a range of selected pages, select the From radio button and enter the starting and ending pages.

5. (Optional) Choose application-specific printing parameters.

Each Mac OS X application provides different panes so that you can configure settings that are specific to that application. You don't have to display any of these extra settings to print a default document, but the power is there to change the look dramatically when necessary. To display these settings, click the drop-down list box in the Print dialog and choose one of these panes. For example, if you're printing from the Address Book, you can choose the Address Book entry from the drop-down list and elect to print a phone list or an e-mail list.

6. When everything is go for launch, click the Print button.

Of course, there are more settings and more functionality to the printing system within Mac OS X, and I cover more complex printing topics in much more detail in Book VI, Chapter 4 — however, I can tell you from my experiences as a consultant and hardware technician that this short introduction to printing will likely suffice for 90 percent of the Mac owners on earth. 'Nuff said.

Chapter 4: Searching Everything with Spotlight

In This Chapter

✔ **Mastering basic Spotlight searching skills**

✔ **Selecting text and keywords for best results**

✔ **Displaying results in the Spotlight window**

✔ **Customizing Spotlight settings in System Preferences**

*T*iger introduces *Spotlight,* Apple's new desktop search technology that you can use to find anything on your computer as quickly as you can type. (Yep, that includes all the documents, Address Book contacts, Mail messages, folders, and drives that your Mac can access.) Remember, this search system is only for your Mac. You can't search stuff on your brother's Atari 800 in Dry Prong, Louisiana. (Not even the folks at Apple are that good.) But if the information is on your Mac's hard drive, or a CD, or on your network, consider it located.

This chapter is your ticket to using this new search technology like a professional techno-wizard from day one. I discuss how Spotlight works, and how you can use it to locate exactly what you want (and present those results like a wine steward shows off a fine vintage).

If you're looking for something on the Internet, you'll need a different kind of sleuth: *Sherlock*, which I cover in the next chapter in this mini-book, is the Tiger tool of choice for Internet searches.

Basic Searching 101

Figure 4-1 illustrates the Spotlight search field, which is always available from the Finder menu bar. Click the magnifying glass icon once, and the Spotlight search box appears.

Figure 4-1:
There's a lot of power behind this single Spotlight search box.

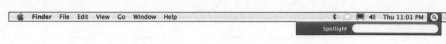

To run a search, simply click in the Spotlight box and begin typing. You'll see matching items appear as soon as you type, as shown in Figure 4-2, and the search results are continually refined while you type the rest of your search criteria. Like the Search box in earlier Finder window toolbars, you don't need to press Return to begin the search.

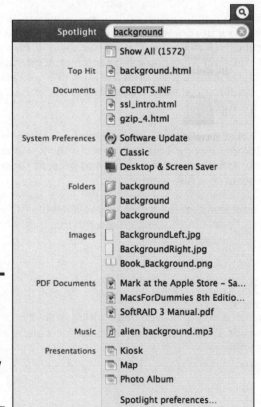

Figure 4-2:
Hey, aren't those System Preference panes in my Spotlight results?

The results of your Spotlight search are presented in the Spotlight menu, which is automatically updated in real time as you continue to type. The top 20 most-relevant items are grouped into categories right on the Spotlight menu, including Messages, Documents, Folders, Images, Contacts, and so on. Spotlight takes a guess at the item that's most likely the match you're looking for, and presents it in the special Top Hit category that always appears first.

To open the Top Hit item like a true Tiger power user, just press ⌘+Return.

Literally any text string is acceptable as a Spotlight search. However, here's a short list of the common search criteria I use every day:

✦ **Names and addresses:** Because Spotlight has access to Tiger's Address Book, you can immediately display contact information using any portion of a name or address.

✦ **E-mail message text:** Need to open a specific e-mail message, but you'd rather not launch Mail and spend time digging through the message list? Enter the person's e-mail address or any text string contained in the message you're looking for.

✦ **File and folder names:** This is the classic search favorite. Spotlight searches your entire system for that one file or folder in the blink of an eye.

✦ **Events:** Yep, Spotlight gives you access to your iCal calendars.

✦ **System Preferences:** Now things start to get *really* interesting! Try typing the word **background** in the Spotlight field. As you can see in Figure 4-2, three of the results are actually System Preference panes! That's right, every setting in System Preferences is referenced in Spotlight. (In this case, the Software Update and Classic panes both contain the word *background* while the desktop background setting is on the Desktop & Screen Saver pane in System Preferences.)

✦ **Metadata:** That's a pretty broad category, but it fits. For example, I like to locate Word documents on my system using the same metadata that's stored in the file, such as the contents of the Comments field in a Word document. Other supported applications include Photoshop images, Excel spreadsheets, Keynote presentations, and other third-party applications that offer a Spotlight plug-in.

To reset the Spotlight search and try another text string, click the X icon that appears at the right side of the Spotlight box. (Of course, you can also backspace to the beginning of the field, but that's a little less elegant.)

After you find the item that you're looking for, you can click it once to

+ Launch it (if the item is an application).

+ Open it in System Preferences (if it's a setting or description on a Preferences pane).

+ Open it within the associated application (if the item is a document or a data item).

+ Display it within a Finder window (if the item is a folder).

 Here is another favorite timesaver: You can display all the files of a particular type on your system by using the file type as the keyword. For example, to provide a list of all images on your system, just use *images* as your keyword — the same goes for *movies* and *audio*, too.

Is Spotlight Really That Cool?

Don't get fooled into simply using Spotlight as another file-'n-folder-name search tool. Sure, it can do that, but Spotlight can also search inside PDF and HTML files, finding matching text that doesn't appear in the name of the file! To wit: a search for *Tiger* on my system pulls up all sorts of items with Tiger in their names, but also files with Tiger in them:

+ *Apple Store SF.ppt* (a PowerPoint presentation that contains several slides containing the text Tiger)

+ *576763 bk01ch03.doc* (a rather cryptically-named Word file chapter of this book that mentions Tiger in several spots)

+ *Conference Call with Bob* (an iCal event pointing to a conference call with my editor about upcoming Tiger book projects)

Notice that not one of these three examples actually has the word *Tiger* occurring anywhere in the title or filename, yet Spotlight found them because they all contain the text *Tiger* therein. That, dear reader, is the true power of Spotlight, and how it can literally guarantee you that you'll never lose another piece of information in the hundreds of thousands of files and folders on your hard drive!

Is Spotlight secure?

So how about all those files, folders, contacts, and events that you *don't* want to appear in Spotlight? What if you're sharing your Mac as a multiuser computer? Will others be able to search for and access your personal information through Spotlight?

Definitely not! The results displayed by Spotlight are controlled by file and folder permissions and your account login, just like the applications that create and display your personal data. For example, you can't access other users' calendars using iCal, and they can't see your Mail messages — only you have access to your data, and only after you've logged in with your username and password. Spotlight works the same way. If a user doesn't normally have access to an item, it simply doesn't appear when that user performs a Spotlight search. (In other words, only you get to see your stuff.)

However, you can even hide certain folders and disks from your own Spotlight searches if necessary. Check out the last section of this chapter for details on setting private locations on your system.

Heck, suppose that all you remember about a file is that you received it in your mail last week or last month. To find it, you can actually type in time periods like *yesterday*, *last week,* or *last month* to see every item that you saved or received within that period. (Boy, howdy, I *love* writing about truly good ideas.)

Be careful, however, when you're considering a search string. Don't forget that Spotlight matches only those items that have *all* the words you enter in the Spotlight box. To return the highest number of possible matches, use the fewest number of words that will identify the item; for example, use *horse* rather than *horse image*, and you're certain to be rewarded with more hits. (On the other hand, if you're looking specifically for a picture of a knight on horseback, a series of keywords like *horse knight image* will shorten your search considerably. It all depends on what you're looking for, and how widely you want to cast your Spotlight net.)

 Because Spotlight functions are a core technology of Mac OS X Tiger — in other words, all sorts of applications can make use of Spotlight throughout the operating system, including the Finder — the Finder window's Search box now shares many of the capabilities of Spotlight. In fact, you can use the time period trick that I mention earlier (entering *yesterday* as a keyword) in the Finder window Search box.

Okay, parents, listen closely: Here's a (somewhat sneaky) Tip that might help you monitor your kid's computer time as well as what your kids are typing/reading in iChat AV:

1. **Enable the iChat transcript feature.**

   a. *From within iChat, choose iChat⇨Preferences.*

   b. *Click Messages.*

   c. *Select the Automatically Save Chat Transcripts check box.*

2. **Click OK to return to iChat.**

   Now you can use Spotlight to search for questionable words, phrases, and names within those iChat transcripts. (For more on iChat AV, turn to Book IV, Chapter 3.)

Expanding Your Search Horizons

I can just hear the announcer's voice now: "But wait, there's more! If you click the Show All menu item at the beginning of your search results, we'll expand your Spotlight menu into the Spotlight Results window!" (Fortunately, you don't have to buy some ridiculous household doo-dad.)

Keyboard mavens will appreciate the Spotlight window shortcut key; and I show you where to specify this shortcut in the last section of this chapter. You can also press Return immediately after typing your search text into the Spotlight box to automatically bring up the Results window.

Figure 4-3 illustrates the window; note the category groups at the upper right. To sort your Spotlight results by a different category, click the desired group. You can even take this sorting stuff a step further, if necessary. To change how items are sorted within each group in the list, click the option that you want under the Sort Within Group By heading.

You can also filter your results listing by the date the items were created or last saved, or by their location on your system (such as your hard drive, your Home folder, or a network server). Images appear as thumbnails, so you can use that most sophisticated search tool — the human eye — to find the picture you're looking for. (If you don't see thumbnail images, click the Thumbnail button on the Images section header.)

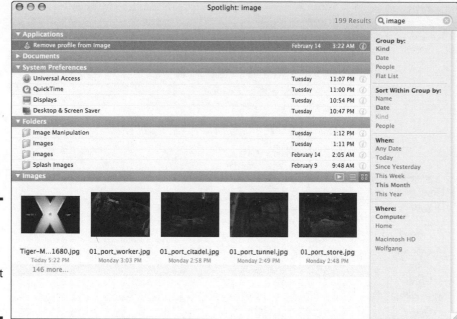

Figure 4-3:
The
spacious
borders of
the Spotlight
Results
window.

 To display more information about any item in the list (without leaving the comfortable confines of the Results window), click the Info icon (lowercase italic *i* in a circle) at the right side of the entry.

Again, when you're ready to open an item, just click it in the Results window.

Customizing Spotlight to Your Taste

You might wonder whether such a revolutionary new Mac OS X feature has its own pane within System Preferences — and you'd be right again. Figure 4-4 shows off the brand-new Spotlight pane within System Preferences: Click the System Preferences icon (look for the light switch) on the Dock, and then click the Spotlight icon (under Personal) to display these settings.

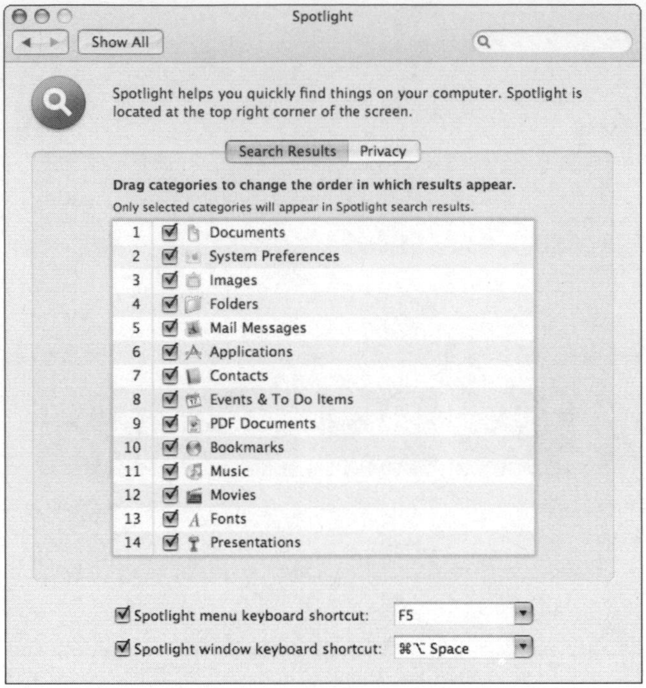

Figure 4-4:
Fine-tune
your
Spotlight
menu and
Results
window
from within
System
Preferences.

Click the Search Results tab to

✦ **Determine which categories appear in the Spotlight menu and Results window.** For example, if you don't use any presentation software on your Mac, you can clear the check box next to Presentations to disable this category (thereby making more room for other categories that you will use).

✦ **Determine the order that categories appear in the Spotlight menu and Results window.** Drag the categories to the order you want them to appear in the Spotlight menu and window. For example, I like the Documents and System Preferences categories to appear higher in the list because I use them most often.

✦ **Specify the Spotlight menu and Spotlight Results window keyboard shortcuts.** You can enable or disable either keyboard shortcut, and choose the key combination from the drop-down list box.

Click the Privacy tab (as shown in Figure 4-5) to specify disks and folders that should never be listed as results in a Spotlight search. I know, I know, I said earlier that Spotlight respected your security, and it does. However, the disks and folders that you add on this list won't appear even if *you* are the one performing the search. (This is a great idea for folders and removable hard drives that you use to store sensitive information like medical records.)

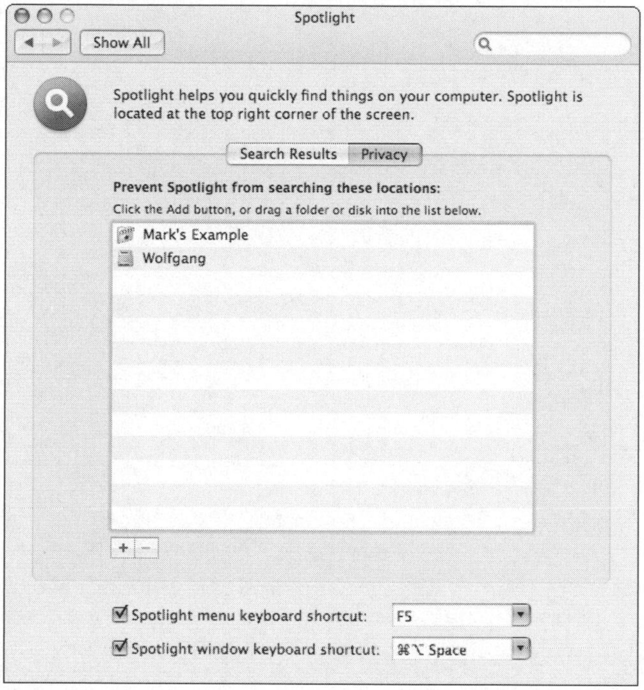

Figure 4-5:
When certain folders and disks must remain private (even from you), add them to this list.

Spotlight helps you quickly find things on your computer. Spotlight is located at the top right corner of the screen.

Search Results | Privacy

Prevent Spotlight from searching these locations:
Click the Add button, or drag a folder or disk into the list below.

Mark's Example
Wolfgang

☑ Spotlight menu keyboard shortcut: F5
☑ Spotlight window keyboard shortcut: ⌘⌥ Space

To add locations that you want to keep private, click the Add button (bearing a plus sign) and navigate to the desired location. Click the location to select it, and then click Choose. (Alternatively, you can drag folders or disks directly from a Finder window and drop them into the pane.)

Chapter 5: Using Sherlock: It's Elementary

In This Chapter

- ✔ Using channels
- ✔ Locating a business
- ✔ Searching for movie listings
- ✔ Checking the definition of a word
- ✔ Following eBay auctions
- ✔ Searching with Internet search engines
- ✔ Tracking stock prices
- ✔ Translating words and phrases
- ✔ Looking up flight schedules

*O*ne of the things that the Internet is *supposed* to provide is (almost) instantaneous access to all sorts of information: news, reference and research material, e-mail addresses, shopping, streaming live video, and even maps that help you chart your way to Grandma's house from wherever you happen to be on the planet. And yes, all that stuff is there, just waiting to be used.

However, actually *finding* anything in the organized chaos that is the Internet is a completely different matter. A favorite e-mail tagline of mine reads as follows:

What good is a Web search engine that returns 324,909,188 "matches"? That's like saying, "Good news, I've located the information you want. It's on Earth."

In this chapter, I introduce to you to the famous sleuth who makes it easy to search for the proverbial needle in the Internet haystack: Sherlock, which is included in Mac OS X. (One note: If you don't have an Internet connection, you can skip this chapter because Sherlock depends entirely upon the Internet while searching for the information that you need. There's always a caveat, right?) And remember that if you're searching for something already on your system, check out the new Tiger search tool, Spotlight. (Read all about your internal sleuth in Book I, Chapter 4.)

Sherlock Is Just Plain Neat

I love Conan Doyle's character Sherlock Holmes — he's one of my favorite fictional figures in literature, as a matter of fact — but even the Bloodhound of Baker Street would be hard pressed to keep up with the great flood of information available online. Apple's Sherlock, on the other hand, was built to do precisely that. To wit:

✦ **Help me, Mr. Wizard!:** Sherlock simplifies the major search engines and allows you to access them all from a single location — no longer do you have to open your Web browser and laboriously visit search engine sites like Lycos. If you find something on a Web site that you want to explore, a simple double-click of the item automatically launches your Web browser and displays that page.

✦ **Real-time, really:** You can also display real-time information by using Sherlock: Access stock prices, news and headlines, your eBay auctions, and such.

✦ **Plug it in:** Sherlock can provide additional services through the use of *plug-ins* — software add-ons offered by companies, libraries, and Apple itself that expand the functionality of Sherlock.

✦ **Show me:** Depending on the type of information you're seeking, Sherlock can display text, graphics, and even video.

Looking for the Scent with the Great Detective

"By Jove, Watson, the game is afoot!" Depending on your installation of Tiger, you can launch our computerized sleuth in two ways:

✦ Clicking its icon on the Dock, which features Holmes' hat and magnifying glass.

✦ Opening the Applications folder on your hard drive and double-clicking the Sherlock icon you'll find there.

To begin, take a look at the Sherlock window itself — Figure 5-1 does the job nicely. The most common window configuration (for the Internet channel) is divided thusly:

✦ Use the **Channel buttons** displayed along the top of the window to quickly switch between different types of searches. To display all the channels on a single page — complete with descriptions — click the Channels button on the toolbar.

✦ In the **Topic or Description box,** type whatever you're searching for. The fields in this area can change depending on the type of search that you're conducting.

Search button

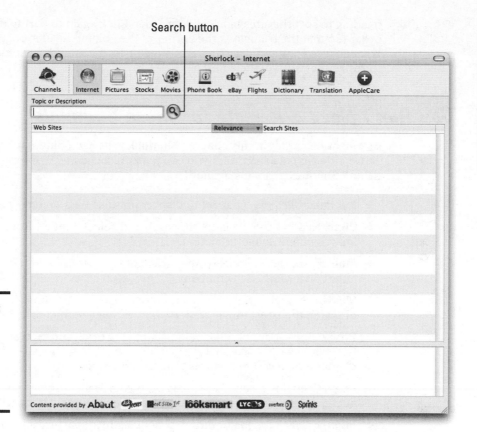

Figure 5-1:
Start the
hunt here
from the
Sherlock
main
window.

✦ Click the **Search button** — the button bearing the suave-looking magnifying glass — to start searching the selected sites. (Alternatively, you
can just poke the Return key.)

✦ The fruits of your search appear in the **results section** — for more information on an item, double-click it.

✦ Clicking an item once often displays a quick summary of the information
in the **summary section.**

Several channels alter the basic look of the Sherlock window, so not every
channel will offer all these controls.

Note the handles — the double lines — that appear in the separator bars.
You can click and drag these handles to resize the dimensions of the channel
button display and the results section.

To sort a column in Sherlock, just click the column's heading button. For
example, if you're looking at your stock portfolio, click the Name column

heading to sort the sites in ascending order. Click again to sort in descending order (so that the triangle at the corner of the column header points down). You can also click and drag the right edge of each column's heading button to resize the width of the column.

You Don't Need a Remote for These Channels

As I mention earlier in this chapter, Sherlock calls each different type (or genre, or class) of search that you can perform a *channel*. For example, the default Sherlock channels include

✦ **Internet:** Click this channel to display popular Web search engines.

✦ **Pictures:** Click this channel to search and select content from the Getty Images online image collection.

✦ **Stocks:** Use this channel to keep track of your stocks and recent headlines concerning each company.

✦ **Movies:** Switch to this channel for movie listings and times in your area or watch the latest movie trailers — now that's techno-*sassy!*

✦ **Phone Book:** Use this channel to search for brick-and-mortar businesses — just like that ponderous paper phone book — and even display a map with directions to help you reach a business.

✦ **eBay:** Click this channel and hang onto your wallet as you traverse *the* auction place to hang out — search and track your auctions with aplomb.

✦ **Flights:** Check the major airline schedules by departure and arrival city, as well as flight information like plane type, altitude, and speed — you can even pinpoint the location of a plane in flight!

✦ **Dictionary:** If you use the Internet for research, this channel is, quite simply, your Holy Grail. From this one location, you can peruse the online versions of the *American Heritage Dictionary, Webster's Revised Unabridged Dictionary,* and other reference works.

✦ **Translation:** Need to know the word for *taxi* in Portuguese? You can translate phrases and words to and from different languages with this channel.

✦ **AppleCare:** Clicking this channel brings you to the Apple Knowledge Base — a virtual gold mine for Sherlock searches — the Macintosh Product Guide and the Apple Web site.

When troubleshooting a Mac OS X issue, fire up Sherlock and use the AppleCare channel to check out keywords potentially related to your problem.

As I mention earlier, you can display all the default channels and a short description of each channel by clicking the Channels button on the Sherlock toolbar. From this Channel panel — yes, I actually wrote that — click a channel icon to begin your search.

To switch channels, just click the desired channel icon at the top of the Sherlock window.

Tracking Businesses, Movies, Definitions, and Auctions

To demonstrate the Fine Art of Search, I show you in this section how to locate a business, how to check movie listings, the definition of the word sleuth, and how to locate a print of Old London on eBay. (Something for everyone there, wouldn't you agree?)

Let your mouse do the walking

First, use Sherlock to locate the address and telephone number for a popular local pizza restaurant. Follow these steps:

1. **Launch Sherlock and then click the Phone Book channel button to display the window that you see in Figure 5-2.**

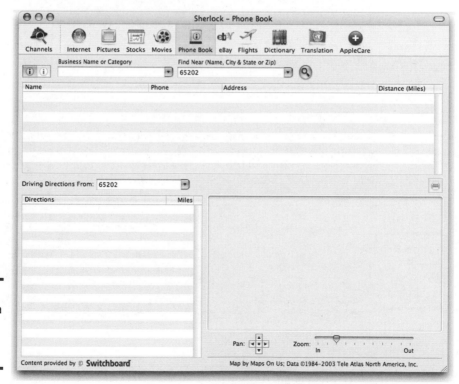

Figure 5-2:
Search for a business with Sherlock.

2. **Type the name** Shakespeare's Pizza **into the Business Name or Category box.**

3. **Type the city and state** Columbia, MO **into the Find Near (Name, City & State or Zip) box and then click the Search button (the magnifying glass button).**

   Figure 5-3 illustrates the results. The business address and phone number is listed, along with the approximate distance in miles from your location.

   By default, Sherlock provides directions starting from your home address (as provided by your card in the Address Book). However, you can click the Driving Directions From drop-down list box to select another starting point for the directions.

   The map display at the lower-right corner can be zoomed by dragging the Zoom slider in the desired direction. To move the map so that you can see additional territory, click the desired direction on the Pan control.

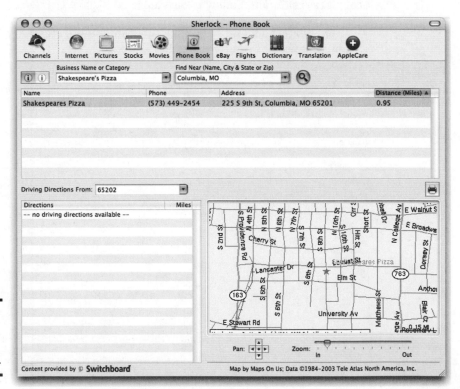

Figure 5-3:
Eureka!
We've
struck pizza.

4. **If the search matches more than one business, click a name in the results section to display the information for that business.**

To print the results of your search, click the Print button.

Scoping local movies

To search local theaters for information on a movie and watch the trailer to boot, follow these steps:

1. **Click the Movies channel button to display the window that you see in Figure 5-4.**

2. **To search by movie name, click the Movies button at the top-left corner of the window; to search by theater name, click the Theaters button.**

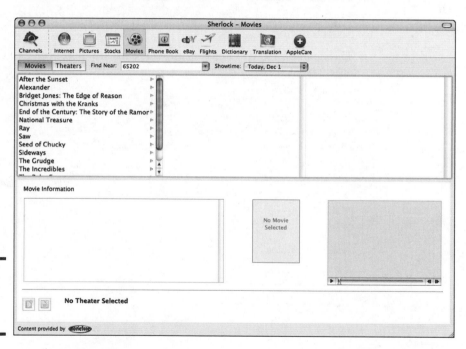

Figure 5-4:
Cinema
searching
simplified.

3. **Click the Showtime drop-down list box and then select the date for your listings.**

By default, today's date is shown.

If necessary, you can also enter a different city/state combination or ZIP code in the Find Near box.

4. **Hey, there's one that looks good — click The Incredibles entry to display the summary text (see Figure 5-5).**

Sherlock automatically begins downloading the poster and QuickTime movie trailer for the film. After the movie downloads, click the Play button in the QuickTime viewer window to watch the trailer.

5. **To display the show times for the selected film, click the desired theater in the center column.**

Consulting Sherlock's dictionary

One of the tasks that I perform most often with Sherlock is searching for word definitions. Follow these steps to find the definition of a word:

1. **Click the Dictionary channel button.**

2. **Type the word** sleuth **into the Word to Define box and then click the Search button.**

The definition and synonyms appear, and you didn't have to turn a single page.

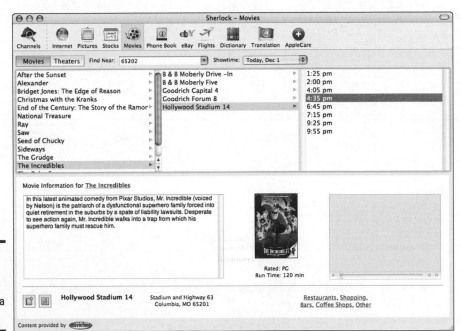

Figure 5-5:
More information on a film is a click away.

3. **To display the definition of any synonyms, click the desired word in the Thesaurus column, and Sherlock provides you with the definition in the summary section, as shown in Figure 5-6.**

   Happy hunting!

Scouring eBay for Old London

To locate a print of London on eBay, follow these steps:

1. **Click the eBay channel button and then click the rectangular Search button (below the Item Title box and to the left of the Track button) to look for items.**

   To track specific auctions, click the Track button instead.

2. **Click the Categories drop-down list to narrow your search to specific categories or leave it set to All Categories to search all of eBay.**

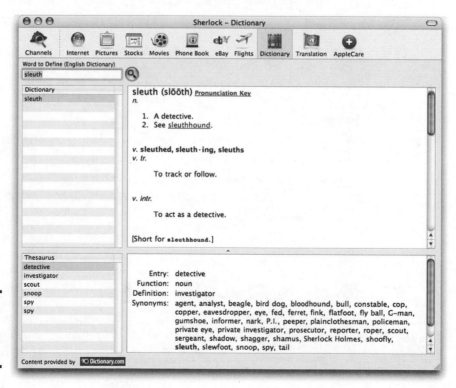

Figure 5-6:
Ferret out
the meaning
of words.

3. **Click the Regions drop-down list to show items from a particular area or leave it set to All Regions to search from any locale.**

4. **To limit the price range for matching items, enter values in the Priced Between boxes.**

5. **Type the words** London print **into the Item Title box and then click the Search button (the one with the magnifying glass).**

   To display matching items by the newest items first or in a particular price order, click the Items Ending First drop-down list box and choose the desired order.

6. **Click any item, and Sherlock updates the summary section with the specific auction information (see Figure 5-7).**

   • **To track this item,** click the Track Listing button at the bottom right of the Sherlock window.

   • **To bid on the item,** double-click the item entry, and Sherlock launches Safari and displays the eBay bidding page for that item.

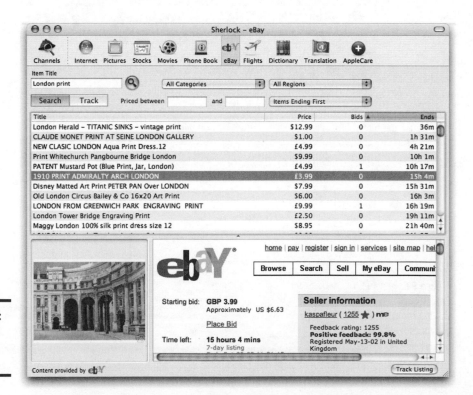

Figure 5-7: Good luck on your bidding!

Using Internet Search Sites

Besides the specialized searches that I present earlier in this chapter, Sherlock can make use of existing Internet search engines. Follow these steps to search the Internet for Web sites:

1. **Click the Internet channel button.**

2. **Type the phrase** Scanners For Dummies **into the Topic or Description box and then click the Search button.**

3. **When you find the perfect match for your search, click that entry to display the summary text (see Figure 5-8).**

Hey, that's quite a coincidence — or is it an obvious plug for another of my books?

4. **To display the entire Web page in all its glory, double-click the entry, and Sherlock launches Safari.**

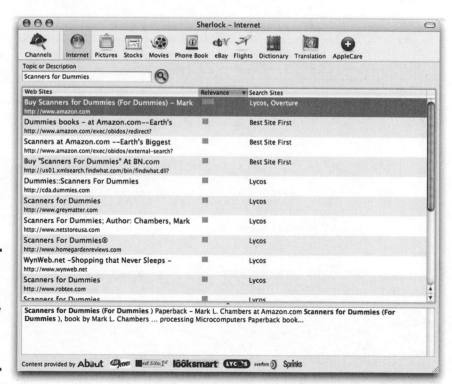

Figure 5-8:
Finding what you need is easy with the Summary section.

Minding Your Portfolio

Next, focus your magnifying glass on your stock portfolio. To display information on a stock, follow these steps:

1. **Click the Stocks channel button.**

2. **Type the word** Apple **(or its ticker symbol** AAPL**) into the Company Name or Ticker Symbol box and then click the Search button.**

   Sherlock displays the latest stock quotation and relevant news headlines concerning the company itself.

3. **To display the text of a news item (or a link to the story on the Web), click the desired headline.**

   Sherlock provides you with the text in the summary section, as shown in Figure 5-9.

4. **To specify a time period for the chart display, click the Chart dropdown list box and pick the desired period.**

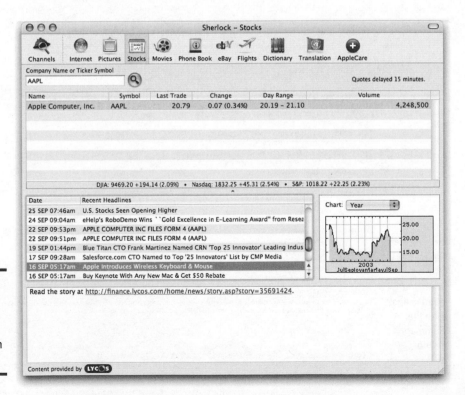

Figure 5-9:
Tracking your Apple stock is a breeze with Sherlock.

Translating 'Twixt Languages

Although Sherlock can't help you with the word for bathroom when you're in the middle of the street in Berlin, you can use the Translation channel to translate words and phrases from the comfort of your computer desk. (And come to think of it, if you have a wireless Internet connection and an iBook, I guess you could use it in the middle of a foreign street!)

Follow these steps to translate words and phrases:

1. **Click the Translation channel button.**

2. **Type the word or phrase that you want to translate into the Original Text box.**

   (Sorry about the very silly line from *Monty Python and the Holy Grail,* but how could I possibly resist?)

3. **Click the language-to-language drop-down list box to specify the starting and ending language for the translation.**

4. **Click the Translate button to translate the text, as shown in Figure 5-10.**

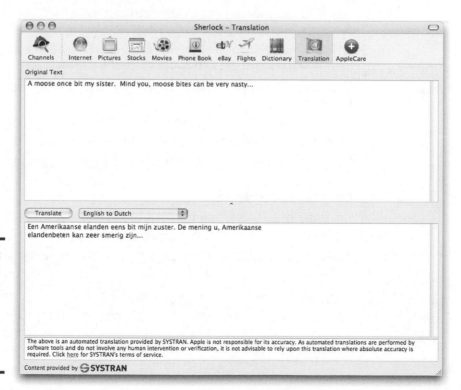

Figure 5-10: I'll bet even Holmes himself wasn't fluent in all these languages!

You can highlight and copy the translated text into the Clipboard and then paste it into your word processor or e-mail application.

Want to experience what I call the *Tower of Babel Effect* (or TBE)? Start with an English phrase, translate it into a second language, and then continue to translate the results to another language or two. Finally, translate the end result back to English and — *voilà!* You'll likely be surprised by just how imprecise different languages can be.

Finding Flight Information

Finally, allow me to demonstrate how you can track flight schedules by using Sherlock — truly, gentle reader, this program is as versatile as Apple claims! Follow these steps:

1. **Click the Flights channel button.**

2. **Click the Airline drop-down list to narrow your search to specific airlines.**

   To display information on a particular flight, type the flight number into the Flight Number box.

3. **To search by departure city, click the Departure City or Airport Code drop-down list and then click the desired location.**

   Note that you can also type a city name or airport code directly into the Departure City or Airport Code list.

4. **To search by arrival city, click the Arrival City or Airport Code drop-down list and then click the desired location.**

   Note that you can also type a city name or airport code directly into the Arrival City or Airport Code list.

5. **Click the Search button.**

6. **Click any flight entry, and Sherlock updates the summary section with the specific flight information, as shown in Figure 5-11.**

   To display any leg of the flight, click the Leg drop-down list box.

Figure 5-11:
Keep track
of your
arrivals and
departures
with the
Flights
channel.

Chapter 6: Keeping Track with the Address Book

In This Chapter

✓ Adding contact cards

✓ Editing contacts

✓ Using contact information throughout Mac OS X

✓ Creating groups

✓ Sending e-mail to a group

✓ Printing contacts

✓ Importing and exporting vCards

Do you have a well-thumbed address book stuck in a drawer of your office desk? Or do you have a wallet or purse stuffed with sticky notes and odd scraps of paper, each of which bears an invaluable e-mail address or phone number? If so, you can finally set yourself free and enjoy the "Paperless Lifestyle" of the new millennium with the revolutionary new Rauncho Digital Address Book! As seen on TV! Only $29.95 — and it doubles as an indestructible garden hose! But wait! If you order now, we'll also send you. . . .

Of course, you and I would tune that stuff out as soon as we heard, "As seen on TV" — but, believe it or not, the Rauncho Digital Address Book does exist (after a fashion), and you already have one if you've installed Mac OS X. It's called the *Address Book,* and in this chapter, I show you how to store and retrieve all your contact data, including iChat information, photographs, and much more.

(And before you ask, operators are *not* standing by.)

Hey, Isn't the Address Book Just a Part of Mail?

It's true that in older versions of Mac OS X, Address Book was relegated to the minor leagues and usually appeared only when you asked for it within Mail. Although it could be run as a separate application, there was no convenient route to the Address Book from the Desktop, so most Mac owners never launched it standalone.

Starting with Mac OS X Panther, however, the Address Book arrived in the limelight, earning a default location in the Dock and available whenever you need it. Although the Address Book can still walk through a meadow hand-in-hand with Mail, it also flirts with other Mac OS X applications and can even handle some basic telephony chores all by itself through the use of Services.

Figure 6-1 illustrates the default face of the Address Book, complete with a personal address card: your own contact information, which you enter within the First Use Wizard that I mention in Book I, Chapter 1. This card carries a special me tag (indicating that it's your personal card) as well as a suave-looking silhouette next to your name in the Name column. Other Mac OS X applications use the data in your card to automatically fill out your personal information in all sorts of documents. (In Figure 6-1, I added a number of well-known friends as well . . . a few TV characters, a composer or two. You know the drill.)

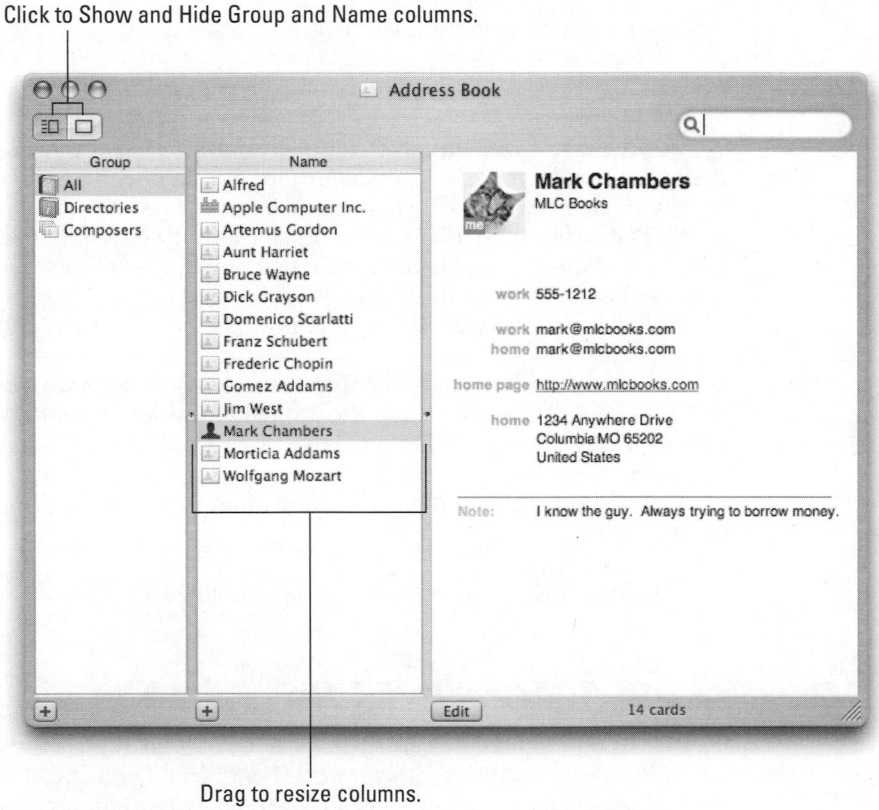

Click to Show and Hide Group and Name columns.

Figure 6-1: Greetings from the Mac OS X Address Book!

Drag to resize columns.

Note those cool little dimples that mark the Group and Name column dividers — click and drag on the dimples, and you can resize the Group and Name columns as well as the display window on the right. Plus, you can click the two buttons at the upper-left corner (underneath the window controls) to hide or show the Group and Name columns.

Entering Contact Information

Unless you've actually met and hired a group of DataElves — see the sidebar "I gotta type (or retype) that stuff?" — you have to add contacts to your Address Book manually. Allow me to demonstrate here how to create a new contact within your Address Book:

1. **Launch Address Book from the Dock by clicking its icon.**

The icon looks like an old-fashioned paper Address Book with an @ symbol on the cover.

2. **Press the ⌘+N shortcut to create a new contact. Alternatively, choose File⇨New Card or click the Add a New Person button at the bottom of the Name column.**

Address Book displays the template that you see in Figure 6-2, with the First name field highlighted and ready for you to type.

3. **Enter the contact's first name and press Tab to move to the Last name field.**

4. **Continue entering the corresponding information in each field, pressing Tab to move through the fields.**

If a field is not applicable (for example, if a person has no home page), just press Tab again to skip it. You can press Return to add extra lines to the Address field.

When you complete certain fields — like the Address field — a plus symbol pops up to the left of the field. That's the Address Book telling you that there are additional versions of the field that you can enter as well. (Think home and work addresses.) Click this plus sign, and you can enter the other version. For example, if you enter an iChat address for the contact at home, the plus sign appears; click it, and then you can enter the contact's work iChat address, too.

5. **To add a photograph to the card, just double-click the thumbnail square next to the person's name (or drag an image from a Finder window on top of the thumbnail square).**

Address Book displays an Open dialog that you can use to select the image.

6. **When you're done, click the Edit button (bottom-center) to save the card.**

You can edit the contents of a card at any time by displaying it and clicking the Edit button at the bottom (or by pressing ⌘+L, or even by clicking Edit and choosing the Edit Card menu item). You can also add new fields to a card, such as birthdays, anniversaries, and the like.

No need to edit a card to add information to the Note field — just click and type.

You can also add contact cards directly to your Address Book from the Mac OS X Mail application — go figure. Within Mail, click the message (to highlight it) from the person whom you want to add, click the friendly Message menu, and then click Add Sender to Address Book, or press ⌘+Y. Naturally, this doesn't add supporting information — just the person's name and e-mail address (and, if they used Mail on their end to send the message and they have a photo attached to their personal card, their photo gets imported as well). Once again, your nimble fingers will have to manually enter the rest. For more on Mail, see Book IV, Chapter 2.

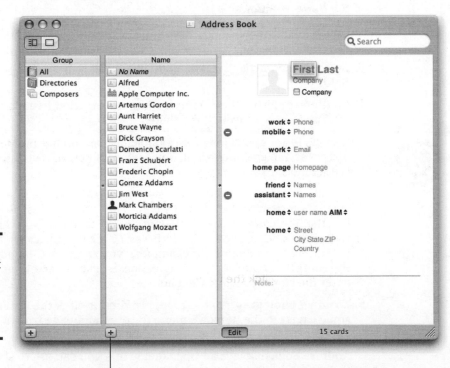

Figure 6-2: "Hey, I don't know anyone named *First Last!*"

Click to add a new person.

"I gotta type (or retype) that stuff?"

In my two decades of travel through the personal computing world, one lovely recurring fantasy shared by computer users keeps cropping up over and over: I call it the *DataElf Phenomenon.* You see, DataElves are the hard-working, silicon-based gnomes in tiny green suspenders who magically enter all the information that you want to track into your database (or Address Book, or Quicken, or whatever). They burrow into your papers and presto! — out pops all that data, neatly typed and . . . whoa, Nellie! Let's stop there.

For some reason, computer users seem to forget that *there are no DataElves.* I wish I had a dime for every time I've heard a heartbroken computer user say, "You mean I have to *type* all that stuff *in?*" (My usual retort is, "Affirmative . . . unless you want to pay me a hideous amount to do it for you.") Make no mistake — adding a lifetime's worth of contact information into your Address Book can be several hours of monotonous and

mind-bendingly boring work, which is another reason why many computer owners still depend on paper to store all those addresses. But take my word for it, dear reader, your effort is worth it — the next time that you sit down to prepare a batch of Christmas cards or you have to find Uncle Milton's telephone number in a hurry, you *will* appreciate the effort that you made to enter contact information into your Address Book. (Just make sure that you — say it with me — *back up your hard drive.*)

By the way, if you've already entered contact information into another PIM (short for Personal Information Manager), you can re-use that data without retyping everything — that is, as long as your old program can export contacts in vCard format. After you export the records, just drag the vCards into the Address Book window to add them, or import them by pressing ⌘+I. (More on this at the end of this chapter.)

Don't forget to add those fax numbers! Tiger can fax from any application — just click File and choose Print (or press ⌘+P) like you always have, and then click the Fax button at the bottom of the Print dialog. Mac OS X automatically fills in the address for you, but only if the contact has a fax number entered as a part of the contact card.

If someone sends you a vCard (look for an attachment with a .vcf extension), consider yourself lucky. Just drag the vCard from the attachment window in Mail and drop it in your Address Book; any information that the person wants you to have is automatically added!

To delete a card, click the unlucky name to display the card, click Edit, and then choose Delete Person.

Using Contact Information

Okay, after you have your contact information in Address Book, what can you actually do with it? Often, all you really need is a quick glance at an address. To display the card for any contact within Address Book, just click the desired entry in the Name column. You can move to the next and previous cards by using the directional arrow buttons at the bottom-right corner of the Address Book window.

But wait, there's more! You can also

✦ **Copy and paste.** The old favorites are still around. You can copy any data from a card (press ⌘+C) and paste it into another open application (press ⌘+V).

✦ **Send an e-mail message.** If you've already read through Chapter 3 of this mini-book, you'll remember the Mac OS X services feature that I tell you about. Click and drag to select any e-mail address on a card; then click the Address Book menu and click the Services menu. Choose Send To. Bingo! Depending on the information that you select, other services might also be available.

✦ **Add an iChat buddy.** From within iChat, click the Buddies menu and then click Add a Buddy to display the dialog that you see in Figure 6-3. From here, you can select a contact card that has an Instant Messenger address and add it to your Buddy List.

Figure 6-3: Adding a new buddy within iChat using the Address Book.

✦ **Export contacts to your iPod (or other applications).** From within the Address Book, select the contacts that you want to export, click File, and then choose Export vCards. Address Book displays a standard Mac OS X Save dialog. Navigate to the location where you want to save the cards (for an iPod connected as a FireWire drive, that's the Contacts folder) and click Save.

✦ **Search amongst your contacts.** If you're searching for a specific person and all you have is a phone number or a fragment of an address, click in the Search field at the top right of the Address Book window and type the text. While you continue to enter characters, Address Book shows you how many contacts contain matching characters and displays just those entries in the Name column. Now that's *sassy!* (And convenient. And fast as all get-out.) Check out Figure 6-4, where many of the characters from my favorite TV shows are gathered — note that a number of very familiar folks share the same address in Gotham City, and I found them by using the Search field.

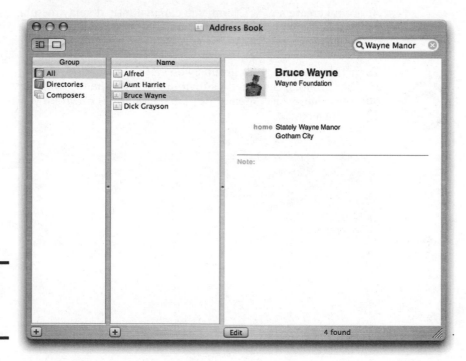

Figure 6-4:
Holy Text
Match,
Batman!

Arranging Your Contact Cards

Address Book also provides you with a method of organizing your cards into groups. A group usually consists of folks with a common link, like your family, friends, co-workers, and others who enjoy yodeling. For example, you could set up a Cell Phone group that you can use when syncing data with your Bluetooth cell phone.

To create a group, choose File⇨New Group or press ⌘+Shift+N. (Using the Hollywood method, click the plus sign button at the bottom of the Group column.) Address Book creates a new entry in the Group column, with a highlighted text box so that you can type the group name (see Figure 6-5). After you type the group name, press Return to save it, and then click and drag the entries that you want to add to the New Group icon.

If you already selected the entries for those contacts that you want to add to the group, choose File⇨New Group from Selection instead. This saves you a step because the group is created and the members are added automatically.

After you create a New Group, you can instantly display members of that group by clicking its icon in the Group column. To return to the display of all your contacts, click the All group button.

To further organize your groups, you can drag and drop a group on top of another group. It becomes a subgroup, which is handy for things like branch offices within your company, or perhaps relatives to whom you're not speaking at the moment.

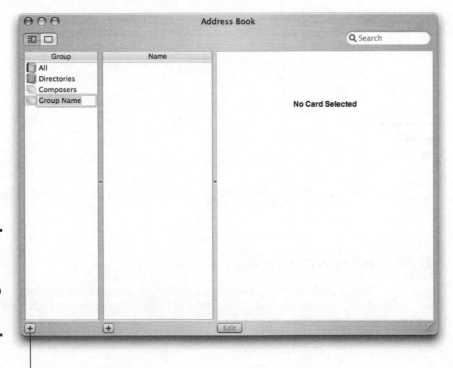

Figure 6-5:
Create a New Group . . . go ahead, I dare you!

Click to add a new group.

Here's another handy feature of an Address Book group: You can send all the members of a group the same e-mail message at once. Within Mail, simply enter the Group name in the To field in the Compose window, and the same message is sent to everyone. Even Gandalf couldn't do that (but my copy editor bets that Dumbledore could).

Using Network Directories

I know, I know, I said earlier that you'd have to enter all your contacts yourself — but I was talking about your personal contacts! You can also access two types of external directories from within Address Book:

✦ If you're a member of a company NetInfo network — and if you don't know, ask your wizened network administrator — you can search network directory servers from within Address Book. These servers are available automatically, so there's no configuration necessary. Sweet.

✦ You can search Internet-based LDAP directories. Sorry, folks, I know that's pretty cryptic, but others have written entire books on this technology. Again, suffice it to say that your network guru can tell you whether LDAP servers are available to you. (In another blazing display of techno-nerd acronym addiction, LDAP stands for *Lightweight Directory Access Protocol.*) With LDAP, you can search a central company directory from anywhere in the world as long as you have an Internet connection. To configure this feature, click Address Book from the menu and choose the Preferences menu item; click the LDAP tab, and then click the button with the plus sign to enter the specific settings for the server that you want to access. Your network administrator or the LDAP server administrator can supply you with these settings.

To search either type of network directory, click the Directories entry in the Group column and use the Search field like you normally would. Matching entries display the person's name, e-mail address, and phone number.

"But hey, Mark, what if I'm not online? My company's LDAP directory isn't much good then, right?" Normally, that's true. If you're a mobile user, LDAP information is only available to you when you're online and the LDAP server is available. Ah, but here's a rocking power user Tip that'll do the trick for iBook and PowerBook owners: To make a person's information always available, search the LDAP database and drag the resulting entry from the Directories window to the All group. You'll import the information to your local Address Book — and you'll see it even when you're not online!

Printing Contacts with Flair

Next, consider how to print your contacts (for those moments when you need an archaic hard copy). Address Book offers two different formats.

By default, Address Book prints on standard US letter-size paper (8½-x-11 inches) in portrait orientation. You can change these settings right from the Print dialog: Choose File➪Print or press ⌘+P. From the Print dialog, you can choose exotic settings such as legal-size paper or landscape orientation.

Follow these steps to print your contacts:

1. **Choose File➪Print or press ⌘+P.**

   Address Book displays the Print dialog.

   If you need more than one copy, click the arrows next to the Copies field to specify the desired number.

   Need labels? We've got 'em! Click the Style drop-down list box and choose Mailing Labels to specify what type of label stock you're using on the Layout panel. Click the Label button to sort your labels by name or postal code, choose a font, select a text color, and add an icon or image to your labels. To switch back to a standard contact list, click Style again and then click Lists.

2. **Select the desired Attributes check boxes to specify which contact card fields you want to appear in your list.**

   The Attributes list appears only if you're printing contacts in Lists style.

3. **Click the Preview button to check the appearance of the list or click the Print button to send the job to the selected printer.**

   Alternatively, you can create a PDF file in a specified location — a handy trick to use if you'd rather not be burdened with paper, but you still need to consult the list or give it to others. (*PDF files* are a special document display format developed by Adobe; they display like a printed document but take up minimal space and can't be edited.) To display the contents of a PDF file in Mac OS X, you need only double-click it in the Finder window, and the built-in Preview application will be happy to oblige.

Swapping Bytes with vCards

A *vCard* is a standard file format for exchanging contacts between programs like Address Book, Microsoft Entourage, Eudora, and the Palm computer desktop. (Heck, if you're lucky enough to have an iPod, you can even store vCard data there.) Think of a vCard as an electronic business card that you can attach to an e-mail message, send via File Transfer Protocol (FTP), or exchange with others by using your cellular phone and palmtop computer. vCard files end with the extension .vcf.

In Address Book, you can create a single vCard containing one or more selected entries by clicking File and choosing Export vCards. Then, like any other Mac OS X Save dialog, just navigate to the spot where you want the file saved, give it a name, and click Save.

To import vCards into Address Book

✦ Drag the vCard files that you've received to Address Book and drop them in the application window.

✦ Alternatively, choose File⇨Import vCards or press ⌘+I. From the Open dialog, navigate to the location of the vCard files that you want to add, select them, and then click Open.

Chapter 7: The Joys of Maintenance

In This Chapter

- ✔ Deleting applications
- ✔ Using Apple System Profiler
- ✔ Using Activity Monitor
- ✔ Using Disk Utility
- ✔ Updating Mac OS X
- ✔ Backing up your system
- ✔ Using a disk defragmenter
- ✔ Using start-up keys in Mac OS X
- ✔ Updating your drivers

_T_he title of this chapter really sounds like a contradiction in terms, doesn't it? The concepts of _joy_ and _maintenance_ will likely be mutually exclusive to you — and it's true that most Mac OS X owners would rather work or play than spend time under the hood, getting all grimy. I understand completely; maintenance is far less sexy than Call of Duty or PowerPoint.

However, if you do want your work or play uninterrupted by lockups and crashes — yes, believe it or not, the Big X can indeed take a dive if it's not cared for — and you'd like your Mac to perform like Lance Armstrong, you've got to get your hands dirty. That means performing regular maintenance on your hardware, Mac OS X, and your all-important applications, documents, and folders.

Like most techno-types, I actually *enjoy* pushing my system to the limit and keeping it running in top form. And who knows — after you become a Tiger power user, you could find yourself bitten by the maintenance bug as well. In this chapter, I cover how to take care of necessary tune-up chores, step-by-step.

Deleting Applications the Common Sense Way

Nothing lasts forever, and that includes your applications. You might no longer need an application or maybe you need to remove it to upgrade to a new version or to reinstall it. Unlike Windows XP, Mac OS X doesn't have an Add or Remove Programs utility for uninstalling software — nor does it need one because virtually all Macintosh applications are self-contained in a single folder or series of nested folders. (And not by accident . . . it's always been a rule for Apple software developers since the first days of the Macintosh.) Therefore, removing an application is usually as easy as deleting the contents of the application folder from your hard drive.

Always check the application's README file and documentation for any special instructions before you delete any application folder. If you've created any documents in that folder that you want to keep, don't forget to move them before you trash the folder and its contents!

Some applications can leave preference files, start-up applications, or driver files in other spots on your disk besides their home folder. When you're uninstalling a program that has support files in other areas, use the Search box in the Finder toolbar to locate other files that might have been created by the application. (I cover this feature in Book II, Chapter 1.)

For example, Figure 7-1 illustrates a Spotlight search that I've run on Microsoft Office 2004. By searching for the word *office,* I've found a number of files created in other folders, like the settings file that's in my Preferences folder. Typically, you'll want to delete the main application folder first and then remove these orphans.

Spring Cleaning, from Allume Systems ($30; www.allume.com), also has the ability to uninstall a program, as well as a feature that can find and remove orphaned files left from past applications.

Figure 7-1:
Locate
support files
after
removing an
application
folder.

Popping the Hood: Using the Apple System Profiler

Need hard information about your hardware? You might need to determine precisely what hardware is installed in your Mac for the following reasons:

✦ **If you're working with a technical support person to solve a problem:** This person will usually request information about your system, such as what processor you're running and how much memory you have.

✦ **If you're evaluating an application before you buy it:** You'll want to check its minimum system requirements against the hardware on your Mac.

✦ **If you're considering an upgrade to your Mac:** You'll likely need to determine how much memory you have, what type it is, and which memory slots are filled. (The same goes for your hard drive and your video card, for those Macs with video card slots.) For more on upgrading your Mac, thumb through Book VI, Chapter 2.

Apple provides Mac OS X with an all-in-one hardware and software display tool, aptly named *Apple System Profiler*, which you can find in the Utilities folder within your Applications folder. You can also reach the Profiler through the Apple menu (). Just click About This Mac and then click the More Info button.) As you can see from Figure 7-2, there's a lot to digest from the System Profiler window.

Like the folders in a Finder window in list view mode, you can expand or collapse each major heading that appears in a Profiler screen. Just click the triangle that appears to the left of each Contents heading to expand or collapse that heading.

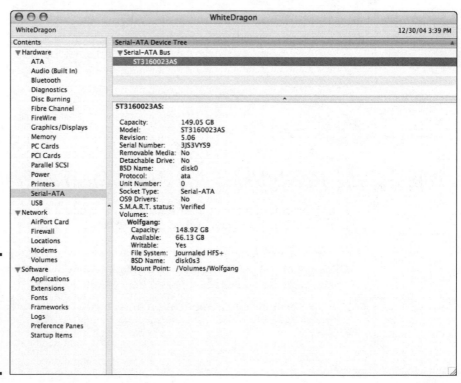

Figure 7-2: You can display an overview of your Mac via System Profiler.

The System Profiler major headings include

✦ **Hardware:** This heading tells you volumes about your hard drives — forgive me — as well as specifics concerning your CD and DVD drives, modem, AirPort and Bluetooth hardware, graphics hardware, AC power settings, and any FireWire and USB devices connected to your system. Figure 7-3 illustrates the information from my USB screen, with many of the devices expanded so that you can see them. (The text you see at the bottom half of the window is the detailed information on the item that's selected.)

✦ **Network:** This heading shows a listing of your network configuration, active network connections, and other assorted network paraphernalia. You'll probably need this screen only when asked by a technical support person for the network protocols that you're using, but it's handy nonetheless. (You'll find details on your network connection here that you can't find anywhere else in Tiger.)

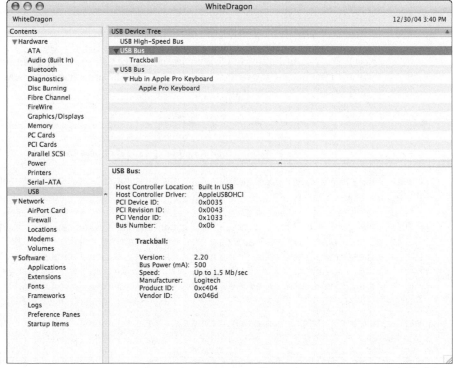

Figure 7-3:
See
information
about the
ports and
connections
on your
Mac.

✦ **Software:** Okay, this heading shows something useful to the average human being! This screen lists all the applications, fonts, and preferences recognized on your start-up volume, along with their version numbers. If you're wondering whether you need to update an application with a *patch file* (to fix bugs in the software) or update a file from the developer, you can look here to check the current version number for the application. You also get a rather boring list of the *extensions* (or drivers) used by Mac OS X applications. Logs are usually valuable only to tech support personnel; they document recent lockups, application crashes, and even system crashes.

Tracking Performance with Activity Monitor

Our next stop in Maintenance City is a useful little application called *Activity Monitor*, which is specially designed to show you just how hard your CPU, hard drives, network equipment, and memory modules are working behind the scenes. To run Activity Monitor, open the Utilities folder in your Applications folder.

To display each different type of usage, click the buttons in the lower half of the window; the lower panel changes to reflect the desired type (see Figure 7-4). For example, if you click System Memory, you see the amount of unused memory; click CPU or Network to display real-time usage of your Mac's CPU and network connections.

Processes *For Dummies*

"Mark, what's that arcane-looking list doing in the middle of the Activity Monitor window in Figure 7-4?" I'm glad you asked. A *process* is a discrete task (either visible or invisible) that Tiger performs in order to run your applications. (Some processes are executed by Tiger just to keep itself running.) For example, the Dock and Finder are actually processes, as are Adobe Acrobat and iPhoto.

You can quit a specific process within Activity Monitor. Just click the offending process in the list and then click the Quit Process button on the Activity Monitor toolbar. But tread carefully, Mr. Holmes, for there's danger afoot. For example, deleting a system process (like the Dock or Finder) can result in *all* of Mac OS X locking up! Therefore, delete a process **only if instructed to do so by a support technician**. From the Apple menu, choose Force Quit to terminate a misbehaving application instead.

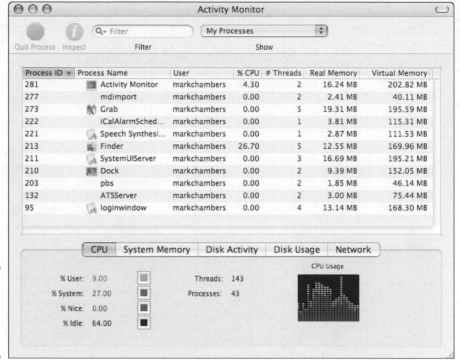

Figure 7-4:
Keep tabs
on Tiger and
what you're
running.

You can also display a separate window with your CPU usage; choose
Window⇨Show CPU Usage or press ⌘+2. There are three different types of
central processing unit (CPU, which is commonly called the "brain" of your
Macintosh) displays available from Activity Monitor:

✦ **Floating CPU window:** This is the smallest display of CPU usage; the
higher the CPU usage, the higher the reading on the monitor. You can
arrange the floating window in horizontal or vertical mode from the
Window menu.

✦ **CPU Usage window:** This is the standard CPU monitoring window, which
uses a blue thermometer-like display. The display works the same as the
floating window.

✦ **CPU History window:** This scrolling display uses different colors to
help indicate the percentage of CPU time being used by your applications (green) and what percentage is being used by Tiger to keep things
running (red). You can use the History window to view CPU usage over
time.

So what's a disk image?

You might have noticed the New Image button on the Disk Utility toolbar (or the image creation commands on the File⇨New submenu). If you're wondering what a *disk image* is, you've come to the right place. Think of a disk image as a file that looks (and acts) like an external storage device within Tiger; for example, a mounted disk image operates much like a CD or DVD, and it can be ejected just like a disc. Images can be read-only (just like a standard CD-ROM or DVD-ROM), or they can be created blank (just like an empty hard drive), ready to accept files and folders that you copy using the Finder.

So what are images used for? They're great for storing data that would normally have to be loaded from a CD or DVD (a great convenience if you don't want to lug optical media along with you during a vacation). Remember, a disk image acts just like removable storage media as far as Tiger's concerned. Many Mac Web sites also offer images as download files because a simple double-click is all that's necessary to automatically mount a disk image. (Software

developers like words like *fast* and *simple* when offering their shareware and demo applications to the public.)

Finally, images are often used to create simple archives of little-used data: The images can be burned to CD/DVD or even copied to other hard drives. Oh, and don't forget the security aspect — you can choose to encrypt the data stored in an image, protecting it from prying eyes. (However, I don't recommend using disk images to create full backups of your Mac's hard drives; more on this elsewhere in the chapter.)

If you're intrigued, I encourage you to click New Image on the Disk Utility toolbar (see Figure 7-10) and create a simple, unencrypted blank disk image on your Desktop. Then you can experiment with it. A disk image can be ejected to unmount it (just like a CD/DVD, an iPod, or a USB Flash drive), and you can delete the image file at any time. (Just remember not to delete it if it contains anything you want to keep, of course . . . but you knew that already.)

Whichever type of display you choose, you can drag the window anywhere that you like on your Mac OS X Desktop. Use the real-time feedback to determine how well your system CPU is performing when you're running applications or performing tasks in Mac OS X. If this meter stays peaked for long periods of time while you're using a range of applications, your processor is running at full capacity.

You can even monitor CPU, network, hard drive, or memory usage right from the Dock! Choose View⇨Dock Icon; then choose what type of real-time graph you want to display in your Dock. (Feeling like a Tiger power user yet? I thought so.) When you're monitoring CPU usage from the Dock, the green portion of the bar indicates the amount of processor time used by application software, and the red portion of the bar indicates the CPU time given to the Mac OS X operating system (just like the CPU History window).

Note, however, that seeing your CPU capacity at its max does not necessarily mean that you need a faster CPU or a new computer. For example, when I'm running memory-ravenous applications such as Photoshop or Premiere, the Activity Monitor on my iMac G5 is often pegged (indicating maximum use) for several seconds at a time. The rest of the time, it barely moves. Whether a computer is actually fast enough for you and the applications that you run is more of a subjective call on your part.

Fixing Things with the Disk Utility

Another important application in your maintenance toolbox is the Disk Utility, which you'll find — no surprise here — in the Utilities folder within your Applications folder. When you first run this program, it looks something like Figure 7-5, displaying all the physical disks and volumes on your system.

The Disk Utility application has its own toolbar that you can toggle on and off. Click the lozenge-shaped button at the upper-right corner of the window to display or hide the toolbar.

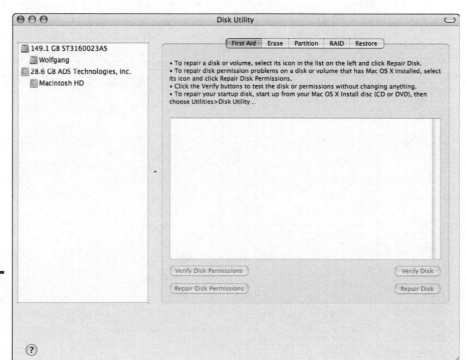

Figure 7-5:
The familiar face of Tiger's Disk Utility.

Displaying the goods on your disks

The volume tree structure on the left of the Disk Utility window lists both the physical disks and the partitions that you've set up. A *partition* is nothing more than another word for *volume*, which is the formatted section of a disk that contains data. A single physical hard drive can contain several partitions. The information display at the bottom of the Disk Utility window contains data about both the volumes and the partitions on your hard drive.

To illustrate: On my system, clicking the drive labeled 149.1 GB (the physical hard drive at the top of the tree) displays a description of the drive itself, including its total capacity, interface (connection type), and whether the drive is internal or external. (See Figure 7-6.)

Clicking the tree entry for Wolfgang, however — that's the name of the partition that I created when I formatted the drive — displays information about the type of formatting, the total capacity of the partition and how much of that is used, and the number of files and folders stored on the partition (as shown at the bottom of Figure 7-7).

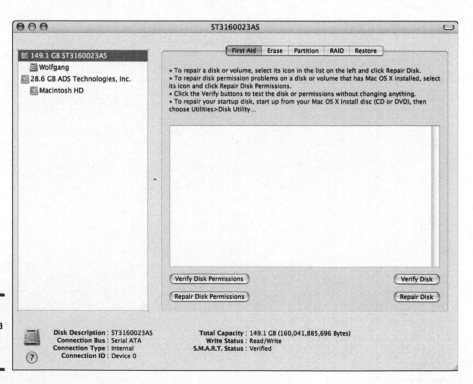

Figure 7-6: Display data on a physical drive.

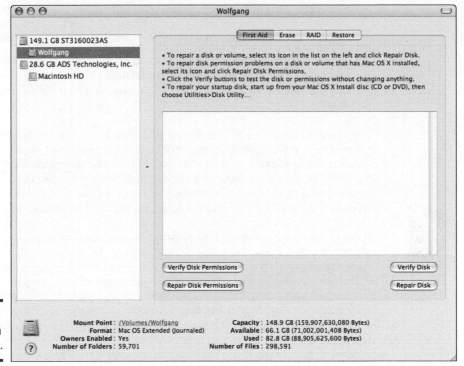

Figure 7-7:
Display data
on a volume.

Playing doctor with First Aid

From the First Aid pane, Disk Utility can be used to verify (or check) any disk (well, *almost* any disk) for errors, as well as repair any errors that it finds. Here are the two exceptions when the buttons are disabled:

✦ **The start-up disk:** Disk Utility can't verify or repair the *start-up disk* — that's Mac talk for the boot drive that contains the Mac OS X system that you're using at the moment — which makes sense if you think about it because that drive is currently being used!

If you have multiple operating systems on multiple disks, you can boot from another Mac OS X installation on another drive to check your current start-up disk. Or, you can boot your system from the original Mac OS X installation CD and run Disk Utility from the Installation menu.

Your start-up disk is *automatically* verified and repaired (if necessary) during the boot procedure, so you really don't need to worry about checking the start-up disk.

✦ **Write-protected disks:** Although you can use the Disk Utility to verify CDs, DVDs, and write-protected removable disk drives (like a write-protected Zip disk), it can't repair them. (Sound of my palm slapping my forehead.)

You also can't repair a disk that has *open* files that are currently being used. If you're running an application from a drive or you've opened a document that's stored on that drive, you won't be able to repair that drive.

You can also elect to verify and repair *permissions* (also called *privileges*) on a disk; these are the read/write permissions that I discuss in detail in Book II, Chapter 6. If you can't save or move a file that you should be able to access, I recommend checking that drive for permissions problems. Unlike fixing disk errors, you can verify and repair permissions on any volume that contains a Mac OS X installation (whether it was used to boot your Mac or not).

In order to verify or repair, you must be logged in as an admin-level user.

To verify or repair a drive, first select the target volume/partition in the list at the left. To check the contents of the drive and display any errors, click the Verify Disk button. Or, to verify the contents of the drive and fix any problems, click the Repair Disk button. (I usually just click Repair Disk because an error-free disk will need no repairs.) Disk Utility displays any status or error messages in the scrolling list; if you've got eagle eyes, you'll note that the window can be resized so that you can expand it to display more messages. (You can also drag the dot between the left and right panes to expand the list.)

I generally check my disks once every two or three days. If your Mac is caught by a power failure or Mac OS X locks up, however, it's a good idea to immediately check disks after you restart your Mac. (Don't forget that the start-up volume is automatically checked and repaired, if necessary.)

A number of very good commercial disk repair utilities are on the market. My favorite is Drive 10 from Micromat ($70; www.micromat.com) — however, Disk Utility does a good job on its own, and it's free.

Erasing without seriously screwing up

"Danger, Will Robinson! Danger!" That's right, Robot, it is indeed very easy to seriously screw up and get *Lost in Erase.* (Man, I can't believe I actually typed such a bad pun. I have no shame.) Anyway, it's time for another of Mark's Maxims. To paraphrase the rules for handling a firearm responsibly:

> *Never* **click this button unless you mean to use it.™**

Figure 7-8 illustrates the Erase controls within Disk Utility. You need erase a disk or volume only when you want to *completely wipe* the contents of that existing disk or volume. You can also erase a rewriteable CD (CD-RW) or DVD (DVD-RW, DVD+RW, or DVD-RAM) from this pane.

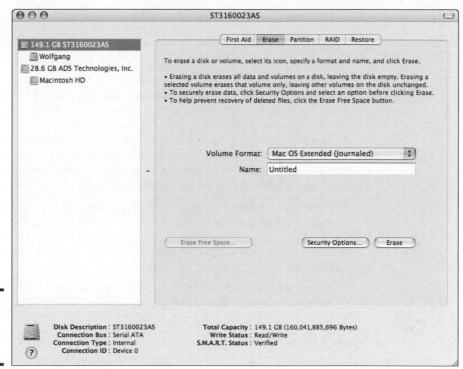

Figure 7-8:
The Disk
Utility Erase
controls.

◆ Erasing an *entire disk* deletes *all volumes* on the disk and creates a single new, empty volume.

◆ Erasing a *volume* only wipes the *contents of that specific volume,* leaving all other volumes on the physical disk untouched.

To erase, follow these steps:

1. **From the Erase panel within Disk Utility, click the disk or volume icon that you want to erase from the list on the left side of the screen.**

2. **Click the format that you want to use from the Volume Format drop-down list.**

Always choose Mac OS Extended (Journaled) entry from the Volume Format list unless you have a specific reason to use the MS-DOS File System (for compatibility with PCs running Windows) or the UNIX File System (for compatibility with UNIX/Linux machines). In some cases, Disk Utility will force you to choose the Mac OS Extended entry instead, but the end result is the same. Note that you do *not* need to format a disk or volume with the MS-DOS File System just to read or write a floppy or a Zip disk from a PC system — Mac OS X recognizes MS-DOS removable media without a problem.

3. In the Name field, type the name for the volume.

If you're erasing an existing volume, the default is the existing name.

4. If you're worried about security, click Security Options and specify the method you want to use.

By default, this is set to Don't Erase Data, so Disk Utility doesn't actually overwrite any data while formatting — instead, it simply trashes the existing directory, rendering that data unreachable. *Or is it?* With some third-party disk utilities, some unscrupulous bum could actually recover your files if you choose, so you can specify alternate, more secure methods of erasing a disk or volume. Unfortunately, these more secure erasure methods can take a horrendous amount of time.

Therefore, it's okay to use the Don't Erase Data option unless you want to make sure, or use the Zero Out Data to take a more secure route with the least amount of extra waiting. For example, you'd want to use the Zero Out Data option if you're selling your Mac on eBay and you're formatting the drive for the new owner.

You can even click Erase Free Space to wipe the supposedly "clean" areas of your drive *before* you format. Man, talk about airtight security! Again, the Zero Out method is the fastest.

5. Click the Erase button.

In the sheet that appears, click Erase to confirm that you do actually want to do the deleterious deed.

Partitioning the right way

From time to time, just about everyone wishes they had additional volumes handy for organizing files and folders, or at least a little extra space on a particular partition. If you find yourself needing another volume on a disk — or if you need to resize the total space on existing volumes on a disk — click the Partition tab within Disk Utility to display the controls that you see in Figure 7-9. (Make sure that you select a disk and not a partition.) From here, you can choose a volume scheme, creating anywhere from 1 to 16 volumes on a single disk.

You can't monkey around with the partitions on a start-up disk because Mac OS X is currently running on that disk. Think about removing your own appendix, and you'll get the idea.

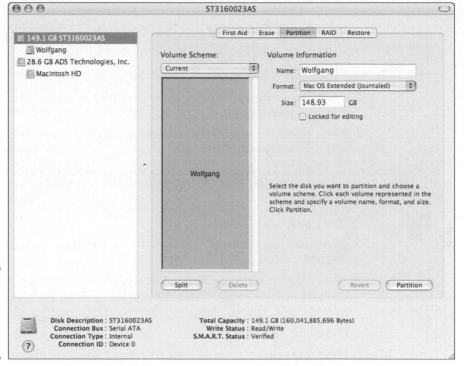

Figure 7-9:
The Disk
Utility
Partitioning
controls.

To set up the partitions on a disk, follow these steps:

1. **From the Partition panel within Disk Utility, click the disk icon (left side of the pane) that you want to partition.**

2. **Click the Volume Scheme drop-down list and choose the total number of volumes that you want on the selected disk.**

3. **Click the first volume block in the partition list (under the Volume Scheme drop-down list) to select it.**

   I have only one for this disk, as you can see.

4. **Click in the Name field and enter the name for the selected volume.**

5. **From the Format drop-down list, choose a format for the volume.**

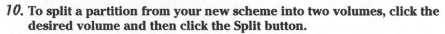

Always use Mac OS Extended or Mac OS Extended (Journaled) from the Format list unless you have a specific reason to use the MS-DOS File System (for compatibility with PCs running Windows) or the UNIX File System (for compatibility with UNIX/Linux machines).

6. **Type a total size for this volume in the Size field.**

7. **After you set up your first volume partition, mark the Locked for Editing check box to prevent any further changes to that volume.**

8. **If you're creating multiple volumes, click the next volume block to select it and repeat Steps 4–7.**

9. **To delete a partition from your new scheme, click the unwanted volume and then click the Delete button to remove it.**

If the partition is locked, you'll need to clear the Locked for editing check box before deleting it.

10. **To split a partition from your new scheme into two volumes, click the desired volume and then click the Split button.**

Some folks create multiple volumes so that they can boot from multiple versions of Tiger — like us author types.

If the partition is locked, you need to clear the Locked for Editing check box before splitting it.

11. **When everything is set to your liking, click the Partition button to begin the process.**

If you suddenly decide against a partition change, click the Revert button to return to the original existing partition scheme.

The Revert button is available only before you click the Partition button!

If you have more than one partition, check out the bar(s) with a handle separating the volumes in the partition list. If you leave all your partitions unlocked (by leaving the Locked for Editing check box disabled), you can click and drag these separator bars to dynamically resize the volumes. This makes it easy to adjust the individual volume sizes for the disk until you get precisely the arrangement you want. If a volume is locked, it can't be resized dynamically in this fashion.

RAID has nothing to do with insects

The final stop on the Disk Utility hayride isn't for everyone — as a matter of fact, only a Mac OS X power user with a roomful of hardware is likely to use it. RAID, *Redundant Array of Independent/Inexpensive Disks,* is actually what it says. In normal human English, a *RAID set* is a group of multiple separate disks, working together as a team. Using RAID can

✦ Improve the speed of your system

✦ Help prevent disk errors from compromising or corrupting your data

The RAID controls within Disk Utility are illustrated in Figure 7-10. (Note that I've turned on the Disk Utility toolbar as well, just to show you what it looks like.) You'll need at least two additional hard drives on your system besides the start-up disk, which I don't recommend that you use in a RAID set.

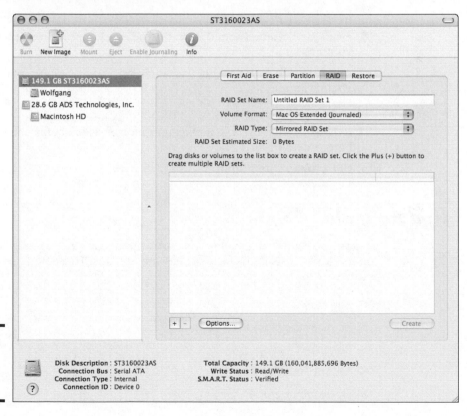

Figure 7-10:
The Disk
Utility RAID
controls.

To set up a RAID array in Mac OS X, follow these steps:

1. **From the RAID tab of Disk Utility, click and drag the disks from the list at the left to the Disk box at the right.**

2. **Click the RAID Type drop-down list to specify the type of RAID that you need.**

   - *Striped RAID Set:* Choosing this can speed up your hard drive performance by splitting data between multiple disks.

   - *Mirrored RAID Set:* Choosing this increases the reliability of your storage by creating a mirror backup of that data across multiple disks.

3. **Click in the RAID Set Name field and type the name for your RAID set.**

4. **From the Volume Format drop-down list, choose a format for the volumes.**

   Always use Mac OS Extended or Mac OS Extended (Journaled) from the Volume Format list unless you have a specific reason to use the MS-DOS File System (for compatibility with PCs running Windows) or the UNIX File System (for compatibility with UNIX/Linux machines). Journaling helps reduce the amount of disk fragmentation and also helps speed up your hard drive's performance.

5. **Click the Create button.**

Updating Mac OS X

As any good software developer should, Apple constantly releases improvements to Mac OS X in the form of software updates. These updates can include all sorts of fun stuff, like

+ Bug fixes
+ Improvements and new features
+ Enhanced drivers
+ Security upgrades
+ Firmware upgrades

Apple makes it easy to keep Mac OS X up-to-date with the Software Update controls in System Preferences (see Figure 7-11). Alternatively, you can choose the Apple menu and then choose Software Update. To check for new updates periodically, enable the Check for Updates check box. Then from the drop-down list box, choose how often you want these updates. (I suggest at least weekly, if not daily.) For a manual check, make sure that you're connected to the Internet and then click the Check Now button.

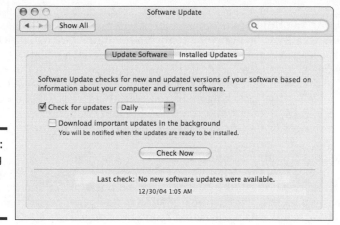

Figure 7-11:
Configuring
Software
Update is
easy.

To download updates automatically, mark the Download Important Updates in the Background check box to enable it; the Big X politely downloads the updates behind the scenes and then alerts you that they're ready to be installed. (With automatic downloading disabled, Mac OS X displays any available updates with short descriptions, and you can toggle the installation of a specific update by enabling or disabling the check boxes next to it.)

I recommend installing all updates, even for hardware that you don't have yet. For example, I always install AirPort updates even though I don't use an AirPort connection at home. The reason? Often, the functionality covered by an update may include system software that you do use, so you'll still benefit from installing it.

After you specify the updates that you want to install, click the Install button to begin the update process. You might have to reboot after everything has been installed.

To see which updates you've already installed, click the Installed Updates tab.

1 Demand That You Back Up Your Hard Drive

I know we're friends, but there's no excuse for not backing up your data. The more valuable and irreplaceable that your documents are, the more heinous it is to risk losing them. (I don't get to use the word *heinous* in many of my books, but it fits really well here.)

Although Apple does include the ability to create *disk images* and restore them in the Disk Utility (see the sidebar titled "So what's a disk image?" earlier in this chapter), I'm not going to recommend that you use disk images for backups. (Insert sound of stunned silence here.) That's because the restore process can be confusing, and the disk image method doesn't offer the level of control that you need when it comes to backing up individual files and folders (or selectively backing up by date or recent use). Only a bona fide backup application gives you such flexibility and convenience . . . and that's why Tiger power users turn to true-blue backup software for help.

If you've subscribed to Apple's .Mac service, a back-up utility is included, but it's not a part of the default Mac OS X package. Therefore, if you're not a .Mac member, you can turn to a commercial back-up application for your salvation — my personal recommendation is Retrospect, from EMC Dantz (www.dantz.com). This well-written "software bungee cord" has saved my posterior more than once.

Using Retrospect is cheap security, but if you can't afford it at the moment, take a second to at least back up your most important documents by copying them to a rewriteable CD or a Zip disk. Don't trust a floppy (if your Mac is actually old enough to sport a floppy drive); they're far too unreliable. With this poor man's backup, even if you lose your entire hard drive, you can still restore what matters the most.

1 Further Demand That You Defragment

Defragmenting your hard drive can significantly improve its performance. Using a defragmenter scans for little chunks of a file that are spread out across the surface of your hard drive and then arranges them to form a contiguous file. After a file has been optimized in this way, it's far easier and faster for Mac OS X to read than reassembling a fragmented file.

However, Apple dropped the ball on this one and didn't include a defragmenter with Mac OS X. Luckily, many third-party disk utilities (like Micromat Drive 10 from www.micromat.com) also includes a defragmenting feature. If you have a defragmenter, I recommend that you use it once a month.

Special Start-Up Keys for Those Special Times

Mac OS X includes a number of special keys that you can use during the boot process. These keys really come in handy when you need to force your operating system to do something that it normally wouldn't, like boot from a CD instead of the hard drive.

+ **To boot from a CD or DVD:** Restart your Mac while pressing the C key. This is a great way to free up your start-up volume when you want to test it or optimize it using a commercial utility.

+ **To eject a recalcitrant disc that doesn't show up on the Desktop:** Restart Mac OS X and hold down the mouse button — or if you have a late-model Mac, press the Media Eject key as soon as you hear that magnificent startup chord.

+ **To force your Mac to boot in Mac OS X:** Hold down the X key while restarting or booting the Mac.

+ **To display a system boot menu:** Hold down the Option key while restarting or booting the Mac, and you can choose which operating system you want to use.

+ **To prevent start-up applications from running during login:** Hold down the Shift key while you click the Login button on the Login screen. If you don't see the Login screen during startup, just hold down Shift while Mac OS X boots until the Finder menu appears.

Crave the Newest Drivers

No chapter on maintenance would be complete without a reminder to keep your hardware drivers current. *Drivers* are simply programs that allow your Mac to control hardware devices, like a video card or a Small Computer System Interface (SCSI) card that you've added to your Mac. The Mac OS X Software Update feature that I discuss earlier in the section "Updating Mac OS X" provides most of the drivers that you'll need for things like printers, USB and FireWire peripherals, and digital cameras, but it's still very important to check those manufacturer Web sites.

Like the software updates from Apple, updated drivers can fix bugs and even add new features to your existing hardware, which is my definition of something for nothing.

Chapter 8: Using Classic Mode

In This Chapter

✔ **Understanding how Classic mode works**

✔ **Locating Classic applications, files, and folders**

✔ **Configuring Classic mode**

✔ **Restarting in Mac OS 9.2**

To someone as familiar as you are with Mac OS X, using applications in Mac OS 9 is like watching an evening of Lawrence Welk — you know that this music *used* to be cutting-edge, and that tap-dancer *used* to be cool, but now it all seems . . . well . . . horribly *wrong*. (I don't mean to offend the champagne-music crowd — Lawrence and the band were really quite good. Perhaps it's those unspeakable robin's-egg blue tuxedos that give me such a headache.)

We're lucky because virtually all of popular Mac applications have been updated for the Big X, but the process isn't yet complete. Most older applications still run only in Classic mode, so if you're using an older Mac and older applications, it's practically a sure thing that sooner or later you'll launch an application, see the bouncing number 9 on the Dock, and realize that means Classic is revving up. For those times, this chapter will prove a soothing balm.

Classic Mode Explained

Let's start with a definition: *Classic mode* is actually an implementation of Mac OS 9 that runs in Mac OS X. Think of it as a virtual session of Mac OS 9 that runs whenever you need it — although you won't actually see the Mac OS 9 session after it boots up. Instead, Classic runs in the background, providing breathing space for applications that wouldn't otherwise run in Mac OS X.

The beauty of Classic is that virtually all older applications run fine in Classic mode, and they have absolutely no idea that they're actually working under Mac OS X. Any problems that you're likely to experience in Classic mode stem from "confused" hardware that can't communicate through ports that are still controlled through Mac OS X, or the same "shared" memory problems that plagued older versions of Mac OS. (Sigh.) In other words, if a lockup could happen in a "real" Mac OS 9 session, it can also happen in Classic mode . . . but luckily, the only thing that would crash is the Classic environment itself, so the rest of your Mac OS X applications should continue working without a hitch. (In fact, you can launch Classic from System Preferences, as I show you later in this chapter, and try to run the Classic application again without wreaking havoc on the rest of Mac OS X.)

If you need to use an application from time to time that simply won't run correctly under Classic mode at all, you might be able to take drastic measures and restart under Mac OS 9, which I demonstrate at the end of this chapter. (Unfortunately, today's Macintosh models won't boot into Mac OS 9, so this is no longer an option for those using recent Mac models based on the G4 processor (as well as all Macs using the G5 processor.)

Tiger no longer installs a Classic System Folder by default on new hardware. If you buy a new Mac and need Classic, you'll have to install it. For instructions on installing a Classic System Folder, crank up Safari and enter this URL: http://docs.info.apple.com/article.html?artnum=86775.

Of Carbon and Cocoa . . .

First, a word about why Classic mode is required in the first place — you can politely brush past this section if you're not interested in the Grand Design, and I'll catch up with you in a paragraph or two.

Still here? Okay. Here's the chop. Mac OS X applications are written by using two software development APIs (nerdspeak for *Application Program Interfaces*). An *API* specifies how a program communicates with the operating system.

Mac OS X recognizes two programming APIs: Carbon and Cocoa. A *Carbon* application runs in both Mac OS 9.2 and Mac OS X. A *Cocoa* application runs only under Mac OS X, such as Microsoft Office 2004. Cocoa applications perform significantly better than Carbon under Mac OS X, and Cocoa's structure allows software developers to finish an application faster.

If a program supports either Carbon or Cocoa, it'll work within Mac OS X (with a Cocoa application providing the better performance). However, if the program is older and was exclusively written for earlier versions of Mac OS without Carbon, it won't run in Mac OS X, and Classic mode automatically launches to run the application in a comfortable environment.

Cranking Up Classic

The four methods of running Classic mode are

✦ **Double-click an application without Cocoa or Carbon support.** In other words, launch an older application. As I mention earlier, you'll see the sprightly bouncing Classic mode icon appear in the Dock, and a minimal progress bar appears (as shown in Figure 8-1). Click the arrow next to the progress bar to expand the Classic window and watch the boot process, just as if you were actually staring at Mac OS 9. After Classic mode loads, the Classic icon disappears from the Dock, the Mac OS 9 boot window/progress bar disappears, and the application menu and window appear.

Figure 8-1:
Starting
Classic
mode with
just the pro-
gress bar.

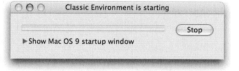

Note that applications running in Classic use the Mac OS 9 menu bar, and Classic mode windows have the older Mac OS 9 window controls. In fact, here's an easy way to tell whether an application is running in Classic mode: Just to look at the Apple logo (🍎) in the top-left corner of the screen! If it's a solid-colored apple, the active application is a native Mac OS X application. On the other hand, if the apple appears as the traditional six-color logo, the active application is running in Classic mode.

✦ **Launch Classic from System Preferences.** Click the System Preferences icon on the Dock and choose Classic settings to display the dialog that you see in Figure 8-2. Click the Start button.

✦ **Launch Classic from the Mac OS X Finder menu bar icon.** If you've enabled the Show Classic Status in Menu Bar check box (on the same Classic settings panel in System Preferences), you get a nifty Classic icon on your menu bar. You can click this menu bar icon to start, stop, or restart Classic mode — or you can click Open Classic Preferences to display the Classic settings panel.

✦ **Configure Classic to run automatically.** To start Classic automatically when you log in to Mac OS X — on a system on which you're the only user, that means when you boot your computer — click the System Preferences icon on the Dock and choose Classic settings. Mark the Start Classic When You Login check box to enable it, and then press ⌘+Q to exit System Preferences and save the change.

Tiger can hide Classic in the background when it runs automatically. Mark the Hide Classic While Starting check box to enable it, and you'll never know that your little friend is alongside you. With this check box disabled, you get the standard Classic startup mode with the progress bar. (Oh, and one more caveat to the "hidden" Classic mode: If you enable the Classic icon on the Finder menu bar, the icon will always let you know that Classic is starting up. The little snitch . . .)

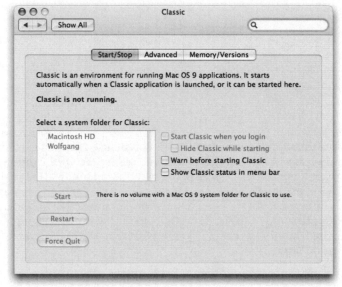

Figure 8-2: Starting Classic mode from within System Preferences.

After Classic mode is running on your Mac, any number of Mac OS Classic applications can use it. You have to launch Classic only once, and it remains running until you log out, Mac OS X is restarted, or Classic mode goes to sleep (more on this nocturnal behavior later in the section "Configuring Classic Mode").

To stop Classic mode — thus freeing up both system RAM (memory) and your processor, as well as improving the performance of other Mac OS X applications — open System Preferences, choose Classic settings, and click Stop on the Start/Stop pane. (Alternatively, if the Classic icon is displayed in your Finder menu bar, just click it and choose Stop Classic from the menu.)

Reaching That Antique Software

If you upgraded from Mac OS version 8 or 9 to Mac OS X, you'll be happy to know that all those legacy applications that you used before are still available. You can find them in a number of places on your system:

✦ **Applications (Mac OS 9) folder:** Mac OS X places all the applications that existed on your drive in the old Applications folder into this new folder — and, in turn, all the new Mac OS X applications added to your system are stored in the Applications folder. Although slightly schizophrenic, it's a great solution that actually works. After you upgrade to Mac OS X, simply look in the Applications folder for your Mac OS X native applications and open the Applications (Mac OS 9) folder for your older stuff.

Many new Mac OS X native applications that use the Carbon API will also install an *alias* (known as a *shortcut* to the Windows crowd) in your Applications (Mac OS 9) folder so that you can easily run them when you restart in Mac OS 9. If a Mac OS X application runs under Mac OS 9 but doesn't automatically create an alias (how rude!), it takes but a second to add the alias yourself in the Applications (Mac OS 9) folder. (For more about aliases, see Book I, Chapter 2.)

✦ **The Mac OS 9 Desktop:** Yep, you heard right, you can still reach the icons and programs on your Mac OS 9 Desktop, including folders and aliases. (Any changes that you make to this "Desktop in a Folder" in Mac OS X will naturally be reflected when you restart in Mac OS 9.)

To reach your Mac OS 9 Desktop items from within the Finder window, open the System Folder. Remember, this is your Mac OS 9 **System Folder,** not the Mac OS X **System** folder (note the whomping big loss of the word *Folder* there; it's important). Within, you'll find the Desktop Folder, which contains the same Mac OS 9 items as the folder on your Desktop. Hang on, I need more Diet Coke . . . it always helps me when I'm nearing a state of confusion.

Configuring Classic Mode

The default System Preferences settings for the Classic environment can be tweaked to enhance performance or to change when Classic starts or how it operates. These settings include the following:

✦ **Startup and Other Options:** Click the Advanced tab to display the options that you see in Figure 8-3. From the drop-down list box, you can elect to start Classic with extensions off or to start the Classic Extensions Manager to individually toggle Control Panels and Extensions on or off. Select the Use Key Combination option and type up to five keys — one at a time — that should be simultaneously pressed when you start Classic (which allows you to simulate Mac OS 9 startup keys). *Note:* These Advanced startup options work only when you launch Classic manually from this panel using the Start Classic button.

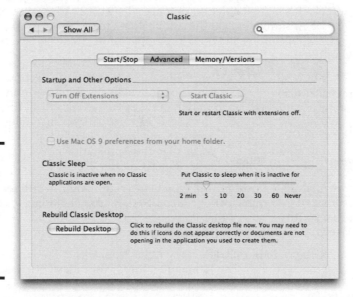

Figure 8-3: The Classic pane includes Advanced settings for in-depth tweaking.

✦ **Putting Classic to sleep:** Click and drag the Classic Sleep slider to specify the amount of inactivity that will trigger the sleep option. When Classic is asleep, it uses much less system memory and doesn't bog down your Mac's CPU. And, when a Classic application is launched, it takes Mac OS X far less time to activate Classic from Sleep mode than it does to start Classic from scratch. To disable the Classic Sleep option, move the slider to Never. After it's running, Classic will continue to remain active in the background until you manually stop it (as I describe earlier in this chapter).

✦ **Rebuilding your Classic Desktop:** Click the Rebuild Desktop button to regenerate the Classic Desktop file. This process stores data on which icons go with which Classic applications. This also sets which types of documents link to which Classic applications. Normally, you need do this only if your Classic applications no longer have the proper icons or if double-clicking a document created with a Classic application no longer launches the proper application.

To see what's running in the Classic environment — something roughly akin to asking, "I wonder how refrigerant is circulated in my central air conditioning system?" — click the Memory/Versions tab of the Classic System Preferences dialog. You'll see how many Classic applications are running, the amount of memory that they're actually using, and the maximum amount of memory that they're allowed to have. To show what's running in the background in Classic mode, mark the Show Background Processes check box to enable it. This dialog also displays the version of Mac OS that Classic is using. (If you're not interested in what's happening behind the curtain in the Classic environment, you can gleefully forget that this tab ever existed in the Classic System Preferences settings.)

Returning to Your Mac OS 9 Roots

If you need to take the plunge and travel back in time, you might be able to restart your Mac in Mac OS 9 for as long as you like — simply change the system Startup Disk! Remember, this ability to restart using Mac OS 9 depends on what model of Macintosh you own. Current Mac models (as well as most produced within the last year or two) can run Mac OS 9 only in Classic mode.

Follow these steps in Mac OS X to return to the days of yore:

1. **Click the System Preferences icon on the Dock.**

2. **Click the Startup Disk icon.**

3. **Click the Mac OS 9 System Folder to select it.**

   Note that if you have multiple installations of Mac OS 9 on your system on different hard drives — as I do — you'll have to choose the proper System Folder on the proper drive. For those with only one Mac OS 9 System Folder, all is well.

4. **Click the Restart button and then click the Save and Restart buttons on the confirmation sheet that appears.**

After you finish your fun in Mac OS 9.2 and you want to return to Mac OS X, follow these steps:

1. **Choose ![apple] ➪Control Panels.**

2. **Choose the Startup Disk submenu item.**

3. **Click the Mac OS X System Folder to select it.**

If you have multiple Mac OS X installations or multiple drives, you can click the triangle next to a drive to expand the display.

4. **Click the Restart button.**

Voilà! You've returned to Wonderland. Say hello to the White Rabbit for me.

Mac OS X also provides two neat "Choose your operating system weapon" startup keys you can use when booting or restarting your system. If you hold down the X key while booting or restarting, your Mac boots into Mac OS X. In fact, the Startup Disk choice in System Preferences is actually changed to the Mac OS X System folder on the current boot drive, so this eliminates the need to follow the steps that I just outlined! (Pretty catchy, huh? Holding down X to start the Big X, I mean.) Alternatively, if you hold down the Option key while booting or restarting, your Mac displays a menu of all the available operating systems on your system, and you can pick one. Note, however, that the Option key does not change your Startup Disk setting, so the next time that you reboot or restart, you revert to the startup operating system that you selected in System Preferences.

Chapter 9: Getting Help for the Big X

In This Chapter

✔ Using the Mac OS X Help Center

✔ Searching for specific help

✔ Getting help in applications

✔ Finding other help resources

Whether the voice echoes from a living room, home office, or college computer lab, it's all too familiar: a call for help. No matter how well written the application or how well designed the operating system, sooner or later you're going to need support. That goes for everyone from the novice to the experienced Mac owner to the occasional e-mail user to the most talented software developer.

In this short but oh-so-important chapter, I lead you through the various help resources available within Mac OS X as well as native Mac OS X applications. I show you how to tap additional resources from Apple, and I also point you to other suppliers of high-quality (and even questionable) assistance from sources on the Internet and in your local area.

Displaying the Help Viewer Window

Your first line of defense is the Mac OS X Help Viewer, as shown in Figure 9-1. To display the Help Viewer from the Finder menu, click Help and choose Mac Help; or, you can press the ⌘+? keyboard shortcut (or, if you think about it, ⌘+Shift+/, or the forward slash key keyboard shortcut). This Help menu is context-sensitive, so it contains different menu items when you're working inside an application.

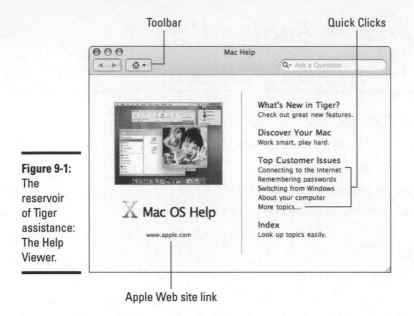

Toolbar   Quick Clicks

Figure 9-1:
The
reservoir
of Tiger
assistance:
The Help
Viewer.

Apple Web site link

As shown in Figure 9-1, the Help Viewer is divided into three sets of controls:

✦ **Toolbar:** The toolbar includes navigational controls (Back, Forward and Help Center buttons) and the Ask a Question (or Search) text box.

✦ **Quick Clicks:** Clicking these links takes you directly to some of the most frequently asked Help topics for the Finder (or the application you're using), such as *Connecting to the Internet* and *Switching from Windows*. To use a Quick Click, just click once on the question that you want to pursue.

✦ **Apple Web site link:** Click this link to display the latest Mac OS X news and the latest Help topics from the Apple Web site.

I know that the Help Viewer looks a little sparse at first glance. However, when you realize how much information has to be covered to help someone with an operating system — check out the size of the book you're holding, for instance — you get an idea of why Mac OS X doesn't try to cover everything on one screen. Instead, you get the one tool that does it all: the Ask a Question text box.

Searching for Specific Stuff

To search for the help topic you need, click in the Ask a Question text box, type one or two words that sum up your question, and press Return. (Although you can ask a full sentence question, I've found that the shorter and more concise your search criteria is, the better the relevance of your return.) Figure 9-2 illustrates a typical set of topics concerning DVD movies.

Note that the topics are sorted by approximate relevance first. Articles taken from the AppleCare Support section of the Apple Web site appear in the Support Articles portion of the window. *Note:* You won't see these articles unless your Mac has an active Internet connection.

To sort the topics alphabetically or by their location within the Help system, click the Topic or Location column headings, respectively. You can click a column heading again to toggle the sort order between ascending and descending.

You can double-click any topic to display the topic text, which will look like the text that you see in Figure 9-3.

Figure 9-2:
The results of a search in Help Viewer.

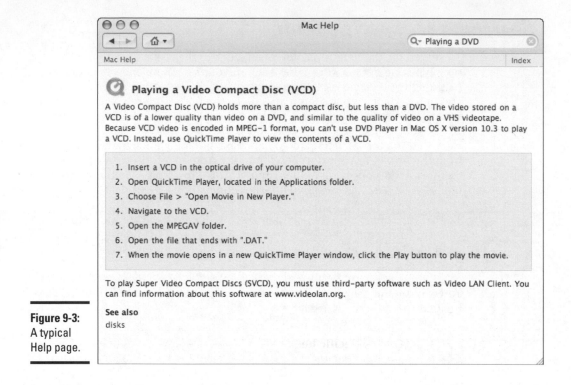

Figure 9-3:
A typical
Help page.

To move back to the previous topic that you chose, click the Back button on the Help Viewer toolbar.

Prodding Apple for the Latest Gossip

As I mention in the earlier section "Displaying the Help Viewer Window," I heartily recommend that you visit the Apple Web site at www.apple.com and surf wildly to and fro. You'll often pick up on news and reviews that you won't find anywhere else on the Internet.

From the opening Web screen, you should click these three links during every visit to the Apple site: the Hot News link on the Apple tab, the Support tab, and the Mac OS X tab. These pages give you

✦ Articles about the latest news from Cupertino

✦ Downloads of the latest Mac OS X freeware, shareware, and demo-ware

✦ The *Knowledge Base* (an online searchable troubleshooting reference)

✦ News about upcoming versions of Mac OS X and Apple applications galore

You'll also find Mac OS X product manuals in Adobe Acrobat PDF format and online discussion forums that cover Mac OS X.

Calling for Help Deep in the Heart of X

A number of different help avenues are available within Mac OS X applications as well. They include

✦ **The Help button:** A number of otherwise upstanding Mac OS X windows, dialogs, and System Preference panes include a Help button, as shown in the lower right of Figure 9-4. Click the button marked with ? to display the text for the settings in that dialog or window.

✦ **Pop-up help for fields and controls:** Most Mac OS X applications display a short line of help text when you hover the mouse pointer on top of a field or control. Sometimes it's just the name of the item; sometimes it's a full descriptive line. Them's the breaks.

✦ **Application-specific help:** Applications typically have their own Help system, which can use the Help Viewer, a separate Help display program, or a HyperText Markup Language (HTML; read that *Web-based*) Help system. Figure 9-5 illustrates the standalone online Help system for Microsoft Internet Explorer.

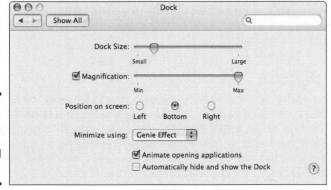

Figure 9-4:
Notice the not-so-well-camouflaged Help button.

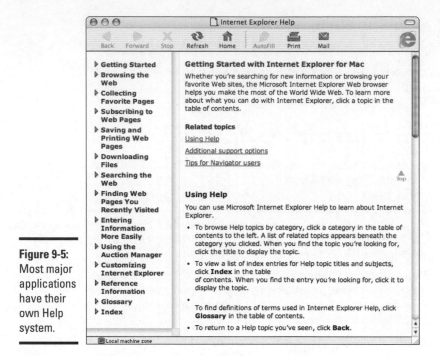

Figure 9-5:
Most major
applications
have their
own Help
system.

Other Resources to Chew On

Although the Help Viewer can take care of just about any question that you
might have about the basic controls and features of Mac OS X, you might
also want to turn to other forms of help when the going gets a little rougher.
In this last section, I cover resources that you can call on when the Help
Viewer just isn't enough.

Voice support

As of this writing, Apple provides voice technical support for Mac OS X. You
can find the number to call in your Mac's printed manuals or online in the
Support section of the Apple Web site. However, exactly when you qualify for
voice support and exactly how long it lasts depends on a number of different
factors, like whether you received Mac OS X when you bought a new machine,
or whether you purchased a support plan from Apple.

You can also try the general online support site at www.info.apple.com —
it's a great starting point for obtaining Mac OS X help.

Mac publications and resource sites

You can refer to a number of great Mac-savvy publications and resources, both printed and online, for help. My favorites include

✦ *Macworld* (www.macworld.com) and *MacAddict* (www.macaddict.com) magazines, both in archaic hard copy and oh-so-slick online versions

✦ MacGamer (www.macgamer.com), the online gaming resource for the Macintosh

✦ VersionTracker (www.versiontracker.com), an online resource for the latest updates on all sorts of Macintosh third-party applications

✦ MacFixIt (www.macfixit.com), a well-respected troubleshooting site devoted to the Mac that offers downloads, news, and discussion areas

In most of my books, I mention specific Internet newsgroups that cater to the topic I'm discussing — however, virtually all the Mac-specific newsgroups around are devoted to illegally swapping pirated games and applications, so I won't be covering them. Also, the help that you receive from individuals in newsgroups is sometimes misguided — and sometimes downright wrong, so take any claims with a grain of salt.

As a general rule, *never* identify yourself or provide your snail-mail or e-mail addresses in a newsgroup post! These messages are public, and they remain hanging around in cyberspace on newsgroup servers for years — you'll be a prime target for spam (or even worse).

Local Mac outlets and user groups

Finally, you can find local resources in any medium- to large-sized town or city: A shop that's authorized by Apple to sell and repair Macintosh computers can usually be counted upon to answer a quick question over the phone or provide more substantial support for a fee. (For example, my local Mac outlet sponsors inexpensive classes for new Mac owners.)

You might also be lucky enough to have a local Macintosh user group that you can join — members can be counted on for free answers to your support questions at meetings and demonstrations. To find a group near you, visit the Apple User Group Support site at www.apple.com/usergroups and use the locator.

Chapter 10: Troubleshooting the X

In This Chapter

✔ **Mastering the scientific approach**

✔ **Using troubleshooting techniques**

✔ **Performing the radical solutions**

✔ **Checking troubleshooting resources**

Mac OS X Tiger is rugged, stable, and reliable — and as you can read earlier in this mini-book (in Chapter 7), practicing regular maintenance can help eliminate problems caused by everything from power failures to faulty software drivers to cats upon the keyboard. However, sooner or later you *will* encounter what I like to call *The Dark Moments* . . . a blank screen, a locked Mac, or an external device that sits there uselessly like an expensive paperweight.

How you handle The Dark Moments defines you as a true Mac OS X power user because most folks seem to fall into one of two categories: Either you panic and beat your head against the wall (which really has little effect on the computer, when you think about it), or you set your brow in grim determination and follow the troubleshooting models that I provide in this chapter to locate (and hopefully fix) the source of the problem.

Don't Panic!

My friend, this is the first — and **most important** — rule of troubleshooting, and yet another of Mark's Maxims:

> **Whatever the problem, you *can* fix it.**™

Most computer owners seem to forget the idea that a hardware or software error can be fixed because they panic — they simply see The Problem, and somehow they feel that they'll never be able to use their computer again.

Although the situation might look grim, don't ignore these facts:

✦ **You don't need to scrap your Mac.** As long as you haven't taken a hammer or a chainsaw to your Mac, the problem is only temporary. Sure, individual components do fail over time — heck, so do people — but the problem is certainly something that can be tracked down and fixed without scrapping your entire computer.

✦ **Don't beat yourself up.** As long as you haven't installed a virus on purpose or deleted half your system files to spite yourself, the problem *isn't* your fault. Sure, it's possible that you might have done something by accident, but don't blame yourself — it happens to everybody.

✦ **Trust your Apple dealer.** As long as an Apple dealer is in your area, you can always get your computer repaired professionally if a component has gone south. (In some cases, professional help is a necessity: For example, I'd be a fool to try to fix a power supply or a monitor on my own because both can pack a heavy electrical punch.)

✦ **Rely on your backup.** As long as you've made a backup — you *did* back up your hard drive, didn't you? — you won't lose much (if any) work. (I harp about backups further in Chapter 7 of this mini-book.)

Commit these facts to head and heart, and you can rest easy while you track down and attack the *real* enemy — whatever's causing the problem.

The Troubleshooting Process

When I first conceived this chapter, I had originally decided to divide this section into separate hardware and software troubleshooting procedures. However, that turned out to be impractical because often you won't know whether a problem is caused by hardware or software until you're practically on top of it.

Therefore, here's the complete 12-step troubleshooting process that I designed while working as a consultant and Macintosh hardware technician for more than a decade. Feel free to add your own embellishments in the margin or include reminders with Post-it Notes.

If you're not sure quite what's producing the error, this process is designed to be *linear* — meaning that it's meant to be followed in order — but if you already know that you're having a problem with one specific peripheral or one specific application, feel free to jump to the steps that concern only hardware or software.

Step 1: Always try a simple shutdown

You'd be amazed at how often a *reboot* (the process of shutting down and restarting) can cure a temporary problem. For example, this can fix the occasional lockup in Mac OS X or a keyboard that's not responding because of a power failure. If possible, make sure that you first close any open documents, or you might lose unsaved work. When troubleshooting, always do a shutdown instead of simply restarting the computer because when Mac OS X shuts down, all the hardware components that make up your system are reset.

If your Mac is locked tight and you can't use the Shut Down command from the Apple menu (🍎), you have two choices. First, press and hold the Power button on your Mac for a few seconds (which turns your computer off). If this doesn't work — and, from time to time, it actually doesn't — you'll have to physically pull the power cord from the wall (or turn off the surge suppressor, if you're using one).

Step 2: Check all cable connections

Check all connections: the AC power cord and the keyboard cord, as well as any modem or network connections and all cable connections to external peripherals. Look for loose connectors — and if you've got a cat or dog, don't forget to check for chew marks. (Yep, that's the voice of experience talking there.) If you've recently replaced a cable — especially a network, Universal Serial Bus (USB), or FireWire cable — replace it with a spare to see whether the problem still occurs.

Step 3: Retrace your steps

If the problem continues to occur, the next step is to consider what you've done in the immediate past that could have affected your Mac. Did you install any new software or have you connected a new peripheral? If your Mac was working fine until you made the change to your system, the problem likely lies in the new hardware or software.

✦ **If you added an external device:** Turn off your Mac and disconnect the peripheral. Then turn on the computer to see whether all proceeds normally. If so, then check the peripheral's documentation and make sure that you correctly installed the *driver* — the software provided by the device manufacturer — and that you connected it properly to the right port. (You can also use System Profiler, which I discuss later in this chapter, to check to see whether your Mac recognizes the external device.) To verify that the cable works, substitute another cable of the same type or try the peripheral on another Mac.

Make it a practice to check the manufacturer's Web site for the latest driver when you get new hardware. The software that ships in the box with your new toy could have been on the shelf for months before being sold, and the manufacturer has probably fine-tuned the driver in the interim.

✦ **If you installed new software or applied an update/patch:** Follow the guidelines in Chapter 7 of this mini-book to uninstall the application and search for any files that it might have installed elsewhere. (Searching by date created and date modified can help you locate files that you recently installed.) If this fixes the problem, it's time to contact the developer and request technical support for the recalcitrant program; you can always re-install the program after the problem has been solved by the developer.

Not all versions of Mac OS X are created equal. If you've recently upgraded to a major or minor new release of Mac OS X, some of the applications that you've been using without trouble for months can suddenly go on the warpath and refuse to work (or exhibit quirky behavior). If this happens, visit the developer's Web site often to look for a patch file that will update the application to work with the new version of Mac OS X.

✦ **If you recently made a change within System Preferences:** It's possible that you've inadvertently "bumped" something. For instance, you might have accidentally changed your modem or network settings or perhaps made a change to your login options. Verify the settings screens that you visited to make sure that everything looks okay. Other locations to check include the Printer Setup Utility (which I discuss in Book VI, Chapter 4) and your Web browser's Preference dialog. (I cover Safari in Book IV, Chapter 5.)

Step 4: Run Disk Utility

Next, run Disk Utility (as shown in Figure 10-1) to check for disk errors and permissions errors — especially permissions errors, which can wreak absolute havoc on just about any application on your hard drive. (Click the Disk Utility icon in the Utilities folder inside your Applications folder. Chapter 7 of this mini-book provides all the details.)

Step 5: Run antivirus software

Run your antivirus software and scan your entire system for viruses, including all system disks and removable disks. Although Mac OS X doesn't come with antivirus protection built in, the world-class program Norton AntiVirus (www.symantec.com) constantly scans each file that you open or download for infections.

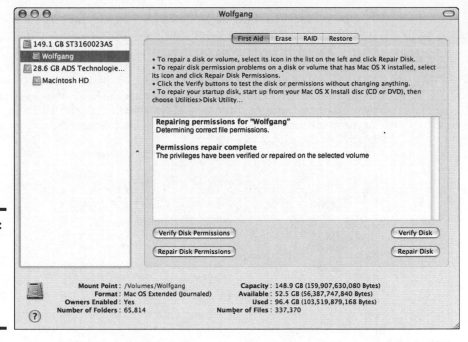

Figure 10-1:
Use Disk
Utility to
check the
integrity of
your drive
and files.

If you haven't already set your antivirus application to automatically update itself, download the latest virus update — usually called a *signature file* or *data file* — to keep your virus protection current.

Step 6: Check the Trash

Check the contents of your Trash to make sure that you haven't inadvertently tossed something important that could be causing trouble for an application. Click the Trash icon on the Dock to open the Trash window and peruse its contents. (*Hint:* Switch to list mode to see the file types.) To restore items to their rightful place, drag them from the Trash back to the correct folder on your hard drive.

Step 7: Check online connections

If you're connected to an Ethernet network, a cable modem, or a digital subscriber line (DSL), check your equipment to make sure that you're currently online and receiving packets normally. Your network system administrator will be happy to help you with this, especially if you're blood relatives.

Step 8: Disable troublesome Login Items

Disable any *Login Items* (called Startup Items in versions of Mac OS X before Tiger) that might be causing trouble. As you can read in Book II, Chapter 3, Login Items are automatically launched as soon as you log in. For example, an older application that doesn't fully support Mac OS X can cause problems if used as a Login Item. You can do this from the Login Items settings in the System Preferences Accounts panel (as shown in Figure 10-2); click the Apple menu, choose System Preferences, click Accounts, and then click the Login Items button.

Figure 10-2:
A misbehaving Login Item can cause you a world of grief.

Unfortunately, if a Login Item doesn't display an error message, your old friend Trial-and-Error is just about the only sure-fire way to detect which item (if any) is causing the problem. Click an item to select it, click the Remove button (marked with a minus sign), and then press ⌘+Q to quit System Preferences. Shut down and reboot your Mac to see whether the problem has been solved. (If not, don't forget to add the item again to the Login Items list.)

You can also disable Login Items entirely when you reboot. If the login window appears when you reboot your computer, hold down the Shift key and then click the Login button. If you don't see the login window when you reboot, hold down the Shift key when you see the progress bar in the startup window and continue to hold down the key until the Finder appears.

Step 9: Turn off your screen saver

Another candidate for intermittent lockups is your screen saver, especially if you're running a shareware effort written by a 12-year-old with a limited attention span. Display your System Preferences, choose Desktop & Screen Saver, and click the Screen Saver button. You can deactivate the saver entirely (by moving the Start Screen Saver slider to Never) or choose the Computer Name saver (which is provided by Apple) from the Screen Savers list.

Step 10: Check for write-protection

If you're running a multi-user ship, check to make sure that another user with administrator access hasn't accidentally write-protected your documents, your application, or its support files. If possible, log in with an administrator account yourself (as I describe in Book II, Chapter 5) and then try running the application or opening the document that you were unable to access under your own ID.

Trying an application under someone else's account is also a great way to determine whether your user-specific Preference file for that application has been corrupted. If you can run the application using another person's account, contact the software developer to see how you can repair or delete a Preference file that's causing problems.

Step 11: Check your System Profiler

If you've reached this point in the troubleshooting process and haven't found the culprit, you've probably experienced a hardware failure in your Macintosh. If possible, display the Hardware category within the Apple System Profiler (see Figure 10-3) and make sure that it's able to recognize and use all the internal drives, ports, and external devices on your Mac. To start the System Profiler, click the Apple menu, choose About This Mac, and then click the More Info button.

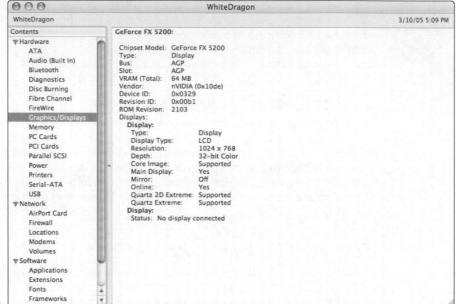

Figure 10-3:
Use System
Profiler to
check the
devices and
ports on
your system.

Step 12: Reboot with the Mac OS X Installation Disc

In case your Mac is in sad shape and won't even boot from its hard drive, here's a last step that you can take before you seek professional assistance: Reboot your Mac from the Mac OS X Installation disc. Hold down the C key immediately after you hear the startup chord (which boots your system from the CD-ROM or DVD-ROM drive) and then run Disk Utility from the Installation Apple menu that appears. Because you've booted the system from the installation disc, you can verify and repair problems with your startup hard drive. (Some new Mac models also come with a diagnostic CD-ROM that can help you pin down hardware problems.) After you're done, restart your system.

Do I Need to Reinstall Mac OS X?

To be honest, this is a difficult question to answer. Technically, you should never *need* to reinstall the Big X, but there's also no reason why you *can't*.

I can only think of two scenarios where reinstalling the operating system will likely solve a problem. One, if your system files have been so heavily corrupted — by a faulty hard drive or a rampaging virus, for example — that you can't boot Mac OS X at all. Two, if the operating system encounters the death-dealing kernel panic on a regular basis. A *kernel panic* displays a dialog that instructs you to restart your Mac (in multiple languages, no less), usually overwriting whatever's on the monitor at the time. (This is analogous to the infamous Windows Blue Screen of Death — I've grown to hate that color of blue with a passion.)

If you receive kernel panics on an ongoing basis, something is really, *really* wrong. Make sure that your documents are copied to a rewriteable CD or network drive and don't overwrite any existing backup that you have with a new backup because the back-up application is likely to lock up as well.

To reinstall, you must reboot from your Mac OS X Installation disc. Hold down the C key immediately after you hear your Mac's startup chord. (Read the earlier section "Step 12: Reboot with the Mac OS X Installation Disc.")

It's Still Not Moving: Troubleshooting Resources

As I mention earlier in this chapter, you can pursue other avenues to get help when you can't solve a troubleshooting problem on your own. Mind you, I'm talking about professional help from sources that you can trust. Although you can find quite a bit of free advice on the Internet (usually on privately run Web sites and in the Internet newsgroups), most of it isn't worth your effort. In fact, some of it is downright wrong. That said, here are some sources that I *do* recommend.

The Mac OS X Help Viewer

Although most Mac OS X owners tend to blow off the Help Viewer when the troubleshooting gets tough, that's never the best course of action. Always take a few moments to search the contents of the Help Viewer — click Help from the Finder menu — to see whether any mention is made of the problem that you've encountered.

The Apple Mac OS X Support site

Home to all manner of support questions and answers, the Mac OS X Support section of the Apple Web site (`www.apple.com/support`) should be your next stop in case of trouble that you can't fix yourself. Topics include

✦ Startup issues

✦ Classic mode problems

✦ Internet and networking problems

✦ Printing problems

You can search the Apple Knowledge Base, download the latest updates and electronic manuals, and participate in Apple-moderated discussion boards from this one central location.

Your local Apple dealer

Naturally, an Apple dealer can provide just about any support that you're likely to need — for a price — but you can usually get the answers to important questions without any coinage changing hands. Your dealer is also well versed in the latest updates and patches that can fix those software incompatibility problems. Check your telephone book for your local dealer.

Book II

Customizing and Sharing

The 5th Wave   By Rich Tennant

"Well, the first day wasn't bad—I lost the Finder, copied a file into the Trash, and sat on my mouse."

Contents at a Glance

Chapter 1: Building the Finder of Your Dreams

In This Chapter

- ✔ Choosing a view mode
- ✔ Modifying the toolbar
- ✔ Searching for files from the toolbar
- ✔ Searching for files with the Find command
- ✔ Changing view options
- ✔ Changing Finder preferences

The Finder is the heart of Mac OS X — and we all know how heart surgeons like to tinker, don't we? (*Ouch.* Start again.)

The Finder is the heart of Mac OS X, and as you might expect, it's highly configurable. You can customize the Finder to present icons, or you can peruse folders with a column view that can pack much more information onscreen at one time. Some folks prefer the default Finder toolbar, and others like to customize it with the applications and features that they use most often.

Decisions like these can help you transform Mac OS X into *Your Personal Operating System* — and every Mac OS X power user worth the title will take the time to apply these changes because an operating system that presents visual information the way that *you* want to see it is easier and more efficient to use.

No need for a hammer or saw — when you're building the Finder of your dreams, the only tool that you need is your mouse!

Will That Be Icons or Buttons . . . or Even Columns?

The default appearance of a window in Mac OS X uses the familiar large-format icons that have been a hallmark of the Macintosh operating system since Day One — but there's no reason why you *have* to use them. (In fact, most Mac OS X power users whom I know consider the icon view mode rather inefficient and slow.) Besides the icon view shown in Figure 1-1, Mac OS X offers two other window view modes: list and column.

Figure 1-1:
A Finder window in icon view mode.

✦ **List view:** *List view* displays the folders on the volume in a hierarchical fashion. To display the contents of a folder, you can either click the right-facing small triangle next to the folder name — it rotates downward to indicate that you've expanded the folder — or you can double-click the folder icon to display the contents in a Finder window. To collapse the contents of the folder, click the small triangle again; it rotates back to face the right. Figure 1-2 illustrates the same Finder window in list view.

You can resize a column by dragging the right edge of the column heading.

✦ **Column view:** Figure 1-3 shows the same window in column view, in which the volumes on your Mac OS X system are displayed on the left. Each column on the right represents a lower level of subfolders. Click the volume, click the desired folder in the first second column to display its contents, and so forth. (Personally, this is my favorite view — thanks, Apple! It's efficient and fast as all get-out.) As you drill deeper, the columns automatically shift to the left. When you click an item (instead of a folder), the Finder displays a preview and a quick summary of the selected item in the rightmost column.

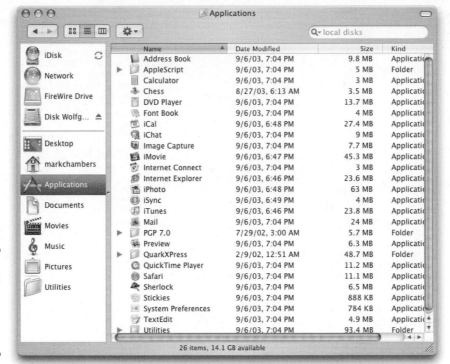

Book II
Chapter 1

Building the Finder
of Your Dreams

Figure 1-2:
The contents
of a Finder
window in
list view
mode.

Each column has its own individual scroll bar (for those really, really big folders), and you can drag the column handle at the bottom of the separators to resize the column width to the left. When you hold down Option and drag a column handle, all the columns are adjusted at once.

Another of my pet peeves is cluttered disks. If you're continually having problems locating files and folders, ask yourself, "Self, do I need to organize? Am I — gasp — *cluttered?*" If your answer is yes, take an hour and organize your files logically into new folders. (Remember, I'm talking your documents and such — not your applications, which are usually where they need to be — in your Applications folder.) Often, documents that you create end up as stragglers, usually located in the root folder of your hard drive, which sooner or later ends up looking like a biker bar after Ladies Night. (The same can be said of many Mac OS X Desktops, too.) By keeping your root folder and Desktop clean and saving your files in organized folders, you'll end up wasting less time searching for files and more time actually *using* them.

To switch between the three modes, click one of the three view mode buttons on the Finder window toolbar (the current view is highlighted) or click the View menu and choose As Icons, As List, or As Columns. Mac OS X places a helpful check mark next to the current view mode. (Keyboard lovers can hold down ⌘ and press the 1, 2, or 3 keys to switch views.)

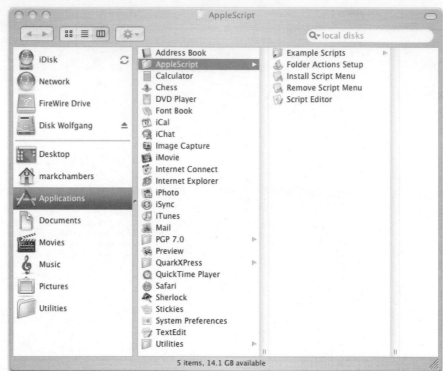

Figure 1-3:
Tiger's
column view
requires
very little
scrolling.

Doing the Toolbar Dance

You can work your customization magic on the Finder toolbar as well! In this section, I show you how to customize that strip of icons across the top of the Finder window that's affectionately called the *toolbar*. Or, if you like, you'll discover how to dismiss it entirely to gain additional real estate for the contents of your Finder window.

Hiding and showing the toolbar

You can toggle the display of the toolbar in an active Finder window in one of three ways:

✦ By clicking the toolbar button located at the upper-right corner of the Finder window

✦ By pressing ⌘+Option+T

✦ By choosing View from the Finder menu and then choosing Hide (or Show) Toolbar

Hiding and showing the status bar

The status bar at the bottom of the Finder window displays a number of helpful informational-type tidbits about the window's contents. Depending on what you've opened, the status bar can include

✦ **Statistics:** See the number of items in the window and the amount of free space remaining on the volume.

✦ **A write-protect icon:** This icon looks like a pencil with a line running through it, as shown in Figure 1-4. This indicates that you don't have write permissions for the contents of the window — or the volume where the contents reside. (Note that this does not necessarily mean that folders at a lower level are write-protected as well.) You'll typically see this icon when you're viewing the contents of a CD or DVD, where everything is write-protected.

**Book II
Chapter 1**

**Building the Finder
of Your Dreams**

Back and Forward buttons

View icons

Action button

Search box

Figure 1-4:
Check the
status bar to
scope out
your write
permissions.

Write-protect icon

✦ **The current automatic icon view setting:** For windows in icon view, the status bar can display either a grid icon (indicating that the icons are set to snap-to-grid) or four tiny icons (indicating that the icons are displayed in a sorted order). You'll discover more about these settings later in the section "Configuring the View Options."

To toggle the display of the status bar, choose View from the Finder menu and then choose Show/Hide Status Bar.

Giving your toolbar big tires and a loud exhaust

The default icons on the toolbar include

✦ **Back and Forward:** Like a Web browser, clicking the Back button moves you to the previous window's contents. If you use the Back button, the Forward button appears. Click this to return to the contents that you had before clicking the Back button.

✦ **View:** Click this control to toggle between the three view modes (icon, list, or column).

✦ **Action:** Click this drop-down list box to display context-sensitive commands for the selected items. In plain English, you'll see the commands that you would see if you hold down Control and click the selection.

✦ **Search:** Okay, I know it's not technically an icon, but the Search box is a member of the default toolbar family nonetheless. You can search for a file or folder using this box — more on this later in the section "Searching for Files from the Toolbar."

But, as one of my favorite bumper stickers so invitingly asks, "Why be normal?" Adding or deleting items from the toolbar is a great way to customize Mac OS X. Follow these steps:

1. **From the active Finder window menu, choose View➪Customize Toolbar to display the sheet that you see in Figure 1-5.**

Along with controls like Back, Forward, and View, you'll find a number of system functions, like Eject and Burn.

2. **To add items to the toolbar, drag them from the Customize Toolbar dialog up to the toolbar at the top of the window.**

To add an item between existing buttons, drop it between the buttons, and they obligingly move aside. If you get exuberant about your toolbar and you add more icons than it can hold, a double-right arrow appears at the right side of the toolbar — a click of the arrow displays a pop-up menu with the icons that won't fit.

In fact, the Customize Toolbar dialog isn't necessary for some toolbar modifications: You can also drag files, folders, and disk volumes directly from the Desktop or other Finder windows and add them to your toolbar at any time. To remove a file, folder, or disk volume from the toolbar, hold down Control and click the icon on the toolbar; then click Remove Item from the pop-up menu — it vanishes like a CEO's ethics.

You can always drag a file or folder into the Sidebar column at the left of the Finder window — the Sidebar column is a separate entity entirely from the toolbar.

3. **To remove an item from the toolbar, drag it off to the center of the window, amongst the other icons.**

4. **Naturally, you can swap item positions. Just click an item, drag it to its new spot, and then release the mouse button.**

5. **To choose the default toolbar configuration or to start over, drag the default bar at the bottom of the window to the toolbar at the top.**

   This is the toolbar equivalent of tapping your ruby slippers together three times and repeating, "There's no place like home."

6. **To toggle between displaying the icons with accompanying text (the default), the icon only, or a text button only, click the Show drop-down list box at the bottom of the Customize Toolbar dialog.**

7. **After you arrange your toolbar as you like, click the Done button.**

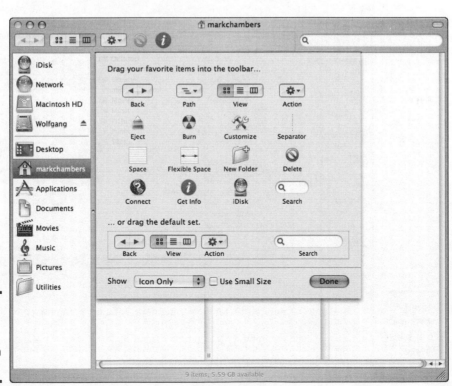

Figure 1-5:
Changing
the toolbar
status quo in
Mac OS X.

Searching for Files from the Toolbar

Need to find a file fast? The default toolbar has just what you need — the *Search field,* which offers the ability to perform a Spotlight search for a string of text within your files (including both filenames and contents). To locate a file with the Search field, follow these steps:

1. **Click in the Search box on the toolbar and type the text that you want to find.**

   It's the text box on the right with the magnifying glass. (The folks at Apple are really, *really* into Sherlock Holmes . . . so am I!) If you need to clear the field and start over again, click the circular X button, which appears only when text is in the Search field.

   Hey, who needs to press Return? The Finder immediately displays the files with names that include the text, as shown in Figure 1-6.

2. **To display the location of a file, click it once. To launch it, double-click the entry.**

   Files can also be moved or copied from the Search results list with the standard drag and Option+drag methods.

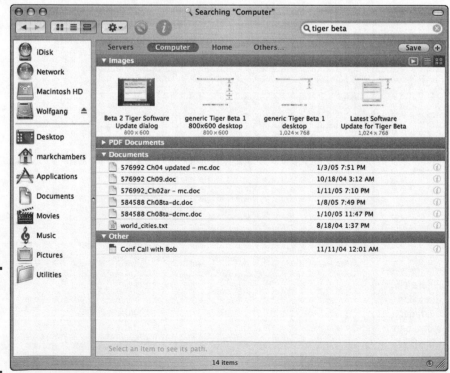

Figure 1-6: Locating a file or folder with the toolbar Search box.

3. **To perform a new search, click the circular X button and type new text in the Search field.**

   To return to your original location in the Finder window, click the Back button on the toolbar.

Searching for Files from the Find Dialog

Although the Search box on the toolbar is all that you'll need to find most files and folders, sometimes you need a little more flexibility and power to locate what you need on your system. To do so, add the Find controls, which you can use to create custom searches with more complex criteria. To locate a file by using the Find controls, follow these steps:

1. **With the Finder active, display the Find controls by pressing ⌘+F (or choose File from the Finder menu and then choose Find).**

   Mac OS X displays the controls that you see in Figure 1-7.

**Book II
Chapter 1**

Building the Finder of Your Dreams

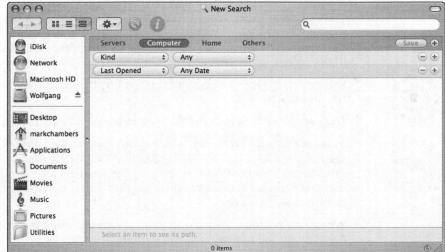

Figure 1-7:
The Find controls add a bit of extra power to a search.

2. **Click the buttons at the top of the list to specify where you want to search.**

   You can choose Computer (your entire system, including network volumes), a local volume, or your Home folder.

3. **To search for a specific filename, click the first drop-down list box in a row and choose Name; then type all or part of the filename in the Contains box.**

   Tiger automatically begins searching as soon as you type at least one character.

   After you locate the file or folder that you need, click the entry name to reveal the location of the matching file or folder. You can also double-click it to launch (or display) it.

4. **If you want to search for a text string within the document itself, click the first drop-down list box in a row and choose Contents. Then type the string to match in the box.**

   The text must appear just as you've typed it, so it's always a good idea to restrict what you're searching for to a minimum of words that you're fairly sure will cause a match. (Content searching is not case-sensitive, though.) Content searching works only when you've generated an index, which I explain later in this section.

5. **To include additional search criteria lines, click the button with the plus sign next to the last criterion line.**

   You can limit your results based on all sorts of rules, including the date that the file or folder was last modified, when it was created, the file type, the size, the extension, or whether the file or folder is marked visible or hidden (such as a system file).

   You can also remove a search criterion line by clicking the button with the minus sign.

6. **To save the search criteria that you selected, click Save.**

   This creates a *Smart Folder*, which (you're gonna *love* this) Tiger automatically updates (in real time) to contain whatever items match the criteria you've saved! You can specify the location for your Smart Folder, and you can also choose to add it to your Finder sidebar for the ultimate in convenience. *Sweet.*

7. **When you're done canvassing your computer, click the Back button in the Find dialog to return to the Finder.**

Configuring the View Options

As I discuss at the beginning of the chapter, you've got a lot of control over how Mac OS X presents files and folders in the Finder. In this section, I cover how you can make further adjustments to the view from your windows. (Pardon me for the ghastly cliché posing as a pun.)

Setting icon view options

First, allow me to provide a little detail on housekeeping in the Big X. After a few hours of work, a Finder window in icon mode can look something like a teenager's room: stuff strewn all over the place, as demonstrated with my Applications folder in Figure 1-8. To restore order to your Desktop, click in any open area of the active window and then choose View⇨Clean Up. This command leaves the icons in approximately the same position but snaps them to an invisible grid so that they're aligned, as shown in Figure 1-9.

After things are in alignment, work with the icon view options. (Naturally, you'll want the active Finder window in icon view first, so choose View⇨As Icons or press ⌘+1.) From the Finder menu, choose View⇨Show View Options — or press that swingin' ⌘+J shortcut — to display the View Options dialog that you see in Figure 1-10. (Remember that these are the options available for icon view; I discuss the options for list and column view later in this chapter.)

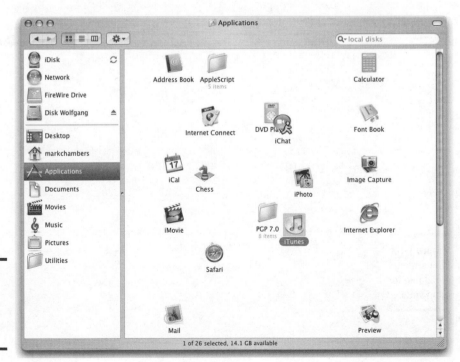

Figure 1-8: Will some-one *please* clean up this mess?

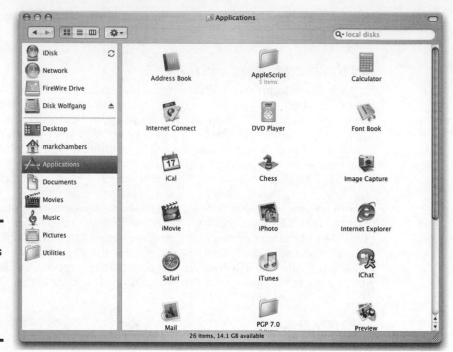

Figure 1-9:
Tidying up is
no problem
with the
Clean Up
menu
command.

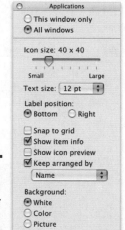

Figure 1-10:
The settings
available for
icon view.

Note these first two radio buttons, which also appear in the list View
Options dialog:

✦ **This Window Only:** Select the This Window Only radio button to apply
the changes that you make only to the Finder window that opens when

you open the selected item — in other words, the item that appears in the window's title bar.

For example, any changes made to the settings in Figure 1-10 will affect only my Applications folder because it was the active Finder window when I pressed ⌘+ J. (You might have noticed that the window name also appears as the title of the View Options dialog.)

✦ **All Windows:** Select the All Windows radio button to apply the changes that you make to *all* Finder windows that you view in your current mode.

Of course, Mac OS X remembers the changes that you make within the View Options dialog, no matter which view mode you're configuring. Now, on to the other changes that you can make from this dialog, which include

**Book II
Chapter 1**

**Building the Finder
of Your Dreams**

✦ **Resizing your Desktop icons:** Click and drag the Icon Size slider to shrink or expand the icons on your Desktop. The icon size is displayed in pixels above the slider.

✦ **Resizing icon label text:** Click the up and down arrows to the right of the Text Size drop-down box to choose the font size (in points) for icon labels.

✦ **Moving icon label text:** Select either the Bottom (default) or the Right radio button to choose between displaying the text under your Desktop icons or to the right of the icons.

✦ **Snap to Grid:** Enable this check box to automatically align icons to a grid within the window, just as if you had used the Clean Up menu command.

✦ **Show Item Info:** With this check box enabled, Mac OS X displays the number of items within each folder in the window.

✦ **Show Icon Preview:** If you enable this check box, the Finder displays icons for image files using a miniature of the actual picture. (A cool feature for those with digital cameras — however, this does take extra processing time because Mac OS X has to load each image file and shrink it down to create the icon.)

✦ **Keep Arranged By:** To sort the display of icons in a window, enable this check box and choose one of the following criteria from its drop-down list: by name, date modified, date created, size, or item type.

✦ **Choosing a background:** To select a background for the window, select one of three radio buttons here:

  • **White:** This is the default.

  • **Color:** Click a color choice from the color block that appears if you make this selection.

  • **Picture:** Select this radio button and then click the Select button to display a standard Open dialog. Navigate to the location where the desired image is stored, click it once to select it, and then click Open.

After all your changes are made and you're ready to return to work, click the dialog's Close button to save your settings.

Setting list view options

If you're viewing the active window in list view, choose View➪Show View Options to display the View Options dialog that you see in Figure 1-11.

Figure 1-11:
List view
settings.

Like in icon view, select from one of the two top radio buttons to apply the changes that you make in this dialog to this window only or to all windows that you view in list mode. The settings include

✦ **Resizing your Desktop icons:** You can choose from two sizes of Desktop icons.

✦ **Resizing icon label text:** Click the up and down arrows to the right of the Text Size drop-down box to choose the font size (in points) for icon labels.

✦ **Show Columns:** Enable the check boxes under this heading to display additional columns in list view, including the date that the item was modified, the creation date, the size, the item type, the version (supplied by most applications), the label color, and any comments that you've added in the Info dialog for that item. (In my personal opinion, the more columns that you add, the more unwieldy the Finder gets, so I advise disabling the display of columns that you won't use.)

✦ **Use Relative Dates:** Enable this check box to display modification dates and creation dates with relative terms, such as *Today* or *Yesterday*. If this freaks you out, disable this check box to force all dates to act like adults.

✦ **Calculate All Sizes:** Enable this check box to have Mac OS X display the actual sizes of folders, including all the files and subfolders they contain. (Handy for figuring out where all your disk space went, no?) *Note:* Using this option takes processing time, so I recommend that you avoid using it unless you really need to see the size.

To save your settings, click the dialog's Close button.

Setting column view options

To make changes to view options in column view mode, choose View⇨Show View Options to display the View Options dialog that you see in Figure 1-12.

You only have three column view options, and any changes that you make to this dialog are always reflected in every column view:

✦ **Resizing icon label text:** Click the Text Size drop-down box to choose the font size (in points) for icon labels.

✦ **Show Icons:** Enable this check box to display icons in the columns. If this option is disabled, the icons don't appear, and you'll gain a little space.

✦ **Show Preview Column:** If this check box is enabled, clicking a file in column mode will display a *thumbnail* (reduced image) and preview information in the right-most column, as shown in Figure 1-13.

If you store a slew of QuickTime movies and digital images on your drive, the Preview column is great. (You can even play a QuickTime movie from the Preview column.)

Click the dialog's Close button to save your settings and return to the Finder.

Book II
Chapter 1

Building the Finder of Your Dreams

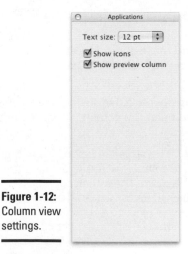

Figure 1-12:
Column view
settings.

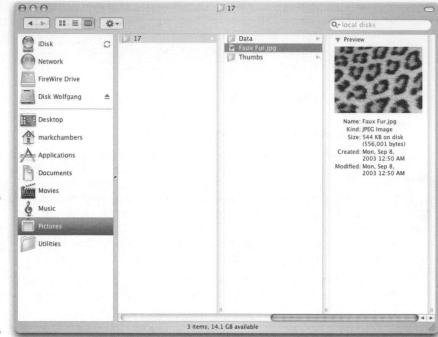

Figure 1-13:
The Preview
column
provides
more
informa-
tion on the
selected file.

Setting Finder Preferences

Finally, you can change a number of settings to customize the Finder itself. From the Finder menu, click Finder and choose the Preferences menu item to display the Finder Preferences dialog that you see in Figure 1-14.

In the General section, the preference settings include

✦ **Displaying icons on the Desktop:** Enable these check boxes to display your hard disks, removable volumes (including CDs, DVDs, and Zip disks), and connected network servers.

✦ **New Finder Windows Open:** Click the drop-down list box to specify the spot where a new Finder window should open. By default, a new window displays the contents of your Home folder.

✦ **Always Open Folders in a New Window:** When this check box is enabled, double-clicking a folder will open it in a new Finder window, as did earlier versions of Mac OS. (If disabled, the contents of the folder appear in the same Finder window, which makes it easier to focus on just the folder you need at the moment.)

✦ **Open New Windows in Column View:** When you enable this check box, each new Finder window that you open automatically uses column view. (If disabled, the new window uses the last view mode you used.)

✦ **Spring-loaded Folders and Windows:** It sounds a little wacky, but using this feature can definitely speed up file copying! If this check box is enabled, you can drag an item on top of a folder — *without* releasing the mouse button — and after a preset time (controlled by the Delay slider), a spring-loaded window appears to show you the folder's contents. At that point, you can either release the mouse button to drop the file inside the folder (upon which the window disappears), or you can drag the icon on top of another subfolder to spring it forth and drill even deeper.

Figure 1-14:
Configure
Finder
prefer-
ences here.

Pssst. Hovering over a folder and pressing the spacebar makes the folder spring open immediately. Pass it on.

The Labels preference panel is a simple one — just click next to each label color to type your own text for that label. (I've gotta recommend red for deadlines and green for contracts . . . call me sentimental.)

From the Sidebar preferences panel, you can choose which default items should appear in the Finder window Sidebar column. Your choices include locations (like your Home and Applications folders), network servers, removable media, the Desktop itself, and — naturally — your hard drives. To add a default item to the Sidebar column, select the corresponding check box to enable it, or disable the check box to banish that item forthwith.

The Advanced preference settings include

✦ **Always Show File Extensions:** If this check box is enabled, the Finder displays the file extensions at the end of filenames, à la Windows. This comes in handy for some applications, where everything from a document to a preference file to the application itself all share the same icon. However, I find extensions distasteful and leave things set with the default of extensions off.

✦ **Show Warning Before Emptying the Trash:** By default, this check box is enabled, and Mac OS X displays a confirmation dialog before allowing you to — in the words of Mac OS X patrons around the world — *toss the Bit Bucket*. If you're interested in speed and trust your judgment (and your mouse finger), you can disable this setting.

After you make the desired changes to the Finder Preferences, click the dialog's Close button to save your settings and return to the Finder.

Chapter 2: Giving Your Desktop the Personal Touch

In This Chapter

✔ Picking your own background

✔ Adding and selecting a screen saver

✔ Choosing menu colors and highlights

✔ Keeping track of things with Stickies

✔ Customizing the Dock

✔ Using Dashboard

✔ Cleaning and sorting the Mac OS X Desktop

"Tweak! Tweak!" It's not the cry of some exotic bird — that's the call of the wild Mac Power User. Power users like to tweak their Mac OS X Desktops just so, with *that* menu color, *this* background, and *those* applications in the Dock. Non-computer types just can't understand the importance of the proper arrangement of your virtual workplace: When things are familiar and customized to your needs, you're more productive, and things get done faster. In fact, if you've set up multiple users on your computer under Mac OS X, the Big X automatically keeps track of each user's Desktop and restores it when that person logs in. (For example, when you use the Mac, you get that background photo of Farrah Fawcett from the '70s while your daughter gets Avril Lavigne.)

In this chapter, I show you what you can do to produce a Desktop that's uniquely your own, including tweaks that you can make to the background and your Desktop icons. I'll also show you how to use Desktop Stickies instead of a forest of paper slips covering your monitor.

With your Mac OS X Desktop clad in the proper harmonious colors — yes, that can be your favorite photo of Elvis himself — and your new Dock icons ready for action, you are indeed prepared for whatever lies ahead in your computing world!

Changing the Background

You might be asking, "Mark, do I really need a custom background?" That depends completely on your personal tastes, but I've yet to meet a computer owner who didn't change his or her background when presented with the opportunity. Favorite backgrounds usually include

✦ Humorous cartoons and photos that can bring a smile to your face (even during the worst workday)

✦ Scenic beauty

✦ Photos of family and friends (or the latest Hollywood heartthrob)

✦ The company logo (not sure it does much for morale, but it does impress the boss)

If you do decide to spruce up your background, you have three choices: You can select one of the default Mac OS X background images, choose a solid color, or specify your own image. All three backgrounds are chosen from the Desktop & Screen Saver panel, located within System Preferences (as illustrated in Figure 2-1).

You can also hold down Control, click the Desktop, and choose Change Desktop Background from the pop-up contextual menu (or right-click, if you're using a mouse with multiple buttons).

Figure 2-1:
To select a background, get thee hence to System Preferences.

Picking something Apple

To choose a background from one of the collections provided by Apple, click one of these groups from the list at the left:

✦ **Apple Images:** These default backgrounds range from simple patterns to somewhat strange and ethereal flux shapes. (You'll have to see them to understand what I mean.)

✦ **Nature:** Scenic beauty: blades of grass, sand dunes, snowy hills . . . that sort of thing.

✦ **Abstract:** Even weirder twisting shapes in flux, this time with bright contrasting colors. Good for a psychiatrist's office.

✦ **Solid Colors:** For those who desire a soothing solid shade — more on this in the next section.

✦ **Pictures Folder:** This displays the images saved in the Pictures folder by the active user.

✦ **Choose Folder:** You can open a folder containing images and display them instead. (I discuss this in more detail in a page or two.)

If you see something you like, click the thumbnail, and Mac OS X displays it in the well and automatically refreshes your background so that you can see what it looks like. (By the way, in the Apple universe, a *well* is a sunken square area that displays an image — in this case, the background image that you've selected.)

Notice your iPhoto albums in the list? That's no accident — Tiger automatically offers your iPhoto Photo Library, so you can choose images from your iPhoto collection!

Book II
Chapter 2

Giving Your Desktop
the Personal Touch

How to annoy friends and confuse co-workers

Never let it be said that I can't dish out revenge when necessary. I don't know whether I should call this a *Tip* or a *Devilish Practical Joke That Will Drive People Nuts* — anyway, it's fun as all get-out. Right before you go to lunch, use the Grab utility in your Applications/Utilities folder to take a snapshot of your Desktop with a number of windows open (or an error dialog with an OK or a Close button) and then save the image to your Pictures folder. Select the image as your Desktop background and then watch others go crazy trying to click those faux windows, buttons, and icons. For an archenemy, try the same trick on *his* Mac! Arrange a slightly embarrassing Desktop on his computer, specify it as the background, and sit back while the fun begins. (Perhaps a Web browser open to a somewhat unusual Web site?)

Mac OS X automatically manipulates how the background appears on your Desktop. If an image conforms to your screen resolution, fine — otherwise, click the drop-down list box next to the well and you can choose to

✦ **Tile the background.** This repeats the image to cover the Desktop. (This is usually done with pattern images to produce a smooth, creamy, seamless look.)

✦ **Fill the screen.** This can be used with a solid color to get uniform coverage. The original aspect ratio of the image is preserved, so it's not stretched.

✦ **Stretch the background to fit the Desktop.** If your Desktop image is smaller than the Desktop acreage, this works, but be warned — if you try to stretch too small of an image over too large a Desktop, the pixilated result can be pretty frightening. (Think of enlarging an old Kodak Instamatic negative to a 16 x 20 poster. Dots, dots, dots.) The original aspect ratio of the image is not preserved, so you might end up with results that look like the funhouse mirrors at a carnival.

✦ **Center the image on the Desktop.** This is my favorite solution for Desktop images that are smaller than your resolution.

Note that this drop-down list appears only if the Desktop picture that you select is not one of the standard Apple images. All the pictures in the Apple Background Images, Nature, Abstract, and Solid Colors categories are automatically scaled to the size of your screen.

 To change your Desktop background automatically on a regular basis, enable the Change Picture check box and then choose the delay period from the corresponding drop-down list box. To display the images in random order, also enable the Random Order check box; otherwise, Mac OS X displays them in the order that they appear in the folder.

I just gotta have lavender

As I mention earlier, for those who want their favorite color without the distraction of an image, one can choose from a selection of solid colors. You can choose from these colors the same way that you'd pick a default Mac OS X background image (as I describe in the previous section).

Selecting your own photo

Finally, you can drag your own image into the well from a Finder window to add your own work of art. To view thumbnails of an entire folder, click the Pictures Folder (to display the contents of your personal Pictures folder) or click Choose Folder to specify any folder on your system. Click the desired thumbnail to embellish your Desktop.

Changing the Screen Saver

Screen savers are another popular item. Because I cover the Screen Saver preferences in Chapter 3 of this mini-book, I'll simply illustrate here how to choose one. Open System Preferences and click the Desktop & Screen Saver icon; then click the Screen Saver tab to display the settings that you see in Figure 2-2.

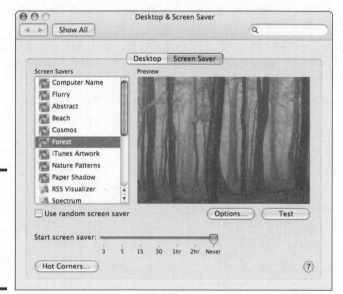

Figure 2-2:
A good screen saver can cancel the effects of a bad boss.

**Book II
Chapter 2**

**Giving Your Desktop
the Personal Touch**

To add a third-party, screen saver module so that everyone can use it on a multi-user system, copy it into the Screen Savers folder within the top-level Library folder.

Click one of the entries in the Screen Savers column to display a thumbnail of the effect. Enabling the Use Random Screen Saver check box, naturally, runs through 'em all. You can also test the appearance of the saver module by clicking the Test button; the screen saver runs until you move the mouse or press a key.

Many screen savers allow you to monkey with their settings. If the Options button is enabled (not grayed out), click it to see how you can change the effects.

Changing Colors in Mac OS X

I can't understand it, but some people just don't appreciate menus with purple highlights! (You can tell a Louisiana State University graduate a mile away.) To specify your own colors for buttons, menus, and windows, follow these steps:

1. **Open System Preferences and click the Appearance icon to display the settings in Figure 2-3.**

2. **Click the Appearance drop-down list and choose the main color choice for your buttons and menus.**

3. **Click the Highlight Color drop-down list and pick the highlight color that will appear when you select text in an application or select an item from a list.**

4. **Press ⌘+Q to exit System Preferences and save your changes.**

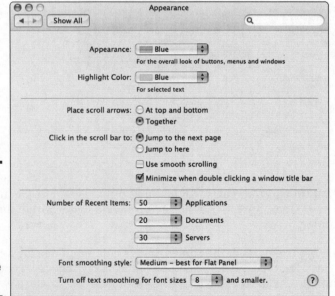

Figure 2-3:
Okay, then, set up your own school colors with the Appearance settings!

Adding Stickies

Stickies are interesting little beasts — I don't know their genus or phyla, but they're certainly handy to have around. To be technical for a moment, a *Stickie* is actually nothing more than a special type of application window, but these windows remain on your Desktop as long as the Stickies application is running.

I use Stickies for anything that a Post-it Note can handle, including

✦ Reminders that you don't want to misplace

✦ Snippets of text that you want to temporarily store while your Mac is turned off (without launching a behemoth like Word or digging for TextEdit)

✦ *Boilerplate* (repeated and standard) text that you're constantly including in your documents, like your address

✦ A quick note that includes someone's e-mail address or phone number

✦ Today's Dilbert cartoon from `www.dilbert.com`

**Book II
Chapter 2**

**Giving Your Desktop
the Personal Touch**

A Stickie can contain data pasted from the Clipboard, or you can simply type directly into the Stickies application window. Stickie windows can include graphics and different fonts and colors. You can even locate specific text from somewhere in your vast collection of Stickies by using the Find command within the Stickies application — just press ⌘+F while the Stickies menu is active to display the Stickies Find dialog. (And you don't use up our bark-covered friends of the forest, either.)

In Book I, I discuss the Mac OS X Services menu — you can make a Stickie note from the Finder Services menu, as well.

Follow these steps to stick your way to success:

1. **Open your Applications folder and run the Stickies application to display the new window that you see in Figure 2-4.**

   The text cursor is already idling in the new window. (The other windows are Stickies, too, but they contain display text from the application. If you like, you can close them.)

2. **Type text in the window or press ⌘+V to paste the contents of the Clipboard into the window.**

   You can also import the contents of an existing file into a Stickie. Just choose File and then choose Import Text to display a standard Open dialog.

3. **You can add text formatting, change the text font, and change the color of the font from the Font menu.**

   From the Note menu, you can also choose to make the Stickie translucent. (No pressing reason; they just look cool.)

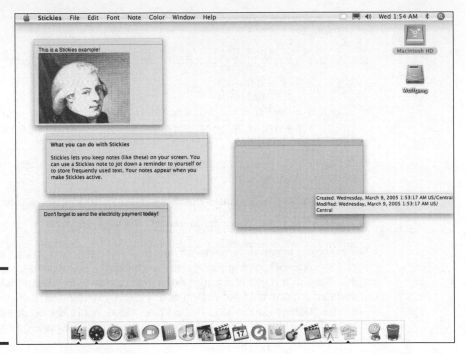

Figure 2-4:
"Look,
Ma, it's a
Stickie!"

4. **To change the Stickie's color, click the Color menu and choose the appropriate hue.**

5. **Resize and drag the Stickie window to the desired location.**

   Press ⌘+M to toggle between a *miniaturized* view (showing only the title bar) and the expanded view.

To automatically run the Stickies application each time you log on, open the Accounts settings in System Preferences and click your account in the list. Click the Startup Items button and add Stickies to the list by clicking the plus button.

To delete a Stickie, simply click the Close button at the upper-left corner of the Stickie window. Or, click the Stickie to make it the active note and then click Close. Stickies display a dialog to confirm that you want to close the note; click Save to save the contents in a file or click the Don't Save button to close the note and discard its contents.

To close the Stickies application completely, click any note and press ⌘+Q. The application remembers the position and contents of each note until you launch it again.

Customizing the Dock

In terms of importance, the *Dock* — the launch pad for applications and documents that appears on your Desktop — ranks right up there with the command center of a modern nuclear submarine. As such, it had better be easy to customize, and naturally, Mac OS X doesn't let you down.

Adding applications and extras to the Dock

Why be satisfied with just the icons that Apple places in the Dock? You can add your own applications, files, and folders to the Dock as well.

✦ **Adding applications:** You can add any application to your Dock by simply dragging its icon into the area to the *left* of the separator line (which appears between applications and folders or documents). The existing Dock icons will obligingly move aside to make a space for it wherever you like.

Attempting to place an application on the right of the separator line sends it to the Trash (if the Trash icon is highlighted when you release the button), so beware.

✦ **Adding files and folders:** Folders and volume icons can be added to the Dock by dragging the icon into the area to the *right* of the separator line. (Attempting to place these to the left of the separator line will open an application with the contents, which usually doesn't work.) To open the location in a Finder window, click and hold the mouse button (or press Control when you click) to display a Dock menu, where you can open documents, run applications, and have other assorted fun, depending on the item you chose. Now that, my friends, is genuine *sassy!*

✦ **Adding Favorites:** You can drag any URL from Safari directly into the area to the right of the separator line. Clicking that icon automatically opens your browser and displays that page. (Safari gets the treatment in Book IV, Chapter 5.)

To remove an icon from the Dock, just click and drag it off the Dock. You get a rather silly (but somehow, strangely satisfying) animated cloud of debris, and the icon is no more. Note, however, that the original application, folder, or volume is *not* deleted — just the Dock icon itself is permanently excused. If you like, you can delete *almost* any of the default icons that Mac OS X installs on the Dock; only the Finder and Trash icons must remain on the Dock.

To set up a Dock icon as a Login Item — without the hassle of opening the Accounts pane in System Preferences — just click a Dock icon and hold the mouse button down until the pop-up menu appears. Then select the Open at Login menu item.

If you can't delete items from the Dock, you're using a *managed* account — that's a standard user account with certain limitations set. (In this case, your account is set to Some Limits, and your administrator has disabled the Modify the Dock check box in your account.) You'll need an admin-level user to log in; then visit the Accounts panel in System Preferences and enable the check box again. For more information on user accounts, see Chapter 5 of this mini-book.

Resizing the Dock

You can change the size of the Dock from the Dock settings in System Preferences — I explain this in more detail in Book II, Chapter 3 — but here's a simpler way to resize the Dock, right from the Desktop.

Move your mouse cursor over the separator line on the Dock; the cursor turns into a funky line with arrows pointing up and down. This is your cue to click and drag while moving the mouse up and down, which expands and shrinks the Dock, respectively.

You can also hold down the Control key and click when the funky line cursor is visible. This allows you to change your Dock preferences without the hassle of opening System Preferences and displaying the Dock settings.

Stick It on the Dashboard

One of Tiger's funkiest new features is *Dashboard,* which you can use to hold widgets and display them with the press of a button. (Okay, I know that sounds a little wacky, but bear with me.) *Widgets* are small applications called *applets* that typically provide only one function. For example, Dashboard comes complete with a calculator, a clock, and a quick-and-simple calendar. You can display and use these widgets at any time by pressing the Dashboard key; by default, that's F12, but you can modify the key on the Dahlsboard & Exposé pane within System Preferences. Tiger also includes a thoughtful Dashboard icon on the Dock, which you can click to display your widgets. (Geez, that sounds kind of racy. Best not to pursue it.)

Figure 2-5 illustrates Dashboard in action. Press the Dashboard key, and the widgets appear, ready for you to use. You can add or delete widgets to your Dashboard by clicking the Add button (which bears a plus sign, naturally) at the lower left corner of the Dashboard screen. When you click the Add button, a scrolling menu strip appears at the bottom of the Dashboard display, and you can drag new widgets directly onto your Dashboard from this menu. It's also easy to rearrange the widgets that are already populating Dashboard by dragging them to the desired spot. (To remove a widget, just click the Add button to display the menu strip, and you'll notice a tiny X button appears next to each widget on your Dashboard; click the X button next to the widget you want to remove, and it vanishes from the display. You can add it back again at any time.) Press the Dashboard key again to return to your Tiger Desktop.

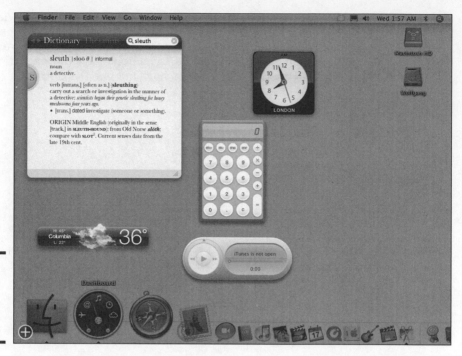

Figure 2-5:
Dashboard
proudly
displays
its widgets.

If you need to use a widget for only a second or two, press the Dashboard key and hold it. When you release the key, you're back to your Desktop.

Apple offers additional widgets that you can download on the Mac OS X download site (www.apple.com/macosx). Third-party software developers also provide both freeware and shareware widgets.

You can also modify the Dashboard key by turning it into a key sequence (a good thing if you're already using an application that thrives on F12). Visit the Dashboard & Exposé pane in System Preferences, and use the Shift, Control, Option, and ⌘ keys in conjunction with the Dashboard key to specify a modifier.

Arranging Your Precious Desktop

Finally, consider the layout of the Desktop itself. You can set the options for icon placement from the Finder View menu. Just like the options for Finder windows that I cover in Chapter 1 of this mini-book, you can clean up and arrange your Desktop by name, date, size, or kind.

The View Options for the Desktop are slightly different than the View Options for a Finder window in icon view. (Garner the scoop on setting these preferences in Chapter 1 of this mini-book.) First, you choose a background for the Finder from System Preferences. Also, you don't have to worry about whether the options are global or not . . . you have but one Desktop, after all.

Chapter 3: Delving under the Hood with System Preferences

In This Chapter

✔ Displaying and customizing settings in System Preferences

✔ Saving your changes

✔ Changing settings

*L*ike the Mac OS 9 Control Panel before it, the System Preferences window is the place to practice behavior modification in Mac OS X. The settings that you specify in System Preferences affect the majority of the applications that you use as well as the hardware that you connect to your Mac, your Internet and network traffic, the appearance and activity on your Desktop, and how Tiger handles money, dates, and languages. Oh, and don't forget your screen saver.

In this chapter, I discuss the many settings in System Preferences. You'll discover what does what and how you can customize the appearance and operation of Mac OS X.

The Preferred Way to Display the Preferences

Apple has made it easy to open the System Preferences window. Just click the System Preferences icon (which looks like a wall light switch, next to the Apple logo) on the Dock, and the window shown in Figure 3-1 appears. You can also open the window by clicking the Apple menu and choosing the System Preferences item.

To display all the System Preferences panels at any time, click the Show All button. You can also use the Back and Forward buttons (in the toolbar's upper-left corner) to move backward and forward through the different panes you've accessed in System Preferences, just like the similar buttons in a Web browser (yes, just like Safari!).

Tiger even allows you to display all the System Preferences panes in alphabetical order, which can make it easier to choose a pane if you're unsure what group it's in. To do so, choose View➪Organize Alphabetically. (Note that you can also select any pane directly from the View menu.)

Figure 3-1:
The System Preferences window is a familiar face to any Tiger user.

Saving Your Preferences

You'll note that there's no Save or Apply button on the System Preferences window. Illustrating the elegant design of Mac OS X, simply quitting System Preferences automatically saves all the changes that you make. (However, some panes in System Preferences have an Apply Now button that you can click to apply your changes immediately.) Like any other Mac OS X application, you can quit the System Preferences window by pressing ⌘+Q or by choosing System Preferences⇨Quit System Preferences.

Searching for Specific Settings

Searching for a single button or check box amidst all the settings in System Preferences might seem like hunting for the proverbial needle in a haystack, but your friends at Apple have added a Search box to the right side of the window toolbar. Click in this Search box and type the setting name, like **screen saver** (or even a word that's generally associated with a setting, like **power** for the Energy Saver settings). Tiger highlights all the icons in System Preferences that have anything to do with the search keywords you entered, as shown in Figure 3-2. You don't even have to press Return!

Hey, I got bonus icons in my window!

Some third-party applications can actually install their own groups within your once-pristine System Preferences window. For example, I have icons for StuffIt, VirusBarrier X, and Déjà Vu in my window. Naturally, I can't document these invited guests in this chapter, but they work the same way as any other group within System Preferences. Click the icon, adjust any settings as necessary, and then close the System Preferences window to save your changes.

To reset the Search field for a different keyword, click the X button that appears at the right of the Search box.

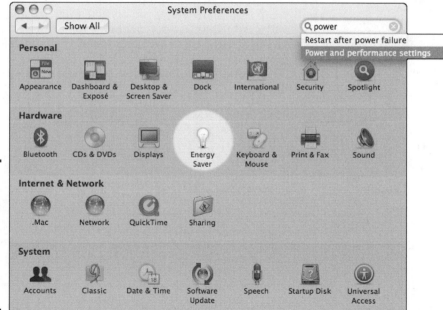

Figure 3-2: System Preferences highlights the categories that contain your search keywords.

Getting Personal

The first stop on your tour of the System Preferences window is the Personal section. No singles ads here — this section is devoted to settings that you make to customize the appearance and operation of your Desktop and login account.

Appearance preferences

The Appearance group appears in Figure 3-3.

These settings are

✦ **Appearance:** From this drop-down list, choose a color to be used for buttons, menus, and windows.

✦ **Highlight Color:** From this drop-down list, choose a color to be used to highlight selected text in fields and drop-down list boxes.

✦ **Place Scroll Arrows:** Select either radio button here to put the scroll bar arrow buttons together (at the bottom of the scroll bar, in the lower-right corner of the window) or at the top and bottom of the scroll bar.

✦ **Click in the Scroll Bar To:** By default, Mac OS X jumps to the next or previous page when you click in an empty portion of the scroll bar. Mark the Jump to Here radio button to scroll the document to the approximate position in relation to where you clicked. (You can also choose smooth scrolling, which looks cool, but many folks think that it's too slow compared with the default scrolling speed.) If you enable the Minimize When Double Clicking a Window Title Bar check box, you can minimize a Finder or application window by simply double-clicking the window's title bar.

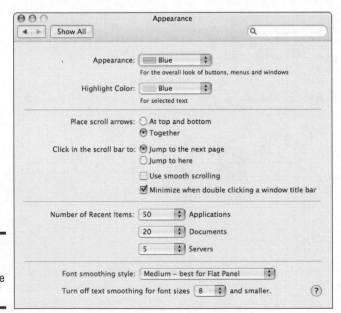

Figure 3-3:
The
Appearance
pane.

✦ **Number of Recent Items:** The default number of recent applications, documents, and servers (available from the Recent Items item in the Apple menu, which you can read more about in Book I, Chapter 3) is 10. To change the default, click any of the drop-down list boxes here and choose up to 50. (Personally, I like 20 or 30 for each.)

✦ **Font Smoothing Style:** Click this drop-down list for choices to make the text on your monitor or flat-panel appear more like the printed page. The best choices are Standard (for a typical CRT monitor) and Medium (for a typical flat-panel LCD display).

✦ **Turn Off Text Smoothing for Font Sizes:** Below a certain point size, text smoothing isn't much good for most onscreen fonts. By default, any font displayed at 8 point or smaller isn't smoothed, which is suitable for a high-end video card and monitor. If you have an older monitor or a low-end video card, you can speed up the display of text by turning off text smoothing for fonts up to 12 point.

Dashboard and Exposé preferences

Figure 3-4 illustrates the Exposé settings — and the Dashboard settings, which are new in Tiger — that you can configure in this group. You can use Exposé to view all the application windows that you're using at one time, so you can select a new active window. Or, you can move all windows aside so that you can see your Desktop. Dashboard presents a number of mini-applications called *widgets,* which you can summon and hide with a single key.

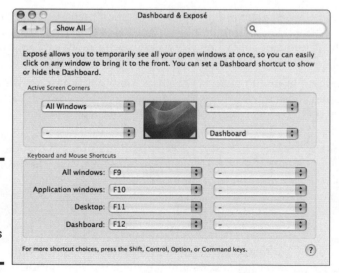

Figure 3-4:
Set your
Dashboard
and Exposé
preferences
here.

The settings here are

✦ **Active Screen Corners:** These four drop-down list boxes operate just like those in the Screen Savers panel, but they control the operation of Tiger's Dashboard and Exposé features. Click one to specify that corner as an All Windows corner (which displays all windows on your Desktop), an Application Windows corner (which displays only the windows from the active application), a Desktop corner (which moves all windows to the outside of the screen to uncover your Desktop), or a Dashboard corner (which displays your Dashboard widgets). Note that you can also set the Screen Saver Start and Disable corners from here.

✦ **Keyboard and Mouse Shortcuts:** Click each drop-down list box to set the key sequences (and mouse button settings) for all three Exposé functions as well as the Dashboard.

Desktop and screen saver preferences

Figure 3-5 illustrates the settings in the Desktop & Screen Saver group.

The settings on the Desktop tab are

✦ **Current Desktop picture:** You can drag a picture from the thumbnail field at the bottom half of the screen and drop it into the *well* (the square box in Figure 3-5) to use it as your Desktop background. To display a different image collection or open a folder of your own images, click the Choose Folder entry in the left column and browse for your heart's desire.

✦ **Layout:** As I explain in Chapter 2 of this mini-book, you can tile your background image, center it, and stretch it to fill the screen. The layout control appears only when you're using your own pictures, so you won't see it if you're using a desktop image supplied by Apple.

✦ **Change Picture:** Enable this check box to change the Desktop background automatically after the delay period that you set, including each time that you log in and each time that your Mac wakes up from sleep mode.

✦ **Random Order:** To display screens randomly, enable the Random Order check box. Otherwise, the backgrounds are displayed in the sequence in which they appear in the thumbnail strip.

Click the Screen Saver tab to see the following settings:

✦ **Screen Savers:** In the Screen Savers list at the left, click the screen saver that you want to display an animated Preview of on the right. To try out the screen saver in full-screen mode, click the Test button. (You can end the test by moving your mouse.) If the screen saver module that you select has any configurable settings, click the Options button to display them. (A screen saver is configurable if the Options button is enabled.)

✦ **Start Screen Saver:** Click and drag the slider here to specify the period of inactivity that will trigger the screen saver. To disable the screen saver, choose the Never setting at the far right of the slider.

✦ **Use Random Screen Saver:** Just what it says — if this check box is enabled, a different screen saver module is used each time that the screen saver is activated.

✦ **Hot Corners:** You can click any of the four drop-down list boxes at the four corners of the screen to specify that corner as an *activation hot corner* (which immediately activates the screen saver) or as a *disabling hot corner* (which prevents the screen saver from activating). As long as the mouse pointer stays in the disabling hot corner, the screen saver will not kick in no matter how long a period of inactivity passes. Note that you can also set the Exposé activation corners from here. (For the scoop on Exposé, see the preceding section, "Dashboard and Exposé preferences.")

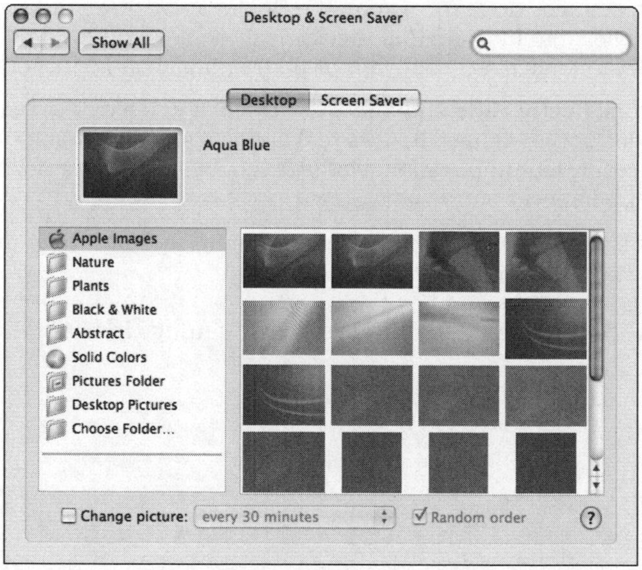

Book II Chapter 3

Figure 3-5:
The Desktop & Screen Saver pane.

Aqua Blue

Apple Images
Nature
Plants
Black & White
Abstract
Solid Colors
Pictures Folder
Desktop Pictures
Choose Folder...

Change picture: every 30 minutes
Random order

Dock preferences

The Dock group is shown in Figure 3-6.

Settings here are

✦ **Dock Size:** Move this slider to change the overall size of the Dock.

✦ **Magnification:** With this check box enabled, a Dock icon will magically expand like the national deficit when you move your mouse cursor over it. You can move the Magnification slider to specify just how much magnification is right for you.

This feature is useful for helping you click a particular Dock icon if you've resized the Dock smaller than its default dimensions or if you have a large number of items on the Dock.

✦ **Position on Screen:** Choose from three radio buttons to make that crazy Dock appear at the left, bottom, or right edge of your Desktop.

✦ **Minimize Using:** By default, Mac OS X animates a window when it's shrunk into the Dock (and when it's expanded back into a full window). From the Minimize Using drop-down list, you can choose from a genie-in-a-bottle effect or a scale-up-or-down-incrementally effect. To demonstrate, choose an effect and then click the Minimize button (the yellow button in the upper-left corner) on the System Preferences window.

✦ **Animate Opening Applications:** By default, Mac OS X has that happy, slam-dancing feeling when you launch an application: The application's icon bounces up and down on the Dock two or three times to draw your attention and indicate that the application is loading. If you find this effervescence overly buoyant or distracting, disable this check box.

✦ **Automatically Hide and Show the Dock:** If you like, the Dock can stay hidden until you need it, thus reclaiming a significant amount of Desktop space for your application windows. Enable this check box to hide the Dock whenever you're not using it.

To display a hidden Dock, move your mouse pointer over the edge of the Desktop where it's hiding.

You can also change these Dock preference settings from the Apple menu.

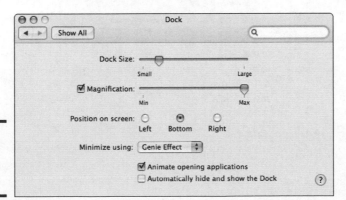

Figure 3-6:
The Dock preference pane.

International preferences

The International group appears in Figure 3-7.

✦ **Language tab:** Choose the preferred order for language use in menus and dialogs as well as the standards that Mac OS X will use for each script style.

✦ **Formats tab:** Find these settings here:

• *Date:* You can select a region and use its date conventions (month-day-year versus day-month-year), or you can build a custom format for both the long date (Saturday, September 24, 2005) and short date (9/24/2005) used throughout Mac OS X. The changes that you make are immediately reflected in the sample box at the left.

• *Time:* Click Customize to select a region to use the preset time conventions. You can choose 12-hour or 24-hour (military) time formats, change the time separator (colons, a period, or a dash), and specify different suffixes for morning (a.m.) and evening (p.m.).

• *Numbers:* These convention settings determine the separators used for large numbers or numbers with decimals, as well as the currency symbol that you want to use and where it appears in a number. You can also choose between standard (US) and metric measurement systems.

✦ **Input Menu tab:** Each check box toggles the keyboard layouts available from the Input menu. You can click the Keyboard Shortcuts button to toggle the shortcuts for switching layouts and input methods.

Security preferences

The Security group is shown in Figure 3-8.

Settings here are

✦ **FileVault:** These controls allow you to set the master password for FileVault encryption within the current user's Home folder, which makes it virtually impossible for others to access those files. Only an admin-level user can set the master password. After the master password has been set, you can click the Turn On FileVault button to enable FileVault encryption for the user who's currently logged in; the user's Login password becomes his FileVault password as well.

✦ **Require Password to Wake This Computer from Sleep or Screen Saver:** If you enable this check box, Mac OS X requires that you enter your log in password before the system returns from a sleep state or exits a screen saver.

Book II
Chapter 3

Delving under the Hood with System Preferences

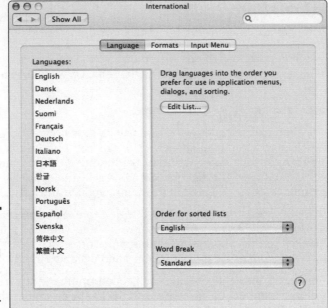

Figure 3-7:
The
International
pane in
System
Preferences.

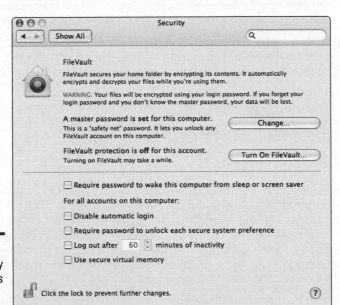

Figure 3-8:
Set Security
preferences
here.

✦ **For All Accounts on This Computer:** If you're an admin-level user, you can set these global security features that affect all user accounts. You can choose to disable the automatic logon feature, force Mac OS X to require a log in password each time that a System Preference pane is opened, automatically log off any user after a certain amount of inactivity, or use secure (encrypted) virtual memory on your hard drive.

Spotlight preferences

The Spotlight group is shown in Figure 3-9.

Settings here are

Book II Chapter 3

Delving under the Hood with System Preferences

✦ **Search Results tab:** You can enable or disable the check boxes next to each of the categories to display or hide each category in the Spotlight search menu and dialog. Click and drag the categories to the order that you prefer. For example, I like to see matching documents immediately after matching applications in the Spotlight dialog, so I dragged Documents to the second position in the list. You can also specify a different keyboard shortcut for the Spotlight menu and window.

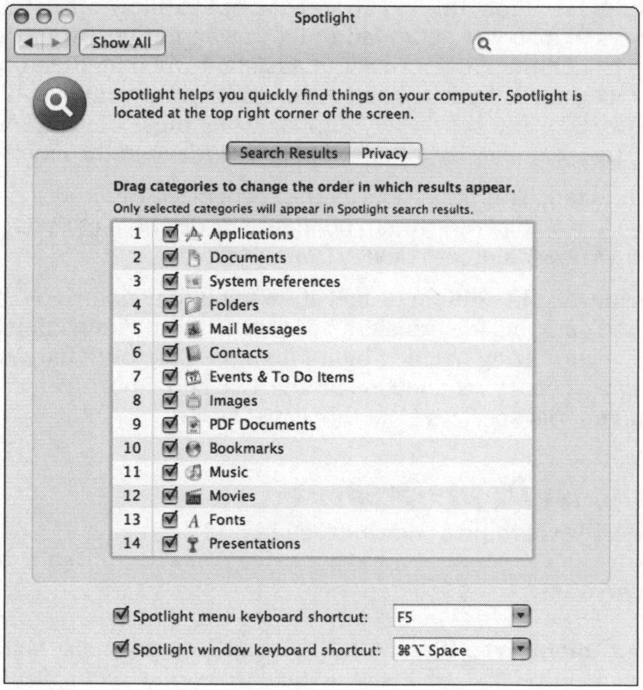

Figure 3-9:
Fine-tune your Spotlight search results here.

⬤⬤⬤		Spotlight			

Spotlight helps you quickly find things on your computer. Spotlight is located at the top right corner of the screen.

Search Results	Privacy

Drag categories to change the order in which results appear.
Only selected categories will appear in Spotlight search results.

1	☑	Applications
2	☑	Documents
3	☑	System Preferences
4	☑	Folders
5	☑	Mail Messages
6	☑	Contacts
7	☑	Events & To Do Items
8	☑	Images
9	☑	PDF Documents
10	☑	Bookmarks
11	☑	Music
12	☑	Movies
13	☑	Fonts
14	☑	Presentations

☑ Spotlight menu keyboard shortcut: `F5`

☑ Spotlight window keyboard shortcut: `⌘⌥ Space`

✦ **Privacy tab:** If you don't want to display the contents of certain folders in the Spotlight — for instance, if you work in a hospital setting, and you can't allow access to patient information and medical records — click the Add button (which carries a plus sign) and specify the folder or disk you want to exclude from Spotlight searches. Alternatively, just drag the folders or disks to exclude into the list from a Finder window.

It's All about the Hardware

The next category, Hardware, allows you to specify settings that affect your Macintosh hardware.

Bluetooth preferences

If your Mac has Bluetooth hardware available, the Bluetooth group shown in Figure 3-10 appears. If you don't have Bluetooth hardware, you'll be blissfully unaware of the existence of this group because the Bluetooth icon won't appear in your System Preferences window.

The choices on this pane include

✦ **Settings tab:** From this panel, you can opt to allow other Bluetooth devices to discover your Mac and also whether you want to automatically launch the Bluetooth Setup Assistant when no Bluetooth devices are recognized. If you're using a Bluetooth mouse and keyboard (as on an iMac G5), you can wake your Mac using these devices. And, if you like, Tiger can display a Bluetooth status menu in the Finder menu bar.

✦ **Devices tab:** This panel lists all the recognized Bluetooth devices in range and also allows you to configure or disconnect them. You can also set up a new Bluetooth device from here.

✦ **Sharing tab:** The Sharing panel allows you to enable and disable incoming and outgoing file transfers over a Bluetooth connection as well as the synchronizing function built into most Bluetooth hardware. If you're using a Bluetooth connection as a virtual serial port, you can add or remove serial services from this panel as well.

CDs and DVDs preferences

The CDs & DVDs group is shown in Figure 3-11.

Choices here are

✦ **When You Insert a Blank CD:** Click this drop-down list box to specify the action that Mac OS X should take when you load a blank CD-R or CD-RW. You can choose to be prompted or to open the Finder, iTunes, or Disk Copy. Additionally, you can open another application that you select, run an AppleScript that you select, or ignore the disc.

Figure 3-10:
The Bluetooth group appears if your Mac is equipped with Bluetooth.

✦ **When You Insert a Blank DVD:** Use this feature to specify the action that your Mac should take when you load a recordable DVD.

✦ **When You Insert a Music CD:** Choices from this drop-down list specify what action Mac OS X should take when you load an audio CD. By default, iTunes is launched.

✦ **When You Insert a Picture CD:** Choices from this drop-down list specify what action Mac OS X should take when you load a picture CD. By default, iPhoto is launched.

✦ **When You Insert a Video DVD:** Choices from this drop-down list specify what action Mac OS X should take when you load a DVD movie. By default, DVD Player is launched.

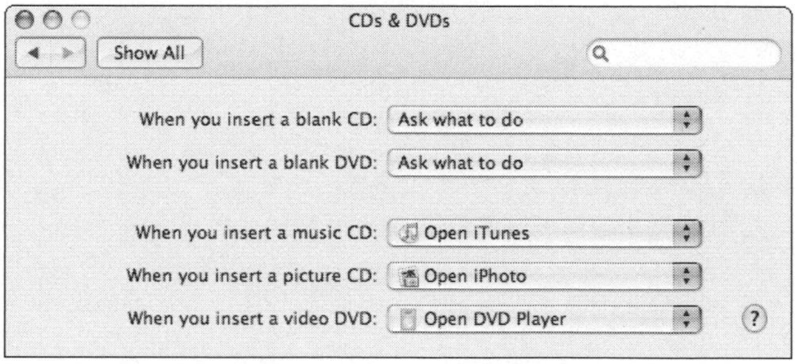

Figure 3-11:
The CD & DVD preferences.

Displays preferences

The Displays group is shown in Figure 3-12.

The two panels here are

✦ **Display tab:** Click the resolution that you want to use from the Resolutions list on the left and then choose the number of colors (from the Colors drop-down list) to display. In most cases, you'll want to use the highest resolution and the highest number of colors. You can also choose a refresh rate (from the, ahem, Refresh Rate drop-down list). Again, generally the higher the refresh rate, the better. Move the Brightness slider to adjust the brightness level of your display. (Note that these settings are different depending on what type of display you're using. For example, a Mac with a CRT monitor has more settings to choose from than a flat-panel LCD system.)

Enable the Show Displays in Menu Bar check box if you'll be switching resolutions and color levels often — this means you, Ms. Image Editor and Mr. Web Designer!

✦ **Color tab:** Click a display color profile that will control the colors on your monitor. To create a custom ColorSync profile and calibrate the colors that you see on your monitor, click the Calibrate button to launch the Display Calibrator. (You can also launch it from your Utilities folder within your Applications folder.) This easy-to-use assistant walks you step-by-step through the process of creating a ColorSync profile matched to your monitor's gamma and white-point values.

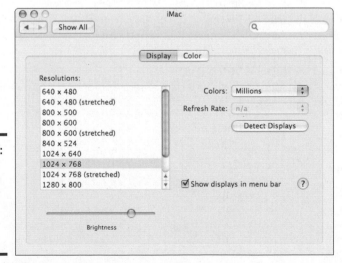

Figure 3-12: Configure your Mac's display settings from this pane.

Energy Saver preferences

The Energy Saver group is shown in Figure 3-13.

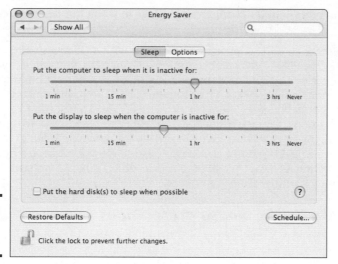

Book II
Chapter 3

Delving under the Hood with System Preferences

Figure 3-13:
The Energy
Saver pane.

The two tabs here are

✦ **Sleep tab:** Move the Put the Computer to Sleep When It Is Inactive For slider to specify when Mac OS X should switch to sleep mode. The Never setting here disables sleep mode entirely. To choose a separate delay period for blanking your monitor, drag the Put the Display to Sleep When the Computer Is Inactive For delay slider to the desired period. You can also power-down the hard drive to conserve energy and prevent wear and tear (an especially good feature for laptop owners).

If you want to start or shut down your Mac at a scheduled time, click the Schedule button. Mark the desired schedule (the Start Up/Wake check box and the Shut Down/Sleep list box) to enable them; then click the up and down arrows next to the time display to set the trigger time. Click OK to return to the Energy Saver pane.

✦ **Options tab:** These settings can toggle events that can wake Tiger from sleep mode, including a ring signal from the modem or a network connection by the network administrator. If you'd like to put your Mac into sleep mode by pressing the Power button, enable the Allow Power Button to Sleep the Computer check box. You can also set Mac OS X to restart automatically after a power failure, which is a good idea if you'll be running a Web or File Transfer Protocol (FTP) server on your machine. (Read more about this in Book VII, Chapter 4.)

Laptop owners can set two separate Energy Saver configurations:

• *Battery Power configuration:* Applies when their Mac is running on battery power)

- *Power Adapter configuration:* Kicks in when the laptop is connected to an AC outlet

If you're running a laptop or a desktop with a G5 processor, you'll see the Processor Performance list box. From here, you can set your Mac's processor to reduce its power consumption and heat buildup. Choose Automatic if you want Tiger to take care of stepping-down your processor's performance whenever possible. *Note:* This setting isn't available for laptops. Choose Highest if you want the best possible performance at all times; this is my favorite setting for use with iMac G5 and Power Mac G5 desktop units. If you want to reduce your laptop's power consumption as far as possible to conserve your battery charge while you're working, choose Reduced.

Keyboard and mouse preferences

The Keyboard & Mouse group is shown in Figure 3-14.

You'll find either three or four panels in this group, depending on whether your Mac has Bluetooth installed. The settings include

✦ **Keyboard tab:** Move the Key Repeat Rate slider to alter the rate at which a keystroke will repeat. You can also adjust the Delay Until Repeat slider to alter how long a key must be held down before it repeats. To test your settings, click in the sample box and hold down a single key.

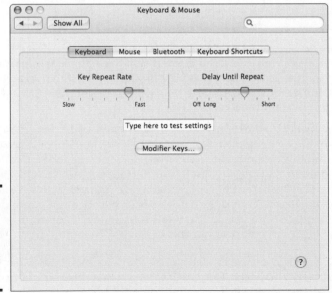

Figure 3-14: The Keyboard & Mouse preferences panel.

✦ **Mouse tab:** Drag the Tracking Speed slider to determine how fast the mouse tracks across your Desktop. You can also drag the Double-Click Speed slider to determine how fast you must click your mouse to cause a double-click — feel free to click in the sample box to test your settings. Drag the Scrolling Speed slider to specify the rate at which the contents of windows will scroll. Lefties might want to change the primary mouse button for aftermarket pointing devices.

✦ **(Optional) Bluetooth tab:** If you're using a Bluetooth mouse or keyboard, you can check the battery level on these devices from this panel. If you don't have a Bluetooth card or external adapter, this tab won't appear.

✦ **Keyboard Shortcuts tab:** If you're a power user who appreciates the lure of the keyboard shortcut, you can edit your shortcuts here.

Looking for even more keyboard customizing possibilities? Select the All Controls radio button on the Keyboard Shortcuts panel to see additional keys to use.

Printing and fax preferences

Figure 3-15 illustrates the Print & Fax preferences.

✦ **Printing tab:** Click the Printer Setup button to launch the Printer Setup Utility, and click the Print Queue button to display the Print Queue window (no great shockers there). To add a new printer, click the Add button, which bears a plus sign. You can read more about printer setup in Book VI, Chapter 4.

The other settings here are

- *Selected Printer in Print Dialog:* Click this drop-down list box to select the installed printer that should act as the default printer throughout your system. If you choose Last Printer Used, Mac OS X uses the printer that received the last print job.

- *Default Paper Size in Page Setup:* Will that be US Letter or Tabloid? Click this drop-down list box to specify the default paper size for future print jobs.

✦ **Sharing tab:** Click this tab to take advantage of Tiger's one-click method of sharing your printers across your network: Enable the Share These Printers with Other Computers check box, and enable the check box next to each printer that you want to share. Mac OS X takes care of the rest. *Nice.*

✦ **Faxing tab:** Click the Faxing button to set up the fax send/receive functions built into Tiger. To receive faxes on your Mac, you must first enable the Receive Faxes on This Computer check box. After faxing has been turned on, you can configure the other settings, which include

- *My Fax Number:* Enter the phone number that others will call to reach your Mac.

- *When a Fax Arrives:* You can determine how many times the phone will ring before your Mac answers the incoming call. By default, Mac OS X saves the incoming fax to your Shared Faxes folder, but you can change that location — or, if you like, you can select an e-mail address where the fax will be sent, or you can choose to print the incoming fax on the printer that you specify. And check this out: If you like, you can send your fax to all three destinations (a disk folder, an e-mail address, and a printer)!

- *Set Up Fax Modem:* Click this button to configure your Mac's internal modem or to select an external USB modem for faxing.

If you send and receive a large number of faxes, make sure you enable the Show Fax Status in Menu Bar check box.

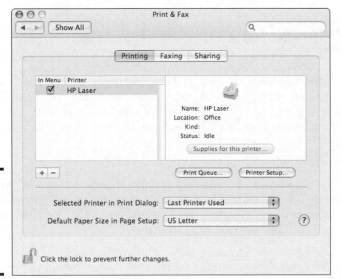

Figure 3-15: Configure faxing and printing using these settings.

Sound preferences

The Sound group is shown in Figure 3-16. To set the overall system audio volume, drag the Output Volume slider. To mute all sound from your Mac, enable the Mute check box. I recommend that you enable the Show Volume in Menu Bar check box, which displays a convenient volume slider menu bar icon.

The three tabs here are

✦ **Sound Effects tab:** From this panel, you can choose the system alert sound and the volume for alerts. You can also choose to mute application and Finder menu sound effects, as well as toggle the sample sound effect when the volume keys are pressed on your Mac's keyboard (or from the Volume slider).

✦ **Output tab:** Use these settings to choose which audio controller your Mac should use for playing sound. Unless you've installed additional audio hardware, this should remain set to Built-in Audio. You can adjust the balance between the left and right channels for the selected output controller.

✦ **Input tab:** These settings allow you to specify an input source. Unless your Mac includes a Line In input source, leave this set to your Internal Microphone. Drag the Input Volume slider to increase or decrease the input signal volume; the input level display provides you with real-time sound levels.

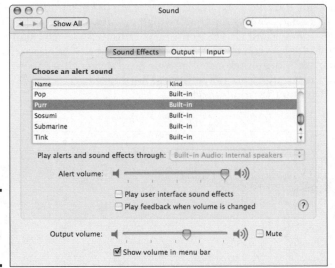

Figure 3-16:
The Sound
preferences
panel.

Sharing the Joy: Internet & Network

Your Internet & Network connections are controlled from the settings in this category.

.Mac preferences

The .Mac group is illustrated in Figure 3-17.

The four panels are

✦ **Account tab:** In the .Mac Member Name and the Password text boxes, respectively, type your .Mac member name and password. If you'd like to subscribe, click the Learn More button to launch your Web browser — you'll be whisked to the .Mac sign-up page. For more information about joining Apple's .Mac service, see Book IV, Chapter 1.

✦ **Sync tab:** If you want to synchronize your computer (or multiple Macintosh computers) with the personal information and data stored online in your .Mac account, select the Synchronize with .Mac check box, and click the drop-down list box to specify manual or automatic synchronization. (To manually sync, click Sync Now.) You can also specify which categories of data you want to sync. Naturally, the fewer categories you choose, the less time it will take to sync. Tiger can display your Sync status in the Finder menu bar.

I recommend that you click the iDisk Syncing Start button to enable Tiger's iDisk syncing function (which creates a local copy of your iDisk on your Mac) and also select the Synchronize Automatically option. This allows iDisk to run much faster because Mac OS X can read and write by using your local iDisk copy on your hard drive. Your Mac will regularly synchronize the data on your local hard drive across the Internet with the iDisk on the Apple server.

Figure 3-17:
Your .Mac account is controlled and configured using these settings.

✦ **iDisk tab:** This tab displays your current iDisk usage and allows you to subscribe for additional space with the Buy More button. You can set your access privileges for your public folder to Read-Only or Read-Write, and you can add a password that others have to enter before they can access your public folder. For a complete description of iDisk, see Book IV, Chapter 4.

✦ **Advanced tab:** From this list, you can see which Macs you've registered for synchronization with your .Mac account. Remember, the actual synchronization settings are found on the Sync panel. To register the computer you're using, click the Register this Computer button.

Network preferences

The Network group is shown in Figure 3-18.

You can create a new Location by clicking the Location drop-down list at the top of the dialog — Mac OS X prompts you for a name — or you can edit your existing Locations by choosing Edit Locations from this list. (Automatic is the default, and it does a pretty good job of figuring out what settings you need.) As I mention in Book I, Chapter 3, creating Locations makes it easy to completely reconfigure your Network preferences when you connect your computer to other networks: for example, when you take your laptop to a branch office. You can also set up Locations to accommodate different ISP dialup telephone numbers in different towns.

Book II
Chapter 3

Delving under the Hood
with System
Preferences

Figure 3-18: The Network preferences panel, showing the Built-in Ethernet settings.

If you need to create a new Location that's very similar to an existing Location, click the Location drop-down list box and choose Edit Locations. Then select the Location that you want to copy and click the Duplicate button. The new Location that you create will contain all the same settings (without several minutes of retyping), so you can easily edit it and make minor changes quickly.

You can choose locations from the Apple menu — a useful trick for laptop road warriors.

When you select Built-in Ethernet from the Show drop-down list box, the tabs displayed are

✦ **TCP/IP:** These settings are provided either automatically (by using Dynamic Host Configuration Protocol [DHCP]) or manually (by using settings provided by your network administrator). For more details on TCP/IP settings, see Book IV, Chapter 1 and Book V, Chapter 2.

✦ **PPPoE:** The settings that you enter here — if necessary — are used for *Point-to-Point Protocol over Ethernet* connections. If you're not using PPPoE to connect to your ISP, you can forget about the settings in this dialog. If you are using PPPoE, see Book IV, Chapter 1 for more details.

✦ **AppleTalk:** If you're connecting your Mac to older Macs or AppleTalk network printers via an AppleTalk network, enable the Make AppleTalk Active check box and choose an active Zone to join from the AppleTalk Zone drop-down list box. Automatic configuration should work in nearly every AppleTalk environment, but if you want to specify the Node ID and Network ID for your computer manually, choose Manually from the Configure drop-down list box.

Note that AppleTalk can be active on only one port within a location. For example, if you have AppleTalk active for Ethernet, you can't select AppleTalk for the wireless port in the same location. (You can, however, define different locations for AirPort and Ethernet, both with AppleTalk active.)

✦ **Proxies:** Network proxy servers are used as part of a firewall configuration to help keep your network secure, but in most cases, changing them can cause you to lose Internet functionality if you enter the wrong settings.

Most folks using a telephone modem, cable modem, or digital subscriber line (DSL) connection should leave these settings alone. Enable and change these settings only at the request of your network administrator.

If you've enabled your Mac OS X firewall and you use FTP to transfer files, enable the Passive FTP Mode check box on the Proxies tab. I recommend that you enable this setting to allow downloading from some Web pages as well.

✦ **Ethernet:** From this panel, you can configure the settings for your Ethernet network interface card. I *strongly* recommend that you leave the Configure drop-down list box set to Automatically (unless specifically told to set things manually by your system administrator or that nice person from Apple tech support).

When you select Internal Modem from the Show drop-down list box, the tabs displayed are

✦ **TCP/IP:** You can configure your Internet connection for Point-to-Point Protocol (PPP), AOL dialup, or enter the settings manually. The Transmission Control Protocol/Internet Protocol (TCP/IP) dialup connection that you choose determines what fields are available. Your ISP will supply you with these settings.

✦ **PPP:** These settings are used for a Point-to-Point Protocol connection over a telephone modem. Again, your ISP will provide you with the right values to enter here. If you're supplied with a secondary telephone number to dial when the primary is busy, enter it into the Alternate Number field.

If you're concerned about who's using your Internet connection — or you want to add an extra layer of security when you dial out — disable the Save Password check box, and Mac OS X will prompt you each time for your Internet account password.

✦ **Proxies:** Some ISPs use proxy servers for their dialup accounts to maintain security, but (as I mention earlier in this section) changing these settings willy-nilly is inviting disaster. Leave them disabled unless given specific instructions on what to set by your ISP.

✦ **Modem:** Click the drop-down Modem list box and choose the brand and model of your modem. If Mac OS X detects an internal modem, it's used by default.

I strongly recommend that you enable both the Enable Error Correction and Compression in Modem and the Wait for Dial Tone Before Dialing check boxes because they will provide you with the best performance and the fastest speeds.

You can also select tone or pulse dialing and whether you want to hear the two modems conversing. (If the caterwauling bothers you, turn off the Sound option.) If you like, Mac OS X can notify you with an alert sound if you receive an incoming call while you're connected to your ISP — just enable the Connection check box on the Modem panel. If you live outside the United States, click the Change button to select the proper Country Setting; this governs how your modem dials your ISP. Finally, I recommend that you enable the Show Modem Status in Menu Bar check box, which gives you a visual reference on your connection status.

When you select Built-in FireWire from the Show drop-down list box, the tabs displayed are

✦ **TCP/IP:** These settings allow you to configure a network connection using TCP/IP over a FireWire connection. The choices here are the same as with the Built-in Ethernet configuration above.

✦ **Proxies:** If you need to configure proxy servers for use over your FireWire network, you'll find the same settings here that I outline earlier for the Built-in Ethernet configuration.

To enable and disable your network ports, click the Show drop-down list box and choose Network Port Configurations. You can enable the On check box to toggle individual ports — for instance, if you don't use your internal modem on your laptop, you can turn it off to conserve power. And you can drag configurations into any desired order to specify which ports Mac OS X should use first when connecting.

QuickTime preferences

The QuickTime group is shown in Figure 3-19. For complete details on QuickTime, streaming media, and viewing movies downloaded from the Web, see Book III, Chapter 7.

If you've purchased a registration code for QuickTime Pro or Player Pro, click the Register tab to enter it.

Figure 3-19:
Configure and register QuickTime from this pane.

The other panels here are

✦ **Browser tab:** These settings determine how QuickTime acts when it's used as a Web browser plug-in. Enable the Play Movies Automatically check box to toggle automatic playback of movies that you've downloaded from the Web. If you'll be viewing downloaded QuickTime movies often, it's a good idea to enable the Save Movies in Disk Cache check box — this improves the playback performance. Drag the Movie Download Cache Size slider to the right to dedicate more hard drive space for movie caching.

✦ **Update tab:** By default, QuickTime checks for new updates automatically, but you can check for new updates immediately by clicking the Update button. You can also add QuickTime enhancement software from other companies by clicking the Install button.

✦ **Streaming tab:** Click the Streaming Speed drop-down list to choose the data transfer speed closest to your connection rate. This optimizes QuickTime's streaming video performance to match your connection.

Click the Instant-On button to enable or disable streaming playback the moment that you start to receive the media (without queuing a significant amount first, which takes time). The faster your Internet connection is, the less time you'll need to queue a media stream. Drag the delay slider to adjust the time delay allowed for caching.

✦ **Advanced tab:** If you've added a software-based music synthesizer (such as Deck or VST) to Mac OS X, you can click Default Synthesizer to use it instead of QuickTime's built-in synthesizer.

When the Enable Kiosk Mode check box is enabled, the options available from the Player window no longer include the ability to save movies or change QuickTime settings. This is a good idea when your kids will be downloading and watching movies from the Web.

If you receive protocol error messages from QuickTime, click the Transport Setup drop-down list box and choose the Automatic setting. Mac OS X will choose the correct transport protocol and port ID for your connection.

If you need to change the MIME file types that QuickTime will play from a Web page, click the MIME Settings button. (These are the different types of multimedia files that you'll encounter on the Web, like video, audio, and photographs.) However, I recommend that you use the default settings because otherwise you might end up downloading a file type that you can't use because you've disabled it.

Often, third-party media players will, in effect, take over the MIME file types from QuickTime. Naturally, this is what you want, *if* you like the new player application. However, if you decide that the new player is not your style, you can return QuickTime to its rightful place as Kahuna of the Web Downloads by displaying the MIME settings, clicking the Use Defaults button, and then clicking OK.

If you play MP3 or MOV files that require secure media keys, you can click the Media Keys button and enter the category and key. To edit a key, select it from the list and click the Edit button. To remove a key from the list, select it and click the Delete button.

Sharing preferences

Figure 3-20 illustrates the Sharing preferences.

Click in the Computer Name text field to change the default network name assigned to your Mac during the installation process. Your current network name is listed, but you can change your network settings by clicking the Edit button.

The three tabs here are

✦ **Services tab:** Each entry in the services list controls a specific type of sharing, including Personal File Sharing (with other Macs), Windows Sharing (with PCs running Windows), Personal Web Sharing, Remote Login, FTP Access, Apple Remote Desktop, Remote Apple Events, and Printer Sharing. To turn on any of these services, enable the On check box for that service. To turn off a service, choose it from the list and click the Stop button that appears.

From a security standpoint, I highly recommend that you enable only those services that you will actually use. A Mark's Maxim to remember:

Poking too many holes in your firewall is *not* a good thing.™

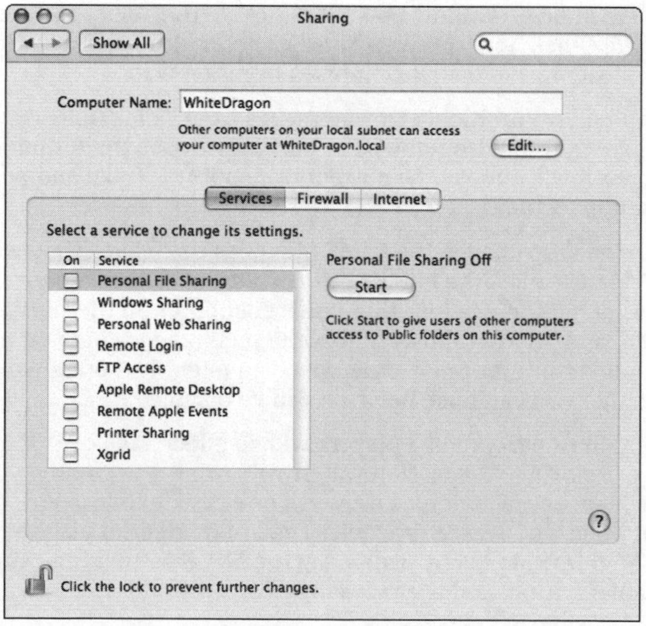

Figure 3-20:
The Sharing preference settings.

✦ **Firewall tab:** As I discuss in Book IV, Chapter 6, Mac OS X includes a built-in firewall, which you can enable from this panel. When the firewall is on, communication to any service not allowed in the list is blocked. (In firewall-speak, these entries are called *rules* because they determine what's allowed to pass through to your Mac.)

After you click Start to enable the firewall, it's easy to enable communications with a service: select the entry in the list and enable the On check box. Click the New button to specify a new rule by entering a port and assigning it a name. After you create a new rule, it appears in the list, and you can toggle it on and off like any of the default rules. Click the Edit button to edit the selected rule; click the Delete button to remove the selected rule.

If you're using an Internet or network connection, I strongly urge you to enable the firewall (but only after you review Book V, Chapter 2). However, if you suddenly can't connect to other computers or share files that you were originally able to share, it's time to review the rules that you've enabled from this panel.

✦ **Internet tab:** If you want to share the Internet connection from this Macintosh, click the port to use in the Share Your Connection From drop-down list box — this will almost always be the Built-in Ethernet option — and then click Start.

**Book II
Chapter 3**

Delving under the Hood with System Preferences

Tweaking the System

The last section of the System Preferences window covers system-wide settings that affect all users and the overall operation of Mac OS X.

Accounts preferences

The Accounts group is illustrated in Figure 3-21.

Each user on your system has an entry in this list. The panels here change, depending on the access level of the selected account. They can include

✦ **Password tab:** Click in these text fields to enter or edit the account name, password, and password hint for the selected user.

Click the Address Book Card button to edit the card that you've marked in the Address Book as My Card. Mac OS X launches the Address Book, and you can edit your card to your heart's content. (For the complete scoop on the Mac OS X Address Book, see Book I, Chapter 6.)

✦ **Picture tab:** From the Picture panel, you can either choose one of the thumbnail images provided by Apple to represent you or click Edit to drag a new image from the Finder.

✦ **Login Items tab:** The applications that you add to this list will launch automatically each time that the current user logs in to Mac OS X. To add an application, click the Add button (which carries a plus sign), navigate to the desired application and select it, and then click the Add button. (Alternatively, you can simply drag an item from a Finder window into the Login Items list.) To remove an application from the list, click to select it and then click the Remove button (which has a minus sign). Each application can be launched in a *hidden state,* meaning that its window doesn't appear on the Desktop. To toggle an item as hidden or visible, enable the Hide check box next to the desired application. The order that Login Items are launched can be changed by dragging entries in the list into the desired sequence.

You can even set up Login Items directly from the Dock! Control-click (or right-click) the desired Dock icon to display the pop-up menu and then click Open at Login.

✦ **Parental Controls tab:** This panel is available only when you're adding or editing a standard-level account. You can choose to assign limitations based on specific applications and the Finder itself. For more information about assigning limitations, refer to Book II, Chapter 5.

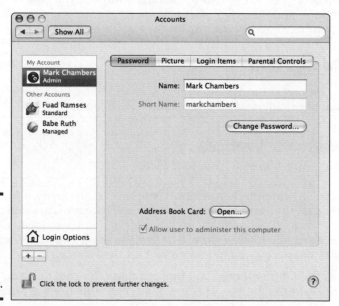

Figure 3-21: Configuring accounts is easy from System Preferences.

A word about the Login Options button (look for the little house icon, lower left). Click it to set a number of global options that control how users log in. For example, you can choose to display either a Name and Password field on the Login screen (which means that the user must actually type in the correct username) or a list of users, from which a person can select a user ID.

(If security is a consideration, use the Name and Password option.) You can also add VoiceOver spoken interface support at the Login screen, making it easier for physically challenged users to log in to this Mac.

If you choose, you can log in automatically as the selected user by clicking the Login Options button and enabling the Automatically Log in As *<Username>* feature.

The Login Options panel also allows you to enable or disable Fast User Switching (which I discuss in Book II, Chapter 5), and you can prevent anyone from restarting or shutting down the Mac from the Login screen by enabling the Hide the Restart and Shut Down Buttons check box.

Classic preferences

Figure 3-22 shows the Classic System Preferences settings.

The three panels here are

✦ **Start/Stop tab:** You can select from multiple Mac OS 9 System folders when launching Classic, and you can elect to start Classic automatically when the current user logs in. (Personally, I don't use Classic often, so I don't run it automatically at login — therefore saving those system resources for my other applications.) If you'd rather be prompted before Classic is launched, enable the Warn Before Starting Classic check box. You can launch Classic manually from this panel by clicking Start; if Classic is encountering problems, you can click the Restart or the Force Quit buttons as well.

Note that you can monitor the status of Classic mode by enabling the Show Classic Status in Menu Bar check box. This can be a boon for those who use many legacy applications from the days of Mac OS 9.

✦ **Advanced tab:** Three special start-up options are available from the drop-down list — and *only* when you use the Start Classic button on this panel. (As you might expect, these options are typically only for debugging and troubleshooting.) You can elect to start Classic with all extensions turned off, or you can open the Extensions Manager to toggle individual extensions on and off within Classic. Finally, you can choose Use Key Combination from the drop-down list to start or restart Classic when you press a shortcut sequence of up to five keys.

To use preferences from the current user's Home folder, enable the Use Mac OS 9 Preferences from Your Home check box. If this is disabled, preferences from the System folder that you choose on the Start/Stop panel are used. You can specify the amount of inactivity before Classic switches to sleep mode, and you can rebuild the Classic Desktop, which is a good idea if custom icons disappear or documents that once had recognized file types are no longer recognized.

✦ **Memory/Versions tab:** This panel displays information on both Classic and the applications that it's running. To show background processes that would normally be invisible, mark the Show Background Applications check box to enable it.

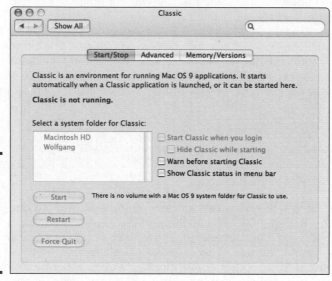

Figure 3-22:
Yep, Classic mode is still around, and it's configured here.

Date and time preferences

Click the System Preferences Date & Time icon to display the settings that you see in Figure 3-23.

The three tabs here are

✦ **Date & Time tab:** To set the current date, click the date within the mini-calendar; to set the system time, click in the field above the clock and type the current time.

You can't set these values manually if you use a network time server. To automatically set your Mac's system time and date from a network time server, enable the Set Date & Time Automatically check box and then choose a server from the drop-down list that corresponds to your location. (Of course, you need an Internet connection to use a network time server.)

✦ **Time Zone tab:** Click your approximate location on the world map to choose a time zone or click the Closest City drop-down list and choose the city that's closest to you (and shares your same time zone).

✦ **Clock tab:** If you enable the Show the Date and Time check box, you can choose to view the time in text or icon format. The clock can appear on the menu bar or in its own window. You can also optionally display seconds, AM/PM, and the day of the week; have the time separator characters flash; or use a clock based on 24 hours. If you choose a clock window, you can even specify the transparency of that window so that it won't interfere with applications behind it.

TIP

Personally, I get a big kick out of my Mac announcing the time on the hour . . . plus, it helps pull me back into the real world. (You've got to eat sooner or later.) Anyway, if you'd like this helpful reminder as well, enable the Announce the Time check box on the Clock panel, and click the drop-down list to select an hour, half-hour, or quarter-hour announcement.

Book II Chapter 3

Delving under the Hood with System Preferences

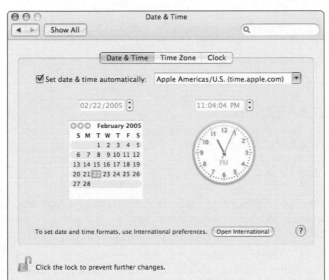

Figure 3-23: The Date & Time preferences pane.

Software Update preferences
The Software Update settings are shown in Figure 3-24. (Oh, and don't forget that you'll need an active Internet connection.)

The two panels here are

✦ **Update Software tab:** I recommend enabling the Check for Updates check box — and I also recommend that you choose Daily or Weekly from the drop-down list box. (You can also elect to download critical updates in the background automatically while you continue working.) To check immediately, click the Check Now button.

✦ **Installed Updates tab:** Click this tab to display a list of the updates that you've already applied to Mac OS X. You can open the list as a log file as well, which allows you to cut and paste text.

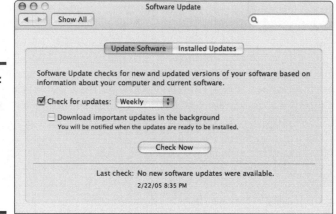

Figure 3-24:
Keep Tiger
up-to-date
with the
controls
in the
Software
Update
group.

Speech preferences

Figure 3-25 illustrates the Speech settings. For a discussion of how these settings are used, visit Book VII, Chapter 3.

The two panels here are

✦ **Speech Recognition tab:** This tab has two tabs of its own: Settings and Commands. With Speakable Items toggled on, you can control Tiger with spoken commands.

  • *Settings tab:* If you have more than one microphone, you can select which one you want to use as well as set the input volume with the Calibrate button. You can change the Listening key (Esc by default) and specify whether your Mac should listen only while the key is pressed or whether the Listening Key toggles listening on and off. You can also change the name of your computer (using the Keyword box) and whether that name is required before a command. From the Play This Sound drop-down list, you can indicate what sound effect Mac OS X will play when it recognizes a speech command. (Optionally, Tiger can confirm the command by speaking it if you enable the Speak Command Acknowledgement check box.)

  • *Commands tab:* Here you can select which types of commands are available as well as whether exact wording of command names is required. Click the self-named button to open the Speakable Items Folder from this panel. Read more about these settings in Book VII, Chapter 3.

✦ **Text to Speech:** Here's a fun panel. Click a voice from the System Voice drop-down list box, and Mac OS X will use that voice to speak to you from dialogs and applications. You can set the Speaking Rate (from Slow to Fast) and play a sample by clicking the Play button. (Try Zarvox, Bubbles, and Pipe Organ.)

The Announce When Alerts are Displayed feature actually speaks the text within alert dialogs; to configure spoken alerts, click the Set Alert Options button. You can optionally add a phrase before the text, which you can choose from the Phrase drop-down list box. To add a phrase to the list, like *Don't Panic!,* choose Edit Phrase List from the list. Move the Delay slider to specify how much time your Mac should wait before reading the dialog to you.

You can also optionally announce when an application wants your attention, and Tiger can speak the text that's currently selected within an application when you press a key that you specify.

This pane also provides a couple of convenient shortcut buttons that take you to other "speech centers" within System Preferences — specifically, the Date & Time and Universal Access panes.

**Book II
Chapter 3**

Delving under the Hood
with System
Preferences

Figure 3-25:
Tiger
includes
highly
configurable
Speech
features.

Startup Disk preferences

Figure 3-26 illustrates the Startup Disk settings.

To select a start-up disk, click the desired start-up folder from the scrolling icon list.

Figure 3-26:
The Startup
Disk pane
within
System
Preferences.

Mac OS 9 System folders have a 9 icon, and Mac OS X folders have the familiar blue X logo. Mac OS X displays the version numbers of each system and
the physical drives where each system resides. Select the Network Startup
icon if you'd like to boot from a System folder on your local network — typically, such a folder is created by your network administrator.

If you're planning on rebooting with an external Universal Serial Bus (USB)
or FireWire start-up disk, that disk must already be connected, powered on,
and recognized by the system before you display these settings.

Tiger introduces a new button on the Startup Disk pane. Click Target Disk
Mode to restart this Mac as a FireWire external hard drive connected to
another computer. (This comes in especially handy when you're upgrading
to a new Mac and you need to move files between the two computers. I've
also used it when the video card in one of my Macs decided to stop working.
This allowed me to make an updated backup copy of the ailing Mac's hard
drive before I sent it off for repair.) You can also restart your Mac and hold
down the T key to invoke Target Disk Mode.

After you click a folder to select it, click the Restart button. Mac OS X con-
firms your choice, and your Mac reboots.

Universal Access preferences

The final group, Universal Access, is shown in Figure 3-27. These settings
modify the display and sound functions within Mac OS X to make them more
friendly to physically challenged users. Note that if you select the VoiceOver
On radio button, Mac OS X speaks the text for all text and buttons onscreen.

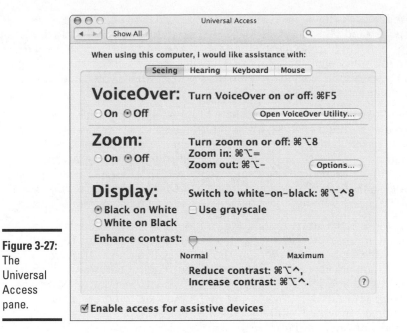

Figure 3-27:
The
Universal
Access
pane.

If you have an assistive device that's recognized by Mac OS X, select the Enable Access for Assistive Devices check box to allow it to be used throughout the operating system.

The four panels here are

✦ **Seeing tab:** These settings make it easier for those with limited vision to use Mac OS X. You can toggle VoiceOver on and off from here; I discuss more on this feature and these settings in Book VII, Chapter 3. To turn on the display Zoom feature, select the Zoom On radio button or press ⌘+Option+8.

To specify how much magnification should be used, click the Options button. From the sheet that appears, you can set the minimum and maximum Zoom magnification increments. From the keyboard, use ⌘+Option+= (equal sign) to zoom in and ⌘+Option+– (minus sign) to zoom out. Optionally, you can display a preview rectangle of the area that will be included when you zoom.

Mac OS X can also smooth images to make them look better when zoomed. If you prefer white text on a black background, select the White on Black radio button (or press the ⌘+Option+Control+8 keyboard shortcut). Note that depending on your display settings, it might be easier on the eyes to use grayscale display mode by selecting the Use Grayscale check box.

✦ **Hearing tab:** If you need additional visual cues to supplement the spoken and audio alerts in Mac OS X, click this tab and enable the Flash the Screen When an Alert Sound Occurs check box. To raise the overall sound volume in Mac OS X, you can click the Adjust Sound button to display the Sound System Preferences settings, where you can drag the Volume slider to the right.

✦ **Keyboard tab:** These settings help those who have trouble pressing keyboard shortcuts or those who often trigger keyboard repeats (repetition of the same character) accidentally. If you mark the Sticky Keys On radio button, you can use *modifier keys* individually that will be grouped together automatically as a single keyboard shortcut. (You can optionally specify that Mac OS X should sound a beep tone when a modifier key is pressed and whether the modifier keys should be displayed onscreen.)

Sticky Keys (a feature that allows you to press the modifier keys in a key sequence one after another instead of all together) can be toggled on from the keyboard by pressing the Shift key five times. Turn Slow Keys on to add a pause (of the length that you specify) between when a key is pressed and when it's actually acted upon within Mac OS X. You can optionally add a key-click sound each time that you press a key. To turn keyboard repeat off entirely, click the Set Key Repeat button, which opens the Keyboard preference settings that I discuss earlier.

✦ **Mouse tab:** With Mouse Keys active, you can use the numeric keypad to move the mouse pointer across your screen. Mouse Keys can be toggled on and off by pressing the Option key five times. Drag the Initial Delay and Maximum Speed sliders to specify how long you must hold down a keypad key before the pointer starts to move, as well as how fast the pointer should move across the screen. The cursor can be resized to make it easier to spot onscreen. You can also click the Open Keyboard Preferences button to turn on Full Keyboard Access.

Chapter 4: You Mean Others Can Use My Mac, Too?

In This Chapter

⮑ **Understanding how multi-user systems work**

⮑ **Configuring login settings**

⮑ **Changing the appearance of the login screen**

⮑ **Tightening security during login**

⮑ **Starting applications automatically when you log in**

Whether you're setting up Mac OS X for use in a public library or simply allowing your 12-year-old to use your Mac in your home office, configuring Tiger for multiple users is a simple task. However, you must also consider the possible downsides of a mismanaged multi-user system: files and folders being shared that you didn't want in the public domain, users logging in as each other, and the very real possibility of accidental file deletion (and worse).

Therefore, in this chapter, I show you how to take those first steps before you open Pandora's Box — setting login options, configuring the personal account that you created when you first installed the operating system, and protecting your stuff. (Network administrators call this security check-up *locking things down*.)

How Multi-User Works on Mac OS X

When you create multiple users in Mac OS X, each person who uses your Macintosh — hence the term *user* — has a separate account (much like an account that you might open at a bank). Mac OS X creates a Home folder for each user and saves that user's preferences independently from other users. When you log in to Mac OS X, you select (or provide) a username and a password, which identifies you. The username/password combination tells Mac OS X which user has logged on — and therefore, which preferences and Home folder to use.

Each account also carries a specific level, which determines how much control the user has over Mac OS X and the computer itself. Without an account with the proper access level, for example, a user might not be able to display many of the panels in System Preferences.

The three account levels are

✦ **Root:** Also called *System Administrator,* this uber-account can change *anything* within Mac OS X — and that's usually A *Very* Bad Thing, so it's actually disabled as a default. (This alone should tell you that the Root account shouldn't be toyed with.) For instance, the Root account can seriously screw up the UNIX subsystem within Mac OS X, or a Root user can delete files within the Mac OS X System Folder.

Enable the System Administrator account and use it only if told to do so by an Apple technical support technician. To enable the Root account, you must launch NetInfo Manager, which is stored in the Utilities folder inside your Applications folder.

✦ **Administrator:** (Or admin for short.) This is the account level that you were assigned when you installed Mac OS X. *Note:* The administrator account should *not* be confused with the System Administrator account!

It's perfectly okay for you or anyone you assign to use an administrator account. An administrator can install applications anywhere on the system, create/edit/delete user accounts, and make changes to all the settings in System Preferences. However, an administrator can't move or delete items from any other user's Home folder, and administrators are barred from modifying or deleting files in the Mac OS X System Folder.

A typical multi-user Mac OS X computer will have only one administrator — like a teacher in a classroom — but technically, you can create as many administrator accounts as you like. If you do need to give someone else this access level, assign it only to a competent, experienced user whom you trust.

✦ **Standard:** A standard user account is the default in Mac OS X. Standard users can install software and save documents only in their Home folders and the Shared folder (which resides in the Users folder), and they can change only certain settings in System Preferences. Thus, they can do little damage to the system as a whole. For example, each of the students in a classroom should be given a standard-level account for the Mac OS X system that they share.

If Parental Controls are applied to a standard account, it becomes a *managed* account, allowing you to fine-tune what a standard account user can do. (I discuss Parental Controls at length in Book II, Chapter 5.)

The next chapter of this mini-book covers the entire process of creating and editing a user account.

Configuring Your Login Screen

Take a look at the changes that you can make to the login process. First, Mac OS X provides three methods of displaying the login screen:

✦ **Logging in with a list:** To log in, click your account username in the list, and the login screen displays the password prompt. Type your password — Mac OS X displays bullet characters to ensure security — and press Return (or click the Log In button).

✦ **Logging in with username and password:** Type your account username in the Name field and press Tab. Then type your password and press Return (or click the Log In button).

✦ **Auto Login:** With Auto Login set, Mac OS X automatically logs in the specified account when you reboot. In effect, you never see the login screen unless you click Log Out from the Apple menu. (Naturally, this is an attractive option to use if your computer is in a secure location — like your office — and you'll be the only one using your Mac.)

To specify which type of login screen you see — if you see one at all — head to System Preferences, click Accounts, and then click the Login Options button.

✦ To set Auto Login, display the Login Options settings and select the Automatically Log in As check box to enable it. Click the account name drop-down list box and choose the account that should automatically log in. When Mac OS X displays the user Name and Password sheet that you see in Figure 4-1, type the corresponding password and then click OK.

Never set the Auto Login feature to an admin-level account unless you're sure to be the only one using your Mac. If the computer is rebooted, you're opening the door for anyone to simply sashay in and wreak havoc!

✦ To determine whether Mac OS X uses a list login screen, you must again visit the Login Options settings panel (see Figure 4-2). Select the List of Users radio button for a list login screen or select the Name and Password radio button for a simple login screen where you must type your username and password.

To change settings specific to your account — no matter what your access level — log in with your account, open System Preferences, and click Accounts. From here, you can change your account password and picture, the card marked as yours within the Address Book, and the Login Items launched automatically when you log in. (Peruse more information on the Address Book in Book I, Chapter 6.)

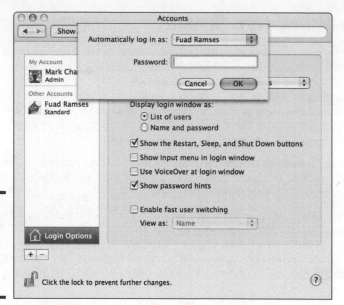

Figure 4-1:
Configuring
Auto Login
from the
Accounts
panel.

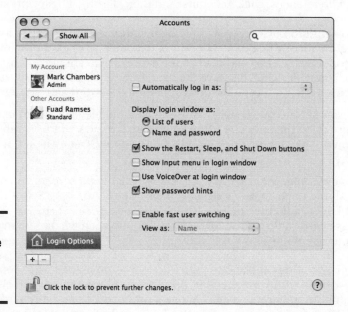

Figure 4-2:
Will that be
a simple or
a list login
screen?

To log out of Mac OS X without restarting or shutting down the computer, choose the Apple menu and then either choose Log Out or just press ⌘+Shift+Q. You'll see the confirmation dialog shown in Figure 4-3. Although Mac OS X will display the login screen after two minutes, someone can still saunter up and click the Cancel button, thereby gaining access to your stuff. Therefore, make it a practice to always click the Log Out button on this screen before your hand leaves the mouse!

**Book II
Chapter 4**

**You Mean
Others Can Use
My Mac, Too?**

Figure 4-3:
Always click Log Out before you leave your Mac.

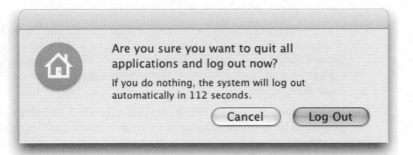

Are you sure you want to quit all applications and log out now?

If you do nothing, the system will log out automatically in 112 seconds.

Cancel   Log Out

You can also enable Fast User Switching from the Login Options panel. This feature allows another user to sit down and log in while the previous user's applications are still running in the background. When you enable switching, Tiger displays the currently active user's name at the right side of the Finder menu bar. Click the name, and a menu appears; click Login Window, and another user can then log in as usual. Even though you're playing musical chairs, the Big X remembers what's running and the state of your Desktop when you last left it. (When you decide to switch back, Tiger prompts you for that account's login password . . . just in case, you understand.)

Locking Things Down

If security is a potential problem and you still need to share a Mac between multiple users, lock things down. To protect Mac OS X from unauthorized use, take care of these potential security holes immediately:

✦ **Disable the Sleep, Restart, and Shut Down buttons.** Any computer can be hacked when it's restarted or turned on, so disable the Restart and Shut Down buttons on the login screen. (After a user has successfully logged in, Mac OS X can be shut down normally by using the menu item or the keyboard shortcuts that I cover earlier.) Open the Accounts panel in System Preferences, click the Login Options button, and enable the Hide the Sleep, Restart, and Shut Down Buttons check box. Press ⌘+Q to quit and save your changes. (You can find more about restarting and shutting down in Book I, Chapter 2.)

✦ **Disable list logins.** With a list login, any potential hacker already knows half the information necessary to gain entry to your system — and often the password is easy to guess. Therefore, set Mac OS X to ask for the username and password on the Login screen, as I describe earlier. This way, someone has to guess both the username and the password, which is a much harder proposition.

✦ **Disable Auto Login.** A true no-brainer. As I mention earlier in the chapter, Auto Login is indeed very convenient. However, all someone has to do is reboot your Mac, and the machine automatically logs in one lucky user! To disable Auto Login, display the Accounts panel in System Preferences and click the Login Options button; then disable the Automatically Log In As *<username>* check box.

✦ **Disable the password hint.** By default, Mac OS X obligingly displays the password hint for an account after three unsuccessful attempts at entering a password. Where security is an issue, this is like serving a hacker a piece of apple pie. Therefore, head to System Preferences, display the Accounts settings, click each user's account in the list, and make sure that the Password Hint box is empty.

✦ **Select passwords intelligently.** Although using your mother's maiden name for a password might seem like a great idea, the best method of selecting a password is to use a completely random group of mixed letters and numbers. If you find a random password too hard to remember, at least add a number after your password, like *dietcoke1* — and no, that is not one of my passwords. (Nice try.)

For even greater security, make at least one password character uppercase, and use a number at the beginning and ending of the password. Or, do the "c001" thing and replace characters with numbers, like the zero that you insert in dietc0ke.

Starting Applications Automatically After Login

Here's one other advantage to logins — each account can have its own selection of applications that run automatically when that user logs in. These applications are *Login Items.* (For the Mac OS 9 old-timers, these are the same as the Startup Items in days gone by.) A caveat or two:

✦ **The users setting their Login Items must be logged in.** Only the user can modify his or her own Login Items.

✦ **Users must have access to System Preferences.** If the person is using a standard-level account, it must allow access to System Preferences.

Ready? Let's begin. Open System Preferences and click Accounts, click your account to select it, and then click Login Items (see Figure 4-4).

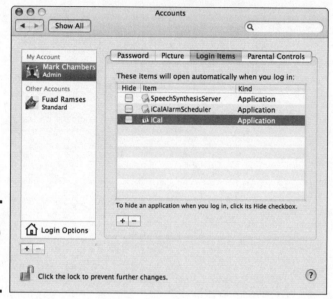

Book II
Chapter 4

You Mean
Others Can Use
My Mac, Too?

Figure 4-4:
Preparing to
launch iCal
every time I
log in.

Including an application in your Login Items list is easy: Click the button with the plus sign to navigate to the desired application, select it, and then click Add. (Alternatively, you can just drag items from a Finder window and drop them directly into the list.) Note that items in the list are launched in order — if something needs to run before something else, you can drag the item entries into any sequence.

To launch the application in hidden mode — which might or might not display it in the Dock, depending on the application itself — click the list entry for the desired item and enable its Hide check box.

Chapter 5: Setting Up
Multi-User Accounts

In This Chapter

✔ **Adding, modifying, and deleting users**

✔ **Setting Parental Controls**

✔ **Avoiding keychains**

*I*n the previous chapter, I introduce you to the different Mac OS X multi-user account levels and the login process. If you're ready to share your Mac with others, you discover how to add new accounts and edit existing accounts in this chapter. Oh, and yes, I also show you how to *frag* — that's multiplayer game-speak for *delete* — accounts that you no longer need. I also demonstrate how to add optional limitations to an individual user account and how to avoid using a keychain (which is supposed to make it easier to store that pocketful of passwords that you've created on the Internet).

Yes, you read correctly. By all that's good and righteous, Mac OS X actually has a feature that I *don't* want you to use. Read on to find out more.

Adding, Editing, and Deleting Users

All multi-user account chores take place in a single System Preferences pane. (Cue James Bond theme song.) The Accounts pane is the star of this chapter, so open System Preferences and click the Accounts icon.

If you haven't added any users to your system yet, the Users list should look like Figure 5-1. You should see only your account, which you set up when you installed Mac OS X, set to administrator (admin) level.

Adding an account

To add a new user account, follow these steps:

1. **In the Accounts pane in System Preferences, click the New User button — which carries a plus sign — to display an empty user record sheet that you see in Figure 5-2.**

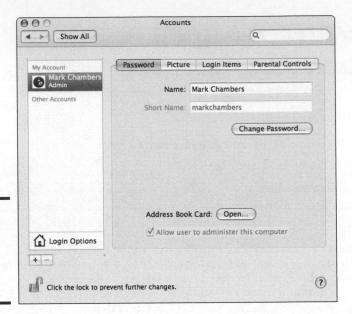

Figure 5-1:
A typical
first look
at the
Accounts
pane.

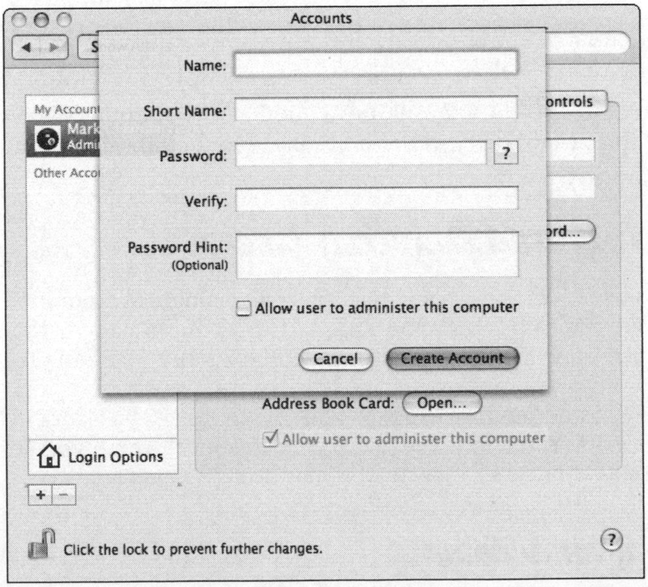

Figure 5-2:
Setting up a
new user
account.

2. **In the Name text box, type the name that you want to display for this account (both in the Accounts list and on the Login screen) and then press Tab to move to the next field.**

Mac OS X automatically generates a short name for use as your screen and Buddy name in iChat AV and various network applications. The short name is also the name of the folder that Mac OS X creates on the computer's hard drive for this user. You can keep the default short name or type a new one, but it must not contain any spaces. For more on iChat AV, jump to Book IV, Chapter 3. (I'll wait for you here.)

3. **Press Tab again.**

4. **In the Password text box, type the password for the new account.**

Click the question mark next to the Password field, and Tiger is happy to display the new Password Assistant, complete with a suggestion. Click the Suggestion drop-down list box to see additional suggestions. You can choose the length of the password, and select from several types: letters and numbers, memorable, or completely random. To insert a password from the Assistant, use ⌘+C to copy the password, click in the Accounts Password text box, and then press ⌘+V (or click the password and drag it to the Accounts Password text box).

As always, when you enter a password or its verification, Mac OS X displays bullet characters for security.

5. **Press Tab, type the password again in the Verify text box, and press Tab again.**

6. **(Optional) If you decide to use the password hint feature that I describe in Book II, Chapter 4, you can enter a short sentence or question in the Password Hint text box.**

The hint is displayed after three unsuccessful attempts at entering the account password.

I recommend that you *do not use this option*. Think about it: Any hack could type in anything three times to get your hint to pop up! If you do use this option, at least make sure that the hint is sufficiently vague!

Press Tab to continue.

7. **To grant this account administrator-level access, enable the Allow User to Administer This Computer check box.**

If this check box remains disabled, the user receives a standard level account.

8. **Click the Create Account button to finish and create the account.**

The new account now shows up in the Accounts list and in the Login screen.

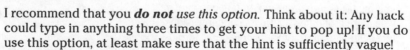

Editing an existing account

If you have administrator access, it's a cinch to make changes to an existing account from the Accounts panel in System Preferences. (Often, this is to assign a personalized account picture, so I'll demonstrate that here.) Follow these steps:

1. **Click the account that you want to change in the Accounts list.**

2. **Edit the settings that you need to change.**

3. **Click the Picture tab to specify the thumbnail image that will appear in the Login list next to the account name.**

   Apple provides a number of good images in the scrolling strip — just click one to select it.

4. **To add your own picture, click Edit to drag a new image from the Finder into the Images well; then click Set.**

   Alternatively, you can click the Snapshot button to grab a picture from your iSight or other video camera connected to your Mac. *Most* cool.

So you like your privacy . . .

These days, everyone's interested in securing their personal files from prying eyes. Granted, this isn't a problem if you're the only one using your Mac. However, if you're sharing a computer in a multi-user environment, you might want a little more protection than just user permissions for those all-important Fantasy Football formations that you'll unleash next season.

Never fear, Tiger offers a feature called *FileVault,* which provides Home folder encryption that should prevent just about anyone except the NSA or FBI from gaining access to the files in your Home folder. You can enable the FileVault feature from the Security panel in System Preferences. Two passwords control access to your Home folder when FileVault is active:

✔ The *Master Password* can unlock any Home folder for *any* user. Only someone with an admin account can set the Master Password. The Master Password must be set before you can turn on the FileVault feature for any account on your system.

✔ Your *Login Password* unlocks your Home folder.

Personally, I love this feature, and I use it on all my Macs running Tiger. Yet there is a risk involved (insert ominous chord here). To wit: *DO NOT* forget your Login Password, and make doggone sure that your Admin user remembers that all-important Master Password! Mac OS X displays a dire warning for anyone who's considering using FileVault: If you forget these passwords, you can't retrieve any data from your Home folder. *Period.* As Jerry Reed says, "It's a gone pecan."

5. After you make the changes (and you've selected just the right image to capture the user's personality — a more difficult task than you might think), press ⌘+Q to save them and close the System Preferences dialog.

Deleting an existing account

To wipe an account from the face of the Earth, follow these steps:

1. **Click the account that you want to delete in the Accounts list.**

2. **Click the Delete User button (which is smartly marked with a minus sign).**

   Mac OS X displays the confirmation sheet that you see in Figure 5-3.

Figure 5-3:
Are you
quite sure
that you
want to
delete this
user?

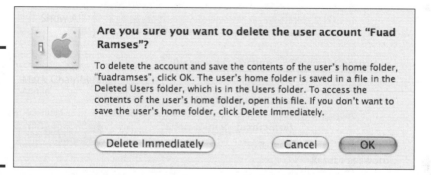

Are you sure you want to delete the user account "Fuad Ramses"?

To delete the account and save the contents of the user's home folder, "fuadramses", click OK. The user's home folder is saved in a file in the Deleted Users folder, which is in the Users folder. To access the contents of the user's home folder, open this file. If you don't want to save the user's home folder, click Delete Immediately.

[Delete Immediately]   (Cancel)   (OK)

Note that the contents of the user's Home folder are saved in a file in the Deleted Users folder (just in case you need to retrieve something). If you're absolutely sure you won't be dating that person again, click the Delete Immediately button (which doesn't save anything in the Deleted Users folder).

3. **Click OK to verify and delete the account or click the Delete Immediately button to zap it completely. Click the Cancel button to abort and return to the Accounts list.**

Tightening Your Security Belt

Administrators are special people. Just ask one; you'll see. Anyway, when an administrator creates or edits the account for a standard-level user, Mac OS X offers a number of levels of specific rights — Parental Controls — that can be assigned on an individual account basis.

Parental Controls are available only for standard-level users; administrators don't need them because an administrator-level account already has access to everything covered by Controls.

When do you need Parental Controls? Here are three likely scenarios:

✦ You're creating accounts for corporate or educational users, and you want to disable certain features of Mac OS X to prevent those folks from doing something dumb. Just tell 'em you're *streamlining the operating system*. (Yeah, that's it.) For example, you might not want that one particular kid making CD copies of *The Illustrated Anarchist's Cookbook* in the classroom while you're gone. Therefore, you disable the ability for that account to burn CDs or DVDs.

✦ In the same environment, you might want to give a specific standard-level account the ability to view all the settings in System Preferences. If Roger in Accounting is both helpful and knowledgeable — oh, and add *trustworthy* in there, too — you might want to give him this capability so that he can make necessary changes to the system while you're on vacation.

✦ You want one or more users to access one — and *only* one — application on the system, or perhaps just two or three applications. To illustrate: In my years as a hospital hardware technician, we had a number of computers that were used solely to display patient records. No Word, no e-mail, nothing but the one program that accessed the medical records database. We called these machines *dumb terminals* although they were actually personal computers. (This trick also works well if you're a parent and you'd like to give your kids access without endangering your valuable files. Just don't call your computer a *dumb terminal* lest your kids take offense. That's experience talking there.) If you want to allow access to a specified selection of applications, you can set them in that account's Controls.

Setting Parental Controls

Time to review what each of the settings does. To display the controls for a standard account, click the account in the list and then click the Parental Controls tab. Tiger includes four different categories of controls, as shown in Figure 5-4:

✦ **Mail:** Click its Configure button to specify the e-mail addresses that this user can exchange mail with. If the Mail check box is disabled here, the user can exchange mail with anyone.

✦ **Finder & System:** These settings (which I discuss in a second) affect what the user can do within Tiger as well as what the Finder itself looks like to that user.

✦ **iChat:** Click this Configure button to specify the instant messaging accounts that this user can chat with. If the iChat check box is disabled here, the user can chat with anyone.

✦ **Safari:** Mark the Safari check box to turn on access controls. The controlled user can access anything in the Safari Bookmarks bar. However, if a user tries to access a site that's not in the Bookmarks bar, he'll get a rather stern dialog box explaining that the site he's trying to visit is off-limits. (Safari also provides an Add Website button in the dialog that adds the site to the Bookmarks bar, but an admin user ID and password must be supplied.)

Figure 5-4:
You can restrict access to many functions within a Standard account.

You can always tell whether an account has been assigned Parental Controls because the account description changes from Standard to Managed in the Accounts list.

Of particular importance are the Finder & System controls. Select the Finder & System check box to enable it, and then click the Configure button to modify these settings:

✦ **Open All System Preferences:** When this check box is enabled, this option allows the user to view any setting throughout System Preferences, just as if the account were administrator-level. However, in order to change a setting, a managed user must still click the padlock (in the lower-left corner of most panes in System Preferences) and enter a valid admin-level username and password to unlock the controls.

✦ **Modify the Dock:** Enable this check box, and the user can remove applications, documents, and folders from the Dock in the Full Finder. (If you don't want the contents of the Dock changing according to the whims of other users, it's a good idea to disable this check box.)

✦ **Administer Printers:** With this check box enabled, the user can modify the printers and printer queues within the Print & Fax pane in System Preferences (as well as the Printer Setup Utility application). If disabled, the user can still print to the default printer and switch to other assigned printers, but can't add or delete printers or manage the Mac OS X print queue.

✦ **Change Password:** Enable this check box to allow the user to change the account password. If the user isn't allowed to open all System Preferences settings, this check box is disabled.

If you're creating a single standard-level account for an entire group of people to use — for example, if you want to leave the machine in kiosk mode in one corner of the office or if everyone in a classroom will use the same account on the machine — I recommend disabling the ability to change the account password. (Oh, and please do me a favor . . . *don't* create a system with just one admin-level account that everyone is supposed to use! Instead, keep your one admin-level account close to your bosom and create a standard-level account for the Unwashed Horde.)

✦ **Burn CDs and DVDs:** Disable this check box to prevent the user from recording CDs or DVDs via the built-in disc recording features in Mac OS X. (Note, however, that if you've loaded a third-party recording program like Toast, the user can still record discs with it.)

✦ **Allow Supporting Programs:** If disabled, an application that the user runs can't automatically invoke another application.

✦ **This User Can Only Use These Applications:** When this option is enabled, you can select the specific applications that will appear to the user. These restrictions are in effect whether the user has access to the Full Finder or just the Simple Finder (which I cover in a second).

To allow access to all the applications in the specified folders — Applications, Utilities, Applications (Mac OS 9), and an empty category titled Other — click the Allow All button (which is the same as disabling the This User Can Only Use These Applications checkbox). To restrict access to all applications, click the Uncheck All button. You can also toggle the restriction on and off for specific applications that Mac OS X finds in these folders; click the triangle icon next to each folder to expand the list and then either mark or clear the Allow check box for the desired applications.

To add a new application to the Allow list, drag its icon from the Finder and drop it in the list within the desired folder. Alternatively, click the Locate button and navigate to it, click the application to select it, and then click Add. After you add an application, it appears in the Others section of the Allow list, and you can toggle access to it on and off like the applications in the named folders. (This is a good reason to use the Other folder, as you can create your own set of applications that you can easily grant or suspend.)

Assigning the Simple Finder

You can restrict your standard-level users even further by assigning them the Simple Finder set of limitations. The default Simple Finder, as shown in Figure 5-5, is a highly simplified version of the regular Mac OS X Finder. The simplified Dock contains only the Finder icon, the Trash, and folders for the user's approved applications, documents, and shared files.

Book II
Chapter 5

Setting Up Multi-
User Accounts

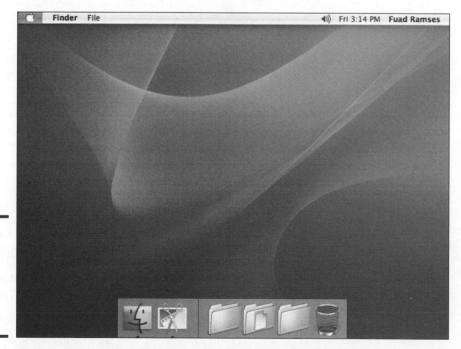

Figure 5-5: Whoa! It's the Simple Finder — less filling, still runs great!

This is the network administrator's idea of a foolproof interface for Mac OS X: A user can access only those system files and resources needed to do a job, with no room for tinkering or goofing off.

A Simple Finder user can still make the jump to the full version of the Finder — click Finder and choose Run Full Finder. The user will have to enter a correct admin-level username and password.

You can also change the Auto Login account from the Accounts panel. Click the Login Options button under the Accounts list, and then enable the Automatically Log in As *<username>* check box to enable it. Click the drop-down list box to choose the account that will automatically log in when Mac OS X starts up. This is yet another good feature for those preparing a Mac for public use — if you set the Auto Login to your public standard-access account, Mac OS X automatically uses the right account if the Mac is rebooted or restarted.

You can always choose Log Out from the Apple menu to log in under your own account. If you need to temporarily disable the Auto Login feature without changing which account it uses, disable the Automatically Log in As *<username>* check box.

Using Keychains — NOT

Before I leave this chapter, I'd like to discuss a Mac OS X feature that's been around since the days of Mac OS 9: the *keychain*. Your account keychain stores all the username/password combinations for Web sites, file servers, File Transfer Protocol (FTP) servers, and the like, allowing you to simply waltz in and start using the service (whatever it is). Sounds handy, doesn't it? And it can be, but you'd better watch your step.

I will be perfectly honest here: I **hate** account keychains. With a passion, mind you. As a consultant, Webmaster, and the SYSOP (an ancient Bulletin Board Service acronym meaning *System Operator*) of an Internet-based online system, I know what a hassle it is for users to remember separate passwords, and I feel that pain. However, three massively big problems are inherent with using keychains:

✦ **Anyone can log on as you.** If your keychain is unlocked, which happens automatically when you log in, all someone has to do is sit at your desk, visit a site or connect with a server, and *bam!* They're on. As *you.* Think about that. And then think how many times you get up from your desk, just for a second, to grab another Diet Coke or a doughnut.

✦ **You'll forget your passwords.** If the keychain file is corrupted — and it can happen — your passwords have gone to Detroit without you. Either you've got them on paper hidden somewhere, they're on your recent backup, or it's time to change your online persona.

✦ **Keychains need yet another stinkin' password.** Yep, that's right — your keychain can be locked (either manually or, with the right settings, automatically), and you have to remember yet another password/passphrase to unlock your keychain. "When, oh when will the madness end?"

From a security standpoint, keychains should be **completely off-limits** for anyone who's interested in maintaining a well-locked-down machine. After all, most folks can completely take care of all their Internet and network connections with a handful of passwords, and that's no big deal for anyone to remember. Unfortunately, Tiger creates a keychain automatically for every user, so you have to monitor (and delete) your keychain data manually. (Sigh.)

However, if you're the only person using your Mac and it resides in your home — personally, I'd prefer a bank vault — and you absolutely *must* use keychains, you can display them all for the current account from the Keychain Access application (see Figure 5-6), conveniently located in Utilities within your Applications folder. Click the Attributes tab and then click an item in the keychain list to display or edit all its information.

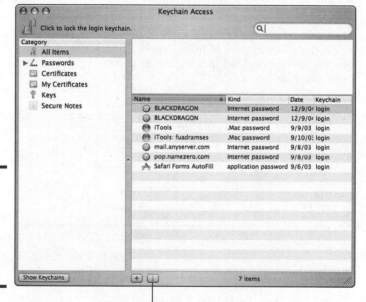

Figure 5-6:
Take my advice — stay away from the allure of keychains.

Click to display information on an Internet password.

Heck, just think about what I just wrote — anyone can display and *edit* server and site information just by launching this application! That includes your nephew Damien — you know, the one who considers himself the hacker extraordinaire. (While I'm at it, I should mention that it's just as bad to set the Auto Login feature — which I discuss earlier in this chapter — to an admin-level account. One reboot, and you're rolling out the red carpet for the little rascal.)

To help lock things down — at least when it comes to your Internet communications — follow this path:

1. **To display your Internet passwords, click the triangle icon next to the Passwords category (upper-left) and then choose Internet.**

2. **Click each Internet password to select it in the list, and then click the lower-case *i* button to display the information on that password in a separate window.**

3. **Click the Access Control tab to display the settings that you see in Figure 5-7, one of which I strongly recommend.**

   To minimize the damage that someone can do with this password, you can enable the Confirm Before Allowing Access radio button. And for yet another level of security, enable the Ask for Keychain Password check box.

   Of course, you're probably thinking, "Well, Mark, that pretty much eliminates the purpose of quick, convenient access without passwords, doesn't it?" Yes, indeed it does, but at least your online identity is somewhat safeguarded.

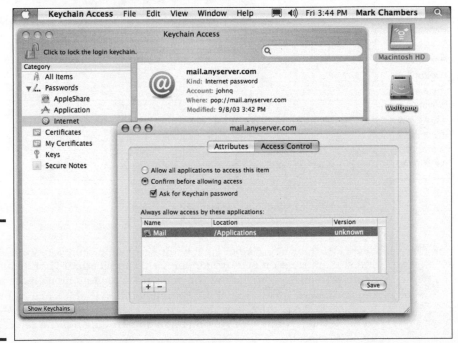

Figure 5-7:
Safe-
guarding a
keychain
rather
dilutes its
usefulness.

Click the plus sign button at the bottom of the Keychain Access window to add a new password. Type a name for the item, the username that you typically type to gain access, and the password for that server or site. Then click Add and cross your fingers.

To display all the keychains you can access, choose Edit⇨Keychain List. To create a brand new keychain, choose File⇨New Keychain. Mac OS X prompts you for the filename for your new keychain file. In the New Keychain dialog that appears, enter a catchy name in the Save As text box. By default, the keychain file is created in the Keychains folder — a good idea — but if you'd like to store it elsewhere, click the down-arrow button next to the Where list box and navigate to the desired folder. When you're ready, click the Create button. Now you need to enter yet another password, type it again to verify it, and click OK.

To lock or unlock your login keychain, click the Lock icon at the top-left of the Keychain Access window. (Unlocking your keychain requires you to enter your login password. Go figure.)

You might be saying to yourself, "Geez, this guy is more than a little paranoid." And yes, dear reader, I suppose that I am. But then again, who's been uploading all those questionable images and MP3 files to the company server . . . using *your* account?

**Book II
Chapter 5**

**Setting Up Multi-
User Accounts**

Chapter 6: Sharing Documents for Fun and Profit

In This Chapter

✔ **Comparing network sharing with multi-user sharing**

✔ **Setting and changing permissions**

✔ **Sharing documents in Microsoft 2004 for the Mac**

✔ **Sharing documents in AppleWorks**

*N*ow here's a topic that any Mac OS X power user can sink fangs into — the idea that a document on a multi-user system can be *everyone's* property, allowing anyone in your family, workgroup, or highly-competitive mob to make whatever changes are necessary, whenever they like.

Of course, potential pitfalls lurk — even in the Apple world, there's no such thing as an operating system that's both powerful *and* perfectly simple. However, I think you'll find that our dear friends from Cupertino have done just about as well as can be expected and that the settings that you use to share documents are fairly easy to understand and use.

Prepare to share!

Sharing over a Network versus Sharing on a Single Mac

First, allow me to clear up what I've found to be a common misconception by using another of Mark's Maxims.

> **Sharing documents on a single computer is fundamentally different from the file sharing that you've used on a network.™**

True, multiple users can share a document over a network, which is a topic that you'll find covered in Book V. But although the results are the same, the way that you share that same document on a single machine betwixt multiple users is a completely different turn of the screw. In this section, I discuss the factoids behind the matter.

No network is required

Although reiterating that no network is required is seemingly the most obvious of statements, many otherwise knowledgeable Mac OS X power users seem to forget that sharing a document over a network requires an active network connection. (Note the word *active* there.) Unless you physically copy the document to your hard drive — which defeats the purpose of document sharing — any loss of network connectivity or any problem with your network account will result in a brick wall and a brightly painted sign reading, "No luck, Jack." (Or perhaps it's flashing neon.)

On the other hand, a document shared on a multi-user Mac in the home or classroom is available whenever you need it. As long as the file is located in the Shared folder, the file privileges are set correctly, and you know the password (if one is used), then — as they say on *Star Trek* — "You have the conn" whether your network connection is active or not.

Relying on a guaranteed lock

Sharing documents over a network can get a tad hairy when multiple users open and edit the document simultaneously. Applications such as Office 2004 for the Mac and AppleWorks have methods of locking the document (giving one person exclusive access) when someone opens it or saves it. However, you always face the possibility that what you're seeing in a shared network document is not exactly what's in the document at that moment.

A multi-user system doesn't need such exquisite complexity. *You're* the one sitting at the keyboard, and *you* have control: This is what network administrators call a *guaranteed lock* on that document file. Refreshing, isn't it?

But wait! Mac OS X Tiger includes a feature called *Fast User Switching* — I discuss it in Book I, Chapter 2 — that allows other users to remain logged in behind the scenes while another user is at the keyboard. Therefore, if you enable Fast User Switching, two users could have the same document open at the same time. To prevent this, you can simply turn off Fast User Switching from the Accounts panel in System Preferences. (Click Accounts, click Login Options, and clear the Enable Fast User Switching check box.)

Most places are off-limits

Network users are often confident that they can blithely copy and move a document from one place to another with the greatest of ease, and that's true. Most shared network documents created by an application — such as a project outline created in Word, for example — carry their own sharing information and document settings internally. Thus, you can move that same file to another folder on your hard drive, and the rest of the network team can still open it. (Um, if they have the network rights to access the new folder, of course.)

This isn't the case when it comes to multi-user documents. As you can read in Chapters 4 and 5 of this mini-book, Mac OS X places a rather tight fence around a standard-level user, allowing that person to access only the contents of certain folders. In this case, your document must be placed in the Shared folder for every standard-level user to be able to open it. If everyone using the document has administrator access, you can then store the file in other spots on your system; as long as the permissions are set, you're set. And speaking of permissions. . . .

Permissions: Law Enforcement for Your Files

Files are shared in Mac OS X according to a set of rules called *permissions,* the *ownership* of the file (typically the person who saved the document the first time), and an access level specified as a *group.* The combination of privileges, ownership, and group determines who can do what with the file.

When you (or the person with the administrator account on your Mac) created your user account, you were automatically granted ownership of your Home folder and everything that it contains as well as any files or folders that you store in the Shared folder or another user's Public folder.

Four possible actions are allowed through permissions:

+ **Read Only:** This action allows the user to open and read the file, which includes copying it to another location.

+ **Read & Write:** This permission grants full access to the file, including opening, reading, editing, saving, and deleting. Read & Write permission also allows the user to copy or move the file to another location.

+ **Write Only (Drop Box):** A neat permission setting that appears only with a folder — it allows access to copy an item to the folder, but not to read any files it contains. (Hence the informal name *Drop Box*, and the + (plus sign) icon added to the folder's icon to identify it.) For example, a drop box is made to order for teachers: Students can submit homework by dragging their work to the teacher's drop box.

+ **No Access:** This is just what it sounds like — the user can't open the file, copy it, or move it.

No matter what permissions you've set, only the System Administrator (or root user) can copy items into another user's Home folder. Take my word on this one: Simply consider that this can't be done, and **stay as far away from the Root/System Administrator account as possible.** (Trust me on this.) Read all about the perils of enabling the System Administrator account in Chapter 4 of this mini-book.

These permissions are set in the Info dialog for a file or folder (always accessible by pressing ⌘+I). If you're setting the permissions for a folder, you can also elect to apply those same settings to all the enclosed items within the folder.

To set permissions, follow these steps:

1. **Click the item to select it, press ⌘+I (or choose Finder➪File) and then choose the Get Info menu item.**

If you have a mouse or trackball with a right button, you can right-click the item and choose Get Info instead. Either way, Mac OS X displays an Info dialog like you see in Figure 6-1.

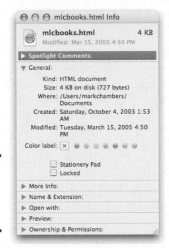

Figure 6-1:
The collapsed Info dialog.

2. **Click the right-facing arrow next to the Ownership & Permissions heading to expand it, as shown in Figure 6-2.**

If necessary, click the right-facing arrow next to the Details subheading to expand it as well.

Because I selected a folder, the Apply to Enclosed Items button appears at the bottom of the section.

3. **If you're the file's owner, you can click the lock icon to change the owner.**

Typically, the Owner drop-down list box is disabled.

The drop-down list box displays all the users with accounts on this machine, as well as some less savory choices such as *nobody, system,* and *unknown.* Don't choose any of these.

Perhaps I should be a little less tactful here: *Never* choose an owner other than yourself or another recognized standard-level user because you can potentially prevent yourself from accessing the file in the future!

4. The first Access drop-down list box determines the access level for the file's owner.

This will likely be set to Read & Write, and it's a good idea to leave it alone. If you're the file's owner, you're likely not a security risk.

5. Assign permissions for an entire group — this is a good idea for limiting specific files and folders to only Administrator access.

Choose the group from the Group drop-down list and select the desired access permission from the second Access drop-down list box.

6. Set the permission for the Others drop-down list (otherwise known as "I'm going to lump everyone else into this category").

If a user isn't the owner of an item and doesn't fit into any group that you've selected, this access permission setting for this file applies to that user.

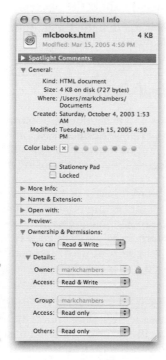

Figure 6-2:
The expanded Info dialog.

7. **If you're setting permissions for a folder, Mac OS X can automatically change the permissions for all the items contained in the folder to the same settings. Click the Apply to Enclosed Items button, and Mac OS X displays the confirmation dialog that you see in Figure 6-3.**

Generally, it's a good idea not to override the permissions for all the items in a folder, so click the Apply to Enclosed Items button only when necessary.

Figure 6-3:
Tiger wants to be sure you're not going permission-crazy.

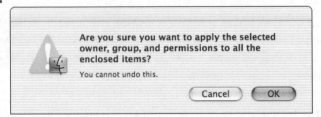

Are you sure you want to apply the selected owner, group, and permissions to all the enclosed items?

You cannot undo this.

Cancel   OK

8. **Click OK to proceed or click Cancel to abort the process.**

9. **After all the permissions are correct, click the Close button to save your changes and return to your friendly Finder.**

Permission and Sharing Do's and Don'ts

After you get the basics of sharing files and assigning permissions under your belt, you need to master when to change permissions and why you should (and shouldn't) modify them. Follow these common-sense guidelines when saving documents, assigning permissions, and choosing access levels:

✦ *Do* **use your Shared folder.** The Shared folder is the center of proper document sharing. I know there's a strong urge to create a new document in your Home folder, but you're just making more work for yourself because you'll end up copying that document from your Home folder to the Shared folder. Instead of an extra step, store a document that's intended to be shared in the Shared folder — where it belongs in the first place.

✦ *Don't* **assign permissions just to protect a file from deletion.** Remember, if all you need to do is prevent anyone (including yourself) from deleting an item, you don't need to go to all the trouble of changing permissions. Instead, just display the Info dialog for the item and select the Locked check box to enable it, which prevents the item from being deleted from the Trash until the Lock status is disabled.

> ✦ *Do* **review the contents of a folder before changing permissions for enclosed items.** That confirmation dialog doesn't appear just for kicks. For example, if you set a highly sensitive, private document with permissions of No Access for everyone but yourself and then you apply less-restrictive permissions globally to the folder that contains the document, you've just removed the No Access permissions, and anyone can open your dirty laundry. (Ouch.) Therefore, make sure that you open the folder and double-check its contents first before applying global permissions to the items it contains.

> ✦ *Don't* **change permissions in the Applications or Utilities folders.** If you have Administrator-level access, you can actually change the permissions for important applications like Mail, Address Book, iTunes, and Safari, as well as their support files. This spells havoc for all users assigned to the standard-access level. Be polite and leave the permissions for these files alone.

> ✦ *Definitely don't* **change System ownership.** Mac OS X is stable and reliable. Part of that stability comes from the protected state of the System folder, as well as a number of other folders on your hard drive. If you displayed the Info dialog for the System folder, you'll see that the Owner is set to *system,* and the Group is set to *wheel* (a term from the UNIX world that encompasses all administrator accounts). Now, promptly close that Info dialog, without making any changes!

> ✦ *Do not* **change any permissions for any files owned by the System unless specifically told to do so by an Apple support technician.** *Do not* monkey with System-owned items.

Sharing Stuff in Office 2004

Many Mac OS X applications offer their own built-in document-sharing features. For example, Microsoft Office 2004 for the Mac includes both file-level and document-sharing features. Because Office 2004 is the most popular productivity suite available for Mac OS X, I discuss these commands in this final section.

Document-sharing features

You'll find a number of commands that help multiple users keep track of changes that have been made in a shared Office document. Probably the most familiar is the Word revision tracking features (heavily used during the development of this book), but there are others as well:

> ✦ **Revision marks:** If several users edit a document, how can you tell who did what? By using *revision marks,* which apply different colors to changes made by different editors, those additions and deletions can be accepted

or rejected individually at a later date. If Johnson in Marketing adds incorrect material, you can easily remove just his changes. In a worst-case scenario, you can actually reject all changes and return the document to its pristine condition.

✦ **Compare Documents:** Using this feature allows you to compare a revised document with the original (if, of course, you still have the original file handy). I use Compare Documents only if revision marks weren't turned on before editing began.

✦ **Comments:** Editors can also converse within a document by using embedded Comments. These don't change the contents of the Word file like revision marks do but store commentary and notes in a behind-the-scenes kind of way. (Think of a Mac OS X Stickie that appears within a document.) Again, the author of each comment is listed, allowing for (sometimes heated) communication within the body of a document.

✦ **Highlighting:** You've heard the old joke about. . . . Well, anyway, a traditional highlighter marker is pretty useless on a computer monitor (leaving a nasty mess for the next user to clean), but Word allows multiple highlighting colors for identifying text. (And for the occasional practical joke — nothing like adding eight different highlighting colors to that important proposal. Just make sure that your résumé is up-to-date.)

File-level sharing features

Along with the document-level sharing commands, you'll also find that Office 2004 applications also offer sharing features that control access to the document file itself.

Password protection

You can add password protection to any Office 2004 document. Follow these steps with a document created within Word, Excel, or PowerPoint:

1. **Choose File⇨Save As.**

2. **In the Save As dialog that appears, click Options to display the Save Preferences panel.**

3. **Click Security to display the Preferences panel that you see in Figure 6-4.**

4. **To password-protect the document, enter a password in the Password to Open field.**

This password must be provided when opening the document.

If you like, you can enter another password in the Password to Modify field. This second password would then also be required to modify the document.

Preferences

Security options for "iMac G5 LEDs.doc"

View
General
Edit
Print
Save
Spelling and Grammar
Track Changes
User Information
Compatibility
File Locations
Security
Note Recording

Password to open:

Password to modify:

☐ Read-only recommended

Protect Document...

Privacy options

☐ Remove personal information from this file on save

☐ Warn before printing, saving or sending a file that contains tracked changes or comments

Macro security

☑ Warn before opening a file that contains macros

Description of preference

Warn before printing, saving or sending a file that contains tracked changes or comments
If a document contains tracked changes or comments, you may want to remove them before you save or distribute it. Do this to minimize your risk of accidentally sharing private information.

Cancel   OK

Book II Chapter 6

Sharing Documents for Fun and Profit

Figure 6-4: Office 2004 offers two types of document passwords.

Both passwords are case-sensitive.

5. **Click OK to save the preference changes and return to your document.**

Versions

If you like, Word can save multiple versions of a document in a single file. Each version is identified by the date and time when it was saved, the user who saved it, and an additional comments line. Choose File➪Versions to display the Versions dialog, from which you can choose to automatically save a new version of the document whenever it's closed. To save a new version immediately, click the Save Now button.

Document protection

Think of the Protect Document dialog in Word, from which you can effectively write-protect certain elements, as an extra level of security in a multi-user environment. In this Office application, you can protect revision marks, comments, and sections of a document containing forms. A password can be added if desired. To display the Protect Document dialog, click Tools in any of the Office 2004 applications and choose Protect Document from the drop-down list that appears.

Password Protection in AppleWorks

Like with Office 2004, you can set a password to prevent other users from opening an AppleWorks document. With the document loaded in AppleWorks version 6, follow these steps:

1. **Choose File⇨Properties to display the document Properties dialog, as shown in Figure 6-5.**

2. **Click the Set Password button and type the password in the Password box that appears.**

3. **AppleWorks displays a verification box in which you need to type the password again.**

   These document passwords are case-sensitive!

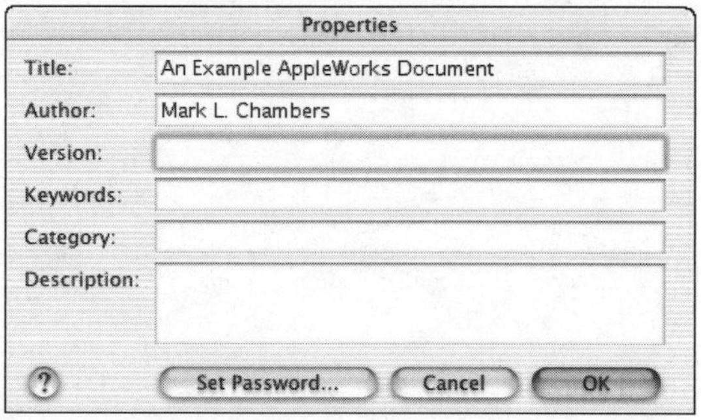

Figure 6-5:
You can password-protect an AppleWorks document.

Properties
Title: An Example AppleWorks Document
Author: Mark L. Chambers
Version:
Keywords:
Category:
Description:
? Set Password... Cancel OK

4. **Click OK to save the password and then click OK to return to your document.**

You can edit or remove the password by repeating this process. Use a blank password to remove password protection.

Book III

The Digital Hub

"I've got some image editing software, so I took the liberty of erasing some of the smudges that kept showing up around the clouds. No need to thank me."

Contents at a Glance

Chapter 1: The World According to Apple

In This Chapter

✔ **Doing things the hub way**

✔ **Digitizing your life**

✔ **Making your digital devices work together**

H uzzah! After years of empty promises of professional-quality media features for home and school — most of them coming from that silly Gates person in Redmond — Apple has taken on the challenge and developed a recipe for digital success.

By using tightly integrated hardware and software (where everything works smoothly together), Apple gives you the ability to easily organize and produce your own multimedia with the iLife suite of digital tools, which includes iMovie HD, iDVD, iPhoto, GarageBand, and iTunes. That same software also provides fantastic editing capabilities. Finally (and this is very important) — to paraphrase Will Smith in the movie *Men in Black*, "Apple makes these programs look *good*."

First, Sliced Bread . . . and Now the Digital Hub

In today's overloaded world of personal electronic devices, people can try to juggle as many as five or six electronic wonders. Each device typically comes with its own software, power adapter, and connectors to the outside world. Although managing one or two devices isn't terribly difficult, as the number of devices increases, so do the headaches. When you have a half-dozen cables, power adapters, and software to cart around, the digital life can become pretty bleak. (And quite heavy. You'll need more than a backpack to lug all that gear around.)

To combat this confusion, Apple came up with the idea of a *digital hub*, whereby your Macintosh acts as the center of an array of electronic devices. By using standardized cables, power requirements, built-in software, and even wireless connections via *Bluetooth* (the standard for short-range wireless communications between devices), the Macintosh — along with its operating system, Mac OS X — goes a long way toward simplifying your interaction with all the electronic gadgets that you use.

Given the hub terminology, think of the digital hub as a wagon wheel. (See Figure 1-1.) At the center of the wheel is your Macintosh. At the end of each spoke is a digital device. Throughout the rest of Book III, I give you the skinny on each device, but this chapter gives you the overview and tells you how they all work together.

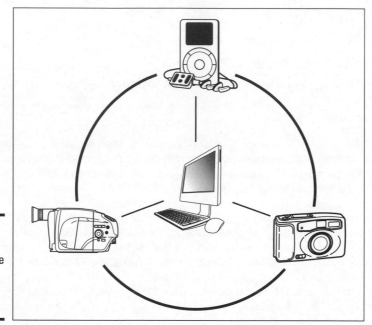

Figure 1-1: Hey, look what's in the center of your digital hub!

What Does Digital Mean, Anyway?

Computers are handy machines. They can process information very quickly and never get bored when asked to do the same task millions of times. The problem is that despite their propensity for reliability and speed, they aren't so hot in the intuition department. You have to tell them how to *do* everything (and most of them only talk to application developers and programmers). Computers know only one thing — numbers — although they do know numbers very, very well.

In fact, *binary* (the language of computers) has only two values — one and zero, which represent *on* and *off*, respectively. (Think of a light switch that toggles: The earliest computers were simply banks of switches that filled up an entire room.) To work with a computer in meaningful ways, you have to describe everything to a computer with numbers — or, if you prefer, *digits*.

By describing audio in numerical digits, you suddenly have something that a computer can work with. Toss a computer as many numbers as you want, and it can handle it. The scientists who figured this out knew that they had a good thing going, so they proceeded to convert anything that they could get their hands on into . . . well . . . digits. (Sorry about the atrocious pun.) Anyway, this resulted in some interesting technologies, most of which you'll surely recognize:

✦ **Audio CDs:** The music is represented as numbers and is stored on a plastic disc.

✦ **Digital video:** Images and sound are stored together on your hard drive or a DVD as one really, *really* long string of numbers.

✦ **Digital fingerprints (no pun intended that time):** Your fingerprint is converted into numerical data, which a computer can use to compare against fingerprint data from other people.

✦ **Automated telephone operators:** When you call a phone operator these days, you often aren't speaking to a real person. Rather, the computer on the other end of the line converts your voice into digits, which it uses to interpret your words. (At other times, I think I'm talking to a real person, but it's hard to tell.)

What Can I Digitize?

As you've probably guessed by now, practically anything can be digitized. As long as you can represent something as numbers, you can digitize that data. Whether it's photographs, video, or audio, your Mac is adept at digitizing data and processing it.

Photographs

Perhaps the most popular of digital devices, the digital camera has transformed photography forever. By using sophisticated electronics, digital cameras convert the image that you see through the camera viewfinder into an image made purely of numbers.

After this numeric information is transferred to your Macintosh, your computer can cut, twist, fade, label, and paint your digital images. Because numbers are the only materials involved, you won't need scissors, paint, or adhesive tape to edit images. (Advertising photographers can say good-bye to the old fashioned airbrush.) Your Macintosh does it all by manipulating those numbers. It cuts down on the messy art supplies and gives you the comfort of being able to go back in time — something that anyone who's not so handy with scissors can appreciate.

Music

As I mention earlier in this chapter, audio CDs are one application of music represented as digital data. The physical CD is just a piece of plastic with a metal coating, but you don't even really need CDs any longer. Your Macintosh can digitize audio for storage on your hard drive, too, which brings up another important point. Not only is digital information palatable to a computer, but it's also very portable. You can store it on any number of storage devices, such as an iPod or an external FireWire drive. (By the way, if you're a musician, you can use GarageBand and external instruments that will turn your Mac into a combination synthesizer, amplifier, and backup band. Mozart would've loved this stuff.)

Video

When you photograph a scene multiple times per second and then replay the sequence, you get (tah-dah!) moving pictures. In the analog (as opposed to digital) world, this would be a strip of celluloid film or a strip of magnetic tape. In the digital world, such a sequence of photographs is called *DV*, or *digital video*. After you take your digital video, you can transfer that data to your Macintosh to further manipulate it: You can edit it and add transitions, text, and other effects.

DVD

Like a CD-ROM or a hard drive, a *DVD* is simply a means of storing digital data. Although you can use it to save many different kinds of data, its most common use is for presenting video content. The Macintosh digital hub can produce DVDs by using any digital information that you give it.

The Software That Drives the Hub

At the heart of your digital hub is your Macintosh. To use and manipulate all the data that arrives at your Mac, your computer needs software, which provides instructions on what to do with the information that you send. Fortunately, Apple has fashioned some of the most attractive and easy-to-use software ever written to help you manipulate and manage your digital lifestyle. The list of software that belongs to the digital hub includes

+ **iPhoto:** Use iPhoto to download, manipulate, and organize your favorite digital photographs. After everything is just so, iPhoto can print them, burn them to disc, or even help you design and order a hardbound album! (For way more on iPhoto, go to Book III, Chapter 3.)

+ **iTunes:** iTunes offers the ability to create and manage your music collection. You can also purchase and download audio tracks from the Apple

Music Store. iTunes can even burn CDs! (Head to Book III, Chapter 2 for more.)

✦ **iMovie HD:** Every film director needs a movie-editing suite. iMovie HD gives you the chance to set up Hollywood in your living room with outstanding results. (For more, see Book III, Chapter 4.)

✦ **iDVD:** As home video moves toward the digital realm, iDVD becomes an essential tool for authoring your own DVD media. Home movies will never be the same! (iDVD is covered in Book III, Chapter 5.)

✦ **GarageBand:** Call it a "music-building" application! Even if you can't play a note, GarageBand makes it easy to create your own original songs — and if you *are* a musician, you can turn your Mac into a production studio. (Turn to Book III, Chapter 6 for more.)

✦ **iCal:** To help keep your hectic digital lifestyle in order, iCal offers complete calendar features. Besides tracking your dates and appointments on your Mac, you can publish calendars on the Web or share them with different parts of the digital hub. (Or, if you've got an iPod like me, you can even download your appointments and carry 'em with you.)

✦ **iSync:** With so many digital devices at your disposal, it gets hard to keep them all straight. *iSync* is software for automatically synchronizing contact and calendar information between cellphones, your personal digital assistant (PDA), an iPod, the Mac OS X Address Book, and iCal.

iPhoto

What good is a camera without a photo album? *iPhoto,* Apple's photography software, serves as a digital photo album. Check out the cool contact sheet view in Figure 1-2. Use it to help you arrange and manage your digital photos. Beyond its functions as a photo album, iPhoto also gives you the ability to touch-up your images through cropping, retouching, scaling, rotating, and red-eye reduction (photographically speaking, not morning-after speaking).

Besides offering editing features, iPhoto also works automatically with your digital camera. Simply plug in the camera to your Mac's Universal Serial Bus (USB) port, and iPhoto knows it's there. Need to transfer photos from the camera to your photo album? iPhoto can do that, too.

When you complete a collection of photographs that you find interesting, use iPhoto to help you publish them on the Internet or even to create your very own coffee-table book. (The latest in high-tech: a paper book.) And for those of you who still want that nifty wallet print to show off at work or a poster to hang on your wall, you can print them with your own printer or order them online through iPhoto. Orders made with iPhoto show up in your mailbox — the US Postal Service physical one outside your domicile — a few days later.

**Book III
Chapter 1**

**The World
According to Apple**

iTunes

To help you wrangle your enormous music collection, Apple offers iTunes (see Figure 1-3). For starters, iTunes is a sophisticated audio player for all your digital audio files. But iTunes is also handy for converting audio tracks from audio CDs to a number of popular digital audio file formats, such as AAC, MP3, and AIFF. After you import or convert your music into computer files, iTunes helps you manage and maintain your music collection. You can even listen to streaming online "radio stations," 24 hours a day.

Figure 1-2:
Use iPhoto to edit and manage your digital photo albums.

Plus, Apple throws in the Apple Music Store with iTunes, where you can preview hundreds of thousands of songs for up to 30 seconds each without spending a dime. If you hear something that you'd like to buy, you can use your credit card to purchase and download your music (either as individual tracks for 99 cents each, or as a complete album for a package price). After the music that you've bought is comfortably nestled in iTunes, you can play it on your Mac, burn it to an audio CD, or download it to your iPod.

Why do I keep harping on the iPod? Well, as a proud owner of one, I'm glad you asked: Apple's *iPod* is a versatile, lightweight audio player with hidden extras that James Bond would covet. It has enough capacity to store your entire collection of music, but it's small enough to fit into your shirt pocket. With iTunes, you can instantly exchange songs between your Macintosh and your iPod. You can also use iTunes to create audio and MP3 CDs for playback elsewhere. And the iPod even works as honest-to-goodness, back-up storage . . . you see, it also functions as a standard external FireWire or USB 2.0 hard drive. It can display text files and play games; you can carry even your Address Book contacts and iCal appointments with you with aplomb. (For the low-down on iPod, peruse Book III, Chapter 2.)

iMovie HD

You needn't restrict yourself to still images: Hook up your digital camcorder to your Mac as well. Use *iMovie HD,* the easy-to-use video editing application shown in Figure 1-4, to create and edit digital movies. With stunning video-editing candy like transitions, sound effects, and video effects, iMovie HD turns your home movies into professional productions that you'll be proud to share with friends and family. Finally, you can have a home movie night without putting everyone to sleep.

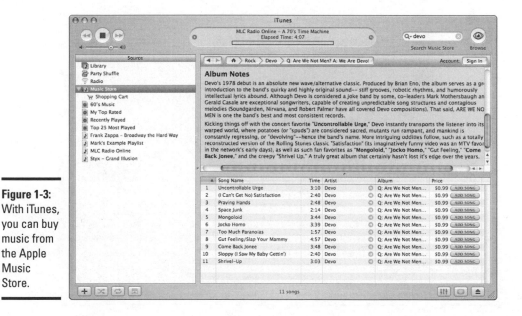

Figure 1-3:
With iTunes, you can buy music from the Apple Music Store.

iDVD

Of course, after you create a video masterpiece, you probably want to save it on a DVD for preservation and future viewing. To help you in your endeav-ors, use iDVD to create — or, as video professionals call it, *author* — DVD movies. With the preset templates, iDVD will have you cranking out stunning DVDs with interactive menus in no time, ready to use with any DVD player.

GarageBand

Imagine the freedom to create your own original music by simply dragging "digital instruments" onto a canvas . . . and then adding your own voice or the lead instrument! After the basic melody is in place, you'd want to be able to edit whatever you like, or even choose different instruments with the click of a mouse. As recently as ten years ago, dear reader, that concept was indeed just a dream. Then, software-based synthesizers and mixing applications brought musicians into the digital age. (The problem was that normal human beings couldn't afford the expensive software or the sample libraries of literally thousands of different instruments.) With the addition of GarageBand, however, the iLife suite provides everything that you need to start making your own music (inexpensively) and then create MP3 files or burn your own audio CDs. And believe me, if I can create a techno track that actually hit the speakers at a local dance club, then *you* can too!

Figure 1-4: iMovie HD can turn you into Hollywood material — let's do lunch.

Can I Use All This Stuff at Once?

What makes the digital hub idea even juicier is that it's an *interoperable* model. Let's pause to appreciate that. (What, you don't speak *engineer?* No problem!) In plain English, the digital hub allows you to use digital media from one part of the hub with another part of the hub. Thus, the individual parts of the digital hub can work together to complement each other. To illustrate, consider some digital sharing scenarios:

✦ You shoot a great photograph of your kids. It's so great, in fact, that you'd like to use it as the title page of your family's home movie. With the digital hub, you can use that same photograph in iMovie HD to create your home flick. When you're done with that, transfer the whole thing to a DVD by using iDVD, and your masterpiece is safe for decades of viewing. One image just worked its way through three parts of the digital hub.

✦ You just recorded a catchy song using GarageBand. You add the song to the soundtrack of the music video that you're creating with iMovie HD. Then you create a fancy opening menu and burn the finished project to DVD with iDVD to show prospective agents. Again, one piece of media has traveled through three parts of the digital hub!

✦ Your band becomes popular and starts to play some impressive gigs. To document your band's rise to stardom, your friend films a concert with a DV camcorder. You use iMovie HD to transfer the video to your Macintosh and create clips of your favorite performances of the concert. After that, it's a simple matter to author to DVD with iDVD, extract the audio from the video for use as an MP3, and grab an image from the video for a band scrapbook that you're creating with iPhoto. Now you've attained honest-to-goodness DHH (shorthand for *Digital Hub Heaven*). You've traversed the entire hub, easily sharing the media along the way.

Lest I forget, I should mention the other advantage of the digital hub: The media that you swap between all your "iApplications" remains in digital form, so it *never loses quality!* In the previous example of shooting a concert, for instance, that concert footage never lost quality while it was being transferred to DVD, converted to MP3, or pasted into your iPhoto album. Unlike archaic VHS tape, you don't have to worry about whether your source is second-generation — and you can forget degradation and that silly tracking control.

Chapter 2: Jamming with iTunes and iPod

In This Chapter

✔ Playing music with your Mac

✔ Arranging and organizing your music collection

✔ Tuning into the world with Internet radio

✔ Sharing your songs across a network

✔ Creating eye candy with the Visualizer

✔ Buying the good stuff from the Apple Music Store

Good news! It's time to throw out your Dad's Hi-Fi from the early '70s (you know, the one with the four-inch speakers that you're embarrassed to show your friends). Every installation of Mac OS X comes with the newest gadget in town: a great stereophonic audio application called *iTunes*. With iTunes, you can listen to your favorite songs, organize your music collection, listen to radio stations from around the world, buy music online, burn CDs, and much more! iTunes has so many features that you'll soon find yourself wondering why you even own a stereo at all. In no time, you'll be pondering how much new speakers with a subwoofer will cost for your Mac.

In this chapter, I show you how to play audio CDs and Internet downloads, but that's just the beginning. You discover how to use iTunes' Library to get one-click access to any song in your collection. I even show you how to tune into Internet radio (and share your favorite songs with others on your network), burn audio CDs (if you have the necessary hardware), plug in your iPod, and buy the latest hits from the iTunes Music Store. (And I demonstrate how to make your iTunes window look just as good as your music sounds.)

Just in case, though, keep your Dad's Hi-Fi . . . it might fetch a hefty sum as an antique on eBay.

What Can I Play on iTunes?

Simply put, iTunes is an audio player; it plays audio files. These files can be in any of many different formats. Some of the more common audio formats that iTunes supports are

+ **MP3:** The small size of MP3 files has made them popular for file trading on the Internet. You can reduce MP3 files to a ridiculously small size (at the expense of audio fidelity), but a typical CD-quality, three-minute pop song in MP3 format has a size of 3–5MB.

+ **AAC:** *AAC* (short for Advanced Audio Coding) is an audio format that's very similar to MP3; in fact, AAC files offer the same recording quality at significantly smaller file sizes. However, this format also supports a built-in copy protection scheme that prevents AAC music from being widely distributed on Macs. (Luckily, you can still burn AAC tracks to an audio CD, just like MP3 tracks.) The tracks that you download from the Apple Music Store are in AAC format.

+ **Apple Lossless:** A recent introduction from Apple, *Apple Lossless* format provides the best compromise between file size and sound quality: These tracks are encoded without loss of quality. However, Apple Lossless tracks are somewhat larger than AAC, so only the most discerning audiophile usually considers this format for their entire music library.

+ **AIFF:** The standard Macintosh audio format produces sound of the absolute highest quality. This high quality, however, also means that the files are pretty doggone huge. A typical pop song in AIFF format has a size of 30–50MB.

+ **WAV:** Not to be outdone, Microsoft created its own audio file format (WAV) that works much like AIFF. It can reproduce sound at higher quality than MP3, but the file sizes are very large, like AIFF.

+ **CD audio:** iTunes can play audio CDs. Because you don't usually store CD audio anywhere but on an audio CD, file size is no big whoop.

+ **Streaming Internet radio:** You can listen to a continuous broadcast of songs from one of tens of thousands of Internet radio stations, with quality levels ranging from what you'd expect from FM radio to the full quality of an audio CD. You can't save the music in iTunes, but it's still great fun. (In fact, I run my own station . . . more on MLC Radio later in the chapter.)

Playing an Audio CD

Playing an audio CD in iTunes is simple. Just insert the CD in your computer's disc tray, close the tray, start iTunes by clicking its icon on the Dock, and click the Play button. (Note that your Mac might be set to automatically launch iTunes when you insert an audio CD.) The iTunes interface resembles that of a traditional cassette or CD player. The main playback controls of the iTunes are Play, Previous Song, Next Song, and the Volume Slider, as shown in Figure 2-1.

Playback controls

Figure 2-1:
The main
playback
controls:
Play,
Previous,
and Next.

Equalizer button

Visuals button

Click the Play button to begin listening to a song. While a song is playing, the Play button toggles to a Stop button. As you might imagine, clicking that button again stops the music. If you don't feel like messing around with a mouse, you can always use the keyboard. The spacebar acts as the Play and Pause buttons. Press the spacebar to begin playback; press it again to stop.

Click the Next Song button to advance to the next song on the CD. The Previous Song button works like the Next Song button but with a slight twist: If a song is currently playing and you click the Previous Song button, iTunes first returns to the beginning of the current song (just like an audio CD player). To advance to the previous song, double-click the Previous Song button. To change the volume of your music, click and drag the volume slider.

Like other Macintosh applications, you can control much of iTunes with the keyboard. Table 2-1 lists some of the more common iTunes keyboard shortcuts.

Table 2-1	Common iTunes Keyboard Shortcuts
Press This Key Combination	*To Do This*
Spacebar	Play the currently selected song if iTunes is idle.
Spacebar	Pauses the music if a song is playing.
Right-arrow key (→)	Advance to the next song.
Left-arrow key (←)	Go back to the beginning of a song. Press a second time to return to the previous song.
⌘+up-arrow key (↑)	Increase the volume of the music.
⌘+down-arrow key (↓)	Decrease the volume of the music.
⌘+Option+down-arrow key (↓)	Mute the audio if any is playing. Press again to play the audio.

Playing a Digital Audio File

In addition to playing audio CDs, iTunes can also play the digital audio files that you download from the Internet or obtain from other sources in the WAV, AAC, Apple Lossless, AIFF, and MP3 file formats. Enjoying a digital audio file is just slightly more complicated than playing a CD. After downloading or saving your audio files to your Mac, open the Finder and navigate to wherever you stored the files. Then simply drag the music files (or an entire folder of music) from the Finder into the Library entry in the iTunes Source list. (The added files appear in the iTunes Library. Think of the Library as a master list of your music. To view the Library, select it in the left-hand column of the iTunes player, as shown in Figure 2-2. Go figure.) Heck, you can also drop a song file from a Finder window and drop it on the iTunes icon in the Dock, which adds it to your Library as well.

If you happened to drop the file on top of a playlist name in the Source list, iTunes adds it to that particular *playlist* as well as the main Library. (More about playlists in a bit.)

To play a song, just double-click it in the Library. Alternatively, you can use the playback controls (Play, Previous Song, Next Song) that I discuss earlier in this chapter (refer to Figure 2-1).

Note that the Source list of iTunes can list up to six possible sources for music:

✦ **Library:** I talk about this in this section.

✦ **iPod:** *Note:* You have to have one connected.

✦ **Music Store:** I discuss this later in the section, "Buying Music the Apple Way."

✦ **Audio CD:** A standard audio CD . . . anything from the Bee Gees to Maroon 5.

✦ **Shared music:** If another Mac on your local network is running iTunes and is set to share part or all of its library, you can connect to the other computer for your music. (Shared music on another Mac appears as a separate named folder in the Source list.)

✦ **Radio:** Think *Internet radio stations,* which I discuss further in the section "iTunes Radio."

Notice also that the Library lists information for each song that you add to it, such as

✦ **Song Name:** The title of the song

✦ **Time:** The length of the song

✦ **Artist:** The artist who performs the song

✦ **Album:** The album on which the song appears

If some of the songs that you're adding don't display anything for the title, album, or artist information, don't panic; most MP3 files have embedded data that iTunes can read. If a song doesn't include any data, you can always add the information to these fields manually. I show you how later in the section, "Setting or changing the song information manually."

Figure 2-2:
The Library
keeps track
of all your
audio files.

Clicking any of the column headings in the Library causes iTunes to reorder the Library according to that category. For example, clicking the Song Name column heading alphabetizes your Library by song title. I click the Time heading often to sort my Library according to the length of the songs. Oh, and you can drag column titles to reorder them any way you like.

Browsing the Library

After you add a few dozen songs to iTunes, viewing the Library can become a task. Although a master list is nice for some purposes, it becomes as cumbersome as an elephant in a subway tunnel if the list is very long. To help out, iTunes can display your Library in another format, too: namely, browsing mode. To view the Library in browsing mode, click the Browse button in the upper right-hand corner of iTunes, as shown in Figure 2-3.

The Browse mode of iTunes displays your library in a compact fashion, organizing your tunes into four sections:

- ✦ Genre
- ✦ Artist
- ✦ Album
- ✦ Song Name

Figure 2-3: Click Browse to view your Library in a more manageable form.

Will I trash my Count Basie?

Novice iTunes users, take note: *iTunes will watch your back when you trash tracks.*

To illustrate: Suppose you delete a song from the Library that's located *only* in the iTunes music folder (which you didn't copy into iTunes from another location on your hard drive). That means you're about to delete the song entirely, and there'll be no copy remaining on your Mac at all. Rest assured, though, that iTunes will promptly prompt you to make sure that you really want to move the file to the Trash. (I get fearful e-mail messages all the time from readers who are loath to delete *anything* from iTunes because they're afraid they'll trash their digital music files completely.)

Remember: If you delete a song from the Library that *also* exists elsewhere on your hard drive (outside the reach of the iTunes music folder), it won't be deleted from your hard drive. In fact, if you mistakenly remove a song that you meant to keep, just drag it back into iTunes from the Finder, or even from the Trash. 'Nuff said.

Selecting an artist from the Artist list causes iTunes to display that artist's albums in the Album list. Select an album from the Album list, and iTunes displays that album's songs in the bottom section of the Browse window. (Those Apple software designers . . . always thinking of you and me.)

Finding songs in your Library

After your collection of audio files grows large, you might have trouble locating that Swedish remix version of "I'm Your Boogie Man." To help you out, iTunes has a built-in Search function. To find a song, type some text into the search field of the main iTunes window. As you type, iTunes tries to find a selection that matches your search text. The search is quite thorough, showing any matching text from the artist, album, song title, and genre fields in the results. For example, if you type **Electronic** into the field, iTunes might return results for the band named *Electronic* or other tunes that you classified as *electronic* in the Genre field. (The section "Know Your Songs" later in this chapter tells you how to classify your songs by genre, among other options.) Click the magnifying glass at the left side of the Search field to restrict the search even more: by Artists, Albums, Composers, and Songs.

Removing old music from the Library

After you spend some time playing songs with iTunes, you might decide that you didn't *really* want to add 40 different versions of "Louie Louie" to your Library. (Personally, I prefer either the original or the cast from the movie *Animal House.*) To remove a song from the Library, click the song to select it and then press the Delete key on your keyboard.

**Book III
Chapter 2**

**Jamming with
iTunes and iPod**

You can also remove a song from the Library by dragging it to the Trash in your Dock.

Keeping Slim Whitman and Slim Shady Apart: Organizing with Playlists

As I mention earlier, the iTunes Library can quickly become a fearsomely huge beastie. Each Library can hold up to 32,000 songs: If your Library grows anywhere near that large, finding all the songs in your lifelong collection of Paul Simon albums is *not* going to be a fun task. Furthermore, with the Library, you're stuck playing songs in the order that iTunes lists them.

To help you organize your music into groups, use the iTunes playlist feature. A *playlist* is a collection of some of your favorite songs from the Library. You can create as many playlists as you want, and each playlist can contain any numbers of songs. Whereas the Library lists all available songs, a playlist displays only the songs that you add to it. Further, any changes that you make to a playlist affect only that playlist, leaving the Library intact.

To create a playlist, you can do any of the following:

✦ **Choose File⇨New Playlist.**

✦ **Press ⌘+N.**

✦ **Choose File⇨New Playlist from Selection.** This creates a new playlist and automatically adds any tracks that are currently selected.

✦ **Click the New Playlist button in the iTunes window** (the plus sign button in the lower-left corner). You get a newly created empty playlist (the toe-tappin' *untitled playlist*).

All playlists appear in the Source list. To help organize your playlists, it's a good idea to . . . well . . . *name* them. (Aren't you glad now that you've got this book?) For example, suppose that you want to plan a party for your polka-loving friends. Instead of running to your computer after each song to change the music, you could create a polka-only playlist. Select and start the playlist at the beginning of the party, and you won't have to worry about changing the music the whole night. (You can concentrate on the accordion.) To load a playlist, select it in the Source list; iTunes displays the songs for that playlist.

The same song can appear in any number of playlists because the songs in a playlist are simply pointers to songs in the Library — not the songs themselves. Add and remove them at will to any playlist, secure in the knowledge

Some playlists are smarter than others

Click the File menu and take a look at a menu command for creating a smart playlist. The contents of a *smart* playlist are automatically created from a specific condition that you set via the Smart Playlist dialog: You can limit the track selection by mundane things like album, genre, or artist; or you can get funky and specify songs that were played last, or by the date you added tracks, or even by the sampling rate or total length of the song. For example, iTunes can create a playlist packed with songs that are shorter than three minutes, so you can fill your iPod Shuffle with more stuff! Ah, but wait, you're not limited to a single criterion. If you want to add other criteria, click the Plus sign at the right side of the dialog, and you get another condition field to refine your selection even further.

You can choose the maximum songs to add to the smart playlist, or limit the size of the playlist by the minutes or hours of play or the number of megabytes or gigabytes the playlist will occupy. (Again, great for automatically gathering as much from your KISS collection that will

fit into a specific amount of space on a CD or your iPod.) Mark the Live Updating check box for the ultimate in convenience. iTunes automatically maintains the contents of the smart playlist to keep it current with your conditions at all times in the future. (If you remove tracks manually from a smart playlist, iTunes adds other tracks that match your conditions.)

Now think about what all these settings mean when combined . . . *whoa.* Here's an example yanked directly from my own iTunes library. I created a smart playlist that selects only those songs in the Rock genre. It's limited to 25 songs, selected by least often played, and live updating is turned on. The playlist is named Tracks I've Gotta Hear because it finds the 25 rock songs (from my collection of 1,654 songs) that I've heard least often! After I listen to a song from this smart playlist, iTunes automatically "freshens" it with another song, allowing me to catch up on the tracks I've been ignoring. Completely, unbelievably *sweet*— and another reason why iTunes is the best music player on Planet Earth!

that the songs will remain safe in the Library. Removing a playlist is simple: Select the playlist in the Source list and then press Delete.

Removing a playlist does not actually delete all those songs from your Library.

Click the *Party Shuffle* playlist, and you'll encounter a random selection of songs taken from your iTunes Library — perfect for your next party! You can change the order of the songs in the Party Shuffle playlist, add songs from your Library, or delete songs that don't fit the scintillating ambience of your gathering. Enjoy!

Know Your Songs

Besides organizing your music into Elvis and non-Elvis playlists, iTunes gives you the option to track your music at the song level. Each song that you add to the Library has a complete set of information associated with it. iTunes displays this information in the Info dialog with the following fields:

✦ **Name:** The name of the song

✦ **Artist:** The name of the artist who performed the song

✦ **Composer:** The name of the astute individual who actually *wrote* the song

✦ **Album:** The album where the song appears

✦ **Grouping:** A group type that you assign

✦ **Year:** The year the artist recorded the song

✦ **BPM:** The beats per minute (which indicates the song's tempo)

✦ **Track Number:** The position of the song on the original album

✦ **Comments:** A text field that can contain any comments on the song

✦ **Genre:** The classification of the song (such as rock, jazz, or pop)

You can display this information by clicking a song name and pressing ⌘+I — the fields appear on the Info tab.

Setting the song information automatically

Each song that you add to the iTunes Library might or might not have song information included with it. If you add music from a commercial audio CD, iTunes connects to a server on the Internet and attempts to find the information for each song on the CD. If you download a song from the Internet, it often comes with some information embedded in the file already; the amount of included information depends on what the creator supplied. (And believe me, it's often misspelled as well — think *Leenard Skeenard.*) If you don't have an Internet connection, iTunes can't access the information and displays generic titles instead.

Setting or changing the song information manually

If iTunes can't find your CD in the online database or someone gives you an MP3 with incomplete or inaccurate information, you can change the information yourself — believe me, you want at least the artist and song name! To view and change the information for a song, perform the following steps:

1. **Select the song in either the Library or a Playlist.**

2. **Press ⌘+I or choose File⇨Get Info.**

3. **Edit the song's information on the Info tab, as shown in Figure 2-4.**

Keep in mind that the more work you put into setting the information of the songs in your Library, the easier it is to browse and use iTunes. Incomplete song information can make it more difficult to find your songs in a hurry. If you prefer, you don't have to change all information about a song (it just makes life easier later if you do). Normally, you can get away with setting only a song's title, artist, and genre. The more information you put in, however, the faster you can locate songs and the easier they are to arrange. iTunes tries to help by automatically retrieving known song information, but sometimes you have to roll up your sleeves and do a little work. (Sorry, but the DataElves are out to lunch.)

Want to add album covers to your song info? Select one (or all) of the songs from a single album in the track list, display the Info dialog, and click the Artwork tab. Now launch Safari, visit Amazon.com, and do a search on the same album. Drag the cover image from the Web page right into the Info dialog, and drop it on top of the image well. When you click OK, the image appears in the Summary pane, and you can display it while your music is playing by pressing ⌘+G, or by pressing the Show or Hide Song Artwork button at the lower left of the iTunes window! (Note that adding large images can significantly increase the size of the song file.)

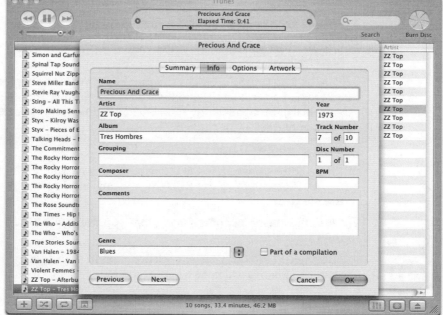

Figure 2-4:
View and
edit song
information
here.

Ripping Audio Files

You don't have to rely on Internet downloads to get audio files: You can create your own MP3, AAC, Apple Lossless, AIFF, and WAV files from your audio CDs with iTunes. The process of converting audio files to different formats is *ripping*. (Audiophiles with technical teeth also call this process *digital extraction*, but they're usually ignored at parties by the popular crowd.) Depending on what hardware or software you use, each has its own unique format preferences. For example, most iPod owners prefer MP3 or AAC files, but your audio CDs are not in that format. Being able to convert files from one format to another is like having a personal translator in the digital world. You don't need to worry if you have the wrong format: You can simply convert it to the format that you need.

The most common type of ripping is to convert CD audio to MP3 format. To rip MP3s from an audio CD, follow these simple steps:

1. **Launch iTunes by clicking its icon on the Dock.**

Alternatively, you can locate it in your Applications folder.

2. **Choose iTunes⇨Preferences.**

3. **In the Preferences window that appears, click the Importing tab.**

4. **Choose MP3 Encoder from the Import Using pop-up menu.**

5. **Choose High Quality (160 Kbps) from the Setting pop-up menu and then click OK.**

This bit rate setting provides the best compromise between quality (it gives you better than CD quality, which is 128 Kbps) and file size (tracks you rip will be significantly smaller than "audiophile" bit rates like 192 Kbps or higher).

6. **Load an audio CD into your Mac.**

The CD title shows up in the iTunes Source list, which is on the left side of the iTunes interface. The CD track listing appears on the right side of the interface.

7. **Clear the check box of any song that you don't want to import from the CD.**

All songs on the CD have a check box next to their title by default. Unmarked songs will not be imported.

Notice that the Browse button changes to Import.

8. **After you select the songs that you want added to the Library, click the Import button.**

Tweaking the Audio for Your Ears

Besides the standard volume controls that I mention earlier in this chapter, iTunes offers a full equalizer. An *equalizer* permits you to alter the volume of various frequencies in your music, allowing you to boost low sounds, lower high sounds, or anything in between. Now you can customize the way that your music sounds and adjust it to your liking.

To open the Equalizer (as shown in Figure 2-5), do one of the following:

✦ Choose Window⇨Equalizer.

✦ Press ⌘+2.

✦ Click the Equalizer button (refer to Figure 2-1).

The Equalizer window has an impressive array of 11 sliders. Use leftmost slider (Preamp) to set the overall level of the Equalizer. The remaining sliders represent various frequencies that the human ear can perceive. Setting a slider to a position in the middle of its travel causes that frequency to play back with no change. Move the slider above the midpoint to boost that frequency; conversely, move the slider below the midpoint to reduce the volume of that frequency.

**Book III
Chapter 2**

**Jamming with
iTunes and iPod**

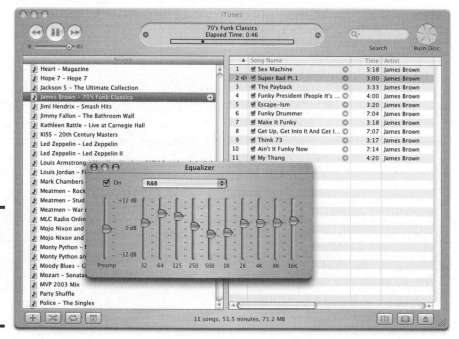

Figure 2-5:
Use the
Equalizer
sliders to
tweak the
sound of
your music.

Continue adjusting the equalizer sliders until your music sounds how you like it. When you close the Equalizer window, iTunes remembers your settings until you change them again. If you prefer to leave frequencies to the experts, the iTunes Equalizer has several predefined settings to match most musical styles. Click the pop-up menu at the top of the Equalizer window to select a genre.

After you adjust the sound to your satisfaction, close the Equalizer window to return to the iTunes interface and relax with those funky custom notes from James Brown.

A New Kind of Radio Station

Besides playing back your favorite audio files, iTunes can also tune in Internet radio stations from around the globe. You can listen to any of a large number of preset stations, seek out lesser-known stations not recognized by iTunes, or even add your favorite stations to your Playlists. This section shows you how to do it all.

iTunes Radio

Although it's not a radio tuner in the strictest sense, iTunes Radio can locate virtual radio stations all over the world that send audio over the Internet — a process usually called *streaming* amongst the "In" Internet crowd. iTunes can track down hundreds of Internet radio stations in a variety of styles with only a few mouse clicks.

To begin listening to Internet radio with iTunes, click the Radio icon located directly beneath the Library icon in the Source list. The result is a list of more than 20 types of radio stations, organized by genre.

What's with the numbers next to the station names?

When choosing an Internet radio station, keep your Internet connection speed in mind. If you're using a broadband DSL or cable connection — or if you're listening at work over your company's high-speed network — you can listen to stations broadcasting at 128 Kbps (or even higher). The higher the bit rate, the better the music sounds.

At 128 Kbps, for example, you're listening to sound that's as good as an audio CD.

However, if you're listening over a dialup modem connection, iTunes can't keep up with audio streaming at higher bit rates, so you'll be limited to stations broadcasting at 56 Kbps or lower.

When you expand a Radio category by clicking its triangle, iTunes queries a tuning server and locates the name and address of dozens of radio stations for that category. Whether you like Elvis or not-Elvis (those passing fads, like new wave, classical, or alternative), there's something here for everyone. The Radio also offers news, sports, and talk radio.

After iTunes fetches the names and descriptions of radio stations, double-click one that you would like to hear. iTunes immediately jumps into action, loads the station, and begins to play it.

Tuning in your own stations

Although iTunes offers you a large list of popular radio stations on the Web, it's by no means comprehensive. Eventually, you might run across a radio station that you'd like to hear, but it's not listed in iTunes. Luckily, iTunes permits you to listen to other stations, too. To listen to a radio station that iTunes doesn't list, you need the station's Web address.

In iTunes, choose Advanced⇨Open Stream (or press ⌘+U). In the Open Stream dialog that appears (as shown in Figure 2-6), enter the URL of your desired radio station and then click OK. Within seconds, iTunes will tune in your station.

Figure 2-6:
Tuning in to
MLC Radio,
my Internet
radio
station.

This particular technology author has a preference for a certain hot Net station: It's `http://12.217.39.187:8000`, the address for *MLC Radio*, which is the Internet radio station I've been running for several years now. I call my station a '70s Time Machine because it includes hundreds of classic hits from 1970–1979, inclusive. You'll hear everything from *Rock and Roll Hoochie Koo* by Rick Derringer to *Moonlight Feels Right* by Starbuck. (Hey, I'm summing up a decade here, so be prepared for both Rush and the Captain and Tenille, too.) The station broadcasts at 128 Kbps, so you'll need a broadband connection to listen. Just follow the steps in the next section to add MLC Radio to your playlists! For more details or additional help connecting to MLC Radio, visit my Web site at `www.mlcbooks.com`.

Radio stations in your Playlists

If you find yourself visiting an online radio station more than once, you'll be glad to know that iTunes supports radio stations in its Playlists. To add a radio station to a Playlist from the Radio, do the following:

1. **Open the category that contains the station that you want to add to your Playlist.**

2. **Locate the station that you would like to add to your Playlist and drag it from the Radio list to the desired Playlist on the left.**

If you haven't created any Playlists yet, see the section "Keeping Slim Whitman and Slim Shady Apart: Organizing with Playlists" earlier in this chapter to find out how.

Adding a radio station that doesn't appear in the Radio list is a bit trickier but possible nonetheless. Even though iTunes allows you to load a radio station URL manually by using the Open Stream command in the Advanced menu, it doesn't give you an easy way to add it to the Playlist. Follow these steps to add a radio station to a Playlist:

1. **Add any radio station from the Radio to your desired Playlist.**

2. **Press ⌘+I or choose File➪Get Info to bring up the information dialog for that station.**

3. **Click the Summary section and change the URL by clicking the Edit URL button.**

4. **Enter the desired URL.**

5. **Name the station to your liking and then click OK.**

This name is just a reminder for yourself. It doesn't change the actual name of the radio station.

iSending iTunes to iPod

If you're lucky enough (like me) to own an iPod, you'll be happy to know that iTunes has features for your personal jukebox as well. *iPods,* Apple's MP3 players, comprise an entire family of portable devices (ranging from $99 to about $399) that can hold anywhere from about 300 songs to literally thousands of songs. This great gadget and those like it have replaced the venerable Sony Discman and Walkman as *the* preferred portable music player.

You connect your iPod to your Macintosh with a FireWire or USB 2.0 cable (which are included, natch). After the iPod is connected, it automatically synchronizes to the Playlists in iTunes. The iPod and the iTunes software communicate with each other and figure out what songs are in your iTunes Library (as compared with the iPod Library). If they discover songs in your iTunes Library that are missing from your iPod, the songs automatically transfer to the iPod. Conversely, if the iPod contains songs that are no longer in iTunes, the iPod automatically removes those files from its drive.

Go back and reread that last sentence above about the iPod **automatically removing** files from its drive. (I'll wait here.) Apple added this feature in an effort to be attentive to copyright concerns. The reasoning is that if you connect your iPod to your friend's computer, you won't be able to transfer songs from the iPod to that computer. Of course, you could always look at it from the marketing perspective as a feature that makes sure your Mac and iPod are always in total sync. Whatever the case, pay close attention and read all warning dialogs when connecting to a Mac other than your own, or you might wipe out your iPod's library.

The best thing I can say about the iPod and iTunes combination is . . . well . . . that there *isn't* anything else to say about them. The auto-sync feature is so easy to use, you forget about it almost immediately.

Sharing Your Music Across Your Network

Ready to share your music — *legally*, mind you — with other folks on your network? You can use the same type of streaming music broadcasting that I mentioned earlier (in the section on Internet radio) to offer your music to other iTunes users across your local network. Follow these steps:

1. **Click iTunes⇨Preferences to open the Preferences dialog.**

2. **Click Sharing.**

3. **Select the Share My Music check box.**

4. **Specify whether you want to share your entire library or only selected playlists.**

Sending music elsewhere with AirTunes

If your Mac has an AirPort Extreme wireless card and you're using an AirPort Express portable wireless Base Station, you can ship your songs right to your Base Station from within iTunes, and from there to your home stereo or boom box! (I get into some serious discussion of AirPort Express in Book V, Chapter 4.)

After your AirPort Express Base Station is plugged in and you connect your home stereo (or a boombox, or a pair of powered stereo speakers) to the stereo mini-jack on the Base Station, you'll see a Speakers pop-up list button appear at the bottom of the iTunes window. (If the Speakers button doesn't appear, choose iTunes⇨Preferences to open the Preferences dialog, and click the Audio tab. Make sure that the Look for Remote Speakers Connected with AirTunes check box is enabled.)

Click the Speakers button, and you can choose to broadcast the music you're playing in iTunes across your wireless network. Ain't technology truly *grand?*

Sharing selected playlists is a good idea for those Meatmen and Sex Pistols fans who work at a cubicle farm in a big corporation.

5. **Enter a name for your shared folder.**

6. **If you want to restrict access to just a few people, select the Require Password check box; then type a password in the text box.**

7. **Click OK.**

Your shared folder will appear within the Source list for all iTunes users who enabled the Look for Shared Music check box on the same pane of the Preferences dialog. Note that the music you share with others can't be imported or copied, so everything stays legal.

Burning Music to Shiny Plastic Circles

Besides being a great audio player, iTunes is adept at creating CDs, too. iTunes makes the process of recording songs to a CD as simple as a few mouse clicks — making the modern version of a compilation (or *mix*) tape is easier than getting a kid to eat ice cream. iTunes lets you burn CDs in one of three formats:

✦ **Audio CD:** This is the typical kind of commercial music CD that you buy at a store. Most typical music audio CDs store 700MB of data, which translates into about 80 minutes of music.

✦ **Data CD:** A standard CD-ROM is recorded with the audio files. This disc can't be played in any standard audio CD player (even if it supports MP3 CDs, which I discuss next). Therefore, you can listen to these songs only by using your Mac and an audio player like iTunes 4, or a PC running Windows.

✦ **MP3 CD:** Like the ordinary computer CD-ROM that I just describe, an MP3 CD holds MP3 files in data format. However, the files are arranged in such a way that they can be recognized by audio CD players that support the MP3 CD format (especially boomboxes and car stereos). Because MP3 files are so much smaller than the digital audio tracks found on traditional audio CDs, you can fit as many as 160 typical 4-minute songs on one disc. These discs can also be played on your Mac via iTunes.

Keep in mind that MP3 CDs are not the same as the standard audio CDs that you buy at the store, and you can't play them in older audio CD players that don't support the MP3 CD format. Rather, this is the kind of archival disc that you burn at home for your own collection.

First things first: Before you burn, you need to set the recording format. Open the iTunes Preferences dialog by choosing iTunes⇨Preferences; then click the Burning tab. Select the desired disc format by enabling the corresponding radio button. Click OK to close the Preferences window when you're finished.

The next step in the CD creation process is to build a playlist (or select an existing playlist that you want to record). If necessary, create a new Playlist and add to it whatever songs you would like to have on the CD. (See the earlier section "Keeping Slim Whitman and Slim Shady Apart: Organizing with Playlists" if you need a refresher.) With the songs in the correct order, select the playlist. When you do, the Browse button changes into a Burn Disc button. Click that button to commence the CD burning process. iTunes will let you know when the recording is complete.

Feasting on iTunes Visuals

By now, you know that iTunes is a feast for the ears, but did you know that it can provide you with eye candy as well? With just a click or two, you can view mind-bending graphics that stretch, move, and pulse with your music, as shown in Figure 2-7.

To begin viewing iTunes visuals, choose Visuals⇨Turn Visual On (or press ⌘+T). Immediately, most of your iTunes interface disappears and begins displaying groovy lava lamp-style animations (like, *sassy*, man). To stop the visuals, choose Visuals⇨Turn Visual Off (or press ⌘+T again). The usual sunny, brushed aluminum face of iTunes returns. You can also turn visuals on or off by clicking the starburst button at the bottom right of the window, as shown in Figure 2-1.

You can also change the viewing size of the iTunes visuals in the Visuals menu. From the Visuals menu, choose Small, Medium, or Large to alter the size of the visual presentation. Similarly, to view the graphics at full screen size, choose Visuals⇨Full Screen (or press ⌘+F). To escape from the Full Screen mode, click the mouse or press Esc.

Figure 2-7:
iTunes can
display
some
awesome
patterns!

You can still control iTunes with the keyboard while the visuals are zooming around your screen. See Table 2-1 earlier in this chapter for a rundown on common keyboard shortcuts.

The iTunes Visualizer has many hidden features. While viewing the Visualizer, press H for Help to see a list of hidden Visualizer settings. Press H again, and the list changes to reveal more hidden functions. Table 2-2 shows the list of settings that you can change.

Table 2-2	**Visualizer Hidden Keyboard Features**	
Press This Key	*To Perform This Action*	*What This Action Does*
H	View a list of hidden features.	Displays the list of shortcuts from this table on the screen.
I	Display song information.	Displays the song's title, artist, and album.
D	Reset settings to default.	Returns all Visualizer settings to a default state.
F	Toggle frame rate display.	Displays how fast your screen is redrawing the animations.
T	Toggle frame rate capping.	Sets the highest permissible frame rate.

Press This Key	To Perform This Action	What This Action Does
M	Select config mode.	Chooses between random, user configuration, and current modes.
0–9	Select user configuration (press Shift to set).	Do you like how a certain animation looks? Save the settings in a user configuration for later.
R	Make new random configuration.	Creates the animations based on a random configuration.
C	Display current configuration.	Shows which configuration is currently in use.

But wait, there are more Easter eggs to be found! Again, while viewing the Visualizer, press one of following keys:

✦ **A:** Changes the Visualizer pattern

✦ **Z:** Changes the Visualizer color scheme

Press either of these keys repeatedly to cycle through the various patterns and color schemes lurking deep within the Visualizer.

Buying Music the Apple Way

Before we wave goodbye to the happy residents of iTunes iSland, I won't forget to mention the hottest spot on the Internet for buying music: the iTunes Music Store, which you can reach from the cozy confines of iTunes. (That is, as long as you have an Internet connection. If you don't, it's time to turn the page to the next chapter.) If you're not in iTunes, go to www.apple.com/itunes/store.

Figure 2-8 illustrates the lobby of this online audio store. Click the Music Store item in the Source list, and after a few moments, you'll be presented with the latest offerings. Click the Choose Genre drop-down list to browse through the store according to musical genre, or click the Power Search link to search by song title, artist, album, or composer. The Back/Forward buttons at the top of the Music Store window operate much like those in Safari, moving you backward or forward in sequence through pages that you've already seen. A click on the Home button (which, through no great coincidence, looks like a miniature house) takes you back to the Store's main page.

To display the details on a specific album or track, just click it. If you're interested in buying just certain tracks (for that perfect road warrior mix), you get to listen to 30 seconds of any track — for free, no less, and at full sound quality. To add a song or album to your Music Store shopping cart, click the Add Song or Add Album button. When you're ready to buy, click the Shopping Cart item in the Source list and then click the Buy Now button. (At the time of this writing, tracks are 99 cents a pop, and an entire album is typically $9.99 . . . what a bargain!)

Figure 2-8: Hmm . . . now where's that Liberace section?

The Music Store creates an account for you based on your e-mail address, and it also keeps secure track of your credit card information for future purchases. After you use the Music Store once, you never have to log in or retype your credit card information again.

The tracks that you download are saved to a separate playlist called Purchased Music. After the download is finished, you can play them, move them to other playlists, burn them to an audio CD, share 'em over your network or ship them to your iPod, just like any other track in your iTunes Library.

Remember all those skeptics who claimed that buying digital audio could never work over the Internet because of piracy issues and high costs? Well, bunkie, hats off to Apple: Once again, our favorite technology leader has done something the *right* way!

Chapter 3: Focusing on iPhoto

In This Chapter

✔ **Importing pictures from your hard drive or digital camera**

✔ **Organizing images with iPhoto**

✔ **Tweaking the appearance of photographs**

✔ **Sharing photos with your friends**

*F*or years, the Macintosh has been the choice of professional photographers for working with digital images — not surprising, considering the Mac's graphical nature. Apple continues this tradition with *iPhoto,* a photography tool for the home user that can help you organize, edit, and even publish your photographs. (It sports more features than a handful of Swiss army knives.) After you shoot your photos with a digital camera, you can import them into iPhoto, edit them, and publish them. You're not limited to photos that you take yourself, either; you can edit, publish, and organize all kinds of digital image files. You can even create a photo album and use the iPhoto interface to order a handsome hard-bound copy shipped to you.

In this chapter, I walk you through an overview of what iPhoto can do. After that, I give you a brief tour of the controls within iPhoto so you can see what features are available to you, including features for managing, printing, and publishing your photos.

What iPhoto Can Do

iPhoto performs many different types of tasks. From your camera to the printed page and everything in between, iPhoto steps you through the process of digital photography:

✦ **Import:** Digital cameras are everywhere these days, so it's important for your Macintosh to quickly and easily connect with them. iPhoto takes the guesswork out of working with a digital camera. Simply plug any supported digital camera into your Mac's USB port, open iPhoto, and click a button or two. (I give you the details later in the section "Importing Images 101.") iPhoto automatically imports the images that you've taken. If iPhoto doesn't recognize your camera, it's likely either out of battery power or is not supported.

✦ **Organize:** Ansel Adams would be shocked that a digital camera has no film (while your kids don't even raise an eyebrow). Instead, most of today's digital cameras use memory modules called *cards,* which are instantly reusable. For that reason, you might find yourself taking many more pictures than usual — and as your collection of photographs grows, you'll need some help keeping them all organized (perennial favorites like paper albums and shoeboxes are out). iPhoto is, at its core, a *digital* photo album that you can use to organize, sort, and search your photographs in seconds. iPhoto offers many great features to help you manage your digital equivalent of a shoebox full of photos. You'll never lose an important photo again.

✦ **Edit:** After you see the images from your camera on your computer monitor, you realize that your dog Lucifer has red eyes (no big surprise there), your ocean pictures are upside down, and the campfire photos are too dark. With a traditional film camera, you'd probably toss that campfire photograph in the trash; thankfully, iPhoto has an array of image-editing tools that make the bad photos good and the good ones better.

✦ **Publish:** With all these photographs on your computer, you decide that it would be nice to pass a few on to Aunt Harriet, post a couple on your Web site, and print the rest. iPhoto guides you through a number of ways to share your photographs with others. From print to the Internet to e-mail to CD-ROM, iPhoto takes away the hassle of working with images on a computer with a simple-to-use interface.

Delving into iPhoto

The iPhoto interface continues in the vein of other iLife *iApps,* using only one window (plus the occasional dialog) to work all its magic. The main iPhoto window is split into three sections: its Toolbar, the Album List, and the Viewer. Figure 3-1 shows the three main sections of the iPhoto window.

✦ **Toolbar:** The iPhoto Toolbar is the main control center for iPhoto. Along the Toolbar is a row of buttons (see Figure 3-1). They give you one-click access to the various modes of iPhoto.

When you change modes, the Toolbar panel changes to reflect the functions available in that mode. For example, click the Edit button to view the editing functions, such as Crop, Adjust, or B & W (black and white). Click the Book button to see the controls necessary to publish a hardcover or soft-cover photo album.

✦ **Source List:** To the left side of the iPhoto interface is the Source list (refer to Figure 3-1). This is where you organize your photo albums, film rolls, and the books you've designed. You can also select any source for viewing or editing.

✦ **Viewer:** The largest portion of the iPhoto interface is the Viewer (also shown in Figure 3-1). The Viewer, where you see your photographs when you browse through photo albums, is also the main window for editing individual images and laying out photo books.

Source list   Viewer

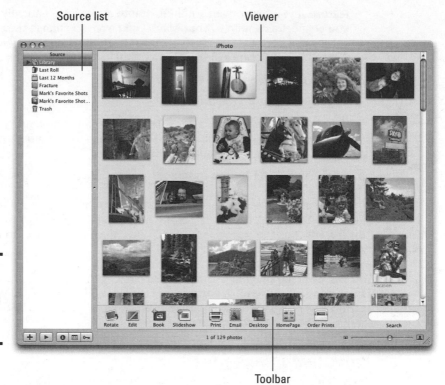

Figure 3-1:
The iPhoto
window has
three main
sections.

Toolbar

Importing Images 101

After you have the iPhoto basics under your belt, it's time to get busy. Before
you do anything else with iPhoto, you need to import some photographs
into it. iPhoto provides a couple of ways to import photos, depending on the
source of the image.

Importing images from a digital camera

To import photographs from your digital camera, follow these simple steps:

1. **Connect your digital camera to your Macintosh.**

   Plug one end of a USB cable into your camera and the other end into
   your Macintosh's USB port. Then prepare your camera to download
   images; for most models, that means simply turning on the camera.

2. **Launch iPhoto.**

   Launch iPhoto by clicking its icon in the Applications folder. The first time
   that you launch iPhoto, you have the option of setting its auto-launch

feature. If you turn on auto-launch, iPhoto starts automatically whenever you connect a camera to your Mac. If you want to change the auto-launch setting at a later date, you can access it from the Preferences menu of Apple's Image Capture utility, also located in the Applications folder.

3. Type a roll name for the imported photos.

4. Type a description for the roll.

If you want to delete the images from your camera's memory card after they're safely in iPhoto, mark the Delete Items from Camera After Importing check box to enable it.

5. Click the Import button to import your photographs from the camera.

While you import images from your camera, iPhoto displays a small preview in the Toolbar panel. iPhoto sticks the newly imported images in the Photo Library, which is the warehouse for all your images, as well as in a separate "virtual" film roll in the Source list.

You can even import short digital video clips from today's digital cameras! These clips are stored like your images, but double-clicking a clip thumbnail in the Viewer plays the clip. And yes, you can drag clips into iMovie HD from the iPhoto Viewer window. *Uber-sassy!*

Importing image files

Besides images that you shot with your digital camera, you can also import any image file on your system into the Photo Library. This could include images that friends have sent you, that you've downloaded off the Internet, or that you've created in a graphics program such as Photoshop. You can import image files in one of two ways:

✦ **Choose File⇨Add to Library:** When you choose this, iPhoto displays a standard Open dialog. From there, you can choose your favorite image files for import. (From the keyboard, press ⌘+O.)

✦ **Drag-and-drop:** Drag files from the Finder and drop them in the iPhoto window. iPhoto instantly adds them to the Photo Library.

If you drag a folder of images into iPhoto, it creates a *film roll* — a familiar method of organizing things, of course — with the folder name as the roll name. Within that roll are all of your images.

iPhoto recognizes a variety of popular graphics formats, so none of your image files will feel left out. You can add images with the following formats:

✦ JPEG

✦ GIF

✦ PICT

✦ PNG

✦ RAW

✦ TIFF

Note that the iPhoto Import function also works with removable hard drives, external CD/DVD drives, and USB Flash drives. If you can move to a location in the Open dialog, you can import from it. (Downright versatile, don't you agree?)

Organizing with Photo Albums

After you build up your Photo Library by importing photographs with your camera, your hard drive, and other storage media, you might become overwhelmed with the volume of images at your disposal. The easiest way to organize your images for quick access is to use the iPhoto Album feature.

Creating a new Photo Album

To create a new Photo Album, do one of the following:

✦ **Choose File➪New Album.**

or

✦ **Click the + button at the bottom of the Photo Album List.**

Either method brings up the New Album sheet, as shown in Figure 3-2. Type the name for your new photo album and click OK.

Note that you can rename your Photo Album anything you like. Just double-click the Album name in the Source List and type the new name.

You can also create a Smart Album from the File menu. A *Smart Album* contains only photos that match certain criteria that you choose, using the keywords and rating that you assign your images. (For example, I have a Smart Album that includes all images with the keyword *Family.*) Other criteria include recent film rolls, text contained in the photo filenames, dates the images were added to iPhoto, and any comments you might have added. iPhoto automatically builds and maintains Smart Albums for you, adding new photos that match the criteria (and deleting those that you remove from your Photo Library). Smart Albums carry a gear icon in the Source list.

**Book III
Chapter 3**

Focusing on iPhoto

Figure 3-2:
Click the +
button to
create a
new Photo
Album.

Adding photos to a Photo Album

After you have your newly created, empty Photo Album in place, add some photographs to it. Click the Photo Library icon in the Source list (refer to Figure 3-1) to view all the images in your collection. Drag any photograph that you want from the Photo Library to your new album in the Source list; iPhoto instantly adds it to the album, without a single drop of glue. (Remember, a Smart Album does all this automatically, behind the scenes, so you never have to add an image manually to a Smart Album.)

"Hey, Mark, isn't this going to use more of my precious hard drive territory?" Don't worry — you're not making copies of the photograph: iPhoto simply creates a reference to the image in the Photo Library and adds it to your Photo Album.

To view the photographs that you've added to a Photo Album, click that album's icon in the Source List. The images instantly appear in the Viewer.

Note the size-changing slider at the lower right corner of the Viewer. You can use it to enlarge or reduce the size of the thumbnail images in the Viewer. (Gee, those good folks in Cupertino think of everything!)

Removing photos from a Photo Album

If you suddenly discover that your boyfriend or girlfriend is now an ex-boyfriend or ex-girlfriend, you'll probably want some way to remove those unwanted photographs from your Photo Album. (Or maybe your relationship is still rock-solid, but you just want to change the location of a photo from one Photo Album to another.) Whatever the case, iPhoto makes it a cinch to remove photographs from a Photo Album. Follow these steps:

1. **Select the Photo Album from the Source list.**

2. **In the Viewer, select the photo that you want to remove from the Photo Album.**

3. **Press Delete.**

Keep in mind that removing a file from a Photo Album doesn't remove it from the Photo Library. (Remember that the Photo Album is just an assortment of links to your photos.) To really remove that image of your "ex," you need to navigate to the Photo Library and delete the picture there, too.

Deleting a Photo Album

It's just as easy to remove a Photo Album (and every image that it contains) from your collection as it is to remove photos from that Photo Album. To delete an entire Photo Album, here's the overly complex, terribly involved process:

1. **Select the Photo Album in the Source list.**

2. **Press Delete.**

Told you it was easy!

If you mistakenly delete a Photo Album, you can immediately use iPhoto's Undo feature. Just press ⌘+Z, and your last action is reversed. However, if you've already gone too far and you can't use Undo to restore an album, you can always re-create it manually because the images that were within that Photo Album still reside in the Photo Library. Simply create the empty Photo Album again (as I demonstrate earlier), open the Photo Library folder in the Finder, and drag the files into the album again.

The Art of Organizing with Keywords

Using Photo Albums is a great way to organize your photo collection, but it's just the start of what iPhoto can do: You can also assign *keywords* to images to help you organize your collection. Keywords give you the opportunity to quickly search through your photos later. You can use iPhoto's standard keywords or create your own. For example, you could organize your photos

**Book III
Chapter 3**

Focusing on iPhoto

according to important family events. Birthday photos would get one keyword; graduation photos would get another. Later you can search for that birthday shot where the cake caught on fire or the graduation where the valedictorian fainted. When you use keywords, they're just a few keystrokes away. Remember this Mark's Maxim:

Using keywords to organize your photos takes time, but it's worth it.™

To begin using the keyword feature, select one or more photos in the Viewer. Then display the Photo Info dialog by choosing Photos➪Get Info — or, for those who prefer fingers, press ⌘+I. Click the Keywords tab, and iPhoto displays the Keywords dialog, as shown in Figure 3-3.

Select the check box next to the keyword that you want to attach to the selected images. When you're done, click the Close button on the Photo Info dialog to save your changes. Straightforward, just like I like it.

iPhoto comes stocked with a handful of useful preset keywords:

✦ Favorite

✦ Family

✦ Kids

✦ Vacation

✦ Birthday

✦ Grayscale

✦ Widescreen

The Checkmark keyword causes a small check mark-in-a-circle icon to appear in the bottom right-hand corner of any image that gets that assignment. For example, you might temporarily mark your favorite photographs with the Checkmark keyword. Then it's a cinch to retrieve just your favorites by searching for the Checkmark keyword.

You can also display the keywords assigned to each photo in the Viewer. (Check out Figure 3-3 to see what this looks like.) Choose View➪Keywords to toggle the display of keywords on and off.

Customizing your own keywords

Besides the keywords that are included in iPhoto by default, you can create a number of custom keywords . . . after all, not everything fits in Family or Birthday. To create your own keywords, follow these steps:

Figure 3-3:
Hey, Archibald, check out the keywords!

1. **Press ⌘+, (comma) to display the Preferences dialog.**

2. **Click the Keywords button on the toolbar.**

3. **Click Add.**

4. **Type your own custom keyword name into the edit box that appears and press Return.**

Note that you can also rename existing keywords (by selecting a keyword and clicking Rename), but keep in mind that they will affect all images that already use that keyword. You can also delete a keyword: Select it in the list and then click Delete from the list.

Searching for keywords

As I mention earlier, the more keywords that you assign, the easier it is to use iPhoto. As your photo collection grows, it can become unmanageable — to help you out, iPhoto lets you search for photos by using the keywords that you assigned to the images. To search for images using keywords, do the following:

1. **Click the Keywords button at the bottom-left corner of the iPhoto window to display the Keywords panel.**

The Keywords button proudly bears the label of a key. (Someone was thinking clearly that day.)

2. **Click as many keywords as you would like to search by.**

3. **When you're done searching, click the Keywords button again to hide the Keywords panel.**

Use the Search tool as a quick and easy way to build a Photo Album. To create a Photo Album of pictures of your wedding, for example, you could search for the keyword Wedding (assuming that you assigned that keyword to your wedding pictures) and then drag the results of the search to a Photo Album in the Album list. Convenient and *sassy* to boot!

Taking Care of Business: Basic Editing

Okay, let's face it: Sometimes mere mortals like you and I don't take the greatest photographs. For those times, iPhoto provides a helping hand with several important editing features with which you can save your dark photos from the Trash and improve "keepers" into honest-to-goodness art.

To begin editing your photographs, select the photo that you want to edit and click the Edit button on the iPhoto toolbar. This displays the Edit panel of the toolbar, as shown in Figure 3-4. (And yes, that's my close personal friend James Brown . . . he likes my soulful '64 Cadillac two-door. Her name is Princess Grace, and she's driven only on weekends.)

Figure 3-4: Click Edit to start fixing your photos.

The editing tools include

✦ **Crop:** This lets you trim off any unwanted edges of the photo and focus on the photo's subject.

✦ **Enhance:** This is a one-click solution that automatically adjusts the color and contrast of the image.

✦ **Red-Eye:** No more vampires! Remove the evil-looking red-eye phenomenon from your photos.

✦ **Retouch:** Remove minor imperfections in photographs by blending them into the surrounding area.

✦ **B & W (black and white):** For that vintage look, you can also convert color pictures to black and white.

✦ **Sepia:** Another antique look, this time in shades of copper and brown.

✦ **Adjust:** These controls allow you to fix photos that are too dark, too light, or washed-out.

✦ **Done:** Click this button when you're done editing, and iPhoto saves your changes and returns you to the thumbnail view.

✦ **Navigation arrows:** Click these to advance to the previous or next image.

Constrain and crop

Sometimes your photos have additional clutter around the edges. To get rid of this problem with traditional photographs, you'd resort to a pair of scissors to cut off the unwanted portion of the image. Professional photographers call this *cropping*. Digital image-editing software packages (including iPhoto) have borrowed this term. The Crop feature of iPhoto gives you the ability to remove unwanted stuff from around the edges of your otherwise perfect photographs, like the strange guy who blundered into the corner of your perfect Grand Canyon composition.

To crop a photo, you must first select what portion of the image that you want to keep by clicking and dragging on the image in the Viewer. As you drag, a rectangle appears indicating what part of the image you want to keep, as shown in Figure 3-5. Everything outside of this rectangle will disappear after a crop operation. (The selection rectangle can be dragged and resized if necessary.)

After you select the portion that you want to remain, click the Crop button in the Edit panel to remove the rest. If you would like to constrain your selection to a specific size, select that size from the Constrain pop-up menu to the left of the Crop button. This lets you resize a photograph according to a preset size. (For example, certain aspect ratios are better for certain media — a 4 x 3 ratio looks best in an iDVD project or a bound book, whereas a 4 x 6 is perfectly proportioned for printing a postcard.)

Figure 3-5:
Click and
drag to
select the
part of the
image that
you want
to keep.

"Hey, I didn't want *that* to happen!" (Yep, time to mention Undo again.) You can always remove any editing change you've just made to an image; just press ⌘+Z or choose Edit➪Undo. iPhoto offers a multiple Undo function, so you can press ⌘+Z multiple times to backtrack through your changes.

Enhance

Things can't get much easier than this. If the colors in your image look drab, you can click the Enhance button to automatically increase (or decrease) the color saturation and automatically improve the contrast within the photo. (Note that this is different from the manual contrast control that I discuss later.) Everything's done for you, so there are no settings to change. To compare the even fresher-smelling photo with the earlier version, press the Control key, and you'll see the un-enhanced image. When you release the Control key, the enhancement is applied again, so you can compare the results.

You can click Enhance more than once to continue your attempts to improve the image, but sooner or later, iPhoto can make no additional adjustments.

The Enhance button only works when no part of an image has been selected with the rectangle (that way, the controls will affect the entire image). If you need to deselect a portion of the photo, just click anywhere in the image outside the selected area, and the selection rectangle disappears like beer at a football game.

Retouch

Do you suffer from spots or specks in an otherwise-perfect image? Click the Retouch button, and the cursor turns into a crosshair; click and drag the cursor across the imperfection in short movements to remove it. Again, you can hold down and release the Control key to compare the retouched version of the image with the fixed photo.

Naturally, Retouch won't add detail to an image, so it won't add highlights to your girlfriend's hair or fix the dented fender on your Harley — instead, it's best used to clean up specks within a solid band of color, like a photo of a sunset. I find Retouch especially handy with pictures that I've scanned from slides and existing photographs.

Adjust

Shooting photographs that look perfect is a tough task, and sometimes things don't work out the way that you plan. If your images turn out too dark or light, iPhoto can help you clean up after the fact. To adjust the brightness and contrast of an image, simply move the Brightness/Contrast sliders until the image looks the way that you want. You'll also find:

✦ **Color adjustment sliders** on the Adjust dialog for fixing tint, temperature, and saturation problems

✦ **A straighten slider** that's boffo for straightening images that are slightly off-kilter

✦ **A sharpness slider** that increases the definition of borders and edges in your image

✦ **Exposure and histogram sliders** that allow you to fine-tune the color and exposure range for an image

Red-eye removal

Have you ever picked up your photographs from the local photo developer only to discover that the subjects in your photographs all look like rather unsettling red-eyed zombies? *Red-eye* is a phenomenon that occurs when the camera captures light reflecting off the retinas of eyeballs. This problem isn't limited only to human eyes, either. Even Spot, your loving canine pal, can have that "Demon Doggy" possessed look! To help exorcise these red-eye problems from your photographs, iPhoto gives you a Red-Eye filter.

To remove red-eye problems in your photographs, click the Red-Eye button and then click in the center of each offending eyeball. Your red-eye problem disappears in an instant. When you're done eradicating red-eye, click the Red-Eye button again.

**Book III
Chapter 3**

Focusing on iPhoto

Black and white, or sepia

In the old days, photographers had to cart around several rolls of film if they wanted to shoot in color, black and white, and sepia. These days, you can simply shoot in color because iPhoto can do the black-and-white or sepia conversion for you. It's really simple, too! Just click the B & W button to convert an image from color to shades of gray, or click Sepia to convert the image to shades of brown and copper.

 If you change your mind and want to revert to a color image, choose Edit⇨ Undo to see colors again. For an interesting artistic effect, you can select just a portion of a photo with the Crop tool and click the B & W or the Sepia button to work your antique magic on just the selected area.

Don't forget to rotate!

Although it's not technically an Edit mode feature, rotation is a sort of edit, so I discuss it here. This feature is useful for viewing those images where you held the camera sideways to fit that tall building into the viewfinder. To rotate an image, simply click the Rotate button at the left-hand side of the Toolbar. The default rotation is in a counter-clockwise direction. Hold the Option key while you click the rotate button to rotate in a clockwise direction.

Producing Your Own Coffee-Table Masterpiece

Computerized photo albums are fun and all, but sometimes people long for the real photo albums of the past. They like to turn pages, put it on the shelf, and view it without a computer screen. For those folks, iPhoto offers a way to create and print your own professional-quality photo album. Use iPhoto to create a Photo Album (the digital kind), tweak its formatting until you're satisfied, and then transmit your finished product via the Internet to a vendor who will print, bind, and send you a copy of your finished album, for a small fee, of course. At the time of this writing, costs ranged from a small soft-cover book with 20 pages for around $4 to a large hard-cover album with 20 pages for about $30.

Here's how to create your own bound work of art:

1. **Create a new Photo Album in iPhoto by choosing File⇨New Album or clicking the + button at the left edge of the Toolbar.**

   The name of the album is editable, so you can name it to your liking.

2. **Click the Photo Library icon at the left side of the iPhoto interface and drag your favorite photos into the new Photo Album.**

   These are the images that appear in your bound photo album.

When preparing a photo album that will be printed on paper, use the highest quality images available. It takes higher-resolution images to look good on paper (as compared with your Mac's monitor).

3. **After you complete the preparation of your Photo Album in iPhoto, select that Photo Album in the Source list by clicking it.**

The Source list appears on the left side of the iPhoto interface.

4. **Click the Book button on the Toolbar.**

5. **iPhoto prompts you to select the size of the book and a theme.**

The choices you make here determine the number of pages and layout scheme, as well as the background graphics for each page. Note that you can also choose double-sided pages for the larger books.

6. **Click Choose Theme.**

iPhoto displays a dialog asking whether you want to layout your photos manually or allow iPhoto to do everything automatically. (The remainder of these steps show the manual process.)

7. **Click Manually.**

In Book mode, the Viewer changes in subtle ways. It displays the current page at the bottom of the display and adds a scrolling row of thumbnail images above it. This row of images represents the remaining images from the selected album that you can add to your book. You can drag any image thumbnail into one of the photo placeholders to add it to the page. You can also click the Page button at the left of the thumbnail strip (looks like a page with a turned-down corner) to display thumbnails of each page in your book. To return to the album image strip, click the Photos button under the Page button.

8. **Rearrange the page order to suit you by dragging the thumbnail of any page from one location to another in the strip.**

9. **In the Book panel below the toolbar, you can adjust a variety of settings for the final book, including the book's theme, page numbers, and comments.**

Besides photos, you can also add text to the pages of your photo album. (Nothing on the order of Stephen King or Tom Clancy — more like captions with short descriptions.) Selecting Show Guides draws faint blue boxes in the Viewer that show where you can add text.

10. **Click any one of the text boxes and begin typing to add text to that page.**

When you're satisfied with the results of the photo book, it's time to publish it.

11. **Click the Buy Book button.**

In a series of dialogs that appear, iPhoto guides you through the final steps to order a bound book. (Don't forget your credit card.)

A fast connection to the Internet like cable or DSL is very handy for this process. The images that you must submit are too large for a slow dialup connection.

Remember, you can also save that book as a PDF file and print it later (either on your own inkjet printer, or a nicer one at the copy shop downtown)!

Sharing Photos with Friends and Family

Besides creating a photo book, iPhoto offers many other ways for you to share your photos. Click the Share menu to see the possibilities (some are also available from the toolbar).

Here are the different ways that you can share your photos with iPhoto:

✦ **Print:** Don't forget about your computer's printer. It's mundane, I know, but you can print photographs from iPhoto with your inkjet or laser printer.

✦ **Slideshow:** Display a slideshow presentation of your photos in iPhoto, complete with background music.

✦ **Email:** Send photos to your friends via e-mail. You'll need an active Internet connection. (Go figure, indeed.) iPhoto will launch your default e-mail client when you're ready to send your photographs.

✦ **Order Prints:** Order photographic quality prints of your favorite images. Kodak prints the photographs for you and will ship them wherever you want them to go.

✦ **Book:** Allows you to order a bound book, as I demonstrate in the previous section.

✦ **HomePage:** Publish your photos on your .Mac Web site.

✦ **.Mac Slides:** Publish your photos as a slide show on your iDisk, where others with .Mac accounts can view it.

✦ **Desktop:** Change your Desktop picture to one of your iPhoto images.

✦ **Burn:** Leads you through the process of recording your images on a blank CD or DVD.

Chapter 4: Making Magic with iMovie HD

In This Chapter

- ✓ Working with iMovie HD controls
- ✓ Adding media to your projects
- ✓ Applying text, transitions, photos, and effects to your movies
- ✓ Adding audio to your movies
- ✓ Sharing your movies in many different formats

Alfred Hitchcock, Stanley Kubrick, George Lucas, and Ridley Scott — those guys are amateurs! Welcome to the exciting world of movie making on your Mac, where *you* call the shots. With iMovie HD, you can try your hand at all aspects of the movie-creating process, including editing and special effects. Built with ease-of-use in mind, iMovie lets you perform full-blown movie production on your Macintosh with a minimum of effort.

Don't let iMovie HD's fancy buttons and flashing lights fool you: This application is a feature-packed tool for serious movie production. The iMovie HD controls work the same as many top-notch, movie-editing tools that professionals use. From basic editing to audio and video effects, iMovie HD has everything that you need to get started creating high-quality movies.

The iMovie HD Window

To launch iMovie HD, either navigate to the Application folder and double-click the iMovie HD icon or click the iMovie HD icon that's hanging out on the Dock. When you first launch iMovie HD, the application displays a top-level dialog from which you can choose to create a new iMovie HD project, open an existing project, or make a Magic iMovie. For now, just click Create a New Project, type a name for your project, and click Create.

You'll notice that the window fills most of the screen, even when it's resized as small as possible (as shown in Figure 4-1). In fact, you can't run iMovie HD at resolutions less than 1024 x 768.

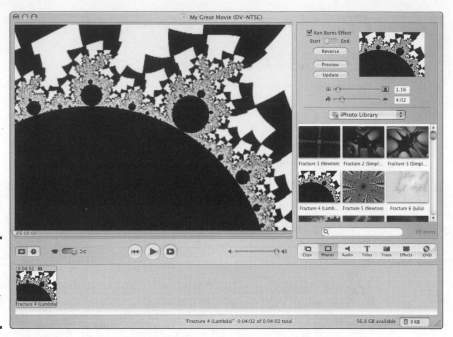

Figure 4-1:
iMovie HD
takes over
most of your
Desktop.

This seemingly rude behavior is actually a requirement. If you think about it, creating and editing a movie requires a *lot* of elbow room (both on your monitor and on your hard drive). To hide the iMovie HD window, press either ⌘+H or ⌘+Tab to switch to other applications that are running. (You can also use the Exposé key, F9.)

You'll notice that the interface consists of three main parts:

✦ **Monitor:** The Monitor is the big, black, square viewer where you watch movies.

✦ **Tool palette:** The iMovie Tool palette appears on the right side of the iMovie HD window. The palette offers one-click access to an array of movie-building tools.

Just above the Tool palette is the Clips pane. The contents of the Clips pane vary, depending on which of the Tool palette buttons you've selected. Clicking the Clips button displays the Clips pane, for example, which is where iMovie HD stores your movie clips for use in full-length movies that you create. A click on Photos allows you to add still images from your iPhoto library (as demonstrated by the versatile Figure 4-1). Clicking the Audio button whisks you to a pane with audio files in it. iMovie stores your audio clips here, which you can also use in any movie that you create.

The Titles, Trans (transitions), and Effects tools let you twist, turn, and label your movies like the pros do. Finally, the iDVD button displays the Chapter List — it's used with iDVD 5, where you can build a DVD movie with your finished masterpiece.

✦ **Viewers:** The viewers are where you compose your movie masterpiece. The two main tabs here are the Clips viewer and the Timeline viewer. I cover these in more detail later.

The Powers of Three

The minimalist approach of iMovie HD provides power with simplicity (something that the average Joe like you and I can appreciate). Instead of the nested windows and cryptic film jargon of traditional movie-editing packages — which also, by the way, tend to cost hundreds or thousands of dollars a pop — iMovie HD reduces the clutter to three elements. Use this trio of tools, and you'll be on your way to movie-making bliss.

Monitor

The Monitor is the largest of all the iMovie HD window elements — it functions just like the video monitor and control deck that a traditional film editor uses. You can think of it as iMovie HD's screen, where you view clips and preview your movie while you edit it. (Check it out in Figure 4-2.) When you launch iMovie for the first time, the Monitor appears black, indicating that you haven't created a movie yet. (Apple is, if anything, eminently sensible.) On subsequent launches of iMovie HD, it displays the most recent movie project.

Nestled directly beneath the iMovie Monitor are the playback controls (see Figure 4-2). Resembling buttons on a conventional DVD player, the iMovie HD playback controls let you play, stop, and return to the beginning of movies that display in the Monitor.

In addition to the buttons that control playback, the Monitor sports other important controls. The *scrubber bar* contains the playback head, which tells you visually where you are in the movie. The *playback head* is a blue triangle positioned directly below the Monitor. While your movie plays, the playback head moves to indicate the current location of playback. The playback head isn't just a visual indicator, though: It also has an important function. You can also click and drag the playback head to move forward or back in the current movie.

All the remaining Monitor button controls affect the playback head's position with one click. Table 4-1 lists the various playback controls and how they affect the playback head's position.

The Monitor

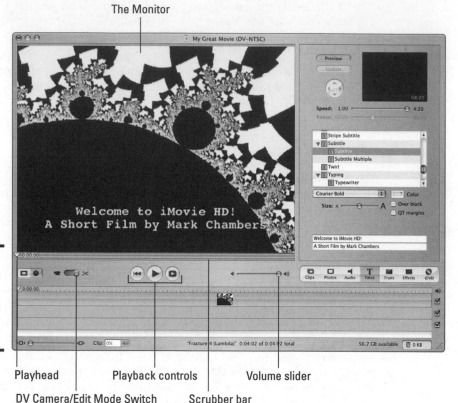

Figure 4-2:
Watch your
movies on
the Monitor
whilst you
edit them.

Playhead   Playback controls   Volume slider

DV Camera/Edit Mode Switch   Scrubber bar

Table 4-1	iMovie's Playback Controls
Control	*What It Does*
Home	Moves the playback head to the beginning of the movie.
Play	Click to begin playing a movie. Click again to stop playback.
Play Full Screen	Plays the current movie in full-screen mode.

The Monitor has two remaining controls that demand attention.

✦ **Volume slider:** Adjusts the volume during movie playback

✦ **DV Camera/Edit Mode switch:** Toggles between video from your camera
and the movie that you're editing with iMovie HD

The DV Camera/Edit Mode switch affects how you import video from a
camera. Read more about this in the upcoming section "Working with Clips
(Not the Paper Kind)."

Palette

The palette occupies the rightmost portion of the iMovie HD window and offers a complete set of tools for creating movies. Divided into seven sections, the palette houses the building blocks that you need to construct your cinematic masterpiece as well as your connection to iDVD. (Refer to Figure 4-1.)

Throughout the creation process, you'll use the tools located in the palette to build the content of your movie. Table 4-2 describes the role that each palette plays in the movie-making process.

Table 4-2	Palette Roles
Palette	*What It Does*
Clips	Stores movie clips from your hard drive in a visual library
Photos	Imports still images from your iPhoto collection
Audio	Gives you audio effects, voiceover tools, and your iTunes audio files
Titles	Offers text editing tools to label and title your movie
Trans	Adds useful video transitions to your movies for professional-looking edits
Effects	Adds stunning visual effects that give your movies an edge
iDVD	Exports your finished movie into iDVD **5**

Viewers

The final stops on the iMovie window tour are the viewers. Located at the bottom of the screen, your trusty *viewers* are the heart of editing operations in iMovie, where you add audio and video clips to construct the perfect movie. As shown in Figure 4-3, they offer a visual representation of the order in which the various clips appear in a movie.

As you can see in Figure 4-3, the viewer interface has two modes:

✦ **Clip viewer:** Displays the sequence of video clips in a movie — this is the mode shown in Figure 4-3.

✦ **Timeline viewer:** Displays the duration and juxtaposition of the various audio and video clips in a movie. (I think it's safe to say that's the only appearance of the word *juxtaposition* in this particular tome.)

Figure 4-3:
Each viewer displays different audio or video information.

Timeline Viewer button

Clip Viewer button   Clip viewer

The Movie-Making Process

After you're on friendly terms with the three main sections of the iMovie HD window, follow the following simple six-step process to create professional looking movies in minutes. I go into more detail about each of these steps in the following sections.

Or, if you need to quickly create a movie, see the upcoming section, "Creating on-the-fly with Magic iMovie."

Making an iMovie the traditional way

Have you got ample time to produce your movie? If there's no imminent deadline, you can follow the hallowed, age-old method of hand-crafting your movie, choosing settings manually, and adding clips, audio, effects, and transitions (as in previous versions of iMovie). To create a movie manually, follow these steps:

1. **Import and edit your movie footage.**

The first step in creating a movie is to import movie clips into iMovie HD, either from your digital video camcorder or from video clips already on your hard drive. You will use these clips to construct a full-length movie.

2. **Add clips from the Clips pane to the Timeline.**

After you prepare your movie clips, you can add them to the movie. By using drag-and-drop, it takes only a few seconds to add the movie segments found in the Clips pane to your full-length movie.

3. **Apply transitions, effects, photos, and text to the movie.**

With your movie clips in place, it's a snap to enhance them with visual effects and transitions. You might also want to spice up the movie with titles and credits.

4. **Import or record audio clips.**

Great movies look even better when accompanied by great audio. You can import audio into iMovie HD from your iTunes audio files, audio files you've created with GarageBand, audio CDs, your iTunes playlists, or even what you've recorded yourself with a microphone.

5. **Add audio from the Audio pane to the Timeline.**

Drag audio clips from the Audio pane to the Timeline to arrange your movie's soundtrack. (And yes, you documentary fans will find it easy to add narration.)

6. **Preview, build, and burn the final product.**

After you build the next *Gone with the Windows* — sorry, couldn't help that one — iMovie HD makes it a snap to preview your creation. Then it's just a few clicks before your project becomes a movie. iMovie helps you distribute your completed movie as well: You can burn it to a CD-ROM, import it into iDVD for use on a movie DVD, or export it into QuickTime for online distribution.

The remainder of this chapter guides you through the details of these steps. Before you know it, you'll be showing that upstart Spielberg a thing or two without setting foot out of your home.

Creating on-the-fly with Magic iMovie

The arrival of iMovie HD includes a new feature, called *Magic iMovie,* that literally reduces all the six standard steps I described to a single dialog and a Create button. Magic iMovie is perfect for those times when speed is of the essence: producing a wedding video immediately after the ceremony, for example, or a video of a school field trip that your teacher can show within minutes of your return to the classroom.

iMovie HD produces the movie automatically, using the movie title you provide, the transition you specify between clips, and the audio soundtrack of your choice. (Naturally, you won't get the chance to be Cecil B. deMille with a Magic iMovie project, but he was never known for the speed of his filmmaking, anyway.) You can optionally choose to send the completed movie directly to iDVD, where you can even use OneStep DVD to create a DVD-video disc automatically! (I swear, if it were any more automatic, your Mac wouldn't need you at all. Of course, with AppleScript, your presence can be eliminated, anyway.)

Here's how to create a Magic iMovie.

1. **Plug in your digital video (DV) camcorder, turn it on, and set it to VCR (or VTR) mode.**

2. **Connect your DV camcorder to your Mac using a FireWire cable.**

3. **Launch iMovie HD, and then click the Make a Magic iMovie button on the opening dialog.**

   If the dialog doesn't appear because you were working on a film, choose File⇨Make a Magic iMovie.

   iMovie HD prompts you for a project name and location as it normally would.

4. **When you see the Magic iMovie dialog, type a name for your movie in the Movie Title box.**

5. **Mark the Use Transitions check box and choose the transition you want (from the drop-down list box) to insert between clips.**

6. **(Optional) Add a soundtrack by enabling the Play a Music Soundtrack check box.**

   To choose the song you want to use, click the Choose Music button to browse your iTunes music library or to select an audio CD that you've loaded.

7. **(Optional) Mark the Send to iDVD check box to send your completed project for later use in iDVD (which Tiger also launches automatically).**

8. **Click Create, sit back, and relax!**

Working with Clips (Not the Paper Kind)

The first step when creating a movie is to add video clips to the Clips pane. These clips usually form the bulk of the video that you use in the completed movie. iMovie HD is flexible in that it permits you to import video clips from more than one source:

✦ **Import from a digital video camcorder:** Connect a DV camcorder to your Macintosh to transfer video.

✦ **Import from files:** Import any DV clip (including high-definition [HD] format) directly from your hard drive. (You can tell a DV clip by its HD DV or DV file type, as shown in the Finder's Info dialog.)

If your favorite movie clip isn't in DV Stream format, you can export it from QuickTime Pro. Then import it into iMovie. See Book III, Chapter 7 for more on QuickTime Pro.

After you import your video, you can perform a variety of editing functions on the clip: You can edit clips together to tell a story; edit mistakes or bad footage; apply audio, transitions, and effects; and even add titles, for that cinematic touch.

Adding clips from media files

iMovie HD allows you to import many different kinds of media files. From graphics to video to audio files, iMovie HD has you covered. Table 4-3 lists the most common file formats that iMovie HD can import into your project.

Table 4-3	File Types That iMovie Understands
File Type	*What It's Used For*
AAC	Compressed audio
AIFF	Audio from an audio CD
MP3	Compressed audio
JPEG	Standard for still images from the Web, scanners, or a digital camera
GIF	Standard for still images from the Web, scanners, or a digital camera
PSD	Images from Photoshop
HD DV	High-definition (widescreen) digital video
MPEG-4	Digital video in MPEG format
DV	Standard digital video (including the feed from your iSight camera)

Book III
Chapter 4

Making Magic with iMovie HD

The file type dictates what happens when you import that file. For example, when you import an image or video file, the file goes directly into the Clips pane. In contrast, importing an audio file automatically places it in the movie at the audio pointer's current location. To import an audio or video file, choose File⇨Import. Select a file to import in the Open dialog and click OK. The imported file appears in the Clips pane or the Audio pane, depending on the file type.

Still images can also be parked on the Clips pane — a holdover from earlier versions of iPhoto, where pictures were handled like static video clips. Therefore, photographs can actually be added to your movie from either the Clips pane (for imported photos) or the Photos pane (for pictures from your iPhoto collection).

Adding clips from your camcorder

Adding clips from your DV camcorder or iSight camera is just as simple as playing a movie. To retrieve video from your camcorder, do the following:

1. **With a FireWire cable, connect a FireWire-compatible camera to your Macintosh and set it to VTR (or Playback) mode.**

   If your camera is not FireWire-compatible, you should be able to buy an adapter. Setting your camera to VTR mode allows remote control of the camcorder by iMovie. If you're not sure how to set VTR mode on your camera, consult its manual.

2. **In iMovie, slide the DV Camera/Edit Mode switch to the Camera position, which is labeled with a miniature camcorder icon (refer to Figure 4-2).**

   This initiates the camera capture mode. When you set this mode, an Import button appears above the Play button.

3. **Find the video.**

   Click the Monitor's playback buttons to locate the video on your camcorder that you wish to import, fast-forwarding or rewinding until you find the correct footage, watching your progress in the Monitor. When you find the video, stop the playback and position the playback head a few seconds prior to the place where the desired video begins. When you're ready, click the Play button again.

4. **When the video that you want to capture appears in the Monitor, click the Import button to begin transferring that video from the camcorder to your Macintosh.**

5. **Stop the video.**

   Click the Import button again to stop the video transfer.

Imported video from a camcorder transfer appears in the Clips pane. Importing multiple clips from your camcorder results in multiple separate clips in iMovie!

Editing video clips

iMovie HD gives you several different ways to edit your video clips. You can copy, trim, and crop your video clips to your heart's content; and if you mess up along the way, an instant fix is but a click away.

Who needs a camcorder?

If you're a serious couch potato — one of those folks who are permanently affixed to their living room furniture, constantly awaiting this TV show or that one — rejoice! Hardware devices are on the market that can capture your favorite programs as digital video, providing you with yet another source of iMovie HD video clips. (The signal can come from a cable-ready TV or from a standard analog video source like a VCR.) After you create a video clip by using one of these video capture devices, you can then import the clip into iMovie HD.

For example, the EyeTV unit from Elgato Systems is practically a complete solution for digitizing analog video: It comes with a built-in, cable-ready TV tuner and a hardware MPEG *encoder* (the hardware that can create a DV stream from analog video). For around $200, EyeTV can provide the somewhat mundane convenience of watching TV on your Mac's monitor, along with the ability to "pause" a live TV show . . . but for me, the *real* treat is creating digital video from all those old VHS family reunion videos that are currently collecting dust in your closet. EyeTV is a Universal Serial Bus (USB) device, so it works with just about any Mac that can run Mac OS X. Each hour of video takes up about 650MB of hard drive space, so a high-capacity 200GB FireWire hard drive suddenly looks most attractive indeed.

For the complete details on EyeTV, visit the Elgato Software Web site at www.elgato.com. And don't forget to honor the copyrights on the material you capture from TV broadcasts, commercial video tapes, and DVDs — consult a lawyer if you plan on distributing any movies that include copyrighted material.

Copying video clips

Sometimes you'll want to work on multiple copies of the same video clip. This gives you the ability to try out different edits on the same piece of footage without altering the original. To duplicate a video clip, do the following:

1. **Select a clip in the Clips pane.**

The selected clip turns blue.

2. **Press ⌘+C or choose Edit⇨Copy.**

3. **Press ⌘+V or choose Edit⇨Paste.**

A new copy of the video clip appears in the Clips pane.

Of course, you can also follow the Macintosh convention of Option-dragging a clip from its cell on the pane to an empty cell or to the Timeline. Doing so makes a copy wherever you release the mouse.

Cropping, splitting, and trimming video clips

Cropping, splitting, and trimming are three important editing functions that iMovie HD affords you. Here's the skinny on these functions:

✦ **Crop:** Deletes everything from the clip except a selected region

✦ **Split:** Breaks a single clip into multiple clips

✦ **Trim:** Deletes a selected region from the clip

To perform any of these functions, you must first select a region of a clip. Choose a clip in the Clips pane. This causes the clip to appear in the Monitor. Position the playback head at the beginning of the region that you wish to select. Then Shift-click anywhere on the scrubber bar to the right of the starting point. (iMovie HD places markers at the edges of the selection, and you can further adjust the selection by dragging them.) A region turns yellow when you select it. After you select a region, perform the editing operation.

✦ **Crop:** Choose Edit⇨Crop. Everything but the selected region disappears.

✦ **Split:** Choose Edit⇨Split Video Clip at Playhead. The clip instantly splits into two clips.

✦ **Trim:** Choose Edit⇨Clear. The selected region disappears. (If you have a section of video selected in the middle of a larger clip, two clips will remain: one with the video before the selection, and one with the video after the selection.)

Naming video clips

As your movie project grows, you'll want to take care to label your clips. This helps to remind you when you return to the project later. It's also a godsend when you begin working on multiple copies of the same clip. Otherwise, you have no easy way to differentiate two identical clips because they appear the same in the Clips pane.

To edit the name of a clip, click the text of the clip name near the clip's bottom edge. When the text appears in a text edit box, type a new name for the clip; then press Return to brand the clip with the new name, pardner. (You can also change the clip name from the Get Info dialog by pressing ⌘+I.)

Basic Composition the iMovie Way

After you import and edit some video clips, it's finally time to begin creating a movie. Adding video to your movie is a simple drag-and-drop operation.

Adding clips to a movie

Before you add clips to your movie, select the desired viewer tab. The Clip viewer displays clips in sequential order, with each clip occupying the same amount of space in the Timeline. The Timeline viewer displays clips with lengths that are relative to their duration. For example, a 30-second clip will appear as half the length of a 60-second clip when you view clips in the Timeline viewer.

To add a clip to your movie, drag it from the Clips pane to the desired location in the Timeline. Constructing a movie is just a matter of repeating this step with the various clips that you want to add to your movie.

Removing clips from a movie

Eventually you'll add a clip that you soon decide doesn't belong in your movie; to delete a clip from a movie, select the clip in the Timeline and press Delete. The clip disappears, and any clips that follow the deleted selection slide to the left to fill the void.

iMovie HD has its own Trash, which appears at the bottom of the application window — you can drag unwanted items from the pane or from the viewers and drop them on top of this icon to delete them. You can empty the iMovie HD Trash at any time by choosing File⇨Empty Trash.

If you mistakenly remove a clip that you intended on keeping, press ⌘+Z or choose Edit⇨Undo to cancel the delete operation.

Rearranging clips in a movie

If you decide at some point that certain clips are in the wrong order, it's a cinch to change. Simply drag a clip in the Clip viewer. Release the mouse when the clip reaches the desired destination; clips in the Timeline will move apart to make room for the nomadic clip.

Transitions for the Masses

Stringing together a bunch of video clips to make a movie is cool stuff, but that's only a small fraction of what iMovie HD can do. Beyond simple editing, iMovie HD offers a set of video transitions for you to use in your movies. *Transitions* are video effects that perform their magic at the point where two clips connect. They help smooth out the joint between the two clips. If you're a television viewer, you see transitions all the time — any time that the screen fades to or from black, you're seeing a transition in action. (Remember the cool swirling bat from the old *Batman* TV series?)

iMovie HD gives you a wide variety of transitions from which to choose. These can be displayed by clicking the Trans (transitions) button in the Tool palette, as shown in Figure 4-4.

Figure 4-4:
A variety of transitions are available within iMovie HD.

Clicking any of the transitions in the Transitions pane causes a brief preview of the effect to automatically play in the preview window at the top of the pane. You can vary the duration of the transition with the Speed slider. The list of available transitions provided free with iMovie HD is short, but it covers most of the basic movie needs:

✦ **Billow:** The view from the first clip shrinks into a grid of circles to reveal the next clip.

✦ **Circle Closing:** Video shrinks with a circular *viewport* (like a lens shutter) to the next clip.

✦ **Circle Opening:** Video expands with a circular viewport to the next clip.

✦ **Cross Dissolve:** Video dissolves from one clip to the next.

✦ **Fade In:** Video fades in from black.

✦ **Fade Out:** Video fades out to black.

✦ **Overlap:** Video fades from one clip to another.

✦ **Push:** Video slides to an edge of the screen over time. Select which edge by clicking the directional arrows that appear when you select the Push transition.

✦ **Radial:** Video wipes in a circular motion around the center, like a radar screen.

✦ **Ripple:** The video from the next clip wipes in a liquid motion across the preceding clip.

✦ **Scale Down:** Video shrinks over time to reveal a clip behind it.

✦ **Twirl:** The first clip spins and shrinks into the center of the screen, while the next clip twirls and expands to fill the frame.

✦ **Warp Out:** Video wipes from the center outward to the next clip.

✦ **Wash In:** Video fades in from white.

✦ **Wash Out:** Video fades out to white.

For those who just can't get enough, Apple offers a number of additional transitions, effects, and audio clips for free at `www.apple.com/imovie`. You can also purchase many transitions and special effects as add-on packages from third-party developers.

To add a transition to your movie, drag the desired transition from the Transitions pane to the Timeline. A transition merges two clips together, so you'll want to drop the transition in an appropriate location — in between two clips. If you change any settings of a transition, make sure to click the Update button. It refreshes the preview of that transition in your movie.

Transitions are a wonderfully subtle way to improve the look of your movie. Use them judiciously to emulate professional movie and television editing. (Too many transitions within a movie can distract your audience from your message — unless, of course, you're filming an episode of *Laugh-In 2005*.) To give you a feel for how the pros do it, pay attention when you watch television or movies and focus on the transitions. Sometimes the simplest transition can have a dramatic effect on a movie.

Even Gone with the Wind Had Titles

Besides transitions, professional movies and videos have text, and lots of it; from the title at the beginning of a movie to the litany of names that scroll by in the credits after the movie, movie editing clearly demands sophisticated text-editing abilities. With over a dozen title styles to choose from, iMovie HD can handle most text tasks that you throw at it.

The Titles pane is where you can find the text features of iMovie HD. Figure 4-5 shows you the basic layout of the Titles pane.

The Titles pane changes to accommodate different amounts of text depending on which title style you choose. Otherwise, the controls for the title styles are identical for each effect. Table 4-4 lists the settings and functions that are common to all title styles.

Figure 4-5:
The Titles pane within iMovie HD.

Table 4-4	Titles Pane Features
Setting	*What It Does*
Speed	Slider that adjusts how quickly the text effect executes.
Pause	Slider that adjusts the length of time that the text remains on the screen after the effect has completed its animation.
Color	Palette pop-up that changes the color of the text in the title style. When you click the Color box, a palette of colors pops up that you can choose from.
Over Black	Check box that displays the text on a black background if checked. If not enabled, a movie appears behind the text.
Font menu	Drop-down list that changes the font that the Title style uses to display the text.
Font size	Slider that increases or decreases the size of the font.
QT Margins	Check box that alters the position of the text based on standardized QuickTime margins.

To begin working with Titles, select a text style from the pane. At the bottom of the Titles pane, you can change the text for any title style, as shown in Figure 4-5. When you alter the text of the style and any of its parameters, the miniature preview at the top of the Titles pane updates to reflect the changes.

After you successfully adapt the text style to match your needs, you can add it to a movie by dragging the title style from the list to the Timeline. When you do, the title appears in the Timeline as a movie segment.

Like deleting a movie clip, removing a title from your movie requires a click of the mouse and one key press. Click the title in the Timeline to select it and then press Delete to remove it from the movie. Should you delete a title accidentally, press ⌘+Z to undo the operation.

What Good Is a Movie without Special Effects?

Although iMovie HD can produce some nice transitions and titles, it doesn't stop there. It also comes stocked with a handful of cool video effects for you to use in your movies.

iMovie HD's stock effects

Click the Effects button to reveal the Effects pane (see Figure 4-6), which houses the various video effects. Selecting an effect from the list causes that effect's controls to appear at the bottom of the Effects pane. The available controls vary based upon the effect.

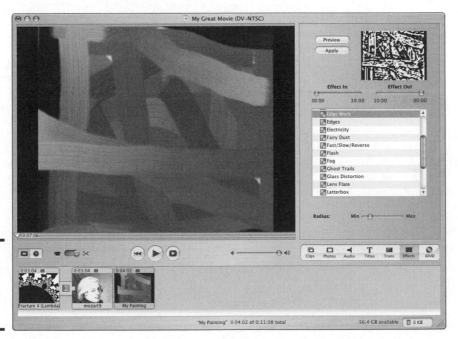

Figure 4-6:
Add effects
to your
movie from
this pane.

Table 4-5 lists the names and features of my favorite built-in iMovie effects. If these effects don't fit the bill for your movie, you'll be happy to know that you can find third-party effects on the Internet, too.

Table 4-5	iMovie Effects
Effect	*What It Does*
Adjust Colors	Tweaks colors to reduce yellow or blue casts; also works great for spooky results.
Aged Film	Gives you that great antique-footage look, with spots and distorted trails across your video.
Black & White	Takes your movie back in time with the nostalgic look of black and white video; good for simulated security camera shots, too.
Brightness & Contrast	Adjusts the brightness and contrast to lighten up a dark movie or to take the edge off harsh footage; when used creatively, also works well for special effects purposes.
Fog	A spooky effect especially made for those horror movie directors (or documenting a British vacation).
Letterbox	Move over, Harry Potter . . . my movie's an instant widescreen sensation.
N-Square	Tiles your clip into four smaller copies, with each taking up a quarter of the screen.
Sepia Tone	Adds a sepia-colored tint on your movie; can give movies rustic, old-fashioned, or romantic moods.
Sharpen	Defines edges in a blurry movie; makes everything look more crisp.
Soft Focus	Makes a movie blurry; fun for I-lost-my-eyeglasses shots.
Rain	Simulates raindrops — anyone for a downpour?

Adding Effects to a movie

To work with Effects in your movies, follow these five easy steps:

1. **In the Timeline, click a movie clip.**

The clip changes to a blue color to indicate that you selected it successfully.

2. **Open the Effects pane by clicking the Effects button in the Tool palette and then select an effect.**

In the Effects pane, choose an effect from the list of available effects by clicking the effect's name.

3. **Adjust the effect.**

From the effect's controls, tweak its settings to suit your needs. The Effect In and Effect Out sliders let you phase in an effect a certain amount of time from the beginning of the clip and then phase it out before it ends. While you adjust the effect's parameters, the results appear in the miniature preview window at the top of the Effects pane.

4. **Preview the effect at full size.**

After you choose and adjust the effect to your liking, you might want to see what it will look like in action. Click the Preview button to see a preview of the effect in the Monitor.

5. **Apply the effect.**

If you're happy with the results of the effects preview, it's easy to permanently add it to the movie clip by clicking the Apply button.

When you apply an effect to a movie clip, iMovie HD begins building the movie effect — the faster your Mac is and the more memory you have, the faster the effect is finished. To track the progress of an effect being built, iMovie HD displays a small red line in the movie clip found in the Timeline. While the build progresses, this red line grows until it spans the entire length of the clip. If you try to preview the clip before it's built, you'll still be able to view it but at a lower quality. This temporary preview permits you to view the effect while iMovie HD builds the real effect.

Hey, There's a Photo in My Video!

Of course, not everything has to move around like Fred Astaire within your frame. You can use still images to begin your film, add a background, or slap an old-fashioned Intermission placard right in the middle of your movie! In fact, iMovie HD includes a cool panning feature called the *Ken Burns Effect*, which is named after the man responsible for all those great documentaries on public television: The camera slowly pans and zooms across a static photograph, bringing motion to your images (and suddenly adding interest to that snapshot of Uncle Milton at the Grand Canyon).

Click the Photos button in the Tool palette to display the Photos pane shown in Figure 4-7. It operates much like the Clips pane — just click and drag an image from the pane to the Timeline or Clip viewer. To display other images from your iPhoto Library (or any of your iPhoto albums), click the drop-down list box and then click the desired album.

Now for the Ken Burns Effect — man, that *really* sounds like an avant-garde jazz group, doesn't it? Anyway, mark the Ken Burns Effect check box to enable it. You can set the duration of the pan and the total zoom throughout the effect. Click the Reverse button to reverse the pan and zoom out instead.

Unlike the other preview windows in iMovie HD, you can click and drag the image in the preview window to set the starting and finishing points for the Ken Burns Effect.

Figure 4-7:
Merging photos with video (sassy, Apple, downright *sassy*)!

Working with Sound

In addition to video and graphics, iMovie HD is adept at working with sound. With iMovie HD, you can use your favorite audio files, music CDs, and microphone to create professional-sounding soundtracks. (Sorry, John Williams is *not* included.)

Adding sound to a movie

All audio that you add to a movie resides in one of the two audio tracks in the Timeline. The audio tracks are visible only in the Timeline viewer tab.

To begin working with audio in iMovie HD, open the Audio pane by clicking the Audio button in the Tool palette. Note that the Audio pane is split into the Audio Library and Voice Recorder sections (which has an input level meter for your microphone and a record button).

Using the built-in sound effects

To get you started with audio in your movies, iMovie gives you a set of prerecorded sound effects, as shown in Figure 4-8. These make great background noises to enhance your movies. To preview any one of the sounds, click the drop-down list at the top of the pane, click iMovie Sound Effects, and then double-click the desired sound.

Figure 4-8:
The Sound
Effects
section
gives you
instant
access to
audio clips.

To add the sound to your movie, drag the sound effect from the Audio pane and drop it on the Timeline at the bottom of the screen. When you do, the audio clip appears in one of the audio tracks for the movie. Feel free to move the sound effect clip anywhere in the track by dragging it, or change the length of the effect by clicking the arrows at the ends of the clip and dragging them. This gives you precise control over when the sound plays so that you can synchronize it with video events.

Adding your own sound effects

If you'd like to add your own sound effects to the Audio pane, you need to do a little work in the Finder. Drag any audio file recognized by iTunes (including your favorite AIFF, AAC, or MP3 files) in the Finder to your Sound Effects folder (which is located in your home folder under Library⇨iMovie⇨Sound Effects).

Restart iMovie HD to see your new sound effects in the Audio pane. With a quick drag, you can add the new audio files to your movie.

Recording voice-overs for your movie

Sometimes you might want to narrate a segment of your movie rather than rely on sound effect files. Fortunately, iMovie HD gives you the ability to do just that. From the Voice Recorder section of the Audio pane, you can record your voice and add it to the audio track of your movie. What's more, you can record your voice as you watch the movie playing in real-time. This allows you to perfectly synchronize any narration you speak with the video onscreen. (Somebody deserves a raise in Cupertino!)

To record your voice, perform the following steps:

1. **Position the playback head at the place in your movie where you'd like to begin recording narration.**

   The playback head tells you where you are in the movie. You can position the playback head in either the Monitor or the Timeline viewer.

2. **Open the Audio pane by clicking the Audio button.**

3. **(Optional) On the Monitor playback controls, click Play.**

   By clicking Play, you are able to view the video in your movie. By watching the video while you narrate, you can synchronize your speech to the video track. This step is optional because you don't have to play a movie while recording a narration. Slower Macs might have trouble playing and recording audio at the same time.

4. **Back in the Audio pane, click the Record Voice button to begin recording.**

   When you speak, the meter in the Audio pane helps you monitor the incoming volume level.

5. **Click Stop in the Audio pane.**

   When you complete the recording process, iMovie HD displays the newly recorded segment in the Timeline. Now you can manipulate the audio in the Timeline just as you would any other movie or audio clip. If you aren't happy with the result, you can always press Delete to remove the audio clip and return to Step 4.

Importing audio from a CD

Wondering about adding music from an audio CD? No problem! To import clips from an audio CD, follow these steps:

1. **Insert an audio CD into your Mac's CD drive.**

2. **Open the iMovie HD Audio pane.**

3. **Click the drop-down list box and click Audio CD.**

   If your Mac is connected to the Internet, the song titles appear in the Audio pane. Without the connection, you see generic track titles, such as Track 01 and Track 02.

4. **Click whichever song you'd like to import into iMovie HD.**

5. **Drag it into your Timeline viewer.**

When you're finished importing a song from an audio CD, it appears in the Timeline in one of the audio tracks.

Removing sound from a movie

To remove an audio clip from your movie, select it in the Timeline and press Delete. Removing an audio clip does not have any effect on the position of other audio clips. This ensures that your audio clips stay in sync with existing video clips.

You can also disable all audio for a track: Just mark the check box at the right of the track to disable it. (This is a good way to temporarily mute the track so you can concentrate on something else.) To vary the volume of an audio or video track, press ⌘+Shift+L to show the volume level lines. To raise or lower the volume of a clip (for that great fade-in or fade-out), drag the line up or down. iMovie HD adds points on the volume level lines to indicate where you make changes.

Completing Your Cinematic Masterpiece

Are you done, Mr. Hitchcock? Congratulations, you've made it through the movie-making process! You've shot, composed, and edited your own movie, but now what? Like any good filmmaker, the goal of creating a movie is to have people watch it — therefore, iMovie HD gives you more than one way to share your movies.

✦ **Digital video camcorder:** Transfer your completed movie back to the camcorder and take it with you.

✦ **HomePage:** Share your movie through your .Mac Web site.

✦ **QuickTime movies:** Millions of Macs and PCs around the world have QuickTime software. These computers can view iMovie HD movies, too! The great part about QuickTime movies is that you can use them in a variety of applications, from Web pages to PowerPoint presentations.

✦ **iDVD:** iMovie can prepare your movies for use with iDVD — including chapter markers, which I discuss shortly. The iDVD application lets you create a DVD. Read more about iDVD in Book III, Chapter 5.

Each type of export has its specific purposes and uses — the medium that you choose depends on your audience, video quality needs, and desired format.

Exporting to a camcorder

To export your completed movie to a DV camcorder, choose File⇨Share. In the dialog that appears, choose Videocamera in the toolbar. iMovie HD presents you with settings for exporting to the camcorder. As the dialog warns you, be sure that your camera is in VTR mode and has a writeable tape in it.

Exporting to QuickTime

QuickTime is a multimedia engine in use on millions of computers everywhere. Its popularity makes it a natural for many different uses:

✦ CD-ROM video

✦ Internet delivery

✦ High-quality playback from hard drive or removable disk

To export your completed movie to a QuickTime file, choose File⇨Share. In the dialog that appears, choose QuickTime from the toolbar. iMovie HD presents you with settings for exporting to QuickTime. From the Compress movie for drop-down list box, choose the option that best fits the intended use of your movie.

Exporting to iDVD

If your movie is destined to be part of an iDVD project, click the iDVD button (in the Tool palette) to display the iDVD pane. Click the Create iDVD Project button, and iMovie HD will save your movie (if necessary) and automatically launch iDVD with your movie as a new iDVD project. Life is good, don't you agree? (For a full discussion of iDVD, run — don't walk — to Chapter 5 of Book III.)

Here's another neat function within the iDVD pane — you can choose to add chapter markers in iMovie HD before you export it to iDVD. (In case you haven't used *markers* while watching DVD movies, they allow you to jump immediately to certain points in the film. For example, each scene in a DVD movie is likely to have a chapter marker assigned to it, so you can jump directly to your favorite scenes.)

To add a chapter marker, move the playback head to the desired spot in the Timeline viewer, click the Add Chapter button, and then enter a name for the chapter marker in the list.

Chapter 5: Burn Those DVDs! Using iDVD 5

A number of years ago, I was witness to yet another proud moment in Apple history: the arrival of a powerful DVD recorder in an affordable computer. The *SuperDrive* was revolutionary because suddenly folks could create and view their own professional-quality DVDs.

Today the tradition continues: Apple includes iDVD 5 **free** with today's SuperDrive-equipped Macs as part of iLife '05. With iDVD, you can easily create beautiful presentations with animation and interactive menus that anyone can watch in a standard DVD player or computer DVD drive. And that, friends and neighbors, is the quintessential definition of *cool*.

In this chapter, I show you the basics of creating your first home-cooked DVD movie — you'll even have fun doing it!

What Am I Doing, Anyway?

Creating a DVD is a unique process: Combining talents in art, video, and presentation, DVD authoring demands that you dabble in all these skills. At its core, a *DVD* is simply a collection of digital video files. Unlike a CD-ROM or videotape, however, a DVD also has a fancy presentation and navigation system built into it. With the DVD authoring tools of iDVD, you can

+ **Create a menu** with buttons, text, animated zones, background music, and images to enable viewers to navigate your DVD.

+ **Add still and moving images** to your DVD.

+ **Burn your DVD** to a disc for permanent storage and distribution to friends, family, and co-workers.

Apple overcomes the complexity of DVD authoring with its powerful iDVD 5 software. Use it to create professional-looking menu systems to present your videos and digital slideshows. Then, when you're ready, a few clicks burn the presentation, videos, and slideshows onto a DVD using your SuperDrive. In fact, iDVD 5 will burn a disc only on a system that has a SuperDrive. (Apologies to the CD-RW crowd.)

Use iDVD to reduce the process of manually creating a DVD to three simple steps:

1. **Customize the Menu.**

The *Menu* of a DVD is the main screen that viewers use to navigate the completed DVD. You can use one of the menus supplied by Apple, or you can create your own.

2. **Add media.**

What's a DVD without movies? Use drag-and-drop to fill your DVD with movie files from iMovie, photographs from iPhoto, and music from iTunes. (Read more on these in Chapter 4, Chapter 3, and Chapter 2 of this mini-book, respectively.)

3. **Preview and burn a DVD.**

You can preview your DVD at any point during the design process. When you're satisfied with the results, slip a blank DVD-R in the drive and click the mouse to burn a finished product.

I go into more detail on each of these steps throughout this chapter.

iDVD 5 includes a new feature called *OneStep DVD*, which makes the entire process of creating a DVD virtually automatic — so much for three simple steps I just listed. (Now those same three steps seem so . . . well, *complex!*) However, you'll lose the creative opportunity of choosing everything yourself, so you might want to do things the manual way after all. I discuss OneStep DVD later in this chapter.

Mastering Menus

As a Macintosh owner, you're no doubt familiar with the term *menu.* When it comes to DVD authoring, however, *menu* takes on a new meaning. Instead of the traditional menus that display when you click toward the top of your screen in Mac OS X, a *DVD Menu* is the name of the entire DVD screen that your viewers will see, including all the buttons that you see.

When you launch the iDVD 5 application, you might immediately see the opening application dialog shown in Figure 5-1. This appears if you didn't have a project file open the last time you closed iDVD. You can choose to create a new project, open an existing project, or begin the OneStep DVD process (which I describe later).

Figure 5-1:
The top-level iDVD 5 application dialog.

If you *did* have a project file open, iDVD loads it automatically, displaying a DVD Menu like the one shown in Figure 5-2. Like that of any commercial DVD movie, you'll see this DVD Menu when you load the completed DVD in your favorite DVD player.

Figure 5-2:
A DVD Menu is the heart of your DVD project.

Four components make up a typical DVD Menu:

✦ **Background image or movie:** The backdrop picture that appears behind all the controls

✦ **Buttons:** Icons that represent the video clips and slideshows on the DVD

✦ **Background music:** The background music that plays while the menu is displayed

✦ **Titles:** Text that appears in your DVD Menu

You can change the look and style of the background, buttons, and titles by using one of the Apple-provided themes, or you can customize all parts of the DVD Menu by using your own images, fonts, and buttons.

Themes

If you can't draw anything from a matchbook cover and you didn't have a single class in graphic arts — like yours truly — you'll be happy to know that iDVD offers several professional-looking, pre-packaged themes for you to use. A *theme* is just a group of settings that determine the look and feel of your DVD Menu. (*Many* thanks, Apple. Especially from those of us who can't draw a stick figure without an eraser handy.)

To view the included themes, click the Customize button in the lower-left corner of the iDVD window. When you do, a drawer pops out from the side of the window, as shown in Figure 5-3.

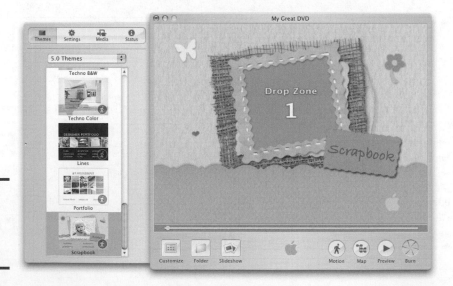

Figure 5-3:
And now presenting the iDVD drawer!

The iDVD drawer contains a panel with buttons, which subdivides the drawer into four sections:

✦ **Themes:** The Themes panel is where you select one of the included themes for your DVD Menu.

✦ **Settings:** Select the Settings panel to tweak the settings of your theme, like the background or audio track.

✦ **Media:** Click this button to organize and import three different types of media. You can choose from Audio (from your hard drive or audio CDs), Photos (images from your iPhoto libraries or other locations on your system), or Movies (manage your existing collection of movie clips or import clips from iMovie HD).

✦ **Status:** The Status tab gives you some extra information about the files in your DVD presentation, like the size of the project. From this tab, you can always see how much space remains on a DVD for you to work with.

Use choices from the Themes and the Settings tabs in the iDVD drawer to personalize your DVD Menu to match your tastes. Start with the Themes panel to choose from a list of professional themes, like Travel Cards, Anime Pop, and Wedding White.

Clicking any one of these themes updates the DVD Menu to reflect your selection. A *theme* contains a background image, a menu audio track, a button style, and settings that affect the onscreen text.

Book III
Chapter 5

Burn Those DVDs!
Using iDVD 5

Most of the animated themes provided by Apple also offer drop zones. A *drop zone* is an area within the menu that can hold a single video clip or still image, which then actually becomes part of the animation itself. For example, the Travel Cards theme has a whopping six drop zones! (Note, however, that a drop zone isn't a link to other content, so you can't use it like a button.) To add a video clip or image to a drop zone, just drag the clip or photo from a Finder window (or the Movie and iPhoto panes within the iDVD drawer, or the iMovie HD window, or the iPhoto window) and drop it on top of the drop zone. To delete the contents of a drop zone, just Control-click (or right-click) the drop zone and click Clear.

A theme includes everything that you need to start building a project, so when you find one that's suitable, you can skip ahead to the section, "Adding Media Files to Your DVD."

On the other hand, if you don't find a theme that fits your needs like a glove, you can customize one of the included themes to match your own style. I'll show you how throughout the rest of this section.

Setting the background

The first thing that you see when you pop your DVD into your DVD player is the background image. The rest of the DVD Menu controls hang out on top of this picture. Besides the beautiful images that iDVD provides in its themes, you're free to use any other image that you prefer: You can use still or motion images as a background and even add background music.

Adding a still background

To change the background of your DVD Menu, perform the following steps:

1. **Click the Customize button in the main iDVD window.**

This opens the iDVD drawer.

2. **Click the Settings tab, as shown in Figure 5-4.**

From here, you can set the various aspects of your DVD Menu.

Figure 5-4:
The menu background is easy to change.

3. **Drag an image from the Finder and drop it into the Background well in the Menu section.**

In Apple-Talk (power user pun intended), a *well* is a box that holds an image or movie — you see a thumbnail preview of its contents. A well also acts as the target for a drag-and-drop operation like this one.

iDVD updates the DVD Menu to reflect your new background choice.

Adding a moving background

The fun doesn't stop there, though. Not only can you use any image from your collection as the backdrop to your DVD Menu, but you can also use any QuickTime movie to animate the background. Outstandingly *sassy!*

Using a movie clip as a background is not the same as adding a clip to a drop zone. Rather, it replaces the original background provided with the theme instead of occupying just a single area within the background, like a drop zone.

When you choose a movie to use as a background, make sure that it's a short clip, preferably no longer than 30 seconds. To make it look really professional, try making the end of the movie clip sync with the beginning of the movie. Because the short clip loops continuously, you don't want too much of a visual difference between the first and last frames of the clip.

To liven up your background with a movie, follow these steps.

1. **Click the Customize button in the main iDVD window.**

   The iDVD drawer opens.

2. **Click the Settings tab.**

   The Settings tab enables you to change the various aspects of your DVD Menu.

3. **Drag a movie from the Finder and drop it into the Background well.**

4. **In the main DVD window, click the Motion button (bottom-right) to see how your background video looks in action.**

5. **Click the Motion button again to stop the background motion.**

Adding audio to your menu

You can make your customized background even cooler — oops, I meant *more professional* — by adding some audio to the mix. To add some background music or audio to your DVD Menu, follow these steps:

1. **Click the Customize button in the main iDVD window.**

   The iDVD drawer opens.

2. **Click the Settings tab.**

   Use choices here to change the background audio that plays while viewing your DVD Menu.

3. **Drag an audio file from the Finder and drop it into the Audio well.**

   iDVD accepts AIFF, MP3, AAC, Apple Lossless, and WAV audio files. If you're a .Mac subscriber, you can download dozens of free, professional-quality audio clips that make good background audio for a DVD.

A word on image dimensions

For best playback results on a standard TV, make sure that your background image has the same dimensions as standard digital video — 640 x 480 pixels. If the dimensions of your image don't match the dimensions of digital video, iDVD will stretch or shrink the image to fit, which might have undesirable effects. When your image is stretched and skewed to fit the DVD Menu, Aunt Harriet might end up looking like Shrek. (Don't forget that you can resize images in iPhoto to help you with this step.)

Because standard TV sets have a different aspect ratio than a digital video clip, activating the Show TV Safe Area option, which you can find under the Advanced menu, is also a good idea. This draws a smaller rectangle within the larger full screen. If you place your buttons within this smaller rectangle and make sure that the important parts of the background image also appear within it, you can be certain that any television will be able to display the DVD properly. Go outside of this "safe area," and you might end up cutting Aunt Harriet's head off in the background image or losing some of your most cherished clips.

You can use QuickTime player or iPhoto to change the dimensions of your background image for import into iDVD. For example, you can use the iPhoto crop feature to alter the overall shape of the image and then resize it within iPhoto. Use the Size setting when you export the image from iPhoto and then save the file in the Pictures folder located in your Home folder so that you can find it easily later. (For more on working in iPhoto, see Book III, Chapter 3.)

If you enjoy a cutting-edge widescreen (16:9) or HD (high-definition) TV display, you naturally might not have the same problem. And because iDVD 5 supports HD video and 16:9 video, maybe prepared to kiss the phrases *pan-and-scan* and *full-screen* goodbye and forget about the Show TV Safe Area feature. If your completed DVD projects are purely for your own enjoyment, that's a great idea. However, don't forget that if you distribute your discs to others with old-fashioned TVs dating back to the archaic '80s and '90s, they might not be pleased with what they see!

4. **Click the Motion button in the main iDVD window (bottom-right) to hear the background audio of your DVD Menu.**

5. **Click the Motion button again to stop the audio.**

When your DVD is complete, your viewers will hear the custom audio play whenever the main DVD Menu is displayed. Here are some suggestions for adding some extra style or mood to your DVD Menu system:

✦ Play a rendition of "Happy Birthday" for a birthday DVD.

✦ Play the "Wedding March" or the song you first danced to as the background for a wedding DVD.

✦ Bring back memories of the family vacation in the backseat of the car with a DVD that plays "99 Bottles of Beer on the Wall" as the background music.

With a little imagination, you can probably come up with numerous ideas to personalize the audio that accompanies your DVD projects.

Adding Media Files to Your DVD

With the background of your DVD Menu in place, it's time to start adding some content to the project — either video or still images. With iDVD, you can add your movies or photographs to a DVD presentation. It's a great way to present and preserve your photographs and videos for years to come . . . never again will your guests groan when you announce that you want to show them home movies.

Adding a Movie Button

iDVD displays video clips in the Menu with small buttons. These Movie Buttons display small previews of the video. To play the video, the user just selects the Button. To create a Movie Button, you need to add some video content to your DVD. To do so, drag a QuickTime movie file from the Finder and drop it into your DVD Menu. If you happen to have iMovie HD open, you can drag a clip from the iMovie HD clip palette into the iDVD window. (Alternatively, open the iDVD drawer and display the Media pane and then click Movies from the drop-down list box — now you can drag clips from your Movies folder.)

Book III
Chapter 5

When you drop a clip into your DVD Menu, a Movie Button appears, as shown in Figure 5-5.

A Movie Button serves two important purposes:

✦ **Preview:** Displays a small thumbnail image of the movie

✦ **Navigation:** Permits a person to navigate the DVD

Burn Those DVDs!
Using iDVD 5

After you drag a movie file into your DVD Menu and create a Movie Button, you can place the button anywhere in the DVD Menu that you wish. To reposition a Movie Button, simply click it and drag it to the desired destination. By default, Movie Buttons snap to an imaginary grid when relocated. To position Movie Buttons outside the confines of this grid, select the Free Position option in the Settings drawer.

An iDVD Menu limits you to 12 buttons. If you'd like to have more than that, add a folder by clicking Folder — which automatically creates a submenu — and drag another 12 movie files into the submenu.

Figure 5-5:
Adding a
button
provides a
link to a
video clip.

Setting the Movie Button style

Like the Menu backgrounds, you can also customize Movie Buttons. To adjust your Movie Buttons, do the following:

1. **Click the Customize button in the main iDVD window.**

The iDVD drawer opens.

2. **Click the Settings tab.**

3. **Click any Movie Button from the DVD Menu to select it.**

When you select a Movie Button, a small slider appears above it. Move this slider to set the default thumbnail picture for that Button in the Menu. If you select the Movie check box, the Movie Button animates in the Menu.

To create a button with a still image instead of a movie clip, drag an image file from a Finder window and drop it on top of the button.

4. **Adjust the button's properties in the Button section of the Settings panel.**

You can customize Movie Buttons in several different ways. Table 5-1 describes the settings and what they do.

Table 5-1	Movie Button Customization Features
Movie Button Property	*What It Does*
Style	Changes the frame shape of the Movie Button.
Snap to Grid	Forces placement of a Movie Button on an imaginary grid.
Free Position	Unlike Snap to Grid, allows Movie Buttons to be placed in a more freeform arrangement.
Transition	Determines the transition that occurs when the button is clicked (before the action occurs).
Size	Adjusts the size of the button and the caption text: Move the slider to the right to increase the button and caption size.

Adding a Slideshow Button

In addition to movies, iDVD 5 gives you the chance to place your favorite digital images on the DVD. In the same way that iDVD handles movies as Movie Buttons in the DVD Menu, you can add a group of images to the Menu as Slideshow Buttons. Slideshow Buttons are nearly identical to Movie Buttons, with one exception: They play back a sequence of digital photographs instead of a movie. Click the Slideshow button at the bottom of the iDVD window to add . . . uh . . . well, a Slideshow Button. (It's not easy to write these books, you know.)

When you add a Slideshow Button, iDVD rearranges the buttons in the DVD Menu to account for the new button.

Add images to the Slideshow

With a new Slideshow Button in place, you can add images to it by following these steps:

1. **Double-click the Slideshow Button that you just added to the Menu to open the Slideshow window.**

2. **To add images to the Slideshow, drag your favorite images from the iDVD drawer (specifically, the Photos section of the Media pane) to the Slideshow window.**

Feel free to drag several photos at once. After the photos are in the Slideshow window, you can drag them around to change their order of appearance.

You can also drag images straight from a Finder window or the iPhoto window itself (if you happen to have it open).

3. **To add some audio, simply drag your favorite audio file from the Finder and drop it on the Audio well within the Slideshow window (or click the drop-down list in the Media pane and click Audio to select an audio track from iTunes).**

4. **When you've completed setting up your Slideshow, click the Return button to return to the main Menu.**

Setting the Slideshow Button preview

Because multiple images comprise a Slideshow, iDVD gives you the opportunity to select which image you want for the DVD preview. To choose an image as the preview, click the Slideshow Button that you added to the Menu to select it. A slider appears above the Slideshow Button. Move this slider to scroll through the various images in the Slideshow. When you find the image that you want to use for the Slideshow Button in the DVD Menu, click the Slideshow Button again to finish the task.

Customizing Titles

Your DVD Menu isn't just a container of images, movies, and sound. It can do text, too! Labeling items in your DVD Menu makes it easier to use, and iDVD makes it a cinch. You can find titles in your DVD Menu in two different locations:

✦ **Main Title:** The main Title usually appears at the top of the DVD Menu. It's the text that uses the largest font.

✦ **Button captions:** Each Movie Button and Slideshow Button has its own caption (a *Title*).

Use a Title to label a video clip with a description or add a date for future reference. As your collection of DVDs grows, you'll be glad that you took the time to properly label your Menu and Movie Buttons.

To change the text of the Title or the captions below Movie Buttons, select the text by clicking it and then click it again to edit it. When you do, a rectangle with a cursor appears to indicate that you can now edit the text. Type the text that you want to appear and then press Return when you're finished.

As I mention earlier in the chapter, you can also customize the font, color, and position of the various Titles by clicking the Customize button at the bottom of the iDVD window. The iDVD drawer appears, and you can click Settings to modify Titles.

Or, you can let iDVD take care of things!

The new OneStep DVD feature in iDVD 5 allows you to plug in your DV camcorder and gawk while *the application itself* imports all the clips you've shot, prepares everything, and then burns the doggone thing — all automatically! And after using OneStep DVD, I can tell you that it does a pretty good job.

OneStep DVD is a neat way of producing a "rough" DVD right after a special event, so that you can give it as a gift (or sell it, if you're in business). Other possibilities include sample presentations on DVD that you can supply to

clients, or a daily DV journal that you distribute among members of your class to keep everyone current on what's happening.

To begin using OneStep DVD, click the OneStep DVD button on the iDVD 5 top-level menu (refer to Figure 5-1). iDVD prompts you to connect the FireWire cable from your DV camcorder, and then to turn on the camcorder and set it in VCR mode. Click OK, and load a blank DVD.

A completed OneStep DVD plays automatically when you load it.

Checking Things Out with a Preview

Hey, you're now a DVD-authoring professional! (Although you're not getting paid like one.) You'll no doubt want to see the results of your efforts. Review your work often to make sure that the results are up to your stellar ambitions. To help you out, iDVD 5 gives you a full-featured Preview mode, in which you can view your DVD creation much as you would with a traditional DVD player. To preview your DVD, just click the Preview button at the bottom right of the main iDVD window.

Previewing your DVD project also gives you the opportunity to check your content. After all, you don't want the "Wedding March" to play in the background of your birthday party footage or "The Old Gray Mare" at your in-laws' anniversary bash. Because you eventually want to commit this DVD presentation to real DVD media, it makes sense to scrupulously preview your presentation; you'll avoid wasting blank DVDs.

The latest version of iDVD is far less finicky about the media you feed it — in fact, if your SuperDrive can record using a specific type of blank DVD, you can bet that iDVD now supports that media as well. Besides DVD-R, iDVD 5 can burn to DVD-RW, DVD+R, and DVD+RW. Remember, however, that your SuperDrive *must* be able to burn that type of disc, too. iDVD can't perform miracles. If you're using a Power Mac G5, an iMac G5, a Mac Mini, or an eMac that's a year old or less, it's a good bet that you can burn DVD-RW, DVD+R, and DVD+RW media, too.

**Book III
Chapter 5**

**Burn Those DVDs!
Using iDVD 5**

Saving and Burning a DVD

After your DVD Menu is complete and the project looks great in Preview, it's time for the final step in the process. iDVD makes it just as easy to burn your DVD as it was to lay out the menu and add media to it.

1. **Click the Burn button at the bottom of the iDVD window to begin recording a DVD.**

   When you click it, the Burn button changes into something that looks like a serious nuclear warning. (No need to run for cover, though. iDVD 5 is powerful . . . but not *that* powerful.)

   iDVD asks you to insert a blank DVD-R into the SuperDrive. When this happens, you might see a message that reads like this:

   ```
   Disc Insertion... Waiting for Device to Become Ready...
   ```

2. **Insert a blank DVD-R into the SuperDrive.**

   As I mention in the previous section, you can use any type of blank DVD media that's supported by your SuperDrive — however, keep in mind that only DVD-Rs are likely to work in older DVD players. The latest generation of DVD players will usually recognize DVD+R media, too.

3. **After you load the disc, wait a moment for iDVD to recognize that the ball is in its court.**

   iDVD begins the process of burning the DVD. The length of this process varies depending on a few factors:

   - **DVD burner speed:** The faster the drive, the shorter the wait

   - **Amount of material:** The more content on your DVD, the longer the wait

   As the burning proceeds, iDVD updates you with progress messages. Don't worry if you don't understand all the messages that it displays. The language of the DVD creation process is a technical one, and sometimes iDVD speaks this language. Just ignore the messages as the burning proceeds.

   Because iDVD has to encode all the content before the burn can take place, it might take a couple of hours to create a DVD. After the first DVD is done, though, iDVD lets you create additional DVDs in a fraction of the time. It will keep asking you for additional discs until you cancel the operation.

   (Insert plug here.) If you want to find out what all these messages mean — as well as how to burn all sorts of data, audio, and exotic CD and DVD formats — I would naturally recommend *CD & DVD Recording For Dummies*, 2nd Edition, by yours truly (Wiley). It's a comprehensive guide to everything optical for both Macs and Windows PCs.

4. **When iDVD completes the burning process, remove the disc from the drive and pop it into any consumer-grade DVD player.**

   Alternatively, you can leave the DVD in the drive, fire up DVD Player by clicking its icon in the Applications folder, and view your new work of art right on your Mac.

Personally, I find that iDVD 5 gives me all the features that I need. If you need industrial-strength DVD authoring, Apple offers DVD Studio Pro 3 software, which allows you to author DVDs like those that you find in the store. The learning curve is a little steeper, naturally, and the application carries a professional price tag hovering around the $500 mark. However, with a little effort, DVD Studio Pro 3 can be mastered by anyone who's an expert at iDVD!

**Book III
Chapter 5**

**Burn Those DVDs!
Using iDVD 5**

Chapter 6: Becoming a Superstar with GarageBand

In This Chapter

↳ **Navigating the GarageBand window**

↳ **Adding tracks and loops to your song**

↳ **Repeating loops and extending your song**

↳ **Adding effects to instruments**

↳ **Exporting your song to iTunes**

When I was a kid, I always thought that *real* rock stars trashed their instruments after a hard night's worth of jamming — you know, like The Who, Led Zeppelin, KISS, and the Rolling Stones. Guitars got set on fire, or pounded into the stage, or thrown into the crowd like beads during a Mardi Gras parade.

I can make my own music now, but you'll never see me trash my instrument because I compose music on my Mac with *GarageBand,* Apple's latest addition to the iLife application suite. You can solo on all sorts of instruments, and even add horns, drums, and a funky bass line for backup . . . all with absolutely no musical experience (and, in my case, very little talent to boot)!

In this chapter, I show you how to create a song using GarageBand, and then you'll make use of that shiny digital hub and listen to your own music in iTunes. (And you know what that means — your own soundtracks in iDVD and iMovie HD.)

Your Digital Instruments Await

Figure 6-1 illustrates the GarageBand window. Doesn't look much like a rock band, does it? Don't worry; these controls will make perfect sense by the end of this chapter. I start with introductions all around:

✦ **The timeline:** This scrolling area might remind you of the timeline in iMovie HD, and the concept is indeed the same: The timeline holds the music loops (more on loops shortly) that you add or record, and scrolls automatically while your song is playing. You can select and move loops effortlessly across your timeline.

✦ **The track list:** Each *track* is a separate instrument that plays one part of your song. In Figure 6-1, the track is a Grand Piano. The track list displays all the instruments you're using. Each track scrolls across the timeline, all the way to the end of your song. Like loops, you can add, delete, or modify tracks as necessary to change the sound of your music.

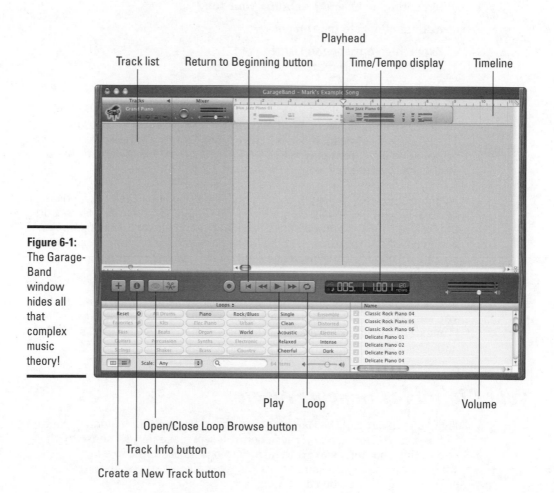

Figure 6-1: The Garage-Band window hides all that complex music theory!

Playhead

Track list   Return to Beginning button   Time/Tempo display   Timeline

Play   Loop   Volume

Open/Close Loop Browse button

Track Info button

Create a New Track button

✦ **Loops:** Each *loop* in your song is the sound of an instrument played in a specific style and tempo. To compose a song, you can drag loops from the Loop Browser into an empty track.

✦ **The playhead:** (Another similarity to iMovie HD, where you also have a playhead that works in the same fashion.) In GarageBand, the *playhead* is a moving vertical line that indicates the notes currently playing in your song as it scrolls by in the timeline. You can change your position in your song by dragging the playhead to a new location.

You can also consider the playhead as the insertion point for new loops, as well as loops and regions of the timeline that you've copied onto the Clipboard — they appear at the current playhead position.

✦ **Play:** This familiar button works just like the Play button in iTunes or the Play button on any audio CD player. As your song plays, the Play button glows blue; to stop the music, press Play again. (If you press Play again, your song starts at the current playhead position.)

✦ **The Create a New Track button:** Most songs you compose have multiple tracks; click this button to add a new track to the list.

✦ **Time/Tempo display:** Musicians — and those that have used software synthesizers before — will immediately recognize this display, which shows the current playhead position in seconds. To change the *tempo* of your song (a fancy word for speed), click the tempo indicator.

✦ **Track info:** Click this button to display more information on an instrument. You can also add effects like Echo from the Info dialog.

✦ **Show/Hide Loop Browser:** This button reveals (or banishes) the Loop Browser at the bottom of the GarageBand window.

✦ **Return to Beginning:** This is a handy button: Click it to jump to the beginning of your song. The playhead automatically returns to the beginning of the timeline.

✦ **Volume:** You get one guess on this one . . . and you're right! Drag the slider to raise or lower the volume.

These main controls are really all you need to start composing your first song. I'll introduce you to other fun stuff throughout the rest of the chapter.

Your First Steps as a Composer

I don't think Mozart began a new work this way, but you can start a new song at any time by pressing ⌘+N. You'll see the New Project dialog shown in Figure 6-2, where you can name your new song and choose the tempo (which determines the speed of the music). Click Create, and the GarageBand window appears.

Figure 6-2:
A new song
in Garage-
Band begins
here.

A song can have only one tempo in GarageBand; however, you can change the tempo at any time.

If you're not a musician, don't fret too much (sorry about that) when it comes to nuances like the time signature (Time) of the song and its key. The defaults of 4/4 (Time) and C Major (Key) are very common in today's popular music. To discover more about time signatures and keys, find a good book on music theory.

Adding a track to the list

You'll notice that a new song is automatically awarded two things: a single track using Grand Piano (must be a favorite of Steve Jobs) and a tiny keyboard window. The keyboard window allows you to record your own loops in the Grand Piano track by clicking notes with your mouse. Unfortunately, this is a rather ponderous chore, so hip musicians prefer to buy a MIDI keyboard or instrument and connect it to the Mac through a USB port. You can choose from all sorts of MIDI instruments; most are keyboards, but I've even seen a MIDI saxophone. Apple offers a 49-key MIDI USB keyboard from M-Audio for around $100. If you add a USB keyboard to your system, the keyboard window won't appear . . . but for now, dismiss the keyboard window by clicking its Close button.

If you actually want to use a Grand Piano in your new song, all is well. However, if you don't need it for your new alternative rock single, click Track in the GarageBand menu and click Delete Track to remove the unnecessary track from the list.

GarageBand provides two basic types of tracks that you can use in your music:

✦ **Real instrument tracks:** A *real instrument track* is an actual audio recording, just like you'd make with a cassette recorder. Real instrument tracks allow you to add your voice or a physical instrument like an electric guitar or flute (with or without a MIDI connection) to your songs.

✦ **Software instrument tracks:** These tracks actually don't exist as conventional audio recordings. Rather, they're constructed from loops (mathematic algorithms that are controlled by GarageBand), but they sound just as good as real instrument tracks. (Think of an old-time piano roll — a sequence of note instructions read by the instrument.)

If you're like me (and can't play an instrument at all), you'll be using software instrument tracks exclusively, and that's what I'll use in this demonstration. (In other words, you and I get to use our ears and creativity, and GarageBand takes care of the rest.)

Your song needs at least one track, so follow these steps to add one:

1. **Click the Add button (which bears a plus sign) at the bottom-left corner of the GarageBand window.**

The New Track dialog, as shown in Figure 6-3, appears.

2. **Click the Software Instrument tab.**

3. **Here's the beginning of the fun part: You get to pick an instrument category from the left column. Click your favorite type of instrument.**

For this track, I pick Bass.

4. **Click the unique instrument from the general category in the right list box.**

In this case, I need a good backup for a James Brown-style funk song, so I pick Slapped Electric Bass, as you can see in Figure 6-3.

Figure 6-3:
Add a new
track to your
song.

5. **Click Create to create the track.**

Your GarageBand window contains the first track for your new song.

If you decide something doesn't work while composing your song, don't forget that you can undo most actions in GarageBand by pressing ⌘+Z immediately afterward.

Selecting and adding instrument loops

If you've followed my example to this point, GarageBand knows what instrument you want in your first track, but the track is empty! To add music to your song, you need to select software instrument loops and add them to your track, using the Loop Browser.

Click the Loop Browser button (which is marked with a cool-looking eye icon) to display the collection of hundreds of loops provided by Apple (see Figure 6-4). The Loop Browser can be displayed using either column or button view mode, and you can toggle between them by clicking the button in the lower-left corner of the Loop Browser. (I use button view mode here.)

Loop Browser button

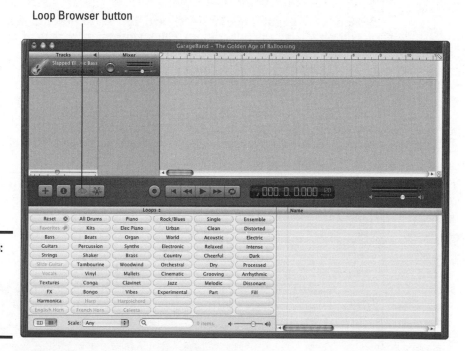

Figure 6-4:
The Loop Browser, shown in button mode.

Because I'm using a bass track in this example, the Bass button is the likely candidate for the best-sounding loops. When you click it, you'll see a list of different loops. Because I'm interested only in the software instruments, click any loop marked with a green musical note icon. I'll pick a favorite of mine: Slap Bass 02.

When you click a loop, GarageBand begins playing it so that you can tell whether that sound is what you're looking for. If you choose another loop in the list, GarageBand switches immediately to the new loop. This is a great way to compare two loops, and you'll quickly find that you can identify just the loop you're looking for in a jiffy.

Check out the familiar-looking Search box at the bottom of the Loop Browser. Click in the box, type a keyword to search for a particular instrument or sound, and then press Return. To reset your search and try another keyword, click the X icon that appears at the right side of the Search box.

Click the Reset button in the Loop Browser to choose another instrument or genre.

You can pick from any category of loops, not just those that are supposed to work the best — there's no rule that says that you can't use a piano loop with your guitar! The instrument stays the same, no matter what type of loop you use, and you can get some really great riffs mixing styles and instruments. Just make sure that you use Software Instrument tracks and software instrument loops, as marked with the green musical note in the Loop Browser.

I use Slap Bass 02 for this song. To add the loop to your track, drag it into your Slapped Electric Bass track and drop it at the very beginning of the timeline. The GarageBand window should now look like Figure 6-5.

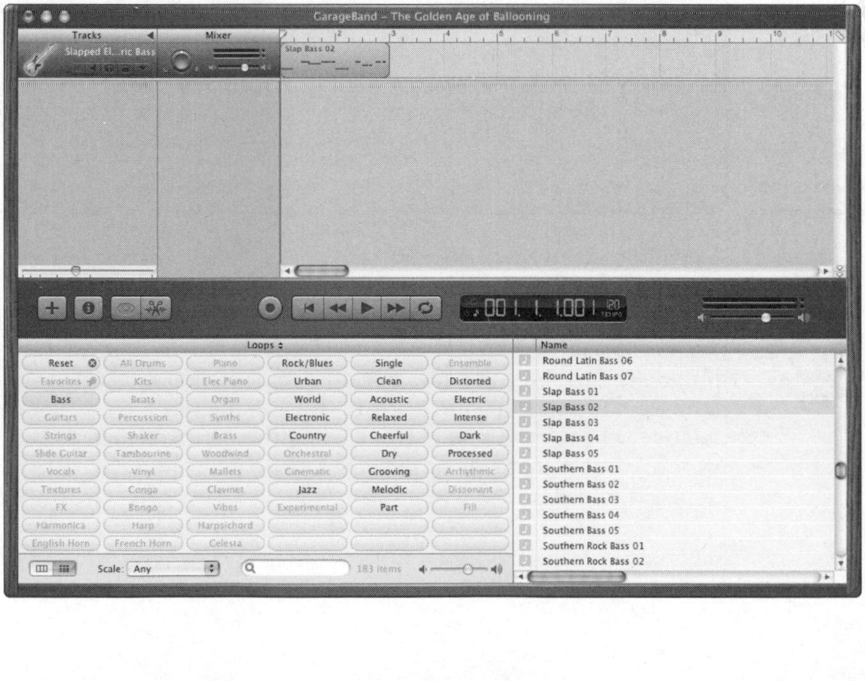

**Book III
Chapter 6**

**Becoming a
Superstar with
GarageBand**

Figure 6-5:
A funky "Seinfeld" bass loop is in the house!

You're not limited to a single loop in each track. You could drag a different loop after the first Slap Bass 02 loop, if you like. However, if you want that same beat throughout your entire song, I'll show you how to extend the beat in a page or two.

Now you're ready to add more tracks — one for each instrument you want in your song — and then you should add at least one loop for each track. A loop can start anywhere in the timeline, so instruments can solo or play simultaneously . . . whatever floats your musical cruise ship. As you can see in Figure 6-6, the Hardest-Working Man in Show Business would be downright proud of my composition so far, with electric guitar, drums, and all-out organ involved!

Figure 6-6: An entire recording session, with four tracks ready to go.

You can mute a track, making it easier to listen to specific tracks and how they work together in your song. Click the tiny speaker button under the track name in the list, and it turns blue to indicate that the track has been muted. To turn off the mute, click the speaker icon again. In the same manner, you can crank up or drop the volume (and even change the stereo balance) of each individual track using the controls next to the track name. After all, a solo instrument deserves to be a little louder!

Editing and moving loops

Even after you add all the instruments and loops, your song isn't finished. Click Play, and you'll find that it probably doesn't last very long. After the playhead moves past the last loop in the timeline, the song is done. What you need is a way to extend the loops and make 'em last longer! There's gotta be a way to do that, right?

Hey, this is an application from Apple. There are actually three ways to extend your song! You can

✦ **Resize the loop.** To change the length of a loop, hover your mouse cursor over either the loop's lower left or right edge. When your cursor changes to a vertical line with an arrow pointing away from the loop, that's your cue to click and drag. As you drag, you'll see that most loops expand to fill the space you're making, repeating the beats in perfect time. If you can't resize the loop, read the following bullet.

✦ **Repeat the loop.** Some loops can't be resized because of the length or the number of beats in the loop; however, these loops can be repeated. Move your mouse cursor over the upper edge of the loop until it turns into a vertical line with a circular arrow, indicating that you can click and repeat the loop. GarageBand automatically adds multiple copies of the same loop, as shown with the Rock Drum kit in Figure 6-7, for as far as you drag the loop.

**Book III
Chapter 6**

**Becoming a
Superstar with
GarageBand**

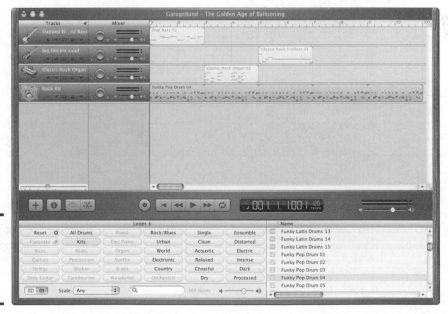

Figure 6-7: Repeating a loop extends your song.

✦ **Add a new loop.** You can switch to a different loop to change the flow of the music. Again, the instrument stays the same, but it's as if your studio musician switches to another style!

Feel free to use Tiger's standard cut and paste editing keys to cut, copy, and paste loops wherever you like on the timeline. Or, you can click a loop and drag it where you want it. Even tracks can be dragged into a different order on the Track list.

Figure 6-8 illustrates my biggest hit — at least among my friends and family members with truly good taste in techno-rock! Notice that several instruments get a chance to solo, giving the music a more complex and interesting sound.

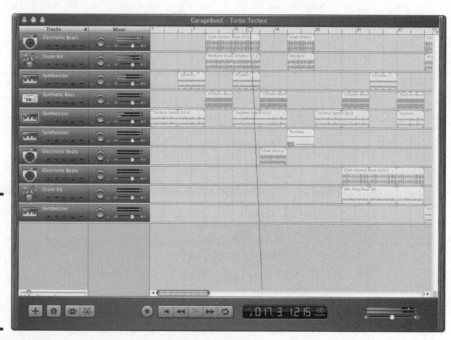

Figure 6-8:
"Turbo Techno" — the author's best work, featured at a real live dance club!

Adding Effects the Easy Way

How would you like to add effects to your music, just like the professionals? No problem! Each instrument in your track list can be customized by adding echo and reverb (great for those wailing guitar solos), or perhaps you'd like to fine-tune the sound of that funky bass line by using GarageBand's built-in equalizer settings.

To make adjustments to a track, follow these steps:

1. **Click the desired track in the track list to select it.**

2. **Click the Track Info button.**

3. **Click the Details triangle at the bottom to display the advanced settings (see Figure 6-9).**

Figure 6-9:
Adding effects to a track to customize the sound of the instrument.

**Book III
Chapter 6**

Becoming a
Superstar with
GarageBand

4. **Mark the check box of each effect you want to add.**

5. **Adjust the effect to your taste.**

   For example, you can change the amount of reverb by dragging the corresponding slider.

6. **(Optional) You can save your changes as a custom instrument for use in later songs. Click the Save Instrument button, and GarageBand prompts you for a name.**

7. **Click the Close button on the Track Info window to return to GarageBand.**

Now you're ready to play your song again to review the changes.

Listening to Your New Hit in iTunes

Yes! Your song is *perfect* — now, how are you going to share it with your adoring public? (Or, more likely, how can you listen to it yourself without having to launch GarageBand every time?) No problem: GarageBand can share the songs you create by exporting them to iTunes. And from there (as you can read throughout this mini-book), you can use your original music in iMovie HD and iDVD.

Your first step is to configure the iTunes preferences within GarageBand. Choose GarageBand➪Preferences, and then click the Export button in the Preference window toolbar to display the settings shown in Figure 6-10. GarageBand supplies defaults for the target playlist within iTunes, as well as the composer and album names to assign to your exported songs. To change these defaults, click in each box and type your own text. GarageBand names each exported song the same as the name you entered when you created the song.

Figure 6-10: Assign playlist, composer, and album names for your exported songs.

After you set your Export preferences, you can create an MP3 file from your song in just two simple steps:

1. **In GarageBand, open the song that you want to share.**

2. **Choose File⇨Export to iTunes.**

iTunes automatically launches and highlights the new (or existing) playlist that contains your new song.

Time to jam! To read more on advanced GarageBand techniques, pick up a copy of *GarageBand For Dummies,* by Bob LeVitus (Wiley).

Chapter 7: No, It's Not Called iQuickTime

In This Chapter

✔ **Viewing movies**

✔ **Listening to audio**

✔ **Converting media to different formats**

✔ **Keeping track of your favorite media**

✔ **Tweaking QuickTime preferences**

*Q*uickTime is a set of exciting technologies that gives you access to the greatest multimedia experience around. Despite its power, don't be surprised if you don't even realize that you're using it sometimes. Built with the average Joe in mind, QuickTime takes multimedia to new heights without forcing its users to become rocket scientists in the process. And dig that *sassy* chrome sheen — not bad for a software application!

QuickTime Can Do That?

QuickTime was created by Apple to perform all sorts of multimedia functions. Although normally associated with movie playback, QuickTime can do much more. Whether movies, audio, animation, or music, QuickTime acts as the main engine that drives all your multimedia needs.

✦ **Media player:** QuickTime's main claim to fame is playing all sorts of media — and I do mean *all* sorts. Table 7-1 lists some of the media types that QuickTime can play.

The real beauty of QuickTime is that it transparently handles playback of all these media formats and more. You don't even really have to know what each of these formats is to play them. QuickTime takes care of that for you.

✦ **File converter:** The world of multimedia includes all kinds of file formats — so many, in fact, that it can take a rocket scientist to figure them all out. Fortunately, beyond its abilities as a world-class media player, QuickTime also has a full suite of conversion tools at its heart. QuickTime can import many kinds of media and spit them back out into practically any other format that it supports. Again, QuickTime handles

the messy details behind the scenes for you. You don't need to know a
.mov file from an .mp4 file to import and export to and from either
format. QuickTime's got you covered.

✦ **Internet media tool:** When it comes to using media from the Internet,
QuickTime is in a league all its own. With its plug-in feature, QuickTime
takes its functionality to the Web browser. In addition to playing the
usual movies and audio files found on the World Wide Web, QuickTime
can play (or display) 3-D scenes and animations. If that weren't enough,
QuickTime even lets you interact with some media. For example, with
QuickTime, you can navigate within 3-D worlds or play Flash games.

Table 7-1	QuickTime Playback Formats
Media Type	*File Types*
Movie	.mov, .avi*, .mpg, .dv, .mp4
Audio	.aiff, .wav, .mp3, .au, .sfil, .aac
Graphics	.jpg, .tif, .pct, .bmp
Music	.mid, .kar
3-D	QTVR (QuickTime Virtual Reality)
Animation	.swf

**Movies in AVI format use a wide range of compression schemes, many of them proprietary (like movies
produced with the DivX plug-in). For this reason, QuickTime might not be able to play some AVI movies
that you download.*

Playing Media with QuickTime

QuickTime makes a world of movies, audio, graphics, and music instantly
available to you. Whether you want to view professional movie trailers or
listen to a garage band's new single, QuickTime faithfully reproduces nearly
any media format that you feed it.

At the center of the action: QuickTime Player

At the heart of QuickTime's playback functionality is the QuickTime Player
application. To launch QuickTime Player, double-click its icon in the Finder.
You can also launch QuickTime Player from the Finder by double-clicking a
media file that QuickTime can play. (See Table 7-1 earlier in this chapter for a
listing of these file types.)

Don't make the mistake of thinking that QuickTime and QuickTime Player are
the same thing: *QuickTime* is a technology that hides in the background waiting for instructions to do something with media; *QuickTime Player* is an application that uses the QuickTime technologies. You'll do media conversions,

playback, and editing with QuickTime Player. What you won't see is the QuickTime technology in action behind the scenes.

You can also launch QuickTime Player from its oh-so-convenient Dock icon. For more on the Dock, read Book II, Chapter 2.

QuickTime has two versions: free or Pro. The main differences between the free and Pro versions of QuickTime lie in the QuickTime Player application itself. The free version just plays media, and the Pro version adds extra features to QuickTime Player, such as converting 'twixt different media formats and full-screen playback. If you're using QuickTime Pro, all items listed in this chapter will work as described.

If, however, you notice that a feature is dimmed out or missing altogether, you might be using the free QuickTime license. To find out whether you're using a free or Pro license, open the System Preferences and navigate to the QuickTime panel. If you've registered as a QuickTime Pro user, you can find its registration information here, as shown in Figure 7-1. If you're not a registered user, you can purchase the upgrade at `www.apple.com/quicktime`. The upgrade will cost you $29.99, at the time of this writing.

Figure 7-1:
Check
System
Preferences
to see
which
license you
have.

Opening QuickTime movies

To begin viewing and hearing — aw, what the heck, how about *absorbing* — multimedia files, choose File⇨Open File from the QuickTime Player application. This isn't the only way to open a file with QuickTime Player, though. Some of the other ways to open files with QuickTime Player are

✦ **Drag a file to the QuickTime Player icon on the Dock.**

✦ **Double-click the media file in the Finder.** If it has a QuickTime-style icon (a blue letter Q), it will automatically open in QuickTime Player.

Operating QuickTime Player

When you open a QuickTime file, QuickTime Player creates a new window to display it. All QuickTime Player windows share some common features.

+ **Close, Minimize, and Zoom controls:** These three controls appear at the top left-hand corner of most windows in Mac OS X. You probably recognize them by their colors: red, yellow, and green, respectively.

+ **Resize handle:** Drag the lower right-hand corner of QuickTime Player to resize its movie for playback. Hold Shift while dragging to break free from constrained resizing. If the document contains sound media only, the window will grow or shrink in a horizontal direction when you resize it.

Any resizing that you perform makes no changes to the original file. QuickTime provides it for your convenience during playback.

Although some window features are common to all QuickTime Player windows, many features depend on the type of media that you wish to play. Table 7-2 lists some of the window features that you might find and the media types associated with those features.

Table 7-2	QuickTime Player Window Features Based on Media
Window Feature	*Media Type That Uses This Feature*
Play button	All time-based media: movies, audio, animations, and MIDI
Rewind button	All time-based media: movies, audio, animations, and MIDI
Fast Forward	All time-based media: movies, audio, animations, and MIDI
Timeline	All time-based media: movies, audio, animations, and MIDI
Volume slider	All media with one or more audio tracks
Audio controls	All media with one or more audio tracks
Video controls	All media with one or more video tracks
Zoom buttons	QTVR 3-D media
Equalizer display	All media with one or more audio tracks

To make your life easier, QuickTime does a lot of work for you behind the scenes each time that it opens a media file. Although you might think that there are different combinations of controls in QuickTime Player, the reality is that the various media windows are more similar than they are different. Figure 7-2 shows the location of various QuickTime Player controls.

Playback controls

Playback head

Video player

Figure 7-2:
QuickTime
Player
sports
different
controls
depending
on the
media you
play.

Audio

Volume slider

Playing media

Playback begins as you might suspect — by clicking the Play button. While a file is playing, the Play button toggles to a Stop button. Click that button to stop playback, which toggles the button back to Play.

Clicking the buttons with double-arrows on them advances the playback head at high speed in the direction of the arrows. If the file has audio in it, you hear the playback at high speed, which sounds like an episode of those helium-inhaling Chipmunks. (Remember? *Meee, I waaant a hooola hooop.*) Despite its comical sound, it's helpful for quickly scanning through a file. Click the buttons with a single arrow to advance to the beginning or end of a file.

You can also advance through the file by dragging the playback head in either direction. This action is permissible while the file is playing or when it's stopped. Unlike when you use the buttons, however, you miss out on the high-speed sound and video.

To adjust the volume of a movie, simply move the volume slider left or right.

You can control playback by using the keyboard as well. Table 7-3 summarizes the keyboard shortcuts for playback.

Table 7-3	Keyboard Shortcuts for Common Playback Functions
Keyboard Shortcut	*What It Does*
Spacebar	Starts or stops the player
Left/right arrow (←/→)	Advances the playback head (either one frame at a time or in slow motion)
Option+←/→	Moves the playback head to the beginning or end of the file
Option+↑/↓	Sets the volume to Maximum and Minimum, respectively
Up/down arrow (↑/↓)	Increases/decreases the volume of the current movie

Advanced playback features

QuickTime Player offers advanced playback features that go beyond simple play and stop functions. Keep in mind, however, that some of the advanced features of QuickTime Player are meant only for registered QuickTime Pro users. The general rule is that registered Pro users of QuickTime Player can modify QuickTime content. If you aren't registered as a QuickTime Pro user, you can take advantage of only playback features in QuickTime Player.

Video playback

To adjust video playback quality, choose Window➪Show A/V Controls or press ⌘+K. When you do, QuickTime presents you with the A/V Controls dialog. The audio and video settings that you can change from this dialog (see Figure 7-3) include

✦ Volume

✦ Bass

✦ Treble

✦ Balance

✦ Brightness

✦ Contrast

✦ Tint

✦ Color

✦ Jog shuttle speed

✦ Playback speed

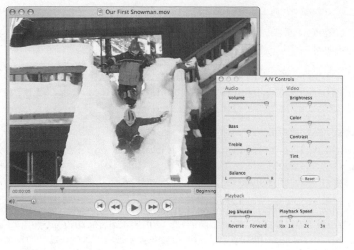

Figure 7-3:
Setting the video controls and audio controls for a movie.

Looping features

Sometimes you might want to play a piece of media more than once. In these situations, you need to loop the playback. To force a movie to loop, choose View➪Loop or press ⌘+L. Press ⌘+L again to turn off looping.

If you want to get fancy, you can also play a movie in a forward direction followed by playback in reverse. Apple calls this *looping back and forth*. To do this, choose View➪Loop Back and Forth.

Movie info

To see more information about the files that you're playing, ask the expert: QuickTime Player. To view basic information about a movie, choose Window➪Show Movie Info or press ⌘+I. The resulting window displays the following data:

✦ **Source:** Location of the file

✦ **Format:** Compressor and dimensions of the file

✦ **FPS:** Preferred rate of playback in frames per second (fps)

✦ **Playing FPS:** Actual rate of playback in fps (available during playback only)

✦ **Data Size:** Size of the file

✦ **Data Rate:** Preferred rate of playback (in bytes per second)

✦ **Current Time:** Position of the playback head (in units of time)

✦ **Duration:** Length of the movie file (in units of time)

+ **Normal Size:** Default movie dimensions

+ **Current Size:** Actual movie dimensions (if you've resized the movie since opening the file)

These bits and pieces of information are *read-only*, which means that you can't change them from the Movie Info window.

Movie properties

In addition to general movie information, you can also peek inside a QuickTime movie to see what makes it tick. To display the Movie Properties window, choose Window⇨Show Movie Properties or press ⌘+J.

The Movie Properties window displays the tracks via the pop-up menu on the top left of the Movie Properties window. Selecting a track causes the pop-up menu on the top right to display a set of properties that pertain to the selected track.

Unlike the Movie Info window, the Movie Properties window does let you change many aspects of a movie. For example, to resize, skew, or even rotate a movie's video track, follow these steps:

1. **With QuickTime Player, open a QuickTime movie.**

2. **Press ⌘+J to open its Movie Properties window.**

3. **From the Tracks pop-up menu of the Properties window, choose the first available Video Track.**

4. **From the Properties pop-up menu, choose Size.**

Back on track

Every file that you open with QuickTime Player consists of one or more tracks. A *track* contains one (and only one) type of media. For example, a typical QuickTime movie might comprise two tracks:

⤳ **Video track:** Stores the video data of the movie

⤳ **Sound track:** Stores the audio data of the movie

In contrast, opening an audio file with QuickTime Player might have only a single sound track. Other files don't have a video or sound track at all: Shockwave and Flash (.swf) files, for example, usually contain only one Flash track. MIDI files have yet another type of track. Luckily, QuickTime makes it simple for you to ignore these technical trivia facts altogether (which most of us prefer).

5. **Click the Adjust button.**

   Red adjustment handles appear in the movie player. Resize and rotate to your heart's content!

6. **After you adjust the track's size to your liking, click the Done button.**

With a similar approach, you can change many other properties of a track, such as Annotations settings.

QuickTime: The Super Converter

QuickTime Pro also makes a great tool for converting media files. As your collection of multimedia grows, you'll eventually find yourself wishing that certain files were in a different format. For example, you might want to convert a QuickTime movie to a digital video (DV) file for use with iMovie. With a few clicks, QuickTime Pro can open a media file in one of dozens of formats and convert it to most any other format that QuickTime understands. To do so, you must import the file into QuickTime and then export it into the format that you prefer.

Importing files

For most operations, you can open a file with QuickTime Player by using the usual File⇨Open File menu item. For some formats, however, this won't work. In these instances, QuickTime gives you the chance to import a file. The difference between *open* and *import* is subtle but important: If QuickTime can natively handle a file's media, you can use the Open menu. If it can't handle a media's data natively, it must import the file. The import process converts the file to a format that QuickTime can use. To start the import process, just choose File⇨Import.

For example, QuickTime doesn't normally display text files. Using the Import command, however, converts a text file into a movie file. Then you can view the text in a traditional movie player window.

Table 7-4 lists the file types that QuickTime can import. For a more comprehensive discussion of the formats you can import, visit the QuickTime area on the Apple Web site at

`www.apple.com/quicktime/products/qt/specifications.html`

Table 7-4	QuickTime Import File Types
Category	*File Types*
Audio	AIFF/AIFC, AAC, Audio CD, MP3, Sound Designer II, System 7 Sound, µLaw (AU), WAV
Video	AVI, DV, Motion JPEG, MPEG-1, MPEG-4
Images	BMP, GIF, JPEG/JFIF, MacPaint, PICT, PNG, Photoshop (with layers), SGI, Targa, FlashPix, TIFF
Animation	3DMF, Animated GIF, FLC/FLI, Flash, PICS
Other	KAR (Karaoke), MIDI, QuickDraw GX, QuickTime Image File, Text

Exporting files

After you open or import a media file, QuickTime Pro will let you export it to one of many formats. For example, you might export a QuickTime movie to an AVI movie for those Windows users who don't have QuickTime installed. To export a movie, choose File⇨Export. In the dialog that appears, select the desired output format from the Export pop-up menu. Each export type also has a set of options. To view them, click the Options button on the right side of the Export dialog.

Make QuickTime the Center of Your Digital Universe

Although QuickTime Player and Pro are great at actively importing, exporting, and altering all kinds of media, most Mac OS X owners don't care about these features. For those who could care less what the media type is for an e-mail attachment, QuickTime transparently handles the chore of displaying the file without having to know all the technical details behind it. With QuickTime as your ally, you can watch the latest *Star Wars* movie trailer, view an image in a Web page, or (if you're like me) you can listen to Bob Hope jaw with Bing Crosby (if you have a collection of classic radio shows in MP3 format). QuickTime makes a great tool for viewing and exploring all sorts of exciting multimedia content.

Favorites

The quickest way to keep track of your media files is with the Favorites menu. It offers one-click access to the media files that you use most. To add a file to the Favorites menu, do the following:

1. **Open your favorite media file.**

2. **Press ⌘+D or choose Window⇨Favorites⇨Add Movie as Favorite.**

Now, anytime you want to watch and/or hear this file, you simply choose it from the Favorites menu.

You can remove files later from the Favorites menu by performing these steps:

1. **Choose Window⇨Favorites⇨Show Favorites.**

2. **In the Favorites window that appears, select the file that you wish to remove.**

3. **Press the Delete key to remove the file from the Favorites menu.**

Free content for all

QuickTime Player offers you one-click access to a variety of multimedia content, including news, entertainment, and educational features. Naturally, an Internet connection is required. To view the QuickTime Player Content Guide, click Window and click Show Content Guide (see Figure 7-4).

Figure 7-4: The QuickTime Player Content Guide appears in a separate window.

Book III Chapter 7

No, It's Not Called iQuickTime

When you do, a new window opens in the Player — this is the Content Guide's main menu. From here, you can click any of the provided links just as you might click a link in a Web page.

TIP

Clicking any item in the Content Guide opens a Web page in your preferred browser.

QuickTime and your browser

QuickTime is equally at home in a Web browser. Like the QuickTime Player application, the QuickTime Web plug-in offers convenient playback utilities directly in your Web browser. To view a movie in a browser window, simply navigate to a Web page that contains a QuickTime movie; QuickTime automatically loads the movie and plays it in the Web page. In many cases, you can even save a movie from a Web page — just click the triangle icon at the far right of the movie controller, or Control-Click/right-click in the movie window. A menu appears, giving you two options to save the movie: Choosing Save As Source saves the file in the format in which you originally downloaded it, and choosing Save As QuickTime Movie converts the file to a QuickTime movie.

To aid your quest for QuickTime content on the Web, Apple hosts a vast array of materials on its site. You can find movie trailers, free tunes from your favorite artists, game trailers, and Internet radio news at this site:

`www.apple.com/quicktime`

Tweaking QuickTime

After you become comfortable with using QuickTime for media playback, you might want to expand your horizons. QuickTime has many features — so many, in fact, that it requires two different Preference windows to handle them all.

Setting QuickTime Player Preferences

To open QuickTime Player Preferences, choose QuickTime Player⇨ Preferences. A General Preferences dialog appears with a number of settings that affect how the QuickTime Player application works.

Working with QuickTime Preferences

To open the Preferences for QuickTime, do one of the following:

✦ Open System Preferences and click on the QuickTime icon.

✦ Using the QuickTime Player application, choose QuickTime Player⇨ QuickTime Preferences.

Click the various tabs of the QuickTime Preferences to change its settings.

Besides the Registration panel, which I discuss at the beginning of the chapter, the QuickTime Preferences consist of four other panels:

◆ **Browser:** To play QuickTime content, your browser uses a QuickTime plug-in. Configure the plug-in's settings here.

◆ **Update:** Wondering whether you have the most current version of QuickTime? Let QuickTime look for you! In this panel, you can force QuickTime to update itself.

◆ **Streaming:** QuickTime can tailor your online multimedia experience to the speed of your Internet connection. Tell QuickTime what speed your connection uses, and it takes care of the rest.

◆ **Advanced:** QuickTime can do music! Select QuickTime's synthesizer in this panel. Click the Media Keys button to set authentication for secure media. You can also click the MIME Settings button to configure the file types recognized by the QuickTime Plug-in.

**Book III
Chapter 7**

No, It's Not Called
iQuickTime

Chapter 8: Turning Your Mac into a DVD Theater

In This Chapter

✔ **What you need to watch DVDs on your Macintosh**

✔ **Using the DVD Player software**

✔ **Mysteries of the hidden controls unearthed!**

All the creative capabilities of the Mac OS X digital hub are a lot of fun, but at some point, you're going to want to take a break from work. In recent years, DVDs have exploded onto the home entertainment scene; because of its high fidelity, convenience, and seemingly limitless storage capacity, the DVD has taken consumers by storm. The idea of an honest-to-goodness theater in your home is now within the grasp of mere mortals (with, coincidentally, merely average budgets). Mac OS X has everything that you'll need to enjoy a night at the movies without ever leaving home. In fact, I can highly recommend the new 20-inch iMac G5 or the 17-inch PowerBook for those wide-screen classics.

The DVD Hardware

Before you watch one second of film, get your setup in order. Playing DVDs requires a bit of hardware; fortunately, most recent Macintosh computers come equipped with the stuff that's necessary to watch DVDs.

To play DVD movies, you'll need either an internal DVD-compatible drive in your Macintosh or an external DVD drive with a FireWire or USB 2.0 connection. *Note:* DVD-ROM drives can only play discs, while others, like the SuperDrive, can both play and record discs. Either type of drive will work fine for watching movies on your Mac.

You can watch any standard DVD that you purchase at your local video store as well as any DVD that you create with iDVD. (For more on iDVD 5, iRead Book III, Chapter 5.)

The DVD Player: It's Truly Shiny

To watch Frodo Baggins, Don Corleone, or James Bond, you'll need DVD player software. Mac OS X comes stocked with the perfect tool for the task: DVD Player.

Apple's DVD Player application is included with Mac OS X — you'll find it within the confines of your Applications folder. But instead of rooting through the Finder, you can launch DVD Player an even easier way: Simply insert a DVD into the drive. As soon as you do, your Mac recognizes the disc and launches DVD Player by default for you. (Time for another round of well-deserved gloating about your choice of personal computer.)

This automatic behavior can be curbed, however. You can control what action Tiger takes (if any) when you load a DVD via the CDs & DVDs panel within System Preferences. For all the details, visit Book II, Chapter 3.

However you choose to start DVD Player, you'll notice that it offers two windows:

✦ **Controller:** The small, silver-colored, remote control-looking interface that holds all the controls for the Player

✦ **Viewer:** The large window where you view your DVD movies

If you're already using a traditional DVD player, you'll be right at home with Apple's DVD Player. Even if you've never used a traditional DVD player, it's not much different than using a software-based audio player like iTunes.

Using the Controller

The *Controller* is the command center of the DVD Player software. Arranged much like a VCR or tape deck, all the familiar controls are present. Check it out in Figure 8-1. (If your controller is facing in the other direction, don't panic — the controller can be switched between horizontal and vertical orientations from the Controls menu.)

Table 8-1 details the fundamental commands present in the DVD Player Controller. Apple software usually has some goodies hidden beneath the surface, and DVD Player is no exception. The controls in DVD Player have a few functions that might not be obvious to the casual user. These are listed in the third column of Table 8-1.

Figure 8-1:
Use the controller for mundane playback chores.

Table 8-1	Basic DVD Controls	
Control Name	*What It Does*	*Other Functions*
Play	Plays the DVD	It also toggles into a Pause button anytime a movie is playing.
Stop	Stops playback of the DVD	
Previous Chapter	Skips to the previous chapter	Click and hold the button to quickly scan through the movie in reverse.
Next Chapter	Skips to the next chapter	Click and hold the button to quickly scan forward through the movie.
Playback Volume	Adjusts the volume of the DVD audio	
Arrow Button	Navigates through the menu items of the DVD	
Enter	Selects the currently highlighted menu item	
Eject	Ejects the DVD from the drive	
Title Menu	Jumps immediately to the DVD's title menu	
Menu	Displays the menu of the current DVD	

Jumping right to the flying-monkey action

Movies on DVD are divided into *chapters* that enable you to jump directly to that point. That way, you can jump right to the scene, say, where the flying monkey guards march into the Wicked Witch's castle in *The Wizard of Oz*. (Or skip that egg-hatching scene in *Alien* that always makes you nauseous.) You can navigate to chapters, play the movie from the beginning, or check out special bonus features (such as trailers and documentaries) from the DVD's main menu.

As I mention earlier, you can switch the Controller between horizontal and vertical orientation, which can make it easier to fit onscreen. Choose Controls➪Use Horizontal Controller (or Use Vertical Controller, depending on the current orientation).

Keep your eyes on the Viewer

As soon as you begin playing around with the DVD Player controls, you'll notice activity in the Viewer window, shown in Figure 8-2.

Figure 8-2: The Viewer is the real star of Tiger's DVD Player.

You can think of the Viewer window as a television inside your Macintosh if it helps, but DVD Player goes one step further. Unlike a television screen, the Viewer has some nice tricks up its sleeve: For example, you can resize the Viewer window by using one of the four sizes listed in the Video menu (half, normal, maximum, and full-screen sizes). This is useful for watching a movie in a small window on your Desktop while you work with other applications. From the keyboard, you can toggle half-size with ⌘+1 (one), normal size with ⌘+2 (two), and maximum size with ⌘+3 (three),

If you're in it for the entertainment factor only, you'll probably want to resize the Viewer to fill the screen. I like to watch movies in full-screen mode, which you can toggle with the ⌘+0 (zero) keyboard shortcut.

Taking Advantage of Additional DVD Features

As anyone with a little DVD experience knows, DVDs can do a lot more than those archaic tapes that you used to feed your VCR. Apple has included several functions that allow you to explore the extra features and content provided with a DVD movie.

Controller extras

To use the additional Controller features, double-click the small tab at the rightmost (or bottom) edge of the DVD Player Controller. When you do, a trick drawer slides out displaying the extra controls. (See Figure 8-3.) You can also display or hide the drawer with the Controls➪Open Control Drawer menu command or by pressing ⌘+] (that's the right bracket key).

Figure 8-3: Expand the controller to view additional controls.

Table 8-2 summarizes the functions that you can perform with these additional controls.

Table 8-2	Additional Controller Features
Control	*What It Does*
Slow Motion (half speed)	Plays a DVD in slow motion at half of the original speed
Step Button (frame speed)	Steps through a DVD in ultra-slow motion, one frame at a time
Return	Navigates to the previous menu
Alternate Tracks - Subtitles	Displays alternate subtitle tracks on the DVD
Alternate Tracks - Audio	Plays alternate audio tracks on the DVD
Alternate Tracks - Video Angle	Displays the current video footage from different camera angles

Although you won't find a Bookmark button on the Controller, DVD Player can set them nonetheless. A *bookmark* is a spot that you specify in a movie that you can return to at any time, like a favorite scene. To set a bookmark at the current spot in the movie, click the Controls menu and click New Bookmark or press ⌘+= (the equal sign key). DVD Player even allows you to name the bookmark so it's easier to remember. To return to a bookmark, choose Go➪Bookmarks and click the desired bookmark.

DVD Player preferences

The DVD Player application has a variety of settings that you can access and adjust via its preferences window. To open the preferences window, choose DVD Player➪Preferences. This brings up the preferences dialog.

This window consists of five panels:

✦ **Player:** Settings that affect how DVD Player operates

✦ **Disc Setup:** Settings for Audio, Subtitles, Language, and the Web

✦ **Full Screen:** Settings that determine your Viewer window configuration

✦ **Windows:** Settings for displaying onscreen information during playback

✦ **Previously Viewed:** Settings that determine what happens when you load a DVD that you've already watched

The advantage of these preference settings is that you can customize your copy of DVD Player to match your needs or desires. (Thanks yet again to the Cupertino Crowd!)

Player

As you can see in Figure 8-4, the Player settings take care of much of the automation within DVD Player.

✦ **When DVD Player Opens:** These two check boxes affect what happens when you launch the DVD Player application. You can force DVD Player to play in full screen mode and automatically begin playback every time you start the application.

✦ **When a Disc Is Inserted:** Besides automatic playback on startup, you can also make DVD Player start playing a disc automatically when the application is already running. (To illustrate: If this check box is disabled, loading a new disc will not automatically start it playing if DVD Player is already running.)

✦ **When Muted:** Do you answer a lot of telephone calls while you sneak a quick DVD movie at work? If so, enable this option . . . if you have to press the Mute button on your keyboard while a movie is playing, DVD Player automatically adds the subtitles/closed captions so that you can keep up with the dialog. ***Super*** *sassy!*

✦ **During iChat with Audio:** Another option for those who like multiple applications at once. If you're watching a DVD and start an audio chat in iChat AV, you can choose to either mute the DVD audio, or pause the DVD playback until you click Play again.

✦ **When Viewer Is Minimized:** Watching a DVD at the office, eh? Enable this check box, and DVD Player automatically pauses the movie when you minimize the DVD Player window. (Managers label this feature *down-right sneaky.*)

Figure 8-4:
Customize those Player options — I dare you!

Disc Setup

The second tab of the Player preferences window consists of these sections:

✦ **Language:** Sprechen Sie Deutsch? DVDs are designed to be multilanguage-aware. Feel like brushing up on your German, Spanish, or Chinese? You can control the language used for the audio, subtitling, and menus in this section.

✦ **Internet:** One lonely setting resides in the Internet section. Some DVDs can access information on the Internet. Mark this check box to allow that function.

✦ **Audio:** Click this drop-down list box to specify the default audio output signal that you'd like to use. You can also choose to disable the Dolby dynamic range compression feature, which might enhance the sound for two-speaker systems.

Multiple languages and Web access are not mandatory features of a DVD, so don't be surprised if you see variations of support when it comes to these settings.

Full Screen

These preference settings control the default screen display settings within DVD Player.

✦ **Controller:** I generally like to hide the Controller after a defined time of inactivity; select the Hide Controller If Inactive For *xx* Seconds check box if you agree. To set the delay period, click in the seconds box and type a new value.

✦ **Displays:** These options specify how DVD Player shares your Desktop with others: politely or downright rude. You can choose to automatically dim other monitors while a movie is playing (if you have more than one display connected to your Mac), and DVD Player can stay in full-screen mode even if another application actually has the active window. Finally, you can choose to remove the menu bar altogether (often called *kiosk mode*), which helps cut down on interruptions and accidents if small hands are nearby — and you can optionally allow Tiger's screen saver to appear on the DVD menu in kiosk mode.

Windows

This panel gives you the chance to configure the behavior of the Controller and status information for the Viewer window.

✦ **Options:** Mark the Display Status Information check box, and DVD Player adds a small text box at the top-left corner of the Viewer window. In this text box, you see the name of the last task that you performed with

DVD Player. For example, click the Stop button to see the word Stop displayed in the Viewer on top of the video beneath it. You can also set the Controller to fade away instead of just disappearing — it's eye candy, but doggone it, it's *good* eye candy!

✦ **Floating Overlays:** If you do decide to display status information, you can click the color buttons to specify the text color for the status information and closed caption text. You can also choose the font for your text. Heck, if your Mac has a powerful-enough video card, you can choose to make these lines of text semitransparent to boot. (Think *Return of the Son of Eye Candy*.)

Previously Viewed

Our final DVD Player Preferences panel controls what happens when you load a disc that you've seen already . . . or perhaps your significant other watched it and didn't tell you. (Insert growling noise here.)

✦ **Start Playing Discs From:** If you have to quit DVD Player for some reason, the application is smart enough to remember where you were . . . and you can choose to begin watching from the beginning, from the last position (where you were when you stopped the last time), or from a default bookmark. Alternatively, just select Always Ask, and DVD Player will prompt you each time that this situation crops up.

✦ **Always Use Disc Settings For:** Enable these check boxes to specify whether DVD Player should use the same settings you used the last time you watched this disc.

Don't forget to click OK to save any changes that you make to your DVD Player preferences.

After you have your DVD Player customized to your liking, get out the popcorn, pull up your favorite recliner, and let the movies roll!

**Book III
Chapter 8**

Turning Your Mac
into a DVD Theater

Book IV

The Typical Internet Stuff

The 5th Wave   By Rich Tennant

"IT'S JUST UNTIL WE GET BACK UP ON THE INTERNET."

Contents at a Glance

Chapter 1: Getting on the Internet

In This Chapter

- Selecting an Internet service provider (ISP)
- Understanding how your Mac gets on the Internet
- Setting up your Internet connection

I'll be honest — the Internet is a terribly complex monster of a network. If you tried to fathom all the data that's exchanged on the Internet and everything that takes place when you check your e-mail for Aunty Joan's fruitcake recipe, your brain would probably melt like a chocolate bar in the Sahara Desert. There's a shoebox *full* of archaic things tucked under the Internet: communications protocols, routing addresses, packets, servers, and other hoo-hah that's beyond the grasp of just about everyone on the planet.

Luckily for regular folks like you and me, Mac OS X closes the trapdoor on all these details, keeping them hidden (as they *should* be). You don't have to worry about them, and the obscure information that you need in order to establish an Internet connection is kept to a minimum. In fact, the happiest computer owners that I've met think that the Internet is a little blinking light on their DSL or cable modem: If the light blinks in the proper manner, all is well. (I don't argue with them.)

In this chapter, I provide help and advice to those who are searching for an on-ramp to the Information Superhighway — and I lead you through the procedure of adding an Internet connection under Mac OS X. (In other words, you'll get your light blinking properly.)

Note: If you entered your Internet configuration information while you were in the First Use Wizard during the installation of Mac OS X — or if you upgraded to Mac OS X from Mac OS 9, and you already had a working Internet connection — *you can skip this chapter!* The information contained herein is only for those who add or change their Internet connectivity *after* installing Mac OS X.

Shopping for an ISP

Before you can connect to the Internet, you must sign up for Internet access. If you already have an ISP (acronym-speak for an *Internet service provider*) or your company provides Internet access, smile quietly to yourself and skip to the next section. Otherwise, hang around while I discuss what to look for in an ISP and how to locate one in your local area.

ISPs are as thick as Louisiana mosquitoes these days, and often they're judged solely by the amount that they charge for basic access. Cost definitely is a factor, but it's not the *only* thing that should determine your choice in a service provider. Consider these guidelines when choosing or switching ISPs:

✦ **Local calling rates:** If you live in a rural area, check to make sure that all prospective ISPs offer local calling rates. Believe me, no matter how much fun and how useful the Internet is, it's not worth hours of long-distance charges. (Oh, and don't forget to make sure that your ISP has local access numbers in the cities that you visit regularly.)

✦ **Broadband service:** Most ISPs now offer digital subscriber line (DSL) and cable modem access. Collectively, these connections are called *broadband* because they offer the fastest method of transferring information to and from the Internet. If you have a home business, a large family, or students — or you telecommute to your office — using broadband can make your life much simpler.

✦ **Quality technical support:** A 24-hour/7-day telephone support line is a godsend for the Internet novice — don't settle for voice support during business hours. Forget e-mail-based support, too; your e-mail application will be dead and gone if your Internet connection gives you problems. (Sound of your palm whacking your forehead.)

✦ **Static IP addresses:** A *static IP address* — the unique number that identifies your computer on the Internet — allows you to set up a professional Web server or File Transfer Protocol (FTP) server. (More on these adventures later in Book VII, Chapter 4.) Most ISPs charge an additional amount for a static IP address, so it's not really a good idea for a typical Mac owner at home. Suffice it to say, however, that a business or organization running a Web server or FTP server will benefit from a static IP address.

✦ **E-mail accounts:** Investigate how many individual accounts that you receive with various ISPs. Also, find out whether you can maintain them yourself through a Web site. If so, that's a good sign. Additionally, if the prospective ISP provides a Web site where you can read and send e-mail messages, you can stay on top of your e-mail even while you're on the road or vacationing halfway across the globe.

✦ **Web space:** If you want your ISP to host your Web site, this is a no-brainer: The more space you get, the better. A minimum of 5MB is acceptable, but most ISPs provide 10MB or 20MB these days. Also, beware of ISPs that charge you for your Web site if it receives a large amount of traffic: It can be expensive to host a popular Web site if you join one of these ISPs.

✦ **Domain name service:** Finally, the better class of ISP also offers a *domain name service,* which allows you to register something like `yournamehere.com`. For the most professional appearance, you can usually pay a yearly fee, and the ISP takes care of all the details in setting up your own `.com` or `.org` domain name.

Locating an ISP is much easier in the modern Internet-savvy world than it was just two or three years ago. In the order that you should try them, here are the tricks that I recommend for finding your local ISPs:

✦ **Check with your cable or telephone companies.** If you're already subscribing to cable service in your area, you're likely to be a candidate for cable Internet access. Also, many local phone companies offer DSL access, but that access area is often limited to certain locations. Call the customer service numbers for these companies and check out what they offer — and don't forget that a broadband cable or DSL connection is always more expensive than an old-fashioned, dialup connection. ("Maude, did you see the Internet bill this month?")

✦ **Get recommendations from friends and neighbors.** Folks love to give free advice: Ask them how much they're paying, how reliable the connection has been, and how well they rate the ISP's technical support.

✦ **Check your phone directory.** Check the phone book for Internet service.

✦ **Investigate ISP Web sites.** If you have Internet access at work, a friend's house, or your local public library, you can surf to The List (`www.thelist.internet.com`) where you can search for ISPs within your area code and location.

Investigating Various Types of Connections

Next, consider the types of connections that are available under Mac OS X to link your Mac to said ISP. You can choose from four pathways to digital freedom:

**Book IV
Chapter 1**

**Getting on
the Internet**

Oh, please! Not ISDN!

If you're thinking, "Hey, Mark, you forgot ISDN!" allow me to reply, "So did everyone else." I don't mean to anger all those prophets who predicted that we'd all be using Integrated Services Digital Network (ISDN) by now, but the truth is that ISDN turned into a joke. Essentially, ISDN was the ancestor of DSL, which actually realized the potential of the idea. ISDN, which was the first broadband connection method to use regular phone lines, was supposed to revolutionize the Internet five or six years back (along with curing male pattern baldness and explaining UFO abductions).

Unfortunately, ISDN technology requires all sorts of very complex and expensive hardware, and it really isn't as fast as all that — most cable modem Internet access is much faster. (Consider what happens to the first entry in just about any technological advance . . . sigh.) ISDN was quickly eclipsed by the other broadband technologies . . . therefore, its abbreviation has come to mean *It Still Does Nothing,* and anyone with an option to use DSL or cable should give ISDN a wide berth.

✦ **A dialup connection:** Old-fashioned, yes. Slow as an arthritic burro, indeed. However, an *analog* (or telephone modem) connection is still the primary method for reaching the Internet for most computer owners. It's the cheapest method available, and all you need for this type of connection is a standard telephone jack and a modem. If you remember your classic iMac commercials, any Mac that can run Mac OS X should have a built-in modem.

✦ **A broadband connection:** Be it through DSL (which uses a standard telephone line) or cable (which uses your cable TV wiring), broadband Internet access is many times faster than a dialup connection. Plus, both these technologies are *always-on,* meaning that your computer is automatically connected to the Internet when you turn it on and that connection stays active. With DSL or cable, there's no squeaky whine that accompanies your modem making a connection each time that you want to check your movie listings Web site. Both DSL and cable require a special piece of hardware (commonly called a *modem,* but it really isn't); this box is usually thrown in as part of your ISP charge. Broadband connections usually require a professional installation, too.

✦ **A satellite connection:** If you're *really* out there — miles and miles away from any cable or DSL phone service — you can still get high-speed Internet access. The price for a satellite connection is usually much steeper than a standard DSL or cable connection, but it's available anywhere you can plant your antenna dish with a clear view of the sky. Plus, a satellite connection is actually faster than other types of broadband access. Older satellite technologies actually required you to use a dialup connection — and the antenna could only receive, not send — but most ISPs that can handle satellite connections now offer satellite systems that both send and receive through the dish.

✦ **A network connection:** The last type of connection concerns those Macs that are part of a local area network (LAN) either at the office or in your home. If your Mac is connected to a LAN that already has Internet access, you don't need an ISP at all, and no other hardware is required: Simply contact your network administrator, buy that important person a steak dinner, and ask to be connected to the Internet. On the other hand, if your network currently has no Internet access, you're back to Square One: You'll need one of the previous three types of connections.

After you connect one of your computers on your network to the Internet, you can use an Internet sharing device to allow all the computers to share that Internet connection. Book V, Chapter 5 goes into all the details on sharing an Internet connection on a network.

Setting Up Your Internet Connection

Okay, so you sign up for Internet access, and your ISP sends you a sheet of paper covered with indecipherable stuff that looks like Egyptian hieroglyphics. Don't worry; those are the settings that you need to connect to your ISP. After you get them in Mac OS X, you should be surfing the Web like an old pro.

Before you jump into this configuration, make sure that you've configured the Internet settings within System Preferences, as I discuss in Book II, Chapter 3. That way, you'll already have entered your default e-mail and Web settings.

Using your internal modem

Follow these steps to set up your Internet connection if you're using your Mac's internal modem:

1. **Click the System Preferences icon on the Dock and choose Network.**

2. **Select Internal Modem from the Show drop-down list.**

3. **Click the TCP/IP tab (as shown in Figure 1-1) and enter the settings for the type of connection that your ISP provides:**

- *If your ISP tells you to use PPP (Point-to-Point Protocol):* Click the Configure IPv4 drop-down list and choose Using PPP. If your ISP provided you with DNS Server or Search Domain addresses, type them now in the corresponding boxes.

- *If you're using AOL:* Click the Configure IPv4 drop-down list and choose AOL Dialup. If AOL provided you with DNS Server or Search Domain addresses, click in the corresponding box and type them now.

- *If you're using a manual connection:* Click the Configure IPv4 drop-down list box and choose Manually. Then click in the IP Address, DNS Servers, and Search Domains fields and enter the respective settings provided by your ISP.

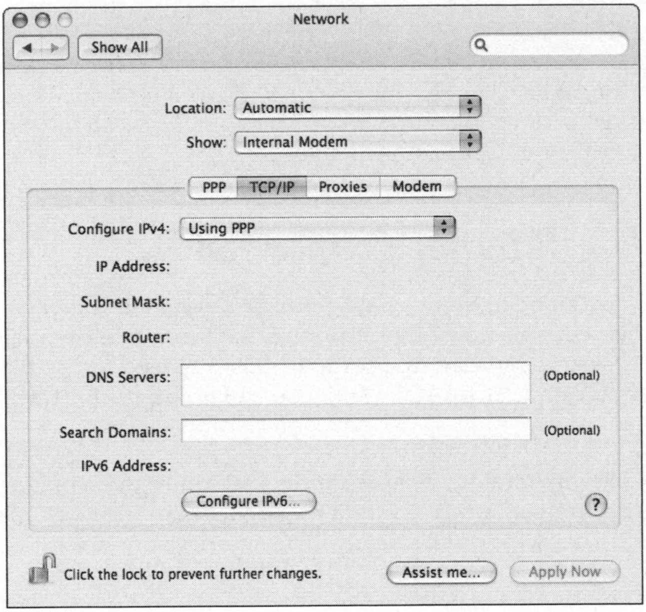

Figure 1-1:
The Network settings for an internal modem Internet connection.

4. **Click the PPP tab to display the settings shown in Figure 1-2.**

5. **In their respective fields, enter the account name, password, telephone number, and (optionally) the service provider name and an alternate telephone number provided by your ISP.**

6. **Press ⌘+Q to exit System Preferences and save your changes.**

In Book V, Chapter 1, I discuss these Internet settings in depth.

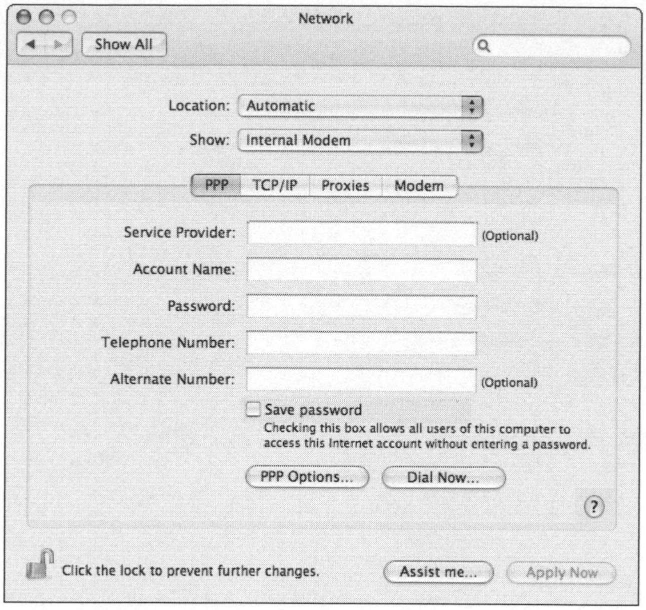

Figure 1-2:
Adding PPP
settings.

Using Ethernet hardware

Follow these steps to set up your Internet connection if you're using a network, cable modem, or DSL connection:

1. **Click the System Preferences icon on the Dock and choose Network.**

2. **Select Built-in Ethernet from the Show drop-down list to display the settings that you see in Figure 1-3.**

3. **Enter the settings for the type of connection that your ISP provides:**

   • *If your ISP tells you to use Dynamic Host Configuration Protocol (DHCP):* Select Using DHCP from the Configure IPv4 drop-down list, and your ISP can automatically set up virtually all the TCP/IP settings for you! (No wonder DHCP is so popular these days.)

   • *If you won't be using DHCP:* Select Manually from the Configure IPv4 drop-down list box. Then enter the settings provided by your ISP in the IP Address, Subnet Mask, Router, and DNS Servers fields.

4. **If your ISP uses PPPoE (Point-to-Point Protocol over Ethernet), click the PPPoE tab to display the settings shown in Figure 1-4.**

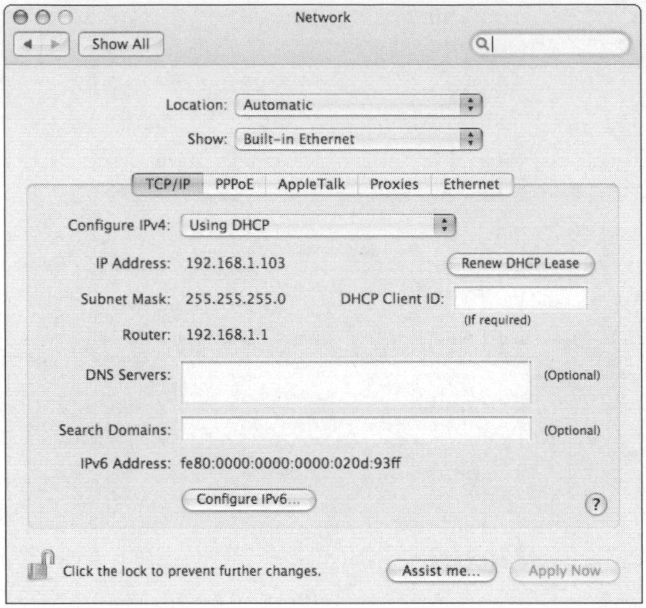

Figure 1-3:
The
Network
settings for
an Ethernet
Internet
connection.

Figure 1-4:
Entering
PPPoE
data —
geez, that
sounds
ridiculous,
doesn't it?

5. **Mark the Connect Using PPPoE check box to enable it and then enter the account name and password.**

   If your ISP includes the Service Provider name and a PPPoE Service Name, you can enter those as well.

6. **To allow everyone who uses your Mac to access the Internet with this account, mark the Save Password check box to enable it.**

   I recommend that you enable the Show PPPoE Status in Menu Bar check box. When you do, Mac OS X displays a menu bar icon that lets you know the status of your PPPoE connection.

7. **Press ⌘+Q to exit System Preferences and save your changes.**

If you need help entering Internet settings or you want to know more about what you're actually doing, I discuss these settings in depth in Book V, Chapter 1.

Connecting with a Dialup ISP (The Hard Way)

Before you leave the serene confines of this chapter, I'd like to demonstrate how to use the Internet Connect application to connect to your ISP via your internal modem. (As I mention earlier in this chapter, most connections made over a network, DSL line, or cable modem won't need to use Internet Connect.) You can also use this application to connect if you're using a DSL line with PPPoE or an AirPort connection. Many ISPs that provide high-speed access for Macs offer PPPoE, which provides more efficient communications than the older PPP protocol that you might have used in the past. Further, if you're using an AirPort wireless connection, you can launch Internet Connect to take advantage of an existing Internet connection available through your wireless network.

To be honest, I always like Mac OS X to connect automatically when I'm using a modem. I hate excess mouse movements, which usually lead to a bad case of Rodent Elbow. To automate your connection, follow these steps:

1. **Re-open the Network settings in System Preferences and choose Internal Modem from the Show drop-down list.**

2. **Click the PPP tab (refer to Figure 1-2), click the PPP Options button, and then enable the Connect Automatically When Needed check box.**

3. **Click OK.**

4. **Press ⌘+Q to exit System Preferences.**

   You can forget about using Internet Connect!

Follow these steps to connect to the Internet manually:

1. **Open your Applications folder, launch the Internet Connect application, and click the Internal Modem toolbar button, which displays the Internal Modem dialog.**

2. **From the Configuration drop-down list box, choose Modem Configuration, Built-in Ethernet (for a DSL PPPoE connection), or AirPort.**

3. **Select the connection options for the hardware that you're using:**

   - *Modem connection:* Type the telephone number provided by your ISP into the Telephone Number text box and then type your password in the Password box (if prompted). I recommend that you enable the Show Modem Status in Menu Bar check box, too.

   - *PPPoE connection:* Type your password in the Password text box (if prompted).

   - *AirPort connection:* If you have an AirPort/AirPort Extreme card installed, click the Turn AirPort On button (if AirPort is currently powered off) and select the network that provides your Internet access from the Network drop-down list box.

4. **Click the Connect button, sit back, and watch the fun!**

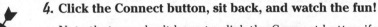

   Note that you don't have to click the Connect button if your AirPort (or AirPort Extreme) Base Station is already connected to your ISP.

Chapter 2: Using Apple Mail

In This Chapter

✓ **Adding and configuring mail accounts**

✓ **Receiving and reading e-mail**

✓ **Sending e-mail**

✓ **Filtering junk mail**

✓ **Opening attachments**

✓ **Configuring Apple Mail**

✓ **Automating Apple Mail**

Okay, how many of you can function without e-mail? Raise your hands. Anyone? Anyone at all?

I suppose that I *can* function without my Internet e-mail, but why should I? Mac OS X includes a very capable and reliable e-mail client, Apple Mail (affectionately called *Mail* by everyone but Bill Gates).

In this chapter, I discuss the features of Apple Mail and show you how everything hums at a perfect C pitch. However, you'll have to sing out, "You've got mail!" yourself. Personally, I think that's a plus, but I show you how you can add any sound that you like.

Know Thy Mail Window

To begin our epic e-mail journey, click the Mail icon on the Dock. Figure 2-1 illustrates the Mail window. Besides the familiar toolbar, which naturally carries buttons specific to Mail, you'll find the following:

✦ **Status bar:** This heading bar at the top of the Mail window displays information about the current folder — typically, how many messages it contains, but other data can be included as well.

✦ **Message list:** This resizable scrolling list box contains all the messages for the folder that you've chosen. To resize the list larger or smaller, drag the handle on the bar that runs across the window. You can also resize the columns in the list by dragging the edges of the column heading buttons.

TIP

To specify which columns appear in the message list, choose View⇨ Columns. From the submenu that appears, you can toggle the display of specific columns. You can also sort the messages in the message list from the View menu; by default, messages are sorted by the Date Received. (Alternatively, use Lazy Mark's method: Just click the column that you want to sort by.)

✦ **Drawer:** The extension to the right of the main Mail window is the Drawer. You can click any of the folders to switch the display in the message list. The Drawer can be hidden or shown from the View menu by clicking the Mailboxes button on the toolbar, or you can press the ⌘+Shift+M keyboard shortcut to hide and show it. The Drawer is also automatically hidden when you maximize the Mail window.

✦ **Preview box:** This resizable scrolling list box displays the contents of the selected message, including both text and any graphics or attachments that Mail recognizes.

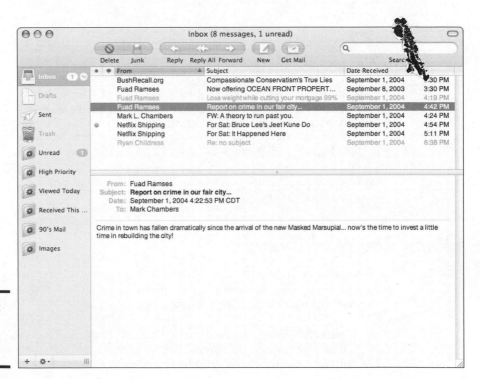

Figure 2-1:
The Apple
Mail
window.

Mail uses the following folders (some of which appear only at certain times):

✦ **Inbox:** Mail you've already received.

✦ **Outbox:** Messages that Mail is waiting to send.

✦ **Drafts:** Draft messages waiting to be completed.

✦ **Sent:** Mail you've already sent.

✦ **Trash:** Deleted mail. Like the Trash in the Dock, you can open this folder and retrieve items that you realize you still need. Alternatively, you can empty the contents of the Trash at any time by pressing the ⌘+K shortcut or by choosing Mailbox➪Erase Deleted Messages.

✦ **Junk:** Junk mail. You can review these messages or retrieve anything you want to keep by choosing Message➪Transfer. After you're sure there's nothing left of value, you can delete the remaining messages straight to the Trash. (Junk mail filtering must be enabled from the Junk Mail settings in Preferences before you'll see this box.)

✦ **Import:** Messages that you've imported from another e-mail application, or an earlier version of Mac OS X Mail.

You can add new personal folders to the Drawer to further organize your messages. Choose Mailbox➪New Mailbox and then type the name for your new folder in the Name box. Click OK to create the new personal folder.

Messages can be dragged from the message list and dropped into the desired folder in the Drawer to transfer them. Alternatively, you can move 'em from the Message list by selecting the messages that you want to move, choosing Message➪Transfer, and then clicking the desired destination folder.

Also note that Spotlight has staked its claim with the Search box at the upper right in the Mail toolbar.

Setting Up Your Account

By default, Mail includes one (or more) of these accounts when you first run it:

✦ **The account that you entered when you first installed Mac OS X:** Go back to the beginning — literally, Book I, Chapter 1 — to read about the first use wizard that I discuss at the beginning of this book. If you entered the information for an e-mail account, it's available.

✦ **Your .Mac account:** If you registered for a .Mac service account, it will be included.

✦ **Upgraded accounts:** If you upgraded an existing Mac OS system, your existing Mail accounts will be added to the Accounts list in Mail.

Speaking of the Accounts list, choose Mail⇨Preferences and click the Accounts button to display the Accounts dialog that you see in Figure 2-2. From here, you can add an account, edit an existing account, or remove an account from Mail. Although most folks still have only one e-mail account, you can use a passel of them. For example, you might use one account for your personal e-mail and one account for your business communications. To switch accounts, just click the account that you want to use from this list to make it the active account.

Figure 2-2:
The Accounts list, where all is made clear (about your e-mail accounts).

Adding an account

To add a new account within Mail, click the Add Account button, which carries a plus sign (see bottom-left, Figure 2-2) to open an Account wizard that leads you through the process. 'Nuff said.

However, I'm a manual kind of guy — at least, that's what I'm told — so I should describe how to add an account from the Preferences dialog. Open the Preferences dialog by clicking Mail and choosing Preferences; then click the Accounts button on the Preferences toolbar. Follow these steps:

1. **Click the Add button at the bottom-left corner of the window, which (also) carries a plus sign.**

2. **On the General Information panel, click the Account Type drop-down list box and choose the protocol type to use for the account.**

   You can select an Apple .Mac account, a Post Office Protocol (POP) account, a Microsoft Exchange account, or an Internet Message Access Protocol (IMAP) account. If you're adding an account from an Internet service provider (ISP), refer to the set-up information that you received to determine which is right. Most ISP accounts are POP accounts.

3. **In the Description field, name the account to identify it within Mail and then press Tab to move to the next field.**

   For example, *Work* or *Mom's ISP* are good choices.

4. **In the Full Name field, type your full name — or, if this is to be an anonymous account, enter whatever you like as your identity — and then press Tab.**

   Messages that you send will appear with this name in the From field in the recipient's e-mail application.

5. **In the User Name field, type the username supplied by your ISP for login to your e-mail account and then press Tab.**

   This is sometimes different from the username and password that you use to connect to the Internet.

6. **In the Password field, type the password supplied by your ISP for login to your e-mail account.**

   Again, this might be different from your connection password.

7. **Click Continue.**

8. **Click Continue on the Account Summary sheet.**

9. **Click Done on the Conclusion sheet.**

   You're done! The new account appears in the Accounts list.

You can specify advanced settings for an account. I cover those in the section "Fine-Tuning Your Post Office," later in this chapter.

Editing an existing account

Need to make changes to an existing account? Choose Mail⇨Preferences and click the account that you want to change. Mail displays the same settings that I explain in the preceding section.

Deleting an account

If you change ISPs or you decide to drop an e-mail account, you can remove it from your Accounts list. Otherwise, Mail can annoy you with error messages when it can no longer connect to the server for that account. Display the Mail Preferences window, select the account that you want to delete, and then click the Remove button (which is graced by a minus sign).

Naturally, Mail will request confirmation before deleting the folders associated with that account. Click OK to verify the deletion, or click the Cancel button to prevent accidental catastrophe.

Receiving and Reading E-Mail Wisdom

The heart and soul of Mail — well, at least the heart, anyway — is receiving and reading stuff from your friends and family. (Later in this chapter, I show you how to avoid the stuff you get promising free prizes, low mortgage rates, and improved . . . um . . . performance. This is a family-oriented book, so that's enough of that.)

After you set up an account (or select an account from the Accounts list), it's time to check for mail. Use any of these methods to check for new mail:

✦ **Click the Get Mail button on the toolbar.**

✦ **Choose Mailbox⇨Get New Mail in All Accounts or press ⌘+Shift+N.**

✦ **Choose Mailbox⇨Get New Mail and then choose the specific account to check from the submenu.**

This is a great way to check for new mail in another account without going through the trouble of making it active in the Preferences window.

Mail can also check for new messages automatically — more on this in the upcoming section, "Checking Mail automatically."

If you do have new mail in the active account, it appears in the Message list (and the Mail icon on the Dock sports a bright red number indicating how many new messages you've received). As you can see in Figure 2-3, new unread messages appear marked with a dot (it's blue) in the first column. The number of unread messages is displayed next to the Inbox folder icon in the Drawer.

Mail also displays the number of new messages that you've received on its Dock icon. If you've hidden the Mail window or sent it to the Dock, you can perform a quick visual check for new mail just by glancing at the Dock.

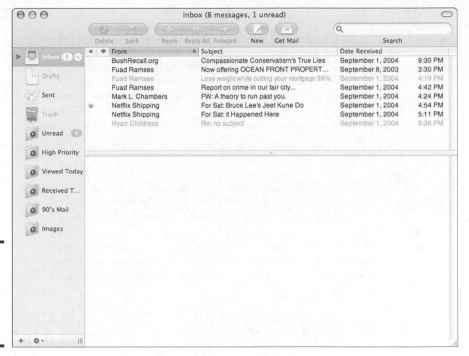

Figure 2-3:
A new message to read. Oh, joy, and no spam!

Reading and deleting your messages

To read any message in the message list, you can either click the desired entry (which displays the contents of the message in the preview box) or you can double-click the entry to open the message in a separate message window, complete with its own toolbar controls.

To quickly scan your mail, click the first message that you want to view in the list, and then press the down-arrow key when you're ready to move to the next message. Mail displays the content of each message in the preview box. To display the previous message in the list, press the up-arrow key.

Mail also allows you to read your messages grouped within threads. A *thread* contains an original message and all related replies, which makes it easy to follow the flow of an e-mail discussion (without bouncing around within your Inbox, searching for the next message in the conversation). Choose View➪ Organize by Thread, and the replies in the current folder are all grouped under the original messages and sorted by date. To expand a thread, click the original message to select it; then press the right-arrow key (or choose View➪Expand All Threads). To collapse a thread, select the original message and press the left-arrow key (or choose View➪Collapse All Threads).

Book IV Chapter 2

Using Apple Mail

Displaying all Mail headers

Mail actually hides the majority of the heading lines that help identify and route an e-mail message to its rightful destination. By default, all you'll see is the *filtered heading,* which includes only the From, Date, To, and Subject fields. This is great unless for some reason you need to display the entire message header in all its arcane madness. If you do, press ⌘+Shift+H. You can toggle back to the filtered heading by pressing the same shortcut.

Hey, why not let Mail *read* you your mail? (That is, if you can drive and listen to your iBook speak at the same time!) Simply select one message or a group of messages and then choose Edit⇨Speech⇨Start Speaking. *Wowsers!*

To delete a message from the message list, click the desired entry to select it and then click the Delete button on the toolbar (or press the Del key). To delete a message from within a message window, click the Delete button on the toolbar.

Replying to mail

What? Aunt Harriet sent you a message because she's forgotten where she parked her car last night? If you happen to know where her priceless '78 Pinto is, you can reply to her and save her the trouble of retracing her steps.

If Aunt Harriet isn't in your Address Book yet, this is a good time to add her. With the message entry selected in the list, choose Message⇨Add Sender to Address Book or just press the convenient ⌘+Y keyboard shortcut. The person's name and e-mail address are automatically added to your Address Book. To add more information in the Address Book, however, you have to open that application separately. (Read through Book I, Chapter 6 for the skinny on the Address Book.)

To reply to a message in Mail, follow these steps:

1. **To respond to a message from the message list, click the desired message entry and then click the Reply button on the toolbar.**

To respond to a message that you've opened in a message window, click the Reply button on the toolbar for the message window.

If a message was addressed not just to you but also to a number of different people, you can send your reply to all of them. Instead of clicking the Reply button, click the Reply All button on the Mail window toolbar. (This is a great way to quickly facilitate a festive gathering, if you get my drift.)

You can also add carbon copies of your message to other new recipients, expanding the party exponentially; more on carbon copies later in the section, "Raise the Little Flag: Sending E-Mail."

If you'd like to send your reply under a different account, click the Account drop-down list box and choose the account. This is a handy method of rerouting a message that you received with your home e-mail account to your office account.

Mail opens the Reply window that you see in Figure 2-4. Note that the address has been automatically added and that the default Subject is Re: *<the original subject>*. Mail automatically adds a separator line in the message body field that reads `On <day><date>at<time>, <addressee> wrote:`, followed by the text of the original message; this is done so that the addressee can remember what the heck he or she wrote in the first place to get you so happy/sad/angry/indifferent. The original text is indented and colored blue to set it apart. If you like, you can click in the Subject line and change the default subject line; otherwise, the cursor is already sitting on the first line of the text box, so you can simply start typing your reply.

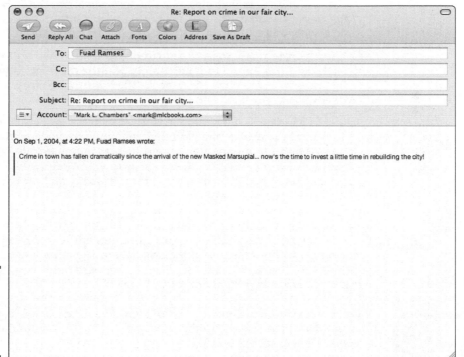

Figure 2-4:
Replying to an incoming e-mail message.

To choose the text from the original message that you want to include in a reply, select the desired text in the original message before you click the Reply button.

2. **After you complete typing your reply, you can select text in the message body and apply different fonts or formatting.**

To change your reply's formatting, click the Fonts button on the message window toolbar. From the window that appears, you can choose the font family, the type size, and formatting such as italic or bold for the selected text. Click the Close button on the Fonts window to continue. (If you like menus, you can also choose Format from the menu and make changes from there.)

To apply color to the selected text, click the Colors button on the message window toolbar and then click anywhere in the color wheel that appears to select that color. You can also vary the hue by moving the slider bar at the right of the Colors window. After you find the color that expresses your inner passion, click the Close button on the Colors window to continue.

3. **To add an attachment, click the Attach button on the toolbar.**

Mail displays a familiar file Open dialog. Navigate to the to-be-attached file, select it, and click the Open button to add it to the message. (More on attachments in the upcoming section, "Attachments on Parade.")

4. **When you're ready to send your reply, you have two options. You can click the Send button to immediately add the message to your Out folder, or you can click the Save As Draft button to store it in your Drafts folder for later editing.**

After a message is moved to the Outbox folder, it is sent either immediately or at the next connection time that you specify in Mail Preferences (more on this in the section, "Checking Mail automatically," later in the chapter). However, saving the message to your Drafts folder will not send it. Read the following section for the skinny on how to send a message stored in your Drafts folder.

When you reply to a message, you can also *forward* your reply to another person (instead of the original sender). The new addressee receives a message containing both the text of the original message that you received and your reply. To forward a message, click the Forward button on the Mail toolbar instead of Reply or Reply to All.

If you don't want to include the text of the original message in a reply, choose Mail⇨Preferences⇨Composing and disable the Quote the Text of the Original Message check box.

Hey, what does MIME mean?

First, a note of explanation about Internet e-mail. (Don't worry about notes; you won't be tested on this stuff.) Decades back, Internet e-mail messages were pure text, composed only of ASCII characters — that means no fancy fonts, colors, or text formatting. However, as more and more folks started using e-mail, the clarion call rang forth across the land for more attractive messages (as well as attachments, which I cover in the section, "Attachments on Parade"). Therefore, the MIME encoding standard was developed. In case you're interested, MIME stands for *Multipurpose Internet Mail Extensions* — a rather cool (and surprisingly understandable) acronym.

Originally, virtually all e-mail programs recognized MIME, but then the Tower of Babel principle kicked in, and now there are actually multiple versions of MIME. Apple Mail uses the most common variant of MIME, so most folks who receive your e-mail should be able to see them in all their glory (even under Windows).

However, if one of your addressees complains that he got a message containing unrecognizable gobbledygook and a heading that mentions MIME, he's using an e-mail client application that either doesn't support MIME or supports a different version. (Of course, that person could have unknowingly turned off MIME support.) You have two possible solutions: You can ask the addressee to double-check whether MIME is enabled on his end in their e-mail application, or you can disable MIME when sending a message to that particular person. When you're composing an original message or a reply, you can use pure text by choosing Format⇨Make Plain Text. (Naturally, this prevents you from doing anything fancy, and files that you attach to a plain text message might not be delivered correctly.)

By default, Mail checks your spelling as you type and also underlines any words that it doesn't recognize. (Very Microsoftian.) I like this feature, but if you find it irritating, you can turn it off. Just choose Mail⇨Preferences⇨ Composing and disable the Check Spelling as I Type check box.

Raise the Little Flag: Sending E-Mail

To compose and send a new message to someone else, follow these steps:

1. **Click the New button on the Mail toolbar or choose File⇨New Message (or avail yourself of the handy ⌘+N keyboard shortcut).**

Mail opens the New Message window that you see in Figure 2-5.

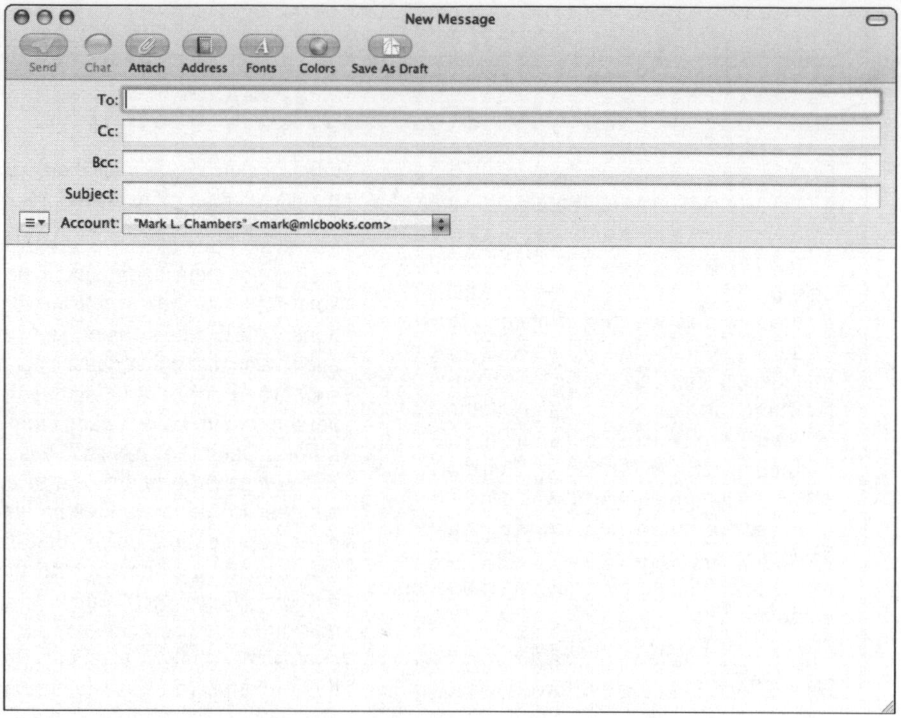

Figure 2-5:
An empty Mail message, waiting to be filled.

2. **Enter the recipient's (To) address by**

- *Typing it in directly.*

- *Pasting it in after copying it to the Clipboard.*

- *Dragging an e-mail address from your Address Book.*

    or

- *(My favorite) Clicking the Address button,* which shows you the scaled-down version of the Address Book (the Addresses window) that you see in Figure 2-6.

From the Addresses window, click the address that you want to use and then click the To button. To pick multiple recipients, hold down the Command (⌘) key while you click the multiple addresses. Click the Close button on the Addresses window to close it and then press Tab.

If you've got a huge number of entries in your Address Book, use the Search field on the Addresses window toolbar, which operates just like the Finder window Search box.

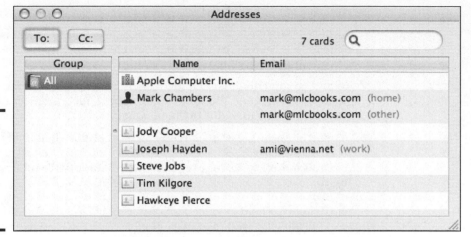

Figure 2-6:
Select an
e-mail
address
from your
Address
Book.

3. **When Mail highlights the Cc field (the spot where you can send optional carbon copies of the message to additional recipients), you can type the addresses directly, use the contents of the Clipboard, or display the Addresses window.**

If you use the Addresses window, select the addresses that you want to use and click the Cc button. Then click the Close button on the Addresses window and press Tab.

Looking for the Blind Carbon Copy (Bcc) field? To display it, choose View⇨Bcc Address Field. (A *blind carbon copy* is a message sent to multiple recipients, just like a regular carbon copy, but the recipients aren't listed when the message is displayed — that way, the other recipients won't know who else got a copy of the message.) You can also click the small drop-down list box at the left side of the Subject field to toggle the display of the Bcc Address Field.

4. **In the Subject field, enter the subject of the message and then press Tab.**

Your text cursor now rests in the first line of the message text box — type, my friend, type like the wind! It's considered good form to keep this line short and relatively to the point.

5. **When you're done typing your message, select any of the text that you've entered and use the toolbar features I describe in the earlier section "Replying to mail" to apply different fonts or formatting.**

Click the Fonts button in the message window toolbar to open a window of formatting choices. (Click its Close button to continue.) If you like menus, you can also click Format and make changes from there.

6. **Add color to any selected text, if you like.**

   Just click the Colors button in the message window toolbar and make choices there; when the hue is perfect, click the Close button on the Colors window to continue.

7. **To add an attachment, click the Attach button on the toolbar, navigate to the to-be-attached file in the dialog that appears, select the file, and then click Open to add it to the message.**

8. **When your new message is ready to post, either click the Send button to immediately add the message to your Out folder or click the Save As Draft button to store it in your Drafts folder (without actually sending it).**

To send a message held in your Drafts folder, click the Drafts folder in the Drawer to display all draft messages. Double-click the message that you want to send, which will display the message window — you can make edits at this point, if you like — and then click the Send button on the message window toolbar.

If you don't have access to an Internet connection at the moment, Mail allows you to work off-line. This way, you can read your unread messages and compose new ones on the road to send later. After you regain your Internet connection, you might need to choose Mailbox⇨Online Status⇨ Go Online (depending on the connection type).

What? You Get Junk Mail, Too?

Spam — it's the Crawling Crud of the Internet, and I hereby send out a lifetime of bad karma to those who spew it. However, chucking the First Amendment is *not* an option, so I guess we'll always have junk mail. (Come to think of it, my paper mailbox is just as full of the stuff.)

Thankfully, the latest version of Apple Mail has a net that you can cast to collect junk mail before you have to read it. The two methods of handling junk mail are

✦ **Manually:** You can mark any message in the message list as Junk Mail. Select the unwanted flotsam in the message list and then click the Junk button on the Mail window toolbar, which marks the message as you see in Figure 2-7. (Ocean-front property in Kansas . . . yeah, right.) If a message is mistakenly marked as junk but you actually want it, display the message in the preview box and then click the Not Junk button at the top of the preview box.

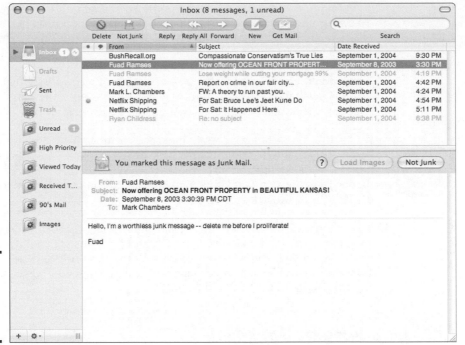

Figure 2-7:
"Be gone,
sludge
demons of
Junk Mail!"

✦ **Automatically:** Apple Mail has a sophisticated Junk Mail filter that you actually train to better recognize what's junk. (Keep reading to discover how.) After you train Mail to recognize spam with a high degree of accuracy, turn it to full Automatic mode, and it will move all those worthless messages to your Junk folder.

You customize and train the Junk Mail filter from the Preferences dialog (available from your trusty Mail menu); click Junk Mail to show the settings. By default, Mail starts in Training mode, using the When Junk Mail Arrives, Leave It in My Inbox option. This means that it takes its best shot at determining what's junk. When you receive more mail and mark more messages as junk (or mark them as *not* junk), you're actually teaching the Junk Mail feature how to winnow the wheat from the chaff. In Training mode, junk messages are not actually moved anywhere — they're just marked with a particularly fitting, grungy brown color.

After you're satisfied that the Junk Mail filter is catching just about everything that it can, display this submenu and choose the Move It to the Junk Mailbox (Automatic) option. Mail creates a Junk folder and prompts you for permission to move all junk messages to this folder. After you review everything in the

**Book IV
Chapter 2**

Using Apple Mail

Junk folder, you can delete what it contains and send it to the Trash folder. To save a message from junkdom, click the Not Junk button in the preview window and then drag the message from the Junk folder message list to the desired folder in the Drawer.

If you don't receive a lot of spam — or you want to be absolutely sure that nothing gets labeled as junk until you review it — click the Enable Junk Mail Filtering check box to disable it. (And good luck.)

By default, Mail exempts certain messages from Junk Mail status based on three criteria: if the sender is in your Address Book, if you've sent the sender a message in the past, or if the message is addressed to you with your full name. To tighten up your Junk Mail filtering to the max, you might want to disable these check boxes as well.

To reset the Junk Mail filter and erase any training that you've done, visit the Junk Mail settings in Preferences again and click Reset. Then click the Yes button to confirm your choice. To display the Junk rule and edit it if necessary, display the Junk Mail settings and click Advanced. (I discuss filtering rules at length at the end of this chapter.)

Attachments on Parade

Attachments are a fun way to transfer files through e-mail. However, remembering these three very important caveats is imperative:

✦ **Attachments can contain viruses.** Even a message attachment that was actually sent by your best friend can contain a virus — either because your friend unwittingly passed one along or because the virus actually took control of your friend's e-mail application and replicated itself automatically. (Ugh.)

Is it a Mark's Maxim, or is it a dire warning? (It's both!)

*Never — I mean never — **send or receive attachments unless you have an up-to-date antivirus scanning application running.**™*

✦ **Corpulent attachments don't make it.** Most corporate and ISP mail servers have a 1–4MB limit for the total size of a message, and the attachment counts toward that final message size. Therefore, I recommend sending a file as an attachment only if it's less than 1MB (or perhaps 2MB) in size. If the recipient's e-mail server sends you an automated message saying that the message was refused because it was too big, this is the problem.

✦ **Not all e-mail applications and firewalls accept attachments.** Not all e-mail programs support attachments in the same way, and others are simply set for pure text messages. Some corporate firewalls even reject messages with attachments. If the message recipient gets the message text but not the attachment, these are the likely reasons.

With that said, it's back to attachments as a beneficial feature. Follow these steps to save an attachment that you receive:

1. **Click the message with an attachment in your message list.**

Having trouble determining which messages have attachments? Choose View➪Columns and then click the Attachments item from the submenu that appears to toggle it on. Now messages with attachments appear with a tiny paper clip icon in the entry.

If Mail recognizes the attachment format, it displays or plays the attachment in the body of the message; if not, the attachment is displayed as a file icon.

2. **To open an attachment that's displayed as a file icon, click the file icon, and then choose Open Attachment from the pop-up menu that appears.**

If you know what application should be used to open the attachment, click the Open With button and choose the correct application from the submenu that appears.

3. **To save an attachment, hold down Control, click the attachment (however it appears in the message), and then choose Save Attachment from the pop-up menu.**

In the Save dialog that appears, navigate to the location where you want to save the file and then click Save.

Fine-Tuning Your Post Office

Like all other Apple software, Mail is easily customized to your liking. In this section, I discuss some of the preferences that you might want to change.

Adding sound

To choose a sound that plays whenever you receive new mail, choose Mail➪Preferences➪General. Either click the New Mail Sound drop-down list box and choose one of the sounds that Apple provides or choose Add/Remove from the drop-down list to choose a sound file from the Sounds folder (which, in turn, is located within your Library folder). Choose None from the drop-down list to disable the new mail sound altogether.

Checking Mail automatically

By default, Mail automatically checks for new mail (and sends any mail in your Out folder) every five minutes. To change this delay period, display the General panel in the Preferences dialog, choose the Check for New Mail drop-down list box, and then choose one of the time periods. To disable automatic mail checking, choose Manually; you can click the Get Mail toolbar button to manually check your mail any time you like.

Automating message deletion

If you like, Mail can be set to automatically delete sent mail and Junk messages (as well as permanently erase messages that you relegate to the Trash). To configure these settings, display the Accounts list in the Preferences window, click the desired account, and then click the Mailboxes Behaviors tab.

To delete Sent messages automatically, enable the Erase Copies of Sent Messages When drop-down list box and choose the delay period or action. You can choose to delete mail after a day, a week, a month, or immediately upon quitting Mail. Alternatively, you can leave this field set to Never, and Mail will never automatically delete any messages from the Sent folder.

To delete Junk messages automatically, click the Erase Messages in the Junk Mailbox When drop-down list box and choose the delay period or action. (They're the same as the options available for Sent mail.)

To delete messages from the Trash, click the Erase Deleted Messages When drop-down list box and choose the delay period or action — again, the choices are the same as those for Sent messages.

Adding signatures

To add a block of text or a graphic to the bottom of your messages as your personal signature, follow these steps:

1. **Choose Mail⇨Preferences⇨Signatures.**

2. **From the Signatures pane that appears, click the Add Signature button.**

3. **Type a descriptive name for the signature in the Description box and then press Tab.**

4. **Type the signature itself in the text entry box or copy the signature to the Clipboard and paste it into the text entry box.**

Because downloading a graphic in a signature takes long — and because some folks still use plain text e-mail — avoid the temptation to include graphics in your signature.

If you enter a block of formatted text, click the Make Plain Text button to reduce those fancy fonts to plain text.

5. **Click OK to save the signature.**

6. **If you have multiple signatures, click the Choose Signature drop-down list to choose which one you want to use or to use them all randomly or in sequence.**

If you use specific signatures for different subjects, you can also enable the Show Signature Menu on Compose Window check box, which allows you to switch signatures from the Compose window.

Changing the status of an account

Sometimes you won't be able to reach one of your accounts. For example, maybe you're on the road with your laptop and you're unable to access your office network. Apple Mail allows you to enable and disable specific accounts without the hassle of deleting an account and then having to add it again.

To disable or enable an account, choose Preferences⇨Accounts and click the desired account; click the Advanced tab and then enable (or clear) the Enable This Account check box as necessary.

If you disable an account, you should also disable the Include When Automatically Checking for New Mail check box to make sure that Mail doesn't display an error message. You can always check any account for new mail by choosing Mailbox⇨Get New Mail and then choosing the desired account name from the submenu.

Automating Your Mail with Rules

Before I leave the beautiful shores of Mail Island — *"GILLIGAN!"* — I'd be remiss if I didn't discuss one of its most powerful features: the ability to create *rules,* which are automated actions that Mail can take. With rules, you can specify criteria that can perform actions such as

✦ Transferring messages from one folder to another

✦ Forwarding messages to another address

✦ Highlighting or deleting messages

To set up a rule, follow these steps:

1. **Choose Mail⇨Preferences and then click the Rules button on the toolbar.**

Mail displays the Rules dialog.

2. **To duplicate an existing rule, highlight it in the list and then click the Duplicate button. (For this demonstration, however, create a rule from scratch by clicking the Add Rule button.)**

3. **In the Description field, type a descriptive name for the new rule and then press Tab to move to the next field.**

4. **Click the If drop-down list to specify whether the rule will be triggered if *any* of the conditions are met or whether *all* conditions must be met.**

5. **Because each rule requires at least one condition, click the target drop-down list boxes to see the target for the condition.**

These include whom the message is from or to, which account received the message, whether the message is marked as junk, and whether the message contains certain content. Select the target for the condition.

6. **Click the Criteria drop-down list box to choose the rule's criteria.**

The contents of this drop-down list box change depending on the condition's target. For example, if you choose From as the target, the criteria include Contains, Does Not Contain, Begins With, and so forth.

7. **Click in the expression box and type the text to use for the condition.**

For example, a completed condition might read

```
Subject Contains Ocean-Front
```

This particular condition will be true if I get an e-mail message with a subject that contains the string Ocean-Front.

8. **Add more conditions by clicking the plus sign button at the right of the first condition.**

To remove any condition from this rule, click the minus sign button next to it. Remember, however, that every rule needs at least one condition.

9. **To specify what actions will be taken after the condition (or conditions) has been met, click the first Perform the Following Actions drop-down list box to see the action that this rule should perform. Then click the second drop-down list box and then select the action for the rule.**

Choices include transferring a message from one folder to another, playing a sound, automatically forwarding the message, deleting it, and marking it as read.

Each rule requires at least one action.

10. **Depending on the action that you select, specify one or more criterion(a) for the action.**

   For instance, if I select Set Color as my action, I must then choose whether to color the text or the background as well as what color to use.

   Like the plus button next to the conditions, you can also click the plus button next to the first action to perform more than one action. To remove an action, click the minus button next to it.

11. **When the rule is complete, click OK to save it.**

   Here's an example of a complex rule:

   If the message was sent by someone in my Address Book *and* the Subject field contains the text `FORWARD ME`, forward the message to the e-mail address `fuadramses@mac.com`.

This is a good example of an automated forwarding rule. With this rule in place and Mail running on Mac OS X, any of my friends, family, or co-workers can forward urgent e-mail to my .Mac account while I'm on vacation. To trigger the rule, all the sender has to do is include the words `FORWARD ME` in the message subject. And if the sender isn't in my Address Book, the rule doesn't trigger, and I can read the message when I get home. Mondo *sassy*.

Each rule in the Rules dialog can be enabled or disabled by toggling the Active check box next to the rule. You can also edit a rule by selecting it in the Rules dialog and then clicking the Edit button. To delete a rule completely from the list, select it and then click the Remove button; Mail will prompt you for confirmation before the deed is done.

Chapter 3: Staying in Touch with iChat AV

In This Chapter

✔ Setting up iChat AV

✔ Changing modes in iChat AV

✔ Adding Buddies

✔ Inviting a Buddy to chat

✔ Sending and receiving files via iChat AV

✔ Ignoring those who deserve to be shunned

*T*hroughout man's history, our drive has been toward communication — from the earliest cave paintings, through written language, to the telegraph, the telephone, and the cellular all-in-one PDA that the guy in the SUV in front of you is using . . . and he's arguing with someone and he's not paying attention and . . . (whump).

So much for the learned and scholarly introduction — forget that silly cellular phone and your complicated calling plan! As long as you have Mac OS X and an Internet connection, you can instantly chat with your friends and family whether they're across the aisle in another cube or halfway across the world. And, by golly, if you both have a Web cam or digital video (DV) camcorder connected to your computers, you'll *see* each other in glorious, full-color video! This modern marvel is *iChat AV,* and it fulfills the decades-old promise of the video telephone quite well, thank you.

In this chapter, I show you how to gab with the following folks:

✦ Others who use iChat AV (either on your local network or on the Internet)

✦ Anyone who uses AIM — that's short for *America Online (AOL) Instant Messaging*

✦ Folks who participate in AOL chat rooms

Configuring iChat

When you first run iChat AV (by clicking the iChat icon in the Dock), you'll be prompted to create an iChat account. Type the first name (your name) that you want to use in the First Name field, press Tab, and then type the surname that you want to use. (Yes, you can even use *Bullwinkle Moose* — just leave out the middle initial *J.*)

By default, iChat AV uses the .Mac account that you set up when you first installed Mac OS X. In this case, your .Mac account name and password are automatically entered for you, and you're good to go. However, if you're already using AIM and you'd like to use your existing AIM account, click the Account Type drop-down list and choose AIM; then enter your AIM name and password instead.

iChat will also set up Bonjour (new name in Tiger) messaging automatically. As you can read in Chapter 1 of Book V, think of *Bonjour* as plug-and-play for your local network. In iChat, Bonjour messaging displays a separate window where you can see (and yak with) anyone on your local network without having to know his iChat name. That's because Bonjour automatically announces all the iChat AV users who are available on your network. If you have others using iChat AV or AIM on your local network, go for this option; if you're not connected to a local network, however, Bonjour messaging isn't necessary. Also, if you're on a public AirPort/AirPort Extreme network or if you're connecting to the Internet with a modem through dialup, I recommend disabling Bonjour messaging. (For all that's cool about AirPort and its faster sibling AirPort Extreme, see Book V, Chapter 4.)

After you finish these configuration necessities, iChat AV displays the Buddy List window (or, if you're using Bonjour messaging, two windows) that you see in Figure 3-1. Remember that your Bonjour window displays only those iChat AV folks on your local network.

A few things to note here about the Buddy List window:

✦ **If you don't like your picture, don't panic.** By default, iChat AV uses your user account thumbnail image as your visual persona. However, you can add a picture to your iChat iDentity — sorry, I couldn't resist that — by dragging an image to the well next to your name at the top of the Buddy List window. If necessary, iChat AV will ask you to position and size the image so that it will fit in the (admittedly limited) space. This picture is then sent along with your words when you chat. In the figures for this chapter, I borrow the smiling face of Wolfgang Amadeus Mozart.

Click your image to display your recent thumbnails. This way, you can even use a different thumbnail image for each of your many moods. (Geez.) Also, you can click Edit Picture from the pop-up menu and capture a new thumbnail with your iSight camera.

✦ **Check out the buttons along the bottom of the Buddy List window.** In order, these buttons are

- **Add a New Buddy** (which I cover in the next section)
- **Start a Text Chat** (plain, old-fashioned chatting via the keyboard)
- **Start an Audio Chat** (chatting with your voice, using microphones)
- **Start a Video Chat** (the ultimate chat, where the parties can both see and hear each other)

Using these buttons can handle about 90 percent of the commands that you need to give while using iChat AV, so use 'em! (Note that the Bonjour window doesn't have an Add a New Buddy button because the Buddy List in the Bonjour window is automatically populated by other iChat AV folks on your local network.)

✦ **Hey, look, there's an iChat menu bar icon!** When you're running iChat AV, the application adds a balloon menu bar icon next to the clock display in the upper-right corner of your screen. Click it to display the options that you see in Figure 3-2. You can change your online/offline status, immediately invite a Buddy for a chat, or display the Buddy List (which I discuss later in the section, "Will You Be My Buddy?"). The menu bar icon appears only if you enable the Show Status in Menu Bar check box. Click iChat in the menu and choose Preferences; then click the General button in the Preference dialog.

Add a New Buddy button

Start a Video Chat button

Start an Audio Chat button

Start a Text Chat button

Figure 3-1: iChat AV and Bonjour instant messaging at its finest.

Figure 3-2:
The iChat
Finder menu
leaps into
action.

Changing Modes in iChat AV

To launch iChat AV, you can click its icon from the Dock or launch it from its iChat AV application icon (which you'll find in your Applications folder). Or, you can click its menu bar icon, which is grayed out when you're offline. If you're not already familiar with the terms *online* and *offline*, here's the scoop: When you're *online,* folks can invite you to chat and communicate with you. When you're *offline,* you're disconnected: iChat AV isn't active, you can't be paged, and you can't chat.

Even when you're offline, you can choose Available from the friendly balloon Finder menu bar icon, which will automatically switch iChat AV to online mode. Or you can click a Buddy name directly, which will automatically switch iChat AV to online mode and open the paging window for that Buddy. (Naturally, you have to have the proper network or Internet connection first.)

You can use another mode, *Away,* whenever iChat AV is running and you're still online but not available. For example, if I'm away from my Mac for a few minutes, I leave iChat AV running but I switch myself to Away mode. My Buddies get a message saying that I'm Away, so they won't bother trying to contact me. When I return to my computer, I simply move my mouse, and iChat AV intelligently inquires as to whether I'd like to return to Available mode. You can also use the menu bar icon to switch from Away to Available (or my other favorite mode, *Twiddling My Thumbs*). Refer to Figure 3-2 to see these choices.

Speaking of modes, you, too, can create a custom mode — like *Bored stiff!* or *Listening to the Pointy-Haired Boss* — and use it instead of the somewhat mundane choices of *Available* and *Away.* To do this, display the Buddy List window, click the word *Available* beneath your name (refer to Figure 3-2), and a drop-down list appears.

To choose an existing mode, click it; modes with a green bullet are online modes, and red bullet modes are offline modes. Click the Custom menu item for either color to open an edit box; type the new mode there and then press Return. The new mode is automatically added to your mode list. You can also switch modes from this drop-down list. (You'll notice in Figure 3-2 that I created a custom mode called *Getting Another Diet Coke...* cAfFeInE fills my life.)

Will You Be My Buddy?

I know that question sounds a little personal, but in iChat AV, a *Buddy* is anyone whom you want to chat with, whether the topic is work related or your personal life. iChat AV keeps track of your Buddies in the Buddy List. You can also add them to your Address Book or use the AIM entry in an Address Book contact to generate a new Buddy identity.

To add a new Buddy, follow these steps:

1. **Choose iChat⇨Buddies⇨Add Buddy, or click the Add Buddy button at the bottom of the iChat AV window and click Add Buddy from the pop-up menu, or press ⌘+Shift+A.**

iChat AV displays the sheet that you see in Figure 3-3.

**Book IV
Chapter 3**

**Staying in Touch
with iChat AV**

Figure 3-3:
Add a buddy
from your
Address
Book.

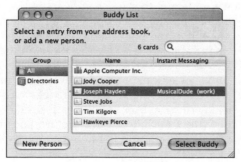

2. **To create a Buddy entry from an Address Book contact who has an Instant Messaging username, click the entry to select it, and then click the Select Buddy button.**

3. **To add a brand-new person who's not already in your Address Book, click the New Person button to display the sheet that you see in Figure 3-4.**

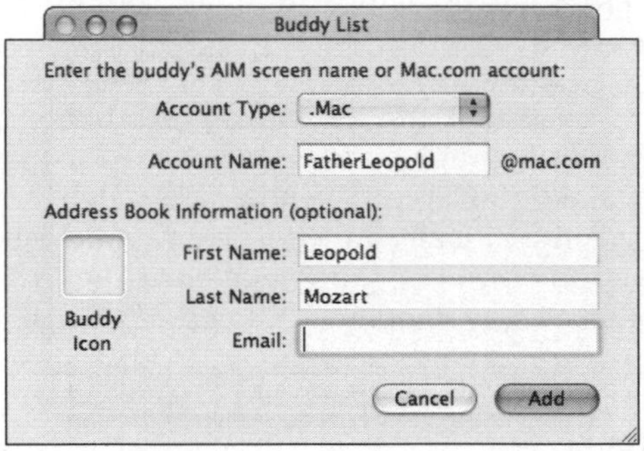

Figure 3-4:
Enter
information
for a new
buddy.

> **Buddy List**
>
> Enter the buddy's AIM screen name or Mac.com account:
>
> Account Type: .Mac
>
> Account Name: FatherLeopold @mac.com
>
> Address Book Information (optional):
>
> Buddy Icon
>
> First Name: Leopold
>
> Last Name: Mozart
>
> Email:
>
> Cancel   Add

4. **In this new sheet, select the proper account type (either .Mac or AIM), press Tab, and then type the person's Instant Messaging account name.**

If you like, you can also add your own picture to represent that person (instead of using the icon that he provides). Just locate the image file that you want to use within a Finder window and drag the image to the Buddy Icon well.

(Optional) You can also enter the person's real name and e-mail address, and iChat AV obligingly creates an entry in your Address Book for your new Buddy. (Apple, you truly rock.)

5. **Click Add to save the Buddy information.**

Even when you add a new Buddy and that name appears in the Buddy List, don't be surprised if the name actually fades out after a few seconds — that indicates that the person is offline and unavailable. You can also tell when a person is available if her name appears with a green bullet in the Buddy List.

You can also specify a number of actions that iChat AV should take if a Buddy logs in or out of Instant Messaging, or if a Buddy changes his or her status to Available. To display these actions, click the desired Buddy's entry in your Buddy List and then press ⌘+Shift+I. Click the drop-down list box at the top of the Info dialog, click Actions, and then choose the event that should trigger the action from the Event drop-down list. Enable the desired check box to specify whether iChat AV should play the sound that you select, speak a line of text, and/or bounce the iChat AV icon on the Dock. (My technical editor prefers, "Elvis has just left the building.")

Chat! Chat, I Say!

Turn your attention to getting the attention of others — through inviting others to chat. Good chatting etiquette implies inviting someone to a conversation rather than barging in unannounced.

If you want to join an AIM chat already in progress, choose File➪Go to Chat (or press ⌘+Shift+G). Depending on the service being used, you might have to specify both the type of chat and the specific chat room name.

At this point, it's time to draw your attention to the green phone and video icons next to each person in your Buddy List (as well as next to your own name at the top of the list). If the green phone icon appears next to both your name and your buddy's name, you can enjoy a two-way audio (or voice) chat. If both you and your buddy are lucky enough to have iSight or DV cameras connected to your Macs, you can jump into a real-time, two-way video chat, complete with audio.

If your Mac has a microphone or video camera hooked up but you don't see these icons, click the Audio menu and make sure that the Microphone Enabled and Camera Enabled menu items are selected.

To invite someone, click the desired Buddy from the Buddy List, click Buddies, and then choose Invite to Chat. (If your pointing thing has two buttons, right-click — or Control-click — on the Buddy in the list and click Invite to Chat.) You can also click directly on the phone or camera icon next to the person's name in your Buddy List. iChat AV displays the Group Chat window that you see in Figure 3-5, which also doubles as an Invitation window.

Figure 3-5:
Inviting that special someone. (Actually, this guy owes me money.)

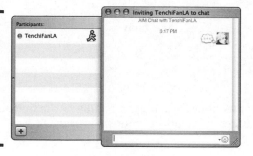

You can invite additional Buddies to enter the chat by clicking the plus button at the bottom left of the Participants list and choosing another Buddy. If the Participants list isn't visible, click the View menu and choose Show Chat Participants.

Type your invitation text into the entry box at the bottom of the window. If you'd like to use bold or italic text, highlight the text and press ⌘+B for Bold (**B**) or ⌘+I for Italic (*I*). You can also add a Smiley face to your invitation text: Click in the desired spot in the text, click the Smiley button to the right of the text entry field, and then choose the proper Smiley from the list. To send the invitation text, press Return.

The recipient of your chat invitation can decline or accept your chat invitation. You'll be notified (as delicately as possible) if the chat has been declined.

To invite a Buddy to an audio chat, select that person in the Buddy List, click the Buddies menu, and then choose Invite to Audio Chat (or One-Way Audio Chat, if only one of you has a microphone). A video invitation works in a similar fashion: Click Buddies and choose either Invite to Video Chat or Invite to One-Way Video Chat, depending on the hardware available.

If the chat is accepted, iChat AV displays a message saying that the Buddy whom you invited has joined the chat, and you now can begin the chat. You don't have to alternate sending messages back and forth between participants — everyone in a chat can compose and send messages at the same time — but I personally like to alternate when I'm chatting one-on-one. See the volley in Figure 3-6. By the way, you might notice that AIM users are represented by the AIM Running Dude icon (unless AOL changes it, or you assign an icon picture of your own as I describe in the previous section).

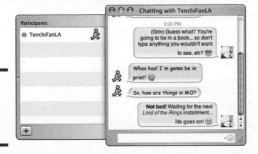

Figure 3-6: A typical chat in progress.

You can resize the Chat window by using the handle at the bottom-right corner, just like most other application windows in Mac OS X.

You can also change fonts and colors while composing a line of text. Simply select the text and then choose Format⇨Show Fonts or Format⇨Show Colors (or press ⌘+T or ⌘+Shift+C) to display the Fonts and Colors windows, respectively. These windows can be resized and moved wherever you like.

To save the discussion in a chat, choose File⇨Save a Copy As. In the dialog that appears, type a name for the chat file, select a location where you want to store the file, and then click Save. To automatically save transcripts of all your chats, choose iChat⇨Preferences and click Messages; then select the Automatically Save Chat Transcripts check box. The transcripts are saved in an iChats folder that's created inside your Documents folder in your Home folder.

When the iChat AV window is active, a number of display choices can be made from the View menu, including

✦ **Show as Text:** Each line that you write and receive in a chat can be displayed in *balloons,* just like your favorite comic — the default — or as simple text.

✦ **Show Names and Pictures:** Each line can be displayed with the individual's picture, just the name, or both the name and picture.

✦ **Background display:** Choose the Set Chat Background menu item to choose a graphic to use for the Chat window. To return to the original appearance, choose the Clear Background menu item.

Click the Buddy List, and the View menu offers a different set of controls: You can sort your Buddy List by first name, last name, or availability; and you can also toggle the display of offline Buddies. These options are also available from the Buddy List toolbar.

To close a chat, click the Close button on the Chat window.

Sending Files with iChat AV

To send a file to a Buddy, click the desired entry in the Buddy List and then choose Buddies⇨Send a File. Alternatively, you can use the ⌘+Option+F keyboard shortcut; right-click and choose Send a File; drag the file from a Finder window to the person's entry in the Buddy List; or even drag the file into the text typing window. (How's that for convenience?) A dialog appears to indicate that the recipient is being offered a file transfer request. If the file request is accepted by your Buddy, the transfer begins and is saved where the recipient specifies on her system.

If a Buddy sends you a file, the Incoming File Request pane appears. You can then either click the Decline button (to decline the file transfer) or the Save File button (to save the incoming file to any spot on your system).

Always check any files that you receive from iChat AV with your antivirus scanning software before you run them!

Eliminating the Riffraff

Here I need to explain something that I hope you won't have to use — what I like to call the *Turkey Filter*. (iChat AV is a little more subtle — you just *ignore* people.)

To ignore someone in a chat group, click her name in the list and choose Buddies⇨Ignore Person. When someone is ignored in a chat group, you won't see anything that she types or have to respond to any file transfer requests from that person.

If only it were that easy to ignore someone when he's standing close to you.

Anyway, if the person becomes a royal pain, you can also choose to *block* that person entirely. That way, the offensive cur won't even know that you're online, and he can't reach you at all. Click the person in the list and choose Buddies⇨Block Person — the deal is done.

Chapter 4: Expanding Your Horizons with iDisk

In This Chapter

✔ Setting up iDisk

✔ Using files and folders on your iDisk

✔ Using public files

*I*f you ask the average Mac owner what's available on the Internet, you'll likely hear benefits such as e-mail, Web surfing, Google, and instant communication via iChat AV. What you probably *won't* hear is, "Convenient, trouble-free storage for my files and folders."

You might have tried to use one of the dozens of storage sites on the Internet that allow you to upload and download files from a personal file area via your Web browser. Unfortunately, these Web-based storage sites are slow in transferring files, lacking in convenience, and typically offer only a small amount of space. As a result, most computer owners decide that the idea of online storage is neat . . . but impractical.

In this chapter, I show you what *real* online storage is all about. I'm talking about *iDisk,* which is the online storage feature that's integrated into the Mac OS X Finder. No jury-rigged Web site is necessary (although you can use one if you're not on a Mac running Mac OS X). I'll admit that online storage won't replace the hard drives on your Mac, but with a .Mac subscription, you can easily make use of online storage for backups and sharing files with your friends . . . from anywhere on the planet!

So how do you actually *use* iDisk? That's the simple part! To use iDisk within Mac OS X, just do what comes naturally — it works like any other removable volume's Finder window. You can copy and move files and folders to and from your iDisk, create new subfolders (except in the Backup, Library, and Software root folders, which are read-only), and delete whatever you don't need.

Grabbing Internet Storage for Your Mac

To set up iDisk on your Mac OS X system, you'll need a .Mac account. You did create one during the installation of the Big X, right? These trial accounts are limited to a maximum of 25MB of storage, and the trial account is active for only 60 days. Therefore, if you decide that you like iDisk, you should subscribe to .Mac; a subscription increases your online treasure chest to 125MB of iDisk storage. To subscribe, visit www.mac.com and follow the prompts to join from there. (At the time of this writing, the subscription fee is $100 per year.)

With a .Mac account active, iDisk is automatically available. To see how much storage you're using and to configure access to your Public folder, open System Preferences, click the .Mac icon, and then click the iDisk button to display the settings that you see in Figure 4-1. (You can also click the Buy More button on this panel to subscribe to Apple's .Mac service, or (if you're already a .Mac subscriber) add more than 125MB of storage.)

Figure 4-1: Your iDisk settings are available from System Preferences.

The iDisk Disk Space bar graph illustrates how much of your current iDisk territory you're using. (Note that the account shown in Figure 4-1 is an evaluation account, so it shows only a total of 25MB.)

You can specify the access privilege level for other .Mac users from this panel as well. Select the Read-Only radio button to prevent any other .Mac user from copying files to your Public folder, or select the Read-Write radio button to allow others to save files there.

Pinning down your iDisk

So where exactly *are* your files kept when you use your iDisk? In earlier versions of Mac OS X, your acre of storage farmland always sat on one of Apple's iDisk *file servers* — perhaps in Cupertino, perhaps elsewhere. These server computers are especially designed to store terabytes (TB) of information (1TB equals 1,000GB), and they're connected to the Internet via high-speed trunk lines. (And yes, they do have a firewall.)

However, you can elect to keep a local copy of your iDisk storage area — usually called a *mirror* — on your Mac's hard drive. (Because Macs have copious hard drives, reserving 125MB is no problem.) Before you scratch your head wondering why you're duplicating your iDisk files on your computer, here's the reason: If you do decide to keep a local copy of your files, you can work on them even when you're not connected to the Internet! Tiger automatically synchronizes any files that you've updated locally with your remote iDisk whenever you connect to the Internet. (If you use multiple Macs at different locations, think about being able to access the latest copies of your files from *any* of them, right from the Finder!)

This nifty mirror also greatly speeds up things when you're browsing the contents of your iDisk or perhaps loading and saving an iDisk document; that's because you're working with your local copy, and Mac OS X updates any changes that you make to the corresponding remote file on the iDisk server. You can tell that things are updating when that funky little yin yang, circular doodad — the thing next to your iDisk in the Finder window — is rotating in its animated fashion. (And yes, I have it on good authority . . . that's what the Apple software developers call it, too.)

You're not required to use a mirror, however. To disable the mirroring feature and return to the remote-only operation of old, click the iDisk Syncing On button on the iDisk settings panel to turn it off. Remember, though, that with the mirroring feature turned off, you must have an Internet connection to use iDisk, and things will move more slowly because you're accessing everything across the Internet.

No matter which privilege level you choose, you can also set a password that other .Mac users must type before they're allowed access to your Public folder — this is the very definition of *A Truly Good Idea*. (More on the Public folder in the next section.)

 If you've already set a password, you can change it by clicking the Set Password button and typing the new word in the Password box. Retype the word in the Confirm box to verify it; then click OK to save the change and return to the .Mac System Preferences panel.

Understanding What's on Your iDisk

Unlike the physical hard drive in your Mac, your iDisk never needs formatting or defragmenting, and you'll never have to check it for errors. However, the structure of an iDisk is fixed, so you can't just go crazy creating your own folders. In fact, you can't create new folders at the *root* — the top level — of your iDisk at all, but you can create new folders inside most of the root folders.

Now that you're thoroughly rooterized, here are the folders that you'll find hanging out in your iDisk:

✦ **Backup:** This is a read-only folder that contains the backup files created with the .Mac Backup application. You can, however, copy the files in this folder to a removable drive on your system for an additional level of safekeeping.

✦ **Documents:** This folder holds any application documents that you want to store . . . things like spreadsheets and letters. No one but you can access these items.

✦ **Library:** Another read-only folder. This spot contains the configuration data and custom settings that you've created for other .Mac features.

✦ **Movies:** QuickTime movies go here — again, you can add the movies stored here to your Web pages. (I cover QuickTime like a blanket in Book III, Chapter 7.)

✦ **Music:** This is the repository for all your iTunes music and playlists, and the contents can be added to your Web pages. (iTunes is the star of Chapter 2 in Book III.) Mine is stuffed full of Mozart, Scarlatti, and that Bach fellow.

✦ **Pictures:** This folder is the vault for your JPEG and GIF images, including those that you want to use with iCards or your Web pages.

✦ **Public:** This is the spot to place files that you specifically want to share with others, either directly through iDisk or with your Web pages. If you've allowed write access, others can copy files to your Public folder as well.

✦ **Sites:** The Web pages that you store here can be created with Apple's HomePage utility — which is available to all .Mac members — or you can use your own Web page design application and copy the completed site files here.

✦ **Software:** Apple provides this read-only folder as a service to .Mac members; it contains a selection of the latest freeware, shareware, and commercial demos for you to enjoy. To try something out, open the Software folder and copy whatever you like to your Mac OS X Desktop. Then you can install and run the application from the local copy of the files.

Opening and Using iDisk

When you're connected to the Internet, you can open your iDisk in one of the following ways:

✦ **From the Finder menu, choose Go⇨iDisk and then choose My iDisk from the submenu or use the ⌘+Shift+I keyboard shortcut.**

✦ **Click the iDisk icon in the Finder Sidebar.**

✦ **Add an iDisk button to your Finder window toolbar by choosing View⇨Customize Toolbar.**

After you add the button, you can click it to connect to your iDisk from anywhere in the Finder.

Your iDisk opens in a new Finder window. After you use one of these methods in a Mac OS X session, your iDisk icon appears on the Mac OS X Desktop; Figure 4-2 shows the iDisk icon on the Desktop, the iDisk contents in a Finder window, and its properties in the Get Info dialog. The iDisk volume icon remains until you shut down or restart your Mac. (Alternatively, you can dismiss the iDisk volume icon from your Desktop using the same method that you eject an external drive: Click the iDisk icon and press ⌘+E, or click the Eject button next to the iDisk icon in the Finder window Sidebar.)

Figure 4-2:
The contents of your iDisk — pretty iNeat, I'm thinking.

If you're using a remote computer with an Internet connection, you can log in to the .Mac page at `www.apple.com` and use your Web browser to access the contents of your iDisk. (Hey, sometimes this is the only choice you have.)

However, you don't actually need to open your iDisk in a Finder window to use it because you can also load and save files directly to your iDisk from within any application. Simply choose your iDisk as you would any of the hard drives on your system when using the application's Load, Save, or Save As commands.

You can also open an iDisk's Public folder — either yours or the Public folder inside another person's iDisk — as if it were an Internet file server. As I explain earlier, if that person has set a password, you need to enter that password to gain access to all of their iDisk folders. From the Finder menu, choose Go⟳iDisk⟳Other User's iDisk (or, to jump directly to their Public folder, choose Go⟳iDisk⟳Other User's Public Folder). If you choose the former, Tiger prompts you for the other person's member name and password; if you pick the latter, you need only enter the other .Mac member's account name.

After you enter a valid iDisk member name (and password, if required), you'll see the .Mac member's Public folder.

You can also use the server address

`http://idisk.mac.com/`*`username`*`-Public?`

to connect to an iDisk from computers running Windows and Linux. Check the Help for your operating system to determine how to connect to a WebDAV server (usually called a *Web folder* in the Windows world). When prompted for your access username and password, use your .Mac account name and password. If you're using Windows XP, Apple has provided an even easier way to open an iDisk Public folder: Use iDisk Utility for Windows, which you can download from `www.mac.com`.

Chapter 5: Going Places with Safari

In This Chapter

- ⌐ Introducing the Safari window and controls
- ⌐ Visiting Web sites with Safari
- ⌐ Moving between sites
- ⌐ Creating and using bookmarks
- ⌐ Receiving files with Safari
- ⌐ Surfing with your tabs showing
- ⌐ Saving Web pages to disk
- ⌐ Protecting your privacy on the Web
- ⌐ Blocking those irritating pop-ups

*W*hen I was designing the Table of Contents for this book, I seriously considered leaving this chapter out. After all, more people use a Web browser now than any other software application. Who really needs a guide to mowing a lawn?

But then again, I suddenly thought of all the hidden features that folks don't know about Apple's Safari browser — for example, the tips and tricks that can help you organize your online visits. It's a little like learning more about the lawn mower itself: Even though you might not need tips on mowing, many people don't know how to remove the spark plug in the winter or how to sharpen the blade so you can handle taller grass. Remember, *magic is nothing more than technology that someone understands.*

In this chapter, I show you how to use those other controls and toolbar buttons in Safari — you know, the ones in addition to the Forward and Back buttons — and you'll discover how to keep track of where you've been and where you'd like to go. (Oh, and did I mention that you'll need an Internet connection?)

One note: Many authors have written entire books on Web browsing. As you might guess, this chapter is far narrower in scope than those books — I've got more ground to cover before dinner — and it doesn't include every one of Safari's features. However, I think the coverage that you find here will explain all that you're likely to need for most surfing sessions.

Pretend You've Never Used This Thing

Figure 5-1 illustrates the Safari window. You can launch Safari directly from the Dock, or you can click the Safari icon within your Applications folder.

Major sections of the Safari window include

✦ **The Address bar:** You'll find the most often-used commands on this toolbar for things like navigation, adding bookmarks, and searching Google. Plus, here you can type or paste the address for Web sites that you'd like to visit. The Address bar can be hidden to provide you with more real estate in your browser window for Web content. To toggle hidden mode, press ⌘+| (the vertical bar right above the backslash) or choose View⇨Address Bar.

Bookmarks bar   Address bar Content window

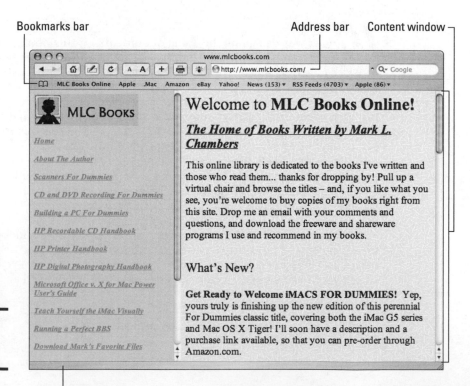

Figure 5-1:
Safari at a glance.

Status bar

✦ **The Bookmarks bar:** Consider this a toolbar that allows you to jump directly to your favorite Web sites with a single click. I show you later in the section "Adding and Using Bookmarks" how to add and remove sites from your Bookmarks bar. For now, remember that you can toggle the display of the Bookmarks bar by choosing View➪Bookmarks Bar, or press ⌘+Shift+B.

✦ **The Content window:** Congratulations! At last, you've waded through all the pre-game show and you've reached the area where Web pages are actually displayed. Like any other window, the Content window can be scrolled; when you minimize Safari to the Dock, you get a *thumbnail* (minimized) image of the Content window.

The Content window often contains underlined text and graphical icons that transport you to other pages when you click them. These under-lined words and icons are *links,* and they make it easy to move from one area of a site to another or to a completely different site.

✦ **The status bar:** The status bar displays information about what the mouse pointer is currently resting upon, like the address for a link or the name of an image; it also updates you on what's happening while a page is loading. To hide or display the status bar, press ⌘+/ (forward slash).

Visiting Web Sites

Here's the stuff that virtually everyone over the age of 5 knows how to do . . . but I get paid by the word, and some folks might just not be aware of all the myriad ways of visiting a site. You can load a Web page from any of the fol-lowing methods:

✦ **Type (or paste) a Web site address into the Address bar and then press Return.**

If you're typing in an address and Safari recognizes the site as one that you've visited in the past, it helps by completing the address for you. If this is a new site, just keep typing.

✦ **Click a Bookmarks entry within Safari.**

✦ **Click the Home button, which takes you to the home page that you specify.**

More on this in the section "Setting Up Your Home Page" later in this chapter.

✦ **Click a page link in Apple Mail or another Internet-savvy application.**

✦ **Click a page link within another Web page.**

**Book IV
Chapter 5**

**Going Places
with Safari**

✦ **Use the Google box in the Address bar.**

Click in the Google box, type the contents that you want to find, and then press Return. Safari presents you with the search results page on Google for the text that you entered. (In case you've been living under the Internet equivalent of a rock for the last couple of years, *Google.com* is the preeminent search site on the Web — people use Google to find everything from used auto parts to ex-spouses.)

✦ **Click a Safari page icon on the Dock or in a Finder window.**

For example, Mac OS X already has an icon in the default Dock that takes you to the Mac OS X page on the Apple Web site. Drag a site from your Bookmarks bar and drop it on the right side of the Dock. Clicking the icon that you add launches Safari and automatically loads that site.

This trick only works on the side of the Dock to the right of the vertical line.

If you minimize Safari to the Dock, you'll see a thumbnail of the page with the Safari logo superimposed on it. Click this thumbnail in the Dock to restore the page to its full glory.

Navigating the Web

A typical Web surfing session is a linear experience — you bop from one page to the next, absorbing the information that you want and discarding the rest. However, after you visit a few sites, you might find that you need to return to where you've been or head to the familiar ground of your home page. Safari offers these navigational controls on the Address bar:

✦ **Back:** Click the Back button (the left-facing arrow) on the toolbar to return to the last page that you visited. Additional clicks take you to previous pages, in reverse order. The Back button is disabled if you haven't visited at least two sites.

✦ **Forward:** If you've clicked the Back button at least once, clicking the Forward button (the right-facing arrow) takes you to the next page (or through the pages) where you originally were, in forward order. The Forward button is disabled if you haven't used the Back button.

✦ **Home:** Click this button (look for the little house) to return to your home page.

Not all these buttons and controls might appear on your Address bar. To display or hide Address bar controls, choose View⇨Customize Address Bar. The sheet that appears works just like the Customize Toolbar sheet within a Finder window: Drag the control you want from the sheet to your Address bar, or drag a control that you don't want from the Address bar to the sheet.

✦ **AutoFill:** If you fill out a lot of forms online — when you're shopping at Web sites, for example — you can click the AutoFill button (which looks like a little text box and a pen) to complete these forms for you. You can set what information is used for AutoFill by choosing Safari⇨Preferences and clicking the AutoFill toolbar button.

To be honest, I'm not a big fan of releasing *any* of my personal information to *any* Web site, so I don't use AutoFill often. If you do decide to use this feature, make sure that the connection is secure (look for the padlock icon in the upper-right corner of the Safari window) and read the site's Privacy Agreement page first to see how your identity data will be treated.

✦ **Text Size:** Shrinks or expands the text on the page, offering smaller, space-saving characters (for the shrinking crowd) or larger, easier-to-read text (for the expanding crowd). Hence the button, which is labeled with a small and large letter A.

✦ **Stop/Reload:** Click Reload (which has a circular arrow) to refresh (reload) the contents of the current page. Although most pages remain static, some pages change their content at regular intervals or after you fill out a form or click a button. By clicking Reload (look for the curvy arrow), you can see what's changed on these pages. (I use Reload every hour or so with CNN.com, for example.) While a page is loading, the Reload button turns into the Stop button — with a little X mark — and you can click it to stop the loading of the content from the current page. This is a real boon when a download takes *foorrevverr,* which can happen when you're trying to visit a very popular or very slow Web site (especially if you're using a dialup modem connection to the Internet). Using Stop is also handy if a page has a number of very large graphics that are going to take a long time to load.

✦ **Add Bookmark:** Click this Address bar button (which carries a plus sign) to add a page to your Bookmarks bar or Bookmarks menu. (More on this in a tad.)

**Book IV
Chapter 5**

**Going Places
with Safari**

✦ **Google Search:** As I mention earlier, you can click in this box and type text that you want to find on the Web via the Google search engine — press Return to display the results. To repeat a recent search, click the down arrow in the Google Search box and select it from the drop-down list.

✦ **Print:** Click this convenient button to print the contents of the Safari window — dig that crazy printer icon!

✦ **Bug:** A rather strange creature, the Safari Bug button makes it easy to alert Apple when you encounter a page that doesn't display properly in Safari. (Software developers call such glitches *bugs* — hence the name.) When you click the Bug button, you'll see a sheet with the settings shown in Figure 5-2; take time to enter a short description of the problem that you're having. (I also enable the Send Screen Shot of Current Page and the Send Source of Current Page check boxes to give the Apple folks more to work with while they're debugging Safari.) Then click the Submit button to send the bug report to Apple.

Figure 5-2:
Have at
thee,
troublesome
buggy page!

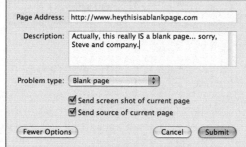

Setting Up Your Home Page

Choosing a home page is one of the easiest methods of speeding up your Web surfing, especially if you're using a dialup modem connection. However, a large percentage of the Mac owners whom I've talked to have never set their own home page, simply using the default home page provided by their browser! With Safari running, take a moment to follow these steps to declare your own freedom to choose your own home page:

1. **If you want to use a specific Web page as your new home page, display it in Safari.**

I recommend electing a page with few graphics or a fast-loading popular site.

2. **Choose Safari⇨Preferences or press ⌘+, (comma).**

3. **Click the General button.**

   You'll see the settings shown in Figure 5-3.

4. **Click the Set to Current Page button.**

5. **Alternatively, click the New Windows Open With drop-down list box and choose Empty Page if you want Safari to open a new window with a blank page.**

   This is the fastest choice of all for a home page.

6. **Click the Close button to exit the Preferences dialog.**

Figure 5-3:
Adding your own home page is an easy change you can make.

Visit your home page at any time by pressing the Home button on the Address bar.

Adding and Using Bookmarks

No doubt about it: Bookmarks make the Web a friendly place. As you collect bookmarks in Safari, you're able to immediately jump from one site to another with a single click on the Bookmarks menu or the buttons on the Bookmarks bar.

Lean, fast, and mean — That's RSS

Well, maybe not *mean* — after all, I don't want you to be afraid of RSS (RDF Site Summary) pages! RSS Web sites display updated information using a shortened list format, rather like a newspaper headline, without unnecessary graphics or silly advertisements. You can tell when a Web site has RSS pages available because Safari displays an RSS icon at the right side of the Address box. (When you click the RSS icon, the Web address switches to a `feed://` prefix — another indication that you're not in Kansas reading HTML pages anymore.)

To display more information about a news item on an RSS page, click the item headline. Safari opens the corresponding Web page — yep, once again you're back in the world of HTML — and you can read the full story. To return to the RSS feed, click the Back button on the Address bar. Naturally, RSS feed pages can be bookmarked. In fact, Apple gives you a number of RSS sites that you can explore immediately.

To customize your RSS display, choose Safari⇨ Preferences, and then click the RSS tab. By default, Safari checks for updated RSS headlines every 30 minutes, but you can change this to an hourly or daily check. (Of course, you can also check for updates manually by reloading the RSS page, just like you would any other Web page.) New articles can be assigned any color you like, and you can specify the amount of time an item should remain on the RSS page after it's published.

To add a bookmark, first navigate to the desired page and then do any of the following:

✦ **Choose Bookmarks⇨Add Bookmark.**

✦ **Press the ⌘+D keyboard shortcut.**

Safari displays a sheet where you can enter the name for the bookmark and also select where it will appear (on the Bookmarks bar or the Bookmarks menu).

✦ **Drag the icon next to the Web address from the Address bar to the Bookmarks bar.**

You can also drag a link on the current page to the Bookmarks bar, but note that doing this only adds a bookmark for the page corresponding to the link — not the current page.

To jump to a bookmark:

✦ **Choose it from the Bookmarks menu.**

If the bookmark is contained in a folder, which I discuss later in this section, move your mouse pointer over the folder name to show its contents and then click the bookmark.

◆ **Click the bookmark on the Bookmarks bar.**

If you've added a large number of items to the Bookmarks bar, click the More icon on the edge of the Bookmarks bar to display the rest of the buttons.

◆ **Click the Show All Bookmarks button (which looks like a small opened book) on the Bookmarks bar and then click the desired bookmark.**

The Bookmarks window that you see in Figure 5-4 appears, where you can review each collection of bookmarks at leisure.

The more bookmarks that you add, the more unwieldy the Bookmarks menu and the Bookmarks window become. To keep things organized, choose Bookmarks⇨Add Bookmark Folder and then type a name for the new folder. With folders, you can organize your bookmarks into *collections,* which appear in the column at the left of the Bookmarks window (or as separate submenus within the Bookmarks menu). You can drag bookmarks within the new folder to help reduce the clutter.

To delete a bookmark or a folder from the Bookmarks window, click it and then press Delete.

Figure 5-4:
The Bookmarks window puts all your bookmarks within easy reach.

Downloading Files

A huge chunk of the fun that you'll find on the Web is the ability to download images and files. If you've visited a site that offers files for downloading, typically you just click the Download button or the download file link, and Safari takes care of the rest. You'll see the Downloads status window, which keeps you updated with the progress of the transfer. While the file is downloading, feel free to continue browsing or even download additional files; the status window helps you keep track of what's going on and when everything will be finished transferring. To display the Download status window from the keyboard, press ⌘+Option+L.

By default, Safari saves any downloaded files on your Mac OS X Desktop, which I like and use. To specify the location where downloaded files are stored — for example, if you'd like to scan them automatically with an antivirus program — follow these steps:

1. **Choose Safari⇨Preferences or press ⌘+, (comma).**

2. **Click the General tab and then click the Save Downloaded Files To drop-down list box.**

3. **Choose Other.**

4. **Navigate to the location where you want the files stored.**

5. **Click the Select button.**

6. **Click the Close button to exit Preferences.**

To download a specific image that appears on a Web page, move your mouse pointer over the image and hold down Control while you click. Then choose Download Image to Disk from the pop-up menu that appears. Safari prompts you for the location where you want to store the file.

Luckily, Safari has matured to the point that it can seamlessly handle virtually any multimedia file type that it encounters. However, if you've downloaded a multimedia file and Safari doesn't seem to be able to play or display it, try loading the file within QuickTime. As you can read in Book III, Chapter 7, *QuickTime* is the Swiss Army knife of multimedia players, and it can recognize a huge number of audio, video, and image formats.

Using Subscriptions and History

To keep track of where you've been, you can display the History list by clicking the History menu. To return to a page in the list, just choose it from the History menu. Note that Safari also arranges older history items by the date you visited the site, so you can easily jump back a couple of days to that page you forgot to bookmark!

In fact, Safari also searches the History list automatically, when it fills in an address that you're typing — that's the feature I mention in the earlier section, "Visiting Web Sites."

If you're worried about security and you'd rather not keep track of where you've been online, I show you how to clear the contents of the History file in the upcoming section, "Handling ancient history."

Tabs Are Your Browsing Friends

Safari also offers *tabbed browsing,* which many folks use to display (and organize) multiple Web pages at one time. For example, if you're doing a bit of comparison shopping for a new piece of hardware between different online stores, tabs are ideal.

When you hold down the ⌘ key and click a link or bookmark using tabs, a tab representing the new page appears under the Bookmarks bar. Just click the tab to switch to that page. (If you don't hold down ⌘, things revert to business as usual, and Safari replaces the contents of the window with the new page.) Figure 5-5 illustrates a number of pages that I've opened in Safari using tabs.

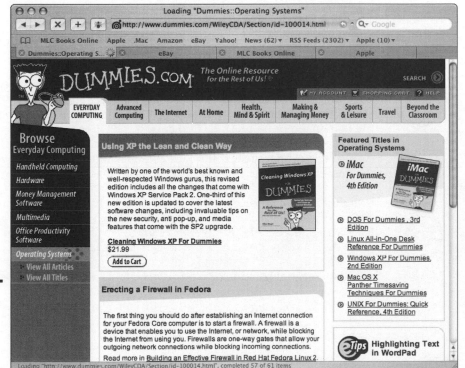

Figure 5-5: Hang on, Martha, we've struck tabs!

To turn on tabbed browsing, choose Safari⇨Preferences to display the Preferences dialog; then click Tabs. From here, select the Enable Tabbed Browsing check box to turn on tabs.

Done with a page? You can remove a tabbed page by clicking the X button next to the tab's title.

Saving Web Pages

If you've encountered a page that you'd like to load later, you can save it to disk in its entirety. (Just the text, mind you, not the images.) Follow these steps:

1. **Display the desired page.**

2. **Choose File⇨Save As.**

3. **In the Save As text field, type a name for the saved page.**

4. **From the Where field, navigate to the location where you want to store the file on your system.**

   To expand the sheet to allow navigation to any location on your system, click the button with the downward arrow.

5. **Click Save to begin the download process.**

   After the Save file has been created, double-click it to load it in Safari.

A quick word about printing a page within Safari: Some combinations of background and text colors might conspire together to render your printed copy practically worthless. In a case like that, use your printer's grayscale setting (if it has one). Alternatively, you can simply click and drag to select the text on the page, press ⌘+C to copy it, and then paste the text into Word or AppleWorks, where you can print the page on a less offensive background (while still keeping the text formatting largely untouched). You can also save the contents of a page as plain text, as I just demonstrated.

If you'd rather mail the contents of a Web page to a friend — or just a link to the page, which is faster to send over a dialup Internet connection — choose File⇨Mail Contents of this Page/Mail Link to this Page. (From the keyboard, press ⌘+I to send the contents in an e-mail message, or press ⌘+Shift+I to send a link in e-mail.) Mail loads automatically, complete with a prepared e-mail message. Just address it to the recipients and then click Send!

Protecting Your Privacy

No chapter on Safari would be complete without a discussion of security, both against outside intrusion from the Internet and prying eyes around your Mac. Hence this last section, which covers protecting your privacy.

Although diminutive, the tiny padlock icon that appears in the top-right corner of the Safari window when you're connected to a secure Web site means a great deal! A *secure site* encrypts the information that you send and receive, making it much harder for those of unscrupulous ideals to obtain things like credit card numbers and personal information.

Yes, there are such things as bad cookies

First, a definition of this ridiculous term: A *cookie,* a small file that a Web site automatically saves on your hard drive, contains information that the site will use on your future visits. For example, a site might save a cookie to preserve your site preferences for the next time or — in the case of a site such as Amazon.com — to identify you automatically and help customize the offerings that you see.

In and of themselves, cookies aren't bad things. Unlike a virus, a cookie file isn't going to replicate itself or wreak havoc on your system, and only the original site can read the cookie that it creates. However, many folks don't appreciate acting as a gracious host for a slew of little snippets of personal information. Also, if you do a large amount of surfing, cookies can occupy a significant amount of your hard drive space over time. (Not to mention that some cookies have highly suggestive names, which could lead to all sorts of conclusions. End of story.)

You can choose to accept all cookies — the default — or you can opt to disable cookies altogether. You can also set Safari to accept all cookies. To change your *Cookie Acceptance Plan* (or CAP, for those who absolutely crave acronyms), follow these steps:

1. **Choose Safari⇨Preferences.**

2. **Click the Security toolbar button.**

Safari displays the preference settings shown in Figure 5-6.

**Book IV
Chapter 5**

**Going Places
with Safari**

Figure 5-6:
Exploring
the contents
of my cookie
jar.

3. **Choose how to accept cookies via these radio button choices:**

   - **Never:** Block cookies entirely.

   - **Always:** Accept all cookies.

   - **Only from Sites You Navigate To:** Personally, I use this default option, which allows sites like Amazon.com to work correctly without allowing a barrage of illicit cookies.

4. **To view the cookies currently on your system, click the Show Cookies button.**

   The site that used that cookie will forget any information that it stored in the file, meaning that you might have to take care of things manually, like providing a password on the site that used to be read automatically from the cookie.

5. **Click the Close button to save your changes.**

Cleaning your cache

Safari speeds up the loading of Web sites by storing often-used images and multimedia files in a temporary storage, or *cache,* folder. Naturally, the files in your cache folder can be displayed (hint), which could lead to assumptions (hint, hint) about the sites you've been visiting (hint, hint, hint). (Tactful, ain't I?)

Luckily, Safari makes it easy to dump the contents of your cache file. Just choose Safari⇨Empty Cache; then click Empty to confirm that you want to clean up your cache.

Handling ancient history

As you might imagine, your History file leaves a very clear set of footprints indicating where you've been on the Web. To delete the contents of the History menu, choose History⇨Clear History.

Another built-in security feature can also help save your sanity: Safari can block those incredibly irritating pop-up advertisement windows that are automatically displayed by some Web sites. (I rank such Webmasters at the same social level as spammers!) Click Safari and choose Block Pop-Up Windows or press ⌘+K — in case you're visiting a site that actually uses pop-up windows to your advantage, you can toggle off the block feature temporarily.

Avoiding those @*!^%$ pop-up ads

I hate pop-up ads, and I'm sure you do, too. To block most of those pop-up windows with advertisements for everything from low-rate mortgages to "sure-thing" Internet casinos, click the Safari menu and click Block Pop-Up Windows to toggle the menu item on.

From time to time, you might run across a Web site that actually does something *constructive* with pop-up windows, like present a download or login prompt. If you need to temporarily deactivate pop-up blocking, press ⌘+K to toggle it off. Then press ⌘+K again to turn pop-up blocking back on after you've finished with the site.

**Book IV
Chapter 5**

**Going Places
with Safari**

Chapter 6: Staying Secure Online

In This Chapter

✔ **Understanding the dangers of going online**

✔ **Using a firewall**

✔ **Avoiding trouble online**

I know that you've heard horror stories about hacking: Big corporations and big government installations seem to be as open to hackers as a public library. Often, you read that even entire identities are being stolen online. When you consider that your Mac can contain very sensitive and private information in your life — such as your Social Security number and financial information — it's enough to make you nervous about turning on your computer long enough to check your eBay auctions.

But how much of that is Hollywood? How truly real is the danger, especially to Mac owners? And how can you protect yourself? The good news is that you can *easily* secure your data from all but the most determined hacker — in fact, depending on the hardware that you're using to connect yourself to the Internet, you might be well guarded right now without even knowing it.

In this chapter, I continue a quest that I've pursued for over a decade now — to make my readers feel comfortable and secure in the online world by explaining the truth about what can happen and telling you how you can protect your system from intrusions.

One quick note: This chapter is written with the home and small business Mac owner in mind. Macs that access the Internet through a larger corporate network are very likely already protected by that knight in shining armor, the network system administrator. (Insert applause here.) Of course, if you're using Mac OS X in your office, you're still welcome to read and follow this material — especially if you have a laptop that could act as a carrier for viruses from home — however, check with your system administrator before you attempt to implement any of the recommendations that I make.

What Can Really Happen?

Before I begin, I want to offer you a moment of reassurance and a little of my personal background to explain that I'm well qualified to be your guide through this online minefield. (After all, you don't want Jerry Lewis lecturing you on how to maintain your Internet security. He's a funny guy, though, convenez-vous?)

✦ I've been running and managing all sorts of online systems since the days of the BBS *(Bulletin Board System),* the text-based dinosaurs that used to rule the online world in the late '80s and early '90s. (In fact, my first book was on this very subject — and it contained a chapter on viruses long before they were the darlings of the techno-media.)

✦ As a consultant, I run Web sites and squash virus attacks for a number of companies and organizations.

✦ I run a popular Internet radio station that serves up '70s hits in CD-quality to anyone with a high-speed DSL or cable Internet connection and a copy of iTunes. (More on this broadcasting revolution in Book III, Chapter 2.)

✦ I keep my own office network of six computers safe from attack while still providing readers all over the world with Web sites and the afore-mentioned radio station and BBS.

With that understood, here's what can happen to you online *without* the right safeguards, on *any* computer:

✦ **Hackers can access shared information on your network.** If you're run-ning an unguarded network, it's possible for others to gain access to your documents and applications or wreak havoc on your system.

✦ **Your system could be infected with a virus or dangerous macro.** Left to their own devices, these misbehaving programs and macro com-mands can delete files or turn your entire hard drive into an empty paperweight.

If it smells phishy . . .

Ever heard of the word *phishing?* It's a recently coined Internet term, so you might not have encountered it yet. Con artists and hackers create Web sites that look just like major online stores — including big names like eBay, PayPal, and Amazon. These turkeys then send out junk e-mail messages that tell you that you must log on to this Web site to refresh or correct your personal information. As you've no doubt already guessed, that information is siphoned off and sold to the highest bidder. *Your* credit card, *your* password, and *your* address. Luckily, if you follow the tips that I give later in this chapter in the section, "A Dose of Common Sense: Things Not to Do Online," you'll avoid these phishing expeditions!

✦ **Unsavory individuals could attempt to contact members of your family.** This kind of attack may take place through iChat AV, e-mail, or Web discussion boards, putting your family's safety at risk.

✦ **Hackers can use your system to attack others.** Your computer can be tricked into helping hackers when they attempt to knock out Web servers and public access File Transfer Protocol (FTP) sites on the Internet. Along the same lines, that innocent Web server that you put online could be misused by spam-spewing, online "entrepreneurs." (Cute name, right?)

✦ **Criminals can attempt to con you out of your credit card or personal information.** The Internet is a prime candidate for identity theft.

To be absolutely honest, some danger is indeed present every time that you or any user of your Macintosh connects to the Internet. However, here's the good news. With the right safeguards, it's literally impossible for most of those worst-case scenarios to happen on your Macintosh, and what remains would be so difficult that even the most die-hard hacker would throw in the towel long before reaching your computer or network.

More of Mark's totally unnecessary computer trivia

The term *hacker* dates far back in the annals of the personal computer — in fact, it originally had nothing to do with networks, the Internet, or illegal activities at all . . . because In The Beginning, there was no public Internet!

"Explain yourself, Chambers!" All right. The original hackers were electronics buffs, ham radio operators, computer hobbyists, and engineers who built (or *hacked*) a working computer out of individual components with a soldering gun and a whole lotta guts. At the time, you didn't simply order a computer from Dell or visit your local Maze o' Wires store in the mall to select your favorite system.

No, I'm talking about the mid-'70s, in the halcyon time before IBM even introduced the IBM PC (and when the only folks using the Internet, which wasn't called that back then, were military folks and researchers). Even the simplest computer — really nothing more than a glorified calculator by today's standards — had to be lovingly assembled by hand. These early personal computers didn't run software as we know it. Instead, you programmed them manually through a bank of switches on the front, and they responded with codes displayed on a bank of lights. (Think about that next time you launch Microsoft Word.)

Today, of course, the need to assemble a computer from individual transistors is nonexistent, and the word *hacker* has an entirely different connotation — but don't be surprised if you meet an older member of your Macintosh user's group who's proud to be an old-fashioned hacker! (Look for the soldering gun, usually worn in a holster like a sidearm.)

**Book IV
Chapter 6**

Staying Secure
Online

And you're using a Macintosh — hackers and virus developers (there's a career for you) are traditionally interested only in "having fun" with PCs running Windows, so the likelihood that Tiger could pick up a virus is far less than it would be if you were using Windows XP. Evidently, Apple just doesn't have the numbers to attract the attention of the Bad Guys . . . yet another reason to enjoy the exclusive nature of the Mac universe! (Heck, I even know a couple of fellow Mac owners who feel they just don't need antivirus protection — but believe me, this is *not* an area where you want to be lax and lazy, and you **still need** an antivirus application! More on antivirus software later in this chapter.)

I also want to point out that virtually everyone reading this book — as well as the guy writing it — really doesn't have anything that's worth a malicious hacking campaign. Things like Quicken data files, saved games of Half-Life 2, and genealogical data might be priceless to us, of course, but most dedicated hackers are after bigger game. Unfortunately, the coverage that the media and Hollywood give to corporate and government attacks can turn even Aunt Harriet more than a little paranoid. Therefore, time for another of Mark's Maxims:

> **It's not really necessary to consider the FBI or Interpol each time you poke your Mac's power button. A few simple precautions are all that's required.™**

"Shields Up, Chekov!"

"Okay, Mark, now I know the real story on what can happen to my computer online. So what do I do to safeguard my Macintosh?" You need but two essential tools to protect your hardware (besides a healthy amount of common sense, which I cover in the upcoming section, "A Dose of Common Sense: Things Not to Do Online"): a firewall and an antivirus program.

Firewall basics

A *firewall* is a piece of hardware or software that essentially builds an impermeable barrier between the computers on your side of the wall (meaning your Mac and any other computers on your network) and all external computers on the other side of the wall (meaning the rest of the Internet).

"But wait a second — if other computers can't reach me and my Mac can't reach them, how can I use the Internet at all?" Ah, that's the beauty of today's firewalls. By using a series of techniques designed to thwart attacks from the outside, a firewall allows you to communicate safely, even monitoring what you send and what you receive for later examination. Figure 6-1 illustrates the basics of a firewall.

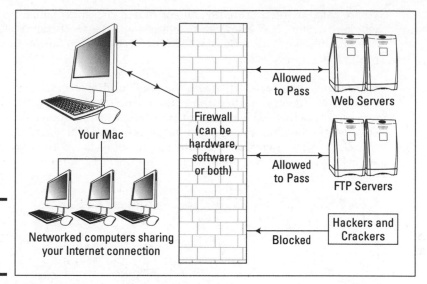

Figure 6-1:
A firewall,
hard at
work.

A firewall sounds grand and incredibly complex and highly technical — and
sometimes it is — but it can also be incredibly simple. For example:

✦ You can spend anywhere from $50 to thousands of dollars installing
sophisticated firewall hardware and/or software.

or

✦ You can activate your firewall by disconnecting your dialup, digital subscriber line (DSL), or cable modem from the wall socket.

Believe it or not, both of those examples technically involve a firewall. In the
first case, the firewall is a physical, tangible presence on the network; in the
second case, the lack of a connection to the Internet actually acts as a firewall. (Think of it as the Air Firewall.) I've spoken to a number of readers who
actually do this — however, if you're running a Web site or downloading a
file from your company's FTP site, yanking the connection when you head
to bed isn't an option. Therefore, most of us will install a physical firewall
through hardware or software.

Do I already have a firewall?

In some cases, you might already be using a hardware firewall and not even
know it. For example, many Internet-sharing devices include a built-in NAT
firewall. NAT stands for *Network Address Translation,* and it's the most effective and popular hardware firewall standard in use by consumer devices. If

you're using an Internet sharing hub or router, check its manual to determine whether it offers NAT as a firewall feature — and if so, turn it on if NAT isn't enabled by default. (See Book V, Chapter 2 for more on Internet sharing, routers, and firewalls.)

For instance, Figure 6-2 illustrates the configuration screen for my Internet router. Note the options to disable port scanning and ping responses, which are two tricks that hackers often use to detect what's often called a *hot computer* — meaning that the computer can be identified and is accessible to attack. (Wireless networks are notoriously hot — for more information on securing your wireless connections, visit Book V, Chapter 4.)

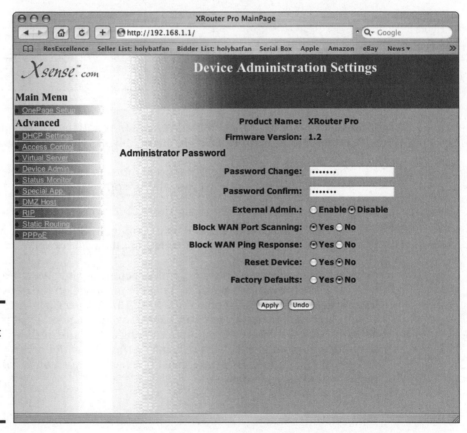

Figure 6-2: My Internet router is set to be downright rude to hackers.

Using the internal Mac OS X firewall

Mac OS X includes a powerful internal firewall called *IPFW.* I'm happy to say that Tiger makes IPFW very simple to use! (In earlier versions of Mac OS X, IPFW — actually a UNIX application — was completely command driven from the Terminal.) The Mac OS X firewall is configured through System Preferences — find more information on setting up IPFW in Book V, Chapter 2.

Using a commercial software firewall

You'll also find a number of popular alternatives to Tiger's built-in firewall on the market. Here are two commercial software firewall applications that are proven to be both effective and easy-to-use:

✦ **Symantec, Norton Personal Firewall, $70 (**www.symantec.com**):** Symantec provides both antivirus and firewall protection for the PC and Macintosh. Frequent updates and top-of-the-line technical support ensure that your firewall stays current and that you can get help when you need it.

✦ **Intego, NetBarrier X, $60 (**www.intego.com**):** NetBarrier X comes with a number of preset configurations that allow you to choose a basic firewall for your network environment with a single click.

Whether you set up IPFW, a shareware firewall, or a commercial firewall, visit a favorite site of mine on the Web: http://grc.com, the home of Gibson Research Corporation. There you'll find the free online utility ShieldsUP!!, which will automatically test just how tight your firewall is and how susceptible your Mac could be to hacker attacks. Visit this site often because this service is updated periodically to reflect new hacking techniques.

Antivirus basics

Next, consider your antivirus protection. *Viruses* are typically transmitted through applications — you run a program, and the virus is activated. (Although not the traditional definition of a virus, both scripts and macros can be used to take control of your system and cause trouble, as well.) Therefore, you need to closely monitor what I call The Big Three:

✦ **Web downloads:** Consider every file that you receive from the Internet as a possible viral threat.

✦ **Removable media:** Viruses can be stored on everything from CD-ROMs and DVD-ROMs to Zip disks and even archaic floppy disks.

✦ **E-mail file attachments:** An application sent to you as an e-mail attachment is an easy doorway to your system.

Horrors! Mac OS X has no built-in antivirus support. (Then again, neither does Windows XP.) However, a good antivirus program will take care of any application that's carrying a virus. Some even handle destructive macros within documents. Make sure that the antivirus program that you choose offers *real-time scanning,* which operates when you download or open a file. Periodic scanning of your entire system is important, too, but only a real-time scanning application like Norton AntiVirus can immediately ensure that the StuffIt archive or the application you just received in your e-mail Inbox is actually free from viruses. (Oh, and don't forget that many of the Software Updates released by Apple for Tiger will plug security holes in our favorite operating system.)

Virus technology continues to evolve over time, just like more beneficial application development. For example, recently a virus has been discovered that's actually contained in a JPEG image file! With a good antivirus application that offers regular updates, you'll continue to keep your system safe from viral attack.

I heartily recommend both Norton AntiVirus from Symantec and Intego's VirusBarrier X (as shown in Figure 6-3). Both programs include automatic updates delivered while you're online to make sure that you're covered against the latest viruses.

Figure 6-3:
Configuring
VirusBarrier
preferences.

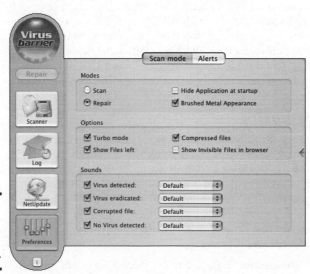

A Dose of Common Sense: Things Not to Do Online

One more powerful weapon that you can use to make sure that your Mac stays safe from unlawful intrusion is this: Practicing common sense on the Internet is just as important as adding a firewall and an antivirus application to Mac OS X.

With this in mind, here's a checklist of things that you should never do while you're online:

✦ **Never download a file from a site you don't trust.** And make sure that your antivirus software is configured to check downloaded files before you open them.

✦ **Never open an e-mail attachment until it's been checked.** Don't give in to temptation, even if the person who sent the message is someone you trust. (Many of today's macro viruses actually replicate themselves by sending copies to the addresses found through the victim's e-mail program. Of course, this problem crops up regularly in the Windows world, but it's been known to happen in the Macintosh community as well.)

✦ **Never enter any personal information in an e-mail message unless you know the recipient.** Sure, I send my mailing address to friends and family, but no one else. In fact, even e-mail can be intercepted by a determined hacker, so if you're sending something truly important, use an encryption application like PGP Personal Desktop (www.pgp.com).

✦ **Never enter any personal information on a Web site provided as a link in an e-mail message.** Don't fall prey to phishing expeditions. Some of these e-mail message/Web site combinations look authentic enough to fool anyone! No reputable online company or store is going to demand or solicit your personal information through e-mail or through a linked Web site. In fact, feel free to contact the company through its *real* Web site and report the phishing attempt!

✦ **Never include any personal information in an Internet newsgroup post.** After all, these posts can be viewed by anyone with a newsgroup account, so there's no such thing as privacy in a newsgroup. (For a glimpse of just how long a newsgroup post can linger in the great Internet continuum, visit www.google.com, click the Groups button, and search for your name. I can pull up newsgroup messages that I posted back in 1995!)

**Book IV
Chapter 6**

Staying Secure Online

✦ **Never buy from an online store that doesn't offer a secure, encrypted connection when you're prompted for your personal information and credit card number.** If you're using Internet Explorer or Netscape, you can tell when you're using a secure connection by checking the status bar at the bottom of the Web browser window: If a small padlock icon appears in the status bar, the connection is encrypted and secure.

If you're using Apple's Safari browser, the padlock icon appears at the top-right corner of the Safari window.

✦ **Never divulge personal information to others over an iChat AV connection.**

✦ **Never use the same password for all your electronic business.** Use different passwords that include both letters and numbers, change them often, and never divulge them to anyone else.

✦ **Never give anyone else administrative access to your Web or FTP server.**

✦ **Never allow any type of remote access to your Macintosh or your network without testing that access first; restrict that access to visitors whom you trust.**

Find more details on securing your network from intrusion — including Internet hacker attacks — in Book V. I cover System Preferences that can affect the security of your system in Book II.

Book V

Networking in Mac OS X

The 5th Wave   By Rich Tennant

@RICHTENNANT

"This part of the test tells us whether you're personally suited to the job of network administrator."

Contents at a Glance

Chapter 1: Setting Up a Small Network

In This Chapter

✔ Finding out what a network is and why you might want one

✔ Setting up the network hardware

✔ Configuring network system preferences

✔ Troubleshooting your network

In the not-so-distant past — I'm talking 10–15 years ago — networks were found only in huge companies that had the money and workforce to pay for and maintain them. But now, as technology rolls on, a home or small office network is both very affordable and relatively easy to create. In this chapter, I introduce you to this helpful beastie: You discover what networks are, what you can do with them, and how to set up a small network of your own for your home or small business.

Networks can be used for many things. Computers exchange all types of data over a network: files that you want to send between computers or to networked printers; streaming audio or video broadcasts; data for multiplayer computer games; or even a private company Web site (typically called an *intranet*). Anything that you can imagine that would involve moving data between multiple computers can be done by using a network.

What Do 1 Need to Set Up My Network?

First, let me define *network*. In a nutshell, a network is a combination of hardware, cables, and software that allows computers and printers to talk to each other. (Heck, you don't even need cables with a wireless network, as I show you in Chapter 4 of this mini-book.) To have a network, you need the right hardware and software. Some of the hardware and most of the software that you'll need probably came with your Mac, depending on which Mac you have. As you progress through this chapter, you'll discover everything that's required to set up your network so that you can pick up any additional parts you need. Any good-sized computer store (either the brick-and-mortar or online variety) has everything that you need to get up and running.

Now, back to the requirements: You need the right hardware and software to make your network sing. This section covers each component with a description about the role that each part plays on the network and other good stuff that you'll want to know to get your network right the first time.

Something to network

Okay, this might be obvious, but I'm nothing if not thorough. The first thing that you need to build a network is . . . well . . . *stuff!* That's right, you need to have devices that you want to network. Most times this will be computers (whether Macs or PCs running Windows/Linux/UNIX), printers, personal digital assistants (PDAs), and other standalone, network-capable devices (such as file servers and shared tape back-up drives).

Network interface card (NIC)

A *network interface card,* or NIC, is a hardware device that your computer uses to talk to the rest of the network. The NIC connects to the network cabling, and it speaks the language of electronics, sending data around the network. Nowadays, most networks use the Ethernet networking protocol, and most NICs are Ethernet-compatible. Most modern Macs have an Ethernet NIC built right in that, in fact, isn't really a card at all but something built right onto the Mac's main system board. If you have an older Mac, say one bought before 1998, you can purchase an add-on NIC at any computer store.

Hub or switch

So you have an assortment of devices in your home or small office that you've decided to network. How do you make them all interconnect? Although you could connect just two computers together by using nothing more than a single crossover cable, you need fancier hardware to connect more than two computers: namely, a hub or a switch. The hub or the switch, used to connect everything, is the focal point of the network. Without a hub or switch, you wouldn't have a network.

Hubs

A *hub* is a small box that has a bunch of Ethernet ports on it. A *port* is really just like an Ethernet NIC on your computer, but a hub or switch has lots of them. Inside, a hub connects all those Ethernet ports so that the talking (sending) wires from each port connect to the listening (receiving) wires on all other ports — therefore, when one computer talks, all others listen. As a side effect of how hubs work, if more than one computer tries to talk at once, a *collision* happens. Collisions are a Bad Thing: The data that was being sent by the two computers is destroyed and has to be re-sent.

Thirty-nine flavors of Ethernet . . . but no Rocky Road

Ethernet standards allow for operation at different speeds. Because the Ethernet standard has improved over time, some older Ethernet devices support only the older (slower) speeds. Ethernet's speed is rated by how much data it can transfer in a second — usually in millions of bits per second, or megabits per second (Mbps). Originally, Ethernet was designed to run at 10 Mbps. Now there are three different speeds of Ethernet: 10 Mbps, 100 Mbps, 1000 Mbps, and even faster.

1000 Mbps Ethernet — also called *Gigabit Ethernet* or just *Gigabit* for short — is still a bit on the expensive side for small home or office networks. All consumer-level Gigabit Ethernet NICs also support running at 10 Mbps or 100 Mbps, so you will hear them called *10/100/1000 Ethernet NICs*. PowerBook G4s and G4/G5 towers come with a 10/100/1000 Ethernet NIC built in, but the iMac, iBook, Mac Mini, and eMac still come with just 10/100 Ethernet NICs built in. Although Gigabit NICs are now priced under $100, most of the devices that can connect Gigabit NICs still cost hundreds of dollars. That fact, coupled with the reality that most computer systems can't really even handle or dish out that much data, makes Gigabit Ethernet a choice for only those wanting an extremely high-end and costly network.

NICs and other Ethernet equipment that only handle 10 Mbps are rapidly becoming obsolete because virtually all the modern NICs and other Ethernet hardware support both 10 Mbps and 100 Mbps. Most times, you will see this labeled as *10/100 Ethernet.* For your home networking, you probably want to invest in 100 Mbps or 10/100 Mbps.

Remember: Keep your eye out for Ethernet NICs and equipment that handle only 100 Mbps. You won't see it much, but be wary because it can't interconnect with 10 Mbps Ethernet NICs and equipment. I advise against buying it — stay compatible, and you'll be a happy puppy.

Although they might seem relatively harmless, collisions can really take a toll on your Ethernet network. When data starts flying around your network, collisions *will* take over and limit the amount of data that you can get through the network. (My technical editor compares this problem with dining in a noisy restaurant while you endeavor to listen to three conversations at once.) Typically you'll only be able to use about 40 percent of the total speed, or *bandwidth,* of the hub. With the cost of switches barely above that of hubs, you really have little reason to get a hub instead of a switch.

Setting up a hub or switch (and therefore giving birth to your network, which sounds more painful than it is) is usually no more difficult than connecting a power cable to the device and then plugging in your computers with their own Ethernet cables. You'll see various lights on the hub — usually a power light indicating that the hub is powered on and operational. You'll also see lights that correspond to each port on the hub — these lights tell you what's going on in the hub. For instance, you normally see the following types of lights:

✦ **Link light:** Each port on a hub should have a link light. *Link lights* simply tell you which ports have something alive connected to a given port: That is, a device is connected and powered on. On hubs that support 10 and 100 Mbps, the speed light is also used to indicate a link, so there isn't a separate link light.

✦ **Speed light:** Each port on the hub should have a speed light. On hubs that support both 10 Mbps and 100 Mbps, this tells you the speed of the device at the other end. Some hubs have different lights for different speeds, and some use a single light and make it different colors for different speeds.

✦ **Activity light:** When one computer speaks, they all hear it. Typically, an entire hub has only one activity light for the entire hub, indicating that someone is speaking. With heavy traffic, the light could appear solid.

✦ **Collision light:** Just like the activity light, collisions affect everything connected to the hub, so logic dictates having only one collision light for the entire hub. This light will flash whenever a collision occurs, which can happen even with only two devices attached. When you add more devices, you get more collisions; if this light stays on most of the time, look into getting a switch (which I describe in the next section).

Switches

A hub is a relatively simple way to connect a bunch of cables to allow computers to talk. (They're not particularly intelligent or efficient creatures.) A hub just receives network data on one port and sends (broadcasts) a copy out through all the other ports. A *switch,* on the other hand, is a more advanced "post office" for your network because a switch uses the information in the network data to eliminate collisions and thus increase the efficiency of your network.

Bear with me whilst I spew techno-talk for a paragraph or two. When an Ethernet switch receives a *frame* — that's the name for a standard unit, or packet, of network data — it reads the label on the frame to see the return address of the computer that sent the frame. In a short amount of time (after being turned on and watching the data move around), a switch learns which computer is located on which port. Then, whenever data comes into the switch, it looks at the *header* (some information on the front of all frames, much like a mailing label on a package that you send) and sees which computer should receive the frame. The switch then sends the frame out the port for that computer only.

This is A Good Thing. Instead of forcing all computers on the network to listen while one Mac speaks (like a hub does) — known as *half-duplex* — a switch can actually send the data directly to the only computer that needs to hear it. This gets rid of the evil collisions, allowing all the computers to speak and talk at the same time *(full-duplex)*. Now, twice as much information can be shoved around because a computer can now send and receive data at the same time. This is a major breakthrough and can happen only on a switch.

Just how much of a performance improvement do you get with a switch compared with a hub? On average, you'll move from a 100 Mbps hub that can handle an average of 5 Mbps of traffic per device (assuming that eight computers are communicating at once) to a 100 Mbps switch that can handle 200 Mbps per device (no matter how many devices are connected). That's a speed increase of 4,000 percent, leading me to another inescapable Mark's Maxim:

> **Buy a switch for your network, and say goodbye to collisions!™**

Cables

Cables are the ties that bind . . . literally. *Cables* are used to connect the NIC card on each computer to the central hardware of the network: namely, hubs (which you don't really want) or switches (which you do want). With a little experience, you'll be a cable-wielding superhero with hundreds of feet of cable draped across every piece of furniture in your place for your first LAN party. (A *LAN party,* by the way, is when way too many techies bring their computers into a very small space, connect them, and play games for 48 hours straight. Oh, and we eat a lot, too. Good stuff!)

Here's the scoop on what kind of cables to use. Technically, you can run 10 Mbps Ethernet over *Cat5* cable (like a super-version of the wire that you use for your telephones). Some networks still use *coaxial* cable (the kind of cable that you use to connect your TV to your cable service), but coaxial is no longer used for home and small office networks like yours or mine. You can run 100 Mbps Ethernet over Cat5 cable or fiber optic cable.

Although you can do 10/100 and most times 100 Mbps Ethernet over Cat5 cable, any new cables that you buy should be Cat5E — which I talk about in the following section — because it is specifically meant to be used with 1000 Mbps Ethernet.

I'm sure that you noticed that the common denominator here is the Cat5 cable. Although you could get by using coaxial cable, it's pretty much gone out of style as a network cable because it's limited to 10 Mbps Ethernet. In fact, it's very hard to find a NIC with a coaxial connection any more. Fiber optic cable, although supporting speeds of 100 Mbps, 1 Gbps, and even 10 Gbps, is much more expensive and more difficult to install.

Hey, did I mention that you can eschew cables entirely? For more information on the lean, mean world of wireless networking, see Chapter 4 of this mini-book.

Be sure to buy *straight-through* Cat5E cables (also called *patch* cables) and not *crossover* cables, which are only used in certain circumstances. Crossover cables are mainly used to connect two computers directly together (to form a tiny, two-computer network), connect a cable/DSL modem directly to a computer, or connect multiple switches.

Cat5 cable supports speeds of 100 Mbps. 1000 Mbps Ethernet, of course, is designed to run ten times faster than that; luckily enough, it was engineered to be compatible with 90 percent of Cat5 installations. Having said that, some Cat5 cable doesn't stick to the stringent specifications that 1000 Mbps Ethernet requires. The newer version of Cat5 cable is *Category 5 Enhanced,* or Cat5E for short. Cat5E is recommended for any new installation because it can easily handle 10/100 Mbps Ethernet and yet can handle 1000 Mbps Ethernet as well. Even if you're using 10/100 Mbps Ethernet, you can upgrade someday to 1000 Mbps without having to worry about upgrading your cabling.

Setting Up Your Network

After you collect the hardware components listed earlier in this chapter, you're ready to connect things. Here's a quick list of things to do to get your network fired up:

1. Find the best location for placing your hub or switch.

To keep costs down, try to place the hub or switch in a location close to a power outlet that's centrally located so that you can use the least amount of cable. If cost isn't an issue, hide the unit in a closet and just run all the cables along the walls to the hub or switch. And if cost *really* isn't an issue, get your house fully wired with Cat5E cable.

2. Plug the hub or switch into the power socket.

Some hubs and switches come on automatically when you plug them in and can never be turned off. Others have a power switch that you need to turn on the first time that you plug them in.

3. Verify that the hub or switch is working by looking at the lights on the front. Check the manual that came with the hub or switch to see what light configuration is normal for that particular unit.

Until you have computers or printers attached to it, you might just have a status light that shows the hub is powered on. But if the lights on your unit don't match up with what the manual says, you could have a bum unit that you need to return.

4. **Verify that all your devices are near enough to the hub or switch to be connected by your cables and then turn them all on.**

5. **Get one of your Cat5E cables and connect one cable from the Ethernet jack on your computer, usually on the side or back, to an open port on the hub or switch.**

   You should see a link light or speed light come on that verifies that the two devices sense each other. (You might also have a link light on your NIC where you plug in the cable, but that depends on the Mac that you're using.)

6. **Repeat Step 5 until each device is attached to the hub or switch.**

Congratulations, you're a network technician! (Don't forget to call your friends and brag.) The first phase of the network, the physical connection, is complete; the next step is the configuration of Mac OS X.

Understanding the Basics of Network Configuration

Take a deep breath, there's no need to panic — in fact, configuring your network software basically involves entering a lot of numbers and other stuff in dialogs. (In fact, most folks can just allow Tiger to take care of network settings automatically.) But just so you'll understand what's involved, this section explains what those numbers are, what they do, and why you ought to know it. Because this is a Mac OS X book, I stick with configuring Macs running the Big X.

TCP/IP

First things first: *Protocol* is just the techno-nerd word for a set of rules or a language. A *protocol* is a language that computers use to communicate. Without protocols, the computers on your network would never be able to speak to each other even though you have NICs, cables, and a hub or a switch. The Internet Protocol (IP) part of the TCP/IP suite is what you're really interested in because it's the most important part of your network configuration chore.

IP addresses

IP addresses are like street addresses for computers on a network. Each computer on the network has an IP address, and it needs to be unique because no other computer can share it. When a computer wants to communicate with another computer, it can simply send the data on the network in a nice package that has its address as well as the address of the computer that it's trying to talk to. (Remember frames? If not, take a refresher in the earlier section, "Switches.")

An IP address is just a number, but it's written in a strange way. (Go figure.) All IP addresses are written as four numbers between 0 and 255 with a dot (period) between them: For instance, a common IP address that you might run into is 192.168.0.1. As everyone knows, engineers can't sleep unless they have three or four ways to write the same thing, including IP addresses. The form shown above — which is by far the most common — is *dotted notation*. Each number, like 192, is an *octet*.

Don't worry too much about this stuff: You don't have to remember terms like *octet* to create your own network. They could be helpful, however, if something goes wrong and you need to place a call to tech support. Plus, you can impress the computer salesperson (gleefully called a *wonk* by Mac power users) at your local Maze 'o Wires store with your mastery of techno-babble.

IP addresses at home versus on the Internet

One very important thing to keep in mind is that the Almighty IP Address Police — *Internet Assigned Numbers Authority* (www.iana.org) — has broken IP addresses into groups. The two main types of IP addresses are public and private:

✦ **Public** IP addresses can be used on the Internet and are unique throughout the whole world.

✦ **Private** IP addresses are used in homes or businesses and cannot be used to talk to the public Internet. Private IP addresses are used over and over by many people and most commonly take the form 192.168.*x.x.*

You will almost always get a public IP address from your Internet service provider (ISP), whether you're using a cable modem, digital subscriber line (DSL), or a regular dialup modem. If you use a cable/DSL router or something like IPNetShareX to share your Internet connection among multiple computers, you'll be using private IP addresses on your network while using a single public IP address to talk to the Internet (more on that later in Book V, Chapter 5).

"Great! I get an IP address, put it into my Network settings in System Preferences, and off I go. Right?" Well, you're close, but here are a few other pieces of information that you might need before you can go surfing around the world:

✦ **Default gateway:** When you send information to other networks —
whether in another building or around the world on the Internet — your
computer needs to know the IP address of the gateway that will forward
your data down the line. The *default gateway* is really just the IP address
of a *router,* which is a device that connects multiple networks. A *gateway*
gets its name because it really is your gateway to all other networks.

✦ **Subnet mask:** A *subnet mask* is a number that helps your computer
know when it needs to send stuff through the router. It's a group of four
octets with dots, just like an IP address, but almost always it uses 0 or
255 as the four octets. Most often, the subnet mask will be 255.255.255.0.
If the wrong number is entered for the subnet mask, it could keep you
from talking to the Internet or even computers on your own network.

Software applications

After you have the hardware in place and you've chosen and configured a
protocol to allow the computers to all talk to each other, you need software
to make use of your new network connections. Time for more good news: A
lot of the software that you'll need to move data on your network is already
included in Mac OS X! Here is a quick list of some of the network software
and protocols already built into Mac OS X and what they're used for:

✦ **FTP:** *File Transfer Protocol* (FTP), part of the TCP/IP protocol suite,
allows computers of any type — Mac, PC, Linux, UNIX, mainframe, or
whatever — to transfer files back and forth between them.

✦ **Telnet:** *Telnet* is also part of the TCP/IP suite — you can use it to remotely
connect to a computer and execute commands on the remote machine.

✦ **Samba:** *Samba,* an open source software suite, enables Mac OS X users
to share files with people using Windows computers and also allows the
Mac user to connect to files that the Windows computers share.

✦ **HTTP:** *HyperText Transfer Protocol* (HTTP), also part of the TCP/IP suite,
is used by Web browsers to provide access to all the various pages on
the World Wide Web.

Configuring Network System Preferences

In this section, I show you how to configure your Mac to communicate with
other computers on a local network.

Using DHCP for automatic IP address assignment

Now I'd like to introduce you to a very dear friend of mine — an abbreviation
that you will soon grow to love, like everyone else who's set up a small Mac

network. *Dynamic Host Configuration Protocol,* or DHCP for short, is a protocol that enables a computer to automatically get all the information that I've talked about to this point. (Check in your Webster's . . . this is the very definition of the word *godsend.*)

You're saying, "Mark, there's gotta be a catch, right?" Well, here's the bad news: Before you can use DHCP, you have to first add a *DHCP server,* which provides other computers on the network with their configuration settings. Here's the good news: Most Internet connection-sharing hardware devices (and software-sharing implementations as well) provide a DHCP server as part of the price of admission. (*Internet connection sharing* allows all your networked computers to access the Internet through a single Internet connection. I cover it more in Book V, Chapter 5.) Even many switches can provide DHCP services these days . . . technology marches on.

If you plan to use Internet connection sharing or you know that you have a DHCP server on your network, you can set up your Mac to automatically obtain the required IP address and information. Open System Preferences from the Dock or the Apple menu and choose Network. From the Network dialog that appears, click the Show drop-down list box and select Built-in Ethernet. Select Using DHCP from the Configure IPv4 drop-down list on the TCP/IP tab. Click the Apply Now button, and Mac OS X will contact the DHCP server to obtain an IP address, a subnet mask, a gateway router IP address, and a Domain Name System (DNS) address. (*DNS servers* convert a human-friendly address like www.yahoo.com to a computer-friendly IP address like 66.218.71.86.)

A few seconds after clicking the Apply Now button, you should see the information come up. Notice the addition underneath IP Address: (*Provided by DHCP Server.*) This lets you know that the process worked and configuration is complete. You might also notice that the DNS information is empty — fear not, Mac OS X is really using DNS information provided by the DHCP server. Press ⌘+Q to quit System Preferences and save your settings.

If you ever make a network change that screws things up, like entering the wrong subnet mask or an IP address that isn't in the same range as others on your LAN, you can always click the Revert button to get back your old settings.

One DHCP server on a network is princely, but two or more DHCP servers on a single network will fight like alley cats and grind everything to a halt. Therefore, if you're considering adding a DHCP server to an existing network, make **doggone** sure that you're not treading on another server's toes. (Ask that network administrator person.)

Manually choosing an IP address range

You say you don't have a DHCP server, and you need to manually assign IP addresses? This configuration means two things: You need to manually configure the Transmission Control Protocol/Internet Protocol (TCP/IP) Properties. Keep in mind that for now, you're not concerned with the Internet — just computers on the local network.

A result of being on a *local* network — because it's not connected to the Internet, it's also called a *private* network — is that you must use IP addresses that are reserved for private network use. You can use a few different ranges of IP addresses, but I recommend that you choose an address range from the 192.168.*x.x* networks. In the next section, I show you how.

Down to business: *I recommend that you use IP addresses in the 192.168.x.x range.* What does this mean exactly? Well, here's the scoop:

+ **Use IP addresses where the first two octets are 192 and 168 (192.168).**

   Octet numbers are conjoined by periods.

+ **For the third octet, choose any number between 1 and 254.**

   It doesn't matter which one you choose as long as you use this same third number on all computers on your network.

+ **For the fourth octet, choose any number between 1 and 254.**

   Make sure that every computer on your local network has a different fourth octet number. This is very important — your network will not work otherwise.

+ **Use 255.255.255.0 as your subnet mask.**

For instance, suppose that you're using three computers on your network. All the IP addresses that you use will start with *192.168.* Next, suppose you choose *123* for the third octet. (Remember that you can choose any number between 1 and 254.) Finally, for the fourth octet, choose the numbers 100, 105, and 110 for the three computers, respectively. (Again, you can choose any numbers between 1 and 254.) The resulting IP addresses used on the three computers are

> 192.168.123.100
>
> 192.168.123.105
>
> 192.168.123.110

By the way, I should mention that there are other range possibilities for reserved private networks — AirPort and AirPort Extreme hardware uses a 10.*x.x.x* network range, for example — but the 192.168.*x.x* range is definitely the most popular and the most common default on Ethernet network hardware.

After you know the IP addresses and the subnet mask that you're going to use, start setting up each computer. Being a nice guy, I'd like to walk you through the process of configuring Mac OS X with the 192.168.123.105 address as an example.

Be sure that you have all the physical portion of your network powered up and connected as outlined in the earlier section "Setting Up Your Network."

1. **Select any of your Macs to start with and open System Preferences (either from the Apple menu or from the Dock).**

2. **From the System Preferences dialog, choose Network.**

    The Network pane appears.

3. **Click Built-in Ethernet in the list and click Configure.**

    The TCP/IP panel should already be active by default; if not, click the TCP/IP button to bring it forward.

4. **Select Manually from the Configure IPv4 drop-down list of the TCP/IP panel.**

    Figure 1-1 shows how things should look at this point.

5. **Enter the IP address for this machine (192.168.123.105 in this example) in the IP Address text box.**

6. **Enter the subnet mask of 255.255.255.0 in the Subnet Mask text box.**

7. **Click the Apply Now button, and your new network settings will take effect.**

8. **Press ⌘+Q to quit System Preferences.**

Repeat this same procedure using the other IP addresses for each of the other Macs that are connected to your network.

Most ISPs also supply DNS server addresses and search domains. If your ISP included DNS server addresses or search domains, don't forget to type them into the corresponding boxes on the TCP/IP panel.

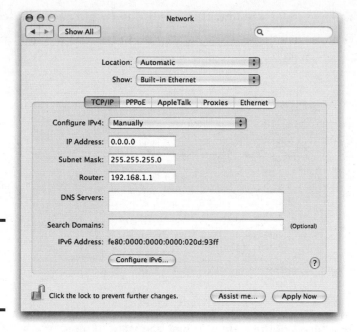

Figure 1-1:
Manually
configuring
TCP/IP
settings.

Verifying Connectivity

After you have your Macs connected and your TCP/IP configuration is done, you need to check to make sure that everything is working. After you have at least two computers on your network, each with a TCP/IP address, you can use a simple little utility called ping to test the connection.

ping is a very simple, yet extremely helpful, utility that's the first connectivity-testing tool out of the box, even for network professionals. When you use the ping utility — referred to as *pinging* something — the application sends out a small packet of data to whatever destination you're trying to reach. When the receiving computer hears the ping, it answers with a ping reply. If the original computer receives the ping reply, you know that the connection between the computers is good.

To ping a computer, you use a little application built in to Mac OS X called *Network Utility,* which allows you to work various network wonders (including checking connectivity, watching the route that your computer takes to get to another computer, and looking up information about Internet domain names). To use Network Utility to check network connectivity, follow these steps:

1. **Open a Finder window, click Applications, and click Utilities.**

2. **Double-click the Network Utility icon to launch the application.**

3. **Click the Ping tab (see Figure 1-2).**

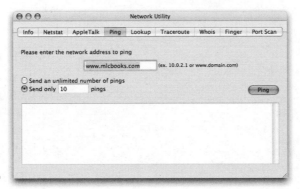

Figure 1-2:
Preparing
to ping. (Can
you say that
with a
straight
face?)

4. **In the Please Enter the Network Address to Ping text field, enter the IP address of the computer that you want to ping.**

5. **To simply verify connectivity, select the Send Only *x* Pings radio button and enter a low number, such as 5, in the text field.**

Five or ten pings are plenty to see whether the connection is good.

6. **Click the Ping button.**

Your Mac sends ping packets to the IP address that you entered.

If the pings are successful, text appears in the text box at the bottom of the Ping tab: one line for each ping reply received from the other computer. The end of each line reads `time=` with a number at the end. That number is the amount of time, in ⅟₁₀₀₀ of a second (milliseconds [ms]), that it took for the ping packet to go from your computer to the other computer and back.

If your ping is unsuccessful, you will see nothing, at least for a little bit. Each ping that you send takes two seconds before it's considered missing in action. So, if you chose five pings, you need to wait ten seconds before you see the results. After all the pings time out — a ping *times out* when it doesn't get returned in the proper amount of time — you see a line of text appear that reads `ping: sendto: No route to host` or `100% packet loss`. Both error messages mean the same thing: All the ping packets that you sent out are now in the packet graveyard, never to be seen again. As you've likely guessed already, this is *not* a good sign for your network connectivity. Look ahead to "Troubleshooting Your New Network" to find out where to begin troubleshooting this problem.

If you can ping all the other computers on your network from one of the computers, you don't need to go to each computer and ping all the others. You can logically assume that all the computers can communicate. For instance, if you can ping computers B, C, and D from computer A, you don't need to bother with ping tests from computer B, C, or D.

After you have your computers configured and you've verified connectivity between them, start doing the fun stuff that a network allows you to do, like sharing data, printing, and (most importantly) playing games with users on other computers.

Troubleshooting Your New Network

After a network is set up and operating, it rarely has problems — still, Murphy sometimes takes charge, and the darn thing just won't work right. When you do have problems with the network, I recommend using a standard, consistent approach to finding and fixing the problem. This section breaks down troubleshooting into two areas:

✦ **The hardware:** The best place to start troubleshooting a network problem is with the actual equipment, such as the NICs, cables, and hubs/switches. (See earlier sections on each equipment type.)

✦ **The software:** The second place to check for problems is in the configuration of the computers on the network, specifically the configuration on the computer(s) having the problem that you're troubleshooting.

Physical problems with your network

Although many things on a network can go bad or cause problems, usually network problems are caused by faulty equipment or wiring. Sometimes it's something as simple as a cable not being plugged in snugly. Looking at the physical cables, connections, and equipment is always the best place to start looking for problems. Here is a quick list of physical things to check while trying to fix network problems:

1. **Make sure that both ends of the network cable are firmly connected.**

First check the end that plugs into the computer and then check the end that connects to the hub/switch.

2. **Turn on the problematic computer to be sure that it's connected to a hub or switch.**

Check the port on the hub/switch to see whether the link/speed light is lit. (Depending on the hub or switch that you have, you might not have a link light. Many hubs and switches use a speed light to indicate a link. Check the manufacturer's manual for your model.) If your computer is on and connected but no link/speed light is lit, try replacing the network cable.

3. **If you replace the network cable and there is still no light, try unplug-ging the cable from the hub/switch and plug it into another port.**

Choose one of the other computers connected to the hub/switch that works, unplug it, and plug the broken computer into that port for test-ing. Occasionally a single port on a hub or switch will go bad; if that hap-pens, just mark it as bad and don't use it anymore. But if all computers connected to the hub/switch stop working, it's probably the hub or switch that has gone south. If the hub/switch is still under warranty, I recommend getting it fixed or replaced.

4. **If you replace the cable, try a different port on the hub, and other computers work fine on that hub/switch, the NIC inside your com-puter has possibly gone bad.**

If you reach this determination, call your local service center to have it looked at and repaired. If you have an older model where the NIC was added instead of built in, you can simply replace the NIC yourself.

The key when troubleshooting physical problems is the link/speed light on the hub or switch. If the link/speed light still won't work, the problem isn't likely a physical problem. You need to start troubleshooting the network configuration on the computer itself.

Network configuration problems

After checking the physical layer, look for problems in the network settings. When using TCP/IP on your network, look for these specific things: the TCP/IP configuration mode, IP address, subnet mask, and router IP address (if you're using a router to connect to the Internet or other networks). To check these settings, choose Apple⇨System Preferences⇨Network to bring up the Network dialog.

1. **Make sure that the Configuration drop-down list on the TCP/IP Properties tab is set to the appropriate option.**

- *Using DHCP:* Select the Using DHCP option only if you're using a cable/DSL modem/router or other DHCP server. Otherwise, set this to Manually.

- *Manually:* If the configuration is set to Manually, check the IP Address, DNS Servers, Router, and Subnet Mask fields to make sure that they're correct. If you're not sure whether your Subnet Mask field entry is correct, you can usually make it the same as other computers on the same network with you. Most times, the subnet mask is 255.255.255.0.

2. **To check your Internet connectivity to the rest of the Internet, try pinging** www.*apple*.com.

   This checks the router and DNS settings.

3. **If you're set up for DHCP and your TCP/IP settings remain blank, make sure that your DHCP server — which could be your cable/DSL modem/router — is turned on and working properly.**

Chapter 2: Using Your Network

In This Chapter

✔ Finding out what you can do with your network

✔ Sharing your files and printers with other Macs

✔ Sharing your files with Windows computers

✔ Accessing files on Windows computers

✔ Configuring the built-in firewall

✔ Remote controlling your Mac from afar

Here's one of those incredibly complex concepts that you always find in these computer books: After you have your network all set up and ready to go, you can do all kinds of things with it. (Now wasn't that utterly painless?) You can use your network to share files, share printers, remotely control your Mac, or even play multi-user games like Call of Duty — my favorite — against other friends. To keep your files safe from unwanted snoops, you can configure the Mac OS X built-in firewall. In this chapter, I cover the basics of file sharing, sharing printers, and using the firewall to protect yourself from intruders.

It's All about (File) Sharing

One of the main reasons for building a network is sharing files between computers. You might even want to set up a *server,* which is a computer with shared files that are always available to anyone on the network. Think of a server as a common file storage area for the rest of the network. Really, any computer that shares files is technically a server because it is serving, so to speak. But usually most people only use the word *server* to mean a computer that's dedicated solely to serving files, printers, and so on for the rest of the network.

Creating an account

Sharing files on your Mac with other Mac users is a piece of cake. Remember, however, that you need to create an account for anyone whom you want to have access to your files. The accounts that you create can only access two folders, shown in Figure 2-1:

✦ **The account's Home folder:** That specific account's Home folder carries a short version of the username that's in the Users folder on your hard drive. Figure 2-1 shows the Home folder, which is noted with an icon that looks like a house, for the chambers account (where *chambers* is the short account name for Mark Chambers). The Home folder icon always bears the short account name for the user who's currently logged in.

Figure 2-1: The location of user folders and the Shared folder on your hard drive.

✦ **The Shared folder:** This folder is also in the Users folder on your hard drive. Anyone with an account on your Mac can access the Shared folder, so it's a great place to keep common files that everyone wants to copy or use.

By the way, here's a quick note about the drive names that you see in these figures. I've never liked that rather mundane *Macintosh HD* moniker, and as I mention elsewhere in the book, I'm a huge (okay, *really* huge) fan of Mozart — hence the drive name Disk Wolfgang. My other drive is an external FireWire drive where I keep all beta builds of upcoming Mac OS X versions . . . and it's thoughtfully named FireWire Drive. (Technology authors can be somewhat eccentric; chalk it up to our techno-nerd beginnings. On the other hand, we never type e-mail messages in ALL CAPITAL LETTERS. That's considered **shouting**, you know.)

To create an account, you need to be logged in as an Admin user. Follow these steps:

1. **Open System Preferences from the Apple menu (🍎) or the Dock.**

2. **Click Accounts under the System section.**

3. **Click the New Account button, which carries a plus sign.**

4. **Fill in the appropriate information, including the name for the account and a password.**

   Note that the name that appears as the short name determines the name of that user's Home folder.

5. **Click Create Account.**

6. **Press ⌘+Q to exit System Preferences.**

I cover creating accounts in greater detail in Book II, Chapter 5 but that's the short version.

Enabling file sharing

When you enable file sharing, your files are exchanged over Transmission Control Protocol/Internet Protocol (TCP/IP) and/or AppleTalk, depending on which protocols you've enabled. (To enable AppleTalk for compatibility with older Macs on your network, see Book V, Chapter 3.)

Regardless of which protocol you use to share your files, follow these steps to turn on sharing:

1. **Open System Preferences either from the Apple menu or from the Dock.**

2. **Click the Sharing icon to open the Sharing Preferences panel.**

3. **On the Services panel, select the Personal File Sharing check box to enable it.**

4. **Click Start.**

   After the computer thinks for a second, you see the message `Personal File Sharing On` appear just above the Stop button. This lets you know that file sharing is enabled.

Connecting to a shared resource

Toward the bottom of the Sharing panel, you can see that other Macintosh users can access your computer at `afp://<ip address>`, where `ip address` is the IP address for your specific computer. When another Mac user wants to connect to your shared files, that person can do the following:

1. **Open the Finder and choose Go⊅Connect to Server.**

2. **After the Connect to Server dialog opens, other Mac users can type** afp://*<ip address>* **(where** `ip address` **is the IP address of your Macintosh) and then click the Connect button.**

   Alternatively, you can choose Go⊅Network and then browse your network for the server name listed at the bottom of the panel.

You can also browse for a shared resource on the Connect to Server dialog. Choose Go⇨Connect to Server or press ⌘+K. Click Browse to locate the shared computer. Note that you might be prompted to choose whether you want to connect as a Guest or a Registered User. To connect to the server as a Registered User, you must supply the right username and password. If you connect as Guest, you don't have to supply a password, but you will have restricted access to only the Public folder for each account on the system that you connect to. If you need to connect as a Registered User, ask an Admin user who controls that Mac to supply you with the correct username and password.

Give the username and password that you created to the person using the other Mac, and he can now access files in that account's Home folder as well as any other Public folders on your computer.

Sharing a Connected Printer

Sharing your printer for others to use is one of the best reasons to have a network. Setting up your Mac to share your printer is very easy under Mac OS X. Here's a quick rundown of what you need to do:

1. **Open System Preferences from the Dock.**

2. **Click the Sharing icon under the Internet & Network section to open the Sharing Preferences dialog.**

3. **On the Services panel, select the Printer Sharing entry.**

4. **Click Start.**

   There will be a slight pause while Mac OS X gets everything ready, but when it's done, you see the message `Printer Sharing On` appear just above the Stop button. This lets you know that printer sharing is enabled.

By default, when you turn on Printer Sharing, Tiger automatically shares all the current printers connected to your Mac. To select which printers can be used for shared printing, click the Print & Fax icon in System Preferences, and then click Sharing. From this panel, you can enable and disable sharing on individual printers.

After Printer Sharing is enabled, follow these steps to connect to that printer from other computers on your network:

1. **Click System Preferences on the Dock.**

2. **Click the Print & Fax icon.**

3. **Click the Add button (which carries a plus sign).**

You might be prompted to add a printer automatically when the Printer Setup Utility opens. Click the Add button to begin the addition. (For more on adding a printer with the Printer Setup Utility, see Book VI, Chapter 4.)

4. **From the Printer List window that opens, click the Add button.**

5. **Click IP Printing on the toolbar.**

6. **Enter the IP address of the Macintosh that's connected to the target printer and then click the Add button.**

Already got the Printer Browser open? Then follow the easier path: Clicking the Default Browser toolbar button displays all the available local shared printers. Click the desired printer and then click Add.

You can also click More Printers at the bottom of the Printer List window to select a printer using Bonjour. Click the drop-down list box at the top of the dialog and choose Bonjour to automatically recognize printers on your local network. Printers just appear in your Printer List automatically. It doesn't get any easier than that!

Sharing Files with Windows Computers

If you've deigned to allow PCs running Windows on your network (a generous gesture to the lower classes), you'll probably want to also share files with those computers. Sharing files with a Windows PC — actually a Windows user — is very similar to sharing files with other Mac users.

Follow these steps:

1. **Click the System Preferences icon on the Dock.**

2. **Click the Sharing icon to open the Sharing Preferences pane.**

3. **On the Services panel, mark the Windows Sharing check box to enable it.**

    After a few moments, you see the message `Windows Sharing On` appear just above the Stop button, confirming that you're now open to connections from the Great Unwashed Windows Horde.

Just like when sharing files with other Mac users, you see a helpful reminder toward the bottom that tells you what the Windows users need to type in order to gain access to your Mac. Also, you might have to enable Windows access on the desired account before it can be used. Click Enable Accounts and then mark the check box next to the account that you want to share with Windows users. Tiger prompts you for your password, smugly inform-ing you that the account password will be stored "in a less secure manner." (Take that, Mr. Gates!)

Accessing File Shares on Windows Computers

If you allow a Windows PC to access your files, you'll also probably want to putter around with files on a Windows PC. Easy!

Accessing files on Windows computers relies on the Samba component (a part of the UNIX foundation of Mac OS X). Follow these steps:

1. **Choose Go⇨Connect to Server from the Finder.**

The Connect to Server dialog opens.

2. **In the Address box, enter** smb://*<ip address>*, **where** `ip address` **is the IP address of the Windows computer that you want to connect to.**

3. **Click the Connect button.**

Depending on the type of account you have on the Windows PC, Mac OS X might display an SMB (Server Message Block) authentication dialog in which you can enter your username and password. (Think security for the Windows crowd.)

4. **Select the desired shared drive to mount from the drop-down list box.**

5. **Mount the shared drive, OS-version-dependent:**

- *If you're accessing a file shared on a Windows 95 or Windows 98 com-puter:* Simply click OK to mount the share.

- *If you're accessing a file shared on a Windows NT, 2000, or XP com-puter:* Click the Authenticate button. Then enter your username and password, click OK, and then click OK again to mount the share.

Using FTP on the Internet

Because File Transfer Protocol (FTP) is a part of the TCP/IP suite, it works on virtually every type of computer (over both the Internet and your local area network). So, assuming that you have your computer connected to the Internet through a modem or a local area network (LAN) connection, everything that I discuss about FTP and how to use it applies to connecting to FTP servers on the Internet as well. When you con-nect to FTP servers on the Internet, you can use the Fully Qualified Domain Name (or FQDN for short) like `ftp.apple.com` instead of an actual IP address. You can also use the FTP server in Mac OS X to make files available to friends on the Internet just as you would to make them available on a LAN.

After you mount the shared drive, you'll see it appear on your Desktop, just like a Mac volume. You can use this drive just like any other drive on your system. To disconnect from the Windows share, you can

✦ **Drag the icon to the Trash on the Dock (which changes to an Eject icon when you start dragging).**

✦ **Press ⌘+E.**

or

✦ **Hold Control, click the icon, and then choose Eject from the menu that appears.**

Using FTP to Access Files

FTP is part of the TCP/IP protocol suite — the hoary acronym FTP stands for *File Transfer Protocol*. FTP is one of the oldest methods for sharing files between computers; however, because it's part of the TCP/IP protocol suite, it can be used on many different kinds of computers, including those running just about any type of strange and arcane operating system. You can still manage to exchange files regardless of whether you're using Mac OS X, Windows, Linux, or UNIX. (Heck, even DOS can join the party.)

FTP is a *client/server* application. In plain English, this means that two pieces make things tick: the *server* (which hosts the connection, rather like a file server) and the *client* (which connects to the server). Mac OS X, thanks to its UNIX foundation, has both an FTP server and client built in. To use FTP, you need a computer running the FTP server software to give others access to files; then the other computer, or client, can connect to the FTP server. After the connection is made, the client can either send files to the server *(uploading)* or get files from the server *(downloading)*. In this section, I cover how to use FTP to give others access to your files as well as talk about the FTP applications that come with Mac OS X.

Using the Mac OS X built-in FTP to share files

One way to give others access to your files is to run an FTP server on your Mac. Mac OS X comes with an FTP server built in, so you just have to activate it. You might wonder why you'd use FTP to share files when you can use Personal File Sharing or Windows File Sharing. The main advantage to FTP is compatibility: Not only can people on your LAN access files, but anyone on the Internet can also access your files, regardless of the type of machine that they're using.

Just like with the other file-sharing methods, you need to create a user account on your computer before someone can connect to and get files from your Mac.

After you have accounts created for the users, you can enable FTP sharing like this:

1. **Click the System Preferences icon on the Dock.**

2. **Click the Sharing icon to open the Sharing Preferences pane.**

3. **Mark the FTP Access check box to enable it.**

You see the message FTP Access On appear above the Stop button, which proclaims that FTP access is enabled. Also you can see toward the bottom of the dialog that people can use ftp://<ip address>, where *ip address* is the IP address of your Mac.

 If you're using an AirPort/AirPort Extreme Base Station or other cable/digital subscriber line (DSL) router to share your Internet connection, you need to place the Mac that you want people on the Internet to access in a *DMZ,* or demilitarized zone. Check your cable/DSL router documentation for more information.

Using FTP from Terminal to transfer files

You can use FTP to transfer files with an FTP server by using the command line interface (CLI); to use the CLI, you need to open a Terminal, or shell, session. To use a Terminal session, click the Terminal icon in the Utilities folder inside the Applications folder. When you open a Terminal session, you're presented with a window that accepts text commands. You'll see a prompt that consists of your computer's name and the folder that you're currently in, followed by your user ID. It's at this prompt where you type various FTP commands.

After you're in the Terminal session, you'll use a series of commands to connect to another computer, move in and out of folders, and transfer files. Following is a list of the basic commands that you need to use FTP as well as a brief description of what each command does.

✦ ftp: This command starts the FTP command line interface session. You can tell that you're in the FTP client application when you see ftp> as your command prompt. This is where you will type all other FTP commands to do things.

✦ open: This command is used to start your connection to another computer. Type this command followed by the IP address of the FTP server that you want to connect to.

✦ ls: Use this command to see a listing of all files and folders in the current folder on the FTP server.

✦ cd: This command allows you to change the folder that you're in. Type *cd <folder>* (where *folder* is a specific folder name) to move into a subfolder on the FTP server. Type **cd ..** (that's c, d, space, and two periods) to go back out a folder level.

✦ lcd: This command acts exactly like cd except that it changes the folder that you're currently in on your local system, not the FTP server. Use this command to put yourself in the folder on the local drive that you want to transfer files to and from.

✦ bin: Type this command to get in binary mode to transfer files that aren't plain text files. (*Always* use binary mode unless you're specifically transferring plain text files.)

✦ ascii: This command puts you in ASCII mode for transferring text files.

✦ get or mget: To retrieve a single file, use the get command followed by the filename of the file that you want to retrieve. If you want to get multiple files at once, use the mget command followed by a filename containing * and/or ? as wildcards.

✦ put or mput: To send a single file, use the put command followed by the filename to send a file to the FTP server. To send multiple files, use the mput command followed by a filename containing * and/or ? as wildcards.

✦ quit: Use the quit command to end your FTP session.

To end a Terminal session and exit Terminal at any time, press ⌘+Q. Terminal will prompt you for confirmation if necessary.

Many FTP servers will only let you send files to certain folders. Most times this folder is named *Upload, Uploads,* or something similar.

Using these commands will enable you to exchange files with an FTP server. Here's an example of how to use these commands within the Terminal window:

1. **Type** ftp **to get into FTP mode.**

2. **Type** open *<ip address>* **to open your connection to the FTP server.**

3. **At this point, you'll be asked for a username and password.**

For many FTP servers, using the username anonymous and your e-mail address as the password is enough to get you logged in. Some sites even allow you to log in without any username or password at all. On secure sites, however, you must use an assigned username and password provided by the administrator of that particular server.

4. Use the `lcd <folder>` (where `folder` is a specific folder name) command to change into the folder on your local drive that you want files to come to/from.

5. Use the `ls` and `cd` commands to place yourself into the desired folder on the FTP server.

6. Use the `ascii` or `bin` commands to set your file transfer mode to ASCII or binary, respectively.

This is important because choosing the wrong type will likely cause the transfer to fail. Unless it's a plain text file, always use binary mode.

7. Use the `get`/`mget`/`put`/`mput` commands to send or receive the desired files.

8. Use the `quit` command to close the connection and exit the FTP session.

Using the Built-in Firewall

A *firewall* watches all the network communications coming into your Mac — it automatically plays the role of security guard, blocking or denying certain network traffic that you want to avoid from reaching your Mac. It acts as another layer of security to help keep you safe from unwanted attacks. That's all well and good, but you must be careful to set up your firewall correctly before you turn it on: A configuration mistake could make your Mac inaccessible from the network.

For instance, if you want to enable FTP access on your Mac but you also want to keep all other traffic from coming into your Mac, you can tell the built-in firewall to only allow FTP traffic. The firewall on the Mac will only block or allow TCP/IP traffic — not AppleTalk — so AppleTalk traffic (which is always from your local network and *not* the Internet anyway) is always able to get in.

When enabled, the firewall blocks all traffic that comes into your Mac. By default, however, the firewall is turned off. So, your first job is to enable the firewall, following these steps:

1. Click the System Preferences icon on the Dock.

2. Click the Sharing icon.

3. Click the Firewall tab to show the settings that you see in Figure 2-2.

4. Click the Start button.

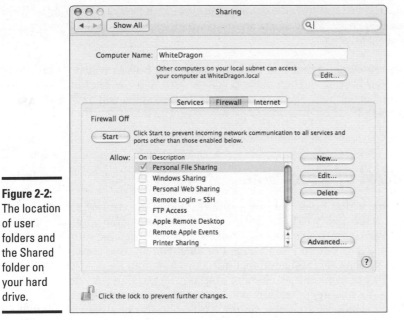

Figure 2-2:
The location of user folders and the Shared folder on your hard drive.

This enables the firewall. And, by default, all incoming TCP/IP traffic is blocked. You must enable each sharing method that you want to be able to use. As you enable different sharing methods, such as Personal File Sharing or FTP Access, notice that under the Firewall tab, those types of traffic now have a check mark in the box for each type of traffic. (In other words, when you turn on a sharing method, the firewall automatically allows traffic for that sharing method. *Most* excellent.)

Sometimes you might want to allow other traffic through your firewall that isn't on the list. At that point, you can click the New button to create a new definition for your firewall to use. The resulting dialog has a drop-down list with some common things that you might want to allow, such as Internet Relay Chat (IRC), I Seek You (ICQ), QuickTime, and MSN Messenger.

If you need to add ports for another application that's not in that drop-down list — for instance, a multiplayer game — you need to select Other from the Port Name drop-down list. Then you can enter a port number, a port range, or a series of ports. You might need to check the documentation for a specific application to see which ports it uses.

Ports are like an extension to an IP address. For example, when you communicate with a Web server, you send a request not only to that Web server's IP address, but you send it on port 80 — the standard port for *HyperText Transfer*

Protocol (HTTP) traffic. Different applications use different port numbers, so you need to check which ports are used when you want to adjust your firewall to allow that traffic.

I highly recommend that you click the Advanced button whilst you're turning on your firewall — then make doggone sure that the Enable Stealth Mode check box is enabled. Hackers and other undesirables will have a much harder time locating your Mac's presence on the Internet with this feature turned on.

Remote Control of Your Mac

Forgive me whilst I wax techno-nerd here: One of the coolest advantages to a network is the ability to take control of one computer from another computer. For example, sometimes you might need to access files on your Mac while you're on a trip, but you don't have Personal File Sharing enabled. What can you do? You can remotely connect into your Mac and then — just as if you were sitting in front of it — enable Personal File Sharing (as I demonstrate earlier in the chapter). Perhaps you have a file on your computer with someone's phone number that you suddenly need on the road — with remote control, it's at your fingertips! (Sigh . . . ah, technology.)

Remotely control your Mac (for free, no less!)

Virtual Network Computer (or VNC, available for many platforms at www. realvnc.com) is a very nice application that enables you to remotely control a computer from pretty much anywhere that has an Internet connection. VNC is easy to install and configure, but the best feature is that it's free. VNC can run on many different platforms, ranging from Windows XP and UNIX on desktop computers and servers to Palm OS and Windows CE on personal digital assistants (PDAs). Wrap your mind around this: You could be at a friend's house on her wireless network and use your PDA to remotely control your Mac at home over the Internet. Pure, undiluted *sassy!*

Some networks have proxies and firewalls that might interfere with VNC's operation. You can remotely control a computer that's behind a firewall or cable/DSL router, but the firewall/router needs to be configured properly. Because the process varies from one manufacturer to the next, check your cable/DSL router manual for instructions on how to do this.

Speaking of firewalls, make sure that you configure the Mac OS X firewall to allow VNC traffic. Follow the steps that I outline in the previous section to allow communications over the port you use for VNC.

How VNC works

In a nutshell, VNC takes the graphical interface on your monitor, turns it into data, and sends it to the computer that you're using to remotely control it. The computer that you're using sends keyboard presses, mouse movements, and clicks to it, acting just the same way it would if you were sitting right in front of it.

A specific version of VNC, called *Share My Desktop* (SMD), is available for Mac OS X. You can download SMD at

www.bombich.com/software/smd.html

There you'll find instructions on how to install and set up SMD. Figure 2-3 shows a screenshot of a Mac running SMD being remotely controlled from a computer running Windows 98.

Figure 2-3:
Yes, bucko, that's my Mac OS X Desktop, accessed remotely via Windows!

Mr. Paranoia speaks again: **Make doggone sure that you set up the password access correctly for SMD, or don't run it!** I can't stress enough how much fun a hacker would have with free remote control over your Mac OS X Desktop.

Remote control of another computer from your Mac

A few different VNC viewers exist for Mac OS X. A *VNC viewer* is just an application you use to remotely control your computer running VNC. You can download them at www.realvnc.com/download.html. If you find yourself on a computer without a VNC viewer — heaven forbid — VNC server actually runs over the Web as well! As long as the computer that you're using has a Web browser that supports Java — which Safari and Internet Explorer do — you can still remotely control your computer.

When you connect to the computer running VNC using a Web browser, the Web server sends a default page that contains a Java applet. That Java applet asks you for the password to connect; upon entering the correct password, it brings up the remote control session right in the Web browser. Good golly, Molly!

Chapter 3: You May Even Need AppleTalk

In This Chapter

- Connecting to a legacy AppleTalk network
- Configuring the AppleTalk network preferences
- Using Mac OS X to access AppleTalk resources

*W*hen emoting concerning networking and Macs, I'd be terribly remiss for not discussing *AppleTalk,* which is the so-called "archaic" communications protocol created years ago by Apple. AppleTalk allows a network of Macs to share files and printers; before the arrival of an Ethernet port, AppleTalk was the cat's meow for connecting Macs. AppleTalk is still used in environments like homes, offices, and college campuses. However, AppleTalk is now disappearing from the corporate world because it simply cannot *scale* (that's administrator-speak for *grow*) to handle large networks like standard Ethernet and Transmission Control Protocol/Internet Protocol (TCP/IP) can.

Although Apple finally made the move to TCP/IP as its primary network protocol — like the rest of the civilized world — Apple still includes support for AppleTalk in Mac OS X Tiger, but it's disabled by default. About the only time when you might need to use AppleTalk is if you find yourself trying to access an existing AppleTalk network (which is practically the definition of the phrase *rare occurrence*) . . . but hey, I like to cover everything in a desktop reference. Therefore, in this chapter, I show you how to enable the AppleTalk protocol on your Mac as well as how to access files and printers on a network that's running AppleTalk.

Setting Up AppleTalk

Just like most network configuration tasks under the Big X, configuring your Mac to use AppleTalk and play well with others in an AppleTalk network isn't very difficult. In this section, I talk about how to configure the settings in the Network dialog of System Preferences so that you can join the file sharing and network printing party.

You can configure AppleTalk on Mac OS X in two ways: manually or automatically. I'll bet you could see this Mark's Maxim coming from a mile away:

> **Automatic is always good.**™

Unless you're given specific AppleTalk settings by a network administrator, I highly recommend using the automatic AppleTalk configuration. However, I cover both methods in this chapter just to be on the safe side. (That's just the kind of guy I am.)

Automatically configuring AppleTalk

To automatically configure AppleTalk, follow these steps.

1. **Choose System Preferences from the Apple menu (** **) or the Dock.**

2. **From the System Preferences window, click Network to open the Network Preferences pane.**

3. **Click the Show drop-down list box and choose Built-in Ethernet (or the connection you're currently using).**

4. **Click the AppleTalk tab to display the AppleTalk settings page.**

5. **Enable the Make AppleTalk Active check box and then click the Apply Now button.**

   Mac OS X defaults to using the automatic AppleTalk configuration mode. Now, I know this is going to be hard to believe, but you're done!

Now your Mac is configured to use the AppleTalk protocol to share and access files and printers. AppleTalk is ready to go as soon as you click the Apply Now button, but you won't notice anything special when you turn on AppleTalk. (Like TCP/IP, AppleTalk is invisible in Mac OS X until you use it.) Check the "Accessing Files and Printers with AppleTalk" section later in this chapter to actually start using AppleTalk to do stuff.

Manually configuring AppleTalk

Although not as simple as using the automatic configuration, manually configuring AppleTalk is quite easy as well. To manually configure AppleTalk, follow these steps:

1. **Choose System Preferences from the Apple menu or the Dock.**

2. **From the System Preferences window that appears, click Network to open the Network Preferences pane.**

A word about Zones

The final option on the AppleTalk settings page is the AppleTalk Zone drop-down list box. (Stick with me here, things are going to get technically flamboyant for a few sentences, but it can't be helped.) *Zones* are logical groupings of computers that an AppleTalk network administrator creates for ease of use. For example, consider a large company that employs many graphic artists: This company has many buildings, but because of how the business has grown, the graphic artists are spread between several different locations in different buildings. An AppleTalk network administrator would likely have created a Graphics Zone that contains all the Macs and servers and printers that make up the graphics department; this way, the artists can get to files on servers or print to printers that are meant for them simply by putting themselves in the Graphics Zone. This works as a handy way to keep people who are physically separate logically grouped into a common area, or *Zone*. (Think of Zones as a convenience thing — they don't help your system performance.)

When you configure AppleTalk, you might or might not need to set the AppleTalk Zone. If you're on a network in which the administrator has configured AppleTalk Zones, you'll see a list of all the Zones by clicking the AppleTalk Zone drop-down list; from there, simply select the name of the Zone that you want to participate in. If you're on a network in which no Zones are configured, the AppleTalk Zone drop-down box will be grayed out and unavailable — and if you can't choose a Zone anyway, don't worry about it. (In other words, don't let your lack of AppleTalk Zones spoil that upcoming trip to Vegas.)

3. **Click the Show drop-down list box and choose Built-in Ethernet (or the connection you're currently using).**

4. **Click the AppleTalk tab to display the AppleTalk settings page.**

5. **From the Configure drop-down list, choose Manually.**

   When you do, two more text boxes appear where you can enter information, as Figure 3-1 illustrates: Node ID and Network ID. Unless you're the network administrator — check to see whether you're surrounded by a glowing aura of authority and wisdom — you must obtain these two ID numbers from that glowing individual who *is* administering your network.

   Use manual configuration only if you're designing an AppleTalk network or you have information from a network administrator on the correct settings to use. If you enter the wrong settings, you won't be able to communicate with other Macs on your network . . . but at least you don't need to worry about blowing something up or watching your Mac melt.

6. **After you enter the appropriate Node ID and Network ID, click the Apply Now button to save those settings.**

Figure 3-1:
Embarking
on manual
preparations
for
AppleTalk.

Accessing Files and Printers with AppleTalk

After you have AppleTalk configured and ready to go, you can share files and printers from your Mac. If you're wondering what to do after AppleTalk is enabled, the following sections show you how to share your files and printers as well as how to access files and printers that others have shared on the network.

Accessing AppleTalk share points

Accessing *share points* — a collection of files that are shared to the network — by using AppleTalk is much like accessing other shared files with Internet Protocol (IP). In this section, I talk about finding AppleTalk servers, connecting to AppleTalk share points, and how to disconnect when you are done. Follow these steps each time when you start your computer or if you get disconnected for any reason.

Even though a server version of Mac OS X exists that is meant to run on corporate servers that do nothing but serve up files and printers to people, in this entire section, I use the word *server* to simply mean any Mac or other computer that has AppleTalk running and is sharing files or printers.

Choosing an AppleTalk server

To choose an AppleTalk server, perform the following steps:

1. **From the Finder, choose Go⇨Connect to Server or press ⌘+K on the keyboard.**

   This brings up the Connect To Server dialog.

2. **From this dialog, click the Browse button.**

   Your Mac searches the local network for any AppleTalk servers and displays a Finder window listing all the available servers.

3. **Double-click the icon representing the appropriate AppleTalk server that contains the share point that you want to access.**

4. **After you choose the AppleTalk server, click the Connect button.**

To help cut down on the time that it takes to connect to this same server in the future, just click the Add button (which proudly bears a plus sign), and the server's path is added to the Favorite Servers list. The next time that you need to connect to that server, you need only double-click the server entry in the Favorite Servers list. (This works for all servers, not just the AppleTalk variety.) Ain't life grand?

Tiger also maintains a list of the servers that you've connected to recently, even if they don't appear in the Favorite Servers list. Click the Recent Servers button (which carries a clock icon) and then click the desired server from the menu. You can also click Recent Items under the Apple menu to show the same servers.

Connecting to the AppleTalk server

Each time you want to access files or printers via AppleTalk, you must connect to the server. To connect to an AppleTalk server, you need to connect as a Guest or, if you have a username and password for that server, as a Registered User. After clicking the Connect button of the Connect to Server dialog, you'll be prompted to choose whether you want to connect as a Guest or a Registered User.

If you're connecting to the server as a Registered User, you must supply the right username and password. If you connect as a Guest, you don't have to supply a password, but (depending on the access rights that have been configured) you might have restricted access only to the Shared folder that appears in the Users folder on each system that you connect to. If you connect as a Registered User, you need to get the correct username and password from the person who is in control of user accounts on a given Mac.

Before you click the Connect button to complete the connection, consider whether you'd like to automate things in the future. If so, enable the Remember Password (Add to Keychain) check box. Enabling this check box saves the username and password for this connection so that you don't have to manually type it in each time that you reconnect to this particular share point (particularly handy if you connect to a share point every time that you use your Mac). However, use this option *only* if your Mac is in a secure location, or if you can be sure that others won't use this connection.

Choosing a share point from the AppleTalk server

Whether or not you chose to play with the connection options, finalize the connection by clicking the Connect button after choosing to log in as a Guest or a Registered User. After you click Connect, you see a list of share points on the AppleTalk server.

Double-click the icon for the share point that you want. You see a network drive appear on your Desktop, which you can treat as you would any other attached drive.

Disconnecting from the share point

When you're done using the share point, you can disconnect from the share point in a few different ways:

✦ **Control+click the network drive Desktop icon and choose Eject from the contextual menu that appears.**

✦ **Click the network drive Desktop icon to highlight it and then choose Eject from the File menu.**

✦ **Click the network drive Desktop icon to highlight it and then press ⌘+E.**

✦ **Click the network drive icon in a Finder window sidebar and click the Eject button next to it.**

✦ **Click and drag the network drive Desktop icon to the Trash on the Dock.** *Hint:* The Trash changes into an Eject icon when dragging a network drive. Simple but *sassy.*

Accessing AppleTalk printers

The other major thing (besides file sharing) that you can do with AppleTalk is to connect to and use AppleTalk network printers. Again, like most things under Mac OS X, it's pretty straightforward and easy.

Adding an AppleTalk printer

Before you can print to an AppleTalk printer, you first need to add that printer to your setup. Follow these steps to add a printer:

1. **Open your hard drive from the Desktop, double-click the Applications folder, double-click the Utilities folder, and then double-click the Printer Setup Utility icon.**

   This opens the Printer Setup Utility.

2. **If you're prompted to add a printer the first time that you open the Printer Setup Utility, as seen in Figure 3-2, click Add to start the process.**

   If you've already opened Printer Setup Utility and have already added printers in the past, you add another network printer by clicking the Add toolbar button.

Figure 3-2:
Adding your first printer in the Printer Setup Utility.

> **You have no printers available.**
> Would you like to add to your list of printers now?
>
> Cancel   Add

3. **Click More Printers.**

4. **From the resulting Printer List sheet, select AppleTalk from the top drop-down box.**

   You see a list of all the AppleTalk shared printers that your Mac sees on the network.

   If you're on a network with more than just the local Zone, you might need to select the appropriate Zone from the second drop-down box before you see the desired printer.

5. **Click the desired printer to select it in the list.**

6. **If necessary, select the proper printer from the Printer Model drop-down list at the bottom of the Printer List dialog.**

   If the Auto Select feature doesn't identify the correct printer, you might have to select the closest match from the Printer Model drop-down list. (Check the printer manufacturer's Web site for updated printer drivers that might be necessary to use this new printer.) Choosing Generic from the list will work with most printers, but (depending on your model) you might be restricted to text-only output and might not have access to special features like tray selection or print quality.

7. **Click the Add button to complete the process.**

You can now treat this as any other printer that could be connected directly to your machine. You can view the print queue and hold, resume, and delete print jobs from the Queue menu.

Removing an AppleTalk printer

Removing an AppleTalk printer that you've connected to is very simple. From the Printer Setup Utility, click once on the printer that you wish to remove and then either click the Delete icon in the Printer Setup Utility toolbar or choose Delete Printer from the Printers menu.

Chapter 4: Going Wireless

In This Chapter

⌐ Finding out how wireless networking works

⌐ Discovering wireless security

⌐ Connecting to other Macs without a wireless access point

⌐ Connecting to and disconnecting from AirPort networks

*N*owadays, wireless connectivity is king. For example, cellphones have gone from being a toy of the technological elite to a permanent fixture on the hip of the common man. The shorts that I'm wearing right now have a special pocket just for a cellphone to ride in; when I'm without my phone, it usually carries a 5th Avenue candy bar. (Perhaps that was too personal . . . sorry.)

Because people have become accustomed to being able to keep in touch wherever they are, they also want to be able to have access to their network, at least within their house or workplace, without the hassle of cables. (Which, by the way, are magnets for pets that enjoy a good chew toy.) This desire for convenience and the advances in wireless technology have combined to bring you the concept of the wireless network (and wireless coffee shops, and wireless access providers, and even wireless gaming centers).

Now you can be connected to your home local area network (LAN) and your shared Internet connection (which I cover in Book V, Chapter 5) from your balcony, deck, lounge chair in the yard, or even your bedroom. In this chapter, I talk about how wireless networks work, and then I give you a lot of information to help you get the right pieces to free yourself — *securely,* mind you — from the world of the wired.

Speaking the Wireless Lingo

Wireless networks aren't all that different from their wired siblings. In this chapter, I discuss some of the features and limitations of wireless networking, but you must first be familiar with a foundation of information.

Because of the technology involved in wireless networks and how things are changing rapidly in this area, you'll find yourself swimming in a sea of acronyms and other techno-babble. Although you don't need to know every little detail to be able to set up your own wireless network, you should know some of these terms so that you can avoid getting stung by hackers or stuck with equipment that's on the verge of obsolescence. Here is a quick list of terms that you'll see on your road to becoming a wireless network guru:

✦ **WLAN:** WLAN stands for *Wireless LAN.* If you've already read previous chapters in this mini-book, a LAN (local area network) is just a bunch of computers and other devices connected together.

✦ **IEEE:** The *Institute of Electrical and Electronics Engineers.* This is an organization that approves standards that allow computers, network equipment, and just about anything else electronic to play nicely together. Sometimes IEEE helps create these standards before approving them, and sometimes it just approves standards that others have produced.

✦ **802.11:** This is the part of the IEEE standards that deals specifically with wireless networking. Although wireless is usually generically referred to as *wireless networks* (or sometimes even *Wi-Fi*), it's all really a wireless form of Ethernet.

✦ **Wireless access point:** A *wireless access point,* or WAP, is a device that allows wireless network devices to connect to a wired Ethernet network.

✦ **Service Set Identifier:** The *Service Set Identifier,* or SSID, is used to tell your computer the name of the wireless network that you want to use.

✦ **Wired Equivalency Protocol:** *Wired Equivalency Protocol,* or WEP, is an encryption that wireless networks can use to keep your wireless network more secure from snoopers and hackers.

✦ **Ad Hoc mode:** An *Ad Hoc* wireless network is one where each wireless device talks directly with all other wireless devices. Apple calls this mode a *computer-to-computer network.*

✦ **Infrastructure mode:** This is where all wireless devices talk to a WAP, and the WAP then talks to other wireless devices and the wired network.

As I cover the different parts of wireless networking and how to set it up, you'll find yourself using these terms over and over. Before you know it, you'll be spouting these wireless-related acronyms like a pro. (No, really. I'm not kidding.)

Figuring Out the Different Flavors of Wireless Ethernet

One of the first things that you might notice when you start looking into wireless networking is the different wireless standards. You should at least be aware that these different standards exist: That way, you can be sure to get wireless network components that will work together because *some of the different wireless standards are not compatible.* (Feel free to photocopy this list and stick it on your fridge door.)

IEEE 802.11b

IEEE 802.11b has another name that you'll likely see on product advertisements, literature, or boxes in stores: *Wi-Fi,* which stands for Wireless Fidelity.
(Kinda like that cutting-edge Hi-Fi stereo from the '60s and '70s, where *Hi-Fi*
stands for *High Fidelity.*) Most folks proclaim Wi-Fi as only 802.11b. Wi-Fi was
the first version of wireless Ethernet. This version of wireless runs at speeds
up to 11 million bits per second, or 11 Mbps. The reason why I say that it
runs at speeds *up to* 11Mbps is because the actual speed that the data is
transferred depends on things like signal strength and quality. When the conditions are such that your signal strength or quality is decreased — such as
an inconvenient concrete wall between you and your AirPort Base Station —
you might find that your wireless connection changes down to 5.5 Mbps,
2 Mbps, or even as slow as 1 Mbps.

Most available wireless Ethernet equipment, including Apple's AirPort network cards and standard-issue AirPort Base Station, uses 802.11b. In fact,
it's time for Mac owners to swell with pride yet again: Apple was the first
computer company to ship 802.11b hardware. (Back then, in 1999, it was the
original AirPort Base Station.) Now, of course, Apple has raised the bar with
AirPort Extreme, which I discuss later in this chapter, and the AirPort
Express mobile Base Station.

In general, Wi-Fi network cards have the ability to communicate with other
Wi-Fi devices and WAPs that are up to 1,000 feet away. Having said that, realize that 1,000 feet is a generous estimate when outdoors on a clear day with
no wind blowing — you see what I'm getting at. In reality, when you set up
your wireless network, things such as walls — especially concrete walls, like
in basements — decrease the distance that you can cover. If you use a WAP,
plan on no more than 150 feet between wireless computers and the WAP.
However, your mileage might vary.

Wireless Ethernet networks operate just like wired Ethernet networks that
use a *hub.* (See Book V, Chapter 1 for more info on hubs.) This means that
the 11 Mbps bandwidth is shared between all computers using it. Collisions
can also occur if more than one computer tries to communicate at the same
time. If you have a lot of people on your wireless network, the network can
and will get noticeably slower because of increased collisions. Remember
that the total bandwidth is shared between the computers on the wireless
network. This applies not only to Wi-Fi but also to the 802.11a (which I cover
in the next section) and the 802.11g standards.

One last thing about 802.11b networking: Wi-Fi uses the 2.4 GHz frequency
range. It actually uses 11 different channels, but they're all around the 2.4 GHz
range. I bring this up because if you're using a 2.4 GHz cordless phone or
even a microwave, using either device can definitely interfere with or even

shut down your wireless network. Keep this in mind when you buy your next phone or wonder why your file transfers stop when you're communing with Orville Redenbacher in the microwave.

802.11a

802.11a is a newer version of wireless Ethernet. No, I didn't get my letters mixed up. For some reason that I don't know (or understand), 802.11b came out first, and 802.11a came out next. (I guess someone ran into a doorframe.) Anyway, 802.11a doesn't have a generally recognized handy nickname like Wi-Fi, so just call it 802.11a.

802.11a isn't all that much different than Wi-Fi, but the few differences make a big impact. First off, 802.11a can run at speeds up to 54 Mbps — almost *five times* faster than Wi-Fi. This is because 802.11a uses the 5 GHz frequency range instead of the cluttered 2.4 GHz range that Wi-Fi uses. The powers that be set aside the 5 GHz range just for wireless networking, so cordless phones and microwaves (or any other wireless devices for that matter) can't interfere with the network. The downside to using the higher 5 GHz range, though, is that the distances that can be covered are even less than that of Wi-Fi — no more than about 60 feet to maintain the highest speeds.

Remember, 802.11a equipment isn't compatible with Wi-Fi or any of the AirPort Base Stations, so don't make the mistake of buying both 802.11b and 802.11a network equipment. Instead, I recommend that you follow the AirPort Extreme course charted by Apple, and use the 802.11g standard (which is backward-compatible with Wi-Fi).

Let's get Extreme: 802.11g

Although some hardware manufacturers have designed equipment that will handle both Wi-Fi and 802.11a, Apple's release of AirPort Extreme provides both the speed of 802.11a and the compatibility with Wi-Fi. That's because it uses the *802.11g* standard, which operates at speeds up to 54 Mbps (like 802.11a) but will also operate at the same frequency ranges and play nicely with existing 802.11b equipment. (Notice that we're heading in the right direction again when it comes to naming conventions. Go figure.)

Oh, and did I mention that Apple is once again the *first* company to offer 802.11g hardware as standard equipment? Feel free to enjoy the Superiority Dance yet again as you use AirPort Extreme.

Naturally, there is a downside: 802.11g returns to that pesky 2.4 GHz range, so your cordless phone and microwave can also wreak the same havoc that they did with your original AirPort equipment.

I should also mention *Bluetooth* — a strange name for a wireless standard, I admit, but it works like a charm. Bluetooth devices use 2.4 GHz as well, but they're designed only for very short distances . . . only about 30 feet. Bluetooth is the future for linking mobile devices (like personal digital assistants and cellphones) and external peripherals (like wireless keyboards and mice) to your Mac. In fact, Bluetooth is a popular feature for the iMac G5, which can turn it into a completely cordless machine — except for the power cord, of course. Tiger provides built-in support for Bluetooth through the iSync application.

Keeping Your Wireless Network Secure

Are you worried about the security of your AirPort wireless network? You *should* be, bunkie. As you might (or might not) know, the government has said that intercepting calls made from wireless phones isn't a violation of privacy. Because of the similarities between wireless phones and wireless networks, it stands to reason that if/when a court has to make a determination, it will most likely determine that it's not illegal for someone in the next apartment or house — or standing right in your street — to listen to and intercept your data from your wireless network.

But before you decide to toss the idea of a wireless network, keep this in mind: Even though it *is* technically possible that someone might camp out on your doorstep in order to gain access to your wireless network, for most home networks, this possibility isn't very probable. Even if someone tries to gain access to your wireless network and perhaps even *sniff* your network — a techno-nerd term meaning to record all the data flying around a network — there isn't a whole lot someone can do with that information.

If a friend invites you for an evening of war driving, think "recreational mobile hacking." *War driving* is the act of driving through neighborhoods in a car equipped with a laptop computer and a wireless network card. The payoff? If the hacker is lucky enough to locate a house with an open wireless network, we're talking free wireless Internet access . . . from the comfort of his car! Again, keep security in mind when installing wireless hardware, and these bozos will get nothing from your network.

You might say, "But I use my credit card on the Internet to buy stuff." Sure, this is a valid concern — however, if you purchase things on the Internet with your credit card, you should already be using a secure connection provided by the Web site for your personal information so that the data you're sending across your wireless network is already encrypted and relatively safe from thieves. (You'll find more on this when I discuss Safari in detail in Book IV, Chapter 5.)

"I have shared my files on my computer. Can the Bad Guys access those shared files?" Another good question, but if you read Book V, Chapter 2, you have to create an account for those whom you want to access your files. Unless the would-be hacker is very good at guessing usernames and passwords, your files are pretty safe, too.

This is not to say that you bear absolutely no risk of being hacked. If a legitimate user on your wireless network connects to your computer and starts transferring a file, a would-be hacker could potentially record all the traffic and then reconstruct the file that was sent from the data that was recorded. In other words, a hacker could grab that user's username and password. That's where WEP comes in.

WEP

Wired Equivalency Protocol, or WEP, is A Good Thing (even if it makes for a silly-sounding acronym). It's an encryption scheme that can be used on your wireless network. WEP is a part of all 802.11 standards, so all your Wi-Fi equipment supports WEP. Apple's implementation of WEP comes in two varieties: 40-bit and 128-bit. The more bits used in the encryption, the more secure (and the better) it is.

To use WEP, you need to select a WEP *key,* which is really just a code word. The longer the key, the better. Also, when making a key, be sure to use something like *ab8sher7234ksief87* (something that's random with letters and numbers) as opposed to something like *mykey* that's easily guessed. If you're using an Ad Hoc wireless network, all the computers need to have their wireless network card configured with the same WEP key in order to communicate. If you're using a WAP to connect to the rest of the network, you need to use the same key on your computers that you've configured on your WAP.

One thing to note about WEP is that it has been *broken,* meaning that someone has figured out how to undo the encryption that WEP provides. For businesses, especially those with sensitive data, WEP is not a good security solution.

However, for home users, WEP works well as a deterrent to keep people out. In order for someone to crack your WEP key, that person needs to record somewhere around 1 million encrypted packets or more. For a business, that might only be an hour or so of monitoring for a hacker, but for most home networks, this could take much longer. Remember that a typical home network carries much less traffic than a business network. So, not only would someone need to pitch a tent outside on your porch, he would need to be able to record at least a million of the packets going over your network and then have the knowledge to crack your encryption key. Although WEP isn't going to ward off the spies at the National Security Agency, it's good enough to protect home networks like yours and mine.

Other security standards

Although all Wi-Fi network equipment supports WEP, a few standards are worth mentioning: LEAP and 802.11n.

Lightweight Extensible Authentication Protocol (LEAP) is a protocol developed by Cisco Systems. To use LEAP, you need to have a server that's set up to enable users to log in to gain permission to the wireless network. After you initially log in (authenticate) to your network, LEAP changes encryption keys on the fly at a time interval that you determine. You could set it so that every 15 minutes, your encryption key is changed: Even if someone is in that hypothetical tent on your front lawn, he would never be able to record enough packets to figure out your key because it changes so often.

Setting up a server so that you can use LEAP isn't something for the novice to attempt. I would encourage you to read up on LEAP only if you are very serious about airtight security on your WLAN. The Cisco Web site (`www.cisco.com`) is a good place to read about LEAP.

All the Apple AirPort 2.0 (and above) and AirPort Extreme wireless network cards and Base Stations are compatible with the Cisco LEAP for higher security.

The other thing worth mentioning is the new upcoming wireless standard from IEEE: 802.11n. Right now, IEEE is still trying to hammer out many of the fine details; however, the final 802.11n standard will probably be based on a system very similar to Cisco's LEAP. After 801.11n is *ratified* (agreed on and finalized) by IEEE, expect to see it integrated with the other 802.11 standards. And did I mention that 802.11n is slated to deliver throughput in excess of 100 Mbps? Don't bet your house that you'll get that kind of speed, though — like the other members of the 802.11 family, that's likely to be a theoretical maximum speed.

Setting Up Your Wireless Network

On to the good stuff. This section describes installing an AirPort Extreme card as well as how to set up an Ad Hoc or infrastructure-based WLAN (wireless LAN).

Installing an AirPort Extreme network card

Some Macs come with an AirPort (802.11b) or AirPort Extreme (802.11b and 802.11g) card built in, especially if you ordered one pre-installed. However, if your Mac doesn't have either type of AirPort card installed, you can usually add one yourself. Naturally, older Macs don't have a slot or antenna for an AirPort card, such as the Indigo iMac with a 350 MHz CPU. However, all Mac models in production at the time of this writing do have a slot for an AirPort card, or have AirPort Extreme functionality built in. You just need to check www.info.apple.com/applespec to see whether your particular Mac can use an AirPort card.

In case you have any issues using AirPort or need more information about anything related to AirPort, check this page at the Apple Web site: www.apple.com/support/airport.

You should be able to use any standard 802.11b Wi-Fi or 802.11g card, but you might run into some issues with drivers and such. Be sure that any non-AirPort/AirPort Extreme card that you might buy is backed up with Mac OS X drivers.

A variety of 802.11b/g wireless network devices are available, many of which come with drivers for the Mac. Some of these devices connect via a Universal Serial Bus (USB), which could be handy if you want to be able to move it between a desktop Power Mac or iMac to an iBook and back (without the hassle of opening the case each time). Before you can set up your wireless network, you have to connect your wireless hardware. Because of the differences between manufacturers, check the installation instructions that come with whichever device that you choose.

After you have your AirPort, AirPort Extreme, or other 802.11b/g wireless network card or device installed, you're ready to connect.

Using non-Apple wireless equipment with AirPort Extreme equipment

Because of Apple's implementation of wireless standards within the AirPort Extreme product line, keep in mind some things when trying to mix Apple wireless equipment with other vendors' 802.11b or 802.11g equipment. As you discover elsewhere in this chapter, using AirPort wireless networks can require a password, which corresponds to the 802.11b/g WEP key for encryption. However, the password that you enter for AirPort networks isn't exactly the same as the WEP key for that same network. If you're using an AirPort network card and are trying to connect to a non-Apple 802.11b WAP, you need to follow a specific procedure. You can find this procedure by going to http://kbase.info.apple.com/index.jsp and searching on the number *106250* (the Apple Knowledge Base article number). If you're using a non-Apple 802.11b network card and are trying to connect to an Apple AirPort Base Station, go to the same URL and search on *106864*. These articles will show you how to convert the Apple AirPort password to a WEP key and vice versa.

You want my opinion? Because of the issues of using non-AirPort 802.11b/g hardware with The Real Thing (AirPort/AirPort Extreme stuff), I recommend that you stick with Apple equipment if possible.

Setting up an Ad Hoc wireless network

Using an Ad Hoc network — also called a *computer-to-computer* network — is a fairly easy thing to accomplish in Mac OS X. Plus, you're not limited to just Macs: With an Ad Hoc network, you can also swap niceties with PCs and PDAs that have 802.11b/g network interface cards (NICs) installed. This Ad Hoc network is great for setting up an impromptu network in a classroom, exchanging recipes and pictures at a family reunion in a park, or blowing your friend up while gaming across the aisle of a Greyhound bus at 70 mph.

To set up an Ad Hoc network, you first have to create the computer-to-computer network on one of your Macs. This takes advantage of the AirPort Software Base Station that's built into Mac OS X. To create a computer-to-computer network, follow these steps:

1. **Click the AirPort status icon on the menu bar.**

If you haven't set Tiger to display your AirPort status in the Finder menu bar, run Internet Connect in your Applications folder and click the AirPort toolbar button. Select the Show AirPort Status in Menu Bar check box to enable it, and then press ⌘+Q to quit Internet Connect. Alternatively, open the Network pane in System Preferences, click the Show drop-down list box, and choose the AirPort entry. You'll see the AirPort Status check box is among these settings as well.

2. **Click the Network drop-down list box and click Create Network to display the dialog that you see in Figure 4-1.**

3. **Enter a name for your network.**

4. **Click Show Options (if necessary) and mark the Enable Encryption check box to turn on WEP encryption.**

Figure 4-1:
Creating a computer-to-computer Wi-Fi network through software. *Excellent.*

Computer to Computer

Please enter the following information to create a Computer to Computer Network:

Name:	Uber–iBook
Channel:	Automatic (11)

☑ Enable encryption (using WEP)

Password:	••••••••••••
Confirm:	••••••••••••
WEP key:	128–bit

The WEP key must be entered as exactly 13 ASCII characters or 26 HEX digits.

(Hide Options) (Cancel) (OK)

5. **Enter a password for your network, and then enter it again to confirm it.**

Although you can leave encryption disabled, I highly recommend that you turn it on and choose a password for that extra bit of security. (Just call me Security Man.) Note that the password must be an exact length (which is determined by whether you choose a 40-bit (5-character) key or a 128-bit (13-character) key).

Out of the 11 channels available for 802.11b networks, channels 1, 6, and 11 are the only ones that don't overlap other channels — and are therefore the best choices to use. If you're close to other WAPs, AirPort Base Stations, or other Ad Hoc networks, you need to try to find a channel that's not being used, or performance can be degraded. (If you have only one access point, it doesn't matter which channel you select — just allow Tiger to automatically select a channel, which is typically Channel 11.)

6. **Click OK.**

Creating a computer-to-computer network gives the illusion of having an AirPort Base Station. So for people to join your network, they would follow the same steps that they would to join any other AirPort network, as I cover in the next section.

Setting up wireless networks with an AirPort Base Station

After one computer is running a computer-to-computer network or you've set up and configured an AirPort/AirPort Extreme Base Station, you're ready to invite other computers with wireless hardware to the party.

Joining in an existing AirPort network

After you have a network set up on one of your wireless-enabled computers, you just need to have the other wireless-enabled computers join that network. You can use the same process, as I describe here, to join any wireless network. Simply click the AirPort status icon on the menu bar, and then select an existing network connection that you'd like to join from the list that appears in the AirPort menu.

If you want to join a network whose name doesn't appear in the list — also called a *closed network* — select Other from the AirPort status menu and then enter the name of the network that you want to join and the password (if any is required). A closed network is another added measure of security — one that's good enough for most people because it's very unlikely that a hacker is going to try to hack a hidden network.

Disconnecting from an AirPort network

To disconnect from an AirPort/AirPort Extreme network, you can turn off your AirPort card altogether, which I cover in the next section. (Simplicity, they say, is an art.) Another way is to simply connect to another AirPort network — but this option is really only useful if you actually *want* to connect to another network.

Turning your AirPort card on or off

You might want to use your Mac, usually your laptop, in a place where your wireless card shouldn't be used, like on an airplane (when they tell you to turn off all cellphones) or in a hospital in an area that doesn't allow cellphones or other wireless devices. Plus, turning off your AirPort/AirPort Extreme card will conserve your notebook's battery life. Being able to turn your AirPort/AirPort Extreme card on and off actually has its uses.

To turn your AirPort card on or off via the AirPort status icon on the menu bar, give it a click and choose Turn AirPort On/Off from the resulting menu.

If you would like to control exactly which wireless network cards can access your wireless network, go to `http://kbase.info.apple.com/index.jsp` and search on *58571,* which is the Apple Knowledge Base article number of a document that explains exactly how to limit access to your network to specific wireless network cards.

Chapter 5: Sharing That Precious Internet Thing

In This Chapter

- ✔ Finding out how Internet sharing works
- ✔ Discovering the difference between hardware and software Internet sharing
- ✔ Connecting your Macs to a cable/DSL router
- ✔ Adding wireless support to your shared Internet connection

Although I discuss lots of fun stuff that you can do with your network in previous chapters, this has to be my favorite: sharing a single Internet connection between all the computers on your network. If you have more than one computer, I'm sure that you've had to deal with the dilemma that pops up whenever more than one person wants or needs to access the Internet at the same time.

Luckily, because most small home and office local area networks (LANs) use our old friend TCP/IP for network communications, connecting an entire network to the Internet isn't as troublesome a task as you might think. In this chapter, I talk about different hardware and software options for sharing your Internet connection as well as how to include your wireless devices.

Sharing the Internet

Sharing a single Internet connection between all your computers can be a boon simply because of the reduced chances of random acts of violence. Internet deprivation can be an ugly thing, you know. Although I won't claim that Internet sharing will save lives, it can indeed save you from headaches and arguments when more than one person wants to use the Internet at once.

Throughout this chapter, I talk a lot about cable modems and Asynchronous Digital Subscriber Line (ADSL) modems. Both of these are high-speed Internet connections — both are relatively inexpensive — that are offered by your local cable company and your local phone company, respectively. The phone company offers different kinds of digital subscriber line (DSL) connections, the most common of which is ADSL. However, because different kinds of DSL connections exist, in this chapter, I refer to them all generically as *DSL*.

To share your Internet connection, you need a few things, so here's a quick checklist:

✦ **An Internet connection:** This could be a dialup Internet connection that's accessed via a standard v.90/v.92 analog telephone modem, or it could be a cable or DSL modem connection.

✦ **A LAN:** You need a standard LAN (which is connected with cables) or a wireless LAN. See Book V, Chapter 1 for more information about setting up a LAN and Book V, Chapter 4 for more on setting up a Wireless LAN (WLAN).

✦ **An Internet-sharing device:** I use the word *device* because the method that you use to share your Internet connection could be software that you run on one of your computers or hardware that is standalone, depending on how you connect to the Internet and what fits your needs best.

When you have these three things ready to go, you can share your Internet connection. However, you need to know some background information to help you choose the right components and get everything up and running.

Using Network Address Translation

You must determine one thing before you start your Internet sharing quest: the set of network Internet Protocol (IP) addresses that you'll use. If you used Book V, Chapter 1 to set up and configure your LAN, you might recall that I suggest a specific range of IP addresses to use on your LAN. In case you missed out on Chapter 1 of this mini-book, I briefly cover this important topic again so that you can share your Internet connection smoothly. (Forgive me if I wax technical, but 'tis only for the moment.)

When talking about IP addresses, the ruling body that tracks IP addresses and where they are used has broken all IP addresses up into two parts:

✦ **Public IP addresses:** *Public* IP addresses are used to communicate on the Internet, and only one device in the entire world can use a given public IP address at any given time.

✦ **Private IP addresses:** *Private* addresses, on the other hand, are supposed to be used only on networks (like your home LAN) and do *not* connect directly to the Internet. Lots of people can use the same private address because their networks never go public: That is, they never access the Internet, so their IP addresses never conflict.

Typically, you'll use addresses in the form of 192.168.*x.x* on your LAN. See Book V, Chapter 1 for an overview of IP addresses and how they work.

You might be wondering to yourself thusly: "If I use private IP addresses on my LAN at home or in the office and I have to use a public IP address to communicate on the Internet, how can my private IP addresses on my LAN communicate with public IP addresses on the Internet?" That is an excellent question, and the answer is *Network Address Translation* (or NAT for short).

NAT acts as a gatekeeper between your private IP addresses on your LAN and the public IP addresses on the Internet. When you connect to the Internet, your Internet service provider (ISP) gives you one — and usually only one — public IP address that can be used on the Internet. Instead of one of your computers using that public IP address and depriving all the other computers on the LAN, the hardware or software that you use to share the Internet will take control of that public IP address. Then, when any computer on your LAN tries to communicate on the Internet, your NAT software/hardware intercepts your communications and readdresses the traffic so that it appears to be coming from your allotted public IP address. (Think of a funnel that collects water from several different sources and then directs all the water into a single stream.)

When the Web site, File Transfer Protocol (FTP) server, or whatever strange Internet intelligence you're using on the Internet replies, it replies to your NAT device. The NAT device remembers which private IP address it should go to on the LAN and sends the information to that computer. See NAT at work in Figure 5-1.

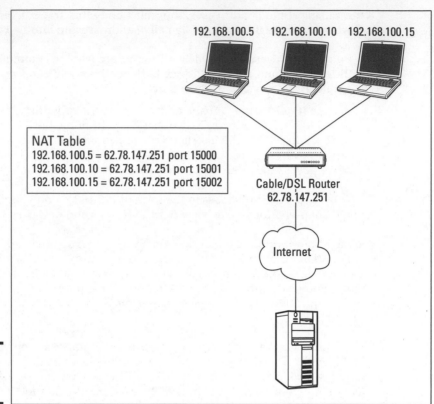

192.168.100.5   192.168.100.10   192.168.100.15

NAT Table
192.168.100.5 = 62.78.147.251 port 15000
192.168.100.10 = 62.78.147.251 port 15001
192.168.100.15 = 62.78.147.251 port 15002

Cable/DSL Router
62.78.147.251

Internet

Figure 5-1:
NAT hard at
work.

Ways to Share Your Internet Connection

After you have an Internet connection and your LAN is set up, you need something to make this NAT thing work. You have two different options to take care of NAT for your shared Internet connection: hardware or software. (Go figure.) Each has pros and cons, so take a look at each option individually.

If you've already read Chapter 4 of this mini-book, you know that Tiger has AirPort software built in. So, if you have an AirPort or AirPort Extreme wireless network card in your Mac and you're using Tiger, you can have your Mac act like an AirPort Base Station for all the wireless computers on your network, which in turn can use a software NAT.

Using hardware for sharing an Internet connection

Probably the most popular way to share an Internet connection is to buy a hardware device that connects to your Internet connection, which then connects to your LAN. These devices are referred to as *cable/DSL routers*. The main downside to a hardware Internet connection-sharing device is that it costs more than a software solution.

Don't let the name throw you: Although these devices are usually used to share cable/DSL connections, many have the ability to use an external analog telephone modem to connect to a standard dialup Internet account.

Cable/DSL routers are nice because they're easy to set up and configure. Too, you can leave them on, which means constant Internet access for those on your LAN. You don't have to worry about turning on another computer to connect to the Internet like you do with a software solution. Sounds like a good spot for a Mark's Maxim: In my opinion, hardware routers are the best choice for sharing your Internet connection, so if you can afford one, you should get one.

> **Hardware routers are the best choice for sharing your Internet connection, so if you can afford one, you should get one!**™

Apple's AirPort and AirPort Extreme Base Stations are not only Wireless Access Points (WAPs) for your network, as I discuss in Chapter 4 of this mini-book, but they also act as Internet connection-sharing devices. (The AirPort Express can't share an Internet connection . . . sorry.) Some flavors of AirPort Base Station have a built-in v.90 modem for sharing a single 56 Kbps connection using a dialup account as well as two Ethernet connections for sharing a high-speed Internet connection: one to connect to a cable/DSL router and one to connect to the LAN.

If you think that a cable/DSL router or an AirPort Extreme Base Station could be the karma pathway for you to achieve your goal of sharing your Internet connection, here are some things to consider when deciding which device to buy for your LAN:

✦ **Do you need a switch?** Most cable/DSL routers have a small 3-, 4-, or 5-port switch built in. Refer to Chapter 1 of this mini-book to discover more about hubs and switches. This multiport capability is nice because the same cable/DSL router that shares your Internet connection is also the centerpiece of your LAN where all your connections meet, thus saving you from having to buy a hub or switch on top of the cost of the cable/DSL router.

Some cable/DSL routers, however, have only a single Ethernet connection to connect to your LAN. So keep in mind that if you choose a device with a single LAN connection, you must supply your own hub or switch that would then connect the cable/DSL router to the rest of your LAN.

✦ **Got modem?** On your cable/DSL router, look for a built-in analog telephone modem, like the one that you find on the more expensive model of AirPort Extreme. If your only Internet connection is through a dialup modem account, you must have this feature if you want to use a hardware device to share your Internet connection. AirPort Extreme is great for this because the modem is built in. Even if you have cable/DSL service, most ISPs also include a dialup account with it. With such a bountiful selection of connections, you can plug in both your cable or DSL service to the cable/DSL router as well as use the dialup account as a backup in case your main service has problems.

✦ **Want a printer with that?** Some cable/DSL routers also have a port for connecting a printer — a great feature to have because it allows you to leave the printer connected and turned on so that anyone on the network can print to it anytime. (This is much better than connecting the printer to a computer and sharing it because then the computer doing the sharing must always be on in order to make the printer available.) Mac OS X can send a print job to a printer by using Bonjour or TCP/IP, so just make sure that your printer is compatible with TCP/IP printing, also called *LPR* (Line Printer Remote).

Using software for sharing an Internet connection

As I mention earlier, if you're using Mac OS X Tiger and have an AirPort or AirPort Extreme wireless network card installed, your Mac can act like an AirPort/AirPort Extreme Base Station, providing both wireless Ethernet connectivity for other computers on the LAN *and* a shared Internet connection.

Tiger also has built-in software that allows a single computer on your network to share its Internet connection with others on the LAN. To share your Internet connection, follow these quick steps:

1. **Click the System Preferences icon on the Dock.**

2. **Click the Sharing icon.**

3. **Click the Internet tab of the Sharing dialog.**

This brings up the settings shown in Figure 5-2.

4. **Click the Share Your Connection From drop-down list and choose Built-in Ethernet.**

5. **Select the Built-in Ethernet check box (in the To Computers Using list) to enable it.**

When you do, you will be issued a warning that enabling this could affect your ISP or violate your agreement with your ISP. In my experiences, this step has never caused any networking problems. However, if you have any doubts, contact your ISP and verify this.

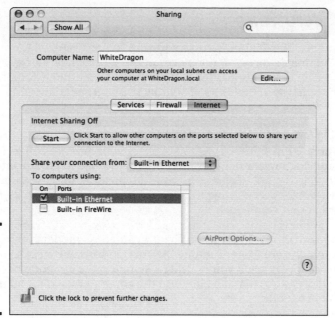

Figure 5-2:
Turning on
Internet
sharing with
Tiger.

6. **Click OK in the warning dialog to continue.**

   You go back to the Sharing dialog, which now has a Start button.

7. **Click Start to enable Internet sharing.**

If you're using a dialup modem to access the Internet, you need to also make sure that the computer that has the modem also has an Ethernet or wireless LAN connection. The iMac is a great example of a computer that can do this because it has both a built-in modem and an Ethernet connection.

If you're using a cable or DSL modem for your Internet connection, the Mac that you want to run the sharing software on should have two Ethernet connections: one to connect to the cable/DSL modem and one to connect to the rest of the LAN.

The main disadvantage to using a software solution for Internet connection sharing is that the computer that connects to the Internet must be turned on and ready to go all the time so that others on the network can get to the Internet. And although the sharing software operates in the background on the machine it's running on, it still chews up some of that Mac's processing power and memory, so it could slow down other applications that you're running on that computer.

Connecting Everything

After you decide whether to use a software or hardware solution, it's time to get your hands dirty: All the pieces of the puzzle must be set up and connected. In this section, I tell you how to connect things for either the software or hardware method of sharing the Internet connection.

Using the software method

When you use the software method to share your Internet connection, one of the computers on your network has both the connection to the Internet and a connection to the LAN. Figure 5-3 shows a typical setup for software Internet sharing, whether you're using a dialup modem account or a cable/DSL modem for your Internet connection.

Keep in mind, though, that when using a cable/DSL modem for your Internet connection, the computer running the sharing software *must* have two Ethernet connections. If you're using a standard dialup modem for Internet access, chances are that it's built into the computer used for sharing the Internet connection.

Using the hardware method

Not only does using a dedicated piece of hardware free one of the Macs on your network from the onerous job of hosting the shared connection, but it also keeps you from having to have more than one Ethernet connection on a single computer if you're using a cable/DSL modem for your Internet access. Figure 5-4 shows how you would connect your devices for hardware Internet sharing by using either a cable/DSL router with a built-in Ethernet switch or a cable/DSL router with a standalone Ethernet hub or switch, like you would need to use AirPort or AirPort Extreme.

If you choose to buy a cable/DSL router that has a built-in Ethernet switch, you can simply connect all your computers on the LAN to the built-in switch. However, if you buy a cable/DSL router that has only a single LAN connection, like AirPort/AirPort Extreme, you must connect that single LAN connection to an external hub or switch in order to get all the computers on the same network.

Regardless of whether you use the hardware or software method to share your Internet connection, all the computers on your LAN — except the one that's doing the sharing if you're using software sharing — should be configured to obtain its IP address automatically through our old friend, Dynamic Host Configuration Protocol (DHCP). (See Chapter 1 of this mini-book for detailed instructions on how to do this in Tiger.) Although it's not a require-ment that you set up your other devices with DHCP, it is recommended unless you understand the IP addressing scheme required by your cable/DSL router and you are willing to set up the addresses manually. You need to follow the instructions that come with the cable/DSL router or software that you pur-chase for detailed information on how to configure that.

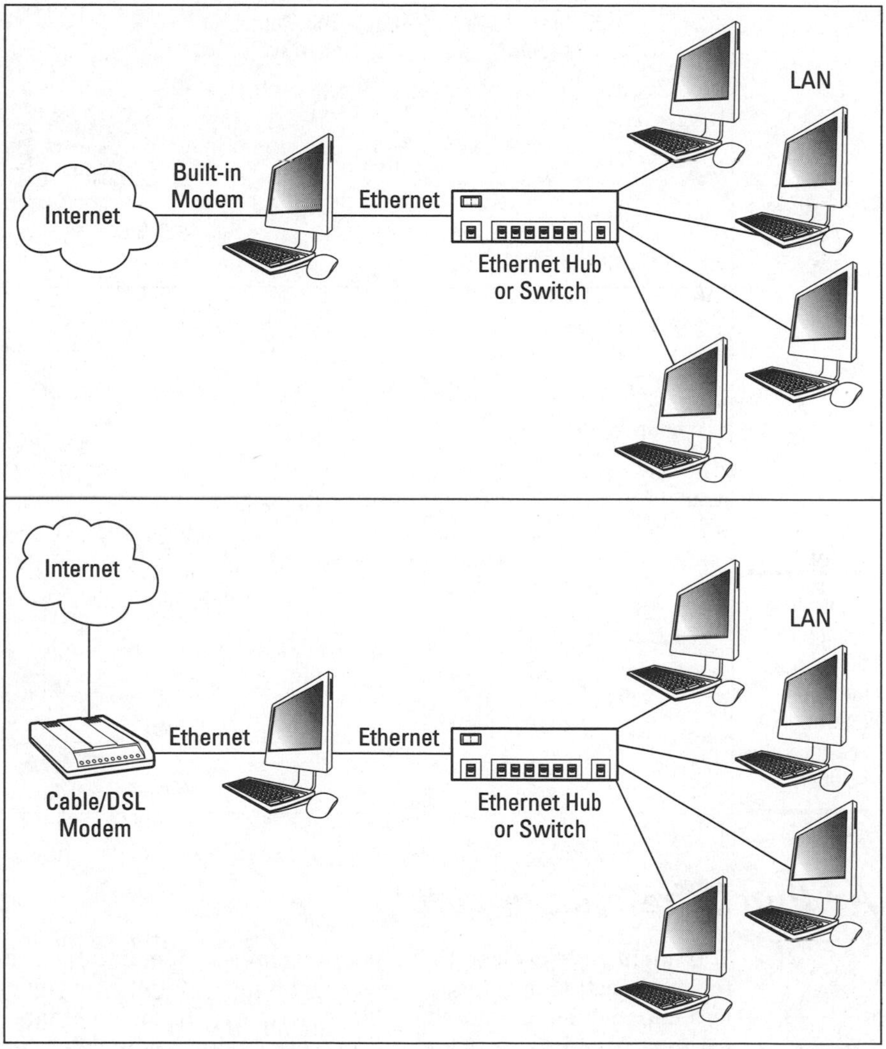

Figure 5-3:
Two
different
configu-
rations for
Internet
sharing
through
software.

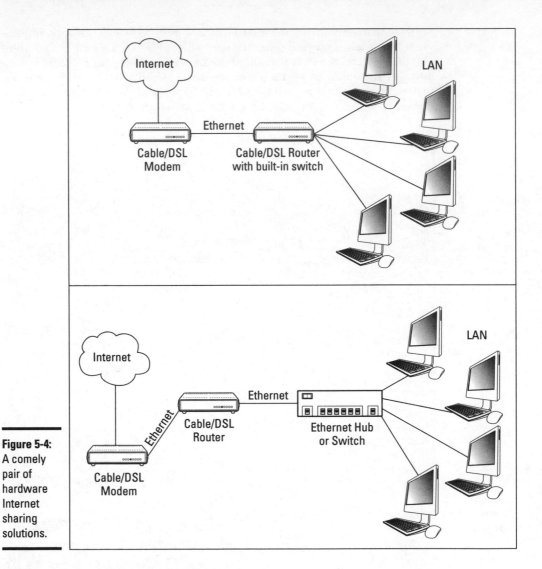

Figure 5-4:
A comely
pair of
hardware
Internet
sharing
solutions.

Adding Wireless Support

You might have noticed that I mention *wireless* here and there in this chapter. This section is going to cover in a bit more detail how you can add wireless capabilities to your shared Internet party. To discover more about how wireless networks work and how to set one up, see Book V, Chapter 4.

Basically, you'll encounter a couple of situations when trying to add wireless capabilities into the mix. Either you already have an Internet connection-sharing mechanism in place (either hardware or software), or you don't yet have your Internet connection shared.

If you already have a cable/DSL router or are using software Internet sharing

If you already have a cable/DSL router or if you're using software Internet sharing, like that built into Tiger, you can simply buy a WAP and connect it to your LAN. Adding a WAP enables anyone using wireless Ethernet access to your network and thus to your shared Internet connection. There are many WAPs that you can buy to add wireless to your network. AirPort and AirPort Extreme are good examples; however, because AirPort also can do Internet sharing, make sure that you *don't* enable the Internet sharing on the AirPort card! (In this case, you don't want or need this feature because it can conflict with your cable/DSL router operation.)

If you do not have a cable/DSL router or an AirPort Base Station

If you don't have a cable/DSL router or an AirPort/AirPort Extreme Base Station for Internet sharing, you have a few options. Each option has an upside and downside.

One option is to get an AirPort or AirPort Extreme Base Station, which provides both wireless access for AirPort-enabled wireless computers and Internet sharing for the entire network. If your Base Station has only a single LAN Ethernet connection and you have more than one computer using wired Ethernet, you must buy an additional hub or switch to connect them.

The other option is to buy a combination cable/DSL router, which has a built-in WAP. Most cable/DSL routers — including the ones that have wireless built in — also have multiple Ethernet ports on them, so connecting computers by using wired Ethernet can be done without buying an external hub or switch.

The final option is that you can use the AirPort software built into Tiger to turn your Mac into an Airport or AirPort Extreme Base Station — that is, if you have an AirPort wireless card on that particular Mac. This is a great, low-cost way to add wireless and Internet sharing to your network. However, many Macs don't come with an AirPort wireless card built in, and you still can eat up processor time and memory by running the AirPort software. For more on wireless networking, read Chapter 4 of this mini-book.

Book VI

Expanding Your System

The 5th Wave   By Rich Tennant

"I asked for software that would biodegrade after it was thrown out, not while it was running."

Contents at a Glance

Chapter 1: Hardware That Will Make You Giddy

In This Chapter

✔ Using digital cameras, digital video camcorders, and scanners

✔ Adding keyboards, trackballs, joysticks, and drawing tablets

✔ Using optical recorders and tape drives

✔ Adding speakers, subwoofers, and MP3 hardware

*H*ardware. We love it. To a Mac power user, new hardware holds all the promise of Christmas morning, whether your new toys are used for business or for pleasure. We pore over magazines and visit our favorite Mac Web sites like clockwork to check on new technology.

These hardware devices don't come cheap, however, forcing you to make the painful decision of deciding which new hardware you really need in order to accomplish what you want and which hardware is a luxury. Also, if you're a new Mac owner, you might not know what's available. For example, I constantly get e-mail from readers, asking, "What can I connect to my new computer?" I guess I could reply, "Why, the kitchen sink!" To that end, I decided to add this chapter to the book to let you know how you can expand the hardware for your Mac OS X Tiger powerhouse.

Each section in this chapter provides a description of what a particular device does, approximately how much it costs, and a set of general guidelines that you can use when shopping. Although this isn't in-depth coverage — after all, the book is supposed to be about Tiger — it will serve to get you started if you've just become a Mac owner. If you're especially interested in a specific piece of hardware, I recommend other books that you can read for the exhaustive details.

Ready? To quote a great line from the first Batman film: "Alfred, let's go shopping!"

Parading Pixels: Digital Cameras, DV Camcorders, and Scanners

The first category of hardware toys revolves around images — hardware for creating original images, capturing images in real-time, and reading images from hard copy.

Digital cameras

A digital camera shares most of the characteristics of a traditional film camera. It looks the same, and you use the same techniques while shooting photographs. The difference is in the end result. With a digital camera, instead of a roll of film that has to be developed, you have an image in JPEG or TIFF format that's stored on a memory card. The contents of the memory card can be downloaded to your Mac from within iPhoto (which I discuss with great pleasure in Book III, Chapter 3), and then the real fun begins. Here are some things that you can do with a digital photograph:

✦ Edit it with an image editor such as Adobe Photoshop

✦ Print it with an inkjet or color laser printer

✦ Record it to a CD or DVD

✦ Add it to a Web page

✦ Print several of them in a coffee-table book (using iPhoto)

✦ Mail it to friends and family

What they cost

Consumer-level digital cameras typically sell for anywhere from $100 (for a 2-megapixel [MP] model) to $500 (for a 6MP camera). *Megapixel* is a general reference to the *resolution* (the size of the image, measured in individual dots called *pixels*) and detail delivered by the camera. Such digital cameras can produce photographs that are well suited for just about any casual shutterbug. Professional digital cameras, which capture far more detail and offer designs that more closely resemble the best SLR film camera, can set you back $1,000 or $2,000. Because of their cost and complexity, I wouldn't recommend them to someone who's just discovered digital photography.

What to look for

Here are some general guidelines that I recommend when selecting a digital camera:

✦ **At least a 3MP camera:** As a general rule, the higher the megapixel value, the better the camera.

✦ **At least a 32MB memory card:** The *memory card* stores the images that you capture.

✦ **A Universal Serial Bus (USB) connection to your Macintosh:** USB is covered in all its glory in Chapter 3 of this mini-book. USB 2.0 is definitely a better choice than a slower USB 1.1 connection.

✦ **An optical zoom feature:** *Optical zoom* allows you to draw closer to subjects that are farther away.

Note that I recommended *optical* zoom there and not *digital* zoom. Essentially, digital zoom is a silly feature that simply resizes a portion of your image, providing a blocky close-up. In fact, an image editor like Photoshop Elements can produce exactly the same result as a camera with digital zoom . . . and it looks as bad. Only an optical zoom results in a sharper magnification of the subject.

✦ **A self-timer:** With a self-timer, your camera can snap a photo automatically, allowing you to finally be seen in your own pictures!

✦ **A manual flash setting:** Although automatic flash is a good thing most of the time, a manual setting allows you to disable your camera's flash for artistic shots (or just to prevent the glare on subjects with polished surfaces).

For a full (even exhaustive) exposé of everything in digital photography, check out *Digital Photos, Movies, & Music Gigabook For Dummies,* edited by some guy named Mark L. Chambers (Wiley). Believe me, if it's got anything to do with digital photography, it's in there!

**Book VI
Chapter 1**

**Hardware That Will
Make You Giddy**

DV camcorders

Like digital cameras, digital video (DV) camcorders are the counterpart to the familiar video camcorder. A *DV camcorder* looks and operates like a VHS camcorder, but you can connect it to your Macintosh via a FireWire cable and download your video clips directly into iMovie. (Chapter 4 of Book III explains all about iMovie, and FireWire is tackled in Chapter 3 of this mini-book.)

Besides the higher quality of digital video, it has a number of other real advantages over analog video:

✦ Digital video can be edited with applications such as iMovie or Adobe Premiere.

✦ Digital video can be recorded to a CD or DVD.

✦ Digital video can be posted for downloading on a Web page.

What they cost

A typical DV camcorder starts at about $400, with the more desirable MiniDV camcorders selling for around $800.

If a DV camcorder is too costly of an investment, you can always convert *analog video* — video from your current VHS camcorder or VCR — into digital video by using an inexpensive device called an *AV converter*.

What to look for

I recommend the following when shopping for a DV camcorder:

✦ **The highest optical zoom in your price range:** Again, like a digital camera, it's important to be able to capture subjects and action when you can't get any closer — think the lion exhibit at the zoo.

✦ **Image stabilization:** This helps steady the picture when you're holding the camcorder without a tripod.

✦ **Onboard effects:** These effects generally include some snazzy things like black and white footage, fades, and wipes.

✦ **AV connectors:** Use these to display your video by connecting the camcorder directly to your TV.

✦ **Support for FireWire (IEEE 1394) connectivity:** For more details on FireWire, see Chapter 3 of this mini-book.

✦ **Digital still mode:** This enables you to take still photographs if your digital camera isn't handy; however, the image quality isn't as good as a bona fide digital camera.

For an in-depth look at digital video, check out *Digital Video For Dummies*, 3rd Edition, by Keith Underdahl (Wiley).

Scanners

Figure 1-1 illustrates a typical flatbed scanner, which is the tool of choice for those Macintosh owners who want to digitize images and text from printed materials. Although you can also connect a sheet-fed scanner, flatbed models are much more versatile and produce better-quality scans.

Images produced by a scanner can be edited, mailed, displayed on the Web, or added to your own documents, just like the images from a digital camera.

Figure 1-1:
The flatbed scanner, King of Digitizing.

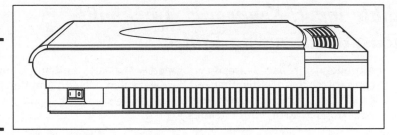

What they cost

A good-quality scanner should cost anywhere from $100–$300, with the best models — featuring the fastest scanning speeds, best color depth, and highest resolutions, or those meant for scanning film negatives — going for anywhere from $500–$1,000.

What to look for

Try to get the following features in a scanner:

+ **The highest color depth that you can afford:** Get a minimum of 48-bit.

+ **The highest resolution that you can afford:** Get a minimum of 1200 dots per inch (dpi) (optical).

+ **Single-pass scanning:** This feature results in a faster scan with less chance of error.

+ **Transparency adapter for scanning film negatives:** If you're a traditional film photographer, you'll find that a transparency adapter turns a standard flatbed scanner into an acceptable negative scanner.

+ **One-touch buttons for e-mailing your scanned images or uploading them to the Web:** These are controls of convenience — pressing one of these buttons automatically scans the item and prepares the image to be e-mailed or uploaded to a Web site.

+ **USB or FireWire connection:** I cover the advantages of both in Chapter 3 of this mini-book.

Another shameless (but good-natured) plug. My best-selling book *Scanners For Dummies,* 2nd Edition (Wiley) offers comprehensive coverage of all types of scanners, as well as chapters devoted to advanced features, image editing, and step-by-step projects.

Incredible Input: Keyboards, Trackballs, Joysticks, and Drawing Tablets

Although your Mac is already equipped with a keyboard and a mouse, you can replace them with enhanced hardware that will add functionality and precision to your work. (Or, you can buy a joystick and spend your days wreaking havoc on your enemies.)

Keyboards

If you're using the latest iMac G5 or G5 tower model, you don't really need to upgrade your keyboard. These new machines come with excellent keyboards already, replete with volume controls and a Media Eject key. However, if you're using an older Macintosh — or you have an iBook or PowerBook and you want to add an external keyboard — you can take advantage of the convenience of a USB keyboard like the one in Figure 1-2.

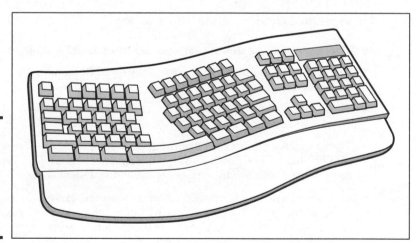

Figure 1-2: An ergonomic upgrade — the aftermarket USB keyboard.

What they cost

Aftermarket (nonstandard-issue) keyboards generally cost anywhere from $30–$100.

What to look for

Look for the following keyboard features when shopping for a keyboard:

✦ **Programmable buttons:** Configure these to launch applications or run macros.

✦ **Additional USB ports:** Use these to turn your keyboard into a USB hub.

✦ **One-touch buttons to launch your browser or e-mail application:** Press one of these buttons to launch your Web browser or Mail.

✦ **Ergonomic wrist pad:** Use these to help prevent wrist strain and repetitive joint injuries.

Trackballs

Some folks prefer using a trackball, like the one shown in Figure 1-3, over a mouse any day. Graphic artists find that trackballs are more precise and offer better control, usually including a secondary button to display contextual menus. (One model on the market has eight buttons. Who needs a keyboard?)

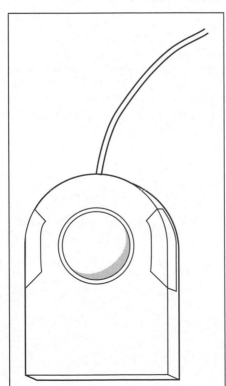

Figure 1-3:
Many Mac power users (myself included) prefer a trackball to a mouse.

What they cost

Trackballs range in price from \$50–\$90. Most are optical (see the following section), so they need little cleaning, and they'll last for many years of precise pointing at things.

What to look for

Look for the following features when shopping for a trackball:

+ **More programmable buttons:** Opt for at least two buttons!

+ **Optical tracking:** An *optical* trackball — one that doesn't use rollers, instead using a photosensitive sensor to record the movement of the ball — is more precise and easier to keep clean.

+ **A scroll wheel:** Use this gizmo to scroll documents up and down.

+ **Ergonomic design:** Look for a wrist pad or slanted buttons.

Joysticks

Game players, unite! For arcade and sports games, using a joystick results in increased maneuverability, more realistic action, higher scores, less wear and tear on your keyboard . . . and just plain more fun. Joysticks range from the traditional USB aircraft controller shown in Figure 1-4 to USB controllers and gamepads that rival anything offered on the PlayStation 2 or the Xbox.

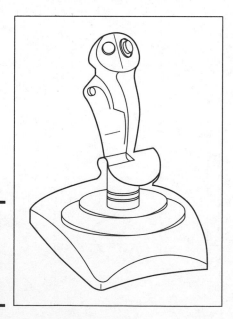

Figure 1-4: The secret weapon of Mac gamers — a joystick.

What they cost

Joysticks vary in price from $30–$120. At the low end, you'll usually find the gamepad-type controllers, and aircraft controllers carry the highest price tag.

What to look for

Get the following features in a joystick:

+ **Yet even more programmable buttons.**

+ **Pitch and yaw controls.** These are for the flight simulator crowd.

+ **Force feedback.** A *force feedback joystick* rumbles and moves in tandem with the action in the game, providing an extra feeling of realism.

Drawing tablets

A drawing tablet like the one you see in Figure 1-5 might be pricey, but if you're a graphic artist or a designer, using a tablet will revolutionize the way that you work with your Mac — especially with the Inkwell technology built into Mac OS X. Rather than use a mouse or trackball to sketch, you can draw on the tablet freehand, just like you would draw on paper or canvas. Tablets can recognize different levels of pressure, allowing applications such as Photoshop and Painter to re-create all sorts of photo-realistic brush effects.

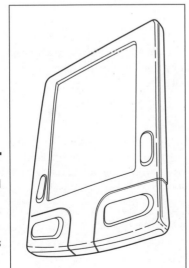

Figure 1-5:
Professional artists and designers swear by the graphics tablet.

What they cost

Depending on the size of the tablet, you'll pay anywhere from around $100 to a whopping $500, depending on the size and the pressure levels that you need.

What to look for

I recommend the following tablet features:

✦ **Programmable buttons:** See a trend here?

✦ **Accessory mouse:** Some high-end tablets include a mouse that you can use along with the tablet.

✦ **A cordless stylus:** Make sure that it doesn't require batteries.

✦ **The highest number of pressure levels possible:** The more levels that the tablet offers, the more subtle and precise your control is over painting effects.

Sublime Storage: CD/DVD Recorders and Tape Drives

I don't include Zip drives in this category because the arrival of cheap, reliable optical storage has rendered a 750MB Zip cartridge obsolete. Even the once-awesome 2.2GB capacity of the original Orb drive seems a little insignificant next to a rewriteable DVD-RW drive, which can store 4.7GB on a single disc.

If you'd like to trade data with another Mac or a PC via floppy disks, you can get an external USB floppy drive for under $50 — however, I personally eschew floppy disks, which are very unreliable and carry a mere 1.44MB of data. Pick up a USB Flash drive instead.

CD and DVD recorders

Virtually all recent Mac models include a rewriteable optical drive — either a CD-RW or the DVD-R SuperDrive — but if your computer is older and didn't come equipped with a recorder, you can always add an external model, like the external DVD-RW drive shown in Figure 1-6.

What they cost

A typical USB or FireWire CD-RW drive costs about $100. A FireWire DVD-RW drive averages about $200.

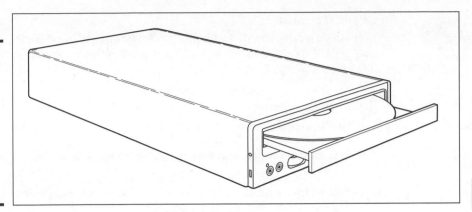

Figure 1-6: An external DVD-RW drive is perfect for backups and recording audio and video.

What to look for

Get the following features in an external CD-RW/DVD-RW drive:

✦ **An internal buffer of at least 2MB:** The larger the buffer, the less chance that you'll encounter recording errors and the faster your drive will burn.

✦ **At least 8X DVD recording speed:** A no-brainer here. The faster the recording speed, the less time you'll wait for the finished disc.

✦ **AC power through the USB 2.0 or FireWire cable:** This eliminates the need for a separate AC power supply.

✦ **Burn-proof technology:** This virtually eliminates recording errors because of multitasking so that you can continue to work on other applications while you record.

Okay, just one more. I'm very proud of another of my books in the *For Dummies* series, *CD & DVD Recording For Dummies,* 2nd Edition (Wiley). It covers everything that you need to know about producing all sorts of discs — everything from basic data and audio CDs to DVDs and more exotic formats such as CD Extra. Mac owners will be happy to know that this book covers the Mac like a blanket, too.

Tape drives

If you're looking for a real high-capacity back-up solution, use a tape drive. A *tape drive* is a storage device that uses a tape cartridge (much like a music cassette). A Travan tape drive (which averages about 40–60GB of storage) is much less expensive than a Digital Audio Tape (DAT) drive, which has a higher capacity of 120GB or more.

What they cost

Travan drives typically range around $500 (storing around 60–80GB per tape), and most DAT drives start at $1,000 (and can store several gigabytes of data on a single tape).

What to look for

Get the following features in a tape drive:

✦ **Hardware data compression:** This provides a faster backup on fewer tapes.

✦ **Automatic head cleaning:** Head cleaning helps reduce errors while writing data (and reading it back later).

✦ **FireWire connection:** A FireWire drive provides much faster data transfer, so your backups take a fraction of the time needed by a USB tape drive.

✦ **A transfer rate of at least 12 Mbps:** The faster the transfer rate, the shorter the time necessary to back up your drive!

Awesome Audio: Subwoofer Systems and MP3 Hardware

Although virtually all Macs ship with speakers, I'll be honest — the "stock" speakers don't measure up to the standards of a true audiophile. For those who really enjoy their music and their game audio, this last section covers the world of Macintosh aftermarket sonic enjoyment.

Subwoofer speaker systems

The ever-popular USB port again comes to your rescue. This time, it enables you to connect a more powerful speaker system with a subwoofer, like the one shown in Figure 1-7. If you've never heard a subwoofer — think chest-rattling *thump, thump, thump* — they provide the basement-level bass that can add power and punch to both your music and your games. Being hit by an asteroid is a rather flat, tinny experience with a pair of battery-powered speakers that you salvaged from your Walkman years ago. With a new set of speakers and a subwoofer, you'll swear that Han Solo is sitting in the cockpit chair next to you!

With the growing importance of the computer as a replacement for your home entertainment center, investing in a more powerful set of speakers will help you enjoy all those audio CDs and MP3s that you've added to your iTunes Playlists. (Read all about iTunes in Book III, Chapter 2.)

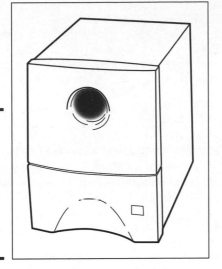

Figure 1-7:
Whether your passion is games or music, a subwoofer delivers the goods.

What they cost

Most USB-powered speakers with a subwoofer are priced below $200, but true audiophiles looking for surround sound can spring for a $500 system that includes several satellite speakers and a subwoofer.

What to look for

Get these features in a subwoofer:

+ **At least 30 watts of power:** The higher the wattage rating, the more powerful the speakers (and the louder your music can be).

+ **Additional headphone jacks and stereo mini-plug input jacks:** Use these for connecting your iPod or MP3 player directly to your speaker system. (Read all about iPods in the next section.)

+ **Magnetic shielding:** This helps prevent your speakers from distorting your monitor display.

MP3 players (well, actually, just the iPod)

I've lusted after Apple's iPod MP3 player ever since it arrived on campus. Depending on which model you get, this incredible device can hold anywhere from 512MB–60GB of MP3 digital audio — that's over 15,000 songs of average length in the 60GB version! Plus, the iPod also acts as your personal data butler by carrying your files; it's an honest-to-goodness, external FireWire drive. (USB 2.0 connectivity is also supported. If you pick up an iPod Shuffle, it acts as a USB Flash drive and supports only USB 2.0.) You can download your contacts and appointments from Mac OS X and view them wherever you go, and some models can now display color photos as well. Just think: Carry your files to and from your office *and* carry Devo and the Dead Kennedys as well! Oh, and did I mention that you can play games with the latest iPod models?

All this fits into a beautiful, stylish package about the size of a pack of cigarettes, with up to a 18-hour lithium rechargeable battery, high-quality earbud headphones, and automatic synchronization with your iTunes MP3 library. (The iPod Shuffle is even smaller — it's about the size of a pack of chewing gum.) Life just doesn't get any better for a technoid like me. If you think that your Mac is a well-designed piece of equipment, you'll understand why this little box is so alluring. (And why I have one now.)

Sure, there are other MP3 players out there, but most of them share the same following problems:

✦ They use digital memory cards, which offer far less capacity than the iPod.

✦ They use standard batteries, or you have to furnish rechargeable batteries (which don't last 18 hours).

✦ They don't operate as an external hard drive, photo slideshow repository, or a contacts/appointment database.

I say forget 'em. The iPod is worth every cent that you'll pay.

The 512MB iPod Shuffle is less than $100 at the time of this writing, while the 4GB iPod mini runs $199 and the 60GB iPod photo model costs $449.

Chapter 2: Add RAM, Hard Drive Space, and Stir

In This Chapter

✔ **Understanding the advantages of extra RAM**

✔ **Shopping for a RAM upgrade**

✔ **Choosing between internal and external hard drives**

✔ **Determining your hard drive needs**

✔ **Shopping for a new hard drive**

✔ **Installing your upgrades**

M ost Macintosh owners will make two upgrades — adding more memory (RAM) and additional hard drive space — during the lifetime of their computers. These two improvements have the greatest effect on the overall performance of Mac OS X. By adding RAM and additional hard drive space, you not only make more elbow room for your applications and documents, but everything runs faster: Think of the Six Million Dollar Man, only a heck of a lot cheaper to operate (and no strange noises accompanying your every move).

In this chapter, I steer you around the hidden potholes along the way for those who aren't well versed in selecting memory modules or weighing the advantages of different types of hard drives. However, if you buy the wrong piece of hardware, remember that using a hammer to make it fit is *not* a workable option.

Adding Memory: Reasons for More RAM

Of all the possible upgrades that you can make to your Macintosh, adding more random access memory (RAM) is the single most cost-effective method of increasing the performance of Mac OS X. (In fact, your machine will likely run faster with more memory than a reasonably faster processor!) Here is exactly what Mac OS X uses available RAM for:

✦ **Applications:** Naturally, Mac OS X needs system RAM to run the applications that you launch. The more memory in your machine, the larger the applications that you can open and the faster they'll run.

✦ **Overhead:** This includes the operating system itself, Classic mode (if it's running), as well as various and sundry buffers and memory areas devoted for temporary work. As you would guess, the more memory here, the merrier. (For more information on the settings that control Classic mode, see Book II, Chapter 3.)

✦ **Virtual memory:** A-ha! Now here's something that I mention lightly and politely in Book I but didn't really amount to a hill of beans until this moment. (Can you tell I'm a big fan of Bing Crosby?) *Virtual memory* allows Mac OS X to use empty hard drive space as temporary system memory, as shown in Figure 2-1. Data is written to your hard drive instead of being stored in RAM, and then it's erased when it's no longer needed. It's a neat trick that's also used by Windows, Linux, and dear old Mac OS 9 (just nowhere near as well as Mac OS X). Virtual memory works automatically within Mac OS X, so you don't have to enable it manually as you did in Mac OS 9.

Figure 2-1: The mysterious beauty of virtual memory — but it still doesn't beat real RAM!

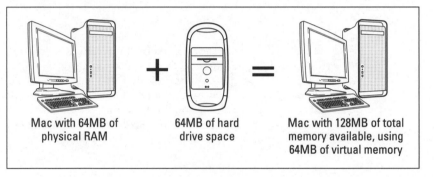

Mac with 64MB of physical RAM   64MB of hard drive space   Mac with 128MB of total memory available, using 64MB of virtual memory

At first, virtual memory sounds like absolute bliss, and it does indeed allow your Macintosh to do things that would otherwise be impossible, like running an application that requires 300MB of RAM in just 128MB of actual physical RAM. However, here come the caveats:

✦ **Virtual memory is slow as molasses in December.** Even today's fastest hard drive is many, *many* times slower than real silicon, so any use of virtual memory instead of RAM slows down Mac OS X significantly.

✦ **Virtual memory abuses your hard drive.** If you've ever run Photoshop on a Windows PC with 64MB of RAM, you're having flashbacks right now — whenever your Macintosh is using virtual memory, your hard drive remains almost constantly active. (Hardware types like myself call this phenomenon *thrashing* because we know what's happening inside that poor hard drive.) Over time, running any computer with insufficient RAM and behemoth applications will result in a significant increase in hard drive wear and tear.

✦ **Virtual memory costs you processing power.** With sufficient RAM, Mac OS X gleefully runs as efficiently as it can — when virtual memory kicks in, however, your Mac has to spend part of its quality time shuttling data to and from the hard drive, which robs your computer of processing power.

The moral of the story is very simple, so it's time for another of Mark's Maxims:

The less that Mac OS X needs to use virtual memory, the better.™

To put it another way, *physical memory* (meaning memory modules) is always a better choice than virtual memory. This is why power users and techno-types crave as much system memory as possible.

A mere two years ago, 128MB of RAM was a quite comfortable figure for most folks, but most of today's Macs can accept at least a whopping 1GB (that's short for *gigabyte,* or 1,024 megabytes) of system RAM. (At the extreme end of the scale, the King Kahuna — Apple's latest Power Mac G5 — can now accommodate an unbelievable **8 gigabytes** of RAM!)

If you'll be keeping your current Macintosh for a few years more, install as much memory as you can afford — you'll thank me every time that Mac OS X Tiger boots.

Book VI
Chapter 2

Add RAM, Hard
Drive Space,
and Stir

Shopping for a RAM Upgrade

Before you click your mouse on some online computer store's Buy button, you need to determine two things that will help you determine which memory module to buy: how much RAM you've already got and how much more your system can handle.

Finding out the current memory in your Mac

Memory modules are made in standard sizes, so you need to determine how much memory you already have and which of your memory slots are filled. To do this, open an old friend you might have used in Mac OS 9, the Apple System Profiler. Here, open System Profiler by clicking the Apple menu, choosing About This Mac, and then clicking the More Info button.

After you launch this application, it takes a few seconds to scan your Macintosh and display all sorts of identifying information about the hardware and software that you're using. Check out the Memory item in the Hardware section. Here you can see exactly how many memory modules you have, what type they are, and how much memory each provides. For example, in

Figure 2-2, my iMac G5 has two memory slots — labeled `DIMM0` and `DIMM1`. One of those slots is filled with a 1GB module, and the other sports a 256MB module, giving me a total physical memory of 1280MB. Jot down the name and contents of each slot on a piece of paper — or, if you're a real Mac OS X power user, add a Stickie to your Desktop with this information. (Stickies are covered in Book II, Chapter 2.)

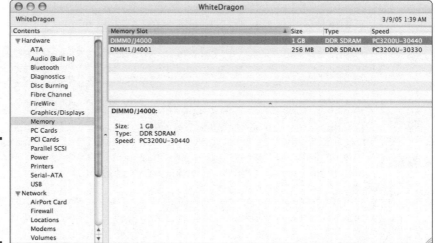

Figure 2-2:
Look under the hood with Apple's System Profiler.

However, on some machines, only one memory module can be upgraded by a mere mortal. For example, on many older iMac G4 models, DIMM0 is an internal module and can be upgraded only by an Apple technician. (Insert sound of harps playing here.)

Unfortunately, this arrangement differs on just about every model of Macintosh ever made — some have more memory slots, and others allow you to upgrade all the system memory instead of just one module. The only way to determine which modules are accessible on your Mac is to identify the exact model of your computer.

Determining the exact model of your computer

Most folks know the type and model of their computers, but there's a catch here, too: Sometimes the memory that you need varies by the processor in your Macintosh. For instance, many different versions of iMacs have been made since the Bondi Blue Beast debuted, and over the course of those years, Apple has made a slew of changes inside. Your eye should be on the actual processor speed and *bus speed* — the transfer speed that data reaches whilst speeding across your motherboard — because they're the identifying factors here. An older iMac with a 333 MHz G3 processor, for example, will use a different type of memory from the latest iMac with a 1.8GHz G5 processor.

Again, your salvation turns out to be Apple System Profiler. Just click the Hardware section to display both the Machine Speed (or *processor speed*) and the Bus Speed. (For example, my machine has a 1.8GHz G5 running at 600 MHz bus speed.) Grab that same piece of paper (or open that same Stickie) and add these two figures to your list.

Now you're armed with the information that you need to go online and buy the right memory — or, if you'd rather work directly with a human being, you can visit your local Apple dealer, present him with the list, and have him order the memory upgrade for you.

Buying memory online is much cheaper. I recommend the following online stores:

Book VI Chapter 2

+ **MacMall:** www.macmall.com

+ **MacWarehouse:** www.cdw.com

+ **MacConnection:** www.macconnection.com

Add RAM, Hard Drive Space, and Stir

The Tao of Hard Drive Territory

Next, turn your attention to the other popular Mac upgrade — adding extra hard drive space. With today's cutting-edge, 3-D games using a gigabyte of space each and Photoshop CS expanding to 500MB, IDC (short for *Insidious Data Creep*) is a growing problem. (Bad pun most certainly intended.)

You can save space by deleting those files and folders you don't need, but what fun is that? To reduce your Mac's waistline before you consider adding more room, I recommend using Spring Cleaning from Allume Systems, which you can find at www.allume.com. It's a great tool for locating duplicates, removing empty folders, and uninstalling old programs that you no longer use.

To determine how much free space remains on a hard drive, click the drive's icon on your Desktop and press ⌘+I to display its information, as shown in Figure 2-3. (I'm a major-league Mozart fan-boy, hence the name of my hard drive.)

As a general rule, the following factors indicate that you're ready to upgrade your hard drive territory:

+ You have less than 2GB of space on your current hard drive.

+ You've cleaned off *all* unnecessary files, and your Mac is still lagging behind in storage.

+ You need to share a large amount of data between computers that aren't on the same network. (Read on to discover why.)

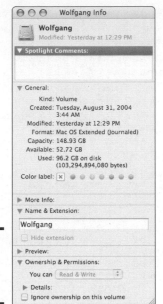

Figure 2-3:
Checking
your drive's
free space.

Internal versus External Storage

Just about everyone who upgrades their existing hard drive does so because
they need extra space; however, you might also need to add a hard drive
to your system that can go mobile whenever necessary. Unlike an *internal*
drive — which resides hidden inside your Mac's case — an *external* drive is
a lean, mean, self-contained traveling storage machine that's perfect for road
warriors.

External drives

External removable cartridge drives, such as a Zip drive, are fine for folks who
have to send cartridges to other locations. Unfortunately, however, the capaci-
ties of these drives are rapidly falling behind conventional, non-removable
external hard drives. Also, most Macs now have either a CD-RW or DVD-R
drive, which basically render Zip technology obsolete. Therefore, if you're
considering an external unit, go with the most popular pick — a high-capacity
non-removable hard drive, which offers the most storage for your dollar.

Most external drives are *shock-mounted* (meaning that they can take more
abuse than an internal hard drive), and they carry their own power supply.
In fact, some external drives actually don't need a separate power supply
because they draw their power through your Mac's Universal Serial Bus
(USB) or FireWire port. (The next chapter in this mini-book tells all about
USB and FireWire.)

External drives also have a number of other advantages:

✦ **No installation hassle:** You can easily install a USB or FireWire drive in seconds. Simply plug in the drive to the proper connector on the side or back of your Mac, connect the power supply (if necessary), and turn it on. (No software installation necessary. As the folks in Cupertino are fond of saying, "Look, Ma — no drivers!")

✦ **No extra space needed:** Many Macs simply don't have the internal space for another drive — laptops, iMacs, and the Mac Mini are good examples. Therefore, if you want to keep your existing internal drive as-is while you're adding more storage, an external drive is your only choice.

✦ **File sharing with ease:** With an external drive, you can share your data between multiple computers or bring your files with you on your next trip.

✦ **Safe from prying eyes:** Unlike an internal drive, external drives are easy to secure. Take your sensitive information home with you or lock it in a safe.

After you plug in an external drive, Mac OS X displays it just like any other hard drive volume. Figure 2-4 illustrates my 30GB FireWire drive in action.

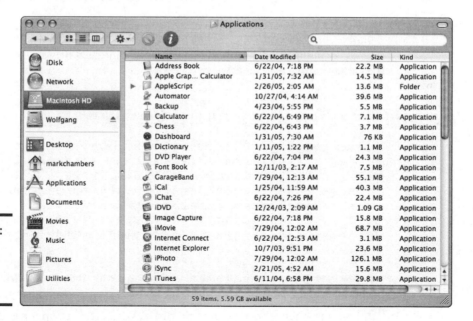

Figure 2-4:
A typical external FireWire drive.

Internal drives

Your other alternative is to upgrade your internal drive, which can be a hassle. Like a memory upgrade, adding or swapping an internal drive involves opening your Mac's case. In fact, it's a somewhat more complex procedure than adding memory.

I usually recommend that folks add a second drive rather than swap out their existing drive. You'll avoid the hassle of backing up and restoring your system on a new drive or (even worse) reinstalling Mac OS X and then reinstalling all the applications that you use. (Swapping a hard drive should be the definition of the word *hassle*.) Instead, add a second drive and leave your current hard drive as-is.

However, here are a number of very important reasons why many Mac owners choose updating internal drives, even with the hassle of swapping:

✦ **They're cheaper.** You'll spend significantly less on an internal drive because it doesn't need the case and additional electronics required by an external drive.

✦ **They're faster.** Even a FireWire or USB 2.0 drive isn't as fast as an internal drive.

✦ **They take up less space in your work area.** An internal drive eliminates the space taken by an external drive, which can range anywhere from the size of a paperback to the size of a hardback book.

After you establish that you are in fact ready for more space — and you've decided whether you want to add an internal drive, an external drive, or (if you enjoy punishment) upgrade your existing internal drive — you're ready to consider how big of a drive you need.

Determining How Much Space You Need

Your next step is to decide just how much hard drive space is enough. I suppose that if your last name is Gates and you live in Redmond, you can probably pick just about any drive on the market. However, I have a family, a mortgage, a car payment, and lust in my heart for the latest computer games; therefore, I must be a little more selective.

I have two hard-and-fast rules that I follow when I'm determining the capacity of a new drive:

1. If you're buying a replacement for your existing drive, shop for a drive with at least twice the capacity of the existing drive (if possible).

2. If you're buying an external USB or FireWire drive, shop for a drive with at least half the capacity of your existing internal drive (if possible).

Those rules seem to work pretty doggone well in most circumstances with these two exceptions: gamers and digital video gurus. These folks need to shoehorn as much space as they possibly can into their systems. If you're a hardcore gamer or if you work primarily with digital video, you need a wheelbarrow's worth of hard drive capacity. Trust me: Buy the biggest hard drive that you can afford.

Shopping for a Hard Drive

Ready to brave the local Wireless Shed superstore (or perhaps its Web site)? Here's a list of guidelines to keep handy while you're shopping for a new internal or external hard drive:

**Book VI
Chapter 2**

**Add RAM, Hard
Drive Space,
and Stir**

✦ **Faster is indeed better.** You'll pay more for a 10,000 revolutions per minute (rpm) drive than a slower 5,400 or 7,200 rpm drive, but the extra cash is worth it. Faster drives can transfer more data to your Mac in less time — and that's especially important for storing digital video.

✦ **Serial ATA and EIDE drives are different.** If you're replacing your internal drive, you have to get the same type of drive that you already have. Again, System Profiler can tell you which type of drive your Mac is currently using.

✦ **Avoid used or refurbished drives.** Hard drives are one of the few components in your computer that still have a large number of moving parts. Therefore, buying a used drive isn't a good idea unless it's priced very low.

Because the prices on new hard drives are constantly dropping, make sure that you check on the price for a new, faster drive of the same capacity before you buy that bargain used drive.

✦ **Pick FireWire over USB 1.*x* every time.** Compared with a FireWire connection, a USB 1.*x* external hard drive is simply a joke when it comes to performance. Because most Macs with USB ports also have FireWire ports, make very sure that you buy a FireWire drive! (If your Mac has USB 2.0 ports, which will show up in System Profiler as well, you can buy a USB 2.0 drive without being embarrassed.)

✦ **Watch the size of the drive when buying internal drives.** Most SATA (short for Serial ATA) and EIDE (Enhanced Integrated Drive Electronics) drives are standard half-height 3.5" units, but check to make sure that you're not investing in a laptop drive — unless, of course, you're upgrading a laptop.

✦ **Do I need SCSI?** In most cases, the answer is *no* — Macs built within the last three or four years all use either EIDE or SATA drives. However, older Macs do use Small Computer System Interface (SCSI) hardware, so make sure that you check before you buy. (SCSI and EIDE are the two different types of internal hard drive interfaces — a fancy word for *connection* — used on Macs that can run Mac OS X.) Again, you can use the Apple

System Profiler to determine what type of drives you have. Click the Hardware category in the Contents column on the left and then click both the ATA and SCSI subcategories to display the information for your hard drives.

Installing Your New Stuff

After you get your memory modules or hard drive, pick from one of two methods of installing them: easy and hard. Guess which method will cost you money?

The easy way

Your Apple dealer can perform either type of hardware installation for you. You can rest easy knowing that the job will be done right, but money will definitely change hands.

Personally, I always recommend that owners of iBooks and PowerBook laptops allow their dealers to install memory upgrades and hard drives because these laptops are much more complex than a desktop, and they're much easier to damage.

The hard way

If you're familiar with the inside of your Macintosh, you can install your own upgrade and save that cash. A memory upgrade is one of the simpler chores to perform, but that doesn't mean that everyone feels comfortable taking the cover off and jumping inside a computer; hard drives are a tad more complex.

If you have a knowledgeable friend or family member who can help you install your hardware, buy him the proverbial NSD (short for *Nice Steak Dinner*) and enlist him in your cause. Even if you still do the work yourself, it's always better to have a second pair of experienced eyes watching, especially if you're a little nervous.

Because the installation procedures for both memory modules and hard drives are different for every model of Mac — heck, even removing the cover on each model of Macintosh involves a different challenge — I can't provide you with any step-by-step procedures in this chapter. Many online stores include installation instructions with their hardware. Other sources for installation instructions include the Apple Web site (www.apple.com) or your Apple dealer. You can use Sherlock (more about this in Book I, Chapter 5) to scan the Internet for installation information for your particular model. However, here are guidelines to follow during the installation:

✦ **Watch out for static electricity.** When opening your Macintosh and handling hardware, make certain that you've touched a metal surface beforehand to discharge any static electricity on your body. (You can also buy a static wrist strap that you can wear while working within the bowels of your Mac.)

✦ **Check the notches on memory modules.** Most types of memory modules have notches cut into the connector. These notches make sure that you can install the module only one way, so make certain that they align properly with the slot.

✦ **Make sure you're using the right memory slot.** As I mention earlier in this chapter, most Macs have multiple memory slots, so check the label on the circuit board to make sure that you're adding the memory to the correct slot. (Naturally, this won't be a problem if you're installing a module into an unoccupied slot.)

✦ **Take good care of older hardware.** If you replace an existing memory module or hard drive with a new one, put the old hardware in the left-over anti-static bag from your new hardware and immediately start thinking of how you'll word your eBay auction . . . *Used 128MB Memory Module for 333MHz iMac,* for example.

✦ **Check your hard drive jumper settings.** If your Mac uses EIDE hard drives, you must set the Master and Slave jumpers correctly on the back (or underside) of the new drive. A *jumper* is simply a tiny metal-and-plastic connector that is used to change the configuration on a hard drive. Setting jumpers indicates to your Mac which drive is the primary drive and which is the secondary drive. (I don't know how engineers got into the whole Master/Slave thing . . . they're normally not quite so exotic when naming things.)

  If you're adding a second drive to a G3 or G4 tower, you'll probably have to change the jumper settings on the original drive as well. (If you're replacing the existing drive, you're in luck; simply duplicate the jumper settings from the old drive and use them on the new drive.) Because the configuration settings are different for each hard drive model, check the drive's documentation for the correct jumper position.

✦ **Leave the cover off while testing.** After you install the upgrade, leave the cover off your Mac while you boot the computer and test to see how well you did. That way, if you have to replace the original hardware for some reason, you won't have to remove the cover a second time.

To determine whether a memory upgrade was successful, you can again turn to the Apple System Profiler. Open the Profiler again and compare the memory overview specifications with the original list that you made earlier. If the total amount of memory has increased and the memory module is recognized, you've done your job well. If not, switch off the Mac and check the module to make sure it's completely seated in the slot.

Chapter 3: Port-o-rama: Using USB and FireWire

In This Chapter

✓ Using FireWire under Mac OS X

✓ Using USB under Mac OS X

✓ Adding a USB or FireWire hub

✓ Troubleshooting FireWire and USB connections

✓ Adding and updating drivers

A pple's list of successes continues to grow over the years — hardware, applications, and (of course) Mac OS X — but the FireWire standard for connecting computers to all sorts of different devices is in a class by itself. That's because FireWire has been universally accepted all over the world as the port of choice for all sorts of digital devices that need a high-speed connection. Even Windows owners have grudgingly admitted that FireWire just plain rocks. Ya gotta love it.

In this chapter, I discuss the importance of FireWire to the digital hub that I discuss in Book III, and I compare it with both version 1.1 and version 2.0 of Intel's Universal Serial Bus (USB) connection technology. I also talk troubleshooting and expansion using a hub.

Appreciating the Advantage of a FireWire Connection

So what's so special about FireWire, anyway? Why does Apple stuff at least one (and usually two) FireWire ports in all its current Macintosh models? Heck, even the *iPod* (Apple's MP3 player, which you can read more about in Book III, Chapter 2) originally used only a FireWire connection. (Its *official* name is IEEE 1394, but even the Cupertino crew doesn't call it that — at least very often.)

First things first. As countless racing fans will tell you, it's all about the *speed,* my friend. The original FireWire 400 port delivers a blazing fast 400 Mbps (megabits per second), which is fast enough for all sorts of peripherals to communicate with your Macintosh. The following list includes a number of hardware toys that are well known for transferring prodigious file sizes:

✦ Digital video (DV) camcorders

✦ High-resolution digital cameras

✦ Scanners and some printers

✦ External hard drives and CD/DVD recorders

✦ Networking between computers

For example, consider the sheer size of a typical digital video clip captured by one of today's DV camcorders. DV buffs commonly transfer several hundred megabytes of footage to their computers at one time. Check out the relative speeds of the different types of ports in Table 3-1, and you'll see a big attraction of FireWire.

Table 3-1	Transfer Speeds for Ports through the Ages	
Port	*Appeared on Personal Computer When*	*Transfer Speed (In Megabits)*
PC Serial	1981	Less than 1 Mbps
PC Parallel	1981	1 Mbps
USB (version 1.1)	1996	12 Mbps
FireWire 400 (version 1)	1996	400 Mbps
USB (version 2.0)	2001	480 Mbps
FireWire 800 (version 2)	2002	800 Mbps

Ouch! Not too hard to figure that one out. Here are three other important benefits to FireWire:

✦ **Control over connection:** This is a 10-cent term that engineers use, meaning that you can control whatever gadget that you've connected using FireWire from your computer. This is pretty neat when you think about it; for example, you can control your DV camcorder from the comfort of your computer keyboard, just as if you were pressing the buttons on the camcorder.

✦ **Hot-swapped:** You don't have to reboot your Mac or restart Mac OS X every time that you plug (or unplug) a FireWire device. Instead, the FireWire peripheral is automatically recognized (as long as the operating system has the correct driver) and ready to transfer.

✦ **Power through the port:** FireWire can provide power to a device through the same wire — typically, there's enough power available for an external drive or recorder — so you don't need an external AC power cord for some FireWire devices. (Apologies to owners of DV camcorders, but those things eat power like a pig eats slop.)

However, FireWire isn't finished evolving yet — the new, cleverly named IEEE 1394 B (called *FireWire 800* by anyone with any sense, including the folks at Apple) is designed to deliver a whopping 800 Mbps. That, dear reader, oughta be fast enough for both you *and* your loved ones. These ports only appear on the top-of-the-line Apple desktop and laptop models at the time of this writing, but if you can afford the best, you'll have to wear racing goggles to use 'em.

Oh, and as you would expect from Apple, the new ports will be backward-compatible with older FireWire hardware. However, the ports aren't exactly the same, so you'll need a plastic port converter to connect FireWire 400 devices to a FireWire 800 port. (Such important little conversion fixtures are commonly called *dongles.* No, I'm not making that up. Ask your favorite techno-nerd.)

Understanding USB and the Tale of Two Point Oh

The other resident port on today's Apple computers is the ubiquitous USB, which is short for *Universal Serial Bus.* (By the way, ubiquitous means *ever-present* or *universal,* which I quickly looked up by using Sherlock — read all about this super sleuth in Book I, Chapter 5.) Although version 1.1 of the USB standard is nowhere near as fast as FireWire, USB has taken the world by storm. It's used for everything from mice to keyboards, speakers, digital cameras, and even external drives and CD recorders. (A friend of mine never misses the chance to point out that USB — which was originally developed by Intel, the makers of the Pentium 4 processor — was given its first wide-spread implementation on the original iMac. *You're welcome,* Intel.)

Unfortunately, those last two are somewhat problematical: Technically, you can add a USB 1.1 external hard drive, but don't expect response times any-where near what you'd enjoy with an internal hard drive. Ditto for a CD recorder — 4X is about the limit for the recording speed with a USB 1.1 con-nection. (Don't even *think* about recording DVDs over a USB 1.1 connection.) Now, compare this performance with that of similar equipment using a FireWire connection, which provides nearly the speed of an internal hard drive and CD and DVD recording at the fastest pace possible.

Like FireWire, USB connections are hot-swappable and provide power over the connection. A USB port also offers a more limited version of Control over Connection as well, making it a good choice for virtually all digital cameras.

The average 2- or 3-megapixel (MP) digital camera creates a JPEG image that's about 400–500K, so USB is the connection of choice for all but the 5MP and 6MP (and higher) camera models. Why is it the connection of choice, even though it's slower than FireWire? Most PCs still don't come standard with FireWire ports, and transferring a 500K file doesn't take that long over USB. (On the other hand, try transferring a 20MB file from a 6MP camera, and FireWire suddenly makes a lot of sense.)

Not to be outdone, a new USB 2.0 specification arrived a couple of years ago that delivers even better performance than the original FireWire standard — USB 2.0 can transfer 480 Mbps. These ports are backward-compatible — meaning they work with the original USB 1.*x* ports as well. (Don't call Apple a snob . . . at the time of this writing, all of the Mac models in Apple's current stable have USB 2.0 ports.)

If you have an expandable tower G3, G4, or G5 machine, you can use an empty Peripheral Component Interconnect (PCI) slot to add USB 2.0 ports to your Mac. For example, Orange Micro sells the OrangeUSB 2.0 Hi-Speed PCI card for about $50 (www.orangemicro.com); you can add a USB 2.0 port to many older laptops by using a PC Card.

Hey, You Need a Hub!

Suppose that you've embraced FireWire and USB and you now have two FireWire drives hanging off the rear end of your Mac — and suddenly you buy an iPod. (Or you get another FireWire device that's as much fun as an iPod, if that's actually possible.) Now you're faced with too many devices for too few ports. You *could* eject a drive and unhook it each time that you want to connect your iPod, but there *must* be a more elegant way to connect. Help!

Enter the hub. Both the FireWire and USB specifications allow you to connect a device called a *hub,* which is really nothing more than a glorified splitter adapter that provides you with additional ports. Note that this device has nothing — repeat, *absolutely nothing* — to do with the network hubs that I discuss in Book V. With a FireWire or USB hub at work, you do lose a port; however, most hubs multiply that port into four or eight ports. Again, all this is transparent, and you don't need to hide anything up your sleeve. Adding a hub is just as plug-and-play easy as adding a regular FireWire/USB device.

I should also mention that FireWire supports *daisy-chaining* — a word that stretches all the way back to the days of the Atari and Commodore computers, when devices had extra ports in the back so that additional stuff could be plugged in. However, not every FireWire drive has a daisy-chain port (also called a *passthru port*). With daisy-chaining, you can theoretically add 63 FireWire devices to your Mac — talk about impressing them at your next Mac user group meeting!

Uh, It's Just Sitting There

Man, I *hate* it when FireWire and USB devices act like boat anchors. FireWire and USB peripherals are so doggone simple that when something goes wrong, it really aggravates you. Fortunately, I've been down those roads many a time before, so in this section, I'll unleash my experience. (That sounds a little frightening, but it's a *good* thing. Really.)

Common FireWire and USB headaches

Because FireWire and USB are so alike in so many ways, I can handle possible troubleshooting solutions for both types of hardware at once:

✦ **Problem:** Every time I turn off or unplug my external peripheral, Mac OS X gets irritated and displays a nasty message saying that I haven't properly disconnected the device.

Solution: This happens because you haven't *ejected* the peripheral. I know that sounds a little strange for a device like an external hard drive or a digital camera, but it's essentially the same reasoning as ejecting a CD or DVD from your Desktop. When you click your USB or FireWire device and hold the mouse button down, you'll see that the Trash icon turns into an Eject icon; drag the device icon to the Eject icon and drop it, and the external device disappears from your Desktop. (You can also click the device icon to select it and press ⌘+E.) At that point, you're safe to turn it off or unplug the FireWire/USB cable.

Book VI
Chapter 3

Port-o-rama: Using
USB and FireWire

If Tiger recognizes the device as an external drive, which is usually the case with a digital camera, external hard drive, or external CD/DVD recorder, you can simply click the Eject button next to the device icon in the Finder window's sidebar.

✦ **Problem:** The device doesn't show a power light.

Solution: Check to make sure that the power cable is connected — unless, of course, you've got a device that's powered through the connection itself. This can sometimes pose its own share of problems, however, when using USB devices. Not all USB ports provide power because some are designed only for connecting mice, keyboards, and joysticks.

To check whether an unpowered USB port is your problem, either connect the device to a USB port on the back of your Mac or connect it to a hub or another computer. If the device works when it's connected to another port, you've found the culprit.

✦ **Problem:** The device shows a power light but just doesn't work.

Solution: This can be because of problems with your cable or your hub. To check, borrow a friend's cables and test to see whether the device works. If you're testing the hub, try connecting the device directly to your Mac using the same cable to see whether it works without the hub.

If you're attempting to connect a FireWire device through another FireWire device, try connecting it directly to see whether it works. If so, the middleman device either needs to be switched on to pass the data through or it doesn't support daisy-chaining at all — in which case, you'll have to connect both devices directly to your Macintosh.

✦ **Problem:** Mac OS X reports that I have a missing driver.

Solution: Check the manufacturer's Web site and download a new copy of the USB or FireWire drivers for your device because they've been corrupted, overwritten, or erased entirely. Because Mac OS X loads the driver for a USB or FireWire device when it's connected, sometimes just unplugging and reconnecting a peripheral will do the trick.

Check those drivers

Speaking of drivers . . . old and worn-out drivers are a sore spot with me. *Drivers* are simply programs that tell Mac OS X how to communicate with your external device. Each new version of Mac OS X contains updated drivers, but make certain that you check for new updates on a regular basis. That means using both the Software Update feature in Mac OS X (which I cover in Book II, Chapter 3) *and* going to the Web sites provided by your USB and FireWire hardware manufacturers.

Chapter 4: I'm Okay, You're a Printer

In This Chapter

✔ **Using the Printer Setup Utility**

✔ **Adding a non-USB printer**

✔ **Managing print jobs**

✔ **Sending and receiving faxes**

✔ **Setting up a shared printer**

Of all the improvements made in Mac OS X over Mac OS 9, one of the most important is the simplified printing process — no Chooser, no strange printer ports . . . just a heap of Universal Serial Bus (USB) and network printing goodness. As I discuss in Book I, Chapter 3, if your USB printer is recognized by Tiger, you can print within seconds of plugging it in, with no muss or fuss. A USB printer is connected physically to your Mac, but you can also send print jobs over the network to a network printer or even to a wireless printer. (Unfortunately, if that network printer is in another room, you *do* have to get up out of your comfortable chair to retrieve your printed document . . . not even Tiger is *that* powerful.)

But what if you want to print to an AppleTalk printer or perhaps send documents to a printer over TCP/IP? (For more on AppleTalk, read Book V, Chapter 3.) To take care of tasks like that, you need to dig a little further — and I do so in this chapter. You also discover here how to use the features of the Printer Setup Utility and how to juggle print jobs like a circus performer.

Meet the Printer Setup Utility

The Printer Setup Utility runs automatically whenever it's needed by Tiger — for example, when you print a document — but you can also run it at any time from two other places:

✦ The Print & Fax pane within System Preferences

✦ The Utilities folder inside your Applications folder

Although the Printer Setup Utility doesn't look like much (as shown in Figure 4-1), power lurks underneath.

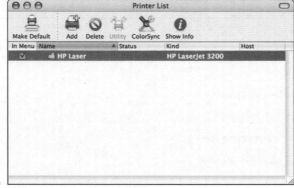

Figure 4-1: The rather plain-looking Printer Setup Utility is actually a rugged adventurer.

If you find the Printer Setup Utility hard to reach and you need to manually launch it often, add it to the Dock (as I show you in Book II, Chapter 2). That way, you can launch it with a single click.

Printer Setup Utility Toolbar Buttons

Along the top of the Printer Setup Utility, you'll find six default toolbar icons. They are

✦ **Make Default:** If you have more than one printer listed in the Printer Setup Utility, you can select which printer Tiger will use by default. *Hint:* The entry for the default printer appears in bold type. Click the desired entry and then click the Make Default icon. (You can also use the ⌘+D keyboard shortcut.)

When you add a new printer to the list, it automatically becomes the default printer. (Some folks like this feature; others would banish the person responsible to Siberia for a decade.)

✦ **Add:** In Book I, Chapter 3, you can read how to add a typical USB printer (both with and without an installed driver). In the next section, I show you how to add a non-USB printer.

"What if I add a printer by clicking the plus sign button on the Print & Fax pane in System Preferences?" Ah, but it's a trick question — System Preferences simply launches the Printer Setup Utility! Hence my coverage of the utility first.

If your USB printer is already *natively supported* (has a preloaded driver in Tiger), you might not need to go through the trouble of clicking the

Add icon on the toolbar. Mac OS X can add a new USB printer automatically, so don't be surprised if your Mac swoops in and does it for you as soon as you plug in a new printer. Also, the manufacturer's installation program for your printer might add the printer for you in a behind-the-scenes way, even if Mac OS X lies dormant.

✦ **Delete:** First click a printer in the list to select it and then click this icon to remove a printer from your list of installed printers. This isn't something that you're likely to do often, but if a printer is no longer available, it helps keep your list nice and tidy.

✦ **Utility:** Clicking this icon displays the model-specific configuration settings and features (if any) that are available for the selected printer. Of course, these settings vary for every printer produced by the hand of Man — they're actually determined by the manufacturer's printer driver — but they usually include actions such as cleaning and alignment, and settings such as print quality.

✦ **ColorSync:** Click this toolbar button to display the color matching controls that are specific for your printer. Graphic artists and print media professionals use *color matching* to make sure that a shade you picked called *Antique Rose* also looks like *Antique Rose* on the printed version. (Wouldn't want *Vamp Red* instead, now would we?)

✦ **Show Info:** From the Printer Setup Utility menu, click the Show Info toolbar button (or press the ⌘+I keyboard shortcut) to display information on the selected printer. You can change the printer name in this list, but you have other options, too. Many Mac printers use the PostScript standard printing language; the dialog displays the PPD (Postscript Printer Description) data files for the printer (the PPD field will be empty if the printer doesn't use PostScript) as well as any installable options, such as a paper feed or scanning upgrade. Click the drop-down list box to display any installable options.

Here are two additional important features that don't seem to rate their own buttons on the Printer Setup Utility toolbar (but would doggone well be there if I were running the show):

✦ **Preferences:** Click the Printer Setup Utility menu and choose Preferences to display the Print & Fax settings within System Preferences (see Figure 4-2). The choices that you make here affect the defaults in all the applications on your system — in this case, for my HP LaserJet printer. Choose the Default Paper Size in Page Setup from the drop-down list for use with all your printers. Click the Selected Printer in Print Dialog list box to pick the default printer that will be used in all your applications. Click the Print Queue button to display the printer queue window, where you can monitor, pause, and stop active print jobs, or display completed jobs.

✦ **Show Jobs:** Click Printers and click Show Jobs (or press ⌘+O) to open the very same printer queue window I just mentioned. Find more on this later in the upcoming section "Managing Your Printing Jobs."

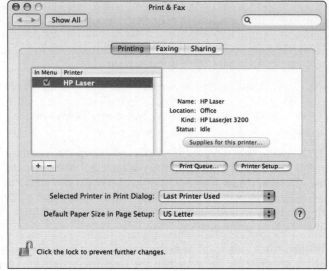

Figure 4-2:
Choose
global
preferences
for the
Printer
Setup Utility.

Adding a Funky Printer

"And what," you might ask, "is a *funky* printer?" Well, you have a number of possibilities, but they all add up to a non-USB connection:

✦ **An AppleTalk printer:** If you're sharing a printer on another Mac by using AppleTalk (or if you have an older printer that supports AppleTalk), you can print to that device. For more on AppleTalk, read Book V, Chapter 3.

✦ **IP printing:** Sending a job to an Internet Protocol (IP) printer actually shoots the document across a network or Internet connection by using a target IP address or domain name. Generally, it's best to have a *static* (unchanging) IP address for a network printer; if the IP address changes often, for example, you'd have to reconfigure your connection to your IP printer each time that it changed.

✦ **Bonjour:** Shared printers on your local network use the built-in Bonjour networking system, which means that they're automatically recognized, and you needn't enter any bothersome settings to reach 'em. (Go, Cupertino!)

✦ **Open Directory:** This connection uses Mac OS X Directory Services to share a printer. If your network uses Directory Services, your network system administrator will have to set up *mappings* (essentially configurations that point the way to a shared printer). Many network system administrators favor Directory Services, which provide a much higher level of security and make it easy to limit access to a printer by user ID or location.

✦ **Windows printing:** "Hey, I get to use the enemy's printers, too?" That's right, as long as a Windows user on your network has shared his printer (via the ubiquitous Windows File and Printer Sharing feature), you can use it. Remember that HP printer of mine? It's actually connected to my PC server. *Sweet.*

✦ **Application printer drivers:** Some printers aren't actually physical devices at all. For example, if you don't want to use Tiger's built-in faxing system, you can print directly to a third-party fax program such as FAXstf X Pro (www.smithmicro.com), which then dials, connects, and sends the document to a fax machine.

Although you can install Adobe Acrobat under Tiger, the operating system provides built-in support for printing documents in Adobe's PDF format (which can then be viewed and printed on any other computer with the Acrobat Reader, or added to your Web site for downloading). In fact, you don't even have to install a PDF print driver or display Printer Setup Utility! To print a document as a file in PDF format, click the PDF drop-down button in the application's Print dialog, navigate to the desired folder and enter a filename, and then click Save.

No matter which type of funky printer you add, it will need a driver installed in the Printers folder, which resides inside your Library folder. (A *driver* is a software program provided by the printer manufacturer that tells Mac OS X how to communicate with your printer.) Also, if the printer is PostScript-compatible, it will need a PPD file installed in your PPD folder, which also appears in the Printers folder. Luckily, Tiger comes complete with a long list of drivers and PPD files already installed and available — bravo, Apple dudes and dudettes!

To add a funky printer, follow these steps:

1. **Launch the manufacturer's installation application, which should copy the driver and PPD files for you.**

If you have to do things the hard way, manually copy the driver file into the Library/Printers folder and then copy the PPD file (if required) into the Library/Printers/PPD folder.

2. **If you're adding a physical printer — instead of an application printer driver — verify that the printer is turned on and accessible.**

If you're printing to a shared printer connected to another Mac, that computer has to be on. Luckily, most network printers (and their computer hosts) remain on all the time.

3. **Launch Printer Setup Utility and then click the Add icon on the toolbar.**

Shared printers using Rendezvous network technology should show up on this list, so you can click the printer to select it, and enter optional name and location labels to help you identify the printer. Click the Print Using drop-down list box and choose the printer model; then click Add.

4. **To add an IP printer, click the IP button on the browser toolbar.**

Click the Protocol drop-down list box to choose the IP printing protocol (typically either IPP or the manufacturer-specific socket protocol). If you have a choice, it's always a good idea to use the manufacturer-specific socket.

Click in the Address box and type the printer's IP address or Domain Name System (DNS) name, which should be provided by your network administrator or the person running the print server. You can use the default queue on the server — which I recommend — or select the Queue check box and type a valid queue name for the server.

If you don't know a valid queue name, you're up a creek — hence, my recommendation to use the default queue.

If you like, you can type a name and location for the remote printer — this is purely for identification purposes. Finally, click the Print Using drop-down list, choose the brand and model of the remote printer, and then click Add.

5. **To add an AppleTalk, Bluetooth, Windows Printing, or application printer driver, click the More Printers button at the bottom of the Printer Browser. Click the top drop-down list box to select the connection type.**

The settings that appear depend on the connection type you choose. If you don't know the correct choice, huddle with your network administrator.

- *AppleTalk:* If you choose AppleTalk, click the second drop-down list and choose the correct AppleTalk Zone. After a scan of the specified Zone, Printer Setup Utility displays the list of printers that it can access from that Zone.

- *Bluetooth:* Choose Bluetooth to display a list of Bluetooth printers that your Mac can recognize. (Remember, Bluetooth devices have a practical range of only 20–30 feet.)

- *Windows Printing:* If you choose Windows Printing, click the second drop-down list and then click the correct Windows workgroup that includes the printer(s) that you want to use. After a scan of the specified workgroup, Printer Setup Utility displays the list of printers that it can access. (Don't forget to thank His Billness later.)

- *Application Name:* If you choose an application name, like FAXstf X Pro, the application's driver will display its own settings. Set the configuration as necessary.

After everything is tuned correctly, click the Printer Model drop-down list and choose the brand and model of the remote printer. Then click Add.

Managing Your Printing Jobs

As I mention earlier in this chapter, you can also exercise some control over the documents — or, in technoid, *print jobs* — that you send to your printer. To display the jobs that are *active* (in line and preparing to print), use one of these methods:

✦ Click Printers on the Printer Setup Utility menu, click a printer in the list, and choose Show Jobs.

✦ Launch the Printer Setup Utility and press ⌘+O.

✦ Open the Print & Fax pane in System Preferences and click the Print Queue button.

Where's the chapter on faxing?

Good question, and here's the answer: Tiger handles faxing so seamlessly that you don't *need* a chapter's worth of instruction! As long as your Mac has either an internal or external analog (dialup) modem connected to a phone line, you're a lean faxing machine.

To fax any open document within an active application, just choose File➪Print or press ⌘+P. Click the PDF button at the bottom of the Print dialog and click Fax PDF. Either type a telephone number directly in the To field, or click the suave-looking button with the profile next to the field and choose a contact with a telephone number from your Address Book. Next, type a dialing prefix if one is necessary to reach an outside line. (Usually, you won't have to select an external modem because virtually all modern Macs have an internal modem.)

If you need a spiffy-looking cover page, select the Cover Page check box. Click in the Comment box directly below it and type whatever you like. You can optionally type a subject as well. When all is ready, you can either click the Preview button to see the fax before you send it,

or throw caution utterly to the wind and click the Fax button. The Printer Setup Utility treats a fax just like any other printed document, so you can cancel it or monitor its progress, as I discuss in the section, "Managing Your Printing Jobs."

Your Mac can also receive faxes. To enable this feature, open System Preferences and click the Print & Fax icon. On the Faxing tab, select the Receive Faxes on This Computer check box. Make sure that you type your fax number into the My Fax Number field and then set the number of rings Tiger should wait before answering the call. You can save your incoming faxes as files within a folder you specify, or e-mail the contents automatically to any e-mail address you like. (Perfect for vacations!) If you like, you can even take the mundane route and print them on your system printer.

If you're going to use your Mac as a fax machine often, I would definitely recommend enabling the Show Fax Status in Menu Bar check box. That way, you can monitor what's happening as your Mac sends and receives throughout the day.

The actions that you can perform from the printer queue window (as shown in Figure 4-3) are

✦ **Delete:** When you click a print job in the list and then click the Delete icon, the print job is removed from the queue. You might need to delete a print job if you discover a mistake in the document while printing.

If the job is currently printing, several additional pages might be printed before the job is finally cancelled. In other words, information already sent to the printer might have to be printed before the cancel request can be processed.

✦ **Hold:** Click the Hold toolbar icon to pause printing of the current print job. The status of the print job changes to Hold.

✦ **Resume:** Click a print job in Hold status in the list and then click the Resume icon to resume printing.

✦ **Stop Jobs:** Click this icon to stop all printing to this printer. Note, however, that unlike using the Delete command, Stop Jobs doesn't *remove* any print jobs from the list. When jobs are stopped, the Stop Jobs icon morphs into Start Jobs — click it to restart all jobs in the queue list.

This is a good feature to use when your printer is about to run out of paper.

✦ **Utility:** Click this icon to display any model-specific configuration settings and features (if any) that are available for the printer assigned to the selected queue.

✦ **Supply Levels:** If your printer supports remote supply monitoring, you can click this icon to display the current levels of ink and paper in your printer. (Thus saving your feet from the wear and tear of walking.)

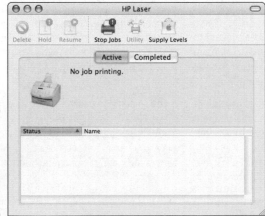

Figure 4-3:
Monitor your print jobs and control them like puppets.

Sharing a Printer across That There Network

Before we leave the Island of Big X Printing, I'd like to show you how to share a printer with others on your local network, using Tiger's super-easy Rendezvous network sharing feature. (Earlier in this chapter, I show you how to connect to other shared printers around you. Here, you're going to share a printer that's connected directly to your Mac.)

If you decide to share your printers, don't be surprised if Mac OS X seems to slow down slightly from time to time. This is because of the processing time necessary for your Mac to store queued documents from other computers. The hard drive activity on your Mac is likely to significantly increase as well.

Once again, turn to the Print & Fax pane within System Preferences. (When it comes to printing, Tiger gives you more than one way to skin a . . . well, you get the idea, even without the bad pun.) To share a printer, click the Sharing tab (as shown in Figure 4-4) and mark the Share These Printers with Other Computers check box. Mark the check box next to each printer you want to share. *Voilà!* You're the guru!

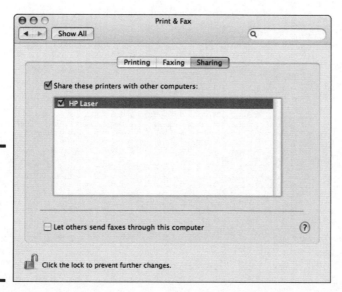

Figure 4-4:
Tiger takes care of everything when you want to share a printer.

"Hey, what about my firewall? And don't I have to do anything on the Sharing pane in System Preferences?" Perhaps you would *if* you were using that Other Operating System — which shall remain nameless here — but you're using Tiger, and everything is set *automatically* for you the moment you click that check box! Tiger automatically opens the correct port in your firewall to allow printer sharing, and even turns on printer sharing for you. (And yes, if you decide not to share your printers and you disable the check box later, Tiger cleans up after you. It disables Printer Sharing and closes the port in your firewall on the Sharing pane in System Preferences.) Super-flippin' *sweet*.

The printers that you specify are available to other computers within the same IP subnet. In other words, someone in your local network is able to use your printers, but no one outside your network has access.

If you haven't already assigned a printer a descriptive name, launch the Printer Setup Utility, select the printer in the list, and press ⌘+I. This displays the Show Info dialog for that particular printer. With Name & Location chosen from the drop-down list, simply enter the name of your printer in the Printer Name text field. You can also identify that printer's location in the Location text field. For example, in an office environment, I like to add the room number to a shared printer name (as well as the Location field).

Chapter 5: Applications That You've (Probably) Gotta Have

In This Chapter

✔ Using Microsoft Office 2004 and AppleWorks

✔ Using disk repair applications

✔ Editing images

✔ Editing digital video

✔ Using Internet applications

✔ Burning discs with Toast

✔ Running Windows with Virtual PC

✔ Adding third-party utilities

✔ Playing games with Mac OS X

*I*n Chapter 1 of this mini-book, I present you with an overview of the most popular hardware that you can add to your Mac — and where there's hardware, software can't be far behind. (Somebody famous said that — I think it was either Bill Gates or Dennis Miller. I consider both of them famous comedians.)

Anyway, Mac OS X comes with a full suite of software tools right out of the box. You get Internet connectivity, disk repair, basic image editing, digital video editing, and — depending on the price that you paid or the Mac model that you bought — even games and a complete set of productivity applications. However, if you're willing to pay for additional features and a manual (at least what passes for a manual in the manufacturer's opinion), you can make all these tasks easier and accomplish them in shorter time.

Read on for an overview to the most popular third-party software applications for Mac OS X: what everyone's using, how much they cost, and why they're (usually) better. But before you drop a *wad* of cash on a fancy new application, though, remember yet another of Mark's Maxims:

> **If a program you already have does everything you really need, you *don't* have to upgrade. Honest and truly.™**

The Trundling Microsoft Mammoth

Yes, I know I've been poking fun at His Gateness for much of this book — you have to admit, he makes a pretty good target — but he *did* pull PC owners out of the character-based world of DOS, and I'll be the first to say that he does get things right from time to time.

For example, I've always been more impressed with Microsoft Office than I have been with Microsoft Windows. (At least Windows XP Professional is a step in the right direction, but it still has a long way to go to match Mac OS X.) Office has long been the productivity suite of choice in the Windows world, and it's also been a popular favorite in years past on the Macintosh side.

A lot of hard work was put into the latest version of Microsoft Office, and it shows. Office 2004 was designed specifically for Mac OS X, using the rules that Apple recommends for the Aqua user interface. As you can see in Figure 5-1, it looks as much like a native Mac OS X application as AppleWorks 6, which is Apple's competing office productivity suite.

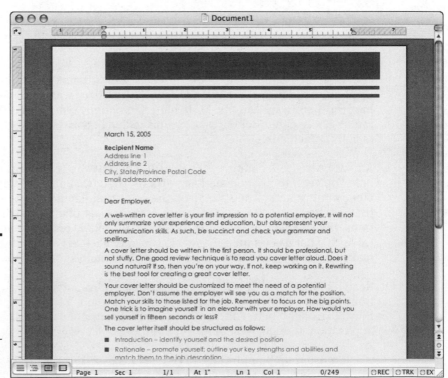

Figure 5-1: Man, that is one good-looking Office. Thanks, Microsoft — and I mean that.

What about AppleWorks?

If you're already using AppleWorks, you might have noticed that the Office applications provide roughly the same features. (The drawing and painting elements of AppleWorks are integrated into the Office 2004 suite.) Therefore, you might wonder whether you should scrap AppleWorks.

Remember my maxim — if the AppleWorks suite that you're familiar with is doing the job, I recommend that you keep it. After all, AppleWorks is a powerful productivity suite on its own, capable of producing results that are easily as good as Office 2004. Also, Apple does provide conversion filters that can allow you to open and save Office documents, so you're not isolated from the Office crowd. If you're still using Mac OS 9 on one or more of your Macs, I should also point out that

Office 2004 doesn't run under Mac OS 9 — but AppleWorks runs like clockwork on both Mac OS 9 and X. (Note that AppleWorks will eventually be phased out by Apple's new iWork suite.)

On the other side of the coin, I *would* recommend that you buy Office if

✔ You prefer the Office 2004 menu design and features.

✔ You'd like to keep most of the same commands replicated in the same places as the Windows version of Office.

✔ You want to seamlessly share documents with co-workers who use Windows Office on your network or through e-mail.

However, like Mac OS X itself, Office 2004 isn't just an attractive exterior. Consider some of the advantages of Office 2004:

✦ **Perfect document compatibility with the Windows version of Office:** You can both read and write documents with transparent ease, no matter which platform gets the file. Documents can be shared between platforms on the same network.

✦ **Mirrored commands:** Both the Windows XP and Mac OS X versions of Office share virtually identical menu items, dialogs, and settings, thus making Mac OS X instantly familiar to anyone who's used Office on a Windows PC.

✦ **Support for native Aqua features:** This includes transparent graphics within your documents, input and confirmation sheets, and palettes for formatting.

✦ **Tons of templates, samples, and support files:** Microsoft doesn't scrimp on ready-to-use documents and templates, as well as additional fonts, clip art, and Web samples.

✦ **Entourage:** *Entourage* (as shown in Figure 5-2) is the Macintosh counterpart to Windows Outlook. It combines most of the same features that you'll find in the Apple Mail, iCal, and Address Book applications. (Read about Apple Mail in Book IV, Chapter 2; read about the Address Book in Book I, Chapter 6.) Use Entourage to participate in Internet newsgroups; it also includes a Mailing List Manager to help you keep track of the deluge of list messages that you receive every day.

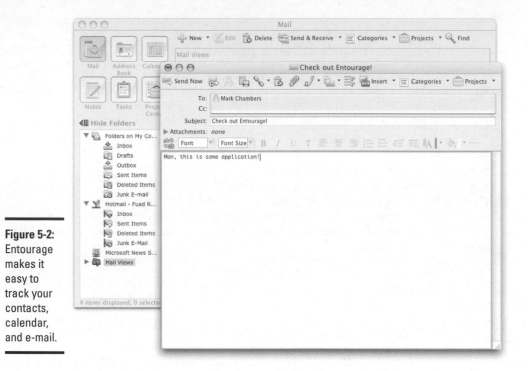

Figure 5-2:
Entourage
makes it
easy to
track your
contacts,
calendar,
and e-mail.

Besides Entourage, Office 2004 includes three other applications:

✦ **Word:** The word processing application that rules the planet

✦ **Excel:** The leading spreadsheet application

✦ **PowerPoint:** A favorite presentation development application

The Office 2004 for Mac Professional Edition suite costs about $500 at the time of this writing. You might save a few dollars if you buy it online from a Web store like Mac Warehouse (www.cdw.com).

Your Mac OS X Toolbox: Drive 10

My favorite native Mac OS X disk repair application is Drive 10 from Micromat (www.micromat.com).

More than just about any other type of application, it's important for a disk maintenance program to be built "from the ground up" for Mac OS X. **Never** attempt to repair a Mac OS X disk in Classic mode, nor should you try to use an older repair utility that was written for use under Mac OS 9.

With Drive 10 (shown in Figure 5-3), you can thoroughly check a hard drive for both *physical* errors (such as faulty electronics or a bad sector on the disk surface) and *logical* errors (incorrect folder data and glitches in the file structure). The Disk Utility that's included with Mac OS X does a fine job of checking the latter, but it doesn't perform the physical testing — and Drive 10 does both.

I should note, however, that Drive 10 doesn't take care of viruses. Pick up a copy of VirusBarrier X (www.intego.com) to protect yourself against viral attack.

Drive 10 also takes care of disk optimization, which is a feature that's been conspicuously absent from Mac OS X ever since the beginning. As I explain earlier in Book I, Chapter 7, defragmenting your disk will result in better performance and a faster system overall.

Drive 10, which will set you back about $70, comes on a self-booting CD-ROM so you can easily fix your startup volume by booting your system from the Drive 10 disc.

Image Editing for the Masses

The only one true King of the Retouching Hill in Mac OS X, Adobe Photoshop (www.adobe.com/products/photoshop) has been the digital-image editing favorite of Mac owners for many years now. Like Office 2004, the newest version of Photoshop (CS) also takes full advantage of the Aqua standard (see Figure 5-4).

**Book VI
Chapter 5**

**Applications That
You've (Probably)
Gotta Have**

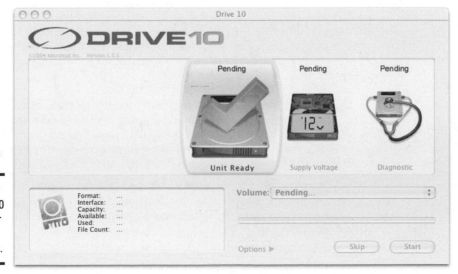

Figure 5-3:
Use Drive 10 to check for all sorts of drive errors.

Figure 5-4:
Photoshop cs includes just about every image tool known to man.

You can find more three-pound Photoshop books on the shelf than politicians in trouble, so it's no surprise that I can't provide you with a sweeping list of its features in this section. However, here's a summary of what you can expect from Adobe's crown jewel:

✦ **Superior editing:** The most sophisticated image editing possible for a digital photograph. If you can accomplish an image-editing task in software, it's very likely that Photoshop can do it. You can even combine and splice parts of different images to produce a new work of art or perhaps distort and liquefy an image to produce a new look.

✦ **Image retouching tools:** These help you rescue images with problems such as overexposure and color imbalance. (You can also use tools like the new Healing brush to erase imperfections in the photograph's subject.)

✦ **Plug-ins:** Photoshop has been a standard for plug-in functionality since it first appeared. If you need features that aren't in the application out of the box, you can add them through third-party plug-ins.

✦ **Web posting:** Prepare images for use on the Web.

✦ **Painting tools:** Use these gems to simulate different types of inks, paints, and brushes on different types of media.

Although Photoshop is a hefty $650 for the full package, Adobe has also created a kid brother, Photoshop Elements, that sells for a mere $90. Designed for the novice or intermediate level photographer, Elements has most of the functionality of the full package that you're likely to need. Elements also provides a number of very helpful wizards to help automate the most common image-editing tasks, as well as one of the most comprehensive Help systems that I've ever used.

The Morass of Digital Video

Two types of applications make up the DV market: *digital video editing* (in which you create a movie) and *DVD mastering* (in which you take that movie and create a DVD movie). You can find a number of great applications on the market in both of these categories, all at different price points and different levels of complexity. They include

✦ **iMovie HD:** I cover this easy-to-use video editing iApp in Book III, Chapter 4. A good choice for any novice, it's usually bundled for free with today's new Mac models, and you get it as part of the iLife suite. You might also receive it with Mac OS X.

✦ **iDVD:** This is the DVD mastering counterpart to iMovie. Although it's a snap to use, it doesn't offer a lot of advanced features. (Book III, Chapter 5 explains iDVD 5 in detail.) Again, you'll receive it free with your Mac if you bought a model with a SuperDrive.

✦ **DVD Studio Pro:** Apple's entry into the ranks of DVD mastering can produce a commercial-quality DVD movie disc, but don't expect any hand-holding or assistants with this application. This is a serious tool for professionals, and it'll set you back $500. With DVD Studio Pro 3 (www.apple.com/dvdstudiopro), you can add interactive, animated menus, subtitles, multiple audio tracks, and Web interactivity to your DVD projects.

✦ **Final Cut Pro HD:** At $1,000, you'd assume Final Cut Pro (www.apple.com/finalcutpro) to be the best DV editing package on the market for Mac OS X . . . and you won't get any argument from me. It offers real-time playback with RT Extreme HD — no waiting for rendering, like you have to within iMovie — and high definition support over a FireWire connection. Sassy.

Yes, It's Really Called "Toast"

Time to turn your attention to a subject near and dear to my heart: recording data CDs, audio CDs, and DVDs on the Macintosh (which I cover in detail in another of my *For Dummies* books, *CD & DVD Recording For Dummies,* 2nd Edition (Wiley). Of course, Mac OS X can burn basic data CDs that you can share with your Windows and UNIX friends without any add-on software. If you have a Mac equipped with a SuperDrive, you can also create standard, cross-platform data DVDs, too. But what if you need an exotic format, like CD Extra, where data and digital audio tracks can co-exist peacefully on one disc? Or perhaps you need a self-booting disc?

There's one clear choice: When you're ready to seriously burn, you're ready for Roxio Toast Titanium (www.roxio.com), the CD and DVD recording choice for millions of Mac owners. (No snickering about the name, please.) Figure 5-5 illustrates this powerhouse of an application, which is an elegant design that's both simple to use and perfectly Aqua. Files, folders, and digital audio tracks that you want to record are simply dropped into the application window.

As for exotic formats, here's a list of what types of discs that you can record with Toast:

✦ Standard data CDs and DVDs

✦ Standard audio CDs

✦ Video CDs

✦ MP3 discs (which store MP3 audio tracks)

✦ Discs recorded from an image file

✦ Mac volumes

✦ Hybrid PC/Mac discs

✦ ISO 9660 discs

✦ Multisession discs

✦ CD Extra discs

Toast works with both internal and external CD and DVD recorders, taking advantage of the latest features on today's drives — in particular, *burn-proof* recording, which can practically eliminate recording errors. You can also copy existing discs, using one or multiple drives.

Toast is quite affordable at $90. You can buy it directly from the Roxio online store at www.roxio.com.

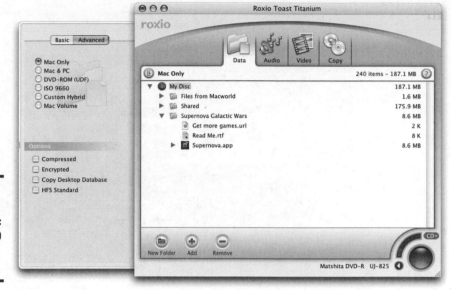

Figure 5-5:
Toast is the
classic Mac
CD and DVD
recording
application.

If You Positively Have to Run Windows . . .

Here's where Mac power users usually start grinning from ear to ear like Santa's elves on the day after Christmas, because — get this — the great Unwashed Windows Horde actually thinks that you *can't* run Windows XP on a Macintosh! Can you believe that? Obviously, they haven't heard of Virtual PC 7 from Microsoft (www.microsoft.com/mac), which without a doubt is one of the coolest applications ever written for the Mac.

No, my friend, your eyes are not deceiving you — you are indeed looking at Windows 2000 running on my iMac G5 in Figure 5-6. Virtual PC 7 (which requires Mac OS X) provides a near-perfect PC environment for any version of Windows from 95 all the way up to XP; literally, Windows has *no* idea that it's not running on a typical piece of PC iron.

Virtual PC simulates everything necessary for you to get the full functionality out of Windows. For example, this jewel automatically (and transparently) handles your Windows Internet connection, network tasks, and CD and DVD access. Heck, it even allows you to use your single-button mouse as a two-button PC mouse (by holding down the Control key while you click). You can run full-screen or run Windows in a window. (Pun joyfully intended.)

If that weren't enough, you can also run multiple operating systems. So, if you need Linux or Windows 2000 along with your XP system, no problem — all it takes is the install disc for those operating systems and the hard drive space to hold 'em. Just plain *sassy*.

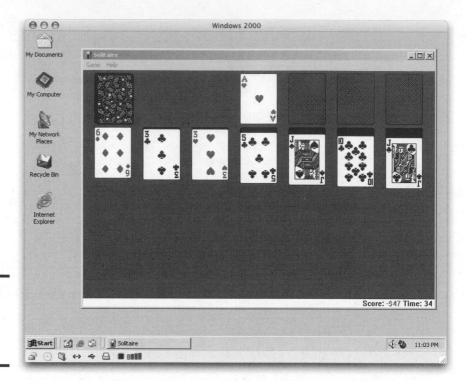

Figure 5-6:
Take *that*,
Bill! I get
to play in
your pool.

Naturally, performance is an issue — and, to be honest, Virtual PC isn't for the PC gamer, even with the newest Macs and their super-duper GeForce and Radeon video cards. Because today's PC games push an actual PC to the limit, they just run too sluggishly on a Mac emulating a PC — they do run, just too slowly. (Also, virtually all of today's blockbuster PC games are also being ported to Mac OS X, so why not just run the Mac version?)

However, when it comes to just about any other type of application, Virtual PC running on a late-model G5 Mac can deliver performance equal to a Pentium 4 PC. The more memory that your Mac has, the more you can give your virtual PC, so it also pays to have 512MB or more of RAM. (And naturally, a dual-processor Mac runs Virtual PC much faster.) I use Virtual PC with niche Windows programs that have never appeared on the Mac as well as native Mac versions of all other applications. Again, you don't need to use Mac to run the Windows version of Photoshop CS because Photoshop CS is also available for the Mac.

If you're tired of the undeserved taunts from your clueless Windows friends, run — don't walk — to your browser and order a copy of Virtual PC 7. The program comes prepackaged with fully licensed copies of several different flavors of Windows and Linux. For example, the version with XP Home costs around $200 — or you can buy a version without an operating system for about $120 and supply your own copy of Windows.

All Hail FileMaker Pro

If databases are the name of your game, you've already been using FileMaker Pro for years (on both Mac and Windows, more than likely). For the uninitiated, *FileMaker Pro* (www.filemakerpro.com) is the premier database creation, editing, and maintenance application for Mac OS X. It comes with dozens of ready-made database templates for business, home, and education use, or you can construct your own database in surprisingly short order.

Right out of the box, FileMaker Pro 7 can create

✦ **Business** databases and forms for inventory, personnel, purchase orders, and product catalogs

✦ **Home** databases for budgeting, recipes, music CDs, DVD movies, family medical records, and event planning

✦ **Education** databases for student records, expense reports, field trip planning, book and multimedia libraries, and class scheduling

FileMaker Pro 7 can add images and multimedia to your database, and you can quickly and easily publish your databases on your Web site by using one of the built-in theme designs. (In fact, visitors to your Web site can update your database online, if you like.) FileMaker Pro can also allow multiple users to share data across your network, no matter whether they're running the Mac or Windows version.

At $299, FileMaker Pro 7 is one of the least expensive — and most powerful — applications that you can buy for the Big X. For a comprehensive yet easy-to-read book on FileMaker Pro 7, check out *FileMaker Pro 7 Bible* by Steven A. Schwartz and Dennis R. Cohen (Wiley).

Utilities That Rock

The next stop on this Cavalcade of Software is an assortment of the absolute best you've-got-to-get-this utility applications. Sooner or later, you're likely going to buy (or register) these utilities because you'll use them every day.

StuffIt

In the Windows world, the Zip archive is the king of archiving formats. An *archive* contains one or more compressed files that you can uncompress whenever you need them. Folks store files in archives to save space on their hard drives; archiving is also a neat way to package an entire folder's worth of files in a single convenient file, which you can attach to an e-mail message or send via File Transfer Protocol (FTP).

On Planet Macintosh, the archiving format of choice is StuffIt. Manage your archives with StuffIt Deluxe, from Allume Systems (www.allume.com), as shown in Figure 5-7. StuffIt Deluxe can both archive and unarchive .sit files (the common name for StuffIt archives) as well as Zip archives from your Windows friends. You can also encrypt the contents of a StuffIt archive for those "sensitive" transfers. The application runs $80 at the Allume Systems online Web store.

Figure 5-7:
Checking the contents of a StuffIt archive.

QuicKeys X

QuicKeys X, from CE Software (www.cesoft.com), is another example of someone's thinking properly. This time, the idea is to automate repetitive tasks by allowing Mac OS X to memorize what you do. Think of QuicKeys X as a system-wide, macro playback application. Unlike AppleScript, however, QuicKeys X works within any application and can play back mouse movement and clicks/double-clicks. (And unlike Automator, which is new in Tiger, you can perform *any* action that you could normally perform within an application by typing.)

I've used QuicKeys X for a number of different tasks, including

✦ Typing a commonly used block of text (like my address) into applications that don't support macros

✦ Launching applications at specific times and dates

✦ Operating menus within programs to automate complex tasks

✦ Launching Classic or choosing a specific startup disk with a single key sequence

QuicKeys X sells for $100 on the CE Software Web site.

BBEdit

Although we all know and love Mac OS X as a graphical operating system, folks still need a powerful text editor for creating and modifying text files. For example, software developers and Webmasters still use text editors daily to write applications or apply a quick fix to the HyperText Markup Language (HTML) that makes up a Web page. (I use a text editor to make minor changes to my Web site, MLC Books Online, without firing up a horrendous Web design application. Talk about overkill!)

At first, you might think of TextEdit, which is the free application that ships with Mac OS X. It's not a bad editor, either, with features that are very similar to Notepad in the Windows environment. However, serious text and code editing requires a more powerful tool, and the text editor of choice for Mac owners is universally considered to be BBEdit, from Bare Bones Software (`www.barebones.com`). Figure 5-8 shows a document open within BBEdit 8.

Bare Bones Software pulls no punches in describing BBEdit — its advertising still proclaims, "It doesn't suck." Gotta give Bare Bones credit; this incredibly popular editor includes features like

✦ **Support for DOS/Windows, Mac, and UNIX text files:** Yes, differences do exist between the platforms, even with a so-called *pure* text file.

✦ **Works with text files up to 2GB in size:** Try that with TextEdit. Hmm . . . on second thought, please don't.

✦ **HTML tools for Web design:** These tools include syntax checking and browser preview.

✦ `grep` **pattern-based, multifile search and replace:** In non-programmer/ non-UNIX English, that means a very sophisticated search-and-replace function that can span more than one text file.

✦ **Syntax coloring:** Use this to help you quickly locate commands and qualifiers in programming languages.

✦ **Built-in FTP transfer commands:** No need to launch a separate FTP application: You can send your files right from within BBEdit.

Figure 5-8:
For editing
text, you'll
find no
better tool
than BBEdit.

You can even expand the functionality of BBEdit with plug-ins, many of which
are free extensions written by programmers and developers specifically for
languages like C/C++, Java/JavaScript, Perl, and Pascal.

BBEdit 8 is available from the Bare Bones Software site for $199.

REALbasic

The final application that I want to mention really isn't a utility as such; how-
ever, you can use it to write your own software, so I guess that it should qualify.
As an ex-COBOL programmer, reluctant Visual Basic shareware developer, and
recalcitrant dBASE coder, I can tell you that REALbasic (from REAL Software)
is definitely the easiest visual drag-and-drop programming environment that
I've ever used. If you want to develop your own productivity applications,
Mac OS X utilities, or — dare I say it? your own game! — award-winning
REALbasic is the way to go.

Development in REALbasic is as simple as designing the application window
by first simply adding controls, text, and multimedia wherever you like. Then
just fill in the blanks, like setting variables and specifying what happens when

the controls are triggered, by using a new implementation of the tried-and-true BASIC language. Of course, some programming knowledge is required but far less than you'd need with Visual Basic. And the results look as good as anything you can accomplish in those so-called *real* programming languages.

Check out these features:

✦ **Cross-platform support** so that you can write your program once and compile it for Linux, Mac OS X, *and* Windows. Code it once; then release three versions with no extra work — this is a *very* superb thing.

✦ **Support for all sorts of multimedia,** including QuickTime.

✦ Ability to **animate and rotate text and objects,** or tap the 3-D power of QuickDraw3D and OpenGL graphics.

✦ Capability to **allow printing, network, and Internet communications** within your application.

✦ **Automation of Microsoft Office applications** and connection of your REALbasic application to business databases (like FileMaker Pro 7).

✦ **Completely royalty-free applications,** so you can give them away or release them as shareware.

REALbasic has been such a popular development tool on the Macintosh that dozens of user-supported Web sites and mailing lists have sprung up, offering all sorts of REALbasic plug-ins, tutorials, and sample code for you to use in your own projects.

I would be seriously remiss if I didn't mention the bestselling *REALbasic For Dummies,* written by Erick Tejkowski (Wiley). I've practically worn out my copy, and it never leaves my desk. If you're looking for a complete tutorial on writing your own applications in REALbasic, I give *REALbasic For Dummies* my highest recommendation!

REALbasic 5.5 comes in two versions — the Standard Edition ($149.95) and the Professional Edition ($449.95). You can order either version from the REAL Software site at www.realsoftware.com.

At Least One Game

To be completely accurate, Mac OS X already comes with at least one game — a very good version of chess, which I cover in the next section — but the Macintosh has never been considered a true gaming platform by most computer owners. Until recently, many popular Windows games were never ported (or converted) for the Mac, and only the most expensive Mac models had the one important component that determines the quality of today's games: a first-rate, 3-D video card.

However, within the last two years or so, all that has changed dramatically. *All* of today's Mac models feature muscle-car-quality video cards that use the NVIDIA GeForce or ATI Radeon chipsets; they can handle the most complex 3-D graphics with ease. Match that with the renewed popularity of the Macintosh as a home computer and the performance of the current crop of G4 and G5 processors, and — wham! Suddenly you've got the best game developers in the business — id Software (`www.idsoftware.com`) and Blizzard (`www.blizzard.com`), to name two — releasing Macintosh versions of their newest games concurrently with the Windows version.

For the gamer in you, allow me to take you on a tour of the best of the new generation of entertainment.

Mac OS X Chess

No mercenaries, no rail guns, and no cities to raze — but chess is still the world's most popular game, and Mac OS X even includes a little 3-D as well. Figure 5-9 illustrates the Chess application at play; you'll find it in your Applications folder.

The game features speech recognition, move hints, take back (or undo) for your last move, and a 2-D or 3-D board. You can also list your games in text form and print them or save games in progress. Maybe it's not a complete set of bells and whistles like commercial chess games, but the price is right, and the play can be quite challenging when you set it at the higher skill levels.

Nanosaur 2

It's not hard to understand why Apple has bundled this 3-D dinosaur adventure game with many of the latest Macintosh models: The graphics are simply out of this world! You have complete three-dimensional freedom, flying a pterodactyl throughout the skies of prehistoric times in search of stolen dinosaur eggs. There's a series of two-player levels as well.

You'll encounter evil in many forms: automated defenses, other dinosaurs, and far worse. There are a wide range of power-ups and weapons in this 3-D shooter. Enemies are smart and hard to beat, and the immersive audio environment is incredible when experienced through a good set of headphones or a speaker system equipped with a subwoofer. (Read about beefing up your sound system in Book VI, Chapter 1.)

Graphics are literally the best you can get on the Mac, using all the tricks offered by those GeForce and Radeon cards. Optional graphics features that will make any Windows gamer nervous include

✦ Highest-quality, 32-bit textures

✦ Resolutions up to 1280 x 800 widescreen

✦ Support for 3-D glasses (both the old-style paper kind and today's latest electronic LCD shutter glasses)

Figure 5-9:
Tiger says,
"How about
a nice game
of chess?"

The game sells for $25 at the Pangea Software site, www.pangeasoft.net. Note: This game comes with a new Mac, not with Tiger.

WarCraft III

To finish my survey of must-have games, I'll end with Blizzard's best: WarCraft III. This heady mixture of RTS (short for real-time strategy) and RPG (short for role-playing game) is yet another sequel in another popular game series. WarCraft III puts you in the boots of human princes, Orc battle generals, undead champions, and elfin lords — in fact, in single player mode, you'll play each of these warrior races in turn. My recommendation: Stick with the Night Elves, my friend.

Combat, however, is only half of the job. Each mission is different; typically, you also have to gather resources by mining gold and cutting trees while you build new structures and train new troops. You can take to the air, buy goods from mercenaries, or even hire goblins to do your dirty work (if you have the gold handy). Spells abound, as do siege weapons and mounted warriors. (Personally, my favorite units have to be the living guardian trees of the Night Elves, which toss boulders. I want one of those — a friendly one, mind you — in my backyard.)

Although visually stunning, WarCraft III is no first-person game. Instead, you view the action from an overhead perspective, as you can see in Figure 5-10. Control is by both keyboard and mouse; the game is easy to learn, but you'll always find someone to kick your posterior in multiplayer games, both over the Internet and across your own local area network (LAN).

You'll find the storyline in this game riveting — it keeps you playing with its twists and turns. Your units include heroes, which are no static figureheads. As they gain experience, you can teach them new skills and outfit them with all sorts of magical items.

You'll pay about $30 online for WarCraft III, and it'll be worth every single penny you spend. (This is a program you'd buy on your own; it does not come with your Mac or with Tiger.) For all the details and some great desktop backgrounds, check the official site at `www.blizzard.com/war3`. (Oh, and don't forget: After you complete the original WarCraft III, you can continue the adventure with the Frozen Throne expansion pack, which sells for around $20 online.)

Figure 5-10: A grand tale of warfare, magic, and alliances — it must be WarCraft III.

Book VII

Advanced Mac OS X

The 5th Wave — By Rich Tennant

"Sure, at first it sounded great—an intuitive network adapter that helps people write memos by finishing their thoughts for them."

Contents at a Glance

Chapter 1: . . . And UNIX Lurks Beneath

In This Chapter

✔ **Why use UNIX?**

✔ **Doing things with the keyboard**

✔ **Introducing UNIX commands**

✔ **Creating text files**

✔ **Exploring deep inside Mac OS X**

As I mention in the first chapter of the book — at the beginning of our Tiger odyssey — UNIX lurks deep beneath the shiny Aqua exterior of Mac OS X. UNIX is a tried-and-true operating system that has been around for decades, since the days when mainframe computers were king. If you don't believe that it's a powerful (and popular) operating system, consider that over half of all Web servers on the Internet use some variety of UNIX as their operating system of choice.

Besides being battle-tested and having a long history, UNIX also offers some fantastic features. Unlike the graphical world of Mac OS X, the keyboard plays an integral role while you're using a UNIX-based operating system. Because UNIX is text-based, you'll find that it has evolved a large set of useful keyboard-driven commands that can perform powerful feats that a mouse user just can't easily equal. This chapter examines the role of the keyboard in UNIX operating systems and describes how to execute standard file system commands. You also discover how to use Apple's additional set of commands and install your own commands (and simple programs) from the Internet.

Why Use the Keyboard?

To begin benefiting from the UNIX underpinnings of Mac OS X, get used to doing things with the keyboard. Although mouse skills can be applied to UNIX, you'll generally find performing UNIX functions faster and easier with the keyboard.

UNIX keyboarding is fast

Why on Earth would any red-blooded Macintosh owner want to leave the comfort of the mouse to use a keyboard? After all, the graphical user interface is what made the Macintosh great in the first place. With the Finder, you can navigate and manage the various files on your hard drive with a few clicks. This sounds simple enough, but for some tasks, using the keyboard can be just as fast, if not faster.

Suppose, for example, that you need to copy a file from somewhere on your hard drive to somewhere else on that same drive. To do so with the Finder, you must first open a Finder window (by clicking the Finder icon on the Dock, or by double-clicking a drive icon on your Desktop). Then, by using a succession of mouse clicks, you navigate to where the file that you wish to copy resides. Next, you might open another Finder window and navigate to the folder where you wish to copy the file. (Note that opening the second Finder window requires pressing ⌘+N; clicking the Finder icon on the Dock does not open a second Finder window.) Finally, you duplicate the original file and drag that copy to its intended destination.

Comparatively, by using the keyboard and the power of UNIX, you can accomplish the same task with a one-line command. For some tasks, the mouse is definitely the way to go, but you can perform some tasks just as quickly, if not faster, with the keyboard. For the skinny on one-line commands, skip down to the upcoming section, "Uncovering the Terminal."

The UNIX keyboard is a powerful beast

So maybe you're not an expert typist, and using the mouse still sounds inviting. For many scenarios, you'd be correct in assuming that a mouse can handle the job just as quickly and easily as a bunch of commands that you have to memorize. Using the keyboard, however, offers some other distinct advantages over the mouse. To allow you to control your computer from the keyboard, all UNIX operating systems offer the *command line tool*. With this tool, you can enter commands one line at a time: hence, its name. Mac OS X ships with the command line application, Terminal. You can find it here:

```
/Applications/Utilities/Terminal
```

One shining feature of the command line is its efficiency. To wit: When you use a mouse, one mouse click is equal to one command. When you use the command line, on the other hand, you aren't limited to entering one command at a time; rather, you can combine commands into a kind of *super-command* (minus the silly cape, but with bulging muscles intact), with each command performing some action of the combined whole. By using the command line, you can string together a whole bunch of commands to do a very complex task.

For example, consider how many times you'd have to click a mouse in the Finder to do the following:

1. Find all files that begin with the letters *MyDocument.*

2. From this list of files, add a number to the beginning of the filename, indicating its size in kilobytes.

3. Save the names of all altered files to a text file.

By using the command line, you could accomplish all these tasks by typing only one super-command: that is, a collection of three simple commands combined to form one instruction. The built-in Terminal program that ships with Mac OS X Tiger gives you everything that you need to start using the command line. I show you how in the section "Uncovering the Terminal," later in this chapter.

Delving farther into super-commands is not for the faint-hearted; things get pretty ugly pretty quickly, and this chapter can only show you the very beginning of the UNIX Yellow Brick Road. Therefore, if your thirst for UNIX dominance so compels you, I invite you to do a little independent study to bone up on the operating system. Pick up a copy of the great book of lore entitled *UNIX For Dummies,* 5th Edition, written by John R. Levine and Margaret Levine Young (Wiley).

Go where no mouse has gone before

The Finder is generally a helpful thing, but it makes many assumptions about how you work. One of these assumptions is that you don't have any need to handle some of the files on your hard drive. As I mention in Book II, Chapter 6, Mac OS X ships with its system files marked Off Limits, and I generally agree with that policy (which keeps anyone from screwing up the delicate innards of Mac OS X). To secure your system files, Apple purposely hides some files from view.

But what road do you take if you actually need to view or modify those system files? Yep, you guessed it: The command line comes to the rescue! You can use the command line to peer inside every nook and cranny of your Mac's vast directory structure on your hard drive. It also has the power to edit files that aren't normally accessible to you. With the command line, you can pretend to be other users — even users with more permissions. By temporarily acting as another more powerful user, you can perform actions with the command line that would be impossible in the Finder. (Just remember to make sure that you know *exactly* what you're doing, or you're working with an Apple technical support person — a wrong move, and it'll be time for an Ominous Chord.)

Book VII
Chapter 1

... And UNIX Lurks
Beneath

Automate to elevate

If all these benefits are beginning to excite you, hold on to your socks! Not only can you perform complex commands with the command line, you can go even one step further: *automation.* If you find yourself using the same set of commands more than once, you're a likely candidate for using automation to save time. Instead of typing the list of commands each time, you can save them to a text file and execute the entire file with only one command. Now that's power!

Of course, you probably don't like doing housekeeping tasks while you're busy on other things, so schedule that list of commands to run in the middle of the night while you're fast asleep. The command line lets you do that, too.

Note that automation of UNIX commands is totally separate from automation of Mac OS X applications with AppleScript and Automator, which I cover in Book VII, Chapter 2.

Remote control

"So, Mark, the command line is the cat's meow for efficiently accessing and working with files on my Mac, and I can use it to automate many operations. Anything else?" I'm glad you asked! By using the command line, you can also send commands to another computer anywhere in the world (as long as you know the right login and password). After you log into another computer, you can use the same commands for the remote computer.

UNIX was created with multiple users in mind. Because computers used to be expensive (and honking huge machines to boot), UNIX was designed so that multiple users could remotely use the same machine simultaneously. In fact, if Mac OS X is your first encounter with UNIX, you might be surprised to know that many UNIX beginners of the past weren't even in the same room, building, state, or even country as the computer that they were using.

Not only can you work with a computer that's in a different physical location, but it's also very fast to do so. Instead of the bandwidth hog that is the Internet, the command line is lean and mean. This permits you to use a remote computer nearly as fast as if it were sitting on the desk in front of you. (This is a great advantage for road warriors who need to tweak a Web, an e-mail, or an FTP server from a continent away.)

Uncovering the Terminal

The best way to learn how to use command line is to jump right in. Mac OS X comes stocked with an application named *Terminal.* The Terminal application is where you enter commands in the command line. It is located in the Utilities folder within the Applications folder on your hard drive — choose Applications⇨Utilities.

Double-click the icon shown in Figure 1-1 to launch Terminal.

Figure 1-1:
Find the
Terminal
application
in your
Utilities
folder.

By the way, feel free to make Terminal more accessible by dragging its icon to the Dock or the toolbar. That way, you won't have to dive this deep into the Applications folder in the future.

What's a prompt?

Upon launch of the Terminal application, you'll immediately notice some text in the window that appears onscreen.

```
Last login: Sun Jun 23 17:51:14 on console
Welcome to Darwin!
[WHITEDRAGON:~] markchambers$
```

As you might guess, this text details the last time that you logged into the Terminal, followed by a greeting from the Darwin underbelly of Mac OS X. (As I mention in Chapter 1 of Book I, *Darwin* is Apple's name for the UNIX underpinnings of Mac OS X.) The last line, however, is the most important one. It's called the *prompt*.

The prompt serves some important functions. First, it lists the current directory, which is listed as ~. A tilde character (~) denotes a user's Home directory. By default, you will always be in your Home folder each time that you begin a new session on the Terminal. After the current directory, the Terminal displays the name of the current user, which is markchambers in this example.

The final character of the prompt is a $. Consider this your cue because immediately after this character is where you enter any command that you wish to execute. Go ahead; don't be shy. Try out your first command by typing **uptime** in the Terminal application. (It's a good idea to type UNIX commands in lowercase.) Your text appears at the location of the cursor, denoted by a small square. If you make a mistake while entering the command, press the Delete key to back up and then type the characters again. (If the typing error is stuck deep in a longer command, press the left- or right-arrow key to move the cursor immediately after the incorrect character and press Delete to back up; then type the correct characters.) After you type the command, press Return to execute it.

```
[WHITEDRAGON:~] markchambers$ uptime
6:24PM  up  2:42, 4 users, load averages: 2.44, 2.38, 1.90
[WHITEDRAGON:~] markchambers$
```

If all goes well, you should see a listing of how long your Mac has been running since the last reboot or login. In the example listing, the computer has been running for 2 hours and 42 minutes (2:42 in line 2). Simple, eh? Immediately following the listing of the uptime command, the Terminal displays another prompt for you to enter more commands. I examine many more commands later in this chapter.

A few commands to get started

Using the command line is simply a matter of entering simple instructions — or *commands* — into the Terminal application and pressing Return to execute them. It's easy to use the command line to navigate through the various folders on your hard drive. You'll become accustomed to using two vital commands: ls and cd. The ls command is shorthand for *list,* and it does just that: It lists the contents of the current directory. Enter **ls** at your prompt, and you should see a listing of your Home folder as shown in Figure 1-2.

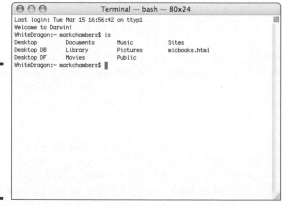

Figure 1-2: See the contents of your Home directory after entering the ls command.

The complementary cd command (lowercase) — which incidentally stands for *change directory* — opens any folder that you specify. It works much the same as double-clicking a folder in the Finder: The difference is that following the cd command, you don't immediately see all of the folder's content.

However, the cd command requires a *parameter* (extra options or information that appear after the command) so that your Mac knows which folder to open.

For example, to open the Documents folder that resides in your Home directory, type **cd Documents** and press Return. When you do, you might be surprised to see another prompt immediately displayed. So where are all the files in the Documents folder? You must enter another command to see what items are in the folder that you just opened. Type **ls** again to see the contents of the Documents folder, as shown in Figure 1-3.

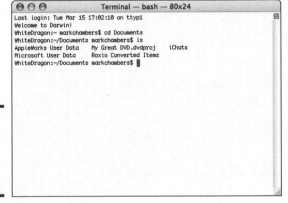

```
●●●             Terminal — bash — 80x24
Last login: Tue Mar 15 17:02:10 on ttyp1
Welcome to Darwin!
WhiteDragon:~ markchambers$ cd Documents
WhiteDragon:~/Documents markchambers$ ls
AppleWorks User Data    My Great DVD.dvdproj    iChats
Microsoft User Data     Roxio Converted Items
WhiteDragon:~/Documents markchambers$ █
```

Figure 1-3:
Use the cd command to switch directories.

If you try to open a folder that has a space in its name, make sure to enclose the folder's name in quotes, like this:

```
cd "My Picture Folder"
```

Read more about using quotes in your commands in the upcoming section, "Command line gotchas."

To return to your Home folder, enter a modified version of the cd command:

```
cd ..
```

This causes your Mac to move back up the folder hierarchy one folder to your Home directory. By using these three simple commands — ls, cd *foldername*, and cd .. — you can traverse your entire hard drive.

After you successfully enter a command, you can recall it by pressing the up-arrow key. Press the up-arrow key again to see the command prior to that, and so forth. This is an extremely useful trick for retyping extra long file paths.

Using the skills you already have

Just because the Terminal is text-based doesn't mean that it doesn't act like a good Macintosh citizen. All the usual Mac features that you know and love are there for you to use. Copy and Paste functions work as you might expect — but only at the prompt position.

Drag-and-drop is also at your disposal. After you play around with the Terminal for a while, you'll find yourself bored to tears typing the long paths that represent the files on your hard drive. To automatically enter the path of a file or folder to a command, simply drag it to the active Terminal window, as shown in Figure 1-4. The file's full path instantly appears at the location of your cursor. (Thanks, Apple!)

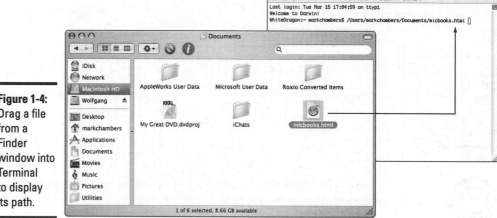

Figure 1-4: Drag a file from a Finder window into Terminal to display its path.

You can even use the mouse while entering commands in the Terminal. Click and drag your mouse over text to select it. From there, you can copy to the Clipboard as you might expect with any other application.

UNIX Commands 101

To use the command line effectively, you need to familiarize yourself with the commands that are available to you. After all, how can you use a tool without knowing what it can do? Despite having to memorize a few commands, UNIX usually makes it easy on you by abbreviating commands, by following a standard grammar (so to speak), and by providing you with extensive documentation for each command.

Anatomy of a UNIX command

UNIX commands can perform many amazing feats. Despite their vast abilities, all commands follow a similar structure:

```
command <optional flag(s)> <optional operand(s)>
```

The simplest form of a UNIX command is the command itself. (For a basic discussion on UNIX commands such as ls, see the earlier section, "A few commands to get started.") You can expand your use of the ls command by appending various *flags,* which are settings that enable or disable optional features for the command. Flags are preceded by a dash (-) and always follow the command. For instance, you can display the contents of a directory as a column of names by tacking on an -l flag to the ls command.

```
ls -l
```

Besides flags, UNIX commands sometimes also have operands. An *operand* is something that is acted upon. For example, instead of just entering the ls command, which lists the current directory, you can add an operand to list a specific directory:

```
ls ~/Documents/myProject/
```

The tilde (~) denotes the user's Home directory.

Sometimes a command can take multiple operands, as is the case when you copy a file. The two operands represent the source file and the destination of the file that you want to copy, separated by a space. The following example copies a text file from the Documents folder to the Desktop folder by using the cp command (short for *copy*).

```
cp ~/Documents/MyDocument ~/Desktop/MyDocument
```

You can also combine flags and operands in the same command. This example displays the contents of a specific folder in list format:

```
ls -l ~/Documents/myProject/
```

Command line gotchas

In earlier sections, I describe a few simple command line functions. All these commands have something in common: You might not have noticed, but every example thus far involved folder names and filenames that contained only alphanumeric characters. Remember what happens if you have a folder name that has a space in it? Try the following example, but don't worry when it won't work.

**Book VII
Chapter 1**

...And UNIX Lurks
Beneath

The cd command stands for *change directory*.

```
cd /Desktop Folder
```

The result is an error message:

```
-bash: cd: /Desktop: No such file or directory
```

The problem is that a space character is not allowed in a path. To get around this problem, simply enclose the path in double quotation marks, like this:

```
cd "/Desktop Folder"
```

Mac OS X lets you use either double *or* single quotation marks to enclose a path with spaces in it. Standard UNIX operating systems, however, use double quotation marks for this purpose.

In a similar vein, you can get the space character to be accepted by a command by adding an escape character. To *escape* a character, add a backslash (\) immediately prior to the character in question. To illustrate, try the last command with an escape character instead. Note that this time, no quotation marks are necessary.

```
cd /Desktop\ Folder
```

You can use either quotes or escape characters because they're interchangeable.

Help is on the way!

By now, you might be wondering how a computer techno-wizard is supposed to keep all these commands straight. Fortunately, you can find generous documentation for nearly every command available to you. To access this built-in help, use the man command. Using the man command (shorthand for *manual*) will display a help file for any command that it knows about. For example, to read the available help information for the ls command, simply type **man ls** at the prompt. Figure 1-5 illustrates the result.

Autocompletion

To speed things along, the bash shell can auto-magically complete your input for you while you type. Although the Terminal permits you to enter commands via the keyboard, it is the shell that interprets those commands. Many kinds of shells are available to UNIX users. The shell that Tiger uses by default is named `bash` — another common shell is named `tcsh`. Use the autocompletion features of `bash` to autocomplete both commands and filenames. To demonstrate, begin by typing the following:

```
cd ~/De
```

Then press the Tab key. This result is that the shell predicts that you will want to type

```
cd ~/Desktop/
```

Of course, if you have another folder that begins with the letters *De* in the same folder, you might need to type a few additional characters. This gives the autocompletion feature more information to help it decide which characters you want to type. In other words, if you don't type enough characters, autocompletion ends up like a detective without enough clues to figure things out.

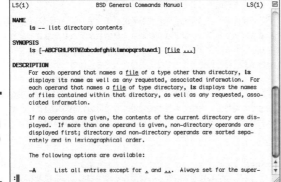

Figure 1-5:
Use the man command to display help information.

Book VII Chapter 1

. . . And UNIX Lurks Beneath

Working with Files

If you've used a computer for any time at all, you're no doubt familiar with the idea of files. Even before the first floppy drive appeared in personal computers, operating systems have stored data in files . . . they date back to the days when a mainframe computer occupied an entire floor of an office building. Mac OS X is no exception, and it's important to understand how Mac OS X arranges them into folders and how you go about accessing them via the command line. This section describes the basic file and folder information that you need to know to tame the beast that is UNIX.

Paths

Before you dive into UNIX commands, you should first know a few facts . . . nasty things, facts, but you can't earn your pair of techno-wizard suspenders without 'em. For starters, as a Mac user, you might not be familiar with how paths work in UNIX. A *path* is simply a textual representation of a folder or file. The simplest path is your Home directory, which is denoted by a tilde character (~) — the tilde character acts as the equivalent of /Users/<your short account name> (in my case, /Users/markchambers). Any folder within the Home directory is represented by the folder's name preceded by a forward slash (/). For example, a document entitled myDoc that resides in the current user's Documents folder would have a path like this:

~/Documents/myDoc

Similarly, a folder named *myFolder* that resides in the current user's Documents folder would have a path like this:

~/Documents/myFolder/

 As you've probably surmised, a *folder* and a *directory* are two different names for the same thing. *Folder* is the name with which most Mac users are familiar, and *directory* is a term that UNIX power users prefer. I use the terms interchangeably throughout the remainder of the chapter.

Because Mac OS X is a multi-user environment, you might sometimes want to work with folders or files somewhere other than in your Home folder. Starting from your Home folder, enter the following command:

cd ..

This will move you to the folder right above your Home folder, which happens to be the Users folder. Using another quick ls command will show you all users who are permitted to use the machine, as shown in Figure 1-6. In this figure, you can see the three users that are allowed to use this machine: markchambers, baberuth, and fuadramses. (By the way, Shared isn't a user — it's a folder with privileges set so that any user can access its contents.)

Enter **cd ..** once again, and you find yourself at the root of your main hard drive. The *root directory* is what you see in the Finder when you double-click your hard drive icon on the desktop. A user's Home directory is represented by a tilde character (~), and the root of the hard drive is denoted by a forward slash (/), as displayed by the prompt:

[WHITEDRAGON:/] markchambers$

```
000          Terminal — bash — 80x24
Last login: Tue Mar 15 17:08:48 on ttyp1
Welcome to Darwin!
WhiteDragon:~ markchambers$ cd ..
WhiteDragon:/Users markchambers$ ls
Shared        baberuth       fuadramses       markchambers
WhiteDragon:/Users markchambers$ █
```

Figure 1-6:
The Users
directory
displays all
usernames
permitted to
use this
Mac.

It's easy to return to your Home directory by following this sequence:

```
[WHITEDRAGON:/] markchambers$ cd Users
[WHITEDRAGON:/Users] markchambers$ cd markchambers
[WHITEDRAGON:~] markchambers$
```

Here's a faster way. Instead of moving through each successive folder until you reach your intended destination, you can specify the path by using just one cd command:

```
[WHITEDRAGON:/] markchambers$ cd /Users/markchambers
[WHITEDRAGON:~] markchambers$
```

Of course, the Home directory is a special folder in that you can also navigate there by simply entering **cd ~**, but the main point here is that you can navigate directly to specific folders by using that folder's path in conjunction with the cd command.

Furthermore, when you navigate your hard drive by using paths, you can jump directly to your desired destination from any place. When you enter **cd ..**, it is in relation to your current position, whereas entering

```
cd /Users/markchambers
```

will always take you to the same directory, regardless of your starting point.

Copying, moving, renaming, and deleting files

After you're comfortable with moving around the hierarchy of your hard drive, it's a cinch to copy, move, and rename files and folders.

**Book VII
Chapter 1**

**. . . And UNIX Lurks
Beneath**

To copy files from the command line, use the cp command. Because using the cp command will copy a file from one place to another, it requires two operands: first the source, and then the destination. For instance, to copy a file from your Home folder to your Documents folder, use the cp command like this:

```
cp ~/MyDocument ~/Desktop/MyDocument
```

Keep in mind that when you copy files, you must have proper permissions to do so. Here's what happens when I try to copy a file from my Desktop to another user's Desktop:

```
[WHITEDRAGON:~] markchambers$ cp ~/Desktop/MyDocument/Users/fuadramses/
    Desktop/MyDocument
```

Denied! Thwarted! Refused!

```
cp: /Users/fuadramses/Desktop/MyDocument: Permission denied
```

If you can't copy to the destination that you desire, you will need to precede the cp command with sudo. Using the sudo command allows you to perform functions as another user. The idea here is that the other user whom you're "emulating" has the necessary privileges to execute the desired copy operation. When you execute the command, the command line will ask you for a password. If you don't know what the password is, you probably shouldn't be using sudo. Your computer's administrator should have given you an appropriate password to use. After you enter the correct password, the command executes as desired.

In case you're curious, sudo stands for *set user and do*. It sets the user to the one that you specify and performs the command that follows the username.

```
sudo cp ~/Desktop/MyDocument /Users/fuadramses/Desktop/MyDocument
Password:
```

A close cousin to the cp (copy) command is the mv (move) command. As you can probably guess, the mv command moves a folder or file from one location to another. (I told you that all this character-based stuff would start to make sense, didn't I?) To demonstrate, this command moves MyDocument from the Desktop folder to the current user's Home folder:

```
mv ~/Desktop/MyDocument ~/MyDocument
```

Ah, but here's the hidden surprise: The `mv` command also functions as a rename command. For instance, to rename a file `MyDocument` on the Desktop to `MyNewDocument`, do this:

```
mv ~/Desktop/MyDocument ~/Desktop/MyNewDocument
```

In this case, you can see that the `mv` command is really copying the original file to the destination and then deleting the original. Because both folders in this example reside in the same folder (`~/Desktop/`), it appears as though the `mv` command has renamed the file.

Again, like the `cp` command, the `mv` command requires that you have proper permissions for the action that you wish to perform. Use the `sudo` command to perform any commands that your current user (as displayed in the prompt) is not allowed to execute. On UNIX systems, not all users are necessarily equal. Some users can perform functions that others can't. This is handy for keeping your child's mitts out of important files on your computer. It also creates a hurdle should you choose to work on files while using your child's restricted user account. The `sudo` command lets you temporarily become another user — presumably one that has permission to perform some function that the current user can't.

What would file manipulation be without the ability to delete files? Never fear; UNIX can delete anything that you throw at it. Use the `rm` (short for *remove*) or `rmdir` (short for *remove directory*) command to delete a folder or file. For example, to delete `MyNewDocument` from the Desktop folder, execute the `rm` command like this:

```
rm ~/Desktop/MyNewDocument
```

Once again, deleting files and folders requires that you have permission to do so. In other words, any time that you manipulate files with the command line, you are required to have the proper permission. If your current user lacks these permissions, using `sudo` will help.

Opening documents and launching applications

Launching applications and opening documents is child's play for a UNIX pro like you. The `open` command does it all. For example, to bring the Finder to the foreground without touching the mouse, use

```
open /System/Library/CoreServices/Finder.app
```

To open a document from the command line, follow a similar scheme. For example, to view an image named `myImage.tif` that's stored in your Documents folder using Preview, try this:

```
open ~/Documents/myImage.tif
```

Useful Commands

Manipulating files and viewing folder content is fun, but the command line is capable of so much more! Now I focus your attention on some of the other useful tasks that you can perform with the command line.

Mac OS X comes stocked with a full set of useful commands. You can discover what commands are installed by viewing the files in `/usr/bin`. Type **cd /usr/bin** to navigate there.

Calendar

One of my favorite command line functions is the `cal` command, which displays a calendar in text form. Simply entering **cal** at the prompt displays a calendar for the current month, as shown in Figure 1-7.

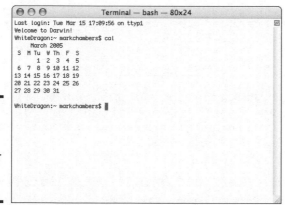

Figure 1-7: Type **cal** to view a calendar for the current month.

Append a number to the `cal` command to display a 12-month calendar for that year. The number that follows the `cal` command is the year for which you'd like to see a calendar. For example, to view a calendar for 1970, type **cal 1970**. The result appears in Figure 1-8.

Terminal — bash — 85x38
WhiteDragon:~ markchambers$ cal 1970
1970
January February March
S M Tu W Th F S S M Tu W Th F S S M Tu W Th F S
1 2 3 1 2 3 4 5 6 7 1 2 3 4 5 6 7
4 5 6 7 8 9 10 8 9 10 11 12 13 14 8 9 10 11 12 13 14
11 12 13 14 15 16 17 15 16 17 18 19 20 21 15 16 17 18 19 20 21
18 19 20 21 22 23 24 22 23 24 25 26 27 28 22 23 24 25 26 27 28
25 26 27 28 29 30 31 29 30 31
April May June
S M Tu W Th F S S M Tu W Th F S S M Tu W Th F S
1 2 3 4 1 2 1 2 3 4 5 6
5 6 7 8 9 10 11 3 4 5 6 7 8 9 7 8 9 10 11 12 13
12 13 14 15 16 17 18 10 11 12 13 14 15 16 14 15 16 17 18 19 20
19 20 21 22 23 24 25 17 18 19 20 21 22 23 21 22 23 24 25 26 27
26 27 28 29 30 24 25 26 27 28 29 30 28 29 30
31
July August September
S M Tu W Th F S S M Tu W Th F S S M Tu W Th F S
1 2 3 4 1 1 2 3 4 5
5 6 7 8 9 10 11 2 3 4 5 6 7 8 6 7 8 9 10 11 12
12 13 14 15 16 17 18 9 10 11 12 13 14 15 13 14 15 16 17 18 19
19 20 21 22 23 24 25 16 17 18 19 20 21 22 20 21 22 23 24 25 26
26 27 28 29 30 31 23 24 25 26 27 28 29 27 28 29 30
30 31
October November December
S M Tu W Th F S S M Tu W Th F S S M Tu W Th F S
1 2 3 1 2 3 4 5 6 7 1 2 3 4 5
4 5 6 7 8 9 10 8 9 10 11 12 13 14 6 7 8 9 10 11 12
11 12 13 14 15 16 17 15 16 17 18 19 20 21 13 14 15 16 17 18 19
18 19 20 21 22 23 24 22 23 24 25 26 27 28 20 21 22 23 24 25 26
25 26 27 28 29 30 31 29 30 27 28 29 30 31
WhiteDragon:~ markchambers$

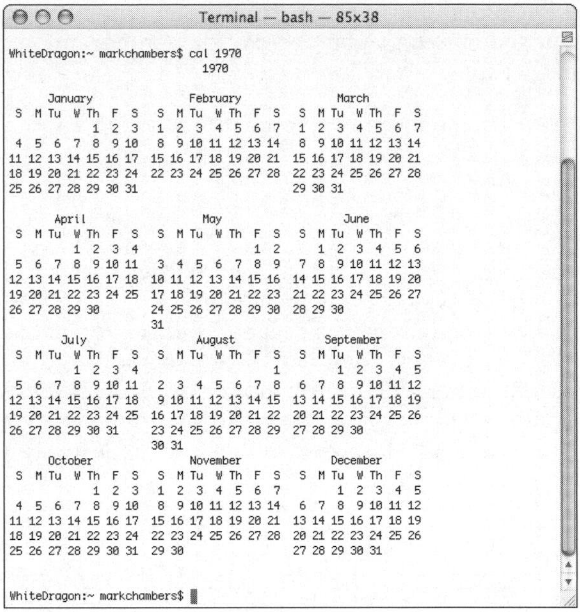

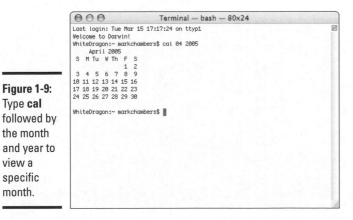

Figure 1-8: Type **cal** followed by a year to view the 12 months of that year.

Append a month number and a year number to display the calendar for that month. For example, to view a calendar for April 2005, type **cal 04 2005**. The result appears in Figure 1-9.

Terminal — bash — 80x24
Last login: Tue Mar 15 17:17:24 on ttyp1
Welcome to Darwin!
WhiteDragon:~ markchambers$ cal 04 2005
April 2005
S M Tu W Th F S
1 2
3 4 5 6 7 8 9
10 11 12 13 14 15 16
17 18 19 20 21 22 23
24 25 26 27 28 29 30
WhiteDragon:~ markchambers$

Figure 1-9: Type **cal** followed by the month and year to view a specific month.

Another useful command that is related to the `cal` command is `date`. Type **date** at the command line to display the day, date, time, and year based on your computer's settings.

```
[WHITEDRAGON:~] markchambers$ date
Mon Jan 10 11:32:20 CDT 2005
```

Processes

Have you ever been curious as to why your hard drive seems to spin and grind on occasion while your system is seemingly inactive? Mac OS X sometimes has a lot of stuff going on behind the scenes. To discover just what your computer is busy doing at any time, use the `top` command to display all the actions that your computer is currently performing, as shown in Figure 1-10. These activities are called *processes;* some are created when you launch applications, and others are simply tasks that Mac OS X has to take care of to keep things running smoothly.

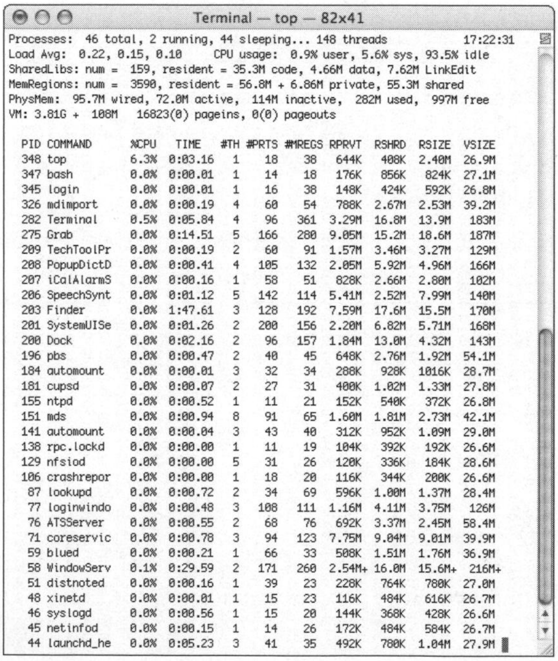


```
Processes:  46 total, 2 running, 44 sleeping... 148 threads          17:22:31
Load Avg:  0.22, 0.15, 0.10     CPU usage:  0.9% user, 5.6% sys, 93.5% idle
SharedLibs: num =  159, resident = 35.3M code, 4.66M data, 7.62M LinkEdit
MemRegions: num =  3590, resident = 56.8M + 6.86M private, 55.3M shared
PhysMem:  95.7M wired, 72.0M active,  114M inactive,  282M used,  997M free
VM: 3.81G +  108M   16823(0) pageins, 0(0) pageouts

  PID COMMAND      %CPU   TIME   #TH #PRTS #MREGS RPRVT  RSHRD  RSIZE  VSIZE
  348 top          6.3%  0:03.16   1    18    38   644K   408K  2.40M  26.9M
  347 bash         0.0%  0:00.01   1    14    18   176K   856K   824K  27.1M
  345 login        0.0%  0:00.01   1    16    38   148K   424K   592K  26.8M
  326 mdimport     0.0%  0:00.19   4    60    54   788K  2.67M  2.53M  39.2M
  282 Terminal     0.5%  0:05.84   4    96   361  3.29M  16.8M  13.9M   183M
  275 Grab         0.0%  0:14.51   5   166   280  9.05M  15.2M  18.6M   187M
  209 TechToolPr   0.0%  0:00.19   2    60    91  1.57M  3.46M  3.27M   129M
  208 PopupDictD   0.0%  0:00.41   4   105   132  2.05M  5.92M  4.96M   166M
  207 iCalAlarmS   0.0%  0:00.16   1    58    51   828K  2.66M  2.80M   102M
  206 SpeechSynt   0.0%  0:01.12   5   142   114  5.41M  2.52M  7.99M   140M
  203 Finder       0.0%  1:47.61   3   128   192  7.59M  17.6M  15.5M   170M
  201 SystemUISe   0.0%  0:01.26   2   200   156  2.20M  6.82M  5.71M   168M
  200 Dock         0.0%  0:02.16   2    96   157  1.84M  13.0M  4.32M   143M
  196 pbs          0.0%  0:00.47   2    40    45   648K  2.76M  1.92M  54.1M
  184 automount    0.0%  0:00.01   3    32    34   288K   928K  1016K  28.7M
  181 cupsd        0.0%  0:00.07   2    27    31   400K  1.02M  1.33M  27.8M
  155 ntpd         0.0%  0:00.52   1    11    21   152K   540K   372K  26.8M
  151 mds          0.0%  0:00.94   8    91    65  1.60M  1.81M  2.73M  42.1M
  141 automount    0.0%  0:00.04   3    43    40   312K   952K  1.09M  29.0M
  138 rpc.lockd    0.0%  0:00.00   1    11    19   104K   392K   192K  26.6M
  129 nfsiod       0.0%  0:00.00   5    31    26   120K   336K   184K  28.6M
  106 crashrepor   0.0%  0:00.00   1    18    20   116K   344K   200K  26.6M
   87 lookupd      0.0%  0:00.72   2    34    69   596K  1.00M  1.37M  28.4M
   77 loginwindo   0.0%  0:00.48   3   108   111  1.16M  4.11M  3.75M   126M
   76 ATSServer    0.0%  0:00.55   2    68    76   692K  3.37M  2.45M  58.4M
   71 coreservic   0.0%  0:00.78   3    94   123  7.75M  9.04M  9.01M  39.9M
   59 blued        0.0%  0:00.21   1    66    33   508K  1.51M  1.76M  36.9M
   58 WindowServ   0.1%  0:29.59   2   171   260  2.54M+ 16.0M  15.6M+  216M+
   51 distnoted    0.0%  0:00.16   1    39    23   228K   764K   780K  27.0M
   48 xinetd       0.0%  0:00.01   1    15    23   116K   484K   616K  26.7M
   46 syslogd      0.0%  0:00.56   1    15    20   144K   368K   428K  26.6M
   45 netinfod     0.0%  0:00.15   1    14    26   172K   484K   584K  26.7M
   44 launchd_he   0.0%  0:05.23   3    41    35   492K   780K  1.04M  27.9M
```

Figure 1-10: The `top` command displays all running processes.

Besides listing the names of the various processes currently in use, `top` also tells you how much of your CPU is being devoted to each process. This lets you know what process is currently hogging all your computing power.

Sometimes a process stalls, effectively freezing that action. By using the `top` command to find the Process ID (PID) of the offending process, you can halt the process. Simply use the `kill` command followed by the PID of the process that you want to stop.

Do *not* go killing processes with a cavalier attitude! Although Mac OS X is extremely stable, removing the wrong process — such as `init` or `mach_init` — is rather like removing a leg from one of those deep-sea drilling platforms: the very definition of Not Good. You could lock up your system and lose whatever you're doing in other applications. If you simply want to shut down a misbehaving program, go graphical again (at least for a moment) and use the Force Quit menu command from the Finder menu.

Like `top`, another handy command for examining process info is `ps` (short for *process*). Most often, you will want to append a few flags to the `ps` command to get the information that you desire. For example, try the following command:

```
ps -aux
```

The `man` page for `ps` explains what each flag means. (Read more about using the `man` command in the earlier section, "Help is on the way!")

UNIX Cadillac Commands

Besides working with files and processes, the command line has all kinds of sophisticated commands. For example, with the command line, you have instant access to a variety of tools for finding files or even stringing together commands.

Finding files

The command line also gives you a number of ways to search for files on your hard drive. The two most commonly used commands are `find` and `locate`.

To use `find`, specify a starting point for the search followed by the name of the file or folder that you wish to find. For example, to find the Fonts folder that belongs to your user, enter the command like this:

```
find ~/ -name "Fonts"
```

You should see at least one result of the `find` command.

```
/Users/markchambers//Library/Fonts
```

One great feature of the `find` command is that you can look for a file or folder in more than one location. Suppose you want to find a file named `MyDocument` that you know resides either in your Documents folder or on your Desktop. For this kind of search, use the `find` command like this:

```
find ~/Documents ~/Desktop\ Folder -name "MyDocument"
```

In this example, you are telling the `find` command which folders it should search when looking for the file named `MyDocument`.

Using pipes

Nearly all UNIX commands can take on greater abilities by using a construct called the *pipe*. A pipe (|) is represented by that funny little vertical line that shows up when you press Shift+\. The pipe routes data from one command to another one that follows — for example, many UNIX commands produce large amounts of information that can't all fit on one page. (You might have noticed this behavior when you used the `locate` command.) Joining two commands or functions together with the pipe command is *piping*. To tame the screens full of text, pipe the `find` function to the `less` command. The `less` command provides data one page at a time.

```
find ~/ -name "Fonts" | less
```

When the results fill up one page, the data stops and waits for you to press any key (except the Q key) to continue. When you reach the end of the results, press Q to quit and return to a command line prompt.

UNIX Programs That Come In Handy

As a Macintosh user, you might be surprised to know that many applications on your hard drive don't reside in one of the typical Applications folders of Mac OS X. These applications, in fact, don't have any graphical user interface like you're accustomed to. They're only accessible from the command line. The remainder of this chapter covers some of these applications.

Text editors

UNIX has many text-editing applications for use at the command line. Some of the more popular ones include `pico`, `vi`, and `emacs`. Each of these text editors has its pros and cons — and thanks to the thorough folks at Apple, because all three are included with Tiger! For my examples here, however, I use `pico` because it's simple to use and sufficient for our needs.

Creating a new document

To create a text file by using `pico`, simply type **pico** at the command line. The result should look like Figure 1-11.

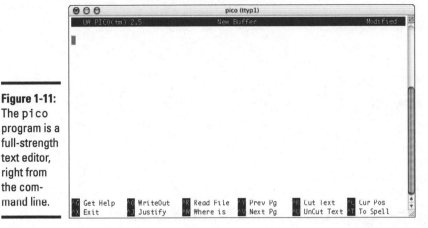

Figure 1-11: The `pico` program is a full-strength text editor, right from the command line.

This is the rough and tumble world of UNIX, which preceded the Macintosh by many years. Perhaps this will also help you to appreciate why the Macintosh was so revolutionary when it was introduced. (You can just hear the designers crowing, "We'll call this a *menu!* Yeah, that's the ticket!" The only graphics that you'd see on your monitor were the comics and sticky notes that you stuck to the bottom.)

At the bottom of the screen is a menu of common commands. Above the menu is a large empty space where you can enter text, much like the word processors that you already know and love. (For those of us that remember the halcyon character-based days of DOS, think older versions of Word and WordPerfect . . . or, if you're a *real* computing dinosaur like I am, consider the original WordStar.) Type some text in that area. Anything will do . . . a letter to a friend, a grocery list, or your school homework.

When you're finished entering your desired text, save the document with the `WriteOut` command in the `pico` menu. Directly next to each command in the `pico` menu is a keyboard sequence used to perform that command. (Refer to the bottom of Figure 1-11.) The ^ character is shorthand for the Control key on your keyboard. Thus, to save a file, press Control+O. This flies in the face of standard Mac keyboard conventions, where the letter *O* is traditionally used to mean *Open*.

After pressing the Control+O sequence, pico prompts you for a filename (see Figure 1-12). Like most UNIX files, you're permitted to enter a simple filename here or a full path to a file. For this example, save the file to your Documents folder, naming it MyPicoDocument.

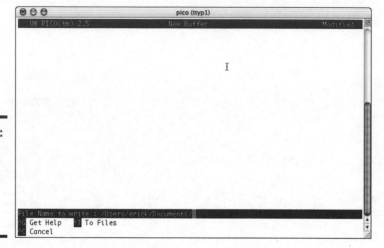

Figure 1-12: When you save your file, pico prompts you for a filename.

After you've completed and saved the document, pressing Control+X will transport you away from Planet Pico and back to the command line.

Networking with the Terminal

Because UNIX isn't a new phenomenon, it has many useful networking abilities built into it. In fact, UNIX was instrumental in creating much of what we now take for granted: e-mail, the Internet, and the World Wide Web. Thus, you will be happy to know that you can communicate over networks with the Terminal in practically any manner that you can dream of . . . and then some!

WWW and FTP

If you've used the Internet for any time, you're probably familiar with the various means to transport data over a network. From FTP (short for *File Transfer Protocol*) and Telnet to e-mail and the Web, UNIX can handle it all. In fact, UNIX has a command for each of these functions (and many more that have passed into historical obscurity). Rather than use each individual command to send and retrieve data with the Terminal, Apple has conveniently provided a command that can handle them all: curl. The curl command is competent at all the standard network protocols. To see it in action, pass a Web address (or URL, to The Enlightened) to the curl command:

```
curl http://www.mlcbooks.com
```

The result is that you will see the HyperText Markup Language (HTML) page that's located at www.mlcbooks.com. Because this isn't particularly useful for most people (it's not very easy to read), you need to add the letter o as a flag. This specifies where you would like to save this file upon download. To save the HTML page to your Home directory, add the -o flag and a path to the destination file.

Don't forget to precede all flags with a hyphen. For this example, it would be -o.

```
curl -o ~/mlcbooks.html http://www.mlcbooks.com
```

If you now perform an ls command, you will see that curl has, in fact, downloaded the HTML found at www.mlcbooks.com and saved it to a file named mlcbooks.html in your Home directory.

The beauty of curl is that it does much more than just retrieve Web pages: It's equally comfortable with FTP transfers. FTP is used to *download* (or receive) files from a server as well as *upload* (or send) them. Like the previous HyperText Transfer Protocol (HTTP) examples, you only have to provide an FTP address in Uniform Resource Locator (URL) format, and curl will take care of the rest. Of course, most people want to save any files that they download via FTP — not view them in the Terminal like I did the HTML file. Therefore, like the previous example, you should add the -o flag and a path to the destination of your download. This time, I download a README file about curl directly from the makers of curl.

```
curl -o ~/Desktop/README.curl
    ftp://ftp.sunet.se/pub/www/utilities/curl/README.curl
```

If you're familiar with FTP, you might be wondering whether curl can upload, too. Yes, indeed! Instead of using the -o flag, you will need to use two flags: -T and -u. The -T flag denotes which file you wish to upload. The -u flag denotes the username and password. Then, specify the FTP destination address of where you want to upload it. Because this example deals with an upload, the remainder of this example is for an imaginary FTP server. In real life, you'd use the appropriate FTP address, username, and password for an FTP server where you are allowed to upload.

```
curl -T /Desktop/README.curl -u username:passwd ftp://ftp.yoursitehere.com
/myfiles/README.curl
```

This example uploads the README.curl file from the Desktop folder that I downloaded earlier to an imaginary FTP server.

**Book VII
Chapter 1**

...And UNIX Lurks
Beneath

How do you spell success? C-u-r-l!

Sure, HTTP and FTP are handy, but did you know that there are many other protocols for network communications? One of the niftier ones is the *Dictionary protocol*. With it, you can look up words from any server that understands the protocol. Suppose, for example, that you would like to know the meaning of the term *CD-ROM*. Enter the following command to find out:

```
curl dict://dict.org/d:CD-ROM
```

The results are shown in Figure 1-13. With curl, Sherlock and your Dictionary Dashboard widget on the same Macintosh, you might never use a "real" paper dictionary again!

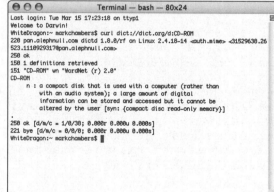

Figure 1-13: The curl tool can even look up words in the dictionary.

Chapter 2: AppleScript Just Plain Rocks

In This Chapter

✓ Simplifying your life with AppleScript

✓ Letting AppleScript create scripts for you

✓ Writing scripts on your own

✓ Using Automator to create your own applications

✓ Searching for AppleScript help elsewhere

*U*sing a Macintosh is supposed to make your life easier — and in many ways, it does. But there's a limit to how much your Mac can do by itself, right? After all, you still have to move the mouse, press keys on the keyboard, and read information on the screen to get things done . . . or *do* you? Why not let your computer do the dull chores — such as renaming a thousand digital photographs from your family vacation and organizing them into folders based on the subject of each photo — for you? Although most people are familiar with controlling their Macs with the mouse and keyboard, few realize that they can operate their machines without touching a key, a mouse button, or even glancing at the screen.

What's So Great about AppleScript?

If one word could describe what AppleScript is all about, it would be *automation*. *AppleScript* is a technology for automating practically any action that you perform with your Macintosh, including both common tasks in the Finder and those that you perform in other applications.

Automate common tasks in the Finder

If you've ever found yourself repeating some task more than once, you're an ideal candidate for becoming an AppleScript techno-wizard. AppleScript is particularly good at taking the boredom and tedium out of using your

Macintosh by performing all sorts of tasks automatically. To illustrate, consider a few jobs that would take a fair amount of time to do by hand but are a snap with AppleScript:

✦ While writing your next best-selling Great American Novel — or *For Dummies* book on Mac OS X — you make a mistake and misnumber the chapters. All the chapters have a filename bearing the chapter number, but they're all off by one. Sure, you could rename each file by hand, but your book is a large tome and renumbering 42 chapters manually doesn't sound like much fun. (Take my word for it. *Please.*) It'll require several minutes and lots of tedious attention on your part, not to mention introduce the likelihood of human error. But wait, there's another way! When using a simple AppleScript of only a few lines of code, you can rename the chapters in seconds whilst you go grab another Diet Coke.

✦ You're a neat individual and think that your Mac should reflect your penchant for order — in fact, you like your Desktop icons to be placed just so. Being left-handed, you prefer the icons over on the left side of the Desktop, like some of those *inferior* operating systems. In this situation, an AppleScript can help you do things that aren't humanly possible; not only can you rapidly rearrange the icons on your Desktop, but you can do so with pixel-point accuracy. Without AppleScript, it would be nearly impossible to precisely align dozens of icons. And if you could, it would take a long time and probably cause you to go blind.

✦ After a font-download binge, you find yourself with hundreds of fonts. You really want to organize them into separate folders based on the date that you downloaded them. AppleScript comes to the rescue again! With a brief script, you could knock out this challenge without ever looking at a single date. Add a couple more lines of code to the script, and AppleScript will take care of creating the folders, too. Right, you know the word: *sassy.*

Automate tasks in other applications

By using AppleScript, you can also often automate your work from beginning to end, despite the fact that you need multiple applications to do so. Look at a few scenarios, and you'll begin to appreciate why AppleScript is such a powerful technology:

✦ You've just completed creating the ultimate library of bagpipe songs in iTunes — no, really! — and you want to share the list with your friends at the next Bagpipers Anonymous meeting. You could easily send everyone in the group an iTunes Playlist, but not everyone in the club has a Macintosh, let alone a computer. This is going to require creating a hard copy for those members without a computer. Because your bagpipe song list contains thousands of songs, you don't want to retype the name of each song. AppleScript can save the day by extracting the song titles for you and compiling them into a list just in time for your meeting.

✦ AppleScript can take care of your computer-owning bagpipe friends, too. With a few extra steps, you can e-mail all of them the list as well.

✦ Being so doggone fond of bagpipes, you want to send your bagpiping friends a special note during the holidays. To help manage your holiday greeting cards, you can create a record in FileMaker Pro or some other database listing the name and address of each person who should receive a card. If you've entered their street addresses in the Contacts section of your e-mail application, AppleScript can aid in transferring the addresses from your e-mail application to the database. Never again will your bagpiping friends miss a holiday greeting . . . and the world is a much better place.

As you can imagine, there are literally thousands of ways that you can use AppleScript to automate your workflow.

Running a Script

The easiest way to get started with AppleScript is to use some scripts that others have already written. *Scripts* are small files that contain a list of commands; this list of commands tells your Mac what function to perform and when to perform it. Fortunately, Apple is kind enough to provide you with several completed scripts with your installation of Tiger. You can find a large cache of scripts in the scripts folder, found in the Library folder, under Scripts.

Many scripts (but not all) end with the extension `.scpt`. Before you get started running scripts, however, you should know a few things first.

Identifying scripts in the field

Each script that you encounter will be in one of these three formats:

✦ **Script application:** Some AppleScripts act much like an application. To use one, simply double-click it in the Finder, and off it goes to perform whatever tasks it was meant to do. Depending on an internal setting of the script, it might quit when it's finished doing its thing. Most often, the script completes its mission and quits. Scripts are typically identified by the icon that you see in Figure 2-1.

✦ **Compiled script:** You might also encounter AppleScripts that won't run without the aid of another application. Apple calls these *compiled scripts.* Although they're not able to execute on their own, they do have the abilities of a script built in. They just require a host application to use them.

✦ **Text file:** In addition to compiled scripts and those that act like applications, a third category of AppleScript that you might encounter is a script stored in a text file. Scripts that are stored in a text file also need a host application before they'll do anything. The main difference between a text file script and a compiled script is that you can read a text file script with any application that can open a text file.

The Script Editor application

Two of the three possible script types (compiled scripts and text files) require some sort of host application before they'll perform any action. Luckily, Tiger provides you with just such a host: the AppleScript Script Editor application, which comes with Mac OS X and can execute any AppleScript with ease. With the Script Editor, you can also do much more, including

✦ View or modify an AppleScript

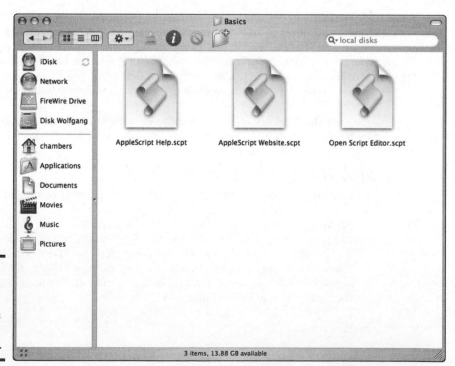

Figure 2-1: A gaggle of typical script icons caught by the camera.

✦ Create a new AppleScript

✦ Check an AppleScript for errors

✦ Save scripts in one of the three possible formats

To launch the Script Editor application, navigate to the AppleScript folder (choose Applications➪AppleScript➪Script Editor) and double-click the Script Editor icon. The Script Editor application displays an empty, script-editing window, as shown in Figure 2-2.

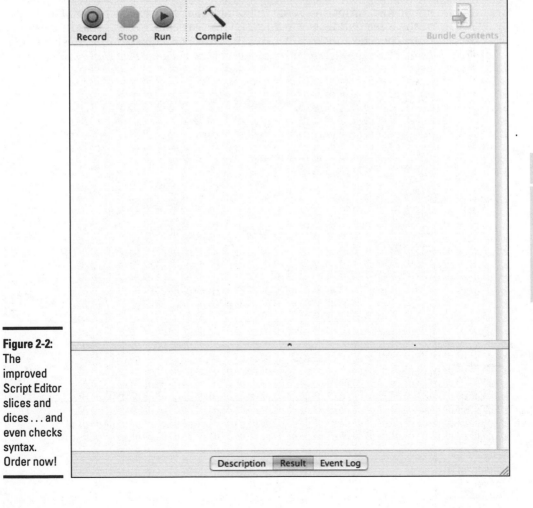

Figure 2-2:
The improved Script Editor slices and dices ... and even checks syntax. Order now!

**Book VII
Chapter 2**

**AppleScript Just
Plain Rocks**

Executing a script

After you have the Script Editor application running, you can run any AppleScript that can you find. To get you started, Apple has conveniently provided a handful of useful scripts. Navigate to the Scripts folder, which is located in the Library folder.

The scripts are divided into folders based on functionality, such as fonts, mail, color, and navigation. For example, open the Internet Services folder, where you'll find a script named `Current Temperature by Zipcode.scpt`. You need an active Internet connection to test this script.

Double-click the script to open it. Because it's a compiled script and not an application script, the Script Editor automatically loads the script and comes to the foreground (see Figure 2-3). This particular script prompts users for their ZIP code and then displays the current temperature, which it retrieves from a Web site. To see the script in action, click the Run button or press ⌘+R.

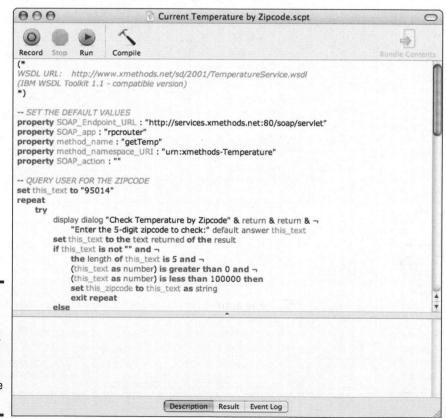

Figure 2-3: Click the Run button in the Editor toolbar to execute the script you've loaded.

Writing Your Own Simple Scripts

Using someone else's scripts is fun and all, but the real joy of AppleScript comes when you create your own. Not only can you customize a script to your own needs and desires, but saving all those keystrokes can really produce a feeling of euphoria. (Okay, perhaps just Tiger power users will actually experience a heightened sense of existence . . . you'll be there soon.)

Create a script without touching a key

You needn't wear a pocket protector or tape the bridge of your glasses to become proficient with AppleScript. In fact, the Script Editor can get you up and running with AppleScript in no time at all. The secret weapon of the AppleScript author is the Record function of the Script Editor. You click the Record button, perform one or more actions in a recordable application, and then return to the Script Editor where you click the Stop button. The Script Editor stores each of your actions and compiles the whole list into an AppleScript.

In *theory,* this is how it should all work, but in reality, finding recordable Macintosh applications is not always so easy. The Finder is, perhaps, the most recordable application on the Mac. Although some other applications support recording, so few do that the Finder could be the only recordable application most Mac users ever see.

Book VII
Chapter 2

To try it yourself, do the following steps to automate actions in the Finder:

1. **Bring Script Editor to the foreground.**

   If Script Editor isn't currently running, double-click its icon in the Finder. If it is running, click its icon on the Dock.

2. **Create a new script by pressing ⌘+N.**

3. **Click the Record button.**

   The Record button is one of four buttons positioned near the top left of a new script window. Refer to Figure 2-3.

4. **Switch to the Finder and perform the actions that you want to automate.**

   When the Finder is active, you can select some icons on the Desktop and move them around, resize any open Finder windows, or navigate to your home directory. Any action that you perform in the Finder should be acceptable fodder for the Script Editor. As you perform tasks in the Finder, the Script Editor automatically generates a script that replicates your actions.

5. **Return to the Script Editor and click the Stop button.**

   To reactivate the Script Editor, click its icon on the Dock. Click the Stop button to cease the recording of your script.

AppleScript Just
Plain Rocks

When you're finished, you should be looking at a complete AppleScript. To test your work, return to the Finder and revert any icons or windows that you might have moved or repositioned. (You don't want to run a script that doesn't appear to have any effect.) Then return to the Script Editor and click the Run button to watch your automated Finder tasks being performed.

Building your own scripts

An AppleScript novice can perform all kinds of amazing feats with the recording features of the Script Editor. Because AppleScript uses a kind of pseudo-English language, it's usually pretty easy to figure out what's going on behind the scenes. Consider the following script for an example:

```
tell app "Finder"
    activate
    set windowList to every window --save list of open windows
    repeat with theWindow in windowList
        tell theWindow
            if collapsed is true then
            --do nothing, because the window is collapsed
            else
                set collapsed to true
            end if
        end tell
    end repeat
end tell
```

(By the way, in the preceding code, I bolded the commands you'll be working with, but they don't have to be bolded for the script to work.) Anyway, the first thing that you might notice about this script is the first line: the `tell` command, which indicates that this script relates to the Finder. This script activates the Finder, creates a list of open windows, and then examines the state of each window: Is it collapsed or not collapsed? (In Tiger, a *collapsed,* or minimized, window appears on the Dock.) If the window is already minimized and on the Dock, nothing happens, and the script continues through the list of windows. If the window isn't minimized, the script collapses it. This continues until the script has examined all open windows. The end result? All open windows end up minimized on the Dock.

Another thing to note about this script is that it has two comments in it (`save list` and `do nothing`). Comments can help you remember what you were thinking months later when you open the script again. Although comments help us humans know what's happening, they don't really have any other function. An AppleScript comment begins with two dashes (`--`).

Here's a big-time Mark's Maxim that every script author should remember:

Comments are your friend!™

One Step Beyond: AppleScript Programming

Creating AppleScripts can soon become very involved, bordering on programming. Don't let that term *programming* scare you away, though. You needn't be a software developer to take advantage of AppleScripts. Apple provides a lot of help to get you started along the AppleScript trail.

Grab the Dictionary

Perhaps the greatest resource for AppleScript novices and experts alike is the AppleScript Dictionary. Although many applications are scriptable, not all are. To be scriptable, an application must contain an AppleScript Dictionary. An AppleScript Dictionary details the various commands and objects of an application that you can access via AppleScript.

The Script Editor application allows you to peer inside an application and view its AppleScript Dictionary. To open an application's Dictionary, choose File➪Open Dictionary. Mac OS X searches through your installed applications and presents you with the Open Dictionary dialog, as shown in Figure 2-4, which lists all applications that have a dictionary and are therefore scriptable.

If you don't see your favorite application in the list, alas, it's probably not scriptable. To make certain, click the Browse button and select the application in question.

After you select an application, the Script Editor displays that application's AppleScript Dictionary. An application's dictionary lists all the features of that application that are scriptable.

Scriptable features are divided into categories, called *Suites,* which you can see on the left side of the AppleScript Dictionary. Every Mac application is supposed to support the Standard Suite, which lists common terms that most applications should support.

Click an item in the Suite on the left side of the Dictionary to view detailed information about its capabilities, as shown in Figure 2-5.

By surveying the various Suites of an application, you begin to see what tasks you can automate. The Finder, with its huge AppleScript Dictionary, is perhaps the most scriptable of all applications.

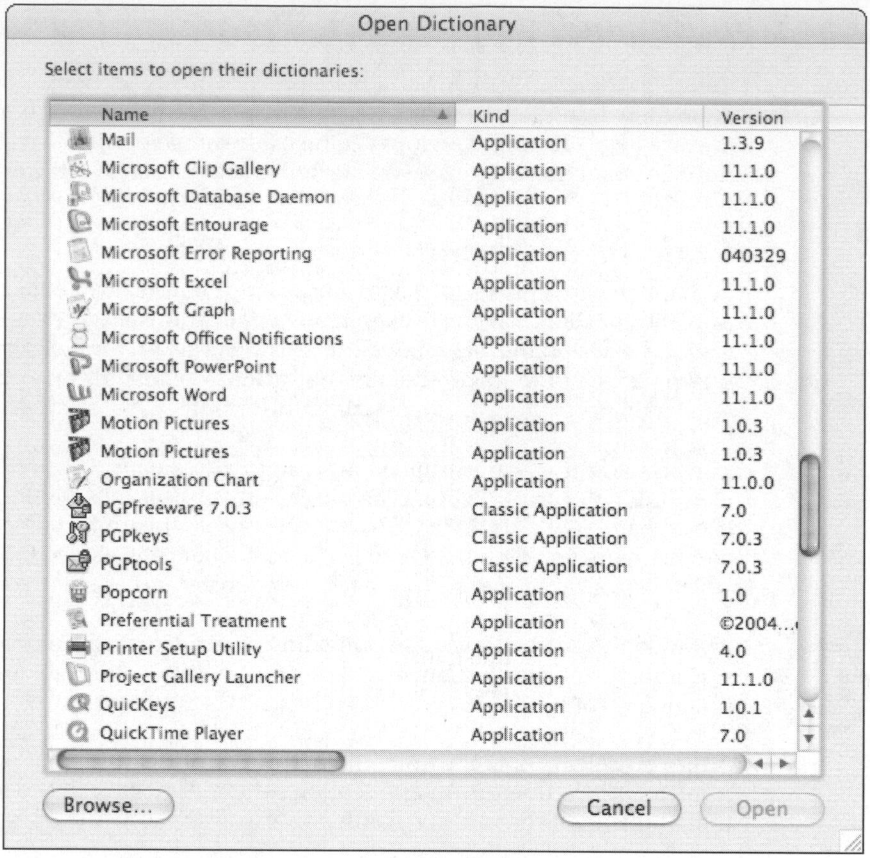

Figure 2-4:
Viewing the
AppleScript
Dictionary
within the
Script Editor.

Anatomy of a simple script

Although a full discussion of AppleScript programming is beyond the scope of this book — after all, we have other things to talk about, too — that doesn't mean that you can't produce some quick and useful scripts. Most AppleScripts begin with a command that addresses the application that you want to automate. Enter this command into a new AppleScript document, which you create by pressing ⌘+N.

```
tell application "Finder"
```

This is like saying, "Hey, Finder, listen up! I'm going to send commands your way!" The double quotes surround the application name that you're addressing in the command.

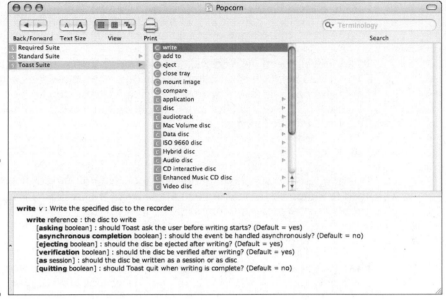

Figure 2-5:
Click an
item in a
Suite to
view details
about its
capabilities
and syntax.

Similarly, after you finish instructing the Finder what tasks you want performed, you must also tell it to stop listening. As such, typical scripts end with

```
end tell
```

With the shell of a script in place, all you have to do is add commands in between the `tell` and `end tell` commands of the script. If you want your script to force an application to the foreground, an `activate` command is usually the first line within the shell of your script.

```
tell application "Finder"
  activate
end tell
```

Believe it or not, this is technically a complete and valid script! It doesn't do much, though, so add some more functionality to make it accomplish something worthwhile. For example, suppose you would like to perform some housekeeping chores each time you log in to your Macintosh. Some desirable tasks might include

✦ Emptying the Trash

✦ Having your Mac say, "Hello!" to you

(Okay, I'll grant that hearing your Mac say, "Hello!" isn't a housekeeping chore, but it makes the whole script that much more fun — and really impresses your visitors, too. No one ever said programming had to be boring!)

To add these functions, you can do so by using a language you already know: English. As I mention earlier, Apple tries (and sometimes succeeds) to make AppleScript as English-like as possible. That way, you don't have to learn some silly computer language; just use your native tongue. For example, to empty the Trash, tell the Finder to do so.

```
empty trash
```

The trickiest line of code might be the speech, and that's only because you need to remember to add quotes. AppleScript thinks that anything without quotes is an AppleScript command.

```
say "Hello!"
```

The result is a super-simple script that anyone can read but that performs two powerful functions. The completed script looks like this:

```
tell app "Finder"
  activate
  empty trash
  say "Hello!"
end tell
```

After you complete the script, choose File➪Save to save your script. Because you want the script to execute and then quit, use the File Format field to save it as an application. Also, make sure that the Stay Open check box is disabled and that the Startup Screen check box is disabled. And don't forget to name your script in the Save As text field.

To have the script automatically run each time you log in to your Mac, save the script anywhere that you wish. (Assign its home folder in the Where field of the Save window.) Open System Preferences by clicking its icon on the Dock, click the Accounts icon, and then click Login Items. Click the Add button (which proudly bears a plus sign) and navigate to your script in the Open dialog that appears. After you click the Add button of the Open dialog, you'll see the script in the Login Items window.

1 Summon Automator — the Silicon Programmer!

Okay, perhaps I've watched too much *Iron Chef* over the years. Anyway, Tiger ushers in a new kid in town — *Automator* (as shown in Figure 2-6) — and he's your own personal robotic AppleScript coder. In fact, Automator can create custom applications that can handle your repetitive tasks. You can even create *workflows,* which are sequential (and repeatable) operations that are performed on the same files or data, and your Automator application can automatically launch whatever applications are necessary to get the job done.

Here's a great example: You work with a service bureau that sends you a CD every week with new product shots for your company's Marketing department. Unfortunately, these images are flat-out *huge* — taken with a 12-megapixel camera — and they're always in the wrong orientation. Before you move them to the Marketing folder on your server, you have to laboriously resize each image and rotate it, and then save the smaller version.

With Automator's help, you can build a custom application that automatically reads each image in the folder, resizes it, rotates it, and even generates a thumbnail image or prints the image, and then moves the massaged images to the proper folder. You would normally have to manually launch Preview to perform the image operations and then use a Finder window to move the new files to the right location. But now, with Automator, a single double-click of your custom application icon does the trick.

You'll find Automator in your Applications folder. Currently, Automator can handle specific tasks within about 20 applications (including the Finder), but both Apple and third-party developers are busy adding new Automator task support to all sorts of new and existing applications.

**Book VII
Chapter 2**

**AppleScript Just
Plain Rocks**

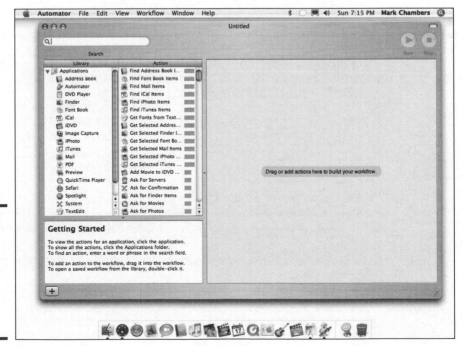

Figure 2-6:
Automator
is a dream
come true
for those
who hate
repetitive
tasks.

To create a simple application using Automator, follow these steps:

1. **Click the desired application in the Library column.**

   Automator displays the actions available within that application.

2. **Drag the desired action into the workflow area (right side of the window).**

3. **Modify any specific settings provided for the action you chose.**

4. **Repeat Steps 1–3 to complete the workflow.**

5. **Click Run (upper right) to test your script.**

   Use sample files while you're fine-tuning your application lest you accidentally do something deleterious to an original (and irreplaceable) file!

   Figure 2-7 illustrates an application that will take care of the earlier example — resizing and rotating a folder full of images, and then moving them to the Pictures folder.

6. **When the application is working as you like, press ⌘+Shift+S to save it.**

7. **In the Save dialog that appears, type a name for your new application.**

8. **Click the File Format drop-down list box and choose Application.**

9. **Click Save.**

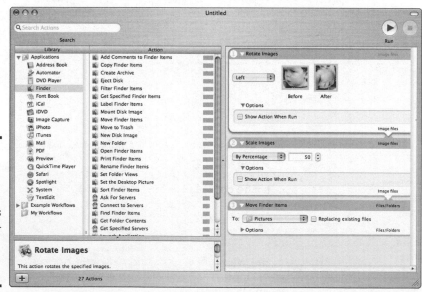

Figure 2-7: Now I'm ready to handle 10 or 1,000 images in a folder — my application does the work!

To find all the actions of a certain type within the Library list, click in the Search box at the left side of the Automator toolbar and type in a keyword, like **save** or **burn**. You don't even need to press Return!

If a task in your Automator application needs different values each time you run it, you can set your application for manual input by selecting the Ask When Run check box in the workflow, which allows your application to prompt you with a dialog requesting the necessary values (like a target folder on your hard drive, or a prefix to add to your images).

Help Is at Your Fingertips

If you would like to explore AppleScript further, you have many resources on hand. Sometimes the easiest way to use AppleScript is to copy existing scripts and modify them as necessary; other times, it's a good idea to read the documentation included in Apple's Help system. Whichever approach you use, with a little practice and guidance, you'll soon be doing stupendous tasks with your Mac.

Built-in AppleScript Help

The most readily available AppleScript reference is built into Mac OS X. Choose Help⇨Mac Help to launch the Mac OS Help Guides from the Finder or choose Help⇨Script Editor Help from the Script Editor. This is a great place to begin your AppleScript exploration. It includes detailed documentation about the AppleScript language and loads of demonstration scripts for you to try (or alter) yourself.

AppleScript on the Web

In addition to the built-in AppleScript help in the Finder, the Internet has much to offer in the way of AppleScript training and examples. Like so many other excellent Web resources, AppleScripts are free!

Not all AppleScripts are created equal: When downloading scripts from the Internet, make sure that they're compatible with Tiger (Mac OS X v. 10.4). Although the majority of scripts made for Mac OS 9 also work with Mac OS X, some simply won't. The converse is also true: Sometimes a script is meant solely for use with Mac OS X.

Apple Computer

The first place on the Web that you should visit for AppleScript help is the Source of All That Is Good, also called the Mother Ship: Apple Computer. Although the built-in OS X help offers a lot, the Apple Web site offers even more scripts, tutorials, and general AppleScript goodness. You can even find a list of all known scriptable applications, which can save you from searching for them with Script Editor. Furthermore, the site maintains an extensive list of links to other useful AppleScript sites.

`www.apple.com/applescript`

ResExcellence

For the hacker in all of us, ResExcellence sports many unique system tweaks, modifications, and outright hacks. Among the ResExcellence bag of tricks is an extensive list of AppleScripts for you to download. Although not geared strictly towards AppleScript, ResExcellence offers many excellent scripts for customizing your Desktop, doing things you didn't think possible, and generally making your Macintosh experience more fulfilling.

`www.resexcellence.com/applescripts/index.shtml`

MacScripter.net

MacScripter.net devotes its site to all Macintosh scripting. Because AppleScript is such a huge part of scripting the Mac OS, you can be certain that there's something here for you. Besides offering up-to-date news on scripting for the Mac OS, MacScripter.net also gives you access to many scripts, information about scripting books, and details on Apple's new AppleScript Studio software, which lets you create AppleScripts with interfaces. The sheer volume of information at this site makes it one you shouldn't skip.

`www.macscripter.net`

Chapter 3: Talking and Writing to Your Macintosh

In This Chapter

✔ Using handwriting recognition to control Mac OS X

✔ Speak to your Mac

✔ Your Mac speaks back

✔ Using VoiceOver to provide feedback in Tiger

*I*f you're a hunt-and-peck typist — leaving you certain that there *must* be some better way to get information into your computer — you'll be happy to know that Apple has you in mind. Since the very first Mac rolled off the assembly line, Apple has had a keen interest in alternative modes of interaction between human and machine. Mac OS X continues in this tradition of alternative computer controls, offering two options for controlling Mac OS X without the keyboard: handwriting and speech.

✦ **Handwriting:** By using a pen and computer tablet, you can enter text into your Mac by simply writing as you would on a sheet of paper.

✦ **Speech:** Talk to your Mac to make it listen and obey your commands. It even talks back!

This chapter guides you through the various options that you have for controlling your Macintosh without using the keyboard. First, I cover the Mac OS X *Inkwell* feature, which you use to write on a tablet to enter data into your computer. (Although it sounds a bit ironic, think of Inkwell as your "digital paper" for the new millennium.) Whatever you write on the tablet appears on the screen as text.

I also take a look at the more space-age speech capabilities available to you in Mac OS X. With your voice, you can command a Macintosh to perform all sorts of interesting feats. And just so you don't get lonely, the Mac will even talk back to you. (Now you can control your computer just like Spock from *Star Trek!*) And Tiger's new VoiceOver feature makes it easy for your Mac to read aloud all sorts of text, including Web pages, Mail messages, and word processing documents.

So, scoot away from your computer, lean that chair back, and let your Mac take care of the rest.

Using Ink with a Tablet

Typing on a keyboard can be a tedious and error-prone experience for even the best typists. To help out, Apple added some useful handwriting features to Mac OS X. Based in part on some of Apple's handheld software for the *Newton* (one of the first personal digital assistants [PDAs], and a product released before its time), the handwriting recognition in Mac OS X gives you the ability to write text on a compatible tablet for use in your favorite applications.

The basic process of working with handwriting on Mac OS X goes like this:

1. **Attach a tablet to your Mac.**

Most tablets use a Universal Serial Bus (USB) connection, so connecting one to your computer is as simple as plugging in the cable from your tablet to the USB port on your Mac.

2. **Write on the tablet with the stylus that accompanies it.**

A *stylus* is the name given the fake "pen" that accompanies most tablets. A stylus doesn't have any ink in it: It's just a pen-shaped tool with a plastic tip meant for writing on a tablet.

3. **Your Mac interprets your handwriting.**

After your Mac recognizes the handwriting, it sends that text to the foremost application at the cursor location where you would normally type with the keyboard. You're spared the whole training bit, too.

You aren't restricted to writing just text on the tablet, naturally. You can use it to control the interface of your Mac as you would a mouse. A tablet also works great for graphics applications like procreate Painter and Adobe Photoshop. Many artists are frustrated when drawing with a mouse; but when you use a tablet, you can feel right at home with the natural pen or brush movements that you've always used.

Although Inkwell pretty much takes care of preparing your Mac for handwriting recognition, it does offer you a few settings in the Inkwell panel within System Preferences. To view the System Preferences, click the System Preferences icon on the Dock. From there, click the Inkwell icon to adjust settings for your tablet.

If you don't have a tablet connected to your Macintosh, you won't be able to view the System Preferences pane for Inkwell. Mac OS X is smart enough to show you only the settings for your current hardware setup.

Computer, Can You Hear Me?

Remember that classic scene from the movie *Star Trek IV: The Voyage Home* where Scotty picks up the mouse on a Macintosh and tries to talk directly to the computer? Since the very early days of the Mac OS, Apple has included some form of speech recognition in their computers. Tiger continues to improve on speech recognition by offering a host of tools that let you get more work done in a shorter amount of time. (We're not to that point yet, Scotty, but we're working on it.)

The Speech Recognition features of Mac OS X let you speak a word, phrase, or sentence. After you've spoken, your Mac goes to work translating what you said — and if it understands the phrase, it then performs an action associated with that phrase. The great part about this system is that you can say any phrase in continuous speech and have your Mac perform any sort of action that you can imagine. In fact, you aren't limited to just one action: You could perform dozens of actions upon speaking a particular phrase.

Before you get started using Speech Recognition, you need a microphone to get sound into your Mac. Most current Macintosh models have a built-in microphone; for example, if you use an iMac G5, your microphone is built into the monitor. PowerBooks and iBooks have a similar microphone built into the screen. If your Mac doesn't have a microphone, connect one to the rear of your Macintosh by plugging it into the microphone jack.

If you're looking for the best quality audio input from your microphone for use with iChat AV, check out a microphone with a USB connection. You'll get far better sound quality than a microphone that connects to your analog jack.

The Speech Recognition tab

To get started with Speech Recognition in Mac OS X, open the System Preferences window by clicking its icon on the Dock and then clicking the Speech icon. This brings up the Speech panel, as shown in Figure 3-1.

You'll find that two tabs comprise the speech settings of Mac OS X:

+ Speech Recognition

+ Text to Speech

In this section, I'm only concerned with the Speech Recognition tab. Later, in the section "Your Mac Talks Back!" I explore the Text to Speech tab.

The Speech Recognition tab consists of two sub-tabs:

✦ **Settings:** The Settings tab provides a number of settings that control how your Mac listens to Its Master's Voice. (Meaning you, friend reader.) From here, you can set the sound input, adjust the key on the keyboard that toggles speech recognition on and off, change microphone settings, and name your computer with a keyword. (You *do* want to call your computer by name like any techno-wizard, don't you?)

✦ **Commands:** When Speech Recognition is active, your Mac can understand any number of commands. From the Commands tab, you tell the Mac what type of command it should expect you to give. You can also specify whether you will be giving the commands word-for-word or whether your Mac should be prepared to interpret paraphrasing. A number of specific applications and menus can be configured with speakable items, like contact names within Tiger's Address Book.

Crowning the Speech Recognition panel are the Speakable Items On and Off radio buttons. You've probably already guessed how to use 'em to switch Speech Recognition features on and off.

When you select the On radio button, the small circular Speech Recognition Feedback window appears on your screen, floating above all other windows. Learn this face well because the Feedback window (also shown in Figure 3-1) is your friend and partner. If you use Speech Recognition often, it'll become a constant companion on your Desktop. (More on it in the next section.)

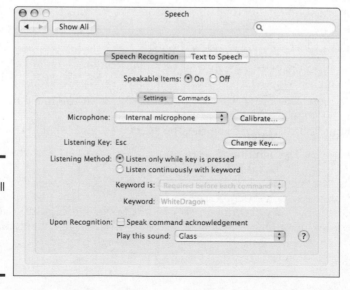

Figure 3-1: Hail and well met, good Speech pane (and Feedback window)!

Feedback window

The Settings panel

At the bottom of the Settings panel is the Upon Recognition section. When your Mac comprehends one of your stentorian commands, you can set it to respond by playing a sound, speaking a confirmation, or both. This is helpful when you're not sure whether your Mac understands you. One hundred percent recognition is not a reality on any computer at this point, so sometimes it helps to have any feedback that you can get. Otherwise, you might feel silly shouting at your machine while it sits there doing nothing. (Or perhaps not, if you're into really cheap anger management.)

You can choose between two styles of listening with the Listening Method options:

✦ **Listen Only While Key Is Pressed:** Speech Recognition works only while the designated key is held down.

✦ **Listen Continuously with Keyword:** When you speak the keyword, listening turns on and remains on.

To change what key must be toggled or held down, click the Change Key button.

Why change the keyword? Instead of saying, "Computer, empty the Trash!" you might prefer, "Elrond, empty the Trash!" This adds a little bit of personality to the interaction and also gives your computer a slightly longer time to react to your command. (As a general rule, the longer the spoken phrase, the more likely your Mac will understand it.) If you select the Listen Continuously with Keyword feature, you can change your computer's name via the Keyword text box.

Finally, you can select the microphone that you want to use from the Microphone drop-down list box on the Settings panel — a great feature if you have more than one microphone connected to your Mac. Click the Calibrate key to adjust the sound volume for better recognition.

The Commands panel

When Speech Recognition is active, your Mac listens for whatever phrases appear in your Speakable Items folder (a directory on your hard drive that holds a number of scripts). The Commands tab (as shown in Figure 3-2) allows you to view the contents of this folder. When you speak a phrase that matches one of these filenames, your Mac automatically executes that script. The script can perform any number of actions, which is what makes Speech Recognition so powerful. Apple includes a large number of scripts with Mac OS X, but you're free to create your own, too.

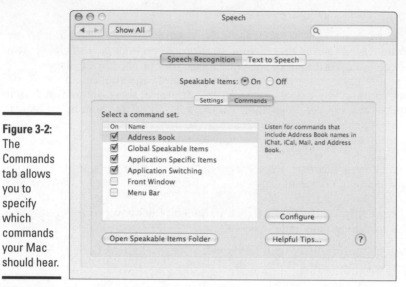

Figure 3-2:
The
Commands
tab allows
you to
specify
which
commands
your Mac
should hear.

To make something speakable, select the item and then speak the command, "Make this speakable." The new speakable command is based upon the item's name.

To view the contents of the Speakable Items folder, click the Open Speakable Items Folder button on the Commands panel. The Finder comes to the foreground and navigates to the folder that holds the scripts. This is handy because each item in the Speakable Items folder is speakable.

To the right of the Open Speakable Items Folder button is another button: Helpful Tips. Click it to get some pointers on how to get the best performance from your microphone.

As I mention in the preceding section, the Speech Recognition features of Mac OS X are not restricted to items in the Speakable Items folder. Any application that supports Speech Recognition is also fair game for your verbal manipulation. To control commands within other applications, use the Commands tab (refer to Figure 3-2). Here you can enable the following check boxes:

✦ Address Book

✦ Global Speakable Items

✦ Application Specific Items

✦ Application Switching

✦ Front Window (requires that you activate assistive devices in the Universal Access panel within System Preferences)

✦ Menu Bar (requires that you activate assistive devices in the Universal Access panel within System Preferences)

Mark any one of these options to allow your Mac to listen to those kinds of commands.

The Feedback window

After you activate Speech Recognition, you'll instantly see the Feedback window. You can click and drag the edge of the window to position it anywhere on your Desktop.

The Feedback window includes controls and displays of its own:

✦ **Microphone Level Meter:** The Feedback window displays indicators to let you know how loud the input to your microphone is.

✦ **Visual Indicator:** The Feedback window displays visual feedback to let you know what mode it is in: idle, listening, or hearing a command. When the microphone is not grayed out but there are no arrows on either side of the microphone, you're in listening mode. When the microphone is flanked by animated arrows, your computer is hearing a command spoken. When Speech Recognition is idle, no arrows are present, and the microphone is grayed out.

✦ **Quick-Access Menu:** You can quickly access the Speech preferences for the System or view the Speech Commands window. Just click the downward-pointing arrow at the bottom of the Feedback window, and a menu appears giving you one-click access to both.

As soon as you disable speech recognition in the System Preferences, the Feedback window disappears.

The Speech Command window

Because Speech Recognition might be listening for different sets of commands from the Finder or many other applications, Mac OS X provides you with a single listing of all commands that you might speak at any given time: the Speech Commands window. To open the Speech Commands window, click the triangle at the bottom of the Feedback window and choose Open Speech Commands Window from the menu that appears.

The Speech Commands window is a simple one, but it serves an important purpose: to let you know what commands Mac OS X understands. The Speech Commands pane, as shown in Figure 3-3, organizes commands into categories that match the settings in the Speech pane of the System Preferences.

**Book VII
Chapter 3**

**Talking and Writing
to Your Macintosh**

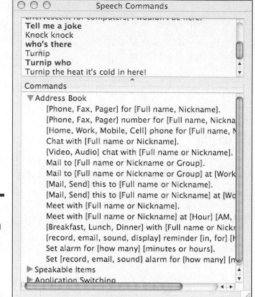

Figure 3-3:
The Speech Commands window, hard at work.

If you launch another application that supports Speech Recognition, Mac OS X adds that application's commands to the Speech Commands window. Speak any of these commands to make your Mac execute that function. For example, Mac OS X ships with speech commands for Address Book, such as "Mail To" and "Video Chat With."

Apple might be a big, serious, computer company — yeah, right — but it isn't without a humorous side! With Speech Recognition enabled, say the phrase, "Tell me a joke." Your Mac will reply with a random joke. Say it again, and your Mac will tell you another joke. (Brace yourself, these jokes were likely written by Windows users . . . they're really, *really* bad.) Oh, and if you get a "Knock, Knock" joke, remember that you have to actually say, "Who's there?"

Your Mac Talks Back!

Mac OS X is great at listening to your speech, but the fun doesn't stop there . . . your Mac can talk to you, too! By using one of the many available voices, you can make your computer talk or even sing. (Not as well as Sinatra, but better than Bob Dylan.) And although Speech Recognition lets you speak to your Macintosh, the new *VoiceOver* feature in Tiger gives your Mac the ability to speak text. This is an especially useful feature because it lets you listen to your e-mails, Web pages, or even your homework — sometimes the eyes need a break. Text-to-speech gives you the opportunity to lean back in your chair or even get up and walk around while still using your Macintosh.

Text-to-speech settings appear in three places within System Preferences: our old friend, the Speech pane; the Date & Time pane; and the VoiceOver settings within the Universal Access pane.

The Text to Speech panel

The text-to-speech engine that comes with Tiger has a collection of many different voices from which to choose; some voices are male, some are female, and some aren't human at all. To select your Mac's voice in Mac OS X, follow these steps:

1. **Click the System Preferences icon on the Dock.**

2. **Click the Speech icon.**

3. **Click the Text to Speech tab, as shown in Figure 3-4.**

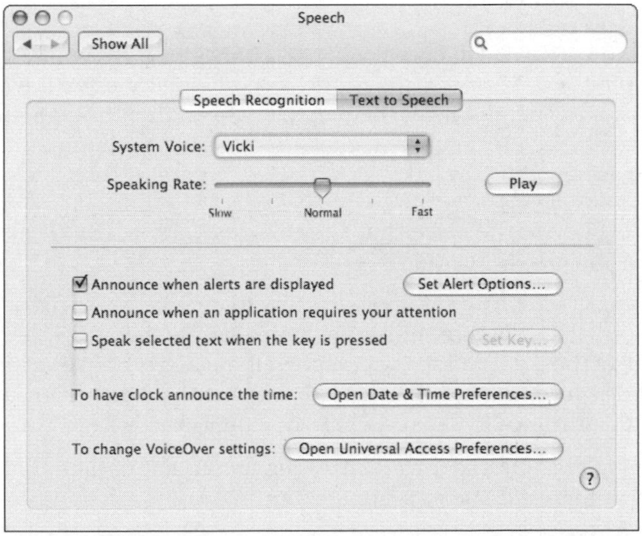

**Book VII
Chapter 3**

Talking and Writing to Your Macintosh

Figure 3-4:
You can select your Mac's voice from the Text to Speech panel.

Click the System Voice drop-down list box to choose a voice for your Mac. To hear the voice, click Play; Tiger speaks a sentence as a demonstration. To the left of the Play button is a slider for adjusting the speed of the speech. Move the slider to the right to increase the speed at which your Mac speaks and to the left to slow it down.

Personally, I think that Bruce, Vicki, Victoria, Kathy, and Ralph have some of the more intelligible voices of the bunch. (I'm a Vicki kinda guy myself.)

Talking alerts

After you select a voice, you have a variety of ways to make your Macintosh speak automatically to you, based on some simple rules. For example, every Mac owner has run into an Alert dialog. (*Alert dialogs* are typically accompanied by a select group of words — better left unspoken — from the human behind the keyboard.) An Alert dialog usually displays some kind of icon from the following list:

✦ **Stop sign:** Indicates that something particularly important requires your attention — usually an error or a dire warning.

✦ **Yield sign:** Signals that you should cautiously proceed; not as severe as the Stop sign, but important nonetheless.

✦ **Notification:** Looks like the profile of a person speaking; displays an informative message, but not a warning. You could use this feature, for example, to have a calendar application alert you when you have a meeting or a deadline.

From the Text to Speech panel, you can choose to have your Mac speak a specific phrase or the contents of the Alert dialog by selecting one of the check boxes at the middle of the panel. If you enable the Announce When Alerts Are Displayed check box, click the Set Alert Options button to set alert-specific options:

✦ **Voice:** Choose the voice that should speak alerts. (By default, it's the voice you choose earlier.)

✦ **Phrase:** Click this drop-down list box to choose a "prefix" phrase that will be spoken before the actual alert text. By default, Tiger speaks the name of the application that displayed the alert, but you can also choose a phrase from the list, or choose to mix up the phrases for a little variety. To add or remove phrases, click the Edit Phrases item.

✦ **Delay:** Drag this slider to control the increment of time that Tiger allows to pass before it speaks.

To hear what your spoken alert settings will sound like in use, click the Play button.

If you click the Play button on the Set Alert Options sheet and don't hear anything right away, remember that it won't begin speaking until the time has elapsed that you set with the Delay slider. To hear the spoken alerts speak as soon as you click the Play button, move the slider to 0 (zero).

Other spoken items

In addition to spoken alerts, you can allow your Mac to speak when other actions occur. Again, these settings are found on the Text to Speech panel. Your Mac can speak in the following circumstances:

✦ **Announce when an application requires your attention:** In case you have your Dock hidden from view, it's not always clear when an application needs your attention. In these instances, Mac OS X will grab your attention via speech.

✦ **Read a selection of text when you press a particular key:** If you have a child who is learning to read, the Mac can help them by reading a selection of text. Kids can learn how to drag and select text often more quickly than they can read that text.

✦ **Announce the time:** Are you like me, constantly getting lost in time while immersed in your work? (Not to mention your favorite game.) I've set my iMac G5 to announce the hour, which always keeps my time sense firmly planted.

The Date & Time panel

There you are, deep in concentration as you finish up the final chapter of your Great American Novel, when you glance at the clock in the Finder menu bar and realize that you were *supposed* to pick up your kids at soccer practice a full hour ago!

You can avoid this shameful lapse of parental responsibility by turning on Tiger's automatic spoken time feature, which is controlled from the Date & Time pane within System Preferences (and is much more effective than a mechanical cuckoo clock). But why go to all the trouble of clicking Show All when you can just click the Open Date & Time Preferences button on the Text to Speech panel? Tiger immediately switches to display the Date & Time panel. You can even click the Clock on the Finder menu bar and click Open Date & Time. (Again, it's all about the convenience when it comes to the geniuses at Apple.)

Mark the Announce the Time check box to enable your Mac to speak the time; then use the Period drop-down list box to choose spoken time at the quarter, half, or full hour. You can also customize the voice for spoken time as well.

After you're done, zip back to the Speech pane by clicking the Back button at the top-left corner of the System Preferences window.

Configuring VoiceOver within the Universal Access panel

With Tiger's VoiceOver utility, your Mac can provide you with all sorts of verbal feedback, creating a spoken English interface with Tiger — a valuable addition to the operating system for the physically impaired. The feedback includes

✦ **Announcing when certain keys are pressed:** Tiger can tell you when a modifier key (like Control, Option, or ⌘) is pressed or when the Caps Lock key is pressed.

✦ **Announcing cursor movements:** You'll hear an audible alert when your mouse cursor switches between windows or when you've clicked on a menu.

✦ **Announcing the position of the VoiceOver cursor:** VoiceOver can audibly identify all operating system controls (like buttons, sliders, and list boxes) by using a special onscreen cursor.

✦ **Reading documents, Web pages, and Mail messages:** VoiceOver can read aloud the contents of all sorts of documents and application windows.

✦ **Speaking the characters you type:** You can set VoiceOver to speak every character or each word you type.

Here is how to enable VoiceOver (or to launch the VoiceOver utility, as shown in Figure 3-5):

1. **Click the Open Universal Access Preferences button on the Text to Speech panel.**

Figure 3-5:
You can customize VoiceOver's audible feedback using the VoiceOver Utility.

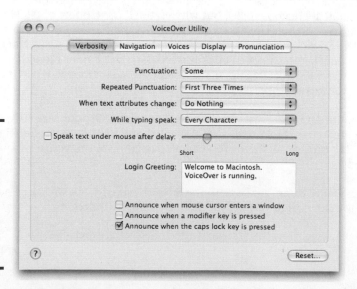

2. **Select the On radio button (or press ⌘+F5) to enable VoiceOver.**

   To customize how VoiceOver operates, click the Open VoiceOver Utility button.

Speaking text through applications

Although VoiceOver provides a comprehensive text-to-speech interface for Mac OS X, it might be more than you need. If you simply want to hear text spoken within your applications, there are a number of alternative methods included in Tiger that don't require VoiceOver.

One of the simplest ways to hear spoken text in Mac OS X is by using the TextEdit application. *TextEdit* is a simple text processor that accompanies every copy of Mac OS X. Besides its handy word processing features, TextEdit can also speak text. This is good for reviewing a document after you've written it by listening to it. To hear spoken text with TextEdit, follow these steps:

1. **Launch TextEdit from the Applications folder.**

   To open the Applications folder, choose Go➪Applications from the Finder. In the window that appears, double-click the TextEdit application.

   This launches the TextEdit application and opens a new document.

2. **Enter some text.**

   Either type some text on the keyboard or paste some into the document from the Clipboard. Here's a favorite example from this book's technical editor (especially when you use the Cellos voice):

   > Billy Gates has lots of cash
   > Lots of cash
   > Lots of cash
   > Billy Gates has lots of cash
   > I'd like $10 please!

3. **Choose Edit➪Speech➪Start Speaking.**

   Your Mac will begin speaking the text from the document. The speech engine has some intelligence, so you can enter dollar amounts (such as $25,423.12) or Roman numerals (such as Chapter XIV), and the speech engine will read them back in plain English. The result of these two strings would be "twenty-five thousand, four-hundred twenty-three dollars, and twelve cents" and "chapter fourteen."

4. **Choose Edit➪Speech➪Stop Speaking.**

   You Mac will stop speaking. It will also stop speaking when it reaches the end of the text.

Speaking text through services

You can also speak text within most applications by using the Services menu, located under the application's named menu. To speak text from an application, first select that text. Then, choose *Application*⇨Services⇨Speech⇨Start Speaking to speak text from many applications (where *Application* is the name of the currently running application). If you don't want to use VoiceOver, this works great for doing things like

✦ Speaking a Web page aloud

✦ Reading your e-mail

✦ Listening to a speech you've written in Pages

As you might expect, choosing *Application*⇨Services⇨Speech⇨Stop Speaking ceases the banter emanating from your Mac's speaker.

Alas, not all applications are created equal. Some applications cannot access the Services offered in the Services menu — if you don't see Speech in the list of services, you're out of luck.

Chapter 4: Hosting a Web Site with Mac OS X

In This Chapter

✔ Creating your own Web site

✔ Using .Mac

✔ Hosting your own Web server

✔ Sharing files with FTP

*I*n the last ten years, surfing the Internet has gone from a nerd's hobby to a fun activity enjoyed by the whole family. For children and grandparents alike, Web surfing has become one of the world's most popular spectator sports — and at some point, you'll probably get the itch to become more involved. Everyone else has a Web site, so why not you?

Creating and hosting your own Web site can be a rewarding experience, and with some help from Apple and Mac OS X, it's a cinch to do. Whether you want to share your favorite eggplant recipes, display pictures of your aubergine Auburn, or just post a purple résumé, Mac OS X has you covered in more ways than one. So put on your seat belts — you're now entering a strange world of servers, mysterious codes, and things that go bump in the Net. No need for alarm, though . . . Apple has made the topic so simple that even a politician can do it.

Building a Site with .Mac

To get you up and running on the Web quickly, Apple offers a suite of online Web-publishing tools. The toolbox, collectively known as *.Mac,* gives you easy and fast access to a variety of Internet functions. A .Mac membership costs $99.95 per year and offers the following features:

✦ **iCards:** Send customized electronic postcards via the Internet.

✦ **HomePage:** Build and edit your own Web site.

✦ **iDisk:** This disk space on Apple's servers is where you can post a Web site or files. (And this is where you store files for use in your own HomePage creations.)

✦ **Backup:** Safeguard your data the right way — across the Internet, or to your Mac's CD or DVD recorder.

✦ **Address Book and iCal sharing:** Store and publish data from your local Address Book and iCal files.

✦ **Email:** This covers Web-based e-mail for your Mac.com e-mail account.

Registering as a .Mac user

You can visit Apple's home on the Internet to register as a .Mac user:

```
www.mac.com
```

To register for your free 60-day trial, you must create a username and password. The username that you select is an important part of the .Mac experience, so choose it carefully. Your username plays a part in your e-mail address, your Web address, your login name, and even the bar code on your forehead. (Okay, the bar code is a joke — for now, anyway — but the rest aren't.) Take a few minutes to carefully plan your .Mac username. It will save you some typing, be easier for your friends to remember, and (like a customized license plate for your car) can convey a certain personality to others on the Web.

Setting up your site with HomePage

After you successfully register as a .Mac user, log in to the .Mac section of the Apple Web site. You can find it on the toolbar at the top of the Web page.

Click the HomePage icon that appears at the left side (or top) of the page. This takes you to the login screen (see Figure 4-1). Enter your username and password that you entered upon registration and click the Enter button.

Figure 4-1:
Log in to
your .Mac
account
here.

HomePage is a complete publishing tool for building Web pages that's actually a Web site itself. HomePage lets you choose from a variety of styles that you can then apply to your Web site within a matter of seconds; because it's template driven, even non-techies can produce impressive-looking Web sites. After you finish designing your Web pages by selecting one of the premade templates, HomePage automatically posts them to your .Mac Web site.

The HomePage interface includes two sections: the Pages section and the Create a Page section. The Pages section (as shown at the top of Figure 4-2) is where you manage the various pages of your site; here you can view a list of all pages on your site as well as password-protect any pages on your site. After you complete your site, you can get spiffy and formal by sending an announcement (click the Announce Site button) to all your friends from the Site section.

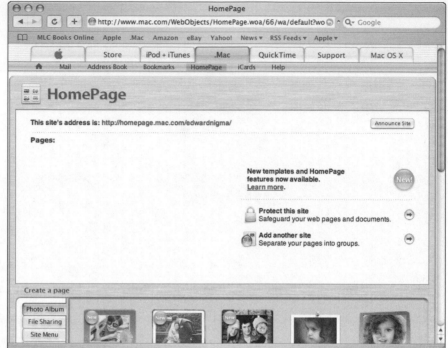

Figure 4-2:
Manage
your existing
Web pages
from here.

Scroll down to the Create a Page section, as shown in Figure 4-3, from which you can directly add a page to your site based on a variety of premade Web page templates. Apple offers a multitude of styles to suit your needs. Click any one of these styles to add it to your Web site. When you do, .Mac walks you through a series of questions that indicate what specific information, graphics, or movies you want on that Web page.

✦ **Photo Album:** Display your favorite photos and images for your friends and family.

✦ **File Sharing:** With HomePage, you can quickly post your favorite files for others to download.

✦ **Site Menu:** This top-level menu design helps visitors navigate quickly around your site.

✦ **iMovie:** Post your home videos or iMovie creations on the Web. (To discover all about iMovie HD, read Book III, Chapter 4.)

✦ **Writing:** Want to update all those close (and not-so-close) relatives on your family's doings? Put out a newspaper or post an online diary.

✦ **Resume:** Looking for a job? A Web-based résumé is a handy tool for impressing prospective employers.

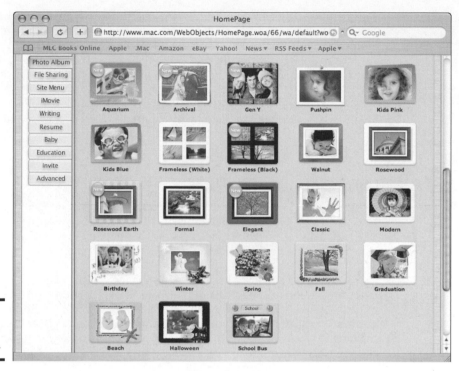

Figure 4-3:
Create new
pages here.

Book VII
Chapter 4

Hosting a Web Site
with Mac OS X

✦ **Baby:** When your bundle of joy arrives, it's a cinch to post photos of
the new baby to your HomePage site. This works great for long-distance
relatives because they can cyber-visit the hospital without leaving home.
It also works well for keeping those curious aunts and uncles out of the
delivery room.

✦ **Education:** Schools are depending more and more on the Internet. To help
the student and the teacher, Apple provides several useful education-
related pages for you to use, including event calendars, homework pages,
and an online school newspaper.

✦ **Invite:** The Web makes for a great tool when it comes to delivering invi-
tations. Gone are the hassles of standing in line at the post office, licking
300 stamps, and having cards lost in the mail. Send your guests a Web-
based invitation. Your guests will thank you. The trees that you save will
thank you. Moreover, your tongue will thank you. The post office, however, might not thank you, but why should it start now?

✦ **Advanced:** Click this tab to add pages you've created with an external
HyperText Markup Language (HTML) editor. (Read more about these
editors in the upcoming sections, "Creating a Home Page with HTML
and iDisk" and "Serving static information.")

Keep adding pages to your site as you see fit. Each type of page has a different layout. If a page requires media like images or movies, for example, HomePage automatically lists all media available on your iDisk. You simply select the desired media file, and HomePage adds them to the current page. The following section elaborates more on iDisk.

After you complete your Web site, you access it by using a URL like this (with *your_username* replaced with your actual username):

`http://homepage.mac.com/`*your_username*

Adding files with iDisk

If you create a Web page with HomePage that requires images or movies, you add them to your site by using iDisk. *iDisk* is a space on Apple's servers designated just for you, where HomePage stores the elements of your site when you add or change Web pages.

You aren't limited to iDisk access via HomePage: Simply choose the iDisk menu from the Finder's Go menu to mount your iDisk. (No need for a saddle — I explain more about mounting volumes in Book I.) When you mount an iDisk, it shows up as an icon on your Desktop, just like you might see when you insert a CD into your Mac. The icon for your iDisk, however, looks like a hard drive with a blue globe on top of it.

With your iDisk mounted, double-click its icon to view its contents. Apple organizes iDisk with a handful of folders that correspond to the page types in HomePage; you can't delete or rename these folders, however. If you need an image for your photo album page, stick it in the Pictures folder. If you need a movie for your Web page, copy it to the Movies folder. When you return to HomePage, your files now appear in the list of items that you can use in a Web page.

Creating a Home Page with HTML and iDisk

For those folks who like driving a car without knowing what goes on under the hood, HomePage is perfect: You just use it to create and post Web pages without knowing what makes it all work. On the other hand, some folks are born mechanics and like to get under the hood. If you're itching to see what goes on behind the scenes, Apple gives you a chance to get your hands dirty. Of course, you don't *have* to use HomePage to work on your Web site. If you're well versed in HTML, you can edit your Web page files on your iDisk just like you would any file on your hard drive.

Within your iDisk, open the Sites folder to see the various files that compose your Web page. If you're an old pro at HTML, you can add your own pages to your iDisk with your favorite text editor. In other words, the iDisk acts much like any other disk that you're accustomed to using. (For all the inside information on iDisk, see Chapter 4 of Book IV.)

As I mention earlier, you can also click the Advanced tab in the Create a Page section to have HomePage assist you in uploading your own pages.

Using Mac OS X Web Sharing

With .Mac, Apple takes care of the Web server for you, but you aren't limited to .Mac: You have other options when it comes to posting Web pages. Mac OS X comes stocked with its own high-powered Web server, so you can run things without .Mac. Consider the advantages, won't you?

✦ **Privacy:** Everyone in the house wants access to the family phone book. You want all computers on your home network to see the telephone list but not the whole world. Posting it on the home network keeps it secure from prying eyes outside your home.

✦ **Your own domain:** Want a name like `www.size14feetphotos.com`? (Don't even think about it, I've already taken it.) Anyway, if you run your own Web server, you can arrange for your own domain name.

✦ **Speed:** Your friend needs a copy of your iMovie HD masterpiece for a class project. Rather than wait for you to post the file to your iDisk, he decides to download it directly from your computer.

✦ **Coolness factor:** It's fun, easy to do, and your mother will truly be proud. Seriously, it is fun and easy to run your own Web server. (And although your mother might not actually give a hoot, companies appreciate employees who know useful skills; therefore, Web server stuff is good to know.)

I love Apache: Confessions of a UNIX Webmaster

Deep in the guts of Mac OS X lies one of the most popular Web servers around: *Apache,* which turns your Macintosh into a full-featured Web server. The Apache Web server is well known around the world and comprises about half of all personal and commercial Web servers in use today. Yes, that's right! You have one of the world's most-used Web servers already installed on your Mac!

Apache's first appealing feature is its price — absolutely free. *Free is sassy!* Free isn't any good without quality, though. Fortunately, Apache is extremely reliable — and combined with the crash-proof Mac OS X, you can be almost certain that your Web server will always be available. Besides being rock-solid and free, Apache sports all the features you'd expect from a top-notch Web server, such as techno-wizard integration with databases and scripting languages. Believe me, it can serve anything you throw at it.

Configuring and running Apache

In addition to all its great qualities, Apache is dead simple to operate in Mac OS X. Open System Preferences and click the Sharing icon; then mark the check box next to Personal Web Sharing to launch Apache. That's it! It doesn't get any easier . . . at least, when it comes to turning on Apache. (See Figure 4-4.)

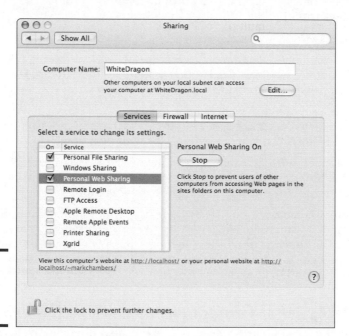

Figure 4-4: Turning on Apache is a cinch.

To begin using your Web server, open a Finder window and navigate to the Sites folder that resides in your Home folder; this is the root of your personal space on the Web server. Any files that you add to this folder are accessible via your Web server.

You might find a file named `index.html` already installed in the Sites folder. This is the default file for your Web site. To view it, open your favorite Web browser and load this URL, replacing *~username* with the username that you're currently using:

```
http://127.0.0.1/~username/
```

The 127.0.0.1 address is a generic Internet Protocol (IP) address, which means *self.* (In other words, your Mac is connecting to itself. Faintly unsettling, but absolutely legal.) You can also use your real IP address, which appears at the bottom of the Sharing panel in the System Preferences when you turn on Personal Web Sharing.

To see the Web page from another computer, you must use the real IP address. The 127.0.0.1 address is merely a convenience for use when you're using the actual machine that runs the Web server.

Because Mac OS X is a multi-user environment, each user can host a Web site. The key is the username found at the end of the URL; replace it with the appropriate username, and you're ready to go. If everything goes smoothly, you should be viewing the default Mac OS X Web page, as shown in Figure 4-5. The default page displays a welcome message and some important information for Web-sharing beginners. Make sure that you read the information carefully.

Book VII Chapter 4

Hosting a Web Site with Mac OS X

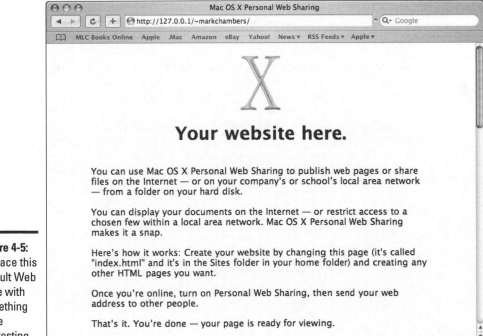

Figure 4-5: Replace this default Web page with something more interesting.

In addition to a main page for any individual that logs in, the Web server also has a global default page. To find the global default page, follow these steps:

1. **Open a new Finder window.**

2. **Double-click the drive that contains your Mac OS X installation.**

3. **Choose Library⇨WebServer⇨Documents.**

Here you'll find dozens of HTML files. These files are the default global home pages for many different languages. For English versions of the Mac OS, this means that the file named `index.html.en` serves as the default home page for the server. To view this file in your browser, try this URL:

```
http://127.0.0.1/
```

Serving static information

To change the default Web page, simply open it in your favorite HTML editor and start changing it. An *HTML editor* is an application that lets you lay out your Web page with what-you-see-is-what-you-get (WYSIWYG) ease. If you're familiar with a word processor, you're well on your way to using an HTML editor. Of the many HTML editors available, VersionTracker (`www.versiontracker.com`) will give you a good head start on finding some of the most popular ones.

You aren't limited only to HTML editors, of course. Many word processors support HTML export — I particularly like Microsoft Word — so it's trés easy to create Web pages with them by simply choosing File⇨Save As.

If you already know HTML (Webmasters might say, "If you can bang out raw HTML code"), you can edit your Web pages by hand. Open the existing `index.html` file with a text editor like TextEdit or BBEdit (`www.barebones.com`) by choosing File⇨Open and change it to suit your needs. For example, a simple Web page might read like this:

```
<html>
<head><title>My First Web Page</title></head>
<body>

Welcome to my Web site!

</body>
</html>
```

Plain old HTML pages are handy for displaying the same information repeatedly. Computer Web-wizards call this type of information *static*. (That is, it doesn't change. Like a fully grown Chia Pet, you can set it once and forget about it.)

Serving information dynamically

Although static displays are good for things like your copy of the Magna Carta or sports stats from the past 20 years, they're not so great for data that changes a lot (usually referred to as *dynamic*, if you hadn't already guessed). Some good examples of dynamic information are the date, the time, your age, or the weather. If you were to display your age on a Web page by using only HTML, you'd have to change it only once every year. This isn't so bad, but consider what happens if you want to post the date on a Web page: Now you have to update the Web page once per day. Add the time, and now you're down to HTML changes every hour, minute, or second, depending on how reliable you want to make the clock. Clearly, you need something besides static HTML for *dynamic* information.

The Apache Web server allows you to use a variety of tools to produce dynamic Web pages. The most basic tool for serving dynamic data is the *Server Side Include*. The Web server executes a small piece of code in your HTML; then the Web server replaces that code with some text and sends the page to whomever requested it. The result is dynamic text in your Web page.

Adding Server Side Includes requires that you perform a few preparatory steps beforehand. To alter Apache settings, you must change text in its settings file. The file is named `httpd.conf` and is located here:

```
/etc/httpd/httpd.conf
```

You probably won't be able to find this file if you go searching for it in the Finder because it's a hidden file. Some text editors like BBEdit can open hidden files, but you might not have that on hand. You do have the Terminal application, though. Launch the Terminal by double-clicking its icon. (You can find it in the Utility folder that resides in your Applications folder.) Book VII, Chapter 1 has more information about the Terminal in case you need a refresher. At the prompt that appears, enter this command:

```
sudo pico /etc/httpd/httpd.conf
```

You are then nudged to provide a password at the following prompt:

```
Password:
```

When prompted for a password, use a password of an administrator account on your machine. If you're the only user, this might be the password of the user that you're currently signed in as. Press Return, and you will be looking at the innards of the Apache setup file. There's a lot of what I call *Programmer Pig Latin* in this file, but don't be discouraged. Scroll down through the file (use the arcane UNIX Control+V key sequence) and look for this chunk of text:

```
# Note that "MultiViews" must be named *explicitly* --- "Options All"
# doesn't give it to you.
#
    Options Indexes FollowSymLinks MultiViews
```

If you don't feel like scrolling through a bunch of text, you can jump to the text by pressing Control+W (shorthand for *where*), entering the text that you want to find (for example: **Options Indexes FollowSymLinks**), and then pressing Return.

Whenever you find the desired text in the file, add the word **Includes** to the end of the last line of this text.

```
# Note that "MultiViews" must be named *explicitly* --- "Options All"
# doesn't give it to you.
#
    Options Indexes FollowSymLinks MultiViews Includes
```

Notice the many pound (#) characters. A pound character denotes a *comment:* Think of comments as notes to yourself that help you remember what the heck you were doing at this point in the file. Techno-wizard coders would say it this way: When a comment character (#) precedes a line, that line of text performs no function. You can use this to your advantage to turn settings on and off for the server. Add a pound character to the beginning of a line, and that function stops working. Remove the character, and the function works again. Continue scrolling through the `httpd.conf` file by using the arrow keys or the Control+W search trick, looking for the following:

```
    # To use server-parsed HTML files
    #
    AddType text/html .shtml
    AddHandler server-parsed .shtml
```

Make sure that no # characters precede the `AddType` and `AddHandler` lines. After you finish, press Control+O, press Return to save the file, and then press Control+X to exit the pico text editor. After you finish editing Apache's settings, you have to restart it for the changes to take effect. Open the System Preferences and click the Internet tab. Deactivate Web Sharing and then reactivate it again.

Next, open your favorite text editor and add some text to a new file:

```
<html>
<head><title>My First Web Page</title></head>
<body>

Welcome to my Web site!<br>
Today's date: <!--#echo var="DATE_LOCAL" -->

</body>
</html>
```

The `<!--#echo var="DATE_LOCAL" -->` part is a Server Side Include. The server understands the `"DATE_LOCAL"` message, and in its place, adds text that displays today's date. Save the text file and give it the name `index.shtml`.

Make sure that you include the `.shtml` extension. It's important for making the Server Side Includes work properly.

Save the file in your global Web folder, located here:

`/Library/WebServer/documents/index.shtml`

Finally, it's time to check out your handiwork and rest your fingers from all this typing. Open a Web browser and navigate to the URL of your global Web folder:

`http://127.0.0.1/index.shtml`

The result should be a Web page that displays today's date. (I know, it's not particularly material for the Louvre at this point, but I think you can appreciate the possibilities.)

If you're not content with appending `.shtml` to your files to take advantage of Server Side Includes, you need to perform another step. When you view your Web site with a Web browser, it's customary to use default pages for a particular directory. For example, when loading the following URL:

`http://127.0.0.1/`

the server looks for a default page to load on the server because you didn't specify one. This is normally a file named `index.html`, which causes problems for Server Side Includes because they require a filename ending with `.shtml`. The easiest way to fix this is to tell the server that `index.shtml` can also be a default page. To fix this discrepancy, reload the Apache configuration file by using this command line:

`sudo pico /etc/httpd/httpd.conf`

If you perform this step within 15 minutes of your last `sudo` command, you won't have to re-enter a password. If it's been longer, you might have to enter the password — I told you in Chapter 1 of this mini-book that UNIX had sophisticated security, didn't I? Then scroll down through the `httpd.conf` file and find this bit of text:

```
# DirectoryIndex: Name of the file or files to use as a pre-written HTML
# directory index.  Separate multiple entries with spaces.
#
<IfModule mod_dir.c>
    DirectoryIndex index.html
</IfModule>
```

Change it by adding `index.shtml` to it:

```
# DirectoryIndex: Name of the file or files to use as a pre-written HTML
# directory index.  Separate multiple entries with spaces.
#
<IfModule mod_dir.c>
    DirectoryIndex index.shtml index.html
</IfModule>
```

Notice that `index.shtml` precedes `index.html`. This line indicates which filenames you can use for the default filename of any folder on the Web server. In this case, I'm forcing `index.shtml` as the default filename before `index.html`. This means that when you load a Web page from your server without specifying a specific file, Apache is going to look for a file named `index.shtml` in that folder first. If it can't find one, it looks for a file named `index.html`. With that change in place, press Control+O to write the file to disk and then press Control+X to quit the pico text editor. To see your work in action, stop and restart Personal Web Sharing on the Sharing pane in System Preferences; then load this URL with your Web browser:

```
http://127.0.0.1/
```

The result should be that your `index.shtml` page loads with Server Side Includes intact.

Server Side Includes can perform a few other simple functions besides the date, including

✦ `DATE_GMT`: Today's date in Greenwich Mean Time.

✦ `DATE_LOCAL`: Today's date in your local time zone. (You're already an expert with this one.)

✦ `DOCUMENT_NAME`: The name of document.

✦ `LAST_MODIFIED`: The date when this document was last modified.

To see them all in action, alter your `index.shtml` file to read like this:

```
<html>
<head><title>My First Web Page</title></head>
<body>

Welcome to my Web site! <br><br>
GMT date: <!--#echo var="DATE_GMT" --> <br>
Today's date: <!--#echo var="DATE_LOCAL" --><br>
Name of this document: <!--#echo var="DOCUMENT_NAME" --><br>
Last Modified: <!--#echo var="LAST_MODIFIED" --><br>

</body>
</html>
```

Reload your Web server's main page to see the results.

Fancier dynamic stuff

Another common use of Server Side Includes gives you a chance to remove whole chunks of your HTML files and put them into another file. (Sounds messy, doesn't it?) You might want to do this for HTML that will appear on each page of your Web site: For example, you might like today's date and the page's last modified date to appear at the bottom of any page of your whole Web site. Webmasters, being the sedentary, nerd-beast crowd that they are, don't want to type this information repeatedly for each HTML page that they create. Furthermore, they don't want to have to retype all that information for every file if it should change. What's a lazy techno-wizard to do? Server Side Includes come to the rescue!

The first step is to modify your main page: in this case, `index.shtml`:

```
<html>
<head><title>My First Web Page</title></head>
<body>

Welcome to my Web site!<br>
<!--#include virtual="footer.shtml"-->

</body>
</html>
```

You might notice that I removed all the Server Side Includes from before and added a new one. The new line

```
<!--#include virtual="footer.shtml"-->
```

tells the Web server to load the file named `footer.shtml` and dump its contents into `index.shtml` in place of this Server Side Include. Save this file.

Next, create a new text file. To the new file, add this code:

```
<center>
<hr width="50%">

Today's date: <!--#echo var="DATE_LOCAL" --><br>
Last Modified: <!--#echo var="LAST_MODIFIED" --><br><br>

</center>
```

If you're familiar with HTML, the first thing that might strike you is that this file doesn't follow proper HTML formatting. Because this file is just a chunk of HTML that's going to be part of a fully formed HTML file, it doesn't need the full treatment. Otherwise, this code is standard HTML with a few Server Side Includes tossed in for good measure. Just to spruce things up a bit, the text is centered with a small horizontal line above it. Save this file, giving it the name footer.shtml.

Now, whenever you want this footer to be at the bottom of any Web page on the server, add the <!--#include virtual="footer.shtml"--> line from before. Besides saving you time from reconstructing the footer each time in an HTML file, you only have to add one line of code, and Server Side Includes take care of the rest. Even better, you can alter the footer file whenever you want, and the changes appear in the HTML of every page that contains the footer.

When bad things happen to good Webmasters

If you have browsed the Web for any time at all, you've no doubt stumbled across a *dead link*. This phenomenon occurs when you attempt to load a Web page that no longer exists on a particular server. If you were lucky and the server still existed, you probably saw a boring error message telling you that the page no longer exists. Apache provides default error messages like this for you, but that doesn't mean you can't improve the messages that your visitors see — a true power user eschews defaults when creativity kicks in!

Open your httpd.conf file for editing with pico like before.

```
sudo pico /etc/httpd/httpd.conf
```

Scroll through the file until you find the ErrorDocument directives.

```
#    2) local redirects
#ErrorDocument 404 /missing.html
#  to redirect to local URL /missing.html
```

Whenever a server can't find a page, it produces a 404 error — also well known as "That Damn Screen" to Web surfers around the world. (Please excuse my clarity there.) In fact, the number *404* has entered popular slang, meaning *dead* or *broken*. Normally, Apache directs itself to a default error message, but by removing one comment (note the now-absent pound character at the beginning of the second line), you can specify which file you would like to display (in the form of a page for the viewer) in the case of a 404 error.

```
#    2) local redirects
ErrorDocument 404 /missing.html
#  to redirect to local URL /missing.html
```

Press Control+O to save the `httpd.conf` file and then press Control+X to exit pico. Now whenever someone comes across a missing Web page on your site, your server will redirect him to a file named `missing.html`. Of course, you also need to create this `missing.html` file. Use your favorite text editor to create a new HTML file. To it, add this code:

```
<html>
<head><title>Uh-oh!</title></head>
<body>

Holy Toledo! <br><br>

We can't find the page you requested. <br>
Would you like to <a href="index.shtml">return to the main page</a>?


<!--#include virtual="footer.shtml"-->

</body>
</html>
```

Save this file, giving it the name `missing.html`. Save it in your Web server's root directory.

```
/Library/WebServer/Documents/missing.html
```

Return to the System Preferences Sharing panel, click the Internet tab, and toggle Web Sharing off and on again. This will force your Web server to read in the changes to the `httpd.conf` file.

To test it out, load a URL that you know doesn't exist. Anything will do.

```
http://1270.0.0.1/some_missing_page_I_forgot_to_add.html
```

If you've configured things properly, you should see a personalized Web error page — this way, perhaps your visitor will chuckle instead of curse when a dead link is encountered.

Index

J

Notes

Notes

Notes

Notes

SINESS, CAREERS & PERSONAL FINANCE

0-7645-5307-0

0-7645-5331-3 *†

Also available:

- Accounting For Dummies †
  0-7645-5314-3
- Business Plans Kit For Dummies †
  0-7645-5365-8
- Cover Letters For Dummies
  0-7645-5224-4
- Frugal Living For Dummies
  0-7645-5403-4
- Leadership For Dummies
  0-7645-5176-0
- Managing For Dummies
  0-7645-1771-6

- Marketing For Dummies
  0-7645-5600-2
- Personal Finance For Dummies *
  0-7645-2590-5
- Project Management For Dummies
  0-7645-5283-X
- Resumes For Dummies †
  0-7645-5471-9
- Selling For Dummies
  0-7645-5363-1
- Small Business Kit For Dummies *†
  0-7645-5093-4

OME & BUSINESS COMPUTER BASICS

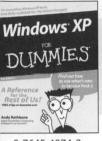

0-7645-4074-2

0-7645-3758-X

Also available:

- ACT! 6 For Dummies
  0-7645-2645-6
- iLife '04 All-in-One Desk Reference
  For Dummies
  0 7645-7347-0
- iPAQ For Dummies
  0-7645-6769-1
- Mac OS X Panther Timesaving
  Techniques For Dummies
  0-7645-5812-9
- Macs For Dummies
  0-7645-5656-8

- Microsoft Money 2004 For Dummies
  0-7645-4195-1
- Office 2003 All-in-One Desk Reference
  For Dummies
  0-7645-3883-7
- Outlook 2003 For Dummies
  0-7645-3759-8
- PCs For Dummies
  0-7645-4074-2
- TiVo For Dummies
  0-7645-6923-6
- Upgrading and Fixing PCs For Dummies
  0-7645-1665-5
- Windows XP Timesaving Techniques
  For Dummies
  0-7645-3748-2

OD, HOME, GARDEN, HOBBIES, MUSIC & PETS

0-7645-5295-3

0-7645-5232-5

Also available:

- Bass Guitar For Dummies
  0-7645-2487-9
- Diabetes Cookbook For Dummies
  0-7645-5230-9
- Gardening For Dummies *
  0-7645-5130-2
- Guitar For Dummies
  0-7645-5106-X
- Holiday Decorating For Dummies
  0-7645-2570-0
- Home Improvement All-in-One
  For Dummies
  0-7645-5680-0

- Knitting For Dummies
  0-7645-5395-X
- Piano For Dummies
  0-7645-5105-1
- Puppies For Dummies
  0-7645-5255-4
- Scrapbooking For Dummies
  0-7645-7208-3
- Senior Dogs For Dummies
  0-7645-5818-8
- Singing For Dummies
  0-7645-2475-5
- 30-Minute Meals For Dummies
  0-7645-2589-1

TERNET & DIGITAL MEDIA

0-7645-1664-7

0-7645-6924-4

Also available:

- 2005 Online Shopping Directory
  For Dummies
  0-7645-7495-7
- CD & DVD Recording For Dummies
  0-7645-5956-7
- eBay For Dummies
  0-7645-5654-1
- Fighting Spam For Dummies
  0-7645-5965-6
- Genealogy Online For Dummies
  0-7645-5964-8
- Google For Dummies
  0-7645-4420-9

- Home Recording For Musicians
  For Dummies
  0-7645-1634-5
- The Internet For Dummies
  0-7645-4173-0
- iPod & iTunes For Dummies
  0-7645-7772-7
- Preventing Identity Theft For Dummies
  0-7645-7336-5
- Pro Tools All-in-One Desk Reference
  For Dummies
  0-7645-5714-9
- Roxio Easy Media Creator For Dummies
  0-7645-7131-1

SPORTS, FITNESS, PARENTING, RELIGION & SPIRITUALITY

0-7645-5146-9

0-7645-5418-2

Also available:

- Adoption For Dummies
  0-7645-5488-3
- Basketball For Dummies
  0-7645-5248-1
- The Bible For Dummies
  0-7645-5296-1
- Buddhism For Dummies
  0-7645-5359-3
- Catholicism For Dummies
  0-7645-5391-7
- Hockey For Dummies
  0-7645-5228-7

- Judaism For Dummies
  0-7645-5299-6
- Martial Arts For Dummies
  0-7645-5358-5
- Pilates For Dummies
  0-7645-5397-6
- Religion For Dummies
  0-7645-5264-3
- Teaching Kids to Read For Dummies
  0-7645-4043-2
- Weight Training For Dummies
  0-7645-5168-X
- Yoga For Dummies
  0-7645-5117-5

TRAVEL

0-7645-5438-7

0-7645-5453-0

Also available:

- Alaska For Dummies
  0-7645-1761-9
- Arizona For Dummies
  0-7645-6938-4
- Cancún and the Yucatán For Dummies
  0-7645-2437-2
- Cruise Vacations For Dummies
  0-7645-6941-4
- Europe For Dummies
  0-7645-5456-5
- Ireland For Dummies
  0-7645-5455-7

- Las Vegas For Dummies
  0-7645-5448-4
- London For Dummies
  0-7645-4277-X
- New York City For Dummies
  0-7645-6945-7
- Paris For Dummies
  0-7645-5494-8
- RV Vacations For Dummies
  0-7645-5443-3
- Walt Disney World & Orlando For Dummi
  0-7645-6943-0

GRAPHICS, DESIGN & WEB DEVELOPMENT

0-7645-4345-8

0-7645-5589-8

Also available:

- Adobe Acrobat 6 PDF For Dummies
  0-7645-3760-1
- Building a Web Site For Dummies
  0-7645-7144-3
- Dreamweaver MX 2004 For Dummies
  0-7645-4342-3
- FrontPage 2003 For Dummies
  0-7645-3882-9
- HTML 4 For Dummies
  0-7645-1995-6
- Illustrator CS For Dummies
  0-7645-4084-X

- Macromedia Flash MX 2004 For Dummi
  0-7645-4358-X
- Photoshop 7 All-in-One Desk
  Reference For Dummies
  0-7645-1667-1
- Photoshop CS Timesaving Technique
  For Dummies
  0-7645-6782-9
- PHP 5 For Dummies
  0-7645-4166-8
- PowerPoint 2003 For Dummies
  0-7645-3908-6
- QuarkXPress 6 For Dummies
  0-7645-2593-X

NETWORKING, SECURITY, PROGRAMMING & DATABASES

0-7645-6852-3

0-7645-5784-X

Also available:

- A+ Certification For Dummies
  0-7645-4187-0
- Access 2003 All-in-One Desk
  Reference For Dummies
  0-7645-3988-4
- Beginning Programming For Dummies
  0-7645-4997-9
- C For Dummies
  0-7645-7068-4
- Firewalls For Dummies
  0-7645-4048-3
- Home Networking For Dummies
  0-7645-42796

- Network Security For Dummies
  0-7645-1679-5
- Networking For Dummies
  0-7645-1677-9
- TCP/IP For Dummies
  0-7645-1760-0
- VBA For Dummies
  0-7645-3989-2
- Wireless All In-One Desk Reference
  For Dummies
  0-7645-7496-5
- Wireless Home Networking For Dummi
  0-7645-3910-8

ALTH & SELF-HELP

0-7645-6820-5 *†

0-7645-2566-2

Also available:
- Alzheimer's For Dummies
  0-7645-3899-3
- Asthma For Dummies
  0-7645-4233-8
- Controlling Cholesterol For Dummies
  0-7645-5440-9
- Depression For Dummies
  0-7645-3900-0
- Dieting For Dummies
  0-7645-4149-8
- Fertility For Dummies
  0-7645-2549-2

- Fibromyalgia For Dummies
  0-7645-5441-7
- Improving Your Memory For Dummies
  0-7645-5435-2
- Pregnancy For Dummies †
  0-7645-4483-7
- Quitting Smoking For Dummies
  0-7645-2629-4
- Relationships For Dummies
  0-7645-5384-4
- Thyroid For Dummies
  0-7645-5385-2

UCATION, HISTORY, REFERENCE & TEST PREPARATION

0-7645-5194-9

0-7645-4186-2

Also available:
- Algebra For Dummies
  0-7645-5325-9
- British History For Dummies
  0-7645-7021-8
- Calculus For Dummies
  0-7645-2498-4
- English Grammar For Dummies
  0-7645-5322-4
- Forensics For Dummies
  0-7645-5580-4
- The GMAT For Dummies
  0-7645-5251-1
- Inglés Para Dummies
  0-7645-5427-1

- Italian For Dummies
  0-7645-5196-5
- Latin For Dummies
  0-7645-5431-X
- Lewis & Clark For Dummies
  0-7645-2545-X
- Research Papers For Dummies
  0-7645-5426-3
- The SAT I For Dummies
  0-7645-7193-1
- Science Fair Projects For Dummies
  0-7645-5460-3
- U.S. History For Dummies
  0-7645-5249-X

Get smart @ dummies.com®

- **Find a full list of Dummies titles**
- **Look into loads of FREE on-site articles**
- **Sign up for FREE eTips e-mailed to you weekly**
- **See what other products carry the Dummies name**
- **Shop directly from the Dummies bookstore**
- **Enter to win new prizes every month!**

eparate Canadian edition also available
eparate U.K. edition also available

ilable wherever books are sold. For more information or to order direct: U.S. customers visit www.dummies.com or call 1-877-762-2974.
. customers visit www.wileyeurope.com or call 0800 243407. Canadian customers visit www.wiley.ca or call 1-800-567-4797.

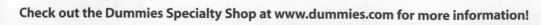